Depending on no-thing

Robert Saltzman

edited by Elena Ascencio Ibáñez
and Rose Youd

new sarum press
united kingdom

DEPENDING ON NO-THING

First edition published October 2019 by New Sarum Press
Footnote material has been added by the editors.

www.facebook.com/4Tbookpage/

New Sarum Press | 6 Folkestone Road | Salisbury | SP2 8JP | United Kingdom
ISBN: 978-1-9993535-9-9
www.newsarumpress.com

Epigraphs

春有百花秋有月 Spring comes with its flowers, autumn with the moon,
夏有涼風冬有雪 summer with breezes, winter with snow;
若無閑事挂心頭 when useless things don't stick in the mind,
更是人間好時節 that is your best season.

—無門慧開 Wu-men Huai-kai

Fear not the pain. Let its weight fall back
into the earth;
for heavy are the mountains, heavy the seas.
The trees you planted in childhood have grown
too heavy. You cannot bring them along.
Give yourselves to the air, to what you cannot hold.

—Rainer Maria Rilke

The adept gives himself up
to whatever the moment brings.
He knows that he is going to die,
and he has nothing left to hold on to:
no illusions in his mind,
no resistances in his body.
He doesn't think about his actions;
they flow from the core of his being.
He holds nothing back from life;
therefore he is ready for death,
as a man is ready for sleep
after a good day's work.

—Lao Tze

Table of contents

Epigraphs iii
About the title ix
Foreword xiii
Introduction xvii

1. A dive 1
2. No one has the answers 5
3. Liberation 7
4. No doer 16
5. A broken staff 18
6. An entity inside me 22
7. Do you feel an oceanic connection? 27
8. The wonderment of being at all 38
9. The Milky Way 41
10. What is truth? 59
11. Myth taken as fact bewilders 70
12. Compassion and self-compassion 72
13. Childhood conditioning 76
14. Speaking truthfully 95
15. Time 98
16. The abysses of vanity and meaninglessness 102
17. Psychotherapy versus spiritual teaching 110
18. Bombarded by thoughts 118
19. The contents of awareness 122
20. I don't want anyone following me 130
21. All the props are crumbling 147
22. A thank you note 152
23. Awake and aware 154
24. Freedom from bondage 157
25. A fresh look at what you need 163
26. Find your own mind 167

27. A block of stone ... 172
28. Psychotic break while awakening ... 175
29. In the midst of this aliveness ... 177
30. We are drawn to shiny things ... 180
31. Observing one's ego ... 186
32. Report from inside a Mooji retreat ... 188
33. "Actual experience" ... 193
34. My search is at a dead end ... 196
35. On meditation ... 199
36. Preconceptual awareness ... 205
37. Imagoes ... 210
38. I'm awake and I know it ... 212
39. What is a spiritual teacher? ... 218
40. Don't throw the baby out with the bathwater ... 220
41. Splitting ... 224
43. Existential suffering ... 229
42. A therapist's misconduct ... 235
43. Loosening the grip of ego ... 242
44. Are we only just flesh and blood? ... 249
45. A human life ends ... 255
46. I am afraid of non-existence ... 261
47. Faith, hope, and prayer ... 270
48. Patience ... 287
49. A light unto oneself ... 294
50. Loneliness ... 299
51. Native trust ... 320
52. Our deepest desire ... 323
53. No one can awaken you ... 332
54. Call off the search ... 335
55. Don't be a donkey ... 338
56. Can you induce your state in others? ... 341
57. Awareness and self-awareness ... 345
58. Knowing and choosing ... 350
59. Watching the movie of our lives ... 357
60. I still suffer ... 359

61. The story of Han-Shan 364
62. Enlightenment and awakening theories 366
63. Crystal healing 379
64. Things are as they are 386
65. Aware of your own enlightenment 389
66. Star gurus 391
67. The chatterbox mind 395
68. *The Power of Now* 397
69. "Be here now" 404
70. Source 406
71. Wash out your bowl 408
72. What is spiritual unfoldment? 410
73. Isn't a teacher irreplaceable? 418
74. The artist versus the art 426
75. Ring around the rosie 433
76. A teacher exploring his sexuality 437
77. Hypocrisy in India 441
78. The grammar of awakening 443
79. *A Course in Miracles* 449
80. Faith 455
81. The snipe hunt 461
82. I am afraid of death 465
83. Dementia 469
84. True human nature 476
85. On suffering 480
86. Existence precedes essence 487
87. Might as well enjoy the show 491
88. Spontaneity 493
89. Hopelessness 498
90. What about protest against oppression? 502
91. Alive and direct 505
92. This is not a test 511
93. *Tabula rasa* 518
94. Philosophical awareness 520
95. To see that you are awake right now 525

96. Nisargadatta and you 535
97. Does psychotherapy reinforce the ego? 537
98. No evidence for "universal consciousness" 539
99. Money and beauty 550
100. Are we just tourists in our little lives? 554
101. The denial of suffering 559
102. A teacher in disguise 564
103. The whirlpool 569
104. The price we pay 573
105. The sense of self 581
106. The myth of Sisyphus 592

About the title

In the 7th century, so the story goes, a humble, illiterate woodcutter, Hui Neng, was delivering a load of firewood when he overheard a man reciting a line from the Diamond Sutra and instantly experienced a powerful awakening.

The words that so moved Hui Neng were these:

"Depending on no thing, you must find your own mind."

Those few words triggered a moment of insight so penetrating that Hui Neng left kith and kin forever to wander in search of his own mind.

Notice that, according to this account, Hui Neng's awakening did not involve *finding* his own mind, but only the venture of *looking* for it *without dependence* on any "thing"—without, that is, reliance on conjectures and speculations about reality, "God," or Brahman, without leaning on theories of so-called "nonduality," without clinging to promises of eternal life, without paths and noble truths, without hanging on the words of so-called masters of the kind my friend John Troy calls "I-dolls," and entirely independent of faith or belief of any kind. A completely open, unimpeded investigation of the kind few have the courage to pursue.

Several years later in his wanders, Hui Neng found himself at the monastery of Master Hongren, the "Fifth Patriarch of Zen." Hongren asked Hui Neng where he was from and why he had come to the monastery. When Hui Neng replied that he had come from the south to study the dharma, Hongren asked how an illiterate southern barbarian like Hui Neng could ever presume to become a Buddha.

Ignoring the insult, as the story is told, Hui Neng replied, "My barbarian body may appear different, but is there a difference in our buddha-nature?" This reply so pleased Hongren that he accepted Hui Neng into the community, but not exactly as a student. Fearing that the well-educated monks would be disconcerted by this man so clearly not of their class, Hongren sent Hui Neng to the kitchen, where he was tasked, as if a character in a fairy tale, with shucking grains of rice from their husks.

Many months passed without Hui Neng's receiving even a word of instruction. He was left to labor in the kitchen untutored. One day, Hongren, who was getting on in years, arranged the manner of his succession in the form of a poetry contest with the winner to receive the insignia of rank—the robe and the bowl—along with the title "Sixth Patriarch." Since one student, the head monk Shen Xiu, stood decidedly above the others, it was assumed he would win, so the other monks did not even try to write poems, but left the challenge to him alone.

Meanwhile, Shen Xiu himself felt uncertain and doubtful of his understanding. He produced a verse but waited until everyone was asleep so that he could write it on the wall surreptitiously.

The body is the Bodhi tree,
Holding heart-mind like a mirror bright.
Never cease to polish it,
And never let the dust alight.

The next morning, Hongren burned some incense and read the verse to his students, directing them to commit it to memory, but later spoke privately with Shen Xiu. He told him that, although he had perhaps reached as far as the gates of wisdom, he had not yet entered, and that he must keep trying to produce a *gatha* worthy of being awarded the insignia of succession.

Meanwhile, in the kitchen, Hui Neng overheard one of the students reciting Shen Xiu's *gatha*. He twigged instantly that it fell short and within minutes produced a verse of his own. That night, illiterate himself, he got one of the students to write his *gatha*, an obvious refutation of Shen Xiu's, on the wall:

The mind of Bodhi has no tree.
There's no support for mirror bright.
Buddha-nature is ever self-clearing.
So where could dust alight?

Hongren knew right away that none of his students could have written such a gem, so it could have come only from Hui Neng. But fearing to upset the order of the monastery by recognizing an uncultured "barbarian," Hongren publicly dismissed Hui Neng's poem as "an insufficient understanding," and instructed the other monks to keep trying.

Nevertheless, late that night, Hongren called Hui Neng into his chambers where he praised the verse, instructed Hui Neng further, bestowed upon him the insignia, and directed Hui Neng to flee forthwith to the mountains and await the proper time to transmit the teachings—otherwise, his life was at peril.

Hui Neng did flee but was followed by a band of dharma students intent on killing him and stealing the robe and bowl. The mountain was steep and harsh, so most of his pursuers gave up the chase. But one of them, a former military commander, Hui Ming, persisted and caught up with Hui Neng at the very summit where he had been hiding. However, instead of attacking and killing Hui Neng as he had planned, Hui Ming found himself bowing deeply. Then, Hui Ming received the teaching, and went on to speak publicly for many years, including this lovely line:

> *"It's not the wind that's moving. It's not the flag that's moving. It's your mind that's moving."*

For me, the story of Hui Neng has a mythic resonance. The tale seems larger than life and replete with symbolism, but somehow, it feels factual too. What if the awakening one seeks is not particularly amenable to an effortful, rigorous process requiring years of training and constant vigilance aimed at "keeping the mirror clean?" What if, like Hui Neng, there are those who need only to hear a very few words, or no words at all, to find the gates of wisdom wide open and always unobstructed *right now*, requiring no *becoming* at all, but only *be*-ing?

That is what I want to discuss in this book you are holding in your hands.

Foreword

Here's a classic Robert Saltzman: "How do you 'try out' 'universal consciousness?' Just *declare* yourself 'universally conscious' and assess how that makes you *feel*? Oh, *please*."[1]

I hope by the time you read this far, you've already read the above paragraph as part of the whole book. Fortunately for you, my reader-friends, a foreword is often one of the last things to be read in any good book; you might have turned to it as a last resort on a long plane journey, or sitting in Waterloo Station on a rainy Sunday evening when the streets glisten with the borrowings of gloomy Dickensian illuminations. Even more fortunately, you may have come to this after reading the book and being subjected to the spray of spiritual bubbles being burst, of pompous people complaining as they sit on whoopee cushions, and of flouted convention as a deluge of fragrant namastes is flushed into common sewers.

Robert is kind enough to call me "friend"—it's one of those friendships where you've never met, but always known each other. So, dear reader-friend, if you are occasionally law-abiding and you're reading this foreword before the actual book, it's a pleasure to meet you and count you in this select company. Robert is closely related, I believe, to a certain small boy who pointed out that the gorgeously arrayed emperor was actually being driven through the streets stark naked.

And yet, at the same time, while ripping apart the defenceless pretensions of a spiritual teacher, he's disarmingly honest and humble. If it's possible for a man to be arrogantly humble, then that man's initials are R.S.

Discussing that famous iconoclast Jiddu Krishnamurti, he points out: "If *4T* goes beyond Krishnamurti's level of discourse—which I think in some ways it may—remember that I had the benefit of his wisdom when I needed it. We are all standing on the shoulders of those who came before." *4T* refers to Robert's first book *The Ten Thousand*

1. See p.555.

Things. If you were lucky enough to see the edition of *4T* with photographs, then I congratulate you for your relationship with Tyche[2].

Why bother to read this book, then, well-written though it is? Of course we can all put it in the bathroom for reading on certain er... occasions, but I would go further. Robert gives a good mental health clear-out to the spiritual "scene". He is attracted to written logic like a moth to a candle flame and glares at an untruth like Medusa uncovered.

He responds to questions with finely attuned intelligent compassion and discusses what really matters to people in real life. Not first-world, armchair, or zen-stool sitters (like myself) but first-world, third-world and all inbetween and around people (also like myself). Grief, dementia, addiction, abusive relationships and... being or even *be*-ing—all the sorts of things I would like to have asked once upon a time.

When it comes to theoretical matters, Robert eschews the god-like, from on-high position of some Victorian *paterfamilias.* Instead he points out the way things are with a compassionately irascible logic —just like you and I might.

This is what I like about Robert's approach—I hope you do too:

> *"Honesty about not knowing is, in my experience, where equanimity is to be found. What we actually know is precious little, so many of us fill the apparent emptiness by pretending that believing is the same as knowing. When one believes without actually knowing, then there is always lingering doubt to deal with—even if only unconsciously—and there is never peace in the struggle between belief and doubt."*

At last! I haven't had to swallow an ocean and strain at a gnat. I don't have to believe in some unproven, unfeeling god-thing and spit out feelings of compassion and common decency like a hair caught at the back of the throat. I don't have to accept the sayings of unsuccessful shysters (or successful ones) because Consciousness has singled them out.

2. I put this in just to show off. *Tyche* is the Ancient Greek Goddess of Fate, Fortune and Luck.

Robert has the ability to hold my interest when he digs deep into what I had always found to be the strangely barren subsoil of the is-ness business, the location of consciousness, the subject and the object, and the self and the Self. I think he stands a good chance of holding your interest too. And if you don't like one chapter, there are plenty to choose from, all with very different focuses.

Please don't assume, though, that I "follow" Robert—we might even fall out one day—but I have seen enough, read enough and been worked on enough to know that this is a book that many of us need; not on the coffee table, not on the bookshelf, but deeply in what I have to call our "hearts."

My only fear is that even though Robert doesn't claim to have final answers to ultimate questions, he might be seen as an unquestioned authority. I hope that doesn't happen, because work such as this is a gift to all of us who are standing at a crossroads, or have trotted off down an unproductive highway and back up again in the hope of finding we know not what.

If a personal deity exists, I will beg Him or Her to bless our endeavours. As it is, I don't always agree with Robert, but I would sacrifice my soul to ensure that people like him write books like this.

Catherine Noyce
Salisbury, October 2019

Introduction

Here I sit, beginning a second book when I never imagined writing the first one. I find myself astounded by the unexpected nature of this aliveness, astonished by this apparently ceaseless bubbling up of phenomena as one moment flows into the next. To feel this aliveness directly puts the lie to any metaphysics that claims to separate real from unreal or otherwise to define *this*.

Before publishing *The Ten Thousand Things*, I'd been engaged for years in conversations with people of diverse backgrounds about freewill, self-determination, destiny, choice, and who are we anyway? Those conversations took place in the intimacy of my psychotherapy practice, on a public webpage devoted to such matters, and more recently on Facebook.

A friend, Catherine Noyce, suggested that I produce a book along the lines of those conversations and that work was published in 2017 as *The Ten Thousand Things*. The first reader of *4T*, as it has become known, was my friend, esteemed Buddhist teacher Dr. Robert K. Hall. Robert loved the book. He told me that it was "destined to become a spiritual classic, like Alan Watts or Krishnamurti." Robert and I are old friends, so I took that appraisal with a grain of salt, but now, two years later, it seems that he had it right—as I said, unexpected and astounding.

Since the publication of *4T*, I have heard from numerous readers, many of whom have said in one way or another that the book had upended a search in which they had been involved for years—a search for what is commonly called spiritual awakening. One comment captures so well the spirit of that book, that I will quote it here:

> *Robert's book... has literally blown away all remaining ideas and beliefs I held about what's true, about what it means to be "awake."*
>
> *A readiness to be my own authority fully, versus following others or hanging onto others' ideas and concepts, arose while reading*

> *the second chapter. A readiness to live in a state of not knowing. A readiness to be a clean slate in every moment and to see for* myself *what is.*
>
> *This brought about a palpable sense of freedom. Robert's writing is unique on this topic, for instead of making* himself *the authority as most do, he prompts* us *to be our* own *authorities. Thank you, Robert!*

You are most welcome. Thanks for that lovely review. Yes, *a clean slate*. Set aside *all* teaching and be your *own* authority, I say. See what *you* see. Be a light unto yourself. Otherwise, I say, you are not yet even fully adult, much less "spiritually advanced."

After replying to questions about *The Ten Thousand Things* in interviews, online meetings, and such, my perspective toward these matters has come into clearer focus, so parts of the present volume build upon the ideas in *4T*, but it's entirely possible to understand and enjoy *this* book without having read *The Ten Thousand Things*. Still, if things I say here seem vague, or indistinct, you can always take a look at *4T* first.

The words in both books aim in the direction of simplicity of vision and the end of hierarchy, but *not* at creating an aura of comfort. If we are honest with ourselves, most of us are stuck in one way or another and could use a bit of a shake-up. So this book is an invitation to let old articles of faith fade away, to eschew dogma, and to be liberated from self-proclaimed experts whose expertise may be more imagined than real anyway. Often, those in the role of teacher are only *self-hypnotized* believers themselves who were put into a trance long ago by *their* teachers.

But the point of this book is not primarily to smash idols, although I am prepared to do that if and when necessary. Here I want to put more emphasis on questions that arise in this form:

> *OK, Robert. I get it. No one is in control. Choice, if it exists at all, pertains only to a little fenced-off area of mind that I call "me." But, having understood that, what does one* do?

If, by "doing," one means taking willful action, I used to say that no one could *do* anything at all—and that's not entirely wrong. In fact, to me, it seems closest to the psychobiological facts, and closest to what I see as "awake"—things are as they are, and cannot be different, including any apparent choosing and deciding. But questions and conversations about *The Ten Thousand Things* reminded me that I myself once regarded awakening as a kind of goal—this was back in the days of reading about Zen and such—and so that outlook shouldn't be ruled out entirely.

I'm not big on methods and practices and certainly don't aim to throw any new fuel atop the already blazing bonfire of becoming, but there are, I think, attitudes that can be useful. What I mean by "attitudes" is not easy to explain. As I mean that word, an attitude cannot be chosen or adopted, but only *recognized* within one's own mind as already part of the scenery. I am thinking now of a kind of attitude I value in myself that I call *intention*—not an intention one *creates*, but one that arises, is noticed, and somehow feels valuable or even essential, so that, whenever the intention makes itself known, it is welcomed, entertained, embraced, and honored.

Speaking personally, I keep finding in the writer of these words an *intention* towards complete candor and honesty, as if these words were a kind of report that should be as accurate as possible. Once an intention like that is recognized and honored, the candor and honesty pretty much take care of themselves. I don't find myself working at candor or trying to improve honesty. The intention, honored, seems sufficient to get the job done. As I said, the subtlety of this phenomenon makes it hard to evoke verbally.

As to whether someone, after hearing about an attitude like that, can notice it in his or her own mind, and then somehow value, honor, and work with it, maybe yes, maybe no. That remains to be seen.

Now some people will call this a book about spirituality—I guess that's where it's shelved in the bookshop—but spirituality is *not* my subject. In fact, the word "spirituality" strikes me strangely. I rarely use that word. If I am honest, I have no idea what that word really *means*, nor how it applies to the question of who and what are we anyway.

In the Biblical view, for example, Yahweh, a creator god, *manufactured* humans from clay or dirt as inanimate objects and then infused those lifeless sculptures with "spirit," whatever *that* is. That is what Alan Watts called the *ceramic view* of the universe, which posits a *god* as the supposed ultimate source of all that exists—including the completely mysterious human intelligence that writes these words and reads them; a god that is the alleged *substrate* of reality, the purported final answer to any question.

But I know Sweet Fanny Adams about the substrate of human intelligence, and not a dicky bird more about the ultimate wellsprings of anything I see, feel, think either. I know *nothing* about that. Nada. Zilch. Zero.

If you try to *envision* such a substrate, your picture is sure to be a mental fabrication. How could it *not* be? If you then call that fabrication "God," or "Universal Mind," or "Source," or "Brahman," you accomplish nothing but self-deception. Naming is *not* knowing. And naming something does not bring it into factual existence. This is a crucial point. The process of naming and *reifying*—which means regarding something abstract as factual as long as there is a word for it—is a process of mind in which we humans engage constantly. It may seem harmless to utter a "positive" word like "Love" or "God" while automatically commodifying (thingifying) it as something *outside* of one's own mind, but that, in my view, is a chief feature of what I call the hypnotic trance.

Humanity, unable to learn anything authentically *factual* about this aliveness, beyond what we see with our own eyes and discover through scientific investigation, has *fabricated* an entire world of superstitious belief to which most of us genuflect in one way or another, often without really noticing our obeisance, so beguiled are we by childhood conditioning, language, custom, and habit. I reject all such fabrications. They have no place in my world.

Accordingly, the subject of this book is neither spirituality nor religion, but ordinary wisdom derived from experience and self-observation—a fact-based approach to the human condition that operates without recourse to metaphysics, esoteric ideas and practices, physical and mental purifications, years of meditation, or any other extraordinary means of "qualifying" to be awake. No *qualifying* is necessary, I say. Only clearing one's mind and *noticing*.

Here is a story I remember once hearing, but I cannot recall where:

> *Layman Pang approached a teacher asking to be shown his true self. The teacher said nothing but just sat silently. Finally, tired of waiting, Pang got up and walked towards the door. Just as he opened the door, the teacher called out, "Oh, Layman Pang."*
>
> *"Yes?" replied Pang.*
>
> *"That's* it,*" said the teacher.*

The Ten Thousand Things ruffled feathers. Some readers found it transgressive. Perhaps it is, but the resistance to authority of that book is *not* vandalism. *Neti, neti, neti*[3]—not this, not this, and not that either—is neither wanton destruction nor disrespect, but a means of cleansing the psychological palate of the stale flavors of other folks' ideas so that the zest of one's *own* mind—one's *native* understanding—can be recognized and savored. That's the idea behind this book too.

I recognize that exposing "Love," "God," and "teachings" as *commodities*—as the *material* of spiritual materialism—can appear unjustly dismissive or deliberately hurtful to those who cling to ideals and who fear being lost without them. That is not my intention, but it may be unavoidable if I speak my mind fully. Nor will I apologize.

In all candor, a casting away of other folks' conceptions, most particularly the impedimenta imposed upon humanity by supposedly authoritative "spiritual" sources, is, I say, the *sine qua non*—the basic prerequisite—of an awakened understanding.

When I say "awake," I do not mean the pronouncements proffered by pundits in the spiritual supermarket, who market their wares as the best way—or in cases of *extreme* idiocy, as the *only* way—to attain the grand consummation, the ultimate acquisition: transcendence, liberation, nonduality, ego-death, universal mind, etcetera. If

3. *Neti neti:* in Hinduism, and in particular Jnana Yoga and Advaita Vedanta, a Sanskrit expression, meaning "not this, not that," or "neither this, nor that."

a path learned from a source like that seems intriguing, or if climbing the stairway to Heaven appears a rewarding project, you won't want to hear much from me, nor would you be *able* to hear much even if you wanted to.

This book is not for everyone, but for those who are familiar already with the staples sold in the metaphysical supermarket and have found them lacking. This book is for those who have the courage to entertain the *Great Doubt*—a radical skepticism towards *all* teaching about ultimate matters and *all* definitions of "reality." Without such basic agnosticism and rejection of dogma out of hand, all the "awakening" in the world may amount to nothing but a self-hypnotic fantasy, a recreation "inwardly" of experiences that one has heard about and now imagines are one's own.

Accordingly, the intention here is not to preach, and certainly not to offer the *next* "Truth"—which, even if I had it, would only deepen the damage already wreaked by years of prescriptions from teachers touting final answers—but to wipe the slate clean of all such pretensions.

Then, having set aside hackneyed preconceptions—like "Everything happens for a reason," or "Only love is real," or "The self in you is the self of God," or "As above, so below," or "Sri Joe Blowji attained the ultimate state"—we are free to participate in the *essence* of the matter, which, I say, has nothing to do with believing or becoming, but only with *be*-ing here and now—free to discard anything that interferes with that *be*-ing, including religion, spirituality, and all that stuff.

The human mind is orders of magnitude more powerful than most of us will admit. Imagination can fashion entire worlds from whole cloth. We can conceive almost anything, and make ourselves believe in it. Fantasy churns out rose-tinted scenarios of enlightenment and transcendence. We all have friends who seem spellbound by all that, but what has a grip on *your* mind?

Having been born in water, a fish never even *notices* water. Likewise, we may fail to notice the atmosphere of mental conditioning in which we are swimming—a conditioning that tells us to strive hard for what we desire. Such efforts may pay dividends in the work-a-day world. We moderns survive in a money economy after all. The tribal days are all but gone on this planet, and one must put food on the table, and clothes on one's back. But the skills and drive needed for making a living—which often requires postponing gratification in the present in exchange for rewards to be enjoyed later—are not useful in discerning the peace of mind that, without striving, is *always* here in *this* moment, and never later. That peace does not need to be earned or deserved, only noticed.

Peace of mind, I am saying, does not have to be attained, nor can it be. Equanimity is a *feeling* that can be recognized *amidst* the chaos of thoughts and emotions, not separate from them, or only when they have been made to calm down or come to an end.

For many of us, a hunger for special states has displaced the natural processes of learning, maturing, and coming to full adulthood, leaving us with a senseless, often desperate chasing after the pot of gold at the end of the rainbow. But one will never *reach* that pot of gold. The end of the rainbow recedes as quickly as we pursue it.

Better to be like the beggar in a different fable about gold—the one Tolstoy told about a panhandler who scrounged for pennies while sitting unknowingly on a box filled with gold coins. At least the mendicant in that story, as wretched as he is, might twig to what he's already sitting on. The fantasized, far-away pots of gold that the leprechauns stashed away can never *be* reached. That gold doesn't exist in the first place.

Once upon a once, without effort and completely exogenous to my usual train of thought, I found myself awake and free—not "happy," but free. I saw that I was not *doing* anything or *creating* anything, but only *participating,* willy-nilly, in a continuous, entirely inexplicable arising—this *aliveness.* I have my ups and downs—we are all just human here, after all—but since then, this perspective that I call "awake," for me, has never left.

Somehow, I had awakened in the manner one hears about. For a time that awakeness was hard to take in. There were *fears* involved: "Who am I to be awake? What if this feeling is only narcissistic delusion?" But gradually this awakeness came to feel natural and ordinary—as plain as day. I went for years without speaking much about this except with Catanya, my partner of more than forty years, and with my friend, Robert Hall, feeling that to speak in such a way might be seen as blowing one's own trumpet, which is *not* my intention.

I speak this way only because I see no other way to discuss these matters. Since I have no dogma to fall back on, whatever I say is personal confession. What else could it be?

OK, then. I've said it. The "A-word." Awake. I find myself *awake.*

Awake is not some "spiritual" attainment. All that hierarchical rubbish. From my perspective, awake is the *natural* state and awakening is not an *acquisition,* not a *commodity,* but a *recognition.*

> *"Oh, Layman Pang."*
> *"Yes?" replied Pang.*
> *"That's* it,*" said the teacher.*

I find myself *here,* fully aware that the suchness of this moment is inevitably just what it is. No one is *making* it be this way. It just *is.* Seen that way, there is nothing left but to get along with *however* it is, and walk on.

To be awake does not require answers to ultimate questions, but, on the contrary, to participate wholeheartedly *without* such answers; and when it sinks in that one really *is* awake, there won't be any questions either.

I've been asked a lot if one can *prepare* gradually to awaken like heating up a kettle until at last, it starts to steam. Maybe. Perhaps one can take in accounts of what others say in satsangs and such, or read old texts and find inspiration there. But I wonder if the analogy of the kettle truly applies. After all, if one keeps heating a kettle, eventually water *will* boil, but is working to boil oneself like heating a kettle?

If you try to bring *yourself* to a boil, and just keep "heating" long enough or with sufficient dedication to a recommended method, will *you* come to a boil inevitably and unavoidably like the water on a hot stove? I don't know. I see plenty of people *trying* to boil, and lots of words about *how* to boil, but not all that much steam.

So I don't know about gradual versus sudden, or whether awakening can be self-initiated like putting water on to boil, or can happen only spontaneously, but that doesn't seem important. I see nothing to judge. Nothing to compare. I came out of the trance the way I did, and that awakening has never ceased. My way is nothing to imitate, nor *can* it be imitated. You get what you get when you get it. These matters can be discussed, but their deepest aspects are not, I say, transferable.

A gradualist might frame coming to awareness as a kind of journey or progressive unfoldment, and I can understand that. But, in my case, gradual and progressive describes better the few years of coming to terms over time with something—the sudden recognition of choiceless awareness—that had been abrupt and undeniable, not progressive or gradual in the least.

The actual first moment of seeing that "Robert" was not doing or choosing anything and never had, felt abrupt, radical, and shocking—a precipitous change of state like the moment when heated water actually boils, like the moment when Hui Neng heard a few words and "got it." The *rest* of Hui Neng's story was the *gradual* part—shucking rice, biding his time, writing his poem, fleeing to the hills.

This dropping away of "myself the agent" was *not* the outcome, I say, of a specific style of meditation, or certain words sufficiently repeated, or psychedelic medication, or special sexual practices, or listening to lectures on nonduality, or . . . This list could go on incessantly—fill in the blanks with the efforts *you* know about. To me now, such methods seem nothing but distractions—ways of *deferring* comprehension until later.

Later never comes. Now is all we have. So if not *now*, when? I love that question!

A *path* is a mishmash of memories projected onto an imagined future. But when the supposed "future" arrives—when an imagined moment suddenly is no longer imagined, but actual—that moment is not at all what one imagined nor could ever have imagined. No one can possibly imagine accurately beforehand the authentic aliveness of *this* moment, *this* actuality, *this* bird in the hand, *this* moment that is all one must deal with and all one ever *can* deal with.

The story of spiritual attainment, of onward and upward, cast as a kind of *Pilgrim's Progress*, serves only to divert attention from the unrepeatable suchness of *this* moment—to paper over the facts of *this* moment with daydreams about the commodities one will acquire later after proper effort. That's the stuff of spiritual teaching: the commodified goal defined, and the path to it laid out. I understand that point of view, but it has nothing to do with awakening of the kind I mean. Nothing.

Keep precisely to paths and practices or wander where you will. Either way, wherever you go, there *you* are. There is just no avoiding being oneself. All you can ever *be* is what you are right now. Just see *that*, and feel free to be as you are.

Part of the material that follows consists of questions I've been asked along with my replies. My replies are truthful, but that does not mean they are "Truth" of the kind bandied about by pundits or propounded as the premises of religions—the kinds of final answers in which one is asked to have faith. I have no such final answers. I have no such faith. And if I spoke that way, I'd want my mouth washed out with soap.

Finally, I want to point to three terms of art from academic philosophy which are helpful to know because they can serve as shorthand for what otherwise would be laborious explanations. I will do the explaining now for those who need it, and then we will all have these three little words to count on later if we need them.

Phenomenology

As its name suggests, phenomenology is the study of "phenomena"—the study of things as they *appear*. I use the word phenomenology broadly to mean the view from a first-person perspective of objects (including the body and the bodies of others), events, thoughts, feelings, the flow of time, and all other *qualia*[4], without inquiring into causes and reasons, but focusing only on direct conscious experience, stripped to the extent possible of presuppositions, value judgments, explications, or interpretations.

4. *Qualia*: phenomenal experiences such as the redness or tartness of an apple.

So the phenomenology of my coffee cup might include its shape, heft, color, etcetera, but not whether it is a "good" cup, which is a value judgment. However, should the thought, "This is a good cup" arise, that thought itself would constitute a phenomenon, albeit of a category different from the category of a physical object like the cup. So that thought itself could be studied phenomenologically too—for example, what does it *feel* like when something is thought to be "good?"

Part of my approach to working with depression focused on exploring with the client the *phenomenology* of the ailment. For example: "What does this depression feel like? Is a cold, empty feeling, as if one barely existed, or more like being weighed down with a burden? Is it a slow, sluggish, heavy feeling, or more like being driven hard by intrusive thoughts?"

Epistemology

This is the study of the origin, nature, and limits of human knowledge—the study of *what* can be known and *how* it can be known, along with a consideration of what gives validity to knowing. For example, if you say, "Jesus awaits you in Heaven," I might reply with an epistemological question: "And you know that *how* exactly?"

Ontology

This is the study of the nature of being, the study of what exists, what it means to exist, and what reality is. The statement, "Everything is made of consciousness" is an *ontological* claim. "Everything is made of quarks" is another. "Dinosaurs walked the Earth along with humans 6,000 years ago" is another venture into ontology, offered inanely by idiots hypnotized by dogma.

If I ask if there is any rice left for dinner, that is an ontological question. I am inquiring into the ontological classification of the rice. Does that rice exist only in *mind* as a hope—which is one ontological condition, or is there actually some rice in the pot—which is a completely different ontological category?

Ontology and epistemology work together. Ontology asks *what* exists and how, and epistemology asks, "How do you *know* that?"

OK then. With those three linguistic arrows in the quiver, let us walk on. What follows is not a one-size-fits-all solution to the eternal mysteries, but only one human's perspective on these matters.

I found myself awake, but that does not make me a spiritual teacher, guru, or guide of any sort. I do not aim at making myself an authority on anything other than my own mind, but at prompting you to be your *own* authority—a light unto yourself.

I speak only for myself, and just say what I see. Take it for what it's worth or reject it out of hand. That's not up to me.

1 - A dive

On Little Cayman Island, the shore drops off so gradually from the beach that here, around half a mile from shore, the sandy bottom is still only around thirty feet below us, its natural whiteness shimmering pale blue through the limpid tropical water as we view it from the skiff. Then with unexpected precipitance, the luminosity of the sand ends suddenly right at the edge of a trench of profound depth with steep sides like an ancient river canyon. It is into that trench we are about to dive.

No one goes to Little Cayman Island to do anything *but* dive—that and a bit of catch and release bonefishing. It's just a small scrap of land with a couple of rustic lodges dedicated to scuba diving and nothing else. My wife and I happen to be the only guests, not just at our lodgings, but perhaps the only guests on the entire island since the other lodge is empty at the moment.

The dive master—a teenage kid—and I had gone out on a few dives previously, and after he saw that I had the knack, he'd led me on a follow the leader chase through some caverns and passageways of the kind where you might get lost if you don't know the way out. It was fairly demanding scuba diving, and the kid had twenty-five years on me, but I kept up. The fast-swimming was a bit out of the ordinary but still within the sport diving limits. The dive arranged for today will be something else entirely. We are about to break all the rules.

He'd proposed a descent into the trench, carrying battery illumination, to visit a black coral forest far below. Black corals are believed to have mystical powers and medicinal properties and nowadays are exploited also in the form of jewelry. This latter use, unfortunately, has led to a depletion of these amazing animals that are among the oldest living creatures on Earth. Individual living specimens of black coral more than 4,000 years old have been found, and living colonies like the forest we were going to see may have been around for thousands of years longer.

There is, however, a small problem. The depth limit for sport diving on regular air is 130 feet, but the coral forest only begins to come into view at twice that and extends perhaps hundreds of feet deeper. Going that deep will be risky—in fact, very risky—but I'm hot to do it. I was, in those days, a bit mad that way. I liked taking chances.

We agree on 280 feet maximum and make the calculations. We'll have only two minutes at that depth. Staying longer would demand a decompression stop on the way up—half an hour hanging on a line fifteen feet down, breathing from extra tanks placed there in advance. Neither of us is up for that. And nitrogen narcosis—the rapture of the deep—will begin to set in at 130 feet or so, getting ever stronger as we descend, so there will be that to deal with as well as the darkness.

Over the side of the boat we go, descending until we are standing on the sand 30 feet down. We check the flashlights, give our gear and gauges one last gander, exchange a thumbs up, and drop into the trench. I face the canyon wall. There's plenty of light here near the surface, and lots to see. The idea is to manage your buoyancy so as to drift slowly downwards while taking it all in. Soon it will be very dark, and the flashlights are all we'll have for seeing.

As we descend, I become aware that the canyon wall contains countless separate niches, large and small, and each of those niches comprises a world of its own—a system of living creatures unique from every other niche. The wall is very close to me—just beyond arm's reach. As I pass one of the larger openings, perhaps the mouth of a cave, a world-class barracuda, maybe five feet long or even more, swims out, seemingly without effort, and stops directly facing the glass covering my eyes, just a foot or so away. He studies me. His stare is emotionless. His rows of fang-like teeth shine in the sunlight still penetrating from above. I feel a momentary frisson, a quick dose of dread. I am larger than his usual prey and don't really expect to be attacked, but he is big and fierce, and I am out of my element here. We drift downwards like that together for a few long seconds. Then in an instant, he is gone.

I become fascinated with the details of each niche. The more I look, the more I see. Every niche is different, and each one constitutes a little interdependent world of its own filled with life. The nitrogen high, just beginning to come on, sparks the feeling that all this *means* something. I don't think I'd ever heard the word "nonduality" back then. That term took off only later, in the 1990s. But all I see seems to fit together seamlessly. Every niche is filled with aliveness—a multitude of individual animate creatures each doing its thing.

Some people like to imagine that no individuals "really" exist. What an idea! Of course we exist. That's what fills the niches—individuals, like that barracuda, all ultimately connected to lives everywhere on Earth, because even the flapping of a flipper half-way 'round the world can affect the environment here in the trench, however impalpably.

Nor do I imagine, as some people seem eager to believe, that the existence of these living creatures depends upon human awareness of them, as if those niches, teeming with life, did not exist until a couple of scuba divers happened upon the scene. Contrary to popular belief, stoked by the foolish declarations of self-described teachers such as Deepak Chopra and his ilk, quantum uncertainty does not speak to this question. Quantum mathematics deals with an infinitesimally tiny level of being, not large objects like corals and barracuda.

Nor are those creatures necessarily an expression of what some people like to call "Universal Mind," which is a concept entertained by *human* minds, not a fact—not by my epistemological lights. Do you know what "Universal Mind" is, or even if such a thing exists? I don't.

Sign on to such metaphysics if you like. I see that wall of life straight on, not through a screen of learned precepts and dogmas such as, "Nothing really exists but consciousness," or, "Only 'God' is real," or, "This is only a dream," etcetera. Those words have nothing to do with the moray eel slithering out from its hidey-hole aiming to devour a tiny scuttling crab, also trying to make a living in his one and only little niche. This is *aliveness*—life and death. If you prefer to pretend otherwise, well, you have every right.

By now I am feeling quite psychedelicized, and tell myself to be sure not to forget my air gauge, my depth gauge, and most of all, the clock. I look to my left, and my companion is there shooting me a

"How's it going?" gesture. I flash him a thumbs up, and we continue drifting downwards.

At 200 feet, we turn on the lights. At 250, I am raging high. Every object revealed in the beam of the flashlight seems to radiate a significance beyond conception. The entire universe seems to be flowing and changing. The second hand on my watch appears to be advancing impossibly slowly, and my eyesight is getting slushy. I am hallucinating too. I feel myself on the verge of an entirely altered state in which there would be no remembering the gauges or the clock.

My companion points his torch down, and there they are, the black corals, extending to the limit of our feeble flashlights and beyond. I won't even attempt to describe the mystery of that moment in the murkiness.

Two minutes later, we begin our ascent, which demands slowness, so the nitrogen dissolved under pressure into our blood can evaporate out little by little without bubbling into joints or the brain. Eventually, our heads break the surface into the tropical afternoon.

Back in the boat, I feel tired but exhilarated. The kid seems happy too. Then it dawns on me that he had made that dive before, perhaps countless times. In his rather empty life on that rather empty island, he'd just been waiting for another diver crazy enough to go down there with him so he could get high.

2 - No one has the answers

Q[5]: Ah, Robert, I have been having a good time working the internet trying to find your writings and interviews on the "I Am" —you are one of the few "realized" without a book! I guess there are more—we just do not know about them, eh?

A: I would never call myself or anyone else "realized." I don't see things that way at all. All of us here are just ordinary human beings. Some of us, it is true, have come to perspectives on the human situation that are not common enough or that are too radical to be called "ordinary," but such views do not and cannot alter one whit the fact that each of us is a natural, standard-issue human being, subject to human psychology, human physiology, and human limitation like everyone else.

None of us knows who or what "I" am, how we got here, what is the source of consciousness, if life has any purpose, etcetera. Those questions may arise, but factual answers to them seem beyond the scope of the human intellect, so we humans have become addicted to inventing answers and addicted to having "faith" in made-up answers. To see this for the first time is to gaze into the face of the sublimity of human limitation, the source of a healthy and realistic humility without which all the knowledge in the world is worse than useless.

Certainly, there are people throughout the ages whose imagination has *created* supposed final answers to such questions as, "Who or what am I?", but they are, I say, either self-deluded, or liars, or both. In my estimation, the wisest among us are those who live without answers to ultimate questions, understanding that each moment is sufficient unto itself.

In my early twenties, I became interested in the philosophy of being and began reading in the wisdom traditions, both Eastern and

5. In any Q&A, if there is more than one questioner, the first one is called "Q," the second "Q2," the third "Q3," etcetera. Some questions have been edited, not for content but for clarity, and some replies have later additions.

Western. For years, my mind was filled with those ideas, but I was not at peace. Then, in my late thirties, I had a sudden awakening that showed me that much of the reading and seeking of my twenties and thirties had been misdirected because it had been done in the belief that there was something to gain by it. There is *nothing* to gain.

In this moment things are as they are and cannot be any different. No one is "doing" this. No one is in control. No one has the answers. Life and the world, including ourselves, arise in a way that is mysterious and unknowable to us humans, and we live and die as we do. The lucky ones find love, compassion, and understanding along the way, but that cannot be obtained by force. You get what you get when you get it.

The idea that there is someone to become "realized," can prevent seeing the simplicity of this. In each moment you see what *you* see and you understand what *you* understand, and that's it. Someone else's understanding, no matter how convincing, cannot be substituted for that.

I am touched by your interest in my work, and I wish you well.

3 - Liberation

Q: Robert, I just listened to an interview you gave and it rubbed me wrong in a good way. It highlighted several precious beliefs that had gone under my radar. Your words were honest, no bullshit, edgy and refreshing. After a ridiculous amount of time spent seeking, I can no longer stomach spiritual teaching and yet the seeking energy rises up, looking for the next something to appease the acute feeling of limbo born by a sensation of freefall amidst the cacophony of experience. I'm wondering if you take questions? I am not interested in a teacher. I'm more inclined toward a clear mirror that allows me to see my bullshit and drop it. Please let me know.

A: Yes, I do take questions and post the better ones along with my replies. Feel free.

Q: Thank you. Four years ago I was in the shower, water raining down, when uneventfully everything shifted slightly and my body erupted with laughter. It was suddenly inexplicably clear that there is only *this* and that "Angelina" is not doing any of it, or responsible for it or choosing it, and neither are you, or you, or you, *ad infinitum*.

This clarity wasn't a thought so much as a shift in view. There is no "God" to appeal to for favors and no enlightened state of perpetual bliss to arrive at after years of celebrated contortions on a pious *zafu* cushion. There is nowhere to go and no one to get there. No meaning to make of all of this and no story to unravel. There's just this unknown arising that the body makes sense of as water trickling down skin in the warmth of a steamy bathroom.

The laughter continued but it wouldn't be true to say that I was laughing. The laughter was a response to the idea that there could *be* an "I" that was laughing. It was a bit like seeing behind the wizard's curtain in Oz but on steroids. It was clear that there was no one doing any of this, but doing still happened and so did trying and all of it. I rumbled with laughter for days. Soon afterward, I became unbelievably sick for the next two and a half years with an obscure illness that resulted in debilitating pain, cognitive impairment, seizures, and exhaustion. It felt as though "I" were being stripped of every identity I had.

The doer was short-circuiting but the habit of trying continued, with hours spent googling solutions, diets, diagnosis, visiting doctor after doctor, refusing drugs, and more. I could no longer work. I tried hard to surrender, which is a laughable contradiction in terms and experience. I gave away my art supplies and coveted possessions. My precious identities crumbled while the habitual doer ran in wild circles trying to reestablish control. The intelligent one could no longer remember even the simplest words much of the time. The athlete stumbled like a drunkard and couldn't exercise more than a bare minimum. When the writer tried to compose even the simplest sentences, the words were incoherent and resulted in a deafening migraine. The good mother had no energy to watch the children play or tuck them into bed or confidently go on a simple outing together. Even the doer was utterly ineffectual at anything more than running hither and yon yelling, "The sky is falling."

In time I realized that I wasn't afraid of death as it is typically conceived, but of the unknown. The unknown, unknowable, raw, razor-edge experience of life unfolding *now*, and the honest clarity that there is no way to move away from this "is-ness," except in chasing illusionary material or spiritual Band-aids that mask this fundamental fear of the unknown mystery that I am, you are, and the whole bawdy cacophony simply is. What is it? No friggin' clue.

When I came across your work and read that you too had your physical ass handed to you with illness, I wondered if you would speak more about that experience? This body has regained much but not by any means all of its former health. It is odd to live with the pretense of "me," all the while knowing that "me" is a social convenience and not a culpable entity endowed with doership from on high. Your perspective is welcome. Thank you.

A: Well, that is a coherent report. I seldom see the details of a sudden awakening put any more clearly than that. My own awakening from the trance of being the doer of my life was not as dramatic as yours, but not entirely dissimilar either, and it was followed, after a few years, by eighteen months of crushing illness, including fevers and chills, night sweats, and hallucinations. When I recovered from that, I felt completely cooked and had no more questions about anything at all.

I have heard from one other person about an awakening followed by serious illness, and there is the rather well-known report from U.G. Krishnamurti along the same lines. Although I had "awakened" a few years earlier, and had no doubts about it really, until the illness, I still struggled to make sense of what had occurred. After recovering—this was in 1991—that struggle was over, apparently for good. Since then, I have simply lived, doing whatever seems necessary, enjoying what I can and suffering what I must.

I feel a deep equanimity that others notice and sometimes comment on. But I do not know if the illness was related to awakening or not. I had been working for years with dangerous chemicals in my darkroom—chemicals from the old days of photography that are seldom used in modern work—and I failed to take the proper precautions, so my illness could have been triggered not in some metaphysical way, but as a result of poisoning. I just don't know and never will.

As for interviews and my writing—what you called "edgy" and "no bullshit"—I just say what I see and never want or need to lie. Frankly, I consider that most of the recognized spiritual teachers are lying. They are lying either to themselves or to their students or both. I am using the word "lying" in a specific way, to mean claiming to be certain of things that one may believe but does not know and cannot know, such as what the "self" is or isn't, or what is the source of human primate consciousness. I don't know if this helps you or not.

Q: I have thought a great deal about your reply, Robert. Thank you for your words and for sharing some of your experience, particularly with regard to not knowing if the illness was metaphysical or a byproduct of chemical poisoning or something else. If anything, the honesty you shared of not knowing is more helpful than all the imagined certainty. As for me, I have not emerged from the illness feeling "cooked." Perhaps parboiled. The experience I described was one of many that have occurred since age twelve—the first lasted for over a month—but the sense of a culpable "me" has always resumed with convincing density. I've come to consider going to the bathroom or grocery shopping or commuting to work on equal par with any "spiritual" experience. All of it is fleeting and none defines the truth of what I am, which remains entirely unknown.

Some experiences are delicious, some bland and some rotten, but nothing lasts. The only difference I can see in the shower experience and subsequent illness from the preceding ones is that the desire for life or myself to be any different doesn't find purchase anymore. I don't believe in that desire for more than a fleeting moment or two, sometimes longer if emotions rev up, but it passes.

The daily grind, however, feels a bit more like limbo than any notion I had of liberation. Nowhere to go and no one to get there, and yet, the energy of "person-ing" remains along with a persistent longing for movement and resolution. It's a bit bizarre and can be isolating within the human story. "Human-ing" feels a bit like watching a very repetitive movie and not being interested in it any longer. Alone in nature, by contrast, it feels like all the body's cells release and it is simply a privilege to consciously appreciate the manifold beauty rising and falling as life.

In nature there doesn't seem to be a "me" requirement—there's no notion of separateness unless I bring it in. Rather, this "me" is a nexus of perception with which, from which, and as which to appreciate life: the bubble of a stream, the song of a bird, the vanilla orange scent of ponderosa pine bark warmed in the sun, the biting chill of an oncoming storm. There is only *this*, and the great privilege of conscious appreciation *of* this and *as* this. A question like "What is it?" doesn't even matter. It *is*. There is no human pretense required to be anything *other* than this. The entire body relaxes. It will live. It will die. No need to be anyone, to impress anyone, or to do anything other than I effortlessly, naturally and holistically "do." Life is living itself. Does that make sense? This is not a belief but a felt release of the tension of human-ing.

A: You write beautifully. As I understand it, you have found yourself in an ongoing condition of non-attachment, which is what you imagined would constitute "liberation," but you don't *feel* liberated. You feel that this cannot be the end of the road that you had always imagined would constitute liberation because you still feel like an ordinary person, longing for movement and resolution.

I understand that. And this is a delicate matter, so I want to emphasize that all I have to offer is my own view based on personal experience. I do not claim that I speak conclusively, but rather honestly and earnestly, in reporting my own phenomenology as a sentient being—not a so-called "realized being," but only *an ordinary human being*—who finds himself awake in the here and now.

That said, in my view those who tout "liberation" as some wondrous condition in which all the pain and uncertainty of human animal life has been "transcended"—leaving only the bliss and joy of endless, deathless existence—either are lying for motives of their own, or have been hypnotized and deluded by exposure to pie in the sky literature, the satsangs of supposed "masters," and all that rigmarole, particularly these days the hocus-pocus called Advaita Vedanta, although that particular form of mumbo-jumbo is not the only culprit.

I do not deny that I find myself in an apparently less-than-usual condition of equanimity which is, in and of itself, a kind of contentment, even in conditions that many people might want to avoid. I don't aim at avoidance, and that "not wanting to avoid" is a chief feature of equanimity.

I say this as one who has faced considerable pain and physical suffering, which is here in the background even now as I write. But this equanimity is not due to being "liberated" from pain and suffering, but rather to having been set free to feel what I feel when I feel it, with the understanding that nothing lasts, neither pain nor pleasure, so that one must and can live each moment as it arises, while watching the moment die away again, only to be replaced by the next moment.

This is like sitting on a beach watching the waves roll in, one after another, after another, after another, after another, after another, endlessly.

So "liberation," if we are going to stick to that word, for me is not the *end* of anything, but just the freedom to participate in this aliveness fully and open-heartedly without expecting it to be one thing or another.

Those who speak of endless joy, pleasure, happiness, etcetera, are only, in my view, bliss-ninnies, whose "liberation" is of the same order as the Christian who is blissed out by the notion of Heaven with Jesus.

The true liberation, in my experience, is feet on the ground, and deal with each moment as it arises without resorting to such escape hatches as "I am not the body," or other such life-denying tripe. This moment is all we must deal with and all we ever *can* deal with, and in that understanding is freedom.

In saying this, I do not mean that I have no feelings of joy. I do have feelings like that, but I don't seek them or even yearn for them. Like the wind in the trees, such feelings are there when they are there, and absent when they are absent, and I am not producing them or controlling them in any way.

I don't know if this helps.

Q: Thank you so much for your open, candid communication. I appreciate it immensely. Speaking from this pinpoint in eternity, there is still seeking here, or more clearly put, the *tendency* to seek, a habit, accompanied by a deep knowing—way deeper than understanding—that there is no one here to seek anything and nothing to attain and nowhere to go. So seeking comes and goes, seeking to be loved, seeking to be healthy, seeking to be loving, seeking to be attractive, yadayada. All that seems to be part of the arising that is Angelina. A habit of trying to be "other" or somehow "better" *within* a groundlessness of I-don't-know, in which the whole idea of "better" or "other" is hilariously absurd.

This groundlessness, for lack of a better word, is the closest thing to a truth I know and there's comfort in it. I don't know what I'm going to say, do, think or feel, and there's no need to change that, even though the desire to change it also arises fairly regularly. I hope that makes sense.

Like you, I too find, after many, many years of reading and seeking, that most teachers are perpetuating a story that doesn't hold true—namely, that there is something to do or fix or some spiritual height to attain, most of which seems to involve bypassing the immediacy of life in favor of some idealized state, however that golden carrot is conceived. You and others have spoken of a personal sense of equanimity. You've also mentioned that your mentor, for lack of a better word, said "That's *not* it" at some point.

I was wondering if by "cooked" you mean that you no longer experience the seeking fluctuations that I do, and if by equanimity you mean that the personality doesn't get revved up anymore? I don't think I've arrived or not arrived. I think this is what *is*, whatever that is, and any effort to move away from this unknown ever-changing now is bullshit, even when that unknown shows up as seeking. Of course, the organism—the body—breathes a sigh of relief whenever that seeking energy drops, as it does when I walk in nature. But trying to *make* it drop is ridiculous. I don't think in terms of awake or liberated anymore, since "I" don't wake up any more than I beat my own heart, but I do wonder if this feeling of limbo settles or if that varies.

A: You are most welcome.

When I say I am not seeking, I do not mean that I won't take an aspirin for a headache as a way of *seeking* to feel better, or that when really ill, I would not consult a physician *seeking* explanations and relief. I am saying that I am not seeking an escape hatch from ordinary mortality or seeking so-called "spiritual" answers to ultimate questions such as "How did this all get here?" or "What is the purpose of life?"

In my view, questions like that *have* no answers that a human primate animal, which is what I identify *"as"*—ha, ha—could possibly come to know. So, in the absence of actual information, weaker minds just make shit up, as they have for eons.

Those fantasies may have had some psychological utility before modern science first came on the scene in the 16th and 17th centuries. After all, we humans do seem to require *some* kind of explanation for phenomena. Wanting explanations is in the DNA. But nowadays, when the field of *natural* explanations keeps widening, to continue grasping at the supposed *supernatural* seems ignorant and superstitious. I have no use for any of it, and I regard the "teachers" of supernatural explanations—for example, "The brain cannot be the source of consciousness because the brain is an object *in* consciousness"—as most often well-intentioned but entirely self-deluded people who imagine that their *beliefs*, which they learned from traditional scriptures or from teachers promulgating those scriptures, constitute *knowledge*.

People have every right to their beliefs of course, no matter how far-fetched, but belief and knowledge are worlds apart, and those who blur the difference or don't care to see it at all, are no better than fools, particularly if they imagine that their views are somehow spiritually advanced. To be clear, someone can be quite intelligent, but also an utter fool when it comes to religion and metaphysics. Think of Mitt Romney and his magic underwear[6].

Since you ask for candor, I must say that I am not seeking the things on your list. I am not seeking to be loved or to be loving. I found love long ago, or it found me—lucky, lucky me—so I don't *need* to seek it. To me, loving seems as natural as breathing, and probably will as long as this heart keeps on beating. To be attractive? Well, I am 74 years old now, and that kind of vanity is no longer entirely practical . . . but you should have seen me 40 years ago. Ha, ha. To be healthy? I do my best to treat this lovely old body respectfully, but most matters of health are beyond my control, so I don't worry much about them. I have been gravely ill more than once, and sometimes for extended periods, which is no fun at all, but at the moment things are OK in that regard. Sooner or later, that entire house of cards must

6. We understand that "magic underwear", also known among Mormons as "the garments" are a two-piece set of underwear, similar to a t-shirt and long johns. The purported magic comes from masonic symbols embroidered onto the chest, navel and knee area. Presidential candidate Romney, an Elder in Mormonism, would neither confirm nor deny that he wore them.

collapse, willy-nilly, and when it does, Sayonara, baby.

As for equanimity, I never chose it. And now I could not choose to be otherwise. I don't try to be equanimous, but people do see it, and even ask me about it. That is a mystery I cannot explain.

If you want my opinion, you feel that you are in limbo, but I know many people who would envy your condition. Limbo, after all, is a lot better than the various rings of Hell, which is where a large portion of humanity seems to reside. You seem in great shape. Just lovely. If you can appreciate how free you already are, the rest—if anything further is even needed—may come to you while you are not even looking for it.

I say this with love.

Q: Oh this is absolutely beautiful. Thank you so much, Robert. I will lean into this and reach out later if more arises. All love and gratitude.

A: You are entirely welcome.

4 - No doer

Q: Hello again, Robert. I have recently been subject to a situation which resulted in my being rid of someone who was toxic. This did not occur as a result of anything I said, did, or intended. It just happened that way and I'm all the better for it.

It is now apparent to me that everything that has ever happened in my life has just happened that way, regardless of my intentions, beliefs, etcetera. The illusion of my mental interpretation of these events has been more clearly seen. I'm now starting to feel more like a passenger in the car rather than the driver. It really is very amusing to see it! I'm like a child with a toy steering wheel in the back seat of a car!

I have listened to interviews with famous people who talk about the events of their lives that led to them being successful. They talk about how anger drove them, love, hate, or whatever driving emotion you could conjure, but it's all bullshit.

A: Hi. That's a useful insight, and I could say a lot about it, but I will confine myself to two points.

Number one: Fame has nothing to do with seeing oneself and the world with wisdom and understanding. Many famous people are simply fools who imagine that their fame constitutes evidence in favor of their world-view. I see this often in so-called spiritual teachers who seem to be ready with an answer to any question and rarely say, "I don't know much or anything about that." Deepak Chopra comes to mind immediately—a classic case of the Dunning-Kruger effect, which is a cognitive bias whereby people who are incompetent at something are totally unable to recognize their incompetence.

Number two: The idea that past experiences could somehow lead to "success" in life (quotes because what "success" means is an endlessly deep question) is not what I would call "bullshit." It is rather the ordinary consensual narrative—a common way of conceiving what "myself" is, and that way may have legs. Cause and effect does seem to operate in some matters, doesn't it?

From my perspective, that kind of narrative—"Poor boy makes good," or whatever, which I have called in *The Ten Thousand Things*, "The story I tell myself"—is not exactly incorrect, but limited. In my view, your discovery that this aliveness unfolds in ways that *defy* narrative is a step forward, but I urge caution. This is difficult ground because "no-doer" can easily become part of a *new* story I tell myself.

If that should occur, then arises the danger of passivity, resignation, and the avoidance of involvement in ordinary matters as an ordinary human—"Ah, well. I'm not the doer, so why work at anything? Effort is pointless." That is not what I call "awake."

As I experience this aliveness, when efforts are needed, efforts take place. The ultimate *source* of such efforts is a mystery to me, but I have no problem saying things such as:

> "I invited my friend Bernard Guy to a Zoom[7] *because* I thought hearing his ideas might be helpful to the kinds of people who follow my work."

Well, from the vantage of your new understanding, the "because" is a bit iffy, isn't it? But I still talk that way. And I might say also that I feel that my work in depth psychology has in some way prepared me for my present work, although by your lights—your very *new* lights—that would be "bullshit."

No blame. I have used the word "bullshit" myself, just much less frequently lately, although I might trot it out in the case of some grinning guru who charges fees to tell you that *you* don't actually exist, only "universal consciousness" *really* exists. Oh, *bullshit*!

In most cases, however, I'd rather not call bullshit. Let's just put it that people must say and do whatever they say and do, however narcissistic and ignorant . . . Deepak. Ha, ha.

---

7. Online group conversations, available on YouTube.

5 - A broken staff

Q: Dear Dr. Robert, you got to me with your idea of nothing to "fix" anymore. This is it, in all its terrifying reality. And this idea of not "getting to choose the movie" kind of dismembers the whole "co-creator" and "manifesting your reality" jargon of the New Age, which is also driving everyone crazy, especially if they want that new car! I have felt as if I have been free of all that for a long time, but the truth of "nothing to fix" is sometimes overwhelmed by the whole spiritual machine grinding out the *next* book, the *next* deck of Tarot Cards, the *next* weekend retreat.

There was a sadhu, I have heard, who was held in high esteem in his town. It was said that the staff he carried was an implement of great power that could heal people who were afflicted. Nevertheless, the sadhu felt that there was something missing in his own life, that his understanding was not complete. He had heard of a man in Poonja, called Papaji, who was said to have the final truth he desired to know, so he traveled to Poonja in hopes of complete enlightenment.

Papaji invited the sadhu into his humble home and asked what he wanted. The sadhu said, "Oh master, I want the final truth." And just as he uttered the word "truth," Papaji reached out, took the magic staff, and broke it in half. Handing the pieces back to the stupefied man, Papaji said, "Good. Now you can go back home and live like an ordinary person."

I may have butchered the story, but I believe that is what you have been trying to do with me, "break my staff."

A: Yes, it's good to break the staff of belief in all that spirituality nonsense. Unsubstantiated beliefs are poison. If we are honest, we know *nothing* for certain, except that in this moment each of us seems to exist as a center of awareness.

There is only now—only ever now—and this experience of existence. As long as you imagine that something *else* must happen for you to "get it," you block yourself from full awareness of *this* present moment, which is all one ever really has. Lost in the trance of becoming, you miss out on *now.*

Nothing is *becoming* anything. The suchness of each moment is a never-to-be-repeated *sui generis*—a thing unto itself—that can become nothing but what it already is. What you are, you already are.

If you overlook *this* moment because you are imagining something better, something higher, something more advanced—perhaps something you imagine learning spiritually at the next retreat or in the pages of the next book —you miss out entirely. With your mind lost in fantasies of becoming, *this* moment is lost forever and can never come back again.

It may be possible to set oneself up as a "co-creator," but only in a limited, make-believe play space. In that mode, one is like a child who imagines that the structure she built with plastic blocks is really a skyscraper. The conceptual co-creator *imagines* having the power to manifest changes in its own being. That is not possible. That *be*-ing already is what it is, and has no power to change itself.

To imagine changing oneself into something it is not now is an illusion that arises due to *splitting.* By "splitting," I mean a psychological defense mechanism that operates by setting up a good, desirable, acceptable "myself" in opposition to a faulty, undesirable, unacceptable "myself." Once that split is ginned up, everything "bad" can be assigned to the "under dog" while the "top dog" avoids scrutiny:

> Top Dog: "You just don't measure up. Other people have it much more together. You really need to work on yourself."
>
> Under Dog: "I know, I know. But it's not my fault. I am doing the best I can."
>
> Top Dog: "You will have to do better. I hate watching you blundering your way through this life—and all that masturbation on top of it. Disgusting!"

> Under Dog: "Well, I have to find some satisfaction in this misery. I am going to die! I can't stand the idea. 'Life is pain and misery, and it's over much too soon' [Woody Allen]. I'm missing out. Help!"

Your previous letters suggested to me that you had understood all that. I do not think I was mistaken, but perhaps there is still an element of confusion about this. At root, "awake" is simply silent knowing, moment by moment—a knowing without a separate knower. There is no *doer* in it. There never was a doer. Reality is what it is *without* any doing required or even possible, except in fantasy. The only freedom I know is to be what you already are—this *aliveness*—moment by moment. If you are always trying to "fix" that, to *improve* it, to *perfect* it, you are sure to end up disappointed or deluded.

No-doer does not mean that one ignores ordinary personal life, including wanting enjoyment or needing to make a living. It only means understanding that what seems to be occurring on that level, the level of ordinary life, is that an apparent person has needs and desires that arise automatically as part of being alive. That is probably what Papaji meant by living "like an ordinary person."

One lives an ordinary life but is not deceived by it. In each moment *myself* dies, and a new myself is born. As foreign as this may seem to the conditioned mind, there is no continuation of myself, but only a projection of dead memories onto an imagined future. The fact of a living, breathing body and one's attachment to that body is normal. It doesn't *need* fixing. Just let it all be what it must be, moment by moment, and you will feel the freedom of awareness beyond attachment.

This is not about being special or attaining anything. It is about being ordinary and just noticing that a human life is transitory, and that in living there is no victory—nothing to gain but the grave. Then one lives freely, step by step, welcoming each moment without fixating on *myself* and what I want and don't want, but rather allowing life to unfold as it must without resisting that unfoldment.

That kind of unattached freefall can seem scary, I know. The fear of missing out if one does not try to be "spiritual" or try to become something special may feel troubling. But reacting to freefall by clinging to a fiction of self-improvement or "salvation" is pure suffering, and does no good anyway. You've been into that kind of suffering for years. Let it go.

Q: You were not mistaken. There is something that knows all that and has known it forever. I do believe I am nearly clear of believing that this spiritual seeking and always trying to be "happy" is real.

When you say that each moment is just what it is and cannot be improved, I believe you, and I can see that for myself. But there is still a little gremlin hiding somewhere that keeps telling me it can't be that simple.

A: I am not saying that your seeking and desiring, including wanting happiness, are not "real." It's *all* real. That's what happens when the magic staff is broken. You see that all you can ever be is yourself, just as you are, moment by moment. That is reality.

Despite the overblown fantasies of what you called "the spiritual machine," there is nothing mystical going on here, nothing occult, nothing esoteric, and nothing to be figured out. Life is life. What else could it be? You live and breathe like any other animal, while thinking and feeling whatever you think and feel. None of that can be "fixed." This aliveness is the playing out of energy, and you *are* that. You *are* this aliveness. If wanting and desiring are part of that, OK. What is, is. Just let it be. There is nothing further to "get."

6 - *An entity inside me*

Q: Hello, Robert. I loved *The Ten Thousand Things.*

Do you no longer feel that there is an entity inside that has a will or makes decisions? Is it a constant experience for you that this aliveness is just a "bubbling up" of feelings, thoughts, and sensations, without an "I" inside here that makes this happen?

A: I have no sensation at all of anything "inside" me. Everything experienced—mental, physical, or emotional—feels part and parcel of the same entirely mysterious happening.

Are you really aware experientially, phenomenologically, of such an entity, or is the "entity inside you" more like an idea you have been trained to believe in, but cannot actually locate or feel if you try?

Q: So that means there isn't even an inside—just a whole, unbroken experience that is completely transitory. Is that right?

A: Well, "*completely*" transitory might be going too far. For me, there is a kind of ongoing sense of being which, as I have detailed elsewhere, is confected of various separate elements, both mental and physiological, but that sense is not under anyone's control. It just *is.* As I said, what I experience is a mystery to me and I have no basis for explaining it to myself, much less to anyone else.

Q2: So the experience of "deciding" when to finally get my butt out of bed on a Sunday morning is also just part of that same mysterious happening. Right?

A: Yes. Countless factors, most of them entirely unconscious, bear upon each moment of apparent decision. Ego-myself gets the news and constructs a story *after the fact* about itself being the decider who "made" a decision. The conscious mental dithering over a "decision" to move a part of the body—keeping to your example, your butt—actually takes place *after* the brain has already prepared to carry out the movement. So, what is experienced as a conscious decision was never a *choice* at all in the ordinary meaning of that word, but a *report* of the resultant—the outcome—of countless negotiations among different parts of the brain and other parts of the body, all connected up on the neuronal level.

This means that while ego-you is still bargaining with itself, carrying out cost/benefit calculations, and thinking about pulling up the covers, your poor old tired butt is already halfway out of bed, all the prep work for that move having taken place already in the brain, unbeknownst to ego-you. There is robust evidence for this in neurology.

The kicker is that these kinds of bargainings, ditherings, and other negotiations with oneself can serve a valuable function in the psychic economy, which is to provide a sense of self-unity and coherence. We *call* that imagined unitary bargainer, ditherer, and negotiator "me" or "myself." But that is only *conscious*-myself, *conditioned*-myself, or *ego*-myself. And, although functioning smoothly in ordinary life may require at least a smidgeon of "ego-myselfness," and, although the human being may require at least *some* illusion of unitary coherence to avoid feeling psychotic, that is not the *real* myself. Awakening, I am saying, involves less dependence on illusion, and more on seeing things as they are.

No one knows ultimately what "the *real* myself" is, but we do understand—*some* of us at least—that most thoughts are never fully conscious; that most sensations are only faintly felt; and that even further in the background, and usually not felt consciously or known at all, are the sensory reports to the brain from every area of the internal organs, bones, and other structures of the body. Unless there is unusual pain or discomfort, those unceasing reports, present even in sleep, go unnoticed by ego-myself, but are a large part of what provides the feeling of "me-ness"—the feeling of the ongoing sense of being that I mentioned before. The apparently coherent "me," supported by the persistence of those reports along with countless other sensory data, both conscious and unconscious, has no *control* over anything. It just *is,* as a part of one's biological constitution.

So, as usual, these questions boil down to what one imagines constitutes "myself." If, like me, you do not fear psychosis and don't worry about cohering psychologically, then you may understand that I feel not like one particular self at all, but more like a sometimes raucous, sometimes tranquil dinner party where the views and opinions flow freely along with the wine. Because in this gathering of "selves," ego-Robert has a pretty good seat at the table, he feels high on the wine of being at all—which emanates from whence he knows not, cannot be explained in the least, but keeps flowing, and never dries up.

Q2: Is there a difference between "I am *be*-ing" and "I am experiencing?"

A: It's best not to get lost in words. Each of us is aware of various objects, feelings, thoughts, emotions, etcetera. As I said, much of that awareness consists of bodily sensations of which we are only barely aware, and those unnamed, under-the-radar sensations give rise to the sense of a human body in space.

The little-known sense of *interoception*—a background awareness of internal organs—is highly influential in creating this sense of being. Normally, one does not consider that facet of "myselfness." If, however, one's attention is captured by a sense that something is amiss—an abnormality in my heartbeat becomes apparent, or a sharp pain in the abdomen—then one notices what was always there, but running in the background.

We call that flow of sensations "I." For example, when certain sensations arising in the gut become pressing enough to come to conscious awareness, one might say, "I'm hungry. Let's have lunch." So it is the *sensations*, previously unnoticed, that are being called "I," but it might be more accurate to call the faculty of conscious awareness "I," and the bodily sensations a *feature* of that awareness, or the *material* of that awareness. This is difficult ground because the body is both an object in awareness and also the living system that gives rise to awareness. If you contemplate that deeply enough, you may find yourself without any more questions.

Q3: Robert, would you say that, due to your having no sensation of anything or anybody inside you, any sense of lack has fallen apart?

A: One might feel a sense of lack in the material world. For example, if I feel thirsty and lack clean water to drink, that would be felt as lacking a vital necessity.

But if you mean a sense of lack on the psychological level, yes, I feel no sense of lack in *be*-ing. I understand that, regardless of social arrangements, friendships, love affairs, etcetera, each of us is essentially alone, living in a vastness of perceptions, feelings, and thoughts that cannot be explained even to oneself, much less to a friend or lover.

If I see that "myself" cannot be explained to anyone, even to myself, that is a turning point. I notice that perceptions, thoughts, and feelings just keep arising as part of this aliveness, and that I am not making them. I become aware that I had been trapped in a self-referential process not of my design, constantly weighing and measuring, continually monitoring my own thoughts and evaluating them as if they were my moral responsibility and a measure of self-worth. When *that* sinks in, the weighing and measuring stops, and things just are *what* they are *when* they are.

This is the freedom of freefall, even if that seems difficult, lonely, or painful at times.

Q4: I would like to add my two cents on this subject. Robert often says something like "You get what you get when you get it." But I have come to see that getting it is not the point. To me, having the sense or a feeling of being a "doer" is not a handicap or inferior, and in no way leads to a loss of quality of life or missing out on some grander or superior way of living.

Each of us is unique, and the way the brain is continuously being configured and conditioned and then reconfigured and reconditioned is, I say, well beyond my conscious understanding or willful control.

Any sense of having control is perhaps an illusion, but it might be worse if one has a sense of *being* controlled, which is more like delusion or hallucination. The sense of doership arises from biographical memory, continuously fed by story-telling or the narrative character of thought.

As long as the illusion of control has not degenerated into a narcissistic, possessive, anxious, depressive or obsessive personality, one can live a very functional life. I mean that, as long as the sense of "I, the doer" remains in the periphery and is not the main focus of attention, we can, I believe, have a high quality of daily living.

Ultimately, the sense of being a doer can be placed somewhere on a spectrum, with total non-doership at one end and total doership at the other. Where we start, or where we dwell momentarily, or where we end on this spectrum, is a mystery not resolved.

For me, I do what I feel like doing, and think what I imagine I am thinking, without worrying about the existence or otherwise of the "ghost in the machine." The same can also be said of the sense of having a free will, I say.

Robert's admonishment that we cannot imitate or wish to live his kind of life was a key turning point in my understanding on this subject, and soon after that my seeking disease stopped there and then.

Robert can and will only do Robert. We have to find and live in our own unique inimitable minds. Every mind is a beauty.

A: Yes! Bravo!

7 - Do you feel an oceanic connection?

Q: Hi, Robert. I am reading *The Ten Thousand Things* for the second time, along with what you post currently and some older writing like the www.dr-robert.com website as well.

In listening to the last group dialogue on Zoom, I was fascinated by your account of the Swedish philosopher who said that human evolution has produced an ability to ask the "big questions" but not the ability to answer them. Could you give me his name again, and elaborate on what you got from reading him?

A: He is Norwegian. His name is Peter Zapfee. I did a rather poor job of discussing him at the meeting. I was feeling ill and about to be really ill. Zapfee and I essentially agree on this matter, although his vision seems a bit darker than mine—but on second thought, that is hard to compare. Neither of us is what you would call optimistic. Ha, ha.

Zapfee's big idea was that we humans have brainpower enough to formulate and *ask* ultimate questions about life, death, God, the self, etcetera, but not enough to *answer* those questions adequately. So, in an attempt to justify the suffering and anxiety that seem part of this aliveness, we have devised modes of *masking* the issue of mortality, such as identifying with family or nationality, attaching ourselves to grand ideas or long-lived institutions, distracting ourselves with constant stimulation, or pursuing the arts in hopes of finding aesthetic justification:

> *"Beauty is truth, truth beauty"—that is all*
> *Ye know on earth, and all ye need to know.*
>
> —John Keats, "Ode on a Grecian Urn"

Q: I was moved as usual by your contributions to that meeting. And I appreciate your efforts to soldier on in the face of illness.

A: Thanks. Soldier on we must, eh?

Q: Have you seen Jill Bolte Taylor's TED talk? She is a neuroscientist who lost the language function during a stroke and found herself functioning totally from the "right hemisphere" in a state of what she termed "nirvana," an oceanic sense of connection with all that is. She says this sense of connection is our birthright as well, and that being able to move from cognitive mind to this state is perhaps the next stage of evolution that will provide a way for humans to move beyond our current state of division and fighting. What do you think of this? Is it similar to the awakening you have had?

A: I have not seen the talk, nor heard of Jill Bolte Taylor otherwise. All of this is so personal. Clearly, *you* do not feel such a connection—otherwise, you would not be asking me this question. So, suppose I told you, "Yes. I do feel an 'oceanic connection.'" What would that mean to you? Since you do not feel such a connection yourself, all you would have is an entirely second-hand, fantasized image based on a couple of words—and the word is *not* the thing. Whereas if you *did* feel such a connection, it would not matter what Jill Bolte Taylor or Robert Saltzman had to say about it.

I like to avoid that kind of language entirely. Let us, I say, move away from daydreams of transcendence and wishful fantasies of peace on Earth, including eschewing the language, opinions, and mental maps of others.

I don't mean that having heard the words, "oceanic connection," you can just throw them away. It's too late for that. And anyway, where would you put them? But you *can* ask yourself what those words mean to *you*. And if you see that words mean nothing except what one *imagines* they mean, and that imagination can run wild when applied to non-physical conceptions, you may lose a craving for the kind of speculation that underlies such discussions. This, Zapfee was saying, is really a craving for an *escape hatch* from the mortal realities of this human animal aliveness: watching oneself suffer and age, eventually to die, without having the foggiest idea of what the meaning of *anything* is—even assuming there *is* a meaning.

> *Once a man receives this fixed bodily form, he holds onto it, waiting for the end. Sometimes clashing with things, sometimes bending before them, he runs his course like a galloping steed, and nothing can stop him. Is he not pathetic? Sweating and laboring to the end of his days . . . never knowing where to look for rest—can you help but pity him? "I'm not dead yet," he says, but what good is that? His body decays, his mind follows it—can you deny that this is a great sorrow? Man's life has always been a muddle like this. How could I be the only muddled one, and other men not muddled?*
>
> —Zhuangzi, also called Chuang Tzu,
> late 4th century B.C.

What I am calling "awakening" involves noticing that this aliveness—this awareness—is not amenable to explanations of any stripe. There is no one, I say, who is not, in one way or another, "muddled." And Zhuangzi's "great sorrow" is not reduced one iota by speculative futurism.

You do not *create* this aliveness. You do not *control* this aliveness. You *are* this aliveness, prior to and independent of ideas such as Jill Bolte Taylor's, who presumably had her personal damaged-brain experience and now wants to whip it up into "the next stage of evolution."

An idea like that may be entertaining, but once you have heard it, so what? How is one supposed to engage in that evolution—have a stroke? Or perhaps one could intentionally damage parts of the brain chemically or with surgery.

What the heart requires, I say, is not conjecture about future more "evolved" states, but breaking open entirely when seeing things as they are *right now,* like Zhuangzi.

This sense of full-on *aliveness* is what one really desires, I say, not ideas *about* it, and not even "salvation" *from* it—although that is precisely what many people seem to be chasing after. In my experience of awakening, all the brainpower consumed formerly in explanation and justification flows instead into *participation*—complete involvement in this never-to-be-repeated moment, *whatever* that entails.

I am not a big fan of Joseph Campbell, who seemed a bit stuck on viewing human life always from a "mythic dimension," but in my view, he got it right with this statement:

> *People say that what we're all seeking is a meaning for life. I don't think that's what we're really seeking. I think that what we're seeking is an experience of . . . the rapture* of being alive.

Yes. Being here at all is a gift too often considered a *problem* requiring finding meaning, explanations, or justifications in order to render it bearable. In that sad view, the *rapture* goes right out the window. Who or what we are, whether or not we are "evolving," and whether this aliveness is only a pale reflection of something "higher," can be discussed endlessly and fruitlessly. Meanwhile, simply *feeling* this aliveness—the unique suchness of each never-to-be-repeated, mysterious moment—outshines desires for power, or pleasure, or even the desire for *meaning*—outshines them in *my* world at least.

When actually engaged in this aliveness *without* trying to explain it, questions such as "Where is it all headed?" "What does it all mean?" or "Who am I?" never even arise. The aliveness *is* the meaning, for whatever that's worth.

I am not at all sure that humans *are* evolving in the way Jill Bolte Taylor used that word. In my view, our current condition reflects accurately what a human primate animal is like and has been like for a long, long, long time. The level of technology in ancient Rome differed from ours, but the human passions that we see in their literature seem very much the same as ours.

Our present cultural arrangements are *not* aberrations from which we will evolve, I say, but expressions of human primate nature. Even assuming that the human mind *is* evolving, evolution occurs on a timescale that none of us can visualize. Ideas may change, and technology will change rapidly, which may modify modes and styles of *outward* behavior; but if more deeply viewed, human behaviors, rooted in emotional needs, aggression, and sexuality, do not change quickly if at all.

I have no use for the daydream of an improved future, neither mine personally nor the so-called "future of humanity" which, frankly, from my present perspective, looks like a slow-motion train wreck. For me, progress, evolution, and all that jazz is just pie in the sky. We humans seem to be killing ourselves a lot quicker than we are "evolving."

According to Elfatih Eltahir, Professor of Hydrology and Climate at MIT, even if the world succeeds in cutting carbon emissions, thus limiting the predicted rise in average global temperatures, large parts of India, where people already die routinely in summer heatwaves, will become so hot they will test the limits of human survivability.

We humans seem to lack any means of facing up to this problem. Our approach is all talk and nothing more. Back in 1992 at the Rio Climate Summit, the talk said that we only had ten years to get climate change under control. During the 27 years since then, that same formulation—"only ten years left"—has been repeated and repeated, and people are still talking that way.

For all our palaver about climate change, we humans cannot, it seems, refrain from blasting around in cars and airplanes just for amusement, just because we can, or ordering goods sent from halfway 'round the world, although those habits are killing the very environment on which we depend for life itself. Most probably, the burning of coal and oil will end eventually not because humans have "evolved," but when there's no more petroleum left in the ground to extract. And the raising of cattle for food—which is also a prime cause of the climate change that is rampaging through this planet—is baked into our minds via countless generations of survival and reproduction, and justified by the self-justifying religious idea that humans were given god-like powers by decree:

> *"God said, Let us make man in our image, after our likeness: and let them have dominion over the fish of the sea, and over the fowl of the air."*

How does one "evolve" out of *that* stupidity?

I am not saying that humans cannot evolve ethically. Perhaps we can. Nor am I saying that we should ignore our bad habits and pernicious behaviors because "that's just the way we are." But the basic ethical principle remains unchanged: do unto others as you would have them do unto you. If you personally can live up to that, wonderful! *Mazel tov!* The human race in general has not and apparently cannot.

All discussion about the "evolution" of our species is a matter of speculation, conjecture, and opinion, not facts in evidence. There *are* no facts in evidence. That is what must be accepted if one is to see things as they are. There are no facts I know of to suggest that humans are going to survive a radical change in the climate. The human race is in serious trouble—just on that score alone—never mind all the *Sturm und Drang* of never-ending territorial wars or the sometimes murderous strife over social issues and matters of self-definition.

To be clear, my view is not one of monolithic pessimism. I am not saying that *everything* is going down the tubes. By some measures, life on Earth has improved for the average human. In my lifetime, poverty on this planet has decreased. There are still far too many people without access to sufficient food and adequate shelter—more than half of us humans live on less than three dollars per day—but this has slowly improved. Humans as a group have more access to medical care, to education, and to other basic necessities than ever before. Part of this is due to technological advances in production and distribution, and part, I think, to greater access to information.

But I and others see no "greater intelligence" managing the show here. As far as we know, we human primates *are* the intelligence calling the tune on this planet, I say, and our destiny, by my best guess—I could be wrong—is self-inflicted extinction.

This is a bit like Zapfee's vision of the human predicament. We seem to possess—some of us at least—intelligence sufficient to make us aware of the problem: increasing population plus increased use of fossil fuel burning and meat eating per capita is a recipe for global climate destruction. We have known about this for a long while now. I was teaching the greenhouse effect to my high school science classes back in 1968, a generation before the Rio Summit. But we seem to lack the intelligence sufficient to overcome our primate animal drives for power, novelty, and self-gratification.

The best intelligence may influence the behavior of some of us, but just as wars don't end until *everyone's* appetite for violence has been temporarily sated, natural drives for the pleasures of wanton consumption seem to win out every time. And so, burn, baby, burn.

Burn not *less* than last year, but more. This crisis worsens minute by minute while the lights burn brightly all night long and jets fill the skies. Carbon emissions in the world have been increasing for years, and are sure to set a new record this year, although we know quite well that it is already too late to stave off certain kinds of severe climate-driven disasters that are just now beginning to make themselves known; and that this will only get worse if we continue on in this way.

We have known for years that, for every day we go on as usual without sharply *decreasing* the burning, the young on this planet and their offspring will live in an increasingly apocalyptic world. Our vaunted intelligence is not coping with this—not one iota. À la Zapfee, we have enough awareness to *notice* the problem, and even to know possible solutions to it, but we do not have intelligence sufficient to *embrace* the solutions.

And this is just the state of human attitudes on the brighter end of the IQ spectrum. At the other end, a bunch of dullards who believe that these facts are somehow still in question, are being deceived by the clever entrepreneurs of energy bent on keeping them ignorant, just as the tobacco companies obfuscated for years about *their* poisonous products. But this issue is a lot more urgent than whether someone dies of self-inflicted cancer.

You may see this view as pessimistic, but I do not think it is. I have been aware of this issue for more than 60 years now, and matters have gotten worse, not better. I am not willing to be caught up in futurist fantasies like Jill Bolte Taylor's. I consider such conjectures to be escapist delusions.

You may wonder how someone who says, "I find myself awake in the here and now" would *care* about what happens 50 years hence. After all, have I not said that the future is just a fantasy and that now is all we have? Yes, I have said that often, but the fanciful, far-away future to which I refer in that regard is not the physical world we call "the environment," but promises about the eventual attainment of "nirvana." I view those promises as escapism because, if nirvana exists, it is here now—so what are you waiting for?

The state of our *physical* environment in the near term—30, 40, 50 years—is a matter that can be approached scientifically, and about which I do care. Present climate models are not 100 percent reliable, but they are not chopped liver either. Predictions from those models will not be perfect, and some of them might even be off the mark, but the future to which they refer is likely to correspond at least roughly to scientific predictions. The power and accuracy of those models are substantiated by the success with which past climate models produced predictions that later proved true, and all the more by applying present models, which are improvements on earlier versions, to past years and comparing the results to actual historical records.

From what I understand, some models predict frequent catastrophic flooding of coastal cities worldwide by 2050, even if we humans do manage to cut back now on the amount of carbon we put into our atmosphere, which we show no signs of doing. Yes, I won't be here personally to witness a world increasingly at odds with the environmental conditions under which we naked apes evolved to survive and upon which we depend, but I already see the beginnings of crunch time. We *all* do, except the numbskulls coached into ignorance by a bunch of depraved John D. Rockefeller clones. So that's one advantage to mortality. I won't be seeing the worst of it. But compassion extends timelessly in all directions, doesn't it?

Right now *is* it for me. I have no life elsewhere in space or time. I find no value, no heart, no *be*-ing in a conjectured future of any kind—and certainly not in an "improved" one. My use of the word "awakening" is not centered on the "oneness" of humanity and the universe all leading to a happy ending, nor is awakening for me some quantum leap into a supposedly higher energy state, or the solution to the human tragedy of which self-destructive overconsumption is one of the main tragic themes.

What I mean by "awake" is living each moment fresh. To see oneself and the world as simply occurring, simply happening, simply flowing, without some character called "I" separate from the flow producing, defining, judging, managing, or controlling it.

If you have the time on Saturday, please drop in on the Zoom meeting and raise these points for discussion by everyone.

Q: Will do. In asking these questions of you, I reveal a desire for a change of state, for the "awakening" you describe. And as a lifelong seeker, I am looking for a *means* to achieve it. I imagine that almost everyone who seeks you out is driven by this desire. But what I find in your work is not a bunch of prescriptions, instructions, methods, or paths, but simply *a description*, as best words can convey, of yourself and how you navigate, from which one can "get it" or not.

A: Yes, I am aware that questions such as yours are motivated by the desire for improvement—the attainment of a condition that one imagines will be "better."

> *Every day in every way I am getting better and better.*
>
> (mantra used in the Émile Coué method of auto-hypnosis, c. 1900)

Countless people have branded themselves leaders, trainers, coaches, tutors, mentors, swamis, savants, gurus, guides, and mahatmas capable of showing the perplexed how to be better off than they are now, step by step. It's not just spiritual teachers who make such claims, but self-improvement mavens of all schools. I have no use for that collection of experts, and certainly, I do not fit into that world.

I have no "wake up" magic to impart. I have attained *nothing*—nothing but ordinary sanity as I define that word for myself—nothing but *my own mind*. If someone asks about something *beyond* sanity, something purportedly "transcendent," I advise finding sanity first and *then* looking for the pot of gold at the end of the rainbow if that is your hankering. If you go at it the other way 'round—transcendence, "God," and all that first—you are asking for a world of delusions in which no sanity will be found. People spend their entire lives in singing such "Loony Tunes," as U.G. Krishnamurti called them.

I have been taken by surprise by how much bite *The Ten Thousand Things* seems to have. By now, two years since its publication, numerous people have written to me about how reading *4T* was "transformative," or "capsized their boat," but I do not know how to account for that. *4T* is not a book of spiritual teaching—not a how-to—but, as you say, only a phenomenological report on the capsizing of *my* boat, and the aftermath. If someone can learn from that, great, but teaching is not the intention. My photographs and writing, including the words I am typing right now, are, for me, only self-expression, not "teaching." This is what I find myself doing, and I can't help it. One must occupy the days somehow.

Enough "spiritual" teaching! Most of it is horseshit, not the imparting of actual information. If you want my advice, stop depending on other people, even the ones called "masters"—*especially* the ones called masters—to teach you anything. Find your *own* mind.

I never met Chögyam Trungpa. I know him only through reading and some reports from people who knew him, including salacious stories of orgies and drunken rampages. He may have been a loose cannon, but he managed to coin the best metaphor yet of what it is like to be awake and know it:

> *It's like you fell out of an airplane. The bad news is that you don't have a parachute. But the good news is that there's no ground.*

The point of words like that is not that someone hearing them should try to *jump* out of the airplane. I can't see how you *could* jump even if you wanted to. The "airplane" is every belief in your mind. When the religious fantasies and all the second-hand self-definitions and self-identification have dried up, run their course, and somehow—who knows how?—you no longer believe in them, you find yourself in freefall with nothing at all to grab onto. All that dogma *was* the airplane.

That's the *bad* news—you have nothing left to believe in, nothing to cling to, no salvation, no escape hatch. But the *good* news is that you are on your own at last. At fucking last. No one telling you what to believe or what to do. And if someone should try to instruct you, it's meaningless. It is one's *own* mind that must be discovered.

Q: The "capsizing" for me was to see how attached I was to "belief," in my case an alternative (to be entirely honest, "superior") set of beliefs. I remember from the EST training, "Life is empty and meaningless, and it's empty and meaningless that it's empty and meaningless" and "You are a machine!" To truly confront these notions can be frightening. Of course, EST, after pulling the rug out from under us, offered us an alternative—which, of course, involved a continued connection to the program, including coming up with more money, in a desire to repeat the experience of "getting it."

A: I have no more use for nihilism like EST than I do for the eternalism of religions. From my perspective, both miss by a mile, and the people who espouse them appear self-satisfied, robotic, and hypnotized by their own beliefs.

Zapfee's vision was dark—perhaps even darker than mine, as I said—but not nihilistic. He raised a real issue: human limitation. The nihilists meet that idea with a foolish fatalism: "Isn't this amusing? Life is a bitch and then you die." That is *not* realism, but avoidance and denial. Meanwhile, the religious ones meet it with unwarranted certainty: "In my 'soul's journey,' this animal aliveness is just a stepping stone."

In the face of that Scylla and Charybdis, what do *you* want to do?

8 - *The wonderment of being at all*

Q: Good morning, Robert. I will bother you only once today. If my understanding is correct, the pains of clinging and attachment are delusions stemming from a failure to understand the nondual nature of reality.

A: Attachments are a normal part of animal life, including human animal life. For example, when an elephant dies, the other elephants in the herd, or *parade*, as a group of elephants is properly called, spend a long time mourning. I would not call that a delusion. After euthanizing my lovely old German shepherd, Tuki, I felt blue for a long time, as if all the joy had gone out of life. In fact, I felt a pain around my heart that lasted for weeks. I would not call that pain delusional either.

The delusion to which I referred consists, as I see it, in imagining that I am somehow *separate* from this aliveness so that I "have" a life. I do not *have* a life. In the same fashion as an elephant or a German shepherd, I am an *expression* of *this aliveness* that manifests in a multitude of forms and ways—in my case, as a human primate.

One may understand nonduality as the interdependence of all and everything, so that no apparently individual entity can exist separated from everything else, but that does *not* mean that one no longer mourns the death of loved ones or tries to live without attachment to mates, children, or friends. It means that one *accepts* life holistically as it appears in each instant, *including* feelings of attachment. *This is a key point.*

All feelings are valid. Awakening does not require avoiding feelings, or even avoiding clinging if that is what arises. Awakening brings the understanding that in this moment nothing can be different from the way it is, *including* one's feelings. You will understand my words here in the way that *you* understand them in *this* moment. You cannot understand them otherwise.

Understanding takes place only right now, and there is no use *trying* to understand. You understand or you don't. Seeing that each of us can understand only what we understand, be what we are, and do what we must, is the birth of compassion. If you see that, you will have to admit that each of us is doing the best that he or she can, and that much of our "doing" is driven by old, inherited, learned programs conducive to survival.

My friend Oscar Moreno, born like me in the 1940s, told me this story from his youth. An elder took him aside and pointed to various people in the room whose personal histories were questionable. "See that one?" the old man asked. "Well, he's a life-long politician who has corrupted every office he ever held. And that one, he's a mechanic who does shoddy work, cheats, and swindles. And that one over there? She'll lie to anyone at the drop of a hat. And her brother, that one over there, keeps selling land he never really owned." And, said Oscar, this talk went on until the old man had unmasked everyone in the room.

Then, Oscar's mentor told him this: "But all of them, and you and me too, have one thing in common—we are all *survivors*. We come from a long line of survivors, and now it is our turn to survive, so be careful before you judge."

That's what I mean by "learned programs conducive to survival." What if "attachment" is one of those learned programs?

Everything is interconnected. "Myself" is not so easily split off from all and everything, *including* ancient drives, the culture in which one was raised, and the programs conducive to survival. This does not mean, as one foolish woman tried to tell me yesterday, that "myself" is only imaginary and that no one actually exists, that inane trope that passes among the ignorant for "nonduality."

Of *course* we exist. If you say you don't, then from whose mouth are those words coming? It's just that "myself" does not exist *independently* of everything else. If she had been even minimally civil in her approach to me, I might have helped her to comprehend this, but no. She could only be what she was in that moment, and, given that I am in the same condition—I can only be myself, like it or not—I felt compassion for her ignorance. Unfortunately for her, one chief aspect of ignorance like hers is obstinacy in *remaining* ignorant. She might spend an entire life trying to believe that she does not exist until one day she really *won't* exist. We call that death.

Compassion without wisdom can be foolish and sentimental. When I had to let Tuki go, it was important to have both compassion for the child in me who was devastated by the loss of a beloved companion, *and* the wisdom to see that loss and death are as much a part of life as pleasure, joy, and all the rest. Only the foolish try to have pleasure without pain or joy without suffering. The wise eat the whole thing and swallow it with gratitude to be having the meal at all.

If we are going to contemplate these high-flown ideas, it behooves us not to use them as an excuse for caring less about day-to-day events by characterizing them as "delusions." One can be lost endlessly in such reductive dead ends of dogma and so miss out on the wonderment of being at all.

To me, a game of fetch with a dog you love seems as real and important as a conversation with a so-called "perfect master"—perhaps *realer,* since dogs actually exist. Regarding "perfect masters," I have doubts.

And if you are *attached* to the dog, that is not any more of a delusion—less of one, I would say—than imagining that by means of attaining "enlightenment" one will be forever immunized against the pain of loss.

9 - The Milky Way

This chapter begins with a discussion of large numbers. In approaching this subject, which is really about consciousness and the human brain, a quantitative perspective seemed unavoidable. But if you find lots of numbers daunting, no worries. Just skim through that part. You will still get the picture. Most of the chapter is number-free.

If one is fortunate enough to be in a place with a good view of the night sky—a high desert far from artificial illumination is ideal—and gazes upwards, one will perceive countless tiny points of light shining forth against the darkness of space. Those points of light are really suns like our Sun, many of them much larger and brighter than ours; and the more closely one looks into that darkness, the more of those suns that we call *stars* one will see.

Those countless stars do not appear uniformly scattered in space. In some places, their multitude seems rather sparse, while in others much more abundant. In a certain area of the sky, the stars become so plentiful that their light seems to run together in a kind of pale white, glowing band, a lacteous highway in the heavens; hence, the *Milky* Way.

The Milky Way is the galaxy that contains our solar system—our Sun and its planets including Earth. A *galaxy* is a vast collection of stars, remnants of stars, gases and other kinds of matter, all bound together gravitationally, often around a central black hole.

Galaxies come in different shapes and sizes, but envisioning the *size* of a galaxy is not feasible. Our galaxy, the Milky Way, is a *spiral galaxy* in the form of a flattened disk, bulging in its center, with arms radiating outwards. Our *solar system* is located on the inner edge of one of those arms, the Orion Arm, which is located some *25,000 light-years* distant from the central bulge. That means the distance a photon, particle of light, would travel in 25,000 years. A distance like that cannot be visualized. We can *talk* about it. Words are easy. But we cannot *grasp* such an immensity of time—25,000 years—much less the vastness of *distance* that a ray of light would cover in such a span of time. To imagine that is not possible. Beyond human capability.

Even so, that distance from Earth to the center of our galaxy is a trifle compared to the magnitude of the almost empty space *between* galaxies. Our nearest neighbor, the Andromeda Galaxy—one of the few that can be seen from Earth with the naked eye—resides at a distance of two and a half *million* light-years from us, meaning that the light of that galaxy we see now—traveling, obviously, at the *speed of light*, which is 300,000 meters or 186,000 miles per second—took two and a half million years to get here from Andromeda. By way of comparison, it takes roughly one second for moonlight to reach Earth.

Two and a half million of anything seems hard to imagine, but two and a half million *years*? Lots of luck with that. And the *distance* that light travels in millions of years—the distance from here to Andromeda—that is a visualization entirely beyond human mental capacity, no matter which human.

Even within a galaxy like ours, the stars are remarkably distant from one another. Out here on the Orion Arm of the Milky Way, our nearest star, Proxima Centauri, lies more than four light-years from us. Near the center of the galaxy, the stars thicken up—it's maybe only half a light-year from one to the next, but that is already a vast distance. The Milky Way appears as a continuous band in our night sky not because its stars are packed closely together—they aren't—but because our galaxy has the shape of a disk. And in observing the Milky Way, we are looking through and across most of the diameter of that disk, and so we see the majority of its three hundred billion stars.

Three hundred billion. That's another unimaginable quantity. We humans lack any way to appreciate, in a phenomenological way, the scale of a number like that. We can say the words *"three hundred billion"* but we can't *feel* anything about that order of magnitude. We have no way to envisage three hundred billion of anything. Our cognitive abilities evolved through eons of contending with ordinary life on Earth—a *handful* of berries and nuts, a *hundred* people in the tribe, not *billions* of anything.

A billion of anything is just too much to imagine. That is one aspect of what I call human limitation. We cannot even rightly conceive a mental image of a *million*, much less a *billion*. We just have no feel for it. We can do the math with numbers as large as we like, or have a computer do it for us, but we cannot grasp *cognitively* what such large numbers actually signify. The best we can do is exercises like this:

> *A ream of paper—500 sheets—is two inches thick. A million sheets would make a stack 400 feet tall.*

To be honest, words like that do not tell me much except that a million is a really big number.

Another approach is to state large numbers in terms of time. For example, to reach a million beats of the heart, one would have to count day and night for a couple of weeks. I will expand on that a bit later.

Not long ago, the number of stars in our galaxy was estimated to be around 100 or 200 billion, about the same as the number of neurons in a human brain; but with better methods of observation, the estimate of stars has increased to the present 300 billion and continues increasing. So there may be more stars in the Milky Way than neurons in a brain, but not by much. And if we consider that each brain cell is connected to the others by many thousands of synapses, we might get a feeling for why it is said that the complexity of the human brain, a gelatinous mass that weighs around three pounds, is far greater than the complexity of our entire galaxy.

In fact, it is said that the human brain is arguably the most complex entity in the known universe. Leaving aside the bulk of those three pounds of jelly and focusing only on the cerebral cortex—which is a coating on the brain only six cells thick, largely responsible for higher intellectual powers (if that layer is damaged, the intellectual powers are damaged as well)—we are looking at perhaps 125 *trillion* synapses, which is more than the number of stars in 1,500 Milky Way galaxies.

I said that a million is hard—impossible, really—to conceive of, let alone a billion, which is a thousand millions. But a trillion is a thousand billions, or a million millions. A concept like 125 *trillion* synapses is so experience-distant as to be essentially meaningless.

Put your fingers on your wrist and take your pulse. Each beat of your heart takes more or less one second. If you sat there counting day and night without ever losing track or missing a beat, in a couple of weeks you would have reached a million beats. But to reach a billion beats, counting day and night, would take 32 *years*. And a trillion beats—well, to get to that number, you would need 32,000 years. This is beyond human comprehension entirely.

Now those numbers may seem huge, and indeed they are huge compared to human comprehension; but compared to certain other numbers, they are paltry. There are orders of numerical magnitude far, far beyond trillions.

I used to play the game called "Go" that originated some 3,000 years ago in China. Go is played on a grid of intersecting lines, 19 by 19, on which black and white stones are placed, one by one, in alternating moves by the two players. The rules of the game are simple, but the number of possible positions as the stones are placed turns out to be 10 to the 170th power, or 10 followed by 170 zeros. That's a quantity which is larger than the number of atoms not just in a *brain*, not just in the Milky Way galaxy, not just in the *Laniakea supercluster—"our"* supercluster, which consists of around 100,000 Milky Ways like ours (but which itself is just one of the ten million or so superclusters in the known universe)—but a quantity larger than the number of atoms in the known universe. Imagine *that*. You can't, I can't, and no one else can either.

In the face of a complexity so beyond the scope of human experience, Go players cannot hope to win by analyzing all the possible outcomes of one move or another, but must resort to intuition and feel, not only contemplating the local area in which the move will be made, but allowing themselves a global, non-rational sense of the entire "universe" comprised of the Go board and its stones.

Beginning in the last century, workers in artificial intelligence who had succeeded in creating chess programs strong enough to beat the best players, turned their efforts to the far greater challenge of devising a program that could play high-level Go. Programs for chess functioned by constructing *search trees*, or *decision trees* as they are also called, of all possible future positions and, through prognostic analysis, choosing the strongest move at each juncture. But that could not be done for Go, in which the number of future positions is a *googol* greater than in chess. (A googol is ten followed by 100 zeros.)

As I wrote earlier, we cannot imagine such a number, but we *can* use the hopeless unimaginability of it to understand why the search tree approach that had worked well for chess could not be applied to Go. All the computing power on Earth could not support a decision tree capable of ascertaining the best point on which to place a Go stone.

Stymied by that limitation, the AI researchers came up with a novel approach. They used the computing power they did have to create a *neural network*, which is a simulacrum in silicon of an organic brain, composed of various layers of *artificial* neurons connected similarly to the way neurons in a brain are connected—connected to both neighboring neurons and far distant ones.

In the development of the chess playing programs based on a search tree approach, the computer was furnished with thousands of the previous games of expert players to use as a basis for rejecting obviously bad moves, so that the parts of the decision tree requiring searching could be narrowed down to only those areas involving moves that were at least reasonable by the standards of the best players. Obvious wrong moves would not even be investigated. But here, in the Google laboratory called "DeepMind," where the AI program for Go, *AlphaGoZero*, was conceived, that kind of narrowing down was *not* the method. It could not *be* the method due to the impossible complexity of Go.

A previous program, *AlphaGo*, had relied on a system of two neural networks, one network to select the next move, and another to predict the eventual winner at each juncture. AlphaGo was given thousands of previous expert games to study and was then left to play against itself. Within hours, the AlphaGo artificial intelligence was playing like an expert, and in 2016 was put up in a match of five games against one of the top players in the world, Lee Sedol. Almost everyone in the world of Go expected Sedol to win all the games, and probably to win easily. Instead, AlphaGo won the first three games—resignations by Sedol, lost the fourth, and won the final game of the five. An astounding performance that left Sedol at one point wandering through the streets muttering to himself.

But that was not enough for the AlphaGo people. In research, nothing is *ever* enough. There is always the *next* thing, the next mountain to climb. And the next mountain in AI involved creating a neural network so powerful that it could begin with no knowledge of Go at all except for the few simple rules of the game: stones are placed wherever one likes—on any empty point—and the winner is the one who manages to enclose more territory than the opponent.

That is all AlphaGoZero was given, the rules of the game. No starting point, no previous games of experts, no plan—*nothing* but the few simple rules—and then was left to play against itself. That is why it was called "*Zero*," meaning starting from scratch.

AlphaGoZero took three days of playing against itself to master the game so thoroughly that when it was put up against the original AlphaGo—the one that had defeated Lee Sedol 4-1—it crushed AlphaGo, winning 100 games in a row while losing none.

But that was still not enough for the AI people. The next step was AlphaZero, an artificial intelligence that could learn in a few hours, starting from scratch, to play *any* game in which chance is not a factor well enough to beat not only any human player but any other computer program on Earth as well—even the ones that were given the advantage of studying past games of human masters.

To underscore this point: *artificial* neurons connected in layers like the neurons in a brain, can *learn* better than living neurons in a human brain—even the best brain—to comprehend shifting patterns and where those patterns are headed. And once having seen the patterns, AI can act intelligently so as to effect desirable changes in those patterns. A current example is the self-driving car where AI is learning to replace human pattern recognition skills, along with the ability to respond to those ever-changing patterns.

Take a moment to remember yourself driving on a high-speed freeway in traffic. Picture the complexity of it and the way decisions are made, primarily unconsciously, to affect the movement of one's own vehicle in relation to countless factors—the road surface and contours, the speed and direction of neighboring vehicles, the responsiveness of one's own vehicle to small movements of hands and feet, possible obstacles in the road, etcetera. Now, those tasks can be managed by an *artificial brain* that is a simulation in electronics of a fleshly brain.

I am writing this with Microsoft Word, a program that can make no decisions. It can only follow the instructions of the operator. That is *not* AI.

When AI drives the car, it *is* making decisions, if we want to use that word, not simply carrying out fixed instructions such as "Turn the steering two degrees to the right and apply 5 percent more power." It has trained *itself* to deal with the work of driving by means of growth and change in its own neural network.

This training might *begin* with observation of a human driver's responses to situations—Robert drives and the AI watches—but soon the training becomes *self-training,* independent of human input, an active creation of neuronal connections. In this so-called "deep learning" the AI teaches *itself* to parse a constant stream of data so as to recognize whether an object in the road ahead is a car, a human, a road sign, or just a shadow. Such distinctions are far too complex to be pre-programmed into any system. They must be *learned.*

Now a neuron in the biological brain functions by generating an electrical pulse called an "action potential" whenever sufficiently stimulated by other neurons. The neurons in our brains are engaged in constant conversation. The *artificial* neurons of an AI work in the same way, not in material detail—the brain uses chemical neurotransmitters, for example, and AI uses tiny pulses of voltage—but functionally.

And yet, despite the similarities, there seems to be a gulf between human intelligence and machine intelligence. In tasks that can be broken down into data, AI shows remarkable intelligence. AI, for instance, can learn to read and evaluate medical scans as well or better than the best physicians. It *teaches itself* by perusing scads of scans—perhaps a million scans in the time a doctor needs to examine one—and recognizing patterns in them that turn out to have diagnostic and even prognostic meaning. So the learning ability, pattern recognition, and predictive aspects of intelligence are highly developed already in AI.

Where human intelligence shows *its* superiority is in the ability to transfer learning that took place in one environment to another, quite different environment immediately, without much further learning being necessary. This might be called "creativity," a combining of elements already at hand into theretofore unimagined configurations. I don't mean the kind of *mechanical* faux creativity in which AI is already way ahead of us humans—the ability, for example, to write a sonata in the style of Chopin or a sonnet à la Shakespeare—but the kind of spontaneous, arriving-as-if-from-nowhere, functioning-outside-the-box kind of creativity, that feels to us humans like "Aha!"

AI is not there yet, nor do we see signs in AI of human emotions such as desire or empathy, and certainly nothing of the self-referential self-awareness that we call human consciousness.

But that does not mean that a system of artificial neurons could *never* be conscious in the way we humans are. Superstition holds that consciousness is a "gift from God." Words like that may be meant literally to claim that humans were lifeless clay until touched by the finger of some zealous deity six thousand years ago. Or less literally—as, for example, in the idea that only Brahman "really" exists, and any intelligence we humans seem to possess originates not in neurons, but as the reflection—a pale reflection—of so-called "universal consciousness," said to be the substrate of all that exists.

I cannot say with epistemological certainty that either of those views is entirely mistaken. In regard to the first, paleontology tells us that there was a time when Earth was entirely barren of organic life, and then, as if from nothing, life arose. So that part could jibe with the "finger of God" idea, if not the six thousand years nonsense that only a brainwashed ninny can believe. I call it nonsense because science can point quite accurately to the point in geologic time when life on Earth began, roughly as many years ago as there are heartbeats in a hundred years: three and a half billion.

But as to the provenance of the original spark of life, no one can explain *that,* so I cannot say with certainty that it *didn't* happen the way the Judeo-Christian Bible claims—assuming that the story of Adam and Eve is taken not literally as religious nuts take it, but more reasonably as myth or metaphor. Nor can I be 100 percent certain that it *didn't* happen the way the Quran of Islam claims, also relying on Adam and Eve, but adding the detail that God disregarded the advice of his angels and Iblis (Satan) when he decided to anoint us human beings as His *khalifah* (vice regents) on Earth. But frankly, to put it mildly, I feel skeptical.

I bring that same dubiosity to Hindu metaphysics. I cannot positively *falsify* those beliefs, but certainly, I see scant evidence for them. And since Vedanta, like the Judeo-Christian-Islamic dogmas, makes big claims, it would need to put forth not just run of the mill *so-called* evidence like ancient texts and personal testimony, but *big* evidence. Without that, we have only the unsubstantiated proclamations of gurus, hocus-pocus logic, and rabbits out of a hat. To be clear, without evidence, all one has is unsubstantiated *belief.*

No one, I say, knows anything about what consciousness "really" is or isn't. In each moment, we experience only what we experience—perceptions, thoughts, and feelings. We may *assume* that those experiences arise and can be split off as the *contents* of an infinite container—so-called "pure consciousness"—that is larger than, separate from, and ontologically distinct from its supposed contents. But that's only dogma. And don't we benighted humans just adore dogma, hierarchies, and splitting off one thing from another!

Since we cannot even know if consciousness *exists* apart from perceptions, feelings, and thoughts, how can we possibly know from whence consciousness derives or whether consciousness is "universal?" Perhaps "Brahman" is just one fantasy, one thought, among countless others.

I am not saying that science can do any better in explaining consciousness, or the origins of life either. Darwin's theory of evolution through natural selection is brilliantly factual as to how all species of life derive from one original living antecedent, but it tells us no more about the ultimate *origin* of life—how the original antecedent came to be—than religion and spirituality do, which is nothing. Zero. Zilch.

Nevertheless, in regards to what occurred once the boiling hot Earth cooled down into a watery world rife with life, Darwin kicks religion's ass all over the lot. Evolution by natural selection is tantamount to fact. Its deniers are all, without exception, numbskulls. We *know,* as well as we can know anything about our world, that the variety of life we see today developed into its present complexity beginning with simple one-celled animals, our ancestors.

Were those earliest living beings *conscious*? Probably, if consciousness means possessed of any awareness at all. Bacteria, being only one cell and so tiny that you'd find a billion of them in a teaspoon of garden soil (another magnitude impossible to conceive, this time of smallness), have no nervous systems and certainly no brains. And yet, via chemical messaging, many species can sense how many other bacteria of their own kind are in the neighborhood—an ability known as "quorum sensing"—and will move away if more are concentrated there than the environment can support. But are those bacteria *self*-conscious? That is hard to imagine.

So apparently consciousness has *evolved,* beginning from the most rudimentary sensitivity to chemical stimuli, into the myriad varieties of animal intelligence that we observe today, including the self-referential self-consciousness of humanity.

Many religious people reject that idea out of hand. Although there are no good arguments at all against the theory of evolution by natural selection *including* the evolution of intelligence, they justify their belief in God, Brahman, or whatever the supposed "substrate" of being is called, by propounding *false* arguments. For example, a favorite assertion of such people claims that faculties such as eyesight could never have evolved, since the human eye, they say, with its ability to focus, is "irreducibly complex." But those who are not wedded to dogma will understand easily how such evolution could have occurred.

The eyesight we now enjoy might have begun with an early ancestor being born, due to the common occurrence of genetic mutation, with a spot on its skin just slightly sensitive to sunlight. In the search for nutrition and thus survival, a new ability, however weak or crude, to sense light and move towards it or away from it if necessary would provide an advantage. Traits that aid in surviving long enough to reproduce, will be passed on to offspring, while those individuals without such traits find themselves at a disadvantage in surviving long enough to reproduce. That is natural selection. So the scions of that ancestor, carrying the new trait of rudimentary photosensitivity, would be advantaged in their competition for nutrition and reproduction. Eventually, the old version of the species—the one without any sensitivity to light—would die out, and thereafter all individuals of that species would carry the new survival advantage.

But naturally, individual members of that species would differ in their sensitivity to light. This is natural genetic variation such as we see in our own species—our intellectual abilities, for example, comprise a spectrum from very dull to very bright, as do physical characteristics such as height, strength, and all the rest. And the individuals towards the end of the spectrum with greater sensitivity to light—the ones with greater *awareness*, that is, of their environment—would tend to reproduce more successfully, thus tilting the balance of development towards more and more photosensitivity. This process might continue until the advent of individuals whose patch of photosensitive skin became acute enough to qualify as a rudimentary eye—and now we are off to the races.

Such natural selection comprises an entirely automatic filtering process in which less effective traits tend to die out, and more useful ones endure. We are—all of us—the progeny of a vast chain of survivors. Billions of years' worth of survivors. The non-survivors *had* no heirs.

It is here where certain religious apologists try to argue that the present-day eye could not have developed along such an axis, but they are fools. Perhaps that absurd six thousand year figure when life supposedly began with Adam and Eve has them bewildered. If one is able to admit the vast stretches of time involved, the process of evolution by natural selection is not hard to fathom.

Evolution does not have to be rapid. Millions of generations might be implicated in the movement from a few photosensitive cells to a creature that could discern faint shadows, thus being able to evade predators, and then millions more until those cells began to specialize further into primitive eyes. If you find yourself balking at accepting the facticity of evolution through mutation and natural selection, ask yourself why? If religion and spirituality are the "why"—if, I mean, you resist the idea that we humans are the evolved offspring of one-celled animals that lived billions of years ago because of some belief about a so-called "God"—you are, I say, hypnotized by dogma. Snap out of it!

There are reasonable hypotheses—educated guesses—about how life might have begun in a lifeless universe. Perhaps lightning strikes in the boiling chemical soup that was Earth's early atmosphere produced the nucleotides that are the constituents of RNA, the vital molecule of early life. This process has been achieved experimentally in laboratories. But still, that is only conjecture. No one *knows* how life began. But we do understand in fairly abundant detail how the earliest forms of life evolved from less complex and capable forms to more complex and capable forms, including us humans. Anyone who denies that is, as I said, hypnotized, mentally deficient, or just plain stubborn.

And right here, precisely on this point, we see the crucial difference between science and religious metaphysics. If one is to be awake and *not* hypnotized, it is imperative to grasp this difference. When the scientific mind makes an educated guess, which is called a "hypothesis," it is understood without a doubt that the guess—the hypothesis—is *only* a guess and not a fact. In science, *facticity* requires overwhelming evidence. No amount of *belief* will suffice. In science, belief is bootless. And in good science, the chief effort is to *falsify* guesses, not to *prove* them. If all efforts to falsify a guess fail, then the hypothesis will be promoted to the status of a *theory*. But a theory is still not considered factual. As more and more attempts to falsify it fail—*and* if the theory is able to predict accurately events in the real world—the theory becomes more "robust," as this is said. If a theory becomes robust enough, then it is taken as tantamount to fact—such as, "The Moon revolves in an orbit around the Earth," or "All species have a common ancestor." In this view, the "theory" of evolution by natural selection is not guesswork, but as factual as the Moon revolving around the Earth.

The religious mind, on the other hand, loves to believe that its guesses are *not* guesses, but *facts.* And here I am not referring only to the Judeo-Christian-Islamic absurdities, but most pointedly to the exhortations of present-day "teachers" of Vedanta who claim, for example, that the brain cannot be the source of consciousness, but is only an object "in" consciousness. If you imagine that a teacher of that view is speaking any "Truth," you are deeply hypnotized, I say. And if the self-described teacher uses logic to prove the point, that would be laughable if not so sad. Logic, unless it is entirely rigorous and exacting, can be used to "prove" anything. The alleged "proofs" in Vedanta are about as negligent and lax as can be imagined. They are shams—full of holes.

You may be feeling that my disdain for religious metaphysics is unfair, or cruel to its teachers and their students, or whatever. You have every right to those feelings. I just say what I see. Please feel free to reject any or all of it. Nevertheless, evolution is a *fact*—as close to a fact as we know—and "universal consciousness," claimed to be unlimited and infinite, is not a fact, but a metaphysical *belief.*

You may like that belief. Perhaps it makes "myself" seem connected to something eternal and "nondual," and that feels warm and fuzzy. Fine by me. To each his or her own. But at least have the courage to admit that you are relying on unverified and unverifiable *beliefs* and personal testimony, not facts.

If we turn our understanding of evolution to the matter of consciousness, it should be easy to grasp how less complex consciousness—such as an early ancestor being *aware* of shadows—can become more complex consciousness. A dog, for example, recognizes the child she loves and distinguishes that child from all other humans. If the child leaves, the dog waits for his return. That is consciousness, is it not?

If you say no, then perhaps, for you, the word *consciousness* means not just awareness (such as the exquisite awareness of their aural environment displayed by my donkeys, whose ears can rotate separately so as to take in two different aural fields simultaneously), but self-referential self-consciousness: "I exist and being me *feels like this*." So on that level of consciousness or awareness—I use those words more or less interchangeably—there is not just existence, but a *phenomenology* of existence. One can discuss what it is *like* to exist. And, if one has a *theory of mind*, as this is called, one may even be able to imagine what it is like for someone else to exist.

Our nearest genetic relatives, the chimpanzees, with whom we share around 99 percent of our DNA, don't talk much. It used to be thought that their anatomy was not speech-ready—otherwise, perhaps they would speak; but that has been debunked. Now we know this is a *brain* thing, due, geneticists say, to their version of just one certain gene—the FOXP2—differing from that of us chatterboxes. But if a chimp *could* speak, would it speak self-referentially, self-consciously, and with the recognition of a theory of mind?

Wow, Robert. You have no idea how tough it is to be a chimp in a world dominated by humans. People are still fucking eating us, for Christ sake, or sticking us in cages and using us as test subjects. Humans supposedly were given dominion over us by their imaginary deity, and we chimps have been in this mess ever since.

I would guess *yes*, that a chimp would speak self-referentially if it could speak, but I don't *know* that. A talking chimp is not a theory, nor even a hypothesis, but only a conjecture. I do *know*, however, that chimps have demonstrated remarkable intelligence, such as the ability to understand words, and to conduct themselves in this world based on reasoning, understanding, foresight, and learning.

Chimps, for example, are one species among a list of animals that intentionally self-medicate. When needing to expel parasites, a chimp will eat nothing but bitter-tasting leaves from a certain kind of bush that, otherwise, it would never use as food. And, in another region where that particular plant does not grow, the chimps will rely on a *different* plant that also has helminthic properties but produced by different chemicals. So this usage of medicinal plants appears to be learned, not innate, behavior. To what extent animal behaviors are instinctual and to what extent learned by observation is unknown, but the scientific consensus seems to be that non-human animals are far more intelligent than most humans—blinded by their speciesist religious twaddle—are willing or able to acknowledge.

I wonder if some of the distance traditionally said to exist between human intelligence and the intelligence of non-human animals is not—partly at least—a failure of humans to know how to evaluate forms of intelligence that are *not* human, but nonetheless exist.

For example, what if the chimpanzees' apparent wisdom in treating themselves with naturally occurring medicine, is a kind of *science* in consonance with the most basic definition of science: a cycle of observing cause and effect, experimenting, learning, discarding, and revising? What if this form of non-human "science" is superior in some ways to the dogmatic medical mythology in which humans seem to become enmeshed?

> *Animals, precisely because of their more limited intellects, might be more doggedly scientific than we are. After all, while animals seem to attend closely to cause and effect, learning from experience, people sometimes indulge a penchant for spinning out grand theories from scant (or no) evidence and then acting on them. Bloodletting, for example, persisted for hundreds of years in Europe even though it almost certainly weakened and killed the sick. It was based on the ancient humoral theory of disease: illness arose when the body's "humors," or essential fluids, were out of harmony, an imbalance corrected by draining blood, among other acts. Other ineffectual and even dangerous treatments include smoking to treat asthma and sexual intercourse with virgins as a cure for syphilis.*
>
> *Animals no doubt blunder in their attempts to self-medicate. But humans seem to be unique in their capacity for clinging to beliefs and theories about the world, even when facing evidence that refutes*

> *them. Consider those religious sects that refuse modern medicine altogether, favoring prayer instead, and whose believers sometimes die as a result. [A chimpanzee] would probably never err in this way, simply because the medicine that chimps practice derives from what they've learned through trial and error, not from untested explanations for how the world works.*
>
> —Moises Velasquez-Manoff, in *The New York Times*

So, here is this *chimp intelligence* that may be engaged in *chimp science*, a science purer than human science since not polluted by dogma, but entirely empirical and 100 percent pragmatic. Now, is this chimp intelligence a "gift from "God?" Is this chimp intelligence a reflection of some overarching, infinite, unlimited, eternal, nondual "Universal Mind?" Or is intelligence neither a bestowal of nor a *reflection* of anything, but an evolved *physical* ability with roots in the survival of the earliest ancestors, culminating so far in certain present-day animals such as humans, chimps, crows, octopuses, dolphins, etcetera?

That is, I say, *an open question*. Except for the knowledge of evolution through natural selection, which is a fairly recent addition to the data, the question about the source of consciousness—assuming that consciousness *has* a source—has been around for thousands of years and remains unanswered. If you think you *know* the answer, how? Upon what epistemology does *your* certainty rest? What are *your* standards for "Truth?"

If one is to notice the "awakeness" that I say is part and parcel of us all, but obscured in most of us by conditioning and clinging to uncorroborated beliefs, the epistemological question is a *crucial* question: what are *your* standards for "Truth?" If your epistemological standards allow that scriptural texts or the assertions of spiritual teachers are a special form of *knowledge*, you are, I say, not awake, but *hypnotized* by custom and tradition. Those texts and assertions are *not* knowledge—not by my epistemological standards—but opinions and conjectures.

Let us suppose that intelligence is *not* a gift from "God," *or* a reflection of "Universal Mind," but has evolved physically just like eyesight, because greater awareness confers advantages in survival and reproduction. There is evidence everywhere for that supposition. We know that cells within early animals had the potential to communicate with one another via electrical pulses and chemical signals. From there, it's just a small step to cells specialized for sending and receiving messages. That's what a brain is—a collection of cells *specialized* for sending and receiving messages connected together so that the whole is more than the sum of its parts.

We *know* that the human brain *evolved* by building upon the architecture of more primitive brains. The limbic cortex in a human brain, for example, is not much different from the same structure in a lizard. Both the lizard and we mammals *inherited* the limbic cortex—which handles basic functions like breathing, balance, and coordination, and survival urges like feeding, mating, and defense—from a common ancestor, fish. The difference between a lizard brain and a mammalian brain is only that the limbic cortex is just about all a lizard has in the brain department; whereas the mammalian brain comprises a far greater size and complexity of neural connections all across the brain, and consequently a spectrum of emotions far beyond, but also *including*, the triplicity of fuck it, fight it, or flee it of a lizard.

This still does not settle the question of the original wellsprings of human intelligence, including the self-referential aspect, possibly shared—I suspect, but do not *know*—by certain other animals. There is always the rather naive claim that the brain is just a receiver of some kind like a radio set, and "God" is the radio station—which, although there is no evidence that I know of, cannot very well be refuted. That's the problem with spiritual beliefs: they are *not* easily refuted. So once they take root, you may be stuck with them far more stickily than you imagine. In fact, I predict that some readers will understand clearly the common sense of my words here, but *still* want to believe in "universal consciousness," whatever *that* means. As I say, you may be stuck more stickily than you know.

Now, as this is a book about finding one's *own* mind, if you remain stuck in that way, you probably won't. We humans, it seems, can have a sane, fact-based understanding of ontology (what does it mean to say that something exists?) and epistemology (what can be known and how can one know it?), or we can wallow in the dubious solace of so-called "faith," but probably not both. When I say "faith," I mean believing what one has been told about existence despite the obvious facts of human intellectual limitation.

Although we do not *know* the origins of human self-awareness, if metaphysical conjecture is set aside so that this matter is viewed not *supernaturally* but *naturalistically*, it seems entirely possible that when a brain reaches a certain level of complexity—a certain plentitude of cross-connected neurons—the capacity for self-awareness *emerges* as a matter of course, as a *natural* outcome.

Emergence means that awareness is not a capacity of any one particular part of the brain, but a synergistic capacity—a capacity that is *more* than the sum of the parts; an ability that arises due to complex interactions *among* the parts. And do recall that the number and complexity of those interactions are on the scale of galaxies. In that view, when enough neurons hook up together, self-awareness comes into being *emergently*—not exogenously as a blessing from a supposed deity, nor as the pale reflection of some Platonic ideal called "universal consciousness," or even more inappropriately, "Love," but as an inevitable concomitant of the inconceivably immense complexity of the neuronal dance.

If self-referential self-awareness is a natural emergent quality of complex systems, then perhaps we will someday converse with an artificial intelligence that *knows* itself to be an AI, can tell us what it is *like* to be an AI, and will say if, like us, it feels awestruck when gazing into the night sky.

10 - What is truth?

Q: Hi, Robert. My question is simple. Many teachers claim to know "Truth," and to be able to bring that Truth to others. Apparently, this has been going on for thousands of years, but you have criticized this as self-deception. So if those spiritual ideas are not Truth, what is? Can we ever know what is true and what is not?

A: That question opens vast panoramas. I will try to be brief. From my perspective, any declarations of absolute truth are doomed to failure. Why? Because, ultimately, at rock bottom, we actually have no idea what anything "really" is, and we have no way of finding out.

In the physical world that we perceive through touch, smell, sound, sight, etcetera, perhaps aided by instruments, the difference between what is true and what is not true often *can* be ascertained. For example, looking into the distance on a hot day, I may see a large body of water—a far-off lake, let's say—but as I try to approach it, the lake disappears. That is because the "lake" was never a lake at all, but a mirage caused by a misinterpretation in mind of sensory data. Such misinterpretations can arise whenever we make assumptions that are not factual.

In the case of a mirage, the faulty assumption is that the refractive index of air—the medium through which light must travel to reach the viewer—is uniform throughout, so that light passes through that air uniformly But that is not the case. When the ground heats up, the air just above it heats up too, and hot air refracts light differently from cold air. So some light from the sky never actually reaches the ground but is bent towards the viewer instead. The viewer does not expect that bending, and so interprets the bent light as if it were a straight-line reflection of an object right at ground level, producing "in awareness" what appears to be a lake.

I put the phrase "in awareness" in scare quotes, because much magical thinking is associated with the word "awareness," and magical thinking gets in the way of seeing things as they are. To me, "awareness" consists of everything seen, felt, thought, and otherwise experienced, without any guarantee that *any* of it is factually true. The word "in" adds another bit of magical thinking to the mix, implying as it does that "awareness" is like a free-standing container just sitting there waiting for something to be poured into it; implying, I mean, that "awareness" is separate from the perceptions, thoughts, and feelings of which one is said to *be* aware. That is an idea I will examine more closely throughout this book.

In *The Republic,* Plato has Socrates describe a cave in which prisoners are chained with their backs to the opening so that all they can see is their own shadows and the shadows of other objects on the wall in front of them. That shadow world, to them, *is* "reality." It is all they know—all of which they are aware. That is what I mean when I say that awareness is no guarantee of truth. We base our entire lives on the data of our senses and have no way of escaping that limitation, even if we understand quite well that our senses may lie, as in the case of a mirage.

I awaken each morning to a world in which I seem to have influence—I can, for example, put the kettle on the stove for morning tea—but that apparent influence is known to me only through data from the senses. I see my hands managing the kettle and lighting the burner. I feel the kettle in my hands. I hear the water boiling. I smell the tea brewing.

And then there is a certain overall sense—a kind of generalized background awareness comprised of numerous sensory data that usually go unnoticed—of which I can become aware, at least partially. It may be, for example, that I am not usually aware of the beating of my heart, but if it loses rhythm, I may notice its disturbed action, which suggests that I had been feeling it all along in the background. In a similar way, my nose is always in my vision (as can be demonstrated by covering one eye), but "tuned out," so to speak. In the variety of awareness called proprioception, there is an ongoing awareness of how my limbs are arranged, which is why I do not have to look down in order to walk forwards. Or I might become aware of a slight headache, or a slightly painful pressure urging me to urinate. For many of us, this ability to sense "myself" leaves little doubt that myself—the person with my name—exists as an entity.

In that view, "Robert" is the one who can put his foot forward without needing to look down (unless, that is, he is walking on the edge of a precipice). But *that* "Robert" is only an assumption based upon sensory data, and, as in the case of the "lake," that assumption could be mistaken.

What if the "Robert" I assume as the center of perception, and the possessor of volition (I *decide* to make tea), is like one of those shadows on the wall of Plato's cave? Suppose I tell you that "Robert" may not actually exist as the center of anything more than self-referential thoughts induced in a brain by inculcation of the beliefs of childhood caregivers and the wider cultural surround? Is that "Truth?"

Or is the slightly different, more religious version "truthier?" In that religious regime, only God (or "Universal Mind" for those averse to naive personification) *really* exists, and "Robert" is nothing more substantial than a pale reflection of that so-called Greater Reality. "Greater than what?" one might ask.

Some people like to avoid that particular philosophical can of worms by sticking to pragmatism: "Truth" is whatever works. So, when I put the kettle on to boil, I do it because I know it's true empirically that a flame will heat water. This works well on the physical level but verges into more questionable territory when people begin to regard as "Truth" whatever makes them feel better.

Don't laugh. That is one of the most common epistemological tests employed by our benighted race. If it makes me *feel* better—which usually means that it helps me cohere psychologically, eases doubts and anxieties, keeps depression at bay, etcetera—then it's *true*. Often this hunger to cohere is disguised by saying that such and such "resonates with me." Such resonance is a sign of emotional *coherence* to be sure, but not, I say, of "Truth"—not in the least.

What does it mean to say that some idea "resonates?" It means that you like hearing it because it fulfills psychological needs by confirming already existing beliefs—the ones which, like the beating of your heart, you *could* notice but usually don't. That's what the new idea resonates *with*—the ideas you already have. You might like to think that the sensation of resonance is a function of intuition—one simply *feels* that the idea is true. From my perspective, that is even a worse test of truth than whether a new idea comports with already existing ideas. At least *ideas* can be critiqued logically—which is not everything, but not nothing either.

For example, a religious believer who survives an accident in which others were killed and attributes her survival to the mercy of God, might be persuaded by logic that her attribution makes no sense. What, after all, of the ones who did not survive? Were they somehow not deserving of mercy? In fact, I have had this discussion with more than one "God" person and was able to make some headway.

But if God's mercy is just my *intuition*—I just feel in my bones that God is all good or that "universal consciousness" is well-intentioned by its very nature—no logic could ever dislodge that belief from my mind, because it was not acquired by logic in the first place. So navigation by means of intuition can lead one far afield indeed. There are no brakes at all on that vehicle. And since we really don't know *what* intuition is or *where* it comes from, why should it qualify as an indicator of "Truth?"

This is not to demean intuition. It has its place. My approach to photography relies on it. But while my photographs may be truly expressive, they are not "Truth."

I wonder if you see the beginnings of the problem. Any idea can be called into doubt, and any can be confirmed, depending on the *epistemology*—the test protocol, explicit or implicit—that one brings to the question. There are numerous aspects to this subject, but I am trying to keep this reply short—otherwise, I'd need to write an entire book about "Truth" and how humans have deluded themselves with that word.

Q: But Robert, doesn't that mean that absolute "Truth" cannot be known, because for that to be known, one would have to have a perfect testing protocol? And you are saying, if I understand you, that no such thing exists.

A: Yes, it is clear to me that the idea of perfect Truth is a religious fantasy that, unfortunately, has infected most of the human race, which continues to pay the price for such foolishness. But my perspective is not merely the kind of postmodernist skepticism that began perhaps with Frederick Nietzsche, and dominates certain popular thought today:

> *Truths are illusions of which we have forgotten that they are illusions, metaphors which have become worn by frequent use and have lost all sensuous vigor . . . Yet we still do not know where the drive to truth comes from, for so far we have only heard about the obligation to be truthful which society imposes in order to exist.*
>
> —"On Truth and Lying in a Non-Moral Sense"

That's good so far as it goes, but tends towards a kind of nihilistic pluralism that holds all truth claims to be equally valid or invalid—you have *your* truth, and I have *mine*—or else a seemingly opposite view that considers truth to be a matter of consensus, the "Fifty million Frenchmen can't be wrong" approach. But is it really the case that all truth claims are equally valid, or that truth is a matter of consensus?

In the physical sense, obviously not. Water either boils when sufficiently warmed, or it doesn't, no matter what anyone says; and "saints" do not produce "sacred ash" or gold rings from thin air no matter how many followers will attest to it. But on a psychological level, such distinctions are not so clear cut. If you think you are a good person, for example, who am I to say you aren't? On what value system do I base my judgment? And if it is just my judgment, just my opinion, what makes it *true*?

As for the idea that the more believers an idea has the "truer" it is, let us consider the plain, entirely testable fact that men have one pair of ribs fewer than women do. I *called* it a "fact," but I lied. It is *not* a fact at all. It is complete nonsense. Both men and women have the same twelve pairs of ribs. Nevertheless, even today, people still believe that canard, which derives from the Biblical fantasy that Eve was created from Adam's rib. Many people nowadays know better, but for centuries, women's extra rib was the consensus view, particularly among Christians who simply assumed that it was true because the Bible said so, and never got around to counting.

I'm about to stick my foot in it here, but why not? Might as well be hung for a sheep as for a lamb, so here goes. Is it really true that a person, having been born with a vagina, not a penis, and whose genotype contains two x chromosomes, who later undergoes gender reassignment surgery, is then a "man?" Who says so? On what is *that* idea based?

Let's leave political correctness out of it. In my view, political correctness really has little or nothing to do with truth, although I do understand that someone might disagree with me entirely on that point, holding political correctness to be the highest form of truth, or at least a necessity in a pluralistic society. And although I am anti-censorship and a lifelong advocate of free speech, it may be that certain aspects of political correctness are a lot more truthful than the kind of "free speech" that has been used over the ages to keep "those people" in their place. These matters are never as self-evident as people like to believe.

To be clear, I am not asking if a transgendered person should be treated as if "they" (I despise that plural for singular locution, but have no substitute to offer) were a man, notwithstanding the genetic facts of the matter. That is another question entirely. In the name of civility and respect, I am willing to call you whatever you ask me to call you, and, if you are a trans man, to stand beside you at the urinals—nothing else makes sense, as I see it. But here I am not discussing social necessities or common decency, but inquiring into the question of whether such a person really is a man *ontologically*—whether a human who was born with female DNA and female sexual equipment, can ever *become* a man in *truth*. As an experiment, try to grapple with that question yourself, and then ask yourself if the purported "truth," advanced by LGTBQ activists, that such a person *is* a man, becomes "truer" if the consensus view "evolves" so as to see it that way.

Can there ever be any "absolute truth" that settles such a

question? I'd say no, and in that, I agree with the French philosopher, Michel Foucault, who advised that we should speak not of a unitary truth that applies across the board, but of *"regimes of truth."* Otherwise, he thought, we might end up latching onto concepts and categories—sexuality and so-called "race" as prime examples—that tend not towards "Truth," but towards inflaming and exacerbating controversies that have little or nothing to do with biological realities, much less metaphysical ones.

In that view, there is a regime of *scientific* truth that is enforced by institutions and other stakeholders; a regime of *spiritual* truth, enforced in the very same way, just by *different* institutions and different stakeholders; a *political* regime likewise enforced by those with skin in the game; an *economic* regime; etcetera.

The idea here is not to decide whether scientific truths are better or more valid than spiritual truths, or vice versa—that is another conversation. Rather it is, first, to understand that a supposed "truth" in one regime may be a falsehood in another, so that finding any absolute, capital T "Truth" seems a far cry; and, second, that controversies about what is true and what is false (for example, the endless, rather foolish debates about "faith" versus atheism) may *seem* on the surface to be about one supposed "truth" versus another, but in fact are much more about which regime, which *epistemology*, which set of rules for determining truth from falsity, should prevail. That is how the struggles among these various separate regimes play out: in struggles over *epistemology*.

One might attempt to bypass all such controversies by defining truth simply as "a statement or a belief that corresponds to the actual state of affairs." So, for example, it is either true or not true that I have a coin in my pocket, and this can be tested. In that view, if I have no coin in my pocket, but claim to have one there, I am either lying or mistaken. The problem here is that many claims cannot be tested like that to see if they correspond to the facts on the ground.

If I like to believe and to teach others that a benign force directs life on Earth, that cannot be tested by comparison to any actual state of affairs. I can observe the actual state of affairs, but observation can never either prove or disprove the bit about the purported benign force. I can *argue* for my belief by pointing, for instance, to the kindness of the maternal instinct, which I may claim is a "reflection of the mind of God;" or I can cast doubt upon the benign force idea, by asking, for instance, how a benign force could allow the horrors we observe everywhere—starving children, rape and murder, endless wars and ethnic strife, abuse of defenseless non-human animals, etcetera—or such supposedly "natural" difficulties like cancers or tornadoes.

Or, if I am an advocate of the scientific regime, I can adduce experimental studies that have tested the efficacy of prayer and found none—found, for example, that prayer makes no difference statistically in health outcomes—so that if there is a benign force, it is moved, apparently, neither by belief in it nor disbelief, nor by entreaties, no matter how sincere.

So, the idea that "goodness" is a basic existential reality can never be shown to be either factually true or factually untrue. That would require an exact definition of "goodness" plus agreement about how that proposition could be tested, which is an *epistemological* debate—and an endless one at that.

For example, a professional spiritual teacher sits on a stage asserting that, if we all knew, as he does, what we "really" are, no child would ever be abused, and no other evils would occur. He is absolutely certain, he says, that brains are not the original source of consciousness, but only "objects *in* consciousness." He is certain too that only "universal consciousness" really exists, and that all evil arises from the false—he says—idea that human beings really exist.

That is an *ontological* claim: God exists, and myself doesn't, or, even if "myself" exists in a certain way, it does not exist on the same absolute ontological level as "The Absolute" or "God," or whatever that so-called oneness is named. That ontology is the primary claim of the branch of Hindu metaphysics called Advaita, which is the source of this teacher's preaching. When someone in the audience questions his assertion about the goodness of oneness—"How do you *know* that?"—the teacher replies that he has determined it, not only by *belief* in Hindu metaphysics, although he has studied that for years with several famous, highly influential teachers, but by "higher reasoning."

Well, that's a buzz kill! How can the cat in the audience, who counts only on *normal* reasoning, continue the conversation after that assertion of special access to hidden knowledge? So, not only is this teacher claiming that he knows about "*The* Truth" (could there not be more than one?) of our essential nature and the absolute nature of reality, but he is claiming too that his epistemology—so-called "higher reasoning"—is the best possible evidence.

This is the regime of the self-described spiritual teachers and gurus. This is *their* epistemology, *their* stakehold, *their* bailiwick, *their* governance. And the people in the audience buy it. They have no access to "higher reasoning" themselves—if they did they would not be sitting there exposing themselves to that repetitious patter. All *they* can do is listen, more or less credulously, to those words from on high about how wonderful and liberating it is to know without a doubt how the universe is really arranged, what is humankind's place in it, and what is our true nature.

To be clear, here I am not calling into question the ideas of Hindu metaphysics. That ontology is, as I said, part of another conversation. At the moment, I am pointing to how such regimes are *enforced*—how the stakeholders grab the epistemological high ground because that's where their *power* is. That may be the power to be paid money for talking or writing books, the egotistical power of being able to influence others, the power of sexual access to young bodies that comes with fame, etcetera.

I am not saying that all spiritual teachers have base motives for their activities. In fact, I have known people who felt good themselves and sincerely desired to share that with others. But we all know how power corrupts and how material necessities can distort good intentions.

Religious metaphysics is a kind of limiting case, since any claim at all can be asserted without any possibility of refutation. But even in science, where refutation of claims *is* possible using ordinary human logic—not the "higher" *jnani*-style variety that to me seems weak at best—the demands of personal success within the regime can distort judgment and overwhelm discernment. I am not speaking here only of scandals in the regime of science, such as the falsifying of data that can garner the same payoffs—money, sex, etcetera—that gurus can grab. However, we are all just human here, I say, and subject to the same kinds of psychological and material pressures, so just as there is corruption in the regime of spirituality, science has its scandals too.

Just recently, a company called Theranos attained a valuation of ten billion dollars—literally a truckload of one-hundred-dollar bills—before their scam fell through. They claimed to have a machine able to diagnose a variety of diseases using only a few drops of blood, but secretly used already existing machines to generate data, and piled more lies on top of that. So there is corruption, cheating, and grifting in all regimes, but it is not corruption of which I speak, but the idea of *truth.*

We are all subject to viewing our world with certainty when there isn't any. In any regime— politics, economics, science, spirituality, ethics, aesthetics, etcetera—there are lay people and experts. The layperson may be clueless and deluded, but no one can be as *deeply* deluded as an expert who suffers from what the French call *déformation professionnelle.* This is a kind of cognitive bias—a distortion of perception and interpretation—stemming from being too caught up in one's training and expertise.

When wrapped up in the robes of one's supposedly maximum competence, one may imagine abilities that do not in fact exist. Or, one may overestimate the scope of one's own regime, and so miss the big picture of this aliveness, which is not just one thing or another nesting neatly in one regime or another, but which is everything we know or ever *can* know. Thus, what may be a *kind* of truth in one regime or another can, in the mind of the expert, be inflated into a universal truth—*the* "Universal Truth."

> *Every specialist, owing to a well-known professional bias, believes that he understands the entire human being, while in reality he only grasps a tiny part of him.*
>
> —Nobel Laureate Alexis Carrel in *Man, The Unknown*

In science, this *déformation professionnelle* may take the form of excluding from consideration anything that cannot be examined with the scientific method. But I am not saying that I *limit* myself to the scientific method or the scientific regime. I am speaking from the standpoint of a skepticism that accepts truth claims only on good evidence—a skepticism that will never accept claims just because they are the consensus, or because they derive from ancient, highly respected or supposedly authoritative sources, or because believing them would make me feel better.

I am completely willing to *entertain* ideas like that—ideas that cannot be tested—but I would never call them "Truth."

11 - Myth taken as fact bewilders

Q: I don't know if you remember me, Robert, but I followed your posts a lot several years back. Then I needed a nice long break from everything that felt like a "teacher." But you did inspire me greatly. So I started looking at your posts again a few months back and what you are saying feels really relatable to me.

Some rather drastic changes have happened in the last few years and it can feel lonely at times, as I don't have anyone to talk to about this stuff besides my husband.

I'm seeing through a lot of things. I can no longer find any permanent "myself." I can't even find a "myself" at all anymore. But that feels really natural and not scary at all. In fact, it feels like a great relief. I can't really find any free will either, which is also OK.

I feel a deep sense of freedom. I gave up all my spiritual beliefs and the comforts that can come with them. I feel very little certainty about anything anymore. In fact, feeling certain about philosophical matters feels painful and boring. If there is anything I feel certain about it's this unmistakable sense of just being. This sense of pure aliveness. It's no longer about someone else's words but my own experience. At times it's really calming and at other times I feel like dancing from all the joy. I don't suffer the way that I used to, either. Rarely do I get caught up in serious stories. I still suffer at times. But to me, that's just life.

I don't usually talk about all of this much publicly as I fear I may come across as "crazy." But I felt like sharing with you because, as I said, it can feel lonely. Thank you for your time. Hoping you are well.

A: That is a lovely message. Thank you for it. I am glad if something I said inspired you to move towards finding the ground of your own being instead of remaining hung up in the foolishness forced upon us humans by superstitious religions and know-it-all spirituality.

In my view, it is not any lack of spirituality that keeps us divided against ourselves, constantly searching for some condition we fantasize will be better than the present moment, but quite the opposite. It is the *over-abundance* of religion and spirituality, foolish deference to authority, and a credulous immersion in magical thinking that keeps us humans enslaved to superstition. This goes not just for Christianity, Islam, and Judaism, but for Vedanta and Buddhism as well. There may be traces of wisdom in all those traditions, but most of what they offer is not wisdom at all, but superstition. Blessed is he or she who can tell the difference.

Some try to exclude Buddhism from that list by asserting that it is not a religion, but as long as Siddhartha Gotama is held up as an infallible, omniscient font of "truth," I am not buying that argument, and I'm tired of hearing it. *Omniscience* is an imagined power of a supposed god, not a human attribute at all. And to imagine that one particular human being from 2,500 years ago knew things then that no one can know today and that nobody will be able to know until the "next Buddha" arrives in the fantasized far away future, seems to me as inane as imagining that Jesus was a divine avatar born of a virgin woman.

Myth taken as myth informs, but myth taken as fact bewilders. Thus one can be deeply bewildered while imagining oneself to be following the correct or true path, and even further bewildered if the path seems to be leading somewhere important. There is fear behind that dogged literalism, I suspect, not wisdom.

No path exists, I say, but the one you blaze yourself, and that can occur only when you are able to live without certainty about ultimate matters. We are all human here. Except in myth, no gods walk this Earth.

As for loneliness, that is the human condition. No one, no matter how close to you, and how determined the efforts such a person might make, will ever fully know your mind; and no matter how you try, you can never fully show it.

In the face of that, kindness to all and compassion for self and other is the best, I say, we human beings can do.

12 - Compassion and self-compassion

Q: I think I have asked this before in different ways, Robert, but I seem to stumble upon the same point, so please indulge me again.

From the point of view of presence, or whatever word you use, how do we deal with emotional suffering such as meaninglessness, powerlessness, and fear of the future? And what is the difference between just *being* with the suffering in the present, and trying to fight back with other emotions—which you would probably say is just a way of distraction from the suffering? I refer not only to my own suffering, but even more to the suffering I see in others. How to help someone? How to help someone to do something about it, to find the right course of action, to come out of that emotional suffering?

A: Well, that's just the point. If you see another's plight and that feels painful, that pain is *your* pain. What you *feel* is *not* a choice. In each moment, things are as they are and cannot be different, including what one feels. However, a feeling lasts but for an instant. You may imagine persistent feelings, but that is an illusion created by connecting the dots, moment by moment, to make what appears to be a fixed picture. If you observe more carefully, you may notice that the picture is *not* fixed, but always changing.

I am speaking here not about the findings of physics and cosmology which investigate various hypotheses of time, space, and causality. Nor am I speaking of Vedanta and other traditional metaphysics that treat conceptions such as "the deathless state" or "oneness" as if they were not just conjectures in changeful human minds, but ontological certainties. Here I am speaking *psychologically*—from the point of view that regards thoughts and feelings as non-stable, ephemeral *phenomena*.

From that angle, nothing is fixed and nothing is certain. There is only this apparent *flow*, like lava pouring from a volcano with no end in sight to the eruption. Any number of conceptual schemas may be overlaid upon this phenomenal flow, but, notwithstanding the claims of experts, none of those schemas is "Truth."

In the non-conceptual phenomenology of this aliveness—which includes perceptions, thoughts, and feelings—there *are* no ultimate explanations. The particular, singular suchness of *this* moment manifests prior to both scientific rationales and the silly certainties of religion. The most *primary* truth, I say, is the personal phenomenology—the living actuality—of one's *own* mind, which in purest form is wordless and far more trenchant than any *idea* about it could ever be.

If explanations are discarded entirely, and concepts about ultimate matters are seen as will-o'-the-wisp notions, not *facts*, then the fleetingness and flow of perceptions, thoughts, and feelings are obvious. This is freefall. There is nothing to hold on to. One sees truly that we are here for our brief moment, we do our little dance, and then we pass away again.

With this always in mind, uncomfortable thoughts and feelings do not dominate *be*-ing, which is prior to thoughts and feelings. In each moment of *be*-ing, I think what I think and feel what I feel, knowing that "myself" is not the author of thoughts and feelings, but more like the noticer of them, the recognizer of them. In each instant, if real-world effort seems required, compassionate or otherwise, and if I am capable of exerting that effort, then I find myself exerting it.

I could equally say, in passive voice, that when situations arise that seem to require effortful responses, and if there is the wherewithal for such effort, then the effort is exerted. That takes the "I" out of it, which is closer to my usual perspective. So that is full *participation* while knowing that *this too shall pass*—that everything passes and nothing remains.

As Chögyam Trungpa put this, "The bad news is that you have fallen out of the airplane and have no parachute… but the good news is that there is no ground."

That is what I mean by "freefall." Thoughts and feelings will not kill you, nor will they save you. In freefall, there is, as my friend Joan Tollifson likes to say, "nothing to grasp."

We humans are a greedy lot. We are hard to satisfy. When events seem gratifying, we wish the moment would never pass, and we may feel anxious or sad at the knowledge that it will. On the other hand, when we are in pain, either physical or psychological, then we can barely wait for that condition to change into something different.

Noticing that human tendency, if we are able to regard what we like as equal to what we dislike—not equal in terms of desirability or satisfaction, but as identical in impermanence; if we see *all* conditions as fugacious, transient, and mortal, then we will be seeing things more as they are instead of how we want them to be.

Q: But what about compassion for others? I feel that it is easier to deal with my own problems and my own pain. In that sphere, I feel somewhat equipped. But when I see someone around me who is suffering... while of course in the end it's me who feels bad about it because those are my own emotions... *[long, long pause]*

A: Compassion may *feel* good and yet be entirely misguided. Compassion is one of those buzz words, you know. Nobody wants to lack *compassion*. But compassion without wisdom can do more harm than good.

Suppose you come upon an accident victim lying in the highway. Hearing her cries of pain, you might want to pick her up and drive her to the hospital. That might *feel* compassionate, but would be all wrong. The correct action—the only *proper* action—is to leave her lying there and call for the experts who know how to move severely injured people.

You can go through this world caring about other people's feelings and all that, and trying to do good. And your involvement might be helpful to a certain person at a certain time but unhelpful or even damaging to another person at another time. And knowing the difference is not always easy.

You hit on something vital in saying that when you react to the suffering of others, "It's me who feels bad about it because those are my own emotions." Yes. That is a key point.

And if your way of dealing with those emotions—which are *your* emotions—involves being "helpful," perhaps by advising the other person what she needs or should do next, that approach may do more harm than good, creating confusion in your mind as well as in the mind of the person you aim to help. The role of rescuer is fraught. It's a lonely, often confusing place.

Whatever you feel right now is yours alone. It doesn't belong to anyone else. You are the one who *knows* the fullness of those feelings—their intricacies and imponderables. *You* are the only witness. No one else feels what you feel. You can *talk* about what you feel, or dance it, or paint it, or sing it, or play it on your guitar, but *your* emotional depths cannot be *known* by anyone *but* you. In that, each of us is totally alone.

So compassion must begin with *self*-compassion. I mean regarding *yourself,* in your pain, your anxiety, your woundedness, and your ultimate aloneness, with love and non-judgmental acceptance. Then, if you feel moved to intervene in the woundedness of another human being, you may be able to intervene with wisdom.

13 - Childhood conditioning

Q: Robert, I don't understand why you discourage meditation. All the great teachers advised meditation. Even the Buddha advised meditation. Have you ever meditated? If you have, did it help you to awaken?

A: Thanks for your question. It is a deep one, about which an entire book could be written. In fact, I have written such a book: *The Ten Thousand Things*. I suggest that anyone with an interest in these matters read it.

If, by meditation, you mean sitting in a certain posture and all that, yes, I have "meditated," but only long enough to get the point—which is that there is no escape from "myself." Whether you sit there consciously "practicing meditation," or you sweat in your garden pulling weeds, "you" are still there. It is important to see that. And if sitting on a cushion in an ashram allows you to see that entirely obvious fact, when you would have missed seeing it if you'd spent that time working in your garden, beautiful! In that case, the ashram by all means. So I don't "discourage" meditation. I only discourage imagining that sitting in a certain way with certain intentions is a magical key to "awakening." It isn't. Not in the least degree.

In the last few days, a couple of people have taken shots at what I am sharing here, both of whom, in different ways, tried to argue that any one way of seeing the world—theirs, for example—is as good as any other—mine, in this case. That, in my view, is bootless. They may be right in an "ultimate" sense, but remaining on that level is only taking cover in cleverness—the kind of cleverness that convinces itself that hatred is as good as compassion, or that suffering does not "really" exist. Holing up in that view—which I call nihilism—is a sure way to remain hypnotized by one's own logical cunning, and so never awakening in the way that I mean that word. Awake, I say, is when you take refuge in nothing at all.

Yes, in some "ultimate" sense, the pain one sees in this world may be illusory, and so the compassion that shares that pain and moves to meet it may be illusory as well. But if pain is illusory, and compassion is illusory, so is everything else—one's body, one's friends, one's interests—including making clever remarks on Facebook—and even being born and dying. The long view may be useful to an extent, but if an idea wipes out the entire experience of living and dying, it is the idea that is illusory, not the living and dying.

If philosophical combat is how someone wants to kill time, OK by me. I'm just not there. I am not just killing time here. I regard these conversations as earnest self-expression and will spend my precious time in that spirit, not in debate and idle speculation.

If you want to be clever and cunning, there are better places for it—places where other "brilliant minds" will get in the game with you. I won't. I am not interested in discussing abstract philosophical matters. I find those conversations fruitless, and only a diversion from the intention here, which is to concentrate on the simplicity of the actual human experience of living and dying.

So the point of meditation is to see beyond escapism—to understand that "myself," just as I am right now, is really *here* in the ashram, in the vegetable garden, or anywhere else, and that trying to escape will not avail.

So, suppose you stop trying to escape. Suppose you say to yourself: "I am really here. Yes, in some ultimate sense that may be an illusion, but saying that, no matter how cleverly, does not make 'myself' go away. I still wake up every morning having to deal with sadness, loneliness, boredom, unfulfilled desires, fear, grief, and all the rest. So, now what? How do I deal with this pain, my pain, and the pain I see everywhere around me? Is there no happiness, no beauty, no relief? Will I never find that space within me that is free, that is filled with peace and love?"

At the risk of being called a Buddhist (I am not—there are wisdom and foolishness to be found in all traditions, and in no tradition as well), and with the proviso that no one knows what the Buddha really said, or even if such a person ever existed historically in the way that

Buddhists take for granted, I will quote the Buddha on this question:

> *Within your own mind, you already have what you need to succeed: the ability to put others ahead of yourself. This is called the wish-fulfilling gem.*

Q2: Hi, Robert. In relation to your quote about the wish-fulfilling gem, what about those who profess to be putting others ahead as based on being driven by some religious/spiritual background? Is this ability to put others ahead of themselves still the wish-fulfilling gem, even if they do so in the belief that they are doing the Lord's work?

Growing up, I had a fundamentalist father who has been going to AA at least five times a week for 50-plus years, and would still defend the Bible and God with all his might if he was ever cornered. For the last fifteen years my younger brother (who has struggled with psychosis) has been going with him and is also a full-fledged member of NA and AA. Also, my mother believes in Jesus and, like Dad, has had some kind of intense early religious conversion experience. Dad had his conversion experience in prison in his early twenties with the help of a chaplain (he's in his mid-seventies now) and both are dead-set believers. Mum's a little more Zen, but Jesus has always been first for her, an extremely personal, unbreakable bond. They both get their strength from their unwavering belief, and this seems to have given them an ability to look after my brother and others "in need."

As for myself, having chiseled away my implanted beliefs and cleared the ground, I don't come from that place. So, in a way, there is a strange distance between us. I tried zazen meditation for a short while some time ago, but these days, since reading *4T*, I enjoy seeing the flow of what arises whilst attention is on the chest area, as recommended in your book. Or a nice cigarette or three chilling in the back garden. Just being quiet, ordinary, speaking sparingly most of the time. And *4T* put a lot of this into perspective for me.

For example, from childhood, I witnessed the subtle manipulations of a narcissistic, psychopathic and extremely charismatic preacher maintain the co-dependency of his "flock" by addressing some of the men of his congregation by their first name, and those "more important" men with the title of "Mr."

A seemingly simple act like this was utilized in full view to psychologically demoralize, and create loyalty and henchmen to do his bidding. With the cultivation of that loyalty/co-dependency, he was able to separate husbands and wives, and the unmarried, partaking himself in some of the separated female company. Demoralize and control. Divide and conquer. He had a myriad of methods for fertilizing and maintaining co-dependency, ensuring indoctrination of the next generation of offspring into "the fellowship" through various means, but always maintaining the hierarchy, with himself as sheepherder and mouthpiece for an imaginary god.

Other less subtle, more heinous examples of developing and maintaining co-dependency, maintaining the loyalty of the seeker and deepening of guru worship in this Alpine country fellowship called "Christ's Place of Restoration," were as follows:

Secret prayer closets behind the main stage for casting out demons during his sermons. His co-dependent minions would be standing on the sidelines waiting for those handpicked or coerced sinners to be taken backstage and prayed over in one of eight padded rooms. Muffled screams would emerge, unleashed by the co-dependent seekers. Children, witnessing the fear-charged atmosphere of their parents' connection with the psychopathic pastor, would tremble in fear themselves, either hoping not to be called to the stage for any reason or fearing forcible indoctrination of the belief that they were special children of God.

Men were made to dig their own graves, with the pastor performing mock death burials to further cement loyalty to him and prepare fearfully for a fictitious Heaven... There was circumcision of some adult men as per biblical instruction... Four- to six-hour sermons were given in a 400-seat Tabernacle Tent, sitting on wooden benches in the middle of a snowy winter, no heating, listening to the rantings of a psychopath and trying not to piss in your pants from holding it in.

And, of course, this mentally unwell, money-grabbing pastor was married to a long-suffering wife, and always had plenty of the congregation's females on stage and off stage, and close by him. Later he was found to have had a child or two with the much younger ones.

A: When they were handing out families, they gave you a doozy. Having started from there, you seem to be doing just great. Congrats.

The quote from Gotama does not speak about professing to put others ahead of oneself. Anyone can profess anything. And the quote is not about some deity watching and judging to see if you really do put others ahead of yourself or not, and who will reward you if you do and punish you if you don't. The wish-fulfilling gem is about what you feel in your heart and how those feelings materialize in action. Since the question was about meditation, the point of the quote is this:

If you wish for inner peace, you can meditate from now until the cows come home, but if that action is based on the self-centered idea of personal "enlightenment," and an end to *your* pain and suffering, such meditation will only deepen the hypnotic trance of separation and self-importance. But in any moment in which you find yourself acting with true concern for another, your desires for peace of mind are granted effortlessly. That's why Gotama called it the wish-fulfilling gem.

Q2: Thanks, Robert. It has been an interesting family to navigate in, and, in many ways, I continue to do so with a vigilance that has grown through the years as I questioned and chiseled away on my own at what has been put in there.

I soaked in so much around me from a young age, yet my awareness and curiosity have been of a very keen quality throughout. Dad has been so one-tracked and hard-headed through the years, particularly with the cult of AA and his savior mentality. I'm definitely not fond of AA and its addictive grip on people's minds. Every now and again I throw a subtle curveball in my young brother's direction, just to give him a sense that NA and AA can hypnotize, and remind him not to fall into mimicking Dad. It's the quiet rascal in me. Such actions on my part certainly don't win me favors with the folks.

I'm not looking to change my parents but, at the same time, I know the reality of acculturation and the trancelike grip that beliefs have had on me. It's been painful at times, but I suppose finding your own mind may or may not be a bit like one imagines. As U.G. Krishnamurti said, "When it comes to touching reality, I'm not surprised either way."

Jiddu Krishnamurti talked about the difference between being lonely and being alone, and the sweetness of aloneness is where I am at. I appreciate your very kind response to my comment. It is very nice to be in the company of someone such as yourself, on your unique page, who understands the many years of quiet and honest inquiring that I have worked through. I know my family have been observing all my explorations through the years, and my relentless willingness to break hypnotic barriers. "Freedom from the known," and "freedom from enlightenment," I wanted to discover for myself, to see if it was possible. It certainly made a few waves in the family and those around me.

I like how you worded your last paragraph where you said, "But in the moment that you find yourself acting with true concern for another..." There is no force in that statement, no coercion to do so based on the background of moral programming. An action that is free from the known. I think of the actions I have taken in situations with my family, and on many occasions how it has not jibed with their strong beliefs; but a lot of my actions came out of true concern in the face of finding my own mind. Choiceless awareness can do that. Once again, Robert, *muchas gracias*.

A: I am so happy to hear this. Thank you for sharing your experience. Finding your own mind is never easy. The incentives are mostly in the wrong direction, and self-honesty can be quite painful. So again, congrats.

Q3: Maybe in a sense what you say is true, but unless you can go to the garden and pull the weeds, only then will the flowers bloom. Meditation tells you how many weeds cloud the original Unconditioned

Awareness. This requires being still for a while and seeing how much out of control your mind actually is. I am afraid that not doing meditation without understanding the essential nature of the mind, will lead one into another trap.

A: As I said in the original post, I am not discouraging meditation. I am pointing out that meditation is not some magic dust that you just sprinkle on an ordinary human to produce an "awakened" human. It doesn't work like that.

If you want someone to tell you that meditation is a magic road to awakening and that everyone ought to meditate constantly, you can find what you are looking for on any shelf in the spiritual supermarket. It comes in all flavors.

My remarks on this page do not pertain to those just dipping a toe into spiritual path-following. Nothing wrong with trying something on to see if it fits. I speak to those readers who have already experimented with meditation, and perhaps other forms of spiritual seeking, but still feel that something is lacking. In this moment, from my perspective, nothing is lacking. So if you feel that something is lacking, and you imagine that meditation is going to fix that, I am pointing out what I regard as the error in that view.

In your case, I would advise this: instead of speaking in generalities, speak about yourself. Are the flowers blooming in your garden or not? If they are not, and you think that meditation is essential to make them bloom, then by all means meditate. But before you sit down again on the magic cushion, you might consider first pulling up the weed that you are calling "the original Unconditioned Awareness." That is a second-hand belief that grew from a seed someone else planted in your mind. You know nothing about Unconditioned Awareness. *Nothing.* If you did, you would not be talking this way. Show me some "unconditioned awareness" if you have any. The idea of controlling a mind that is "out of control" is about as conditioned as it gets.

And I should point out that certain flowers—wildflowers—bloom in many places without anyone weeding anything. Maybe you could think of me as a wildflower, one with a few thorns. Ha, ha.

Q3: I don't think I could have awakened without meditation, and the big mistake I made was thinking that awakening would automatically remove the underlying vasanas[8]. Eradicating the vasanas takes time, and the ego loves not having to do anything. Getting something for nothing is one of the biggest human delusions. And as one of my teachers is fond of saying: "There is no path, but only for those who have completed it."

A: I put it slightly differently in *4T*:

> *The only path is the one you blaze for yourself, and that is seen only in retrospect.*

Q3: True. That I agree with completely. Mr. Krishnamurti would agree also with that statement.

A: Aha. At last! The sun comes up and illuminates the landscape. Jiddu was not a fan of teachers either, including teachers of so-called meditation, as you probably know. In fact, when asked about spirituality and the teachers of it, he often advised something akin to what I am saying here: ignore them and "Be a light unto yourself," as he put it.

I understand how frightening that idea is to many of us. It can feel daunting to live and die without being able to resort to experts on how to go about that, or what it all means—a bit like taking Mommy and Daddy away from a child and leaving the child to fend for itself. Nonetheless, that's really the way it is.

Q4: Nothing to do? No practice? No meditation? Really?

A: Is that really what you got from my words? I'd say my mention of the wish-fulfilling gem points at a kind of practice. Or is the only "practice" you know to sit like a stone so that *you* can become "enlightened?" Snap out of it, boy!

---

8. *Vasana*: a behavioural tendency or karmic imprint which influences the present behaviour of a person.

Q5: Seeing you interviewed on *Buddha at the Gas Pump*[9] was a real eye-opener for me. You said some things that helped me to allow my intentions to arise without the usual judgment. However, when you said, "Most people are fools," that remark really hurt me. I'd say most people aren't fools but are hypnotized, and we have accepted misinformation. I am happy that you have accepted me on your Facebook page as I love what you are trying to convey.

A: Hi. Thank you. I am sorry you were hurt by my saying that "most people are fools." I understand how that could seem harsh and demeaning. Perhaps it would have been better to have said, "Some people are fools, and the many others who seem a lot *like* fools, are really only hypnotized."

And, of course, I was not referring to you personally, since I know nothing at all about your beliefs and intellect. However, the majority of humans are fools, from my perspective, who not only believe in all manner of nonsense but intend to go on believing it no matter what. There is no point in discussing these matters with such people. You'd only be wasting your breath. As Yogi Berra once said—or maybe it was Dizzy Dean—about arguing with a baseball umpire, "Might as well try to argue with a stump."

This point of view that sees an irredeemable foolishness in many humans, elitist as it may seem, is not at all unique to me. In fact, it is shared by many if not most intelligent humans, and always has been since the beginnings of history. We have this which was written on a tablet 3,300 years ago:

> *True wisdom is less presuming than folly. The wise man doubteth often, and changeth his mind; the fool is obstinate, and doubteth not; he knoweth all things but his own ignorance.*
>
> —Amenhotep IV (Egyptian Pharaoh, died 1336 BC)

Now, in a certain way we are *all* fools; we are, after all, all human. But that does not mean we are all equal in our foolishness.

9. See https://BATGAP.com/robert-saltzman/

It may be painful for you to hear someone like me who seems to be loving and compassionate also express ideas that sound elitist, but, if I speak honestly, I can't help it. That's really the way this world of men and women looks to me: an occasional person of wisdom standing out like a brilliant, amazing flower among the weeds of ignorance and stupidity.

Who, after all, do you think is buying all that garbage they sell on TV: the plastic food, the poisonous medicine, the hypnotic politics? Who are those 40,000 people paying to sit in a baseball stadium listening to the short con of Pastor Joel ("Send money") Osteen? Who are the nincompoops buying photographs of Mooji's feet in the gift shop? It ain't me, babe.

Q6: I just started reading *4T*, and your words are confirming and underscoring many things that have crept up on me over the last few years. It's nice to know I'm crazy in a sane way. Thanks for the confirmation.

A: Perhaps by the time you have finished *4T* you will know that you are sane in a crazy way. Ha, ha.

Q7: If my "spiritual" friends were to ask me, the ones I've shared a "path" with—well, I'm not so sure I could be so direct with them. I tried that once. She cried. So, mainly I keep it to myself and a very few others.

A: It's best not to lecture. I am not proselytizing here but responding honestly to questions. If someone asks you a question, be honest if you can. But unless directly asked, kindness trumps "teaching" every time. Or, to look at this from another angle, don't kick out anyone's crutches unless you are requested explicitly to do so.

Q8: Well put. Yep, that's been my approach. I especially like the crutches analogy. Looking back, I can see where there were a few who urged me to let go of mine. I was too sure of myself and of what I thought I "knew," so I just kept on amassing that good old spiritual knowledge. At some point, it was like I was standing on a precipice where behind me was all my acquired knowledge and before me was the great unknown. It dawned upon me I was using all that learned knowledge as a safety net, protecting me from falling into that great unknown. I got tired of fooling myself. I can't tell if I let go, or if letting go happened and I had no volition about it. No matter. Years ago, a friend I trust said: "Be careful you don't become a spiritual teacher." I found that odd at the time because I thought he was something of one. Now I know better. At least, I think I do. "Kindness trumps teaching" is my motto for today. Thanks.

A: Yes. A good motto for any day. Kindness is the flowering of understanding.

Q9: Robert, you seem to speak mostly to people who have gone down the philosophical path and have come up empty-handed, challenging them to put down the concepts that have failed them. For those who are still clutching at concepts, your words, such as "fool," will be met with resistance and I can understand why. Some teachers try to meet someone where they are and gradually break down barriers. Others slap them in the face. You can be harsh, but I can tell it's from love. Grateful here!

A: That's right. Thanks.

My work here is not aimed at newbies. They have other fish to fry, and some of those fish may be exactly the ones I debunk here. There is a time for everything, even foolishness. The time for "Robert" is when you are coming to the end of doctrinal religion and marketplace "spirituality." You have seen some of your conditioning, and suspect that so-called "spiritual paths" may not be so much a way out of that conditioning as a subtle way of defending and continuing it—a way of fortifying the sense of "myself the doer, the practitioner, the accomplisher, the obtainer." You have had enough of teachers. And as far as slapping people in the face, sure, I will resort to that if necessary, but only if you ask for it. Ha, ha.

Q10: Robert, when you say, "so-called 'spiritual paths' may not be so much a way out of that conditioning as a subtle way of defending and continuing it," I am intrigued by that idea. Would you give an example, please?

A: Sure. Suppose you were born in Oklahoma and raised a Southern Baptist, completely certain that "God" watches everything you do and say, and will reward you in Heaven if you are "saved," but that you will go to Hell and burn forever if you are not. The existence of Hell and the idea of burning there if you mess up, to you, seems completely factual and frightens you terribly. You feel absolutely certain that Jesus is the only way to avoid Hell, and so, driven by fear, you take Jesus as your "personal savior"—the one who will "save" you from hellfire as long as you "love" him sufficiently. You were taught, and completely believe, that all other religions are false and their followers will be in Hell the moment they stop breathing.

Now, as an adult, you begin to have doubts. You begin to investigate other philosophies, other world-views, other religions. You come upon the work of, for example, Marianne Williamson—maybe you saw her on Oprah's TV show—and somehow her words appeal to you. She's gentle and nice-looking, the polar opposite of the fire and brimstone preacher of your childhood. You like it when she says, "Love is what we are born with. Fear is what we learn. The spiritual journey is the unlearning of fear and prejudices and the acceptance of love back in our hearts."

That seems so much better than the scary sermons of your childhood, so you begin to follow Marianne; and many of the things she says are lovely and make sense. You find yourself allowing her to guide you along the path she has set out, which does involve seeing through some conditioning. The fear of Hell you learned as a child—the fear that you are inadequate and sinful by nature—she may encourage you to "unlearn." And it never even occurs to you that the entire basis for her teaching—which comes straight out of *A Course in Miracles*[10]—is that you are a "child of God."

10. See Chapter 79, "A Course in Miracles."

So that part of your conditioning—the "God" part—is never examined. On the contrary, *she helps you to defend it from questioning* by reiterating it as an indubitable truth, on no more evidence than that offered by the fire and brimstone idiot who messed with your innocent, naive, trusting child's mind in the first place.

Are you "a child of God?" What is the meaning of that? Am I really a "child" and always will be, or is there a time of authentic adulthood when imaginary Daddies or Mommies are *not* part of the picture, and I must face this existential aloneness on my own steam only?

If you are really interested in investigating your conditioning, a prime question would be, "I was raised to fear God and love Jesus [good cop, bad cop routine], but what if there is no God? Then what am I?" But you never get that far. On the new "path," God is just *assumed*. It was put in your mind by the Baptists and now is being reinforced by Marianne, who is lost in her own rather bizarre career as a motivational speaker, counselor to the Kardashians and other celebrities—and now, as I write this, as a totally unqualified Presidential candidate. And that is comfortable—so much more comfortable than a real existential exploration into the nature of "myself."

Ex-Christians are often unreasonably attracted to Vedanta for the same reason. You get to keep the God idea of your childhood conditioning, but just call it something else like "universal consciousness," which is a popular trope that may refer to nothing at all but a concept invented by humans. Is consciousness really "infinite, universal, and unlimited," or is consciousness an emergent property of brains? That is an open question to people who are not indoctrinated, but a settled one to teachers like Rupert Spira, and others like him who spout that dogma right out of the *Bhagavad Gita* as if it were automatically factual because they say it is.

Q9: Thanks Robert, I admit slight disappointment when I got to the end of *4T*. I mean, I wanted a tidbit to take away, and you left me high and dry. All the countless tidbits and glimpses have faded so it's time to face the music. Thanks for the push!

A: You are most welcome ("Thanks for nothing, Robert." Ha, ha.). A friend of mine gave the manuscript of *4T* to a big wheel in the publishing biz with a view towards seeing if she would get behind it. When my friend asked her what she thought, she replied, "Oh, I really liked it. The writing is great. But when I got to the end, I said to myself, 'Yes, but what does one do?'"

Q9: Yes. Seven steps would have been nice, or ten, or twelve. Something.

A: The interesting thing is that I keep hearing from people who read the book, looking, as usual, for answers, and who found that, instead of adding to their pile of answers from sages, they were left without any questions. Each time I hear that from someone, I feel like saying, "Yes!" with a fist-pump.

Q9: Yes, I know how they feel. There are no steps to take.

A: Right. No steps. This is it. There is no path from here to here. I have every right to be just as I am right now in this moment without feeling that something must be "fixed"—unless, of course, the way I am in this moment *includes* feeling that something must be fixed. In that case, I have every right to try to fix it. No no-nos nohow.

Q10: All these dialogues, I take them with my morning coffee, great way to start the day! Many years of meditating, retreats, all that stuff. They seem now like the struggling of a lost teenager rather than a middle-aged adult. Thank you, Robert, for the straight-talking, gutsy, no bullshit discussion. Love.

A: My pleasure. I got into psychotherapy as a profession years ago because I liked getting below the surface of lies and artifice, and these conversations seem to be another version of that approach: "Let us not talk falsely now, for the hour is getting late."

Q2: Something happened to you, like Jiddu Krishnamurti's process and U.G. Krishnamurti's calamity, that seems to have gone beyond the wiping clean of the glass and so seeing out clearly. This body-flushing illness that you underwent is a rarity in itself. Is there a difference between the ordinary wiping away of illusions and the illness you went through?

A: Perhaps. I have been asked that often. I don't know. A close friend of U.G.'s told me that I remind him of U.G., and we do seem to concur on some rather radical views. He also told me that, beneath his tough exterior that brooked no bullshit, U.G. was generous and kind which, along with honest, are my favorite traits.

The dramatic wake-up I described in *4T* was followed six years later by a year and a half of profound illness, including many days of pain and nights of fevers, sweats, and bizarre hallucinations. In one recurrent dream, I was working on the roof of a tall building when I began to slip. The roof was metal and so I could not get a grip to stop myself from sliding off the edge. Just as I neared the edge, I would awake soaked in sweat. Premonitions of death and one's powerlessness in the face of it. When I recovered from that illness, I was left without questions of any sort, and without the need to "realize" anything or become anything along the lines of "enlightenment."

I felt then, and still do now, that this very moment is *it*, all one ever has—so the yearning for something else, something better, something transcendental, is a fool's errand. This puts me beyond the confines of aspirational spirituality entirely, which outsider position I do seem to have in common with both U.G. and Jiddu.

But I don't actually know what Jiddu's personal experiences were like, nor U.G.'s for that matter, although I suspect that U.G.'s were closer to mine than Jiddu's were. After all, Jiddu was mentored from childhood by spiritualists and mystics who believed that his alleged aura indicated him as the next vehicle for Lord Maitreya[11], and so he would serve as the next "World Teacher." That sounds a lot more like the Dalai Lama's childhood than mine. Ha, ha.

11. In Theosophy, the Maitreya or Lord Maitreya is an advanced spiritual entity and high-ranking member of a hidden spiritual hierarchy.

As for U.G., he had been deeply influenced by Hinduism, and his awakening to the "natural state," as he called it, was a rejection of all that, and of all spiritual teachers, including Ramana Maharshi, whose status as some kind of all-seeing jnani I also reject.

I never knew much about Ramana until recently. I was asked for my thoughts on something he said, so I read up on him. I like some of what he had to say, but certainly not all of it. I wrote about this in *The Ten Thousand Things*. I see the adoration and the way in which his every word is regarded as infallible, and can only shake my head at such foolishness. But he did seem to be a kind and friendly sort and loved to hug non-human animals, which I love too, so I imagine we would have gotten along just fine.

As U.G. told his Ramana Maharshi story, at the age of 21 he went to Ramana and asked, "This thing called *moksha*[12], can you give it to me?"

Maharshi, according to U.G., replied, "I can give it, but can you take it?"

This reply, U.G. said, appeared to be pure arrogance. It sounds like it to me too, and reminds me of the nonsense coming out of the mouths of Ramana wannabes who foolishly imagine that their hero spoke only "Truth," which they are now equipped to "teach." Oh, what rubbish!

According to U.G., Maharshi's words, and the attitude with which he spoke them, showed him the vanity in the very idea of *giving "moksha,"* and so put him "on the right track."

Nowadays, I would say the same. The idea of "giving" *moksha* is some crazy Hindu superstition. But in my innocent American upbringing, I had never heard of *moksha* and, unlike U.G., at 21, I was not thinking spiritually. I was a college senior, rowing on the crew, reading piles of books, messing around with psychedelics, and chasing women.

Nonetheless, something happened to my mind fifteen years later that clarified it pretty damn quick—a lot quicker than following

12. *Moksha:* generally speaking, release from the cycle of death and rebirth; in Advaita Vedanta, release from illusion; and in Dvaita Vedanta, eternal loving union with Vishnu.

some "path"—so perhaps there is some commonality. I just really don't know.

Be that as it may, I understand effortlessly what both of those men were saying, which puts me at odds—just as it put both of them at odds—with the countless teachers of religion and spirituality, *none* of whom either Krishnamurti respected or could abide. And, like both of them, I am not afraid to speak my mind. I just say what I see—take it or leave it. Neither agreement nor disagreement, neither approval nor disapproval, mean anything to me at all.

On that last point, I will quote Charles Bukowski:

> *We're all going to die, all of us, what a circus! That alone should make us love each other but it doesn't. We are terrorized and flattened by trivialities, we are eaten up by nothing.*

And part of the "nothing" that we are eaten up by is the striving to deny death by papering it over with spiritual beliefs. Forget all that folderol, I say; eschew that trumpery no matter whose mouth it is coming out of. See this aliveness for what it is, rather than as you wish it were, or as some "teacher" tells you it is, and you are free, including free to die right now *before* you attain "*moksha*." That freedom is timeless, and there is no path to it. That is my "message," and no teacher taught it to me.

You probably know that Jiddu was actually enthroned as the "World Teacher." He was appointed head of the Order of the Star in the East by Annie Besant and began to lecture. But when his beloved younger brother died of tuberculosis—and this after Jiddu had been assured by Besant and C.W. Leadbeater, his promoters and handlers, that the boy would *not* die, could not *possibly* die—Jiddu, entirely disillusioned, dissolved the Order with these words:

> *I maintain that Truth is a pathless land, and you cannot approach it by any path whatsoever, by any religion, by any sect. That is my point of view, and I adhere to that absolutely and unconditionally. Truth, being limitless, unconditioned, unapproachable by any path*

> *whatsoever, cannot be organized; nor should any organization be formed to lead or to coerce people along any particular path. If you first understand that, then you will see how impossible it is to organize a belief. A belief is purely an individual matter, and you cannot and must not organize it. If you do, it becomes dead, crystallized; it becomes a creed, a sect, a religion, to be imposed on others. This is what everyone throughout the world is attempting to do. Truth is narrowed down and made a plaything for those who are weak...*

Q3: Thank you for taking the time to respond, Robert. I would like to ask you if Jiddu's words, "seeing clearly out of the window", or as you put it "chiseling away" acquired beliefs and cultural gods until all that's left is your own mind, is what you would call awakening, and whether from your perspective, finding your own mind could be considered as being as awake as you'll ever be?

Is there a distinction to be made between "seeing clearly out of the window," and the occurrence of a possible total flushing of the millions of years of what thought/culture has put in the very cells?

Jiddu always talked about the *total* flowering of the human and I took his words to heart, into my very marrow. I've felt it must be possible. U.G.'s story involves a "*total* transformation." I see what appears to be a total flowering or total transformation with Jiddu, U.G. and yourself. This is not sentimentality or putting anyone on a pedestal. Fuck that.

I recall you saying in an interview, that "if you are happy with your life, don't try to awaken, you won't like it." U.G. said things like that too. I feel that your experience is closely aligned with U.G.'s "calamity," but I suppose there is no litmus test for a total flushing away of culture. So, in short, does "seeing this aliveness for what it is" mean, as you said, that "you are as awake as you will ever be," or does that require the flushing of all that has been acquired culturally over thousands of years?

A: It is true that I have said things along the lines of "if you see such and such, you are as awake as you will ever be," but that is a kind of rhetorical device—a writer getting a bit carried away by language. Truthfully, I know nothing about "ever be." I only know right now.

I do not think I can be or should be compared to U.G., Jiddu, or any other apparently awake human. I find myself awake on my terms, not theirs. They both had their own lives to suffer, just as I have mine. I understand what you are trying to do in looking for concurrence in those you consider awake, but I don't think it will work. Even if you find some, this will still always be about you and what *you* make of this aliveness, silently, in your own heart of hearts.

As for flushing away the entire weight of human genetic inheritance, language, tradition, etcetera, that is far too grandiose a notion for me even to imagine. I don't see things that way at all. For me, freedom is not about trying to flush all that away, but about *seeing it in the first place*—really *seeing* it: the fear, the longing, the constant judgment, the inner psychological violence, the pressures of group mind, the religious inanities, etcetera. And being OK with it, and especially being OK *without* it as it leaves.

On this last point, it is important to understand that as shame leaves, pride goes with it; as group mind goes, and tradition, and religion, nothing is left to cling to, so one is forever in freefall without a parachute. That is why I said that "if you are happy with your life, don't try to awaken, you won't like it." I like it, but I have strange tastes. Ha. Ha.

We are all just human here. There is no escape from that, I am saying, and when one stops *trying* to escape, something that had been tightly clenched relaxes. It's like accepting what actually *is*, accepting things just as they are, not as we wish they were or could be—except that no one can "do" acceptance on this level. It just happens when and if it does.

In that relaxation, this evanescent, transitory aliveness we are—this *aliveness* that is always here, regardless of what one believes or doesn't believe—is obvious and completely mortal.

14 - Speaking truthfully

Q: Robert, *The Ten Thousand Things* is the best book I ever read, and I studied comparative literature! You get an inspired vibe from *Siddhartha*, but *4T* takes over the whole train you are reading it in, including the landscape scenery out the window.

A: Lovely. Thank you. That praise may be a bit hyperbolic, but I do appreciate the way you bracketed *The Ten Thousand Things* with Hesse's *Siddhartha*. That reminded me of the many versions of the Buddha story, Hesse's being one of them, in which the details of a great psychological discovery are all but buried in the fictional drama of a pampered rich boy determined to find himself.

Although scholars mostly agree that 2,600 years ago a man called Siddhartha actually existed, son of the Hindu Raja of the Sakyan clan that resided in the foothills of the Himalayas, most of the rest of the story is legendary and mythical. So the greatness of that story, in my view, resides not in the fictional details of struggle and transcendence that are apocryphal at best, but in the *Abhidharma*, the philosophical and psychological aspects of what is now called "Buddhism."

The crux of *Abhidharma*—which is, in my view, the marrow of the matter—concerns the way in which a "myself" as the fixed experiencer of changeful sentient experiences is *constructed* from various elements (a body; sensory perceptions, such as sight, sound, feeling, etcetera; mind or intellect; consciousness or awareness; mental formations, such as thoughts and memories; and many other factors) which are not necessarily related to one another at all, but from which an imaginary sense of "presence," that we have been taught and learned to call "me," is created unconsciously.

If this sense of *presence*—which so many "spiritual" people imagine is the gold standard, but which is, I say, a kind of fictional papering over of freefall with nowhere to land—is understood as a confection of elements, not a unitary "self," then the *person* can be recognized not as a *thing*, but as a *process*—an ongoing, unconscious assembling of largely unrelated information into an apparently permanent "myself," out of thin air so to speak.

My own awakening led me to understand how little we know—how little we *can* know—about who or what we *really* are. And from that perspective, most "spiritual teaching" appears to me, to borrow Shakespeare's excellent words, like "a tale told by an idiot, full of sound and fury, signifying nothing." Fuck yes! That nails it. I see this with an unceasing clarity, and couldn't *not* see it even if I tried. We humans walk around with all kinds of images in our minds that we take to be real when they are only fictions, and this includes all the supposed "verities" such as God, Love, Source, universal consciousness, and all the rest.

But how this vision swirled around and emerged as *4T* seems mystifying and incomprehensible. In the light of readers' reports, such as yours, the book seems imbued with some clarifying energy that I cannot quite fathom. Yes, I am clear myself on this inability of us humans to know final answers to ultimate questions and have been for years now, but I still cannot make out how that clarity was converted into words that seem to speak directly to so many readers.

The Buddha was a heavy cat, to be sure. His ideas were shocking, completely upsetting the apple cart of the spiritual practices of his day. And the shock waves continue—even if, unfortunately, his pointing to the psychological aspects of this aliveness is mostly overlooked, and his message of the universality of the human position is converted routinely into something truly sad: adulation and emulation in the vain hope of using them to "end suffering"—one's *own* suffering. That seems so sad.

The spiritual seekers claim to be searching for "Truth," but for the most part that's a lie. The majority of them don't want truth at all, particularly the self-evident, ongoing truth of living and dying without an escape hatch. What they really seek is to *feel* better—less anxious, less depressed, less frightened—so they will glom on to any so-called teaching, true or not, that promises escape from human biological realities; and they will put the teacher of that escapism on a pedestal to be emulated as if the teacher had some "enlightenment magic."

Since the publication of *4T,* I am getting some of that adoration myself, and it hurts to be misunderstood that way. That is why I say I don't want anyone following me. Be a light unto yourself. Find your *own* mind. If something you hear from me clears the space for that, good. I'm all for seeing what arises in the emptiness of open space. But that's not about me— it's about you.

When you make an ordinary human being into a "master" worthy of emulation, you sell yourself short, and so push out of your reach what might actually be within your grasp. I don't mean you personally. I did not take your comment that way, hyperbolic though it may be. I have had my mind blown by a book or two myself.

Q: The wonderful discernment found in *4T,* in my view, is that you show the classic assumption of the fixed "me" to be false without replacing it with the alleged "There *is* no 'me'" of nonduality. Therefore, it became possible to see that the "me" is always changing and so neither fixed *nor* non-existent. That understanding ended a long period of doubtful questioning about my particular "me," and led me to start speaking truthfully, instead of speaking about "Truth."

Anyway, my assessment was not hyperbole. This is the best book I've ever read. So, Ten Thousand thanks!

A: You really did get that. Great. Thanks.

15 - Time

Q: I find it fascinating that you are both a photographer and possessed of this extraordinary ability to communicate what it's all about, what being awake means. I am sure there is a connection. An innate ability to stop, or see through the illusion of, time and capture what is there in front of you, clearly and succinctly without embellishment. What you do is very poetic, Robert, very beautiful.

If you would ever care to comment about time and its appearance, I'd love to read that. *4T* is wonderful by the way.

A: Thank you.

At the most fundamental level of physical reality, there may be no time at all. I don't want to get too far into the weeds here but, briefly, since Einstein's general relativity, it has been known that time is not a fixed constant, but is relative to the observer. This is not merely speculative or conjectural, but can be demonstrated by actual physical experiments. For example, if two very accurate clocks are perfectly synchronized, and then one is placed on the floor while the other is kept on a table in the same room, they will soon fall out of sync. The clock on the table will run more slowly. Why? Because it is further from the Earth's gravity! Even though the difference is infinitesimal, it can be measured experimentally.

Once quantum mechanics enters the picture, this matter becomes even more arcane. Einstein's mathematics governs relatively large structures, whereas quantum mathematics applies to the world of unimaginably tiny sub-atomic particles. Although abstruse, quantum mechanics, like general relativity, is not speculative but factual and verifiable. Not only can quantum mechanics be demonstrated experimentally, but that mathematics is used widely in practical applications such as computers, the atomic clocks, and GPS (Global Positioning Satellites). The 130-year-old, platinum-iridium cylinder, stored in Paris, that until now has been the world standard for the kilogram, was just retired, replaced by a number based on quantum mechanical measurement of quadrillions of light particles.

However, although both quantum math and the mathematics of Einstein's general relativity are both used successfully in real-world applications, and sometimes even used together in the same application, they are not interchangeable. Indeed, there are ways in which those two mathematical models of the physical universe diverge sharply.

Forty years ago or so, John Wheeler and the late Bryce DeWitt attempted to reconcile that divergence—to unify relativity and quantum mechanics—by developing a mathematics that would apply to both equally well. This became known as the Wheeler-DeWitt equation. It has not been proven, so it is still speculative, but if it is correct, there is no place in it, and no need either, for time. In Wheeler and DeWitt's mathematical unification of general relativity and quantum mechanics, the fundamental description of the universe is timeless.

In that view—which, as I said, remains to be proven—it is not just that time is *relative,* which is a *fact* on the macro level, but that time does not actually exist at all. According to the Wheeler-DeWitt equation, the physical world could run in reverse, like a movie projected backward, just as easily as it runs apparently forward.

In my interview with Rick Archer [13], I recommended the author Carlo Rovelli. If you are interested in reading more about these matters, that is a good place to start. Carlo writes beautifully. I find his work an elegant pleasure, even in translation.

So in the physical world, time may or may not exist, and events can run "backward" as easily as "forward" (scare quotes because in that view there is no backward and forward—no direction at all). So far, no one really knows.

Wheeler-DeWitt is speculation about the *material* world, but there is another world entirely, and that is the *subjective* world, by which I mean the world that you and I experience from moment to moment.

Here I do not refer to the speculative world of religion and spirituality, in which everyday experience is considered "unreal," and

13. See https://BATGAP.com/robert-saltzman/

only "God," or whatever term is used, is real. I mean the world of *human* experience: yours and mine, prior to metaphysics. I do not mean a "spiritual" world that you have heard about second-hand, or read about—which, unfortunately, has so many humans walking around in a kind of hypnotic trance—but the actual moment-to-moment *feeling* of this *aliveness*. This "unmitigated aliveness," as I put it in *The Ten Thousand Things*.

In that world, time obviously exists as observable changes, and the arrow of time points in only one direction. Unlike the world of the Wheeler-DeWitt equation, in *my* world—my *subjective* world—you cannot unscramble an egg, or go back in time even one second. Nor, unlike the world of Einstein's mathematics, would anyone notice that clocks run more slowly on a mountain top than at sea level. It is true that they do, but the difference is far too small to be perceived on a human subjective level.

Some people imagine an objective world, but I say the *subjective* world is the world in which awake human *be*-ing actually occurs, actually exists. In this world, *my* world, the arrow of time clearly exists.

I do not mean the kind of time that clocks measure. I do not mean minutes and hours. Minutes and hours exist only relatively, in relation to the movement of something else: the pendulum of a clock, for example, or the phases of the moon. I mean that *subjectively* we feel that everything is changing and cannot "unchange." For example, a puppy is born, grows into an active dog, ages, and dies. Or, I put a seed in the ground, a shoot comes up, the shoot becomes a sapling, the sapling grows into a tree, and a hurricane blows the tree down. One may miss the dog, or long to see that tree standing where it used to be, but there is no way to have them back again.

That "no way to have them back again" is what we call "mortality," or "impermanence;" and impermanence is what religion and spirituality try to deny by speculating about a "myself" that is *not* mortal like the dog or the tree, but immortal like "Heaven with Jesus," or the kind of so-called self-realization in which "I and Brahman are one and the same." From my perspective all that is wishful chit-chat.

But, someone might ask, "What about Buddhism? Doesn't

Buddhism teach impermanence?" Well, that's what I saw in it—along with the nonexistence or "emptiness" of an imagined unitary "self." But many who call themselves "Buddhists" seem to miss that part entirely. Instead, they fantasize a state of perfection—the condition of a "Buddha"—that for them exists only conceptually, not in fact, but that they strive to attain "later." The human mind seems to be hell-bent on self-deception.

There is, I say, no such future state at all. There is only *this* moment and its indescribable suchness. And the "Buddha" they imagine never existed, except mythologically.

As for photography, the camera sees the world in a way that no human being ever will. The camera can freeze "this moment" forever. My love for the medium involves that very property and the way it informs our human subjectivity. This is from a 1990 interview in *The Taos Review*:

> *I might say to the model, "Stretch your arm up," or something like that. I'm not doing this because I'm thinking, "This isn't composed properly." My decision is based on something that is much deeper than composition. I'm looking for a feeling, and it is unmistakable. When there is really something there that works for me, suddenly I feel a tremendous calmness. It's as if time has stopped.*

I have heard about a similar feeling from artists in other media. For example, a jazz horn player once told me that when improvising, he could get into a "zone" in which, although he might be playing at bebop speed, he felt that he had forever to arrive at the next note.

16 - The abysses of vanity and meaninglessness

Q: May I please ask, is it possible to understand that "myself" is a way for the brain to give a feeling of continuity of experience, being the psychological glia cells, the connective tissue of "lifeing," as it were, yet fear death all the same?

A: I don't know anything about glia cells, but even if I were an expert on the subject, I do not think that understanding consciousness as physical processes is at all helpful in dealing with painful thoughts and emotions. Unless one is in total denial, the pain is there, and it does not matter, in my view, whether glia cells are responsible for that pain, or bad behavior in a so-called "past life," or if "God" is punishing you for your sins, such as failing to believe in "Him."

The fact is that most humans fear death, which—although some try to deny it—most likely means ceasing to exist at all. This, psychologist Donald Winnicott said, was one of the two primal fears, meaning fears we are born with. The other is fear of falling forever.

When I say that I find myself awake, I mean that I do not take refuge in explanations—neither physical explanations like glia cells, nor metaphysical explanations like "Everything happens for a reason"—but that I am present to and welcoming of each moment of life, *prior to* reasons, theories, commentary, or justifications. I mean life as it is right now, *before* hearing the explanations—which must fall short of really explaining anything no matter what they say. This presence to each moment often demands feeling emotions that others consider "negative," and so try to avoid. As my old mom used to say—although she was talking about growing old, not the radical awakeness of which I speak, and quoting Bette Davis—"It's not for sissies."

I am not saying that I never indulge in escapism. I love books and movies, for example, even "lightweight" ones, and it's fun to lose myself in them. I mean that I am attached to no overarching structure of justification such as patriotism or religion, nor to any philosophical system that claims to provide "meaning" in a life that probably ends in complete personal extinction. I live with self-awareness without trying to make sense of it.

I did not create this situation, and I have no way of "solving" it. Nor, in my view, does any other human being, past or present, provide a way of solving it. This includes Jesus, the Buddha, and all the other spiritual heroes of humanity. Self-reflection plus mortality, I say, equals the paradox that just won't go away, no matter *who* or *what* you think you are.

The Norwegian author, Peter Wessel Zapfee, theorized that humans are born with an overdeveloped skill—self-awareness—that is not needed for survival, and so does not really fit into nature's design. I am reading about Zapfee in a book by Thomas Ligotti called *The Conspiracy Against The Human Race*. We humans, Zapfee thought, endowed with this unneeded self-awareness, crave to understand matters such as life and death, but, due to human limitation, that craving cannot be honestly appeased. We *know* about death but cannot *explain* it. In other words, nature has given humanity a desire that nature cannot satisfy.

Faced with this hunger that cannot be fulfilled, Zapfee thought, most humans—almost all humans, he said—spend their time trying to not *be* human. I am in accord with this observation entirely. It is one that I made myself repeatedly long before encountering Zapfee's work.

I wrote about this at length in *The Ten Thousand Things*, pointing out that, since the "final answers" offered by religions such as Hinduism and Christianity are *not* facts, but conjectures—pure fantasies actually—most so-called spirituality boils down to simple escapism. So, in my view, religion serves mostly as a mechanism of defense against primal fears that human animals experience due to possessing a self-awareness, including an awareness of mortality, that our brother and sister animals seem to lack. In short, we *know* we are going to die, and don't like the idea, so we invent psychological defenses and escape hatches.

Now, Zapfee described four defense mechanisms that we humans use to blunt our foreknowledge of death:

1. **Isolation**—Just put death and other disturbing thoughts out of your mind entirely. This is what, in *4T,* I call "denial."

2. **Anchoring**—Develop attachment to a system of beliefs, values, or ideals that seems to *justify* a life that ends in personal extinction. For example, one might be anchored to a patriotic love of country, hopes for the distant future, a political agenda, a family, an institution, etcetera. And if we can arrive at regarding these as "Truth," we may feel, as Zapfee put it, "official, authentic, and safe in our beds."

3. **Distraction**—Quoting Ligotti here, "To keep our minds unreflective of a world of horrors, we distract them with a world of trifling or momentous trash. The most operant method for furthering the conspiracy, it is in continuous employ and demands only that people keep their eyes on the ball—or their television sets, their government's foreign policy, their science projects, their careers, their place in society or the universe, etcetera."

4. **Sublimation**—The refocusing of energy and distancing oneself from the actual tragedy—or horror, depending on point of view—of the human primate situation by viewing existence from an aesthetic outlook, like writers, poets, painters—and, dare I say it, *photographers;* or a philosophical one, so that "the worst fortunes of humanity are presented in a stylized and removed manner as entertainment," as Zapfee put it.

From that perspective, my writing about this, however honest, is a form of sublimation, but at least I am aware of it.

Q. Is it possible to live and not do any of those in your opinion, Robert?

A: That remains to be seen. Anyway, I see no reason to be absolute about it. Soft-pedaling the first two, while resorting to some use of three and four, while acknowledging to oneself that even number four is a way of finessing the situation, would already be a huge step forward.

Of course, the paradox and irony in the idea of "a step forward" should be apparent. In this game, you can't win, which is what "spiritual" people cannot admit to themselves. We all lose everything sooner or later. Nothing that I think I have, nothing that I think I am, has any permanence whatsoever. It never did, and it never will.

When you admit to yourself, without fingers crossed behind your back and without looking for the escape hatch, that there is no *way* to win—that the entire game ends in personal extinction—you find yourself *here*. How can I possibly make this any clearer?

Q2: Imagine if Zapfee had relocated to Mexico like you and lived in the sunshine. Perhaps he'd have written a gentler message more in line with your work. You seem to point to the same understanding as Zapfee, so why do I feel that your version is gentler?

A: Zapfee and I agree on a couple of basics, it seems, and they are the kinds of basics that many others regard as "dark." For example, Zapfee said, "Man is the ultimate tragic being because he has learned enough about the Earth to realize the Earth would be better off without the presence of humankind."

Now perhaps in the 1930s that sounded "dark," but I'd say the same myself right now, and not call it "dark" at all, but simply accurate; and I bet I could get plenty of agreement on that. We humans are destroying ourselves and the natural balance of this planet.

As Horace Walpole said, "This world is a comedy to those who think and a tragedy to those who feel." Since I both think *and* feel, this world is both a tragedy *and* a comedy to me. Fortunately, since I can both laugh *and* cry, I don't feel overwhelmed by consciousness, but at times awareness sure can hurt.

Nevertheless, being *fully* human, which is another way of saying "*awake*," demands a tolerance for looking into the abysses—particularly the abysses of vanity and of meaninglessness—which many of our fellow humans avoid at all cost. That is what I understand Zapfee to have been saying.

I just recalled this passage from Chapter 11 of *The Ten Thousand*

Things, written before I'd come across Zapfee, with which I imagine he would concur, if he were around today to read my work as I did his:

> *The human brain has evolved to a complexity greater than that of most other animals. (I say "most" because in the case of large-brained animals that don't need to invent or build anything in order to survive—cetaceans, for instance—we don't know what they think or how bright they may be.) The human neural complexity seems to leave available a surplus of brain-power which may be devoted to self-justification, self-aggrandizement, religious fantasy, and other such cogitation. But all of that is a fool's errand in my book.*
>
> *Fear of death—a terror at the idea of not being at all—along with apprehensions about falling into depression if one admits that living and breathing seem to lack any larger meaning, keeps many of us humans hypnotized and striving for "victory," but all we really know is that we are here now. The rest, I say, is stories we tell ourselves to cope with pain, fear, and yearning.*

Q3: Of Donald Winnicott's two primal fears, the fear of death is readily apparent, but I am not so clear about the fear of falling forever. Are you able to say something about how that manifests in the average person's life?

A: Yes. It is noticed even in newborn infants as an automatic clutching at anything they can get their hands on. Later, this is seen as what Zapfee called "anchoring."

From my perspective of not knowing answers to ultimate questions—what J. Krishnamurti called "freedom from the known"—I find it really strange to see people clutching at so-called "truths" ("Jesus is Lord," or "You were never born, so you will never die," etcetera) when it seems obvious—obvious to me, at least—that what is being expressed is the fear of *having* no anchor, of having nothing they can grab onto to keep from falling forever into the void of not knowing.

Q4: Thank you for adding me to your page, Robert. Stumbling across your many conversations, thoughts, ideas, and responses, I've come to the conclusion that I'm very much stuck. I am going to be 40 this year and have come to the conclusion that nothing really matters anymore. "Ashes to ashes, dust to dust," from Earth we come and to Earth we return.

As much as we try to give meaning to life, it's all lies. Coming to this conclusion has really impacted my life, in that I'm almost unwilling to remain a party to the human race, to partake in the lies, to indulge in fantasy. I am definitely not suicidal but feel very much alone and without that escape I once called "God" to bless my life with strength to endure. I almost wish I hadn't picked the scab that's called the mystery of life. Seems to be more of a burden than anything.

A: Yes. I understand completely. So, with your mind liberated from the strained rationalizations and protestations of hope and faith that frightened humans force themselves to swear by, you are free to say to yourself, "OK. Nothing lasts. Impermanence is the name of the game. Now, with that in mind, what do *I* want to do?"

That may seem bleak, but if you give it a chance, you may see the beauty in impermanence. For me, this very impermanence itself is a *source* of beauty.

> *I am a child, I'll last a while*
> *You can't conceive of the pleasure in my smile*
>
> —Neil Young

I wish you all the best.

Q5: My understanding of *The Ten Thousand Things,* and the general tenor of the posts and teachings, is to focus less on the ideas that you present—the material or non-material nature of consciousness, etcetera—but rather, to be willing to look at the idols of fancy that we have erected to insulate us against the stark truth of the moment. Aside from the beauty and freedom that may result, there is first lots of junk to wade through, to look at, and to hopefully become more intimate with. Things like death and hate and vengeance and all the other disgusting parts that comprise our humanness.

That seems to be where the true teachers say the treasure lies. Not in the ephemeral, or in the peak experiences, or in the hints of oneness or flavors of grace that make our egos happy, but when we sit in the muck and the hate and find the beauty and love in that. In my experience, that's where lasting healing is. The other stuff can be sweet, but it never lasts. And those peak experiences can become gods unto themselves, which is always dangerous. I don't think it's possible to return to one's essential nature without being willing to go through hell.

I like that quote, Robert, from your mother who says, "It's not for sissies". That's right on. Seems like a lovely woman. Thanks for being out there.

R: That is an excellent statement. My mom was a lovely woman, and brilliant. She died recently at 99. She was doing well still, but fell and hit her head, and that was all she wrote. She loved *4T.* She'd have liked this book.

When one is not looking for an escape hatch, but finds oneself participating in whatever thoughts, feelings, perceptions, etcetera, make up the constituents of *this* very moment, without any hope that things will get "better," including that one will eventually be enlightened, then one is *here*. And it is only *here* that anything true, anything real—anything that is not escapism and fantasy—will be found.

So whereas most of the "teaching" points elsewhere—points, I mean, to an improved condition that you will attain "eventually" by *following* the teaching, heeding the instructions, imitating the teacher—I point only to what you are right now in this moment. The one who is reading these words is *it*, and there *is* no other. "Oh, Layman Pang?"

[Ten weeks later] Reading through this conversation, I was touched again by your comment, Q5. You have my marrow.

Q5: Thanks for that, Robert. I was fortunate enough to have had a teacher who encouraged me to do away with idols and any thoughts of specialness; not that they don't still creep up and try to make a mess of things. He died a few years ago and the process has certainly continued. Your thoughts and words on these matters have served to cook me more thoroughly, it seems. I have been having these rather profound moments of not feeling at all separate from my experience. Lovely in the most ordinary of ways. And it seems as if ordinary is the way to go. I also like that you used the word "bliss-ninny" in your book. My teacher used the same word!

17 - Psychotherapy versus spiritual teaching

Q: During your interview with Rick Archer [14], you made a distinction between psychotherapy and spiritual teaching. Don't they overlap? Isn't psychotherapy done for the sake of getting people better ready to awaken, or whatever you want to call it, to the unknowable? To help people become less depressed and anxious, for example, and thereby more alive?

Also, I'd rather see large sums of money go into the pockets of people that put something positive into the world about loving each other than have it sit in a bank.

Thanks for doing the interview with Rick—you have a unique take.

A: You are most welcome.

I may be doing a kind of teaching here, but it is not *spiritual* teaching. As I said in the very first chapter of *The Ten Thousand Things:*

> *Skepticism is not the right word for my apathy toward religion and spirituality. Having seen the emptiness of supposed answers to ultimate questions, I view those answers as elements in the domain of unsubstantiated magical thinking. Magical thinking holds no interest for me—none. I don't know if a conscious, overarching principle or so-called "Supreme Being" exists or not, and I don't care. I know what I know right now from this present perspective, and that is precious little.*

So, what I call "awake" has nothing to do with spirituality, as most people understand that word. You can be 100 percent "spiritual" while remaining entirely hypnotized. I see that condition all the time. I could make a list of so-called "spiritual teachers" who fit right into that category, as I see it.

---

14. See https://BATGAP.com/robert-saltzman/

You seem to assume that the kind of "holy business" I criticize—in which a self-proclaimed "self-realized" person tells you how you can become "realized" too, by just getting with the program (all is consciousness, you are one with God, and Love is all there is) while in the meantime emptying your bank account into his or hers—constitutes putting "something positive into the world." I don't see things that way. Why assume that talking about God or "universal consciousness" is "positive?" It might be nothing of the kind.

Those who have something worth teaching rarely come by big bucks doing it. Honest information is extended to those who are ready to deal with it, which has nothing to do with who can pay for it or who can't. The true teachers I have known gave away as much as possible. Since you saw the *BATGAP* interview [15] and that whole discussion, I won't expand further on it here; but like so many things in life, you either see this or you don't.

A friend of mine puts it this way: "When I pass a plate, it will have something good to eat on it."

Now the kind of "teaching"—if you want to call it that—that I am doing here is *not* psychotherapy because the object is different. My intention here is not to help people feel better or to adjust better to the demands of ordinary life, but to point out, as directly as I can, the hypnotic trance of belief and credulity in which so many of us are spending our days. Seeing that might make someone feel worse for all I know. And by the way, psychotherapy is rarely, if ever, "done for the sake of getting people better ready to awaken to the unknowable."

If you ask me a question, I reply with complete candor, without considering the possible effects of my reply. Whether my words make you feel better or not is not my concern. You may go to psychotherapy aiming to feel better. My present work is *not* that.

Psychotherapy is a healing art that is centered on the needs of the patient, whether those needs involve "awakening," or not. In doing therapy, I would never put all my cards on the table as I do here. The cards to be put on the table in psychotherapy are the *patient's* cards, *not* the therapist's.

15. *Buddha at the Gas Pump*–see, again, https://BATGAP.com/robert-saltzman/

Most often, people come to therapy with no intention of awakening in the way we are using that word here, but to feel less frightened, less depressed or anxious, more able to function in relationships, work, sexuality, etcetera. It is not the job of the therapist to "awaken" them, but to meet *those* needs.

When I speak here of awakening, that is not about helping people to become "less depressed and anxious," as you imagine, but to encourage all of us to see things as they are in each unique moment. When awake you might feel depressed—you might *feel* anything at all—but you will understand that what you feel *is* you, so you will *not* be trying to escape those feelings.

Q2: When you say, "My intention here is *not* to help people *feel* better, but to point out, as directly as I can, the hypnotic trance of belief and credulity in which so many of us are spending our days," that is classic cognitive behavioral therapy—the questioning of mistaken beliefs. Also, when you say that you aren't out to help people feel better with your "non-spiritual" teaching, but to feel whatever they feel, that is classic cognitive processing therapy. When you say that as a psychotherapist you are meeting people's needs to feel better and that you use the patient's cards rather than the therapist's, that is empathic, compassionate listening, which I would call a spiritual quality. And where do you get the desire to meet your patients' needs for feeling less depressed, anxious, etcetera? I suspect it's not just because you want to make a living, but because your heart and passion are in it, just like Byron Katie, Adyashanti, etcetera.

A: Yes, I was trained in therapy techniques, so it is no surprise that I use them without even thinking about it. That is what the French call the *déformation professionnelle*. And you are correct that, for me, psychotherapy was a calling, not a business. I altered my entire life radically so as to be able to do that work, so I appreciate your recognizing my sincerity and honest compassion for those in pain. But you may be missing the crux of what I have to say. And please do not put me in a conceptual box with the likes of Adyashanti, who seems to be practicing psychotherapy without a license or proper training either, opening people up publicly and then just leaving them that way, standing at a microphone with tears in their eyes. Is that really "*spiritual* teaching," or is it more like an old medicine show?

I don't know anything about Byron Katie other than her name. As for Adyashanti, I am not questioning his sincerity. I have no information about that but, frankly, the "Adya" I saw in some video clips appeared unfocused and "new-agey," and I wonder about people who change their names to Hindu-sounding ones and then start to teach. What is the message in that procedure? Nothing good, I think.

You may feel just peachy after listening to "Adya" telling you how great it is to be enlightened, and explaining how you can be that way too. Perhaps you now have a new sense of purpose and possibility. But contact highs don't last.

Since I am retired from my work as a psychotherapist, I have no need for healing artifice or considering the possible effects of my words. Now, I just speak from the heart—speak my *mind*, I mean. In many Asian languages, the word for mind is the same as the word for heart—*kokoro* in Japanese, for example—which is what makes work on oneself feasible: to find one's *own* mind, one's *own* heart.

Q3: Often what you say and what Adyashanti says is the same thing. I think your styles are somewhat different, but you have very similar realizations.

A: I cannot agree. We may see certain things in common, but from my perspective, there is a crucial difference right on the fault line. Promises, promises. I will not abet that.

Q3: Robert, by "promises, promises," you mean any language that suggests or implies some better knowledge or experience in the future may or can exist (and therefore merits pursuing)?

A: That is part of it. The idea of progress in the matter of *be*-ing creates a trance state through hypnotic suggestion.

I have never met Adyashanti. For all I know, he might be a nice guy and we'd get along fine. The same applies to Rupert and others. I am not sitting in judgment of one particular personality or another. It is the protocol of big-time spiritual teaching and the credulity with which it is approached that to me seems so destructive. In my view, calling it "teaching" is a bit much. It's a lot more like show business.

There can be progress in learning—a second language, for example, or how to use a camera—but if you observe the crowds at the feet of one of these rock-star teachers, you will see not progress and learning, as much as mass hypnosis. You will see repeat customers who actually believe that the more time they spend with "Adya," the closer they will be to *it*.

But that is nonsense. As Alan Watts once put it, "This is like a game of tag. *You're* it."

It is here right now. It *always* is. Obviously. Wherever *you* are, *it* is. Where else could it be? If *you* are here, *it* is here. *You* are it, and nothing Adyashanti says about *his* trip has jack shit to do with that. Listening to someone's descriptions of so-called "Truth" takes you away from *it,* I say, and *that* is what has to be seen.

The fantasy of "spiritual progress"—requiring plenty of retreats, books, videos, etcetera—is a disaster. There is no progress from here to here. You get what you get when *you* get it, and "when" is always right now. Or you don't get it, and nothing "Adya" says is going to give it to you. Ignore all that spiritual fantasy trip of future attainment, is what I am saying. Just put it out of your mind and be a light unto yourself right now.

"Progress" in the matter of *be*-ing is a lie. It is little more than distraction and entertainment, which is why it generates such big bucks. Meanwhile, straight talk without woo-woo is not for sale, and if it were, few people would buy it. Entertainment is the name of the game, and walling off recognition of impermanence and mortality for as long as possible.

Q4: Robert, I was struck by your bio. I've met several people in these groups who were therapists but stopped practicing after their awakening because it stopped making sense to them or they lost the energy for it. It seems rarer to have an awakening first and then practice psychotherapy.

How did you manage to get through graduate school in psychology after already seeing through the self? Did it ever drive you crazy? Did you ever feel at risk of getting stuck in the personal perspective again, or was your training a good way to work out the kinks and conditioning?

Without getting into my story, I am somewhat conflicted personally and professionally between psychological healing and awakening, so I am interested in your perspective.

A: Awakening, I like to say, never ends. A "myself" may hear about so-called "universal consciousness" or "Source"—which is a religious belief, not a fact—and attempt to identify with that, thus imagining her- or himself to be "unchanging," while the imagined "outside world" of objects and events is in constant flux. "Myself" may even imagine itself equipped to advocate for that point of view, employing logic, appeal to tradition and authority, or special "higher reasoning."

But "myself" is *always* changing, I say, flowing right along with everything it fantasizes itself to be separate from, and which it imagines observing from a changeless, fixed position. Only dead things are changeless. This aliveness is ephemeral, I say—entirely transitory.

I draw no clear boundary between psychological healing and awakening. Everyone is different. The pursuit of "enlightenment" or claims to be enlightened or to be the student of an enlightened teacher, might be indications of narcissistic illness. A case like that—and I have seen some—calls for fact-based, strong-minded psychotherapy, not satsangs about how ordinary life is "unreal" but how lovely it is to be "awake." Narcissistic personalities are not healed by "spirituality," but only gratified by it—just another way to feel "special." Better a bit of tough love in cases like that.

There is the story of the student and the teacher who are walking together. The student is touting his fresh understanding, waxing smug and self-satisfied about how he now understands that the material world is only a dream to be transcended, a mere fantasy of ego, and blah, blah, blah. At last, the old teacher can bear not a syllable more of this horseshit. She takes the student by the elbows and kicks him hard right in the shins.

"Ow, ow, ow," cries the student. "Why'd you do that?"

"How's that for a dream?" the teacher replies.

From my perspective, most religion and received metaphysics incorporates elements of self-hypnosis in service of papering over undesired thoughts and fears, particularly the fear of impermanence and mortality. Frequent repetition of unsubstantiated beliefs, voiced either outwardly or tacitly to oneself, constitutes a highly potent mode of self-hypnotism.

It is a simple and testable psychological fact that the more a proposition is repeated, the more readily it is believed, true or not. Once *that* is taken into account, the question arises of what is so fearsome as to demand the constant repetition of unsubstantiated "spiritual" beliefs as a means of self-calming. That locus of fear, in my experience, *can* be determined if one is open to seeing it, which may occur in successful psychotherapy.

Labels and categories, I say, cannot fathom the mysteries of selflessness. Don't be deceived by experts making claims about being able to teach you *how* to awaken. "Selflessness" is not an attainment to be summoned up or manipulated, nor can "shedding the ego" be taught, any more than one can be taught how to fall in love.

Give some thought to *splitting*. I mean constantly dividing experience in half: a spiritual world on the one hand and a material world on the other. Are there really two separate worlds, one true and the other illusionary? Or is that bifurcated view a reflection or projection of the split in one's *own* mind, the division in one's *own* psyche?

Then, turn your attention to the disordered functioning of that mind, filled with voices in seeming conversation—often judgmental and self-justifying in the manner of Gestalt psychology's "top dog/ under dog" confrontations. This is a mindset that runs deep among us humans naturally anyway, and is commonly reinforced by a robust set of early childhood conditioning about authority and kowtowing to authority. Only some lobsters seem able to climb out of *that* pot, no matter what words are said and by whom.

So for me, psychotherapy—an examination of I and Thou—and philosophical healing through questions about form and emptiness, appear as features of one and the same dance, a dance of improvisation. We are all dancing as best we can, or, if that seems a bit rosy and optimistic, we are all dancing as we do. *Samsara* [16]*is* nirvana—in my view, at least.

As a student in mid-life, for me, graduate school was fun and highly informative. It was heartwarming too. My teachers loved me and I loved them.

16. *Samsara*: meaning literally, "perpetual wandering"; the cycle of death and rebirth to which life in the material world is bound.

18 - Bombarded by thoughts

I met Joan Tollifson for the first time on video chat after she had read *The Ten Thousand Things*. Subsequently, she shared with me the following words from her late teacher, Toni Packer. I'd not heard of Toni before that, but recognized instantly that Toni and I have something in common:

> *When there's a moment of no sense of "me," why not leave it alone completely, come what may? When a fearful thought or feeling arises in an instant, it can also be gone in an instant, even before it has triggered the thirty thousand chemicals throughout the body. There is just a vulnerable being exposed, alone, without knowing, without a word. Maybe it's a moment of dying to all the impulses to know, to protect, to maintain, to continue. Not knowing is dying. And at the same time being wholly alive.*
>
> —from *The Light of Discovery* by Toni Packer

Q. Robert, I am wondering about the concept that thought "arises." In my experience thought feels more like a constant "bombardment" within the space of consciousness.

A: If the flow of thought feels like a bombardment, you may be taking thoughts too personally. They do come and go, after all, flowing like water, not dropping like bombs. What real harm can they do?

Imagine sitting on the bank of a river on a lovely summer's day, far from the madding crowd. Your feet are bare and you've worked your toes into the mud. You breathe deeply, taking in the sweet air redolent with the perfume of a thousand flowers. Birds are singing... But even amidst this wonder, "myself" is still there—in your case feeling bombarded.

From that feeling of vulnerability—the lack of any means of escape from the stream of consciousness that flows uncontrollably—a new thought bubbles up about how to find a method of immunity against what feels like a bombardment. That seems logical but rarely seems to work. What does work, I have found, is understanding that "myself"—the "me" feeling bombarded—is not separate from, nor more permanent than the thoughts, feelings, and physical experiences that constitute the apparent bombardment. "Myself" *is* a thought, no different from the thoughts that in your case feel like a bombardment.

The apparent bombardment and the "myself" supposedly under attack, are part and parcel of the same mind, and it's *all* impermanent—the thoughts, the feelings, the physical experiences—*all* of it. All of it is dying just as it is born—no staying power at all.

This transitoriness, this impermanence, is a plain fact, but one most of us routinely elide. We prefer to feel that the world around me is always changing, but that "I" am unceasingly myself, the same as always, the fantasized changeless "witness" or "presence." That illusion of permanence is only smoke and mirrors, but we *like* that illusion and allow religion, spirituality, along with other habits and customs of society, to keep the illusion fresh, because the *truth*—that we are dying and being reborn in every moment of our lives without ever *getting* anywhere but closer to personal extinction—can feel intolerable.

"Myself" consists of thoughts and feelings that are never the same from one moment to the next. Don't take my word for it. Check it out for yourself. Noticing this ceaseless, ever-changing flow does not require years of meditation. A few moments of sincere investigation reveal it.

If one is frightened by impermanence and sees that perceptions, thoughts, and feelings have no staying power, one may rely on the physical body—which is changing too, but much more slowly than perceptions, thoughts, and feelings—as a kind of anchor to affirm one's existence as a "person."

In that view, "I" is a name, a physical form, and the autobiography of that form. Although the autobiography is *constructed* of thoughts, and although we know that thoughts are impermanent, we ignore that information and imagine a permanent, persistent "myself" who *has* thoughts.

That tactic of *splitting,* of creating an artificial separation between thought and thinker, is part of the lie. Thoughts are not *had* by "myself"—they *are* "myself." Those thoughts, along with perceptions, feelings, the body, and the awareness of all that, comprise one seamless happening that cannot be separated into thoughts and a "haver" of thoughts. The separate "myself" that *has* thoughts is a ghost in the machine, a lie.

That lie is repeated unconsciously, over and over and over again. And each reiteration adds to the creation and maintenance of a *self-image*. There are two self-images actually: the one I hang around my own neck but hide from others, and the one I burnish and refine to show the world.

Many of us understand that the public self-image is a lie—perhaps one we need in order to survive in this cruel world ("It's showtime, folks")—but far fewer see that the *private* self-image is no less a lie. If we have an instant of awareness without that lie—a time when, as Toni Packer put it, "There's a moment of no sense of 'me'"—in that moment, we are *free*. There is nothing to live up to, nothing to maintain, nothing to do.

In that moment, something dies, yet it is not "myself" that dies, but only the *false images* of myself. The ongoing *aliveness* will still be here, but the self-images, at least for that moment, are not. If one is fortunate, the self-images, having been subjected to that moment of being seen through as illusory, will never return in full force, or may not return at all. And that, I am saying, is freedom.

This dying to self-images—the frames one has hung around one's own neck—can at times feel fearsome or poignantly sad, but that's where all the beauty is too. We never really have a proper eye for ourselves, our loved ones, or this astounding world of ours, until we embrace our oft-hidden understanding that none of it *lasts*. The "myself-image" that once felt so firm and lasting, falls apart, leaving a kind of emptiness in its wake.

We may not always *remember* that no detail of this aliveness lasts for more than a trice—some of us do remember, many more don't—but we all have at least *felt* it, I am sure.

When Toni says, "There is just a vulnerable being exposed, alone, without knowing, without a word," I find myself in accord entirely. That's *just* how this feels. And I like the way she puts it. It's firm but gentle—the way we best treat *ourselves*, I say.

So "Why *not* leave it alone completely, come what may?" What choice does one have anyway? Either we live "exposed, alone, without knowing, without a word," or under the spell of some hypnotic anodyne, some dogmatic "teaching."

19 - The contents of awareness

Q: Robert, I am the contents of awareness. Is that right?

A: No, I would not say that. The idea of separating awareness from its so-called "contents" is a favorite fiction of escapists who try to finesse the vicissitudes of ordinary primate human life by making themselves believe that nothing one sees or feels is "real." In that view, only consciousness is real, and the supposed contents of consciousness—perceptions, feelings, thoughts, etcetera—are only "appearances."

I don't buy a word of it. Consciousness and the so-called "contents of consciousness" are one and the same, and cannot *be* separated. If you doubt this, just experiment for yourself. Try to find "pure consciousness," free of any "appearances." I'll bet you can't.

Even if you somehow managed to convince yourself that the entire world of perceptions, feelings, and thoughts is only a mirage, "you" will still be there imagining that it is only a mirage.

This is like a joke but, baffled by the weight of scripture, tradition, and their own reluctance to participate fully in this dance we call life, the escapists don't get it. They listen with dead seriousness to the claims of gurus as if every word emanating from the mouth of one self-described teacher or another were automatically "Truth"—just because it can be linked to what some previous teacher taught, which is what his or her teacher taught, etcetera. And they never subject any of it to epistemological scrutiny. If a particularly bright or courageous student tries to apply a little acid to the so-called "gold," he or she is quickly subdued with "higher reasoning" or other tricks of the trade. The teacher may be sincere, but just mistaken, or hypnotized by too much reverence for *his* teacher or *her* teacher.

Q2: Hi, Robert. I'd contend that attention can bind to awareness apart from content, but in a manner of noticing something that is underlying: meaning the content is still there, but you're looking through the content to see the "pure" awareness.

A: Well, at the risk of getting all bollixed up in words, when you say, "You're looking through the content to *see* the 'pure awareness,'" that sounds to me like double-talk. Seeing *is* awareness, isn't it? On what basis do you split them so that "pure awareness" is *seen*? Seen by what or whom? And what do you mean by saying that "attention can bind to awareness?" Are not attention and awareness just two different names for the process of *noticing*?

These false distinctions are what I call *splitting*. First, you split attention from awareness as if they were two different things, when those are just two different names for the *same* thing. And then you suddenly drop a third factor into the mix—a "you" that *sees* awareness—like pulling a rabbit out of a hat.

What is needed here—forgive me my directness—is not a "contention," but an *investigation* that must begin by confessing ignorance: "I know nothing about 'pure awareness.' It's a phrase I heard, just a couple of words that stoke my imagination and whip up the fantasy factory."

What if the energy behind your "contention" is less about understanding, and more a desire to *justify* and reify the "*you*" that you pulled out of the hat? What if the muddled-up words are a back-door way of sneaking a concocted *permanent* "myself" into this schema —a *separate,* free-standing "you" that is so large and so stable that it can *look for* so-called "pure awareness," *see* it, and *distinguish* it from attention and from objects? That is a rather omniscient "myself" you have cooked up, it seems to me, larger than life and in the realm of fantasy.

For me, awareness is whatever is noticed here and now, which *is* attention. Noticing and attention are two words for the same thing. As I experience this aliveness, I see what I notice and notice what I see; I hear what I notice and notice what I hear; I feel what I notice and notice what I feel. And that *is* awareness. No noticing, no awareness. No awareness, no noticing.

But we seem to be near the limit of the usefulness of words to illuminate this matter, so, in any case, I reject the following spiritual tropes:

1. I am pure awareness.
2. Nothing real ever changes, and nothing that changes is real.
3. I was never born and so I can never die.
4. There is no such thing as a person.
5. The brain is just an "appearance" in consciousness.
6. I and Brahman are one and the same.

I reject them, but I am not saying that you should. As I see it, you will believe whatever you believe, and I can't stop you.

Q3. Hi Robert. I'm a little confused. You say in your book—which is the very best I have ever read on these matters by the way—"Whatever you feel, think, and see *is* you. There is no choice in the matter—no escaping *you*. That is what I mean by the word 'awakening'—a sudden awareness, quite undeniable, that everything you see, feel, and think *is* you."

Is that somehow different from the content of awareness being asked about here?

A: Hi. Thank you for your appreciation of *4T*.

Often, confusion arises due to the limitations of language, primarily the subject/verb/object structure that implies a doer, what the doer does, and to what or to whom the doer does it. So, for example, in the ordinary sentence form, "I see Spot run," we have "I" over here (subject) doing seeing (verb) of "Spot" over there (object).

I am simply pointing out that, although language divides such happenings into three pieces, any apparent "happening" is really only one indivisible process. I like to call that process "this aliveness."

The feeling of being "Robert" is this aliveness, the ability to see is this aliveness, and the image of Spot in the mind is this aliveness. It's *all* this aliveness.

Or, approached from another angle, one might say that what is seen cannot be separated from seeing, nor can the seer be separated from seeing. So seer, seeing, and seen—subject, verb, object—are all of a piece, a single happening. From either point of view, it should be clear that awareness and its supposed "contents" are not separable. Without awareness, there are no contents, and without contents, there is no awareness.

Some people try to say that a completely empty awareness exists already just waiting to be filled with contents. This is sometimes called "pure consciousness." I don't buy it. Show it to me and I might believe you.

Q3: Thank you, Robert. That helps. I have just read *4T* again and keep returning to the part about co-dependent mutuality. It's more than just understanding the words on the page, I think. I am so glad I have the book.

A: Yes, the words on the page are like a guidebook to a city. You may have the book in your pocket, but you still have to walk the streets for yourself. And the guidebook may be mistaken or out of date for all you know.

Q4: Been there. Done that. I followed Nisargadatta and one of his disciples closely and was convinced that I had "set up camp" in "the Absolute." But life kept sneaking back in and upsetting things! What a funny thing. Breaking camp and accepting and enjoying life as it flows without judgment is the real "Camp Freedom." Thanks, Robert, for putting a completely fresh perspective on this amazing life!

A: You are most welcome. "But life kept sneaking back in and upsetting things!" Right. Lucky you.

"The Absolute" is not a fact, but part of an ancient belief system. Nisargadatta is saying nothing new, nothing personal. Apparently, he was rather bright, but his "teaching" is not particularly special or notably intelligent, but really just classical Advaita Vedanta which he learned from his teacher, who had learned it from his teacher, who had learned it from his teacher, etcetera. The metaphors he used in his lectures, gold rings and such, came straight out of books.

Nisargadatta had every right to his beliefs, of course, just as we all do, but why should *his* beliefs be *your* beliefs or mine? He may have been called "Maharaj," but so what? He had his life, I have mine, and you have yours.

The real freedom is when you *don't* believe and when you *don't* let others explain and define this aliveness for you, not when you do. Then you can see things afresh, as they arise, without using someone else's answers to cover up and paper over the emptiness of not knowing final answers to ultimate questions.

Does "the Absolute," in the sense that Nisargadatta seems to have been using that term, exist? I don't know, and I don't *need* to know. Suppose it does—then what? Does that mean I don't feel sad when my dog dies?

Q5: And to add one more coin to the tip jar, we only need to *believe* in something when we don't know it exists, or else why would we need to *believe* it? My left foot is as it is not because I believe it is but because I can't avoid its presence in my life. But of course, beliefs are very big, have always been, and always will be for most folks. Their beliefs are what keeps them from terror or despair. Then, they need to *defend* their beliefs, and we're all in deep trouble.

A: Yes.

Q6: Robert, you stated in *4T* that you said things in the past that you would not say today. So I'm wondering, are there things you are saying today that you may express differently in the future? In other words, do you feel your expression of your perspective, if not the awakened perspective itself, will deepen or become more nuanced?

A: Since you have read *4T*, I assume you remember Chapter 3, called "Awakening Never Ends." That title implies that one's outlook, even among the putative "awake" ones, is nothing fixed. On the other hand, I have just celebrated my 74th birthday, so perhaps I have already reached and passed the apogee of my abilities for nuance. Brains do age you know, and what I say next year might be *less* nuanced, not more. As of now, this is the best I can do. Anyway, we'll always have Paris. Ha, ha.

Q6: I guess what I am alluding to is that everyone's awakening has a context. Even the context "I reject all contexts" is a context, no? Your very potent bonk on my head has caused me to notice some unexamined assumptions. Thanks for that. But I don't want to replace the assumptions I now have let go with yours, as fluid as they may be. I see I must go it alone. But I guess that's the way it works. The teacher teaches himself out of a job.

A: I don't know if a teacher teaches herself or himself out of a job. Frankly, I don't see a lot of that in the spiritual marketplace, where the more followers one has and can keep, the greater the prestige and lucre.

Mostly, in that milieu, teachers offer their *concepts* of what "myself" is, which varies according to what system is being taught, and then offer the student methods and practices designed to "help" the student to arrive at "realizing" that concept. But, according to most of those systems, that "realizing" might take years—or even more than one lifetime for a Theravadin Buddhist—and so teachers gather groups of devotees who follow them like sheep, always imagining that the teacher really "*knows*."

I saw this lovely cartoon once. A long line of sheep is stretched out behind the leader. The second sheep in line stops in his tracks, turns to the great mass of sheep behind him, and calls out, "Hey, this thing is a tumbleweed. We've been following a tumbleweed!"

For example, if you go to a teacher of Vedanta, you will be told that only Brahman (Spirit or "universal consciousness") "really" exists, and that the world of humans, cockatoos, pine forests, and galaxies is only "an appearance." This, you will be told, can be demonstrated logically, albeit not entirely, because only a long course of serious, progressive meditative practice can prepare the mind sufficiently to be able to understand that "higher logic" acutely enough to make the leap to "enlightenment."

Thus, the relationship with the teacher is likely to go on for many years until the student "realizes" what the teacher is teaching, which means coming to see the world the way the teacher does. Sometimes, a particularly bright student notices that the emperor has no clothes. That noticing is a great moment for the erstwhile student. No more student, no more books, no more teacher's dirty looks.

These self-appointed teachers are mostly parroting traditional metaphysics, which they claim is more "real" than what the rest of us see with our own eyes.

I don't *want* anyone to see things as I do. Quite the opposite: I hope that people will find views of these matters authentically for themselves, free of the weight of spiritual tradition, scripture, or submission to hierarchal authority.

That is why I keep saying that I am *not* a spiritual teacher, and I mean it. I may have certain things to teach, but not any established, orthodox view of what "myself" is or isn't, nor how to "awaken" by any path or method at all. I am saying one thing, and one thing only, and as soon as you grasp it fully—not just logically, but psychologically—you are done with me. You don't *need* me for anything. But we can still get coffee. Ha, Ha.

The Ten Thousand Things is an extended circumambulation of that one thing—a 360 degree walk around the matter, seeing it from different angles, so that people with different capacities and experiences may find one angle or another that opens the door for them.

I am happy to hear that you are prepared to "go it alone." Of *course* you must go it alone! All of us are always going it alone. There is no alternative to going it alone, but that fact is occluded by all this spirituality mumbo-jumbo.

Why do I say there is no alternative? After all, isn't faith in the guru an alternative to going it alone? No, it isn't. If you have faith in the guru, that faith is based on your belief that the guru knows things you don't know but must learn from him or her. But that belief is *your* belief based on *your* judgment, *your* assessment. If you project a sense of authority upon a teacher, it is *your* authority that is being projected. It's *all* you. It always was, and it always will be. Depending on nothing, find your *own* mind.

From *4T*, Chapter 24:

> *Those who view another human being—the guru—as an authority on the question of who or what "myself" is, make that judgment from ignorance. If you don't know what "myself" is, how will you know whether the guru's explanation is truth or nonsense? After all, different gurus say different things, and those debates never end.*
>
> *For one reason or another—perhaps charisma, perhaps because the guru's name attracts many followers, perhaps because the guru seems to be promising something "spiritual," and thus "desirable"—some listeners will consider a guru's words to be indubitable "Truth." But regarding another human being as a conclusive expert in these matters is foolish on the face of it—a judgment from ignorance, as I said.*
>
> *The guru may appear authoritative, but ultimately, your opinions about these matters must rely only upon your own authority, not the guru's, for if you find someone to treat as an expert, it is upon your discernment such a person appears to be worthy of belief. That bestowal of authority upon the guru can only be a projection of your own level of understanding. It is your judgment after all that has deemed that person an authority. It is your opinion, your reckoning, your sanction—do you see that? At root level, this all comes down to you and what you perceive, feel, and think.*

20 - I don't want anyone following me

Q: I watched a video of Bentinho Massaro saying "Fuck your relationships, fuck your family, fuck all that shit," and there's a guy well on in years nodding submissively and approvingly as he listens. Now that's what really intrigues me. How on earth does someone like Bentinho get a following? How does that work? What makes people so gullible? I mean you seem to be the real deal, and I can't even follow you. Ha, ha.

A: Well, that's the difference right there. I don't *want* anyone to follow me. The very nature of my understanding precludes a hierarchy of leaders and followers. Whether we recognize it or not, we are all in this together—all in the very same boat. I talk about my experience and my perspective, but not with the idea that anyone will follow or imitate that. No one could, even if someone wanted to. My words are self-expression, not "teaching." Someone may learn from my words just as I have learned from the words of others, but learning is a personal matter. I cannot *give* you learning, even if I try. Some things can be taught, but self-understanding is not transferrable. Self-understanding occurs only in your *own* mind.

The aliveness we call "myself" is a mystery without final answers, so following others who claim to have such answers can lead only to an exacerbation of ignorance—a deepening of the trance of transcendence, by which I mean the fantasy that there is a known and teachable means of gaining an escape from the biological facts of life.

Transcendence of the human condition is a fallacy, a fantasy, a fraud. This right now is it, I say. And *this* is melting away like the morning dew in the first rays of the sun. The idea of getting somewhere "else" is a folly foisted upon eager students by self-proclaimed teachers—once eager students themselves—who bought into so-called "spirituality." Why do I put the scare quotes around the word "spirituality?" Because it is a *nonsense* word. I have no idea what it means.

Does "spirituality" mean that there is a world of unseen "spirits" interpenetrating *this* world—the world we see and feel? That is what our distant ancestors believed, and some say it today, albeit they have no evidence, but only repeat rumors heard from others. That kind of magical thinking goes back to the cave painting days when hunters would carve or paint images of animals on the walls, and then repeatedly attack those representations with the points of their spears. We know that because the marks of those attacks are still visible among the lines of the images.

Or does spirituality mean that a god created *you* for a specific purpose, which is to find "Him" in this life and follow the rules that He has set down, so that by following them you will earn a ticket to an eternity in Heaven with Him? What arrant nonsense! When I think how many otherwise mentally intact humans believe that drivel, I feel a mixture of melancholy and wonderment at such ignorance.

The ones who say, "Of course I don't think of God as an old man in the sky. When I say 'God,' I mean all and everything, or the universe, or 'nonduality'", seem more confused to me. At least the naive, childish believers in "Him" use the word "God" sincerely. They may be intellectually challenged, but they are not hypocritical, and their credulity may be all they have. But the ones who define "God" as "all that exists" are living with fingers crossed behind their backs. If you mean the universe or all that exists, then *say* that.

Clinging to the word "God" is superstitious nonsense, like trying to avoid stepping on the cracks in a sidewalk. You don't *really* believe that your mother's back will break if you fail to avoid the cracks, nor do you *really* believe in the idea of a god who created this vast universe and made Earth this one special place where one particular species of primates—but not any other animals—have "souls" that require saving; a god who makes rules, demands obedience, watches and judges, hears prayers and responds. You are pretty sure that such fodder for the simpletons can't be true, but, just in case there is something to it, you cling to the phony insurance of Pascal's wager. And don't tell me that the image of "God" is a "metaphor." A metaphor for what?

I try to avoid exposing the sincerely religious to my skepticism. I don't want to hurt them, and hearing words from me cannot possibly do them any good. But when someone like that—a naive believer in the religion of his or her childhood indoctrination—does come upon my point of view, he or she may react by pitying me because I am not "saved." I don't mind. I understand that. Some try to preach to me. If only they could see how deeply benighted such preaching sounds to my ear—a dismal clatter of one inane idea rattling against the next.

My experience with the other type—the ones who imagine that the word "God" has some philosophical utility—is more complex. From them, I don't get preaching so much as invitations to debate. I used to have some patience for that kind of discussion—at least it might help me to clarify my own perspectives—but nowadays, I rarely take the bait. Mostly, I say what I see and leave it at that. The majority—even some who say they like my point of view—will misunderstand me, and continue to comfort themselves with half-baked metaphysics anyway.

Now and then someone really *does* get it, and that is a joy. For example, this from a reader in Austria:

> *"Reading* 4T *for the first time gave me a headache, as I wanted to grasp it all at once. Only months later it all fell into place, or still is falling into place and probably will always be. And now I can approach the whole idea of a non-permanent self and non-permanent world from my gut feeling, from my heart. This feels so liberating."*

Many who can be satisfied with half-baked metaphysics will find just what they desire with a Bentinho, a Mooji, or someone of that ilk. For me, those shenanigans are just a crying shame. Other self-proclaimed teachers seem to offer better approaches. I mean a Rupert, an Eckhart, an Adyashanti, or someone of that caliber. I am willing to take people like that seriously. Some of their views could be useful—not useful to me perhaps, but to someone. Still, at times, they too seem hypnotized by dogma, self-deluded, and driven to collect followers—which I view as a bad sign. Most assuredly, they are being carefully marketed as cash cows. Real sages and truth-tellers don't *want* people paying to sit at their feet.

What, you ask, makes people so gullible? Fear, I'd say—fear of impermanence, and fear of missing out on the promised "deathless, changeless state" with the power to trump biology. Deathless? Changeless? Really? And you know that how?

As my Austrian reader has discovered, when you really see that "myself" is a mixture of countless fragments, many of which have no staying power at all, and is in no way a changeless, unitary "thing," then you find that each instant of actual awakeness is a kind of death. Like it or not, there is no going back, not even one millisecond. Nothing can be repeated or retained. It's now or never.

This very moment is *sui generis*—a thing unto itself—a never to be repeated once-upon-once. That is not some spiritual mumbo-jumbo. That is my actual living experience. That's what I mean by "awake." Someone may want to be awake "like Robert," but that's not possible. You can only be awake like *yourself*, right now in this moment, or not. Awake is not a matter of degree, but of a clear-cut, night-and-day difference in perspective. Unless you are a light unto yourself, which is part of what I mean by "awake," you will be hypnotized by someone else's version of "reality." To me, this is entirely obvious, but somehow, for others, the hankering to transcend biology, impermanence, and mortality occludes the transparency of *this* moment with vain hopes for something "better" in the next.

To be a light unto oneself is a main theme of *The Ten Thousand Things*, stated explicitly right at the beginning in Chapter 1:

> *Following others will not lead to seeing myself and the world as the mystery they are. Quite the opposite. Awakening is when you don't follow.*

Q: Yes, Robert. I understand. It's amazing what people will follow. I went to a concert last night, and the band was awful, singing praises about the devil and such, but nonetheless, they had a massive following.

Q2: The major difference with a band, of course, is that, whatever bilge they are singing about, they are not offering themselves as saviors and asking people to follow them slavishly. They may be stupid, as many death metal bands are, but they are not creepy cults.

A: Precisely, Q2. I am glad you raised that point. Anyone who claims to be able to *teach* enlightenment or awakening, or call it what you will, risks becoming the cynosure of a cult. Regardless of the details of the teaching, if it promises an escape hatch from the anxieties, pains, boredom, ennui, apparent meaninglessness, and all the rest of what people find unsatisfactory about this aliveness, there will be many customers willing to buy that—to have something delivered to them like a commodity, without real suffering on their part beyond whatever demands are placed upon them by the teacher.

If one *really* wants to understand, much more is required, I say, than just handing over some money, or kissing someone's feet.

A certain kind of person imagines that to be the customer in that kind of transaction is a privilege or a blessing. The instructions of the so-called "master" are seen as a shortcut: "I pay to attend the retreat, and then everything I need to know will be explained to me." Attractive young people may try to cut to the head of the line by offering to have sex with the teacher. Then, they imagine, the supposed transfer of *shakti, satya, prajna,* direct wisdom, or call it what you like, will be even quicker and more powerful than just paying in cash to sit there listening to a lecture. That kind of sex may be gratifying for the teacher, but it is ultimately demeaning to the student; and in a setup like that, any pretensions to honesty fly right out the window.

The entire landscape of spiritual teaching past and present is littered with examples of abuse, ill-treatment, and lies. As long as one imagines that there is some sacred, holy, or faultless aspect in the words of those who call themselves spiritual teachers, those perversities will be swept under the carpet until finally, the shit hits the fan, as it did for Bubba Free John (Adi Da), Rajneesh (Osho), Muktananda, Satchidananda, Yogananda, Sai Baba, Bikram Choudhury, Andrew Cohen, Sogyal Rinpoche, Sakyong Mipham, Noah Levine, Bentinho Massaro, et al.

To be clear, I have no first-hand knowledge of bad behavior involving any of those people, but stories about them all have been published widely and confirmed by various witnesses.

Back in the 1980s, I wrote about the case of Osel Tendzin, the successor to Chögyam Trungpa. I did have inside information about that situation. Tendzin was diagnosed with AIDS but continued having sex with many of his students, both male and female, without advising them of the risk. In many of those encounters, Osel passed on the virus to students and consequently to their unknowing spouses and partners. When *that* scandal came to light, it was accompanied by a grotesque controversy over whether Trungpa had told Tendzin or not told him—there was testimony on both sides of the question—that he could carry on having sex with his students confidently, because as long as he kept up his esoteric *Vajra* practices, no one could be infected. You can't make this shit up.

Due to the AIDS factor, that is a particularly lurid case. But even if less salacious, the way that power differentials between teacher and student are used to procure sexual gratification in exchange for a leg up (sorry) on the teaching, is commonplace, and entirely regrettable in my view.

As for the money aspect, many teaching operations are carried out along the lines of the most modern business models aimed at branding, growth, and "revenue enhancement," just like any other for-profit operation. That, in my view, is also entirely regrettable. Wisdom has no price, and those who charge large fees for discussing it probably don't have the real thing in the first place. Or, if they do, they are acting like spiritual sex-workers who may offer some cheap, counterfeit "love" to the rubes, but who save the real thing for their personal lives, the lives the customers never see.

Suffice it to say that the teacher in such a setup, motivated by the material, sexual, and other narcissistic gratifications that being "the one" can provide, has every incentive to recruit and retain followers/customers. That, in my opinion, is already perverse. If you are really free yourself, why do you *want* followers and want to keep their numbers growing? Why do you *care* how many followers you have? You care because they pay.

The famous Sri Nisargadatta, who inspired so many contemporary teachers like Eckhart Tolle, Deepak Chopra, and Wayne Dyer, had few followers and earned his own livelihood as a shopkeeper. That man shared his point of view in a small attic room, refusing to accept money or gifts of any kind in exchange for that teaching. Eckhart, Deepak, and Wayne, I observe, are not so scrupulous. They are all about the bread, and in it to win it, although it is Nisargadatta's ideas, misunderstood and watered-down, that they are selling. Why do I say "misunderstood?" Because Nisargadatta himself said that only one person ever understood what he was saying. The rest only *imagined* understanding, and still do.

You might ask, "Robert, why do you focus so much on the *money* aspect of the spiritual supermarket?" I suppose that's because I have seen that, once a high-gain business model is the focus, veracity goes right out the window. It must, because fulsome honesty rarely leads to the kind of popularity that gins up six- or seven-figure profits. Cashing in big requires a painless, palatable product—something that goes down easy—not the troublesome truths of transience.

Spiritual seekers, who are the clients of these so-called teachers, *claim* to want "Truth," but they are *lying* to themselves. It is not "Truth" they are after, but a reduction in anxiety, an improvement in the way they feel, a purpose and a meaning to this aliveness beyond living itself. And most of all, they want and are willing to pay for the promise of a path that leads to transcendence of or escape from mortality and human limitation—which is flat-out nonsense, I say.

Before continuing, I want to say that I am not questioning the *sincerity* of one particular self-described teacher or another. Probably some of the ones I have mentioned here and elsewhere, along with others I have not mentioned, are sincere in wanting to convey a certain message that they take to be "Truth" and, in some cases, parts of a message like that might be reasonable.

But even if their intent is sincere, they seem equally earnest, or even more, in believing that they ought to be *paid* for teaching, so that their *job description* is "spiritual teacher," which I find an absurd designation. A mind like that says to itself, "If I had to work otherwise to pay my bills, I would not have the time to teach, to travel, to conduct retreats, etcetera." So, it is clear that making a living from spiritual teaching is the intention right from the start, and no bones about it. Selling sex is said to be the world's oldest profession. If it is, priestcraft is right behind.

As someone who has provided professional services for pay—I practiced depth psychotherapy for twenty years or so—I feel well-equipped to comment on this point. I cannot view conversations like this about our ultimate existential being as a "professional service." To provide therapy is one matter. This is *not* that. The questions that arise here, and are part of *4T*, need another approach entirely—one based on coming clean about all one does *not* know and never will know. The only valid "spiritual teaching" I can imagine would say something along these lines:

> *No one knows what any of this is. No one ever has. We find ourselves alive and aware without knowing how or why, if there even* is *a why. Our brains invent questions that they are not powerful enough to answer. A great deal about this aliveness must remain always beyond our ken. The deepest questions* have *no final answers but must remain open. To accept final answers is to be deceived. No one is an expert in the art of living, which is an art of improvisation, not certainty. Now, with that in mind, what do* you *want to do?*

Just watch one of these professional teachers at work, sitting on the throne, surrounded by the paying customers, and often plenty of flowers and portraits of famous gurus in whose "lineage" they claim to belong—what foolishness. If asked a question, how often does one of these self-described teachers say something like, "I don't know. I'm not sure. To be honest, I have no idea about that. Maybe no one does or ever did?" Your chances of hearing a reply like that are either slim or none, and Slim, it seems, just left town.

Relentless certainty is a chief feature of the product. The customers pay to have their doubts assuaged, not aggravated.

I was sent a video of one of the most highly regarded contemporary teachers in which he was asked why evils such as child abuse exist. Well, this cat twisted himself into knots trying to answer that ancient, insoluble question, smiling all the while—his stagecraft seemed obvious—as if in those dulcet, carefully modulated tones, interrupted by oh-so-thoughtful pauses, he was proffering profundities instead of tendering tired tropes.

Rather than saying, "I don't know *why* there is evil in the world"—which would have been simple and honest—this man occupied ten minutes riffing on "universal consciousness." When the questioner, exasperated by that performance, interrupted to ask for something more concrete—which I admired as a sign of acumen—this supposed "teacher" just twisted himself into the next grandiloquent knot. He seemed to be up for anything but saying, "I don't *know.*" Equivocation on that level would be difficult to parody, but the teacher was deadly serious, and nothing funny about it.

I did not think this famous teacher was *lying* exactly, but is just deluded himself by the religious dogma of nonduality which *claims* much explicatory power but actually *explains* nothing. So, his answer to the question of why evil exists was not an intentional fib, but the common misapprehension that religious *beliefs* can explain observable *facts*. From his perspective, he *did* have that answer: the one that was poured into his ear while sitting at *his* teacher's feet.

Q: "Why did the plane crash?"
A: "Oh, simple. It was God's will."

But even if he *had* felt uncertain, his glibness, that never missed a beat, suggested that he would never let on publicly. He might justify such an evasion with the argument, "My job is to present and convey the 'teaching'—not to be entirely candid about my own mind."

I can see the attraction of that angle. It must be fairly relaxing to be able to stick to "Love is all there is," or whatever platitude applies, while concealing—perhaps even from oneself—a mind that comprises thoughts and emotions that have nothing to do with love.

My friend, Dr. Robert K. Hall, and I have had wonderfully deep conversations over the years. Robert, as previous readers know, spent many years as a Buddhist teacher and a Gestalt psychologist who trained with Fritz Perls himself, so we always had plenty to talk about.

If you have read *The Ten Thousand Things*, you may recall a conversation where Robert and I were discussing the desire to know "the self." Robert said that after a lifetime of looking, he had found nothing (no-thing). The self, he meant, is empty at its core, so if you search for a lasting, permanent self, it's not there. Like peeling an onion, if you keep at it long enough, you end up with nothing. I agreed that I too had found no-thing, and added, "So all of this religion, all the practice, all this talk about noble truths and such, is just a wall they build to keep out nothing." Robert laughed and nodded his head yes.

Robert is in hospice care now and near the end, so our conversations are even more candid than before, which was already pretty wide-open. I asked Robert what he thought about spiritual teaching now that he is no longer involved. "Well," he said. "It's a good way of passing time, and it might make someone feel better, but that's about it. I don't see that it *leads* anywhere at all." Robert, you are a beacon of honesty.

Another such beacon was Alan Watts, who never claimed to be a spiritual teacher, and certainly not "enlightened." In fact, Alan often said that, being an ordinary chap, he had no obligation to act like a saint, and he didn't. People tried to make a cult leader of him, but he would have none of it:

> *I'm an entertainer. That is to say, in the same sense, that when you go to a concert and you listen to someone play Mozart, he has nothing to sell except the sound of the music. He doesn't want to convert you to anything. He doesn't want you to join an organization in favor of Mozart's music as opposed to, say, Beethoven's. And I approach you in the same spirit as a musician with his piano or a violinist with his violin. I just want you to enjoy a point of view that I enjoy.*

Thank you, Alan. That is my intention too. I'm an ordinary human primate animal who, like others before me, finds himself awake. Since "awake" seems to be a point of view that people imagine is desirable and claim to be seeking, I am willing to speak about it in a simple way, but my words are phenomenology, *not* instruction. I have no "wake up magic." I'm expressing how I see things, not telling others how to see them. Whatever I may say, the intention is not to collect followers, but to encourage finding one's own mind. In finding your *own* mind, you *will* be enjoying the point of view that I enjoy, but in your own way.

Recently, the guru who calls himself Mooji has been accused of the same kinds of sexual transgressions and other forms of power-tripping that have brought down a few once-powerful men in this era of "me too," when at least *some* chronic abusers of girls and women are being unmasked. Along with those allegations, which are multiple enough to be at least credible, the cult atmosphere that surrounds this man has been exposed, including people kissing his feet, and even worshipping him as "God on Earth," which he encourages, although lately, probably because of increased scrutiny, he pretends not to, and even has lawyers threatening people who report that he does encourage it.

These cult members are not bowing to Mooji's *ideas*, which are pretty much the same old platitudes about "love" and nonduality, but to his *person*—a sign of mental disorder and derangement, both on the followers' part, and on Mooji's. That is why a setup like this is called "a cult of *person*ality."

A friend of mine knows Mooji. She jumped to his defense. "He's not like that," she said. "He does not *want* people kissing his feet or worshipping him."

I replied, "You know this guy personally, and I don't, but in his public persona, he seems to manifest all the characteristics of what a friend of mine calls an 'I-doll.'"

If you really don't *want* to be the I-doll at the center of a cult, and if you *really* don't want anyone kissing your feet, it should be a simple matter to end it. No big deal. "Hey," you tell them, "I may have something worth saying, but I'm no god and neither is anyone else. Get off your knees. Do *not* try to kiss my feet. Do *not* call me 'master.' Do *not* say that I am God on Earth. Listen to what I have to say, and then go home and live your own life."

But that's a bootless business model. Why admit to being an ordinary human being when you are paid well to pretend to be a holy man in the lineage of Ramana Maharshi (who, incidentally, *had* no lineage)? Why say "stop," when you have willing women hanging on your words, and can sell photographs of your feet and samples of the earth you have stepped on in the gift shop? (I am not making that up.)

By the way, what's with this foot fetish anyway? Why kiss his *feet*? Can someone who knows more about Eastern religions than I do explain that to me? Why not, for example, kiss his ass?

Well, my friend flipped out and went on a tirade. That was entirely unexpected. Somehow, in her eyes, Tony Moo is above reproach. In her view, Mooji *can't* be just another bad penny holy man, so instead of seeing the cult for what it is, she disparages the reporter who wrote the "fake news" outing Mooji's bad behavior.

Yes, reporters can get stories wrong, but a generalization like that cannot neutralize specifics such as the ones in the reports, particularly when there is corroboration from various ex-followers. This *I-doll*, it seems, has feet of clay. There it is again, the *foot* thing. Go figure.

Q3: If I understand right, everything is just happening—following, not following, awakening, dreaming. So, who cares? In this oneness, who is there to care?

A: *Really?* Are you actually saying you don't care about *anything*? Are you really saying that, no matter what, it's all the same to you? Or are you projecting some kind of nihilistic theory you picked up somewhere onto actual human *be*-ing? Speaking personally, I care about lots of things. If you ask, "Who is there to care?" the answer is "Robert. I care." I care about every word in this reply, for example. If *you* really *don't* care, how about a dog shit sandwich on rye for lunch?

I am *not* talking here about "this oneness," as you put it, nor saying that we are "all one." I am saying we are all in the same boat, which is not the same thing at all. In *this* boat, the vessel of life in which we all are sailing, each of us abides for a time, and then dies and is thrown overboard—burial at sea, so to speak—while the boat sails on. So, "myself" is a passing biological phenomenon. But to notice that "myself" is transient and impermanent is not the same thing as saying, "No person really exists, so who cares?" That attempt to erase any boundaries at all between I and thou—or between peanut butter and dog shit—is a form of spiritual self-hypnosis. Snap out of it.

Q4: I see we have another victim of the folk theory of nondual enlightenment—holding on to it tightly, hoping to find themselves one with the universe some day, all the while being polluted with a constellation of ideas about what enlightenment is like as an experience, that is certain to keep them in ignorance. It's the reason why actual enlightenment is so rare: everyone's beliefs about it have them blinded to what's always right in front of them as their entirely ordinary, mundane awareness.

But that doesn't sell, does it? That doesn't make you special. It's not exotic. Not enough Sanskrit mumbo-jumbo or ancient gurus who were probably just as creepy as the ones we call out today. Nope. You can't be cool if enlightenment is no big deal, and gurus can't get rich, so the cycle continues and people stay in abject ignorance, despite knowing all the fancy words and reciting all the magic chants.

A: Thank you. That's well seen. I will be more succinct: leave so-called spirituality to the ninnies, wake up to what is always right here right now, and you may get a glimpse.

Q5: Would you say more about how duality obviously exists? I have been taught that seeing life dualistically is an illusion, and there is really only one "thing."

A: Sure. Imaginary/real, up/down, light/dark, dead/alive—all of that is duality. We live in a world of duality. In regards to the *material* world, that should be obvious: tall bamboo, short bamboo. On a more *psychological* level, happy/sad, fearful/confident, outgoing/introverted—the list is endless—are all dualistic opposites. The word "spiritual" is entirely dualistic. If there are ideas or experiences that are "spiritual," then there must be ones that are *not* spiritual.

No matter what motivates the attempt, you will never erase by fiat—by just *claiming* so-called nonduality—the obvious differences between one thing and another, including one person and another. If you consider that so-and-so is "realized"—as presumably was the person who *taught* you that duality is an illusion, whatever you mean by the word "taught"—then that implies that others are unrealized. So the term "realized" implies duality as soon as it is spoken.

The idea of "nonduality" is a religious concept—largely a Hindu religious concept—*not* a fact. And it is a concept that confuses people to the bizarre extreme that they deny the evidence of their senses and the thoughts and feelings of their *own* minds, replacing all that with second-hand ideas.

I am old enough now to have watched the notion of "nonduality" manipulated into a marketable mania. That term was barely ever heard until the 1990s. Now "nonduality" is a gimmick, a sales tool, a brand. If you tend towards materialism, you can now buy a "Cosmic Nonduality Mala," and that string of magic beads, advertised on the internet, probably costs less than a Skype session, also sold on the internet, with someone who purports to "teach" nonduality. The beads might work better too.

To see things as they are requires rejecting "nonduality" entirely, I say. Just forget what you were taught about nonduality or anything else. Find your *own* mind. Personally, I never even think about nonduality unless someone asks me. What is, is. And that is neither, I say, dualistic nor nondualistic. It just is.

Q5: Well, Robert, you wrote this: "To the extent that there even is a 'myself' separate from thoughts, feelings, and perceptions, they just bounce around as they will, like a beach ball in a rapids, while I, being just another thought, albeit a repetitive, habitual one—a *pet* thought, so to speak—just bounce around with the rest. It's *all* me. That's what thoughts, feelings, and perceptions are: me. In my experience, there is no 'self' apart from that. Others, I know, believe differently."

So, Robert, if there is no "myself" separate from thoughts, feelings, etcetera, then why does it matter what one thinks or feels?

A: I wrote that in the context of saying that no one is standing apart from thoughts, feelings, and perceptions *controlling* them. That is one aspect. But to say that because no one can *control* feelings means that it does not *matter* what one feels—that, for example, hatred is the same as compassion—is quite another aspect entirely. Of *course* it matters. It does to me at least.

And lacking control over the arising of perceptions, thoughts, and feelings certainly does not suggest that "Robert" does not exist at all, which is what the silly nonduality students are trying to make themselves believe. In the mistaken notion that selling themselves on such silliness will stifle their suffering, they pretend that "myself" is only a figment or a misunderstanding. That kind of pretense will not stifle suffering, but only deepen it, I say.

This is difficult ground. Many people I have known who try to explore these matters—including some well-known teachers—become disoriented and end up clutching at conceptual maps—the map, for example, of "No person really exists." That statement may make sense from a certain angle, but to apply it across the board as a final "Truth" makes no sense at all. Do you really want to deny that "myself" as an individual focus of perceptions, thoughts, and feelings, exists? If so, that is a disorientation from which it is difficult to recover, and I have seen it taken to absurd lengths such as, for example, avoiding the personal pronoun "I" entirely: not "I feel that... ," but "Here it is felt that..."

Well, here it is felt that talking that way is inane.

If you ask me "Who or what *are* you, Robert?" I will reply, "I am a human being." If I were to say, as the self-described teachers try to claim, "I am pure awareness," that would be a lie. No, people are *not* "pure awareness." Pure awareness does not have opinions, *or* students, and certainly does not need lunch money from them. If you are paying to sit there listening to such drivel—including such idiotic classics as "Thought is not real, only love is real"—snap out of it.

And beware believing everything that a self-described "teacher"—even an illustrious, celebrated one—tells you. Jiddu Krishnamurti, who had many worthwhile things to communicate, was famous for his so-called "secret," which many tried to copy in a kind of imitative stoicism. His secret was "I don't mind what happens." But in that, JK was lying. As a look into his biography will reveal, he was a man of *many* preferences. He *did* mind. We *all* do. Stoicism, which I recommend as a valid approach to ordinary living, is one thing. From that perspective, I will enjoy what I can enjoy, and endure the rest. But that is *not* the same as not *caring*.

"What's for lunch?"

"Well, you have a choice between a bean burrito and a warmed-over vomit ragout. Which do you want?"

"Oh, I don't care."

So Krishnamurti, whose ideas inspired me when I first heard them, and whom I still admire on that level, was a liar. He professed to have no interest in sex—which his followers took to be a sign of spiritual enlightenment and tried to emulate, sometimes destroying marriages in the process. But JK's claims to sexual asceticism were pure, unadulterated horseshit.

According to Radha Rajagopal Sloss, author of *Lives in the Shadow with J. Krishnamurti*, the famous "celibate" carried on a 25-year schtupping festival with a married woman (Sloss's mother), including cooking up false accusations of embezzlement against the woman's husband (Sloss's father), which the author called "a personal vendetta fueled by passions of the heart." So not just secret sex, but other lies as well, and nasty lies at that.

There is a capital lesson here: *eschew emulation*.

Krishnamurti voiced some lovely ideas—for example, "The seer *is* the seen"—but he was no saint, nor an "enlightened master." To quote my friend John Troy again: "Take the message, and leave the messenger."

Q5: This seems to be a matter of perspective. If you look from the position of the mind you are the wave. If you look from the position of the flow of experience you are the ocean. To speak from both positions in the same sentence is difficult.

A: No. "You" are *not* the ocean, and *you* will never speak from the perspective of the ocean. That is the kind of spiritual lie people have been taught to tell themselves, I say. You may disagree, and if you do, fine by me. To each her or his own. But what is the difference between "the mind" and "the flow of experience?" Is there a difference?

Q6: But, Robert, isn't the well-worn ocean/wave idea useful as a metaphor, pointing to the notion that we appear to be separate entities, even though ultimately the entire universe is one mysterious happening, one that cannot possibly be described or explained?

A: Yes, it might be useful on that level. However, to say that the universe is one mysterious happening, does not mean that "I" am everything, which is what people try to make of that idea. That is not wisdom, but solipsism.

To stick with the ocean analogy, if there were not an ocean, there could not be any such thing as a fish. So, the fish depends upon an ocean for its survival, but that does not mean that a fish *is* an ocean. A fish is *not* an ocean. A fish is a fish and an *ocean* is an ocean. They are *not* the same. Nor does the ocean *require* the fish. If you take the ocean away, there won't be any fish. But if you take the fish away, the ocean does not disappear. It might be a *different* ocean without that particular fish, but it would still be there.

I am not quibbling. This is *not* a small point. Some people actually imagine that the universe is "inside" them, and, without their consciousness of it, the universe would not exist. That is, I say, delusional. Do you really imagine that the moon exists only when you look at it?

21 - All the props are crumbling

Q: From an early age we are indoctrinated into the notion that life is a journey, maybe even a Hero's Journey of some kind. For the first few years of our lives, we are allowed to just wing it, but pretty soon we are told we have to perform well in school, pass exams, get into a good school, and climb up the ladder of achievement. In our teens, we have to consider a career or a trade and a means of making money to support ourselves. We are encouraged to enter into financial debt, first for our education, and then for the house we live in. We will be asked to choose a mate, have children, rise to the top of our chosen field, be successful, and all the rest of it.

In all this, there is an implied destination, and a false promise: get the job, make the money, choose the partner, have the children—and happiness and prosperity will be delivered. The reality, hidden in plain sight, is that the only destination is the grave. All success ultimately ends in failure, either through disgrace or senility, or both. But this destination is never explicated.

All romantic movies end when the boy gets the girl, or the hero rides off into the sunset—and we never see what happens next: the discord and the arguments, the dirty nappies, the sleepless nights, the infidelities, or the gunslinger waking up the next day to cold coffee and a lame horse. And it seems that much of the spiritual quest is a variation on this theme. If I stare at the wall long enough, or recite the Koran or the sutras fervently enough, chant enough and understand enough, I will one day be ushered into the True Life, the life in which I will finally be affirmed, suffering will end, and Paradise will be regained. Of course, that won't happen today, because I'm not pure enough, worthy enough, practiced enough, wise enough, surrendered enough, analyzed enough. All I need is more time. Tomorrow, maybe.

This is the life of the caterpillar, as you used it in your metaphor, Robert:

What the caterpillar calls "my death," the rest of the world calls a butterfly.

What you are shouting about from the rooftops is the life of the butterfly, in which this fantasy and every other "journey" fantasy has been seen through and discarded. Which, sadly, from the caterpillar's perspective, seems like a fate worse than death, or death itself; or as you say, can feel like either personal annihilation or falling forever.

So now I find myself between a rock and a very hard place. Having seen this much, I cannot turn back, but two angels with flaming swords guard the entrance to the butterfly's realm where you seem to live. I've seen, at least partially, through the illusion of the caterpillar's journey, and not yet supped on the nectar that only the butterfly can taste. And from this perspective, the life of the butterfly appears only as fatalistic, nihilistic, deterministic, depressing, and a source of despair.

Facing that, the logical thing to do is argue with the messenger; tell him it isn't so, prove him wrong, find a flaw in his reasoning or in his character, or see him as an exception to the rule. That way I can go about business as usual and resume the search, find a more amenable and less contrary guru. But I've seen through that dodge too, and all I'm left with is a faint appearance, to paraphrase Bucke[17], of light upon the horizon, but not yet the full sun.

The majority of people live in total darkness, unaware, blissfully or otherwise, of that sun's existence. A tiny minority bask in the full rays of the sun. And poor unfortunates such as I live with the faint glow in the East of light heralding the rising of a sun as yet unseen—which can easily turn back into another quest, another push for the summit, another ten-day retreat, a renewal of vows. Or I can simply take a stand exactly where I am and say, "Fuck it. I honestly can't think of anything else to do. In the meantime, I'll do a little yoga. It might soothe my frayed nerves." Haha! And off we go again. Another turn on the merry-go-round!

17. Richard Maurice Bucke (1837-1902) was a prominent Canadian psychiatrist who headed the provincial Asylum for the Insane in London, Ontario. His best-known work is *Cosmic Consciousness: A Study in the Evolution of the Human Mind.*

A: Good writing. Strong images.

Yes, you certainly are stuck between a rock and a hard place, and it's all in your mind. This suffering you express so eloquently is predictable. It is what people like me foresee when we advise forgetting all about "awakening" unless you are willing to see it through to the end.

"See it through to the *end*" may seem to refer to a journey, but that's not the idea. The end and the beginning are the same "place"—here and now. Here and now is all there is. This is so obvious that saying it seems superfluous, but somehow, although you have heard it countless times, it will not quite sink in.

The difference between those of us who "bask in the full rays of the sun" and "poor unfortunates" such as yourself, has nothing to do with any journey, nor is it a question of so-called spirituality. Paths and practices, nonduality, devotion to the master, and the rest of that stuff, is only the rigmarole in which caterpillars immerse themselves to keep from noticing what is plain and simple to every butterfly whoever flapped a wing: here and now is all we get. Awake, profoundly hypnotized, or anywhere in between, this existence is fleeting, without permanence of any kind. You have *this* moment.

See things as they are. Notice the transience—the death and dying, the passing on and the passing away—that is obvious wherever one looks. Just comprehend fully that one day, like any other living being, you will have to turn your face to the wall and die. If that day is not *this* day, then why waste *this* day in chasing after the pot of gold at the end of the rainbow? There *may* be such a pot of gold, but I wouldn't bet five cents on that proposition.

Q: So all the props are crumbling. The various beliefs about a loving protecting God, or a divine incarnation in female form, the Great Mother, are being seen through. All hope engendered by the possibility of escaping through "enlightenment" or whatever, is being dashed on the rocks. And what I'm confronted with—on this side of the metamorphosis from caterpillar to butterfly—is the very terror from which I have been trying to escape. Because I don't yet have the butterfly's perspective, all your words do is further unmask the fear without assuaging it at all.

To the caterpillar, your words are cold comfort. I can see now how the gurus are peddling snake oil. If they were to simply say, "Life is shit, anything can happen and then you die," they wouldn't have many punters coming back.

A: My words are not intended to be cold comfort, hot comfort, or any other kind of comfort. Nor would I ever say that life is shit. This aliveness as a human primate animal can be painful and challenging at times—even excruciating in some unfortunate situations—but if one is lucky enough to have at least the bare necessities of food, clothing, and shelter, along with the right outlook, there is an ineffable beauty to be noticed right here in the mundane. And an artist like you should know that. You *do* know it. It is only your fear of mortality—which is, after all, just the way of all flesh—that keeps you from delighting in that beauty.

To see a World in a Grain of Sand
And a Heaven in a Wild Flower

—William Blake

If fantasies of *future* glories are what you desire, you can find that flummery on any shelf in the spiritual supermarket. Just bring money and credulity, and the "teachers" will sell you as much future glory as you like.

Apropos, don't take this "butterfly" thing too far. There is an element of truth to it, but everyone, caterpillar *or* butterfly, must suffer in one way or another; and sooner or later everything must crumble away and disappear.

You see "now" as filled with terror. Are you truly *terrified* sitting there at your keyboard writing to me? Why? Is it mortality that frightens you—the notion of not being at all? For me, the thought of death is no more frightening than the idea of drifting off into sleep after a long day. As living seems so painful for you, I'd think you would relish the idea that you won't have to be at it forever.

Of course, no one can say for certain that "myself" ceases to exist at the death of the body and brain. But if that's the way it is—and there is a lot more evidence for that view than for the unsubstantiated fairy tales about life *after* death—you won't be around to regret anything anyway, including that the "myself" you once were no longer exists.

As soon as you admit to yourself that *nothing* is permanent—neither pain nor pleasure, and certainly not "myself"—you can relax, for then there is nothing complex or esoteric to attain. You can welcome each moment without fixating on what you want and don't want. You can allow things to be as they are.

Will that make you happy? I don't have the slightest idea. But betwixt and between, where you are presently—one foot in and one foot out—certainly doesn't seem to be doing much for you, so why would you want to stay in that straddle?

Q: The terror of now. Haha, that's exactly right. The difficulty with this for me is that there is nobody around here who bears witness to the fact that now is OK. Everybody is running from it as fast as they can. Including me. Haha.

A: Yes. That is the only difference between you and "Robert." I'm not running. This is it.

22 - A thank you note

Dear Robert, this is not a question, but a thank you note. I write this letter not knowing if I will send it or not. It's the first time that I put these words on paper or write to someone about these matters.

When I first heard your interview on *Buddha at the Gas Pump*[18], I didn't know who you were, and I don't know why I watched it in the first place, as I only watched interviews if I already knew something about that person's work. Then I saw the few presentations that you have online and I bought your book.

A funny thing happened when I was reading *The Ten Thousand Things* and watching your Zoom gatherings. I developed a love/hate relationship with you and your book. I didn't want to read it anymore—but I couldn't stop reading it. I didn't want to be watching those Zooms, but I did watch all of them. So funny, right?

I have read several authors and seen numerous presentations, supposedly on these matters. I have been focused on these matters (I don't know how to call it anymore) for about twenty years now. And then boom—suddenly you stop all of that for me. Reading your book and listening to you stopped the search.

The identification that I had with the searcher for so long stopped. You took away my beliefs and I saw myself with empty hands. Motherless. And I hated you for that.

Then I saw myself rapidly building another identity (I felt like the character from *The Terminator,* rapidly assembling all the pieces and carrying on with what I was doing). But it wasn't the same. It doesn't mean I like the reality movie I'm in. I don't. It doesn't mean the searcher has died. I don't know that. And I don't really care. I am not troubled with that anymore.

I know now that I wasn't searching for the "Truth." I was trying to escape my reality movie, the suffering, the feeling of loneliness, feeling less than, or that something is wrong with me. The fear of

18. See https://BATGAP.com/robert-saltzman

impermanence. The feeling of anxiety, afraid of life and events out of my control. But I know now, really know—not through the intellect but as a genuine acceptance—that nothing was in my control anyway. I happened to stumble into all this like Alice down the rabbit hole.

I'm reading your book for the third time. Now I underline phrases and circle words, and I smile. Here I am doing it again. But now I don't mind.

I look at people and at events differently. Not because of them or because I'm a very understanding person (I'm not), but because now I'm gentle with me, gentle with myself.

I see your pictures and I feel the love for life itself. I see you with your donkeys and I feel the entanglement of life. One life, not two. I see the tears in your eyes when you answer some people at the gatherings, and I feel the reality of fellowship. And I love you for that.

I write this letter to thank you for shattering my world. For urging me to find my own mind, my own authority.

Yours sincerely,
Teresa
(*Sorry for my grammar: I'm not a native English speaker.*)

(Robert): Hello, Teresa. What a beautiful letter. Clear as a bell. It gets right to the heart of the matter. "I see you with your donkeys and I feel the entanglement of life. One life, not two." Yes. The *entanglement.* The inevitable entanglement. Perfect.

If English is not your first language, I'd like to see how you write in your mother tongue. I feel touched by your appreciation and heartened to hear that my work has moved you in this way. Thank you. Walk on.

23 - Awake and aware

Q: Hi, Robert. Thanks for sharing your insightful exchanges with us here on Facebook, and also for putting out *4T*, which my wife and I are reading and discussing together at the moment.

We both just read Chapter 23, "Choiceless Awareness", regarding Ramana Maharshi's invocation to focus on the "I am." One of the things one comes up against in Advaita circles is the notion of "awareness without objects," said to be the condition in which we should ideally be living on a permanent basis.

There is, of course, the discussion about whether objects apparently or inherently exist—but maybe we can leave that aside, and just look at the notion of awareness without objects.

In my own experience of day to day living, whether sitting quietly or engaged in whatever activity, no such state has ever been experienced. The idea of awareness without objects makes no sense to me, and probably has as much survival chance as a fish out of water—though I imagine that there really are fish out of water, lasting for a few rather unpleasant minutes, while awareness without objects may not exist at all. Perhaps you could say something about this from your perspective, if you can find the time and are so inclined.

Thanks again and be well.

A: Hi. Thank you. You are most welcome.

One can spend a lifetime trying to experience the world according to the claims of others. Since you are asking me to share my perspective, it's really quite simple. I have no need for Vedanta or any other belief system, and I am not *trying* to experience *anything* beyond the vastness of this aliveness and all it contains.

Just as a boat chained to the dock cannot even begin her journey on the seven seas, a human mind that clings to a pre-existing system of beliefs will never even notice the mysterious immensity of being.

I find myself awake, aware, and devoid of desires to become or attain anything that is not here now. Each moment is rich beyond words, and all the more so if we meet it without preconceptions about the so-called "Truth."

I have no idea what awareness "really" is, from whence it comes, or of what it consists. I see many fellow humans laboring to convince themselves that, behind this apparent chaos of pain, fear, loss, disease, insubstantiality, emptiness, and mortality, lies a pure, featureless "thing"—consciousness—which is undying and unchanging; and which is what one "really" is, so that the "I" of experience, including suffering, is only a figment.

But in my understanding, pain, fear, loss, and all the other "negatives," are simply part of living as a human primate animal. Those feelings arise if and as they do, just like the "positives" such as pleasure, joy, peace of mind, creativity, love, etcetera. Trying to have one without the other is, I say, a fool's errand.

When I open my eyes in the morning, I find a world of objects, feelings, perceptions, and thoughts, complete and intact. I do not have to try to create that world, any more than I have to try to circulate my blood or grow my hair. The world just happens, and I could not prevent that happening even if I wanted to.

So one's ordinary, everyday experience conflicts completely with the claims of Vedanta—which can never be lived out or lived through directly, but only *heard about* from others and credulously believed.

Even assuming that the entire material world does not "really" exist but is only a kind of dream, one's direct experience still does not accord with the claims of Vedanta. For within the so-called "dream" are countless happenings of various kinds—sights, sounds, thoughts, etcetera—and those experiences cannot be made to go away. You can *call* that a dream, but naming it that way neither explains any of it, nor explains any of it away.

Advaita Vedanta has become faddishly popular among "spiritual" people, who imagine that—if only they could experience that Brahman alone is real, and that the universe is not real but only *maya* (illusion) or *lila* (divine play), and that Brahman and *Atman* (the individual self) are one and the same (which is what the so-called jnanis claim)—then they would be "saved" from impermanence, loss, and mortality.

Extraordinary claims demand extraordinary evidence, but, apart from dogma and testimony, I don't see much evidence at all for the claims of Vedanta—not even ordinary evidence. I hear you saying that you don't see much evidence either.

As always, I am just reporting my view of these matters, not telling anyone what to believe or disbelieve.

Does that help?

Q2: How refreshing: "I'm not telling anyone what to believe or disbelieve." Robert, sometimes I marvel at your simplicity and its brilliance. I am reading *The Ten Thousand Things* currently, and loving it. Thank you, thank you, thank you.

A: You are most welcome. I am so happy to hear that you love *4T*.

The simplicity is not really "my" simplicity, but the ordinariness of being what one is, rather than striving to become what some other human being tells you that you *should* be.

The condition of what I call "awakeness" only seems extraordinary when seen from the point of view that imagines that, in order to be "awake," one must become something "better" or "more advanced" than one is right now in the present. Since something different from what one is right now is literally *unattainable* (obviously, one can only ever be what one is right now—not something different, no matter how seemingly desirable), all kinds of "spiritual" fantasies arise—and the *fantasies* are the complexity. See that and be free, free to be as you are.

In each moment, what is, is and does not have to be attained, or believed in, but only noticed.

24 - Freedom from bondage

Q: I suppose that all I need to know from you is that it is true, that there is freedom from bondage to be had in this life. You have answered in the affirmative. This is of capital importance, because almost everyone, including the religions and their priests, want to tell me that it is not true; that life simply must be endured, that I must make the best of a bad lot. I know that the goal is not to be reached at some future time, in some other place. But it is crucial to know that someone, somewhere has reached it. Is this another self-deception?

A: What do you mean by "bondage?"

Q: A sense of being not quite right, Robert. Something missing, something lacking, restlessness, discontent, a sense of dread, sometimes acute, but always in the background. This has been added since childhood, probably since around the time of puberty, and has spurred the search for something to relieve it—addictions, distractions, the spiritual quest.

A: OK. So if I have this right, what you experience as bondage is a collection of various features—the "negative" ones—of a personality that you imagine was grafted onto an original child's personality around the age of puberty.

Probably that is not entirely true. Personality is a combination of nature (inherited tendencies transmitted via DNA) plus nurture (outside influences). So others, who had roughly the same kinds of childhood influences as yours, but a different *inherited* nature, experience neither your sense of dread, nor any desire to be liberated from it. Some people are naturally more anxious and less sanguine than others right from birth. Any mother of several children will be able to say something like, "Little Bobby was an easy baby, but his brother was fussy and cranky."

And the *added* discomfort did not begin, as you imagine, at puberty, I would guess, but probably much earlier—at the point around two or three years of age at which children begin to experience themselves as a "someone," a person apart, a "myself."

That identification as a separate "myself" arises *partly* due to training and enculturation—for example, the parent takes the child to a mirror, and, pointing to the child's reflection, says, "See, that's *you*," thereby instantly welding the child to an identity which depends on seeing "myself" as a body and as an image of the body—but not entirely. Not all of personality has to do with enculturation. One is *born* with tendencies, both the generalized human ones and those more specific to that particular individual.

The ancient Greeks spoke of the four "temperaments" that are the luck of the DNA draw: sanguine (pleasure-seeking and sociable), choleric (ambitious and leader-like), melancholic (analytical and literal), and phlegmatic (relaxed and thoughtful). In that view, just as all colors can be created by mixing cyan, magenta, yellow, and black in various proportions, personality types depend on the proportions of temperaments in the mix.

But how personality develops is not the point here. I touch on it just to clear away some misconceptions which could interfere with understanding what I will say next. Understanding this matter, assuming you really want to, will require a painful stretch—including the radical abandonment of long-held beliefs which, in my experience, very few humans *care* to abandon, no matter how uncomfortable they feel in their own skins. And, honestly, I don't know if you are either willing or able to abandon your present beliefs about who and what you are. I certainly would not want to bet on it.

In fact, if I had to bet, I'd wager that you will read what follows, *misunderstand* it, and then, having altered it to match your requirements and satisfaction, file it away comfortably in the bin called "I understand this."

But I could be wrong. Perhaps whatever words follow will be a wake-up call for you. That's not in my control. I reply to questions if they are respectfully put to me as yours have been, but I have no attachment to the effect my replies might have, nor am I engaged in "teaching." For me, this kind of discourse is just self-expression. I have no questions myself about these matters, so the questions of others are stimulating to me in a way—it's entertaining to see what will be written. I let my mind go where it will as if we were sitting face to face talking, and just type.

Now when I asked you to tell me what you meant by bondage, you responded with a list of certain features of your personality—the ones you consider painful or uncomfortable—but you left out a great deal of what a personality contains. How about the "positive" features, the ones of which you are proud or upon which you rely? Why are those not seen as "bondage?"

This is a common misunderstanding. Your desire—which you share with most people I have met who even get as far with this as you have—seems to entail clearing away the "negative" parts of personality while keeping the "positive" ones. In other words, you want to keep on being a "myself," pretty much as you are now, except a "better" myself—freer and happier. That's not a bad goal actually. I practiced psychotherapy for many years, and feeling freer and happier was a chief objective in much of that work.

But what you are calling "freedom from bondage" is not *about* improvement. It's not about feeling happier. The actual situation is far more radical than that. And this is where most folks, when encountering someone who talks like me, get off the bus.

Most self-described "spiritual" people want nothing to do with a perspective like mine. They want to be promised everything that psychotherapy promises, and *more*. They want to be led along a fantasized path to a state of bliss, perfect freedom, endless joy, or whatever. That is not, I say, what awakening is about—not at all. So if you want that, you don't want me.

The matter of so-called bondage is quite simple, and I can lay it out in words that you will understand in a fashion—although certainly not with complete clarity, for if I could do that, I would already have done it, and you would not *have* any questions.

Something in us absolutely hates hearing all this. The kinds of things I say threaten to upset the entire applecart. And it is hard to actually *want* one's applecart upset, so the resistance is massive even if something in us would like to be done with these endless questions.

Questions are a chief method of *remaining* in bondage, because each time a question is formulated, the apparent *asker* of questions or *formulator* of judgments and opinions (I say "apparent" because who knows, really, where words come from?) is made to seem firm and permanent. Since there is never an end to the questions that can be devised, the asker can cling to the fallacious feeling that there will never be an end to *him* or *her*.

If you are able to grasp what I will say next, you will *not* be freed from bondage at all, but only left with a terribly frightening job to do, and it is a job no one else can do for you. Only you.

Bondage is *not* oppression by a collection of various negative personality traits such as the ones you mentioned, so that if those negatives could just be removed everything would then be lovely. In that fantasy, you would still be "myself," but a *better* myself, a happy and free myself, no longer inclined to self-condemnation, fear, desire, and the endless search for relief through escapism. That fantasy *is* the bondage. The desire to continue to be "me"—but without the "bad" parts, the painful parts, the shameful parts—*is* the bondage.

Bondage, if we must use that word, is the very idea that there is a "myself" in any way separate from the negatives—the self-judgment, the unfulfilled desires, the fear, the terror of mortality, and all the rest. If freedom from bondage is desired, that idea—that there is a "myself" separate from all that—will have to *die*. And most likely that would be a prolonged and messy death.

One can intuit all this. I can intuit that I am as hung up and "bound" by the things I am proud of as I am by the ones I find embarrassing or shameful. But that intuition is not exactly a thought, and so language—which can express thoughts, but not intuitions—becomes inadequate. I can *tell* you that I find myself awake, but I cannot explain exactly what that means or what it is like. I can say, however, that neither pride nor shame is part of it.

What you *now* consider "myself"—a *person* with a past and a future—although necessary socially perhaps, is an illusion, a kind of waking dream. Whether that dream is a nightmare or a castle in the air, as long as the character in the dream is not seen *as* empty of any fixed existence, one will never be free from bondage. The illusion of a fixed and separate self that can *become* "awakened" *is* the bondage. No matter the details, that illusion *is* the bondage. Some people say that there is no bondage, that you are free right now, but don't know it. I understand that point of view. I have even voiced such ideas myself, but it can be confusing to think that way. After all, if you don't *feel* free, then how can it be said that you *are* free?

Some dreams are pleasant, some are not, but if one is dreaming, one is *not* awake. The *content* of the dream is irrelevant to the matter of bondage and awakening from so-called bondage—except that pleasant dreams can leave one feeling complacent and unmotivated to awaken from them, whereas uncomfortable dreams may impel investigations such as yours.

If someone dreams that he or she is personally in touch with "higher consciousness"—as so many foolish "teachers" seem to be dreaming, and even presume to instruct others—that might *feel* pretty cool, but it's no less bondage than feeling that one is a total dunce. Those are two ends of the same dream spectrum. Two sides of the same coin.

From my vantage, there *is* no bondage, nor any freedom from bondage. What is, is—including everything one perceives, feels, and thinks—and what *is* cannot be any different from the *way* it is. To the mind of understanding, that's fine. Nothing *needs* "liberation." I don't feel bound by anything at all. Bondage is a detail of *your* dream, and a borrowed detail at that, right out of the books filled with spirituality chit-chat. Others have different dreams—dreams that hang *them* up.

So the "terribly frightening job" I mentioned involves noticing that your entire self-image—*all* of it, not just the "negative" aspects—is a sham. It is a sham because the "myself" you imagine as the *doer* of your life, that which suffers all the ills you mentioned, has no permanent existence at all, but is little more than a social convention. That self is a *false* self.

That self has no ability to choose anything. No ability to decide anything. No ability to change anything. All of those imagined powers are *part* of the dream. And people keep dreaming such dreams because they would rather have dream powers than no powers at all.

The "dream-you" has no power to choose to awaken, or to choose anything else, any more than the dreamer of a nighttime dream has any actual powers in *that* dream. And there's the rub.

This is often considered a paradox, but from my perspective it is not a paradox at all, but just the way things are.

You may keep dreaming along with most of humanity, or you may awaken to the facts of the matter—which requires a total, unwavering focus upon what is true. Not what some teacher *tells* you is true, and you just *believe* it—but what is true for *you* here and now, without trying to change it into something else or escape from it entirely.

My experience of this *aliveness* is that each moment is *sui generis*—a thing unto itself—and moments are not really connected in the way many of us routinely imagine. In my world, one might feel dissatisfied with how things are in *this* moment—but in the next, without having tried to *change* anything, feel gratitude for being at all. And not the slightest trace of any of it, neither dissatisfaction nor gratitude, can be saved or retained for more than a split second.

We do not produce our thoughts and feelings, and we cannot keep them. It's all transitory, all passing away as soon as it arises.

In a way, this "non-bondage" is like living in a wind tunnel or standing in a rapids. In the face of such evanescence and transitoriness, there *is* no chronic dissatisfaction, no ongoing self-judgment, no guilt, no shame. Soon this entire mess will come to a halt, and one's cares will vanish with one's final exhale. Meanwhile, in the words of the cartoon hero Popeye to his skinny-marincky girlfriend Olive Oyl, "I yam what I yam."

So if there is to be dissatisfaction with "myself," at least let it be dissatisfaction with the sham nature of the *entire* dream—not just the "bad" parts.

25 - *A fresh look at what you need*

Q: Dear Dr. Saltzman, thank you so much for graciously accepting my friend request despite our never having met. I consider it a true honor to connect with you here, and am very thankful for all aspects of your work.

I am a 56-year-old former mental health counselor who lives in Chattanooga, Tennessee. I have been on the spiritual path my entire adult life, most recently focused on contemporary nonduality teachings, which somehow led to my stumbling upon your book, of which I have just completed my first read.

The Ten Thousand Things comprises some of the most cogent, thoughtful, and penetrating responses to the deep issues of living that I have ever encountered. Your book seems to have dispelled most of the remaining fantasies I've tried to hold onto regarding the existence of personal agency or anything one could remotely call a soul; and has radically changed the focus of my experience, from a search to simply being the ever-changing flow of thoughts, feelings, and perceptions.

Although *4T* has answered the big-picture questions for me, I wanted to ask, to whatever extent you can answer, how, if at all, this way of seeing plays out in the face of the attempt to resolve apparently recalcitrant personal challenges? In my case, the overarching story driving the spiritual search was having lost all my family connections early in life, and—despite spending years of effort trying everything I could think of, including getting a graduate education—never having found my footing with work and finances, which in turn has led to constant fear of winding up homeless and dying in the streets.

In addition, despite my having done a great deal of therapy and personal growth work over the years, and feeling myself to be a basically worthwhile person, I have been frustrated at never having had any success in forming lasting relationships, romantic or otherwise. So I find myself feeling perpetually alone, struggling to meet my basic needs, with few options available for improving my situation; and very little sense of relief, hope, or progress in between, constantly bracing for total destruction.

What little sense of hope I have been able to summon to this point has come purely from my immersion in various self-help strategies and spiritual practices, and the belief that somehow all my efforts would eventually pay off, resulting in a more relaxed and stable situation that would at least allow me to live out my remaining years in some level of enjoyment.

Now, I have finally confronted the total uselessness of those efforts (except perhaps, as you might say, to get me to this point where I can let them all go). However, there yet remains a part of me that continues to say, "Ok, but what now? Where does this freedom leave me in terms of dealing with my challenges?"

Of course, I realize that you can't tell me what to do, but I would just like to ask if you could clarify for me whether I understand correctly that, in choiceless awareness, it really can be as simple as the old Zen poem says:

Sitting quietly, doing nothing
Spring comes and the grass grows

Since, truly, there appears to be nothing more I can do in practical terms to improve my situation, I would at least like to have confidence that there is, in reality, never anything to worry about. I would be very appreciative if you could provide any additional insights that might help me to gain clarity in light of the specific issues I'm dealing with here.

This is the gist of my dilemma, as I see it, but I would be happy to expand on any part of it upon request. Thank you again, sir, for whatever help you can be in helping me sort this out, once and for all.

A: Hello. Thank you for your message and your appreciation of my work.

First, let me say that I understand your situation, and I feel for you. I imagine that to feel alone and frightened of the future is not easy.

You are asking if I can give you "confidence that there is, in reality, never anything to worry about." I am sorry to say I cannot do that. And if I did offer you something like that, I would only be compounding the problem by adding a new belief in what "Robert" says to the already great weight of beliefs that you are now throwing off like the impediments they are.

If worries are there, they are there until they aren't. No one is *making* worries, and no one can choose to stop them either. Spiritual beliefs and self-help programs do not end worries, but only try to explain them away or sweep them under the rug—which can make matters all the worse.

In his classic book *Cutting Through Spiritual Materialism*, Chögyam Trungpa pointed to the human tendency to imagine spirituality as a method of self-improvement—as a way of refining, developing, and protecting the ego; as a way of transforming "myself" into something *better*, something *more evolved*. In the extreme case, this tendency takes the form of, as it is often said, "transcending the ego"—while, presumably, "I" am still there to enjoy being me—which seems a strange idea indeed.

A bit later, in the 1980s, the psychologist John Welwood wrote about what he called "spiritual bypassing," by which he meant using spiritual practices and beliefs to avoid dealing with painful feelings and unmet developmental needs—which, like an ostrich putting its head in the sand to avoid seeing reality, does nothing to deal with such feelings and needs, but only shirks them.

So now, having come across my book, which "dispelled most of the remaining fantasies I've tried to hold onto regarding the existence of personal agency or anything one could remotely call a soul," as you put it, you are faced with the practical truths to which both of those men pointed.

As Trungpa was saying, freedom is not about making the sense of self *better*, but of seeing the *emptiness* of "myself." And as Welwood was saying, we human primate animals have real-world problems and real-world needs. Merely clinging to beliefs—such as "Everything is only an illusion" (Hindu spirituality), or that an ultimately benign

God is watching and protecting us (Judeo-Christian-Islamic spirituality), or "Visualization will get me what I want" (pop spirituality like *The Secret*) —will not meet those needs, except in fantasy.

That kind of spirituality is bogus, but the *needs* are real. You have mentioned two pressing needs. First, you find yourself friendless and without companionship. I am sorry to hear that, but that is not a condition cast in concrete. That can change; and if it is going to change, it will require that *you* reach out somehow to others. I am not saying that is easy for you. I understand that it is not easy for you. If it were, you'd already be doing it. But please consider ways in which you might. One classic way is volunteering to help others in some program already organized to do that work.

As for your material worries, I find it difficult to believe that someone who writes with such obvious intelligence and insight would have to be fearfully indigent. Is there no way you can use your skills to earn at least enough money to put the specter of homelessness out of the picture? Please try to look into this. Again, I am not saying this is easy for you. I understand full well that it isn't.

To underline what I am saying, I am happy to hear that my book has opened your mind in this way, but please don't misunderstand my words about "myself" being an "ever-changing flow of thoughts, feelings, and perceptions," as you put it, as indicating that "myself" is without needs on the quotidian, everyday, practical level. On that level, needs must be met, which may require changes in perspective and intention. I understand that no one can simply choose or decide to change perspective and intention—indeed, that is one theme of my book—but we are all influenced by everything we see, hear, feel, or otherwise experience. So I hope that my words here will influence you in that way.

To be clear, I am encouraging you to take a *fresh look* at what you need, and then to find ordinary ways—not philosophical or spiritual ones—of meeting those needs.

Sending love,
Robert

26 - Find your own mind

Q: My question relates to teachers of nonduality who state, unequivocally, that there is nothing anyone can do, that no practice or technique can be of benefit to spiritual awakening. I don't think I've heard any nonduality teacher say the opposite. However, this idea or perspective is totally contrary to my own experience.

I could understand if someone was to say, "I personally did not follow a path or technique, but I cannot say that there isn't one." But this total, almost stubborn attitude that there cannot ever be one, confuses me slightly. And it is the origin of this that I am seeking to understand.

With this idea being so commonplace in nonduality teaching, I wonder whether it is now simply traditional? The established philosophy states there is no method, and thus many believe there is nothing that can be done, so nothing *is* done. And when some still say they have "woken up," it seems the belief is legitimized and a self-fulfilling prophecy is born.

If it were only one or two people, then I might wonder whether it's just a matter of those who did not follow a path or technique taking their lack of a method as proof that there isn't one for anyone. But as this idea is so widespread, I feel the reason may be wider too.

The other half of this is that the belief is so deep-seated that, even when a person demonstrates a technique, it tends to be dismissed out of hand as nonsense by both the teachers I've spoken with as well as any seekers. People don't seem to even want to *hear* of a technique or teaching that may help.

What do you think about this, Robert? You seem more open-minded than most, so I'd love to hear your thoughts on this.

A: Well, I am not a teacher of nonduality, nor a believer in that concept either, but just an awake human being who has no commitment at all to any spiritual ideas, so-called "nondual" or otherwise. From my perspective, "spirituality," including nonduality, is mostly frightened human beings making a big deal out of life and death, as if talking about it endlessly would take the sting out of it.

Honestly, I see no division at all between what is "spiritual" and what isn't. When people ask me about spirituality, I feel like the 9th-century Zen teacher who, when asked "What is Buddha?," replied, "The shit stick in the latrine."

Any "teaching" that I might appear to be offering comes down to one simple point: *no one can define for you who or what you are*. No one. Not Buddha, not Jesus, not Ramana Maharshi, not Rupert Spira, not Adyashanti, not yours truly. No one. It does not matter *what* those people believed. All of them were–some of them still are–human beings just like you. You must find your *own* mind, not theirs.

If you are interested in awakening, it is advisable, I say, to begin by discarding *all* beliefs you may have acquired, no matter what their source. Just wipe the slate clean and make your own inquiry, starting from scratch without depending on anyone or anything at all. Forget concepts. Forget what others claim to have known. Forget what *you* know.

I explored this approach in detail in my book, *The Ten Thousand Things*, and I encourage you to read that.

My awakening took place over a ten-year stretch more or less, from the occasion of an initial *satori*; through a period of severe illness; and then, after recovering from that illness, an interval of several years, during which my ordinary personality became integrated with the phenomenology of continually noticing that "Robert" was not really doing or deciding anything and never had, except in fantasy. I could now not forget that even if I tried. But I can't teach that, and no one can imitate it either.

As for technique, I had a mentor who suggested a method, a very simple practice, and I followed it for a time. He advised me to "remember myself," to keep coming back to simple *be*-ing without questions or explanations. The suggested practice was to say to myself whenever I could recall, "I am," meaning "I exist." There was no so-called "inquiry" involved in this approach... So not "*Who* am I?"—not

"*What* am I?"—but just plain old "I am." That is a technique. I used it for a time, and now never even think about it. It's like a medicine I once took but now do not need or want.

But even such a simple practice will not be helpful if one imagines the practice as a "path." It is *not* a path. There *is* no path from here to here. Even if you thought there was a path—suppose, for example, you now regard "I am" as a path—you have no power to *choose* to follow it or to avoid following it. A mentor can put an idea in your mind, but that is like leading a horse to water. The mentor cannot drink the water for you. Drink or no drink, you are exactly where you find yourself *right now*.

If you see *that*—that thoughts are not chosen but arise autonomously; and yet, those selfsame unchosen thoughts are what *guide* so-called "choices"—that is the recognition of what I call "awake." Then you are free—free to flow.

You can hear that from me, and understand it logically, but you can't *will* yourself to wake up—because you don't know what that is, and there is no way but first-hand experience to understand what it is. Words from an awake perspective, including an emphasis on the inevitability of human limitation (a theme I often raise), may seem to point in one direction or another, but the actual *experience* of a welcoming openness to each moment without seeking fulfillment of desires and without particular focus on "myself"—which is what I mean by awake—can only be alluded to at best. Nothing central to that view, I say, can be delivered or "transmitted," no matter how eagerly it is wanted.

When I first came out to myself as "awake," I had a time of ambivalence. I kept it to myself for years. I feared that speaking about "awakening" from a first-person perspective—not what some traditional teaching says, but what I actually experience from minute to minute—could be taken the wrong way. I could be taken as another imagined spokesperson or salesperson for the proverbial carrot that donkeys are always chasing after, which is the last role I'd want to occupy.

I tried, but could not find a better angle or better language than straight talk to discuss these matters, and that straight talk included the A-word. Since I have no religious or philosophical dogma to fall back on, everything I say is only personal confession, and I can't *prove* a word of it. Whether you see me as foolish or as an object of admiration or anything else, is not the point. The point is *you*—not "Robert." It is your *own* mind you must find, a mind at peace with itself even in apparent turbulence, a mind that is not always looking forward to the next thing or analyzing the past, but that is fully alive here and now.

That is the message. Depending on no "thing," find your *own* mind. For once, give yourself a break. Step out of the hierarchy entirely. Let go all the precepts, articles of faith, and second-hand so-called "knowledge" and be yourself just as you are. Open yourself as best you can to *this* moment—not what some dead cat said about it all. You can't help hearing all that stuff, and some of it might be OK, but not if you get caught up in it.

The equanimity that I am calling *awake* is not transferrable. It's not an acquisition, but a *noticing* within oneself of something honest and rock-bottom. This is not a received "Truth" that you have to believe in, but your *own* understanding and experience. That is what is needed, I say—not some schematic diagram of "reality" from on high that's as dead and dry as a cardboard box for lunch. There is no path, no royal-road but the one you discover in silence, I say.

But those are words, and words are not enough, any more than you can eat the menu for dinner. And that is the problem with the nonduality industry—and make no mistake: it *is* an industry. A reader of mine called it the "insufficiency industry." In that business model, words are the *merchandise*—clever words, slogans really. But words are not enough, and quickly become an impediment to those who fixate on them.

So if awakening is really what you desire, forget about so-called "nonduality." Just put it out of your mind entirely. Don't listen to what those self-appointed teachers say. Live by your own lights, without depending upon the ideas of others, or depending on anything else. Find your *own* mind without the explanatory structures of Christianity, Buddhism, Islam, Hinduism, or any other so-called "Truth" imposed upon it.

That suggestion may not sound sexy, like retreats and gatherings with "teachers" who will tell you what "myself" is and isn't—but depending on no-thing to find your own mind, is the only real "technique" I know.

Thirty years and more
I worked to nullify myself.
Now I leap the leap of death.
The ground churns up.
The skies spin round.

—The death poem of Rankei Doryu (c. 1213 – 1278)

27 - A block of stone

Yesterday, replying to a question about whether any techniques could promote awakening, I said this: I have no techniques to teach, nor do I rely on any myself. The only teaching that I can offer comes down to one simple point: no one can define for you who or what you are. *No one.* Not Buddha, not Jesus, not Ramana Maharshi, not Adya, not Rupert, not Eckhart, not Tony Moo, not yours truly. No one. *It does not matter in the least what those people believed.* All of them were or are human beings just like you. You must find your *own* mind, not learn to imitate theirs.

Today, in thinking about finding your own mind, I recalled the story of the sculptor who was exhibiting a work carved from stone—the image of an elephant, perfect in every detail.

"How do you manage to do that?" he was asked.

"Very simple," he replied. "I take a block of stone, and just chisel away everything that does not look like an elephant."

Well, that seems a useful approach to finding your own mind. Just chisel away all the beliefs imposed upon you as a child, religious and otherwise, whether you consider them true or not. Then chisel away all the beliefs about "reality" that you have acquired subsequently from authorities such as spiritual teachers, supposedly sacred texts, etcetera. Keep chiseling until there is no acquired knowledge left. Keep chiseling until all that remains is what you actually feel, think, and observe right now in this very moment. That is what I mean by your *own* mind.

Q: Watch out, Robert! Some of those "teachers" are going to start calling you a chiseler. I love the analogy, but it leaves unanswered the question: who is to do this chiseling?

A: Yes, I knew that when I posted it, but it's a good start, and that "who" question will never be answered in words. That question is part and parcel of finding your own mind—a question of seeing that "myself" is not something, but not nothing either. As for the self-appointed, self-proclaimed teachers, if they don't like hearing that the emperor has no clothes, that's not my problem. I love going naked.

Q2: How does one go about chiseling beliefs stored in the subconscious if they are not available to focal awareness?

A: One doesn't. But you might find enough work in the *conscious* arena to keep you busy for a while.

Q3: As long as one is a doer and caught up in doing, I guess we understand only technique and how-to manuals. Anything else is so alien that most possibly it won't be comprehended.

So does a technique help? I think there are too many people nowadays just parroting the no-technique nothing-to-be-done stance, who have never in their life made an earnest effort.

A: Yes. If an effort seems called for, make the effort by all means. Don't let another human preaching from a throne about "No person really exists" and other such silly tropes steal your life from you. As my amigo John says, "The remedy is exhausting all remedies."

Q4: Chiseling, chipping, peeling away. While listening to authorities who wrote books, took to the stage and had massive followers, I overlooked my *own* mind, which I imagined was insufficient. I was afraid to fully credit my *own* experiences. I was looking for the sense of "Yes, *that* is it!" Not "*This* is it," but "*That* is it." It was Robert who affirmed my *own* experience, which I had missed for so long while trying to be a good follower. People still don't want to see how messy and exploitative this massive spiritual marketing has become.

A: Well, I'll bet it feels good to be out of *that* dark part of the forest. Ha, ha.

Q5: Lovely suggestion, Robert. I visualize myself clearing my kitchen table by sweeping my arm over that table and letting everything crash onto the floor. It may sound wacky, but that is my feeling regarding the end of spirituality—*all* of it! It has stopped. All the questions are gone—questions that are and always will be out of our ability to answer.

A: Lucky you.

28 - *Psychotic break while awakening*

Q: Robert, what keeps a person from having a severe psychotic break during this time of awakening? I feel as if I have no choice about any of this. Out of the blue, something rushes up and totally wipes me out.

I was in a very dark place yesterday. All I can say is I was not entirely lost, but there were thoughts of really being done with it all. They were very old thoughts and emotions. I am not really joking here when I say that it would be OK for me to go. But I will hasten to add that I have no intention to make that happen.

Jed McKenna is right about this one thing concerning awakening: "It's rabid, feverish, clawing madness to stop being a lie, regardless of the price, come Heaven or Hell." The only thing is, in this moment, I don't give a flying fuck about any of it. If I could, I'd crawl right back into a comfortable lie, wrap the denial blankie around me as tight as possible, stick my thumb in my mouth, and go to sleep.

Words of encouragement are welcome. Thanks for listening.

Q2[19]: To me, what this person is going through is such a crucial, momentous juncture, clearly missed if one fills it again with anything.

In my experience, as we find ourselves letting go of ego-structures with all that comes with that, which is what makes up the familiar sense of self, we see that its nature is empty, since it is actually conceptual and not ultimately real. That is when we feel the emptiness, the void—which we will *"a*-void" if we still can. Yet the sense of emptiness is really just the revelation of the immateriality of these structures. As one stays with the emptiness, it reveals itself as spaciousness, which eventually then brings out the fullness inherent in it.

It may seem that I've moved from one place to another, but that's not what happens. If I experience myself as an actual presence, I just see one thing dissolving into another in the midst of my presence. If

19. Bernard Guy, Robert's companion in several public Zoom meetings, available on YouTube.

I'm identified with the structures, then it will feel as if I'm disintegrating. This impression is only because my attention is focused on a certain part of me, and so I'm not experiencing my totality. I do not fall apart or disappear, although it feels that way if my ego-identity is the part of me that I'm identified with.

A: Hi, Bernard. Thanks for sharing that. On point, as usual.

Yes, the instant of the immediate (unmediated, no middle-man) recognition of the "terror of the situation" arrives, unexpectedly, as a gift. It may seem a fierce kind of gift, as in this case, but it can be a gift nevertheless, and a boon that comes only to some of us.

So many of us seem lost in religious credulity, materialism, hedonism, unremitting debates, and whatever other escapist refuges we can find, and *stay* lost that way for a lifetime. To appreciate fully one's essential solitude—along with one's absolute inability to fathom it—is the gift that just keeps on giving.

That said, Q1, you have asked for words of encouragement, and although Bernard supplied some in saying that, "I do not fall apart or disappear," you may not be feeling so sanguine at the moment. I feel your pain, and suicidal urges should not be ignored. The wish to be wrapped up in a security blanket is a message worth heeding too. As you have mentioned psychosis, you might think about finding some therapeutic help during this dark period, even if that is just a wise friend with whom this pain can be shared. If that is not available, or insufficient, I would recommend some professional counseling, even if the counselor knows little or nothing about the Jed McKenna angle. Be well.

29 - *In the midst of this aliveness*

My dear friend, Bernard Dov Wisser, brilliant artist, passed away recently. Here's a dialogue with him from 2011 (when I was still working in psychotherapy) that seems worth sharing:

Bernard: I guess if things and events are illusions and nothing happens by choice, even if knowing and awareness are always present, no one can be held responsible for anything. Moreover, if one can't choose, then psychotherapy must be a farce, because as I understand psychotherapy, its purpose is to make someone aware of their conditioned or programmed patterns of perception and behavioral responses; also, to bring their attention (although, according to you, one can't choose what to attend to) to their actual feelings/impulses in the present, so that they can make better behavioral choices. Oh, wait. I forgot. That would be learning—and there is no one there to learn.

So when you are sitting with a client in therapy, you are not there, and not making choices; and the client is not there, to end their suffering by learning something about themselves and their ideas of reality—which the absolutist model sort of denies is possible.

You know I love you, Robert, and I have come to some of the same ontological (for want of a better term) conclusions as you. But I can't operate from that absolute position you are espousing, for that absolute type of non-conceptual approach, it seems, brings us right back to an extremely cognitive approach to life.

One is working when one meditates, although you may call the work letting go, but, in my experience, there is nothing in the growing life that is *not* a result of letting go/not letting go. And it's sort of spinning one's wheels, to keep transmitting wisdom, when choice does not exist, effort is useless, and learning is an illusion.

I have the same problem with your transmission—which I am sure involves inner-effort (yes, I know inner-outer is a no-no—as I have with Jiddu Krishnamurti, although I have come to the same ultimate conclusions as both of you guys. Somewhere, once having reached those conclusions, one has to go into that empty space, dear friend, and let the heart have a big say in how to transmit that which may be helpful.

A: Things are not as dire as you are painting them. Not at all. Yes, praise and blame, I say, are illusions stemming from the false idea that one day a "person" is born and is forever after accountable for every thought and behavior. But, when doing therapy, if the client believes in those illusions, I must respect that belief—it is his or her world view, after all, that constitutes the material of the therapy, not mine.

Occasionally, a client will come to the deeper understanding that I express in my writing. But even if that does not occur explicitly in the context of the therapy, the tacit understanding I bring to the work very likely relieves a lot of guilt and shame, wordlessly and silently. My understanding of self and other, of I and thou, pretty much leaves the heart in a permanently wide-open condition. That is my experience with it anyway.

I am not saying that anything is a no-no, Bernard. There *are* no no-nos in knowing. Whatever is felt, thought, perceived, and believed, seems real to the mind that apprehends it. I would never dispute that.

What I write here is neither proof of anything nor disproof, but merely personal confession. My posts here on Facebook and elsewhere—just like my face-to-face therapy work, or personal relations—express actual experience and understanding; not something drawn from books and teachers, but a living knowing.

After being drawn into this little "nonduality" global village more or less by chance—a couple of interviews, *et voilà!*—I saw that quotations from supposed masters seemed to make up a large part of the daily conversation. To me, parroting dead masters feels like a dry and moribund procedure indeed—far from inspiring in any way, and you can't even ask them any questions. So I find myself confessing my own ongoing comprehension of the great mystery—the comprehension not of a "master," but of an ordinary person who lives an ordinary life, does ordinary work, etcetera.

Nothing I say should be taken as a rejection of ordinary experience. I am all for it and participate happily in whatever arises.

Bernard: You just said what I knew about you, Robert, but I thought it was important for you to clarify it, which you have just done here so well. Thank you for taking the trouble to answer my comment. I do get tired of "spiritual" shoppers spouting other people's words, when all they have truly experienced and gotten high on *are* the words, not the experiences the words might signify.

A: Yes. All of us have heard many of these things said or read them in books. At one time, I read *Tao Te Ching, Diamond Sutra, Heart Sutra, Lin Chi, Hui Neng,* and found beauty in all of it.

But hearing and reading are not the same as *knowing*. You cannot, after all, eat the menu. And you cannot even ask the menu a question, any more than you can ask one of those dead masters a question. That's why it feels important that we ordinary, living humans affirm and share our understanding in the midst of this aliveness.

Q: A beautiful conversation, Robert. Thank you for sharing it. I have heard you say often that, although "awake," you are only an ordinary person living an ordinary life. Frankly, your point of view seems a bit beyond "ordinary," but taking you at your word, what do you mean by living an ordinary life?

A: I mean living step by step, doing whatever seems necessary from moment to moment, without imagining that there is something "special" to attain and without fixating on "myself" and what I want or don't want.

30 - We are drawn to shiny things

Q: Dear Robert, there's one area in which I am deeply inquiring now, about which you seem clear, but I am not. You say, I think, that there is no one here to make choices, so no choices are ever really made. Neuroscience seems to back that up, showing us that pre-decision activity happens, and decisions are already made unconsciously within us by the time we are aware of them. I understand this. And yet I have a different experience.

I experience making bold choices for myself, even against many internal pressures. Let me cite two straightforward scenarios. For one, I went to AA and got sober many years ago. This entailed choosing a positive action over a self-destructive habit time and again. For my second scenario, I cite years of psychotherapy in which I made choice after choice to confront or integrate or be present with difficult material. *Something* is choosing and it has a beneficial effect on my whole experience of myself. What do you think is going on here? Thank you.

A: Hi. As I experience this, most of the "mystery" is not really mysterious, or not more so than anything else we perceive, as much as it is an artifact of one's point of view—the separation of "myself" from everything else that arises, implicit in using the word "I."

From that point of view, an entity called "Robert" seems to exist in more or less fixed form, and seemingly makes decisions and choices. Most humans I have known simply assume that point of view to be factually true, and so live as if it were true. I understand that, but I don't see things that way. For me, that point of view is one among many, and far from the "truest" one.

For me, the deepest wellsprings of choices and decisions are unknown to me and always will be. Yes, one might have the *feeling* of choosing—the feeling of preferring one thing and not another, or, as in remaining sober, the feeling of struggling to *not* do something—but feelings like those are only the surfacing, the welling up, of desires and aversions that I never chose, and had no way of choosing. I wonder if you see this?

For example, you offer me my choice of either vanilla ice cream or strawberry. I take vanilla. Then you would say, "Robert chose vanilla." OK, but that is true only when viewed from the outside; when you, an observer, see Robert's *behavior* and just assume by habit that the behavior you observe is the outcome of *choice*. But, inwardly, subjectively, although there might have been *feelings* of choosing and deciding, there never was a separate "decider" operating apart from desires, aversions, and all the other contents of mind, known and unknown.

I asked for vanilla simply because I like it better than strawberry. I never *chose* to like it better; I just do. So the apparent "choice" is only an expression of the desires and aversions that already existed, and how the tensions among them played out prior to any consciousness or awareness of them.

"OK," you might say, "I get that, Robert. But what if I learned that vanilla ice cream has health benefits that strawberry lacks, so I choose vanilla on that basis—not because I like it more, but because I want to be as healthy as possible? What then?"

"Well," I'd ask, "what made you put health foremost on the preferences list? When did you 'decide' *that*?"

Other people have different priorities, also unchosen. Someone might say, "Life is short, any way you slice it. I'm going to eat whatever tastes good to me. And if that shortens my life a bit, so be it." You can extend this understanding to any so-called choice: safe sex, risky athletics, drugs and alcohol, whatever.

I have seen and understood that the apparent ability to choose depends not on fact, but upon *belief*—belief in a separate chooser, a little homunculus sitting somewhere behind your eyes who takes in information, weighs it, measures it, and evaluates it, finally coming up with a so-called choice or decision.

That, I am saying, is a fantasy that has little to do with how the human brain works. In fact, thoughts and feelings arise from a neuronal storm that takes place all over the brain, not in one centralized area called "myself," and a complex negotiation among countless neurons produces a resultant that is expressed in behavior as a *so-called* "choice." Then "myself" takes the credit or assigns itself guilt and blame for the "choice" that never was a choice.

Religious people don't like this idea because it leaves God, or Brahman, out of the equation. Yes. God has nothing to do with this. God is not an established fact, but an idea in human minds passed from generation to generation superstitiously. If someone wants to believe in God, or "oneness," or "universal consciousness," or "Love," and expresses that belief by claiming that brains do not "really" exist, but are only secondary phenomena—secondary to consciousness—fine by me. Knock yourself out. But I see no evidence at all for that view, and a *great deal of evidence* for the view that brains come first, and that consciousness is an emergent property of brains of sufficient complexity.

Choosing and deciding appear necessary only as long as we believe they are. In all honesty, I have not made a choice or taken a decision in years. In each moment, I feel what I feel, and find myself doing what seems necessary—or often just doing what I do, necessary or not. And these doings are immediate and without dithering. That is what I mean by freedom.

The more one views this question with open curiosity, the more, I find, choice does not even seem possible. Consequently, I find myself free to participate wholeheartedly in each moment of life—blissful, painful, or anything in between—*without* choosing. Free of dither, one is "in the zone," or "present," or whatever words are used.

I am clear that any "decisions" I find myself apparently facing were already decided (whether milliseconds ago, or decades ago) before "Robert" ever becomes fully aware of any necessity to choose, so that perhaps "Robert" can *imagine* choosing (I don't), but has no footing for actually choosing.

Conscious dithering provides no additional information. Decisions, if that is even the right word for them, occur off stage, and Robert gets to see the show subsequently when the curtain goes up. We call the rising of the curtain "the coming to consciousness" that an apparent choice is required, but that is only a story we tell ourselves. The "chooser" is a ghost in the machine. In each moment, I am saying, we think, feel, and do what we must. There is never an option. That's why I say that no one is to blame, nor is anyone worthy of praise.

> *We are drawn to shiny things in the same wild way our ancestors were overcome by a compulsion to forage for honey. A theory that has found favor among research psychologists (supported, in part, by a study that monitored babies' enthusiasm for licking plates with glossy finishes) is that our attraction to sparkle is derived from an innate need to seek out fresh water.*
>
> —*Caity Weaver, New York Times,* December 22, 2018

"Innate need. Drawn to. The same wild way." That is *not* the language of choice. This does not mean that gathering information and considering possible alternatives is useless. The process of decision is complex, and so perhaps is space and time as well, so no one should presume to have all the facts. It means that dithering and agonizing as if there were some *separate* "decider" is fallacious and useless.

At best, we humans can be aware of such likes, dislikes, cravings, and necessities that are visible superficially. We will never see the vastness lying beneath or behind all that, in the unconscious sectors of this totality of conditioned mind. All the psychotherapy in the world won't open a gate in *that* barrier. We do not get to see beyond that barrier, I say, no matter what the self-appointed "teachers" claim.

Even to recognize the gateless barrier brings a kind of psychological freedom. For the less I imagine that I *must* choose, or even that I *can* choose, the clearer the picture of the cravings, fears, desires, and aversions that, taken together, trigger anxiety about choosing "correctly." In that clarity, I say, resides peace of mind, compassion for self and other, and the equanimity that so many people seek in "spirituality."

Spirituality may not be the best place to look for the peace of mind one seeks. In my view, what most of us *really* want is not some schematic diagram of "reality," nor explanations of the inexplicable, nor a "path" that leads eventually to the pot of gold at the end of the rainbow, but rather to feel the suchness, the once-upon-a-oneness *right now* of this *aliveness*—the immediacy and poignancy of *being* this aliveness. The *enchantment* of being, of having a place at the table.

I rarely dither or agonize over anything. Since I am not focused on "choosing," or even imagining that I have the power to choose, I get a feeling for what is necessary moment by moment, as the outcome of the neuronal dance—the resulting vector of forces mostly invisible to "Robert"—is revealed. Robert, I am saying, cannot choose, nor even be sure what the real issues are in the vastness of all that he cannot know and never will.

Preference is *not* choice. The two should not be confused. I might prefer one thing or another, but I cannot choose *what* to prefer. Preferences—which are the source material of so-called "choice"—simply exist, whether we like them or not. No one gets to decide *what* to prefer. The "what" just comes upon us like fate. This cannot properly be put into words, albeit many over the centuries have tried. I like these words from a friend: "We *have* will. It's the only one we follow. In that sense, there is no choice."

Regarding your examples, lots of people just like you have tried AA and were *not* able to quit drinking, although they entered into the program with that intention. If it worked for you, I would not say that it worked because you *chose* to make it work day by day—I would just say that it did work. That's the way the cookie crumbled in your life.

Someone else just like you might have wanted to stop drinking as keenly as you did, or more, but couldn't. That is not because that person *chose* to fail at sobriety, but because that is what occurred in the crumbling of *that* cookie.

As for psychotherapy, you were presented with difficult material, and you worked with it to the extent you could and did (which, by the way, might not have been as totally and fully as you might imagine) not because you *chose* to, but because that was the totality of your being at the time. No one gets to *choose* who to be. Being oneself is unavoidable. Things are as they are, including oneself. You can put a mask on "myself," but that does not make it disappear.

Q2: What you refer to as decisions made off stage is basically subconscious mind, and psychology has already ventured into it. It is possible today to unhook from your habitual patterns governed more by your subconscious mind through techniques like NLP. One can start from where one is. As long as someone is identified as a person, she or he needs to be aware of all the unseen forces that have a hold over her or him. Without untying all those knots, can one really know the truth and find freedom? One cannot conclude that one truly doesn't exist just because someone explains it be so. It has to be a final conclusion as a fact.

A: I do not think you have understood my post. What I am saying here is that "all those knots" will never *be* untied. Many of them—most of them, actually—cannot even be seen and known, much less "untied."

Neuro-Linguistic Programming is a technique of limited value for which practitioners make wildly exaggerated claims. It does seem helpful for some cases of Post-Traumatic Stress Disorder, and less so for other issues, but certainly is no panacea. And, crucially, NLP does not reveal any "knots" or any other details of the subconscious, any more than aspirin can reveal the underlying causes of a headache.

You say psychology has already ventured into the subconscious mind. Yes. But only to a minor extent, and only by inference. Most of that material has been and remains invisible to us, and yet, there is where much of the "deciding" gets done.

31 - Observing one's ego

Q: Hola, Robert. Where is the line between observing one's own ego in action and disassociation? I'm asking because, as I "allow" (I don't know if you'd say that) my thoughts and feelings to show up and stay for as long as they do without rejecting the difficult ones, sometimes I feel I might become too blasé, indifferent, or detached from thoughts and feelings and the causes and meaning behind them. I am afraid that I might see thoughts and feelings as just part of this body/mind organism, without seeing them as my own personal expression that might be meaningful.

I aspire to nothing more than being human. I don't want to neglect my feelings—I want to embrace them, even my shame about some of them, or my fear of them. I don't want to challenge thoughts and feelings as not spiritual enough, nor inconvenient; and if I do, I want to be aware of that too, of the judging. I don't want to miss out on finding my own mind, as you say, or cover over my own psychological makeup and defense mechanisms by experiencing indifference instead.

How do you see this? I know I am *thinking* a lot here, rather than just plain feeling the world out. I do not want to just be "aware"—I want to properly *feel* whatever is going on and embrace my humanness... come through the other end... see what's there when I'm open to everything. Although sometimes I'd like to just get on with life, and not be so emotional about everything.

A: Hi. You used the word "I" a lot in that question. There is nothing wrong with that. We all must use the word "I," and also think about "myself" a lot. That is part of life. But I wonder if you have ever thought deeply about what you mean when you say the word "I." In other words, who *is* that?

You speak of "I" as someone who has thoughts and feelings that she does not want to neglect. But is there actually an "I" that is separate from thoughts and feelings, and so *has* them? Is there really an "I" that can *choose* to think thoughts or not think them? Is there really an "I" that can decide to feel feelings or not feel them? Or are thoughts and feelings—whatever is thought and felt—moment by moment, beyond anyone's control?

Can you actually *choose* to "observe your ego?" Or does that kind of noticing just occur from time to time, if and when it does, as the unplanned bubbling to awareness of a *desire* to observe, or the haphazard happening of *remembering* to observe? What about all the times in a day when you are *not* observing—when you are *not remembering* to observe or be "mindful?" What is happening then? Where is "I" then? And even if you could choose to "observe your ego," who or what would be making such observations?

I suggest looking into this matter, particularly my last question. If you do, many of your ideas about ego and dissociation may answer themselves.

32 - Report from inside a Mooji retreat

The following is a report I received from a reader who took his copy of The Ten Thousand Things *to a week-long spiritual retreat:*

Hi Robert. I don't know if you remember me, but we spoke in a Zoom meeting. I also wrote to you once, and you replied beautifully. First of all, I want to express my gratitude to you for your honesty, wisdom and clarity. Anyway, I just wanted to share a few things with you. If you post this on your book page, please keep this anonymous.

When I started to read your book, something was already shifting inside me in terms of my beliefs. I was part way through the book when I received an e-mail saying that I had been chosen by lottery to attend a silent retreat with Mooji. As I told you before, I have been his sincere devotee for years.

Well, I hesitated; didn't know if I should go or not. Your book had already changed many of my ideas about this entire spirituality and guru business. But there was still some residue I guess. Somehow I booked the retreat, thinking that I could go and see what happened; see the whole thing with new eyes without putting him on a pedestal. It would be a way of seeing if the retreat would have the same effects on me as the three holy retreats with Mooji that I had attended before.

And here I am in his ashram right now in a silent retreat. It has been four days of complete silence now. So three more days to go, but I already see what's going on here. Holy shit, holy fuck, this is pure horseshit.

I remember you and John Troy talking about branding, stagecraft, and the other techniques of the holy men. I see it clearly right here and now. The music before the satsangs, the flowers, the incense, the reverent tones of voice, etcetera. I wonder what it would be like if Mooji entered the hall accompanied by some hip-hop—music by 50 Cent, or maybe something by Snoop Dogg.

I see so clearly now that is all a set-up, a way of putting people into a satsang mood, a devotional mood. They use many objects and methods here to create this constant atmosphere of sacredness and holiness.

So now, attending the daily satsangs is like a tragic comedy or a humorous tragedy. Miserable, desperate, wounded people, naive and innocent, searching for the so-called "Truth." They all look at Mooji so lovingly, desperately watching his mouth—the horse's mouth. They literally grovel at his feet while he fills their minds with nonsense.

Unchanging awareness. You are not the body. Detachment. And all spoken as if he is a great and perfect authority who knows everything. What I observe now is this guy's great emotional talents. He induces a powerful emotional field, especially about love. Osho used sex to gather the attention of the masses. Mooji uses love, a great power, even if it doesn't sell as much as sex.

Mooji is an emotional romantic of Advaita. I don't think his manipulation of his followers is entirely intentional, though. He seems lost in deep illusions himself and needs the followers to support his fantasies. He has probably created a world for himself where he is the *satguru* or whatever, the one who God moves through. I don't think he is aware of that delusion. It appears that he really believes it.

I guess that he had an experience of awakening, which moved him to give up everything, become god-addicted, and inject himself with beliefs, and what he calls surrender. But underneath all that, it appears to me, he wanted to be special, important, or powerful.

He started from zero, I have heard, trying to earn a living as a street artist in Jamaica. With twenty years of dedication and hard work, he's made a success as a guru like any other well-run business or company, so it's no surprise that he gets the attention of seekers and gets their money. He's really good at it. I was fooled at first, but now I see that he is just a guy like any of us, making a living doing what he does best. But people don't see it that way because of their projections onto him.

So many things are coming clear to me during these days in the retreat. Sometimes I feel angry at seeing all this deception. But then I say to myself that there is no doer. All of this so-called holiness is just the way it is. I wish I had the guts to go to the microphone and speak to Mooji directly. I'd stand up and tell him to read your book... But then I tell myself to relax and take it easy. I am the anxious type, so if I spoke up I'd probably make a mess of it. If I spoke up like that, I would want to speak from my own deepest being. Right now I am not that confident.

Actually, before coming to the retreat, I already knew that I could not buy this guru stuff anymore. There is nothing this guy can teach me when it comes to ultimate questions or truth. But this is a nice quiet environment to read *4T,* to contemplate my own mind, and to enjoy my time here as a holiday.

In reading *4T* here, I can see and confirm in myself the things you express, Robert. This is so beautiful. I contemplated no-doer, and can actually *see* that there is no doer. Everything just happens. It just is. I am able to feel right now that "myself" is this flow of thoughts, feelings, perceptions, just as you wrote. Even these words I am writing right now, I don't know where they come from.

This is all we have. Here and now. This life is a mystery, this aliveness is unspeakable. It is beautiful. Impermanence is inevitable. And that's it.

At the end, everything is OK and I am enjoying my time here. Thank you, Robert. The more I understand your book, the more gratitude I feel. I love you.

Thank you for pulling me out of this searching, this seeking, this guru imitation. Otherwise, I might be like one of these miserable people at this retreat right now, going deeper into the hypnosis of this guru business and maybe wasting my life that way.

A: Ha, ha. Thanks for the amusing report from inside the Mooji retreat. It's a nice piece of writing. I visualized a cartoon and laughed out loud: Mooji pontificating from his throne while someone runs from the back of the room to the microphone waving a copy of *4T.*

Your report hits two important points. The first is the setup—the stagecraft and all that. It's *highly* instructive to see through that. That kind of setup is *intentionally* hypnotic, even if not called hypnosis. The second is your observation that Mooji seems genuine in believing what he is saying.

Yes. I have heard that from someone else who knows him well. Of course, there are out–and-out charlatans in the spirituality business now, just as in all eras. Some have had massive followings. But I cast no such aspersions on Mooji. He may be, as you perceive him, entirely sincere. I have no way of assessing his motives, and scant interest either. I've never been the *bhakti*[20] type myself.

As you point out, chasing money and the other perquisites of success can corrupt or distort what might have begun more innocently. But my critique of the spirituality business is not really focused on the motives of the players themselves, financial or otherwise. We are all just human here after all, and we all need to feed, clothe, and shelter ourselves somehow. If the best someone can do is preach for a living, or for that matter, beg for alms by the side of a freeway entrance, so be it.

Mostly, I am pointing out the irony of humans thirsting after certainty and security in a situation—this aliveness—that offers none. This hankering, I say, gives rise to an unreasoning credulity that confers upon the figure in the chair some special powers—such as, for example, the power of "Love," as in Mooji's case—and even presumes that figure to be in possession of some secret inside information about "reality."

That projection of one's own aliveness, one's *own* mind, is, I am saying, a form of deep ignorance. No one is an expert in the art of living, which is an art of improvisation—not Mooji, nor Robert Saltzman, nor anyone else. And no one knows *anything* about ultimate matters. Nada. Zilch. Zero. Those who *claim* to know are lying to you and often to themselves as well, as you suspect Mooji may be.

To be alive and needy, the way *all* animals are needy, presents challenges to us all. If living and dying were an easy matter, catching on to some bit of so-called "spirituality" would not seem important. But driven by the suffering inherent in any life, along with generalized

20. *Bhakti*: in Indian religions "emotional devotionalism", particularly to a personal god or to spiritual ideas.

anxiety and the fear that without "spiritual" goals, life and death might feel depressingly meaningless, many of us seek answers where there are none. And regardless of motives, high-minded or corrupt, there are always those willing to provide those answers. *Caveat emptor.*

I have seen countless people brandishing their second-hand non-dual beliefs like talismans against anxiety and depression. One may need to resort to that. That's not for me to judge. Anxiety and depression are tough nuts to crack, and I am not interested in kicking out anyone's crutches unless I can provide something better. So if kissing Mooji's feet works for someone, I may be saddened by that spectacle, but I have little interest in intervening. Similarly, if someone needs to be told that "myself" is "undying," and that one can "realize" that permanence and "reside" in it, it's easy nowadays to find self-described experts to tell you that. Sign up and pay here.

My communications are not directed towards people who want those kinds of answers. I don't have them and would never lie and say I do.

You and I, we've been through that
And this is not our fate
So let's stop talking falsely now
The hour's getting late.

—Bob Dylan

There may *be* something permanent, but if there is, we humans have no way of knowing anything about that. We can know here and now, I am saying, and that's the limit. For those who care to find freedom, stop heeding the directions and instructions of others, I say. There is no freedom in imitation and none at all in being a devotee. *Find your own mind right here and right now.*

Thanks again for your clear report and your appreciation of my words.

33 - *"Actual experience"*

Q: Hi, Robert. In a Facebook group, I read the following:

> *The term "actual experience" is used to refer to experience "right now," rather than stories about experience in some imagined other time. Actual experience is experience right now, without the thought stories. So it is sight, sound, smell, sensation, taste, and the simple knowing of thought, at face value.*
>
> *What thought says is not experience. This is evidenced by the fact that you cannot taste the word "sweet." So, when looking at actual experience, you are looking at raw experience* without *what thought says. If it's actual experience, it will be present "now," as something other than what thought says. For example, when pain is showing up, in actual experience, you know it's there, as a sensation of "ouch". When "pain" is showing up as just thought, there is no sensation of "ouch." So, to check whether you are reporting actual experience, it will be something that is "now," and it will be sight, sound, smell, sensation, or taste. If it is just what thought says, without referring to sight, sound, smell, sensation or taste, it is not actual experience.*

Which seems fine, but here's the rub: that definition means that everything which is not sight, sound, taste, touch, smell is designated as "a thought story," and therefore not "true" in the sense of "Indescribable Nowness" (colors, shapes, tastes, sensations, aromas, etcetera), if I can put it like that.

I mean, without thought, or if thought is doubted as "not true," where are "you?" Obviously, "awareness," or whatever term is used to mean "myself," is totally abstract; just a word. But then what is it that agrees? That discerns? That knows? That can judge? That appears to be writing these words? Is it thought?

The duality of thought/language implies a "thing," but "I" am not a thing. By a process of logical deduction based on "sight," "sound," "taste," "sensation, or "aroma," it is none of those. Even the label "human being" would not be supported in terms of how so-called "actual experience" in this case is being defined.

Would you please comment?

A: I am not sure that the distinction between "the simple knowing of thought" and "what thought says" is particularly helpful. It seems impossible to draw that line. As soon as one is aware of thought, one is aware of what thought says. What is one to do—erase that? How?

A better approach, it seems to me, is to stop distinguishing between thought, the content of thoughts, and the thinker of thoughts. Those are not three separate "things," but rather one process—just three different ways of viewing that process, or three different words for the same thing.

No one is in control of that process. The "myself" who imagines getting control of thought, or separating thought from "real experience," is a fiction. And so, in my view, people who seek "liberation" by means of making such distinctions are only fooling themselves. They are trying to liberate a fictional character. There is no such "liberation." There is only what exists right now—and thought is part of that, not separate from it.

No one is making sights, sounds, etcetera, *or* thoughts, and no one is in control of any of that.

A false sense of control arises when one creates a fictional limited area in which one imagines being "in control." For example, I force myself to sit still and "meditate," while telling myself that "meditation" involves letting thoughts arise as they do and pass away again without following them, which is one common instruction.

That procedure *sounds* good, and may even have a calming effect which might feel pleasant—but where did the *idea* of meditation come from in the first place? Did "I" create it? Of *course* not. "Meditation" was imposed upon me culturally, like "God" or "enlightenment." And where did the desire to go along with that procedure—*which is a form of thought*—come from in the first place? Did "I" create it? Of *course* not. All of that just flows along as it does. Another brain may be exposed to the same book extolling meditation as the "path to enlightenment" and have no interest in that all. No one chooses any of that. The "chooser," separate from "the world," is a fantasy.

Q: Yes, but in the Facebook group, if one would mention the "brain," one would be asked to provide evidence that a brain actually exists.

A: I have no interest in intellectual masturbation.

Q: Exactly! Because there is no way of proving anything apart from what is right now.

A: Life is short and involves real suffering. In the face of that, my interests are love, wisdom, and compassion.

Q: Yes. Mine too.

34 - My search is at a dead end

Dear Robert, I want to thank you for taking the time to write *The Ten Thousand Things* and share it with the world. It is a beautiful book. I deeply appreciate the direct and honest way you address the questions you were asked in *4T.* I also appreciate that you are willing to be friends and share with people on Facebook. I was hoping to get your input on a few things.

I spent fifteen years in active addiction (overdoses, hospitals, psych wards, rehabs, jail, homeless, etcetera). I thought I was a hopeless and worthless being and my only way out was death.

Somehow, I survived and, at the age of 30, I woke up in the ICU completely worn out. I was not afraid of death, but of continuing to live this miserable kind of life. I didn't know what to do, so I just started doing what people told me to do (detox, sober living house, NA meetings, sponsor, 12 Steps, etcetera). And it helped. I stayed clean and slowly learned how to deal with life.

In recovery, I was encouraged to develop my "spirituality." I was attracted to Buddhism and meditation. I started reading every book about Buddhism or meditation that I could get my hands on. I started meditating daily by myself (had no idea what I was doing). All of this seemed to help me to deal with life. I started attending a Zen meditation group and continued reading an absurd amount of "spiritual" books. So that is more or less what I have been doing the last two or three years.

Today I feel like I'm at a point where I don't think reading any more books is going to help. I have a daily meditation practice, but I'm not sure that is leading anywhere either (nowhere to go—I know!). I also continue to be very active in NA and recovery-related service work. I work at a substance abuse treatment center, I volunteer with a collegiate recovery program, I am getting ready to start a graduate counseling program, etcetera.

My motivation for all of this at first was just to escape the hell of active addiction and to learn how to deal with life. At some point along the way, I think my reasons for "searching" changed, although I suppose it is still about find relief from suffering. I feel that my "search" is at a dead end, and it is kind of a depressing place to be. And yet I still find myself reaching for the next book that will have all the answers.

Should I stop reading all these books? Should I stop this "searching" and just live my life? Can you force yourself to stop "searching?" I would appreciate any feedback you are willing to provide. Thank you once again for *4T*. It is a treasure.

A: Hi. Good letter. You are most welcome. A close relative of mine was addicted to alcohol and narcotics and has been in recovery for many years, drug-free, so I have plenty of inside knowledge about AA, NA, etcetera. If that works for you, I encourage you strongly to keep working in that way. You will help yourself and others. As the Buddha is reputed to have said:

> *When you raise a lamp to light the way for others, you illuminate your own path as well.*

Relief from suffering is at the heart not just of *your* search, but of everyone's. That is *why* we search. We find the present unsatisfactory, and expect to improve matters by some means or another.

As I see this, an important point to understand is this: you may be able to improve outward circumstances through effort, but no matter what, "myself" will always be there. You cannot run away from yourself. Wherever you go, there "you" are. You cannot run away from this moment and whatever it contains, like it or not.

So this is not a question of forcing anything, but of seeing that—in *this* moment—things are as they are and cannot be any different. In seeing that clearly, the search stops, not because "myself" brings it to a stop—that is not possible—but because in that seeing, the search stops by itself.

The search involves taking an idealized image of happiness and satisfaction and holding it out in front of oneself, the way you might hold a carrot out in front of a donkey to get the donkey to walk. Perhaps you recall reading that passage in *The Ten Thousand Things*. But sane living is not like a donkey chasing after future satisfaction that never comes—not like chasing after the pot of gold at the end of the rainbow. Sane living is one moment after another, after another, after another, after another...

Just be as you are in *this* moment. Think what you think, feel what you feel, care for whatever seems necessary right now, and the "future" will take care of itself.

So I would never tell you that you should stop searching. I would tell you to understand that the present moment is the only moment you have to deal with, and the only moment you ever *can* deal with.

In your experience as a recovering addict, you have learned to take it one day at a time. With that as background, you may be ready to take it just one moment at a time.

I am glad to hear from you and glad that my book has been helpful. I wish you all the best.

35 - On meditation

Q: If I understand you correctly, you are saying that things are the way they are and there is nothing to attain. But I am concerned about the proverbial "monkey mind," the mind that can't stop spinning. Obviously, if the mind is spinning right now, it is what it is. However, I wonder if you can suggest a practice or other advice to reduce the spinning? I believe some use meditation for this.

As I have gotten older and I have less to focus on, I notice my mind tends to run a bit more amok than it used to. I don't know if my brain is bored or what, or maybe I just never paid attention before.

A: In and of itself, there is nothing wrong with formal meditation practice, and it may be helpful to some people some of the time. When I say *formal* practice, I mean, for example, sitting quietly and intentionally observing the breath.

However, that is not a procedure without dangers. Often meditators begin to imagine that their willful "practice" has revealed a permanent "myself"—an "I am" that is an uninvolved "witness" to thoughts, feelings, and perceptions; a "myself" *separate* from experience that is *only* observing thoughts or *only* watching the breath. That is a kind of delusion, which often includes the notion that remaining habitually in this role of "witness/observer" will lead to awakening or "enlightenment." In my experience, nothing could be further from the truth.

Quoting from a 2011 interview I did with *Nonduality Magazine*:

> *Unfortunately, many spiritual seekers, on hearing the idea of a witness, immediately split off part of the ordinary, automatic ego, and make that split-off part—which is really still just ego in disguise—their "witness." Since that splitting creates a seemingly separate point of view which can appear "spiritual," one can be lost in that kind of false witnessing for years. Often this happens to*

successful "meditators," who love to assume the so-called witness position, becoming increasingly isolated from ordinary life, while believing that the greater that isolation becomes, the more "progress" they are making. This is not progress at all, but a trap, a cul de sac.

So, if putting attention on the breath helps you to calm down, no problem. I have used that trick myself at times. Just don't imagine that you are doing something special or achieving something "spiritual" when you meditate, and you won't become confused.

Q2: So many people seem to find it difficult to grasp the fact that the point of meditation is not to get anywhere: it is to wake up to where we are right now, moment to moment. It's not about achieving a particular state. It's about being with what is, good, bad or indifferent. This moment has already arrived and it is what it is, whether we like it or not. "Breathe, and let be."

Q3: While I agree that meditation is not about getting anywhere, if it calms and tones the autonomic nervous system, that might be enough. After all the only reason we seek "enlightenment" is to reduce our suffering. One wouldn't, for example, say there is no point in taking regular exercise because it doesn't lead to enlightenment. Every little bit helps!

Q2: Well, at least for me, a greater sense of calm and clarity of mind seem to be welcome by-products of my meditation practice, but they are not goals. I have met many people for whom meditation has become another form of striving. Some of them actually believe that daily meditation will lead to enlightenment. It sounds like just another story to me.

Q4: I seem to recall Alan Watts saying something like meditation is best as a medicine and not a diet.

Q2: Watts also said that he rarely sat and meditated. He preferred walking meditation.

Q4: Indeed. "Doing it" the Alan Watts way is walking, lying, and sitting. Quite the opposite experience from the one I had at a Zen priory, which was a freaking nightmare.

A: To continue with Q3's analogy: sure, "taking exercise" may be healthier than just lying around on the sofa, but those are not the only modes. There is also a really beautiful kind of "exercise" that just happens in the course of ordinary *be*-ing. In that mode, exercise is not the focus, but a by-product of the real focus—which is living freely and engaging in ordinary tasks. I love to swim in the ocean, for example, but I don't swim for "exercise." I swim because I love being in the ocean.

When I walk around all day with my camera, I am not "taking" exercise—I am "taking" photographs. (I never use that phrase, actually. I prefer to say I am "capturing images.")

Whether one meditates intentionally or not is rather unimportant. Trivial really. The crux of the matter involves whether, on the one hand, one is living with a goal in mind ("enlightenment" or "liberation" or so-called "self-realization," that one will eventually attain through devoted and lengthy practice), or, on the other hand, one is simply *be*-ing—living consciously as this aliveness, no matter what "activity" may be front and center. *Be*-ing is not about attaining anything.

Many, if not most, of the "serious meditators" I have known are lost in a goal-oriented trance of transcendence. We regulars here on this timeline have had to endure their preaching often, and how they love to try to educate poor old Robert!

There *is* no "eventually." This is it. Always was, always will be, whether we know that or not. So if there is to be awakeness and freedom, it's only here and now.

Q5: I don't know that anyone can grok what you are describing, Robert, unless they have already grokked it—a bit of a catch-22. If I have never experienced what you describe, I am left with imagining it. If I have, then what you say is self-evident, to me. Talking about this is tricky but worth the effort anyway, and you offer the closest description I have come across that fits with my experience. Although for me it's not permanent state—but then what is? And that's precisely the point, isn't it? The state is not a "state" really, because it keeps changing.

A: Yes. I am not pointing to a fixed state. The aspect of impermanence—of being born anew in each moment—has always made speaking of these matters difficult.

At this point, I have heard from dozens of people who told me that reading *The Ten Thousand Things* had been "life-changing," or words to that effect. At first, that seemed a bit too rosy; but when I investigated some of those cases, it did appear that some actual living understanding had occurred—not just a contact high, but a new, freer perspective.

So apparently the present form of communication does have value, at least for certain minds. I hear many people demeaning the use of words or pointing to the paradoxical nature of verbal communication—and of course, I get that. But dismissing the value of verbal communication out of hand seems, from my perspective, to be throwing the baby out with the bathwater.

Q5: Yes, Robert. The way you express your experience is as clear as it can possibly be. I often describe the sensation I have when hearing or reading words that are super, hyper-precise as water dissolving sugar. Does that make sense? Suddenly something—thought—that was thick and dark, dissolves and vanishes into the past and nothing replaces it. Then there is just open silence and the unknown of the next moment.

Q6: It seems that even Krishnamurti was saying that, if one tries to practice meditation as bare awareness or choiceless awareness, one is making a choice. This seems to be a kind of catch-22.

A: All that can feel or seem like a paradoxical catch-22 when viewed from the perspective of desiring to *do* something, which is what a "practice" is.

The key to this matter is that one does *not* practice choiceless awareness—indeed, one *cannot*. That is not possible. That is why it is called *choiceless*—no "myself" is doing it, no "myself" is making it, no "myself" is choosing it. It is what it is, prior to likes and dislikes.

Instead, one might practice noticing one's habit of believing and taking refuge in certain ideas and modes of behavior because they are comforting, because they seem to give "meaning" to life, because they fill the void, etcetera.

Those ideas and modes are the "impediments" to be discarded moment by moment, until the instant arrives when one sees and feels with sufficient profundity one's essential aloneness in the universe, even those of us fortunate enough to have friends and families.

In a state like that—grounded and empty, with no expectations and no beliefs in salvation of any sort—there is no catch-22 at all. Everything simply is what it is, just as it always has been and always will be. One understands easily that each moment is *sui generis*—a thing unto itself—undefinable, entirely transitory, carrying no guarantees of any kind.

In that frame of mind—a frame of emptiness and hopelessness—it is entirely obvious that pain and pleasure, happiness and sadness, desire and aversion, annoyance and satisfaction, ignorance and understanding, *are* "my life," flowing like a river, constantly moving and changing, leaving no possibility of hanging on to anything.

Q6: Chögyam Trungpa said, "Meditation is not a matter of trying to achieve ecstasy, spiritual bliss, or tranquility, nor is it attempting to become a better person. It is simply the creation of a space in which we are able to expose and undo our neurotic games, our self-deceptions, our hidden fears, and hopes." What do you make of that, Robert?

A: Trungpa's book *Cutting Through Spiritual Materialism* is one of the few on the subject that is worth reading in my opinion, so I will always appreciate that. And that quote is something akin to what I might say myself. Trungpa could be brilliant, but I do not think his is a wholesome story; perhaps he was one of those who could talk the talk, but not walk the walk.

My view on meditation is dead simple. At a certain time, the learned technique of sitting quietly observing with dispassion whatever arises may bear worthwhile fruit, assuming it is approached properly and without an ulterior motive. Trungpa was good on that subject, a proper approach to meditation.

I would never discourage anyone from sitting quietly and allowing mind to manifest unimpeded. However, if one imagines meditation as a "path" that leads deeper and deeper into the mind, until one at last transcends human limitation and rises above human ignorance, that is the magical thinking to which I refer.

Human limitation is a fact, and human ignorance will never end, not en masse and not even personally. No one is ignorance-free, I say. What we don't know is orders of magnitude greater than what we do know or ever can know. The universe is expanding, including all the growing edges of understanding who and what we are.

So the *jnani* is lying to herself or himself; and anyone who regards a fellow human being as a "perfect master," is delusional. Identifying oneself as a "seeker, a "meditator," a "*sannyasi*," a "stream enterer," or whatever frame one hangs around one's own neck like an albatross, simply abets and deepens the ignorance. Certain meditators I have known are among the dullest, most undiscerning, most self-hypnotized people I have ever encountered.

If Trungpa believed that he had undone his neurotic games and self-deception, he was off the wall. His behaviors, seen fairly, were both highly neurotic and frequently abusive. So, I say, anyone who has either Trungpa or meditation on a pedestal is worshipping false idols. Time to call in the iconoclast. Oh, I see you already did.

36 - Preconceptual awareness

Q: Robert, you really do have your work cut out for you here. I don't envy you.

Although the term "now" refers to *this* moment, in order to be awakened, one must recognize that the source of one's sense of being is derived from one's preconceptual awareness. Just noting that this is the now, or that there is a now, is utterly meaningless, Eckhart Tolle be damned.

A: Well said. And this has nothing to do with so-called "nonduality," or any other flavor of the decade either. This is so simple, and yet missed by almost everyone who seeks "realization." Until one sees it, seeking will never end.

This may be part of what Nisargadatta tried to communicate, Ramana Maharshi too—but almost everyone who went to see those guys missed it entirely. And this includes the self-appointed "teachers" who now hang images of those two men as part of the stage set for their satsangs, as if wisdom will just rub off on them if they manage to identify themselves as "in the lineage" of someone who was wise.

The ignorance that has grown up around the words of Nisargadatta is astounding. Just this morning some fool sent me a private message that had not even one personal word from him—not even a greeting—but only a long quotation from *I Am That*, as if reading that dead letter was supposed to help "Robert." You are right: I really *do* have my work cut out for me here! Ha, ha.

Like children attracted to shiny objects, everyone gloms on to the "I will never die" aspects of Nisargadatta's talks, because that is where the *fear* is; and so they never even notice the crux of what that man was saying.

From an interview with David Godman:

Nisargadatta: *Why do I waste my time with you people? Why does no one ever understand what I am saying?*

Godman: *In all the years that you have been teaching, how many people have truly understood and experienced your teachings?*

Nisargadatta: *One. Maurice Frydman.*

Yes, there *is* something to be "realized," and it is surpassingly simple: all you see, think, feel, perceive, understand, experience—whatever you call it—derives from a source that can *never* be made consciously apparent, no matter what hoops you jump through. That source—no matter what you may believe—is a mystery beyond your ken, and beyond Nisargadatta's too, regardless of how much comfort he found in identifying with "the Absolute."

The real *jnani*, I say, is not someone who *knows* the source of consciousness, but someone who sees the *mystery* of this aliveness called "myself" for what it is: living and dying *without* knowing.

All one's seeing, hearing, feeling, perceiving, etcetera, arises "preconceptually," as you put it. "You"—the self-conscious "you"—are *not* making that or doing that. It just happens. And it happens before you can do fuck all about it.

No one is in control here. Each moment just *is* what it is. When Nisargadatta advised investigating the source of the feeling "I Am," that may be what he meant his listeners to discover: That "am-ness" is not *doing* anything. But none of them, with one exception, ever did. One! And that same blindness continues today among those who read about Nisargadatta and imagine that now they understand something "deep."

So you can keep telling yourself, "I am in the now." You can meditate with the goal of *being* in the now. You can pray, chant, whirl around like a dervish, bow to the guru—whatever. But by the time the "now" actually becomes apparent to you, it has already come and gone.

Your so-called "understanding" is only a projection of the past onto the present. If you aim to be "enlightened," you have, I am saying, royally fucked yourself. There *is* no eventual enlightenment. This is it, and there is nothing you can do about it. If you imagine something else, you are bewildered by the bewitchment of becoming, trapped in the trance of transcendence. Snap out of it!

Of course, those with spiritual ambitions hate this idea because it leaves them high and dry—without methods or practices, without goals, without cherished beliefs, without spiritual heroes—and completely out of control.

The traffickers in the spiritual marketplace hate the idea even more, because it leaves them with nothing special to sell; and for them, the bottom line is the point of this ruckus.

The real "Power of Now" is really a *disempowerment*, a total and complete *disenthronement* of the so-called "person"—the "myself" whose ambition it is to "awaken."

Q3: Dude, I like you. You're right on.

A: Thank you. I just went to your timeline and saw that you featured Ta-Nehisi Coates. So if he is your idea of a dude who is right on, obviously you have good taste in thinkers, and your compliment to me is now doubly appreciated. His are the best words on so-called "race" since James Baldwin, who was my Ta-Nehisi Coates back in the day (I was born in 1945). And the best thing about Ta-Nehisi is that he says it plainly, without getting all tangled up in it. That's high art.

Q3: Thank you. I had one prominent "nonduality teacher" unfriend me after I started sharing openly my feelings about white supremacy. He wrote the words "white privilege" (in quotes) when he explained to me my narrow thinking about life, and how the is-ness of being doesn't see color, etcetera. I was baffled. I remain amazed at folks who make a really decent living off telling people there's somewhere they can escape to, and denying simple obvious injustice to fellow humans that is happening every day in front of us.

But it was good, it clarified my understanding about what matters to me, and what I need not waste time on anymore. Truth is the simplest thing there is, and I'm really glad that there's nowhere to escape to. That is where my peace and freedom came from—not from achieving some enlightenment certificate, but from the exhausting uphill-to-nowhere climb finally ending.

A: Yes. Beautiful. Any philosophy that denies the obvious realities of the human situation—realities, I mean, that are plain as day to any open-hearted human being—is pure nonsense. If an idea interferes with kindness and compassion—not just towards humans, but to any sentient being—there can be no "truth" in it, no matter what some self-appointed teacher may claim.

If a concept pretends to rationalize the suffering of racism, gender discrimination, misogyny, homelessness, hunger, sexual exploitation, poverty, illness, war and other violence, natural disasters, and all the rest, the "teacher" of that concept is either deluded, or a greedy profiteer. And, either way, scared shitless to actually embody this aliveness we all are. Such people are half-dead, no matter how good their words may sound.

I should add that, for me, so-called "race" is a lie, and science backs this up. Factually, among humans, there is only one race: the human race. But that does not mean that *racism* does not exist. Obviously, it not only exists but is baked into cultural and economic arrangements all over this planet. As for white privilege, anyone who denies that is either a blind numbskull, or a knave who is benefiting from it, or both.

Q3. I am so glad you know that. Thank you

Q4. Robert, you said: "If an idea interferes with kindness and compassion—not just towards humans, but to any sentient being—there can be no 'truth' in it, no matter what some 'teacher' may claim."

This idea is so right on, but I think it's one that gets lost in the insanity of so-called spirituality. At the end of the day, is one universally kind? Not nice, but kind? There's no philosophy in that, just experience and living. That's when it gets real.

It's also a really threatening thought, because we are so good at rationalizing and justifying our insane cruelty—especially in these circles—in the name of nonduality, illusion, or whatever. But many folks don't want to hear that because it's too scary.

Truth asks for everything. Not one shred of my silly story can remain. It all has to go. And I think we know that on some level. But damn! The defenses that get erected against the disappearance of the ego are wild. That must be why some of the comments in your direction are pointed and crazy, or intentionally mean, or coming from a distorted view. You scare people, Robert. You really do. But I think that's a good thing. This isn't easy. To deny the terror is to fool oneself. I know it grips me, that's for damn sure. Be well.

A: Thank you. That's right. This aliveness and its free expression do scare some people. That's why they cling to concepts. Nonduality is a concept like that. Concepts can be discussed forever without needing to put any skin in the game at all—but when this aliveness is cut, it bleeds.

The ego doesn't disappear. It just melts.

37 - Imagoes

Q: I'm just using your space to help myself. I find myself still scared, to be honest, about my own views on God and religion. I'm working on that. It feels important to let that fear go.

A: All of us have been taught things by our parents and other authority figures before we reached the age of reason—before, that is, having the capacity to subject those ideas to any critical examination. So such ideas simply etched themselves into our brains immediately, without ever being assessed, doubted, or called into question.

Those ideas are part of our parental "imagoes" (*imago* is a psychology term for images of Mommy and Daddy which are "*introjected*"—google these words if you want to go deeper into this).

The *imagoes* feel to us like parts of our essential selves. We may believe that they *are* our essential selves. Unless we are able to find a sense of freedom in the aloneness and insecurity of *not* knowing, we depend upon those imagoes for the illusion of security they seem to provide. That is why it can feel so frightening to have one's so-called *values* called into question, even by one's own logical aspect.

The myth of a "heavenly father" who hears my prayers and cares for me is an extension of—a projection of—an actual human parental imago—which may explain the childishness with which otherwise intelligent people approach religion.

The spiritual teacher as an object of devotion is another such pseudo-imago, so you treat that person like Daddy or Mommy, craving affection and displaying obedience. I am not saying that acting out this rather infantile stage of development can be avoided, but imagining that it has anything to do with "Truth" or "enlightenment" is a sad mistake. Anyone who allows you to adore him or her in that way is not helping you at all, but only misleading you.

As for your own honesty, there is no hurry to any of this. Things happen in their own time. You cannot simply decide to "do" honesty.

Nor can anyone simply *decide* to let fear go. When understanding changes, feelings change and behavior changes without anyone *doing* anything.

Relax. Be as you are. Allow understanding to unfold organically, without, insofar as possible, clinging to anything—and this includes clinging to the idea of awakening or becoming enlightened.

Awake and *enlightened* are words that refer to ideas one can discuss endlessly. Prior to discussion, this aliveness unfolds organically. Participate while you are part of it.

38 - I'm awake and I know it

Q: Now that you have successfully helped many of us dispel the myth of spirituality, perhaps you can do the same for psychology. Have I been hypnotized into believing in the myth of the subconscious mind, and the way one's core beliefs—aka self-image or self-concept—got formed in early childhood, and thereafter form the heavily filtered lens through which all subsequent experience is processed and assimilated?

Does awakening dispel this insidious myth as clearly as it does spirituality? After all, how could there be a "self-image" if there actually is no "myself" to begin with?

Most importantly, will dispelling the myth of the psyche release me from its imagined effects, such as various compulsions; aversion to hard work (especially house cleaning); buying stuff online on impulse and subsequently returning it a few days later, then buying it again and feeling like I'm out of control and/or batshit crazy, etcetera?

Sometimes I feel like a puppet being jerked around against my will by these imagined subconscious urges and impulses. Please tell me it is possible to wake up from this malodorous puppet show and begin behaving in a rational, orderly, mature manner, and never again feel compelled to overeat, drink, buy stuff I don't need, etcetera.

Please tell me you and your awakened brethren are paragons of wisdom and rationality, and that there are no hidden compartments of mind to cause trouble; that there is in reality a continuum of awareness to which you have complete and unfettered access, and of which you have total understanding and control.

A: You call the subconscious mind a "myth," but I wonder why. Clearly, there are a host of desires, drives, impulses, fears, etcetera, that influence conscious perception without themselves being directly accessible to conscious awareness. Very likely, some of those drives are present at birth or even earlier, *in utero*. So why do you assume that they "got formed in early childhood?" Some did, some didn't.

Take sexuality as an example, a drive that is common not just to humans but to many other animals. If I see an attractive woman (attractive to *me*, I mean—to each his or her own), I may say to myself, "What a babe," and that will be my *conscious* experience. But the basic drives underlying my sense of attraction to "babeness" will *not* be accessible to me. Those are *subconscious* drives, and I—this particular manifestation of aliveness—was *born* with them. Those sexual drives are not "formed in early childhood," although they certainly may be channeled and modified by life experiences in early childhood and later as well.

Are we clear on that much? The subconscious—those aspects of mind that are not accessible directly to conscious awareness—can be demonstrated to exist (post-hypnotic suggestion, for example, reveals this, and so does psychoanalysis); and at least some of those aspects are *present from birth*, and common species-wide.

If you have ever startled when glimpsing a scrap of rope on the ground or a root that appeared to be a snake, you will have felt the *conscious* expression of the *subconscious* fear of snakes that we primates—not just we humans, but *all* primates—carry around with us. *Conscious* fear of snakes—based on the fact that a snake may be venomous and so should be avoided—is another matter entirely. If you happen to live in a place that has no venomous snakes, you will still startle at the sight of a snake. You may be able to reason yourself out of a *conscious* fear of snakes, but you cannot reason yourself out of being startled by even a snake-like rope. Can you say "hardwired?"

Now, you say that I have helped to dispel the myth of spirituality, so I assume that you have read *The Ten Thousand Things*, but perhaps I am mistaken. In a way, your question suggests that you have not read it, or at least that you did not understand what you read.

I have never said that there is no "myself." In fact, I said just the opposite throughout the book, stressing repeatedly that "myself" comprises the totality of seeing, feeling, thinking, and otherwise experiencing. So it is *not* that "myself" is nonexistent, but that no *free-standing* "myself" exists apart from, separate from, or as the experiencer of seeing, feeling, thinking, and all that.

For example, in Chapter 7:

> *But saying that myself is always changing does not mean that myself is nonexistent, as some people like to imagine. Clearly "myself" exists in various ways, but does not have the permanence that many of us presume. The "myself" of yesterday, or even of the last instant, is gone and can never come back again. The arrow of time points in only one direction; there is no going back, no reversing time except in fantasy or delusion.*

Now if you are plagued by behaviors you wish you did not have to repeat, I don't see that advice from the "paragons of wisdom and rationality"—that almost sounds sarcastic—will fix that for you. Many of those behaviors sound like addiction to dopamine spikes—which some people get from standing at the top of a ski jump, or anticipating making a daring bluff in a poker game.

In all honesty, I had a bit of that addiction once. I liked physical risk and dopamine-stimulating drugs, particularly at the same time, but that seems to have passed. I rarely overeat, nor overindulge in alcohol or other drugs, nor buy things compulsively, nor do I have a problem carrying out daily tasks as necessary. For me, it's all part of the flow; and washing dishes or whatever, as dopamine-free as that work might be, is fine by me.

Is that willingness to go with the flow an aspect of awakeness? Perhaps. I really don't know. Nor do I speak for all my "awakened brethren," those "paragons of wisdom and rationality," as you put it. I speak only for myself and do not claim to be a paragon of either wisdom or rationality, but only report that I am awake and know it.

Q2: Why is it I can read something like the excerpt from Chapter 7, get it—and two hours later I am back to my old way of thinking?

A: What is the old way of thinking that you find yourself going back to?

Q2: I guess it's the sense that you are the author of your thoughts. It can seem that way because you perceive them and they are so personal. But weirdly, trying to answer that question is causing a little short-circuiting here. Maybe *everything* encountered is perceived and personal? Omygosh, is it as obvious as that?

A: Aha! It is pretty obvious if you see it. If you take your thoughts personally, they will *feel* personal. If you see that they are just thoughts, and meanwhile life goes on, there may be a sense of freedom in that: the "author" and "the thoughts" are two names for the same thing—*this*.

For you, the "old way" to which you keep returning is what I call *splitting*—the feeling that there is a person, "myself," who is the *creator* of thoughts. Whereas I am saying that, for me, thoughts, thinking, and thinker are not three different happenings, but three different words for the same happening: this *aliveness*. Unless you need to believe in a god of some kind—which I don't—there *is* no creator of this aliveness. It just *is,* and its manifestations are naturally occurring, not caused by some imaginary "myself."

From that perspective, "Robert" is only a thought—a bevy of thoughts, actually, some stickily habitual; while, on the contrary, *this aliveness* is *not* a thought, but the matrix of all thought, all perception, all feeling—*including* the feeling of being a "myself."

Without thoughts, there *is* no thinker. And thoughts are not "created," I am saying, they just *are*; they just *exist* as one aspect of this aliveness. No one *makes* thoughts; they arise spontaneously. Sit for five minutes observing your own mind, and this will be obvious.

Now the foregoing words refer to something entirely real—real to *me,* I mean. I am not talking theory or quoting "spirituality." I have no use for spirituality, most of which is only conjecture *masquerading* as "Truth." Explanations for the inexplicable and conjectures about the unimaginable: Bah! Humbug!

My words in *The Ten Thousand Things,* and here as well, are an attempt at evoking the sensation of *be*-ing that I call "awake." But just because you can understand those words on the level of ordinary language does not guarantee that you will experience that same sensation. *Be*-ing is quite beyond language. Try to describe the flavor of a peach. You can't; and even if you came up with some words, reading them would not make me *taste* the peach.

So hearing a description is one thing, and experiencing what is being described is quite another. Language is best when applied to factual matters. Difficulties arise when trying to discuss "awakeness," which is not a "thing" but simply ordinary awareness—the same general awareness that many or most of us enjoy—unobstructed by theories, conjectures, and speculations about the *source* of all this, what "God" expects of us, or whatever.

Those who are *awake* in the sense that I use that word see that it's no big deal. One has seen into animal mortality and human intellectual limitation and that has given birth to ordinary humility:

> *I am here for this brief time only. I know nothing about any purpose to this aliveness beyond the living of it. For me, the babbling of experts on that question is like a joke they are playing on themselves and their followers. So here I am, naked and alone, without answers to ultimate questions, and completely disinclined to expect any from others.*

In a frame of mind like that, one meets each moment afresh, grateful that there is something rather than nothing. Grateful to be here at all. Grateful for consciousness, which is the ticket to this show, and amazed and astounded at the prodigiousness of the show itself. Its vastness is incomprehensible—a jewel of infinite facets.

This mind-blowing theater of awareness, I find, is best enjoyed when attention is not focused upon "myself" and what I like and don't like, but on what is. Prior to like/dislike judgments, prior to religion and metaphysics, and without nursing hopes of future glory, this actuality beyond comprehension is right before our very eyes in plain sight… if we want it.

Sometimes, those who begin to awaken become overstimulated and begin to preach. I have done a little of that but, luckily for me, very little. Something always held me back, and now I feel thankful for that. This understanding was not spent on outward gratification, nor used to make a buck. There may be those who awaken and preach humbly, without certainty of anything but their own experience, and without being overstimulated or driven by eternal gratifications. But if there are, I say, they are not common. Usually preaching about "reality" goes awry. Most of it is far too hyped-up by claims of certainty and truth, when no one really *knows* anything at all in the realm of being and existence.

Unfortunately, overamped claims like that are just what certain people are dying to believe in. So, motivated by fear of missing out on "liberation," and driven by the fantasy of "transcending" impermanence and mortality, they are easily hypnotized into seeking step-by-step what they already are right now. They are riding around on a donkey searching for a donkey.

A few readers of *4T* have reported experiencing the perspective from which that book is written, after which their previous point of view—myself "in here" and the world "out there"—no longer applied. That is what I call waking up or snapping out of the hypnotic trance:

> *"Wow! I have been looking everywhere for a donkey, and here I am riding on one, and always have been. This is too simple. This is like a joke. How could I have missed this?"*

Perhaps what you are calling "short-circuiting" is an *adumbration* of that awakeness. Excuse the rare word. It just happens to express precisely what I want to say. I studied Latin as a child is my excuse.

Adumbration: a foreshadowing or prefiguration; an omen, trace, hint, signal, or sign.

39 - What is a spiritual teacher?

Q: I have always wondered about the phenomenon of a "spiritual teacher," but not of course about a math teacher. How can someone assume that spiritual teacher role, which implies that he has attained some kind of awakening that others do not have; and so it is his mission in life to enlighten the poor ones who suffer so much due to the basic ignorance that he has gone beyond?

What gives that person the courage to try to save others from ignorance? How does he know, I mean, that he has something which he can give others?

A: This, it seems to me, is not so much a question about the role or identity called "spiritual teacher"—which is really only one version of the authority figure—but more a question about how one reacts to assertions of special, esoteric, inside information.

No matter what the subject, a teacher of it needs to have mastered it personally. You don't wonder about a math teacher because, except at the highest levels of mathematical inquiry, which can be quite mysterious, ordinary mathematics is very much cut and dried. One can determine easily if a calculus lesson or a lecture on plane geometry is valid or not, and thus determine right away if the teacher is any good. But mathematics is an extreme case. In many matters, advice from others must be taken with a grain of salt—and in many cases, have salt poured all over it.

A spiritual teacher problem arises, it seems to me, when the teaching involves assertions that the teacher cannot possibly know to be true, but has learned to "teach," the way a parrot learns to imitate speech without really saying anything meaningful.

The teacher may even believe herself to have attained some advanced, esoteric level or even to be "enlightened." In my view, that kind of "teaching" is not worthy of respect. However, I do not disrespect spiritual teaching when the teacher limits herself to what she really knows and understands. People may benefit from that kind of teaching.

For example, Elena Ascencio Ibáñez, the editor of *The Ten Thousand Things* and co-editor of the present volume, is a dharma teacher; and I respect her teaching because she speaks from the heart and does not claim to know final answers to ultimate matters. So when Elena leads a group in meditation, she is helping them to calm down, get off the high horse, and, naked and unprotected by spiritual dogma, crawl around on the ground for a while—the ground of being, where she is willing to crawl around herself. That can be helpful for certain people at certain times.

Elena does not say that she is teaching how to attain enlightenment, nirvana, freedom from rebirth, or any of that stuff. Why? Because she does not *know* about nirvana or how to attain it. Some old texts discuss that, and even map out supposed paths to it; but if Elena taught that, she would be teaching hearsay—which could be nonsense for all she knows.

Suppose I tell you that the compassion I feel—both self-compassion and compassion for others—is born of looking straight into the face of human limitation, born of seeing that I have no final answers to ultimate questions, and that no one else does either. Would you take that assertion on *faith*, thereby making me an *expert* on compassion and human limitation?

You might be tempted, because making me an authority would allow you to avoid a painful on-going investigation of your *own* human limitation and your *own* lack of compassion. Then, having circumvented the endless freefall of "ignorance" from which spiritual teachers claim to be there to "save" you, you could simply *imitate* what you see in me by "*practicing*" compassion—which has nothing to do with *actual* compassion at all, any more than a plastic flower is a rose.

But if you are willing to *test* the proposition that regarding one's own foibles and limitations with *self-compassion* opens the door to compassion for the foibles and limitations of everyone else—not just *believe* that or have *faith* in it, but subject it to serious scrutiny within your own being—then words like that might be worth hearing, whether you call them *spiritual* teaching or not.

40 - Don't throw the baby out with the bathwater

Q: A questioner told you that he had been to many teachers, but now feels that everything he heard from them was nonsense. You advised him not to throw the baby out with the bathwater.

Now, my question is the following: since discovering your work, I read everything you write—not just *The Ten Thousand Things*, but all your online posts as well—and I watch your interviews and Zoom meetings. It has become impossible to listen or read almost anything or anyone else in this field. I have no more interest in what any teacher has to say, whoever it may be—Rupert, Mooji, Nisargadatta, Ramana, none of them.

Sometimes a friend advises me to read something by someone I've never read before. Last week it was Jed McKenna. I gave it a try but it just isn't doing any good. Some things others write make sense of course, but most just don't—and I now question everything. How can they know what they claim is "Truth" and not self-delusion or hypnotic trance? Whatever I read from you, though, makes sense, resonates deeply, and makes me feel radical and like rejecting everything else.

I want to find my own mind. But maybe my mind is not open to any teacher or teaching, and I too am throwing the baby out with the bathwater. Maybe something those teachers have to say might open my mind a bit. Nevertheless, it is very freeing to not listen or read, any of them anymore. I have found one person I regard as my mentor, since everything he says just makes sense. That one is you, Robert. Any thoughts on this?

A: Yes. As for mentorship, you could do a lot worse. Ha, ha.

But seriously, what I have to say is not at all like those people you mentioned, and that is what must be understood. They all speak about a so-called "Truth" that comes directly from Advaita Vedanta, and I reject that so-called "Truth" entirely without replacing it with another.

Let's stop talking about capital T "Truth" and, instead, just speak truthfully. That is a far less grandiose project, more in keeping with the intellectual and cognitive abilities we humans really have.

Unlike those men you mentioned, I speak only and entirely about my own experience, without filtering it through a lens of Vedic thought or any other dogma. If I tell you such and such, it will be a *report*, an item of personal phenomenology—not a "*teaching*." That is the difference, and, in my view, that difference makes *all* the difference.

But making these reports, and criticizing the old religions and their so-called "truths," is risky business. On the one hand, "eyes wide open" feels too good, too *real*, too wondrous not to speak of. On the other hand, if I sit in a chair at the front of the room calling for snapping out of the trance of transcendence, I hazard becoming *part* of another kind of trance—and that I would never want to see.

I do not see this as a defect in my message. I feel just fine about telling people that, in my opinion, the teachers you mentioned (and others) speak with too much assurance, when an open mind can see easily that no one has all the answers to ultimate questions. But there is something inherent in my speaking this way that risks my being misunderstood, risks my becoming an authority when I am not that at all, but only an awake human.

As Marshall McLuhan, a 20th-century contemporary of mine, said, "The medium *is* the message." In service of crafting a pithy epigram, perhaps McLuhan exaggerated somewhat, but the format—the *medium*—does become at least *part* of the message, and perhaps the "Saltzman speaks" format may involve unintended but ticklish consequences for certain listeners.

I am happy to hear that you enjoy my work, and I do encourage throwing out the bathwater of religious dogma, but don't throw the baby—which is *your* baby, *your own mind*—out with it. You can *hear* me, but you can't *be* me.

Where I part company with those men you mentioned, and with spirituality and religion in general, is the idea of a *hierarchy* founded on the belief that consciousness derives from God, who is the only true reality; and that the ideas, feelings, and experiences of us humans are not "real," but only at best "relatively real." I think that is backward. It is more likely, I feel, that humans *created* "God," not the other way around.

To be clear, those traditions and the contemporary teachers of them do not always use the word "God." Sometimes they call it Brahman, or "The Absolute," or "universal consciousness," or "Oneness" or "Source" or "Nonduality." But the idea is the same, regardless of the name.

To me, the idea that there is a "real" world and a "relative world" is highly suspect. That appears to me as an example of an archaic psychological defense mechanism called *splitting*. According to that view, Brahman or God is infinite, changeless, timeless, and completely conscious, and it alone is real—because anything that changes (like you, me, and the mango tree outside my window) cannot *be* real.

I see no evidence for that view at all. It is purely a *religious* axiom—a dictum to be accepted *without* evidence. The worst part of that traditional Hindu teaching is the presentation of the Brahman concept as an unquestionable certainty. It is *not* a certainty by my epistemological standards, but an unsupported assertion. And the logic used to advocate for it or explain it to seekers of "enlightenment" is shaky at best. Anyway, logic can be used to "prove" any proposition. Zeno of Elea, a Greek philosopher who lived 2,500 years ago, "proved" that Achilles could never overtake a tortoise given a headstart in a foot race:

> *In a race, the quickest runner can never overtake the slowest, since the pursuer must first reach the point whence the pursued started, so that the slower must always hold a lead.*

Still, despite his manner of pontificating in the manner of a so-called *jnani*, as if his pronouncements were automatically "Truth" just because he said so, this advice from Nisargadatta made perfect sense when I first came across it:

> *There is nothing to practice. To know yourself, be yourself. To be*

yourself, stop imagining yourself to be this or that. Just be. Let your true nature emerge. Don't disturb your mind with seeking.

If you desire teaching, that's as good as it gets, in my view. I could not say it better myself.

So please understand: I do think my work here, a phenomenology of awakened *be*-ing, is worth hearing. If I didn't, I would not talk about it. But I am not the only intelligent voice on the planet. Far from it.

And in that regard, why limit your reading to a Jed McKenna, or your video-watching to some cat having his feet kissed, when you could be learning wonderful things that are *not* about so-called "spirituality?" Things that have nothing to do with cults, but, in my opinion, are more inspiring and mind-expanding than almost anything any spiritual teacher *ever* said? Try reading something from Robert Sapolsky, Carlo Rovelli, Brian Greene, or Carl Sagan. Or have a look at *The Cosmos* videos narrated by Neil deGrasse Tyson.

41 - Splitting

Q: *The Ten Thousand Things* continues to surprise me with what unfolds from the mysteries of its gifts. Thanks again for simply being there to write it and share it. I didn't want to let go. I resisted. Yet letting go occurred as if spontaneously.

I see now that our longing, our hurt, and unfulfilled desires are an appearance and in a sense illusory, and that there is no real self to hold on to suffering.

There is no denying the occurrence of longing, hurt, and unfulfilled desires, and no need to. By virtue of their appearance, they belong for the entire length of their stay. I honor them as guests within awareness. Even though they hurt. Even as we wish for them to leave.

What saves us isn't denial, or an attempt to wish a thing away. No, our relief is found in the search for the one who suffers. It's this inquiry that leads to a profound sense of relaxation in the discovery of the absence not of suffering, but of the sufferer.

What we find is simply space or, better said, our *own* spaciousness, that allows for all things to be exactly as they are. Until they change. Until something new appears. And that too belongs within our capacity to hold all things.

And I want to thank you for taking the time to read my messages. I appreciate being able to share with you where I find myself from moment to moment, inspired, and simply writing what comes to me. And much of it right now is largely connected to *The Ten Thousand Things*. For me, *4T* isn't instructive or even transformative. For me, it is a source of self-revelation.

Each time I read this book, I find one more notion, one more concept, one more subtle belief that I've clung to unexamined. And that's the important issue. Not just to let go for the sake of letting go, but to find out if a belief is true, to find out if it serves a purpose, or if it is just something I'm carrying along like unneeded baggage, because someone else in years past gave it to me.

So here I am in this moment, sharing this with you, Robert. I am not insulated from pain or suffering, nor am I free of faults that seem to need forgiveness. I am just awake. And in this awakeness, I find a difference from the way things were before. It's not that I don't try to correct myself, to take what seems the proper course of action, or even to avoid pain and suffering. It's just that all of that occurs within the larger context of awareness. I am awake to all that happens. And it's enough to simply be.

By the way, when people visit my blog and ask for the source of my inspiration, or what my words may mean, I always smile to myself and just write: "Read *The Ten Thousand Things* by Robert Saltzman. It's on Amazon. Let's talk after."

A: Hi. Thanks for your kind comments. You said, "our longing, our hurt, and lost desires are an appearance and in a sense illusory... there is no real self to hold to suffering." I am not saying this is wrong, but I am not at all sure that "our longing, our hurt, and lost desires" are *only* illusory. That just sounds to me a bit too close to boilerplate Vedanta. If *all* our feelings are illusory, and our thoughts as well, then what would constitute what you are calling the "real self?"

Is the "real self" an unfeeling, unthinking nothingness? I cannot quite picture that, and the idea seems far removed from my actual experience. For me, thoughts and feelings are part and parcel of "myself"—not some aberration to be avoided or explained away. I feel extremely reluctant to say that there is a "self" apart from experience—*independent* of experience—although I know that some spiritual traditions encourage that belief.

The concept of a self apart from experience is what I call *splitting*, by which I mean the notion that there is a *real* myself—Brahman, or God, or "Source"—and then there is ordinary human experience, which is not "real" like "God," but only illusory.

If human experience is inevitably illusory, then on what basis can one say that the supposed "real self"—God or whatever, which, after all, is a *feature* of human thought—is *not* illusory?

Some people imagine that "God" preexisted humans, and *made* humans. I find the reverse much more likely: humans made "God," as the explanation for a universe they could not comprehend. They then split themselves off psychologically from their creation, thereby dividing the psyche in two: the defective, unreal "me" part of psyche, and the perfect, real "God" part of psyche.

This split is only conceptual, but leaves many people—the same ones to whom "God" or "Source," or "universal consciousness" seems an indisputable "fact"—feeling that something must be healed or fixed by means of "spiritual practice." As I see this, a cooked-up metaphysics is the source of the split, and it is the metaphysics that needs healing, not "myself." To be clear: it is the conceptual split that needs healing, not "myself," which, being an expression of this aliveness, specifically a primate human expression, naturally suffers and feels pain, and that's the way it is.

There are, of course, traditions that do not split "myself" into false and real. The perspectives of those traditions are much closer to my actual experience than those such as Advaita Vedanta that seem to encourage splitting, dissociation, and disembodiment.

I just had an extended dialogue[21] with a woman who complained that reading *The Ten Thousand Things* made her feel "sad," so that, after a few chapters, she had to stop reading. She then wanted to debate with me about my questioning of the value of popular spiritual teachers, mentioning specifically Robert Adams, who she said had been an important force in her life. She asked why I was "dissing" him, and what I had against him.

"I have nothing against Adams personally," I replied. "But he is what I call a 'wild fox spirit.' Apparently, her "sadness" at reading my ideas had not allowed her to get that far in the book. A wild fox spirit is someone who makes definitive pronouncements about so-called "Truth," when that person has no basis for such statements except tradition and hearsay. That term comes from a famous Zen story:

Whenever Master Dahui gave a dharma talk, an odd old man would stand in the back and listen in silence. He usually left right after the

21. See Chapter 98, "No evidence for 'universal consciousness'."

talk, but one day he lingered, so Dahui approached him and asked, "Who are you?"

The old boy replied, "I am not actually a human being. I was the dharma teacher on this mountain at the time of Kashyapa Buddha. One day a student asked me, 'Does a person who practices with great devotion still fall into cause and effect?' I said to him, 'No, such a person doesn't.' Because I uttered those words I was reborn again and again as a wild fox for five hundred lifetimes."

"But what does Robert Adams say that you object to?" she wanted to know.

Here is an example of what I consider arrant nonsense from Robert Adams:

If you know about the mind, you will know what you have to get rid of. The mind doesn't really exist.

Really, Mr. Adams? And you know that *how*? Other traditions say that mind is *all* that exists, so what makes that view false and yours "Truth?" As I have said elsewhere, that entire "lineage"—Robert Adams to Francis Lucille to Rupert Spira—has been a disaster of axiom posing as certitude; of initial claims being assigned an automatic facticity backed up by the silly logic of Vedanta, which purports to evoke Brahman by prattling about how the bracelets and rings in this world are all made of gold, and if we melted them down, we would know that. What is this—play school for ninnies?

There may be Brahman for all I know, but if there is, those guys don't know anything more about it than I do, and gold rings and other forms of "higher reasoning" are only hocus-pocus.

Q: Thank you for your reply, Robert. This is exactly why I make return visits to *The Ten Thousand Things*. It's those fine points, little hang-ups we find ourselves attached to without conscious thought. By themselves, singularly, maybe they mean nothing. But they do add up to a very subtle form of clinging that at the very least should be examined. I appreciate your pointing to them.

I write from where I find myself. I feel inspired in this awakening, and the more I examine my thoughts with a critical eye, the clearer this inspiration feels. In no way does this increasing clarity invalidate my previous writing—indeed it honors it by guiding those ideas to greater clarity. This is the real value of my continued reading of *The Ten Thousand Things.* As you've stated many times, awakening never ends. Thank you, my friend.

A: Yes indeed. Awakening never ends. Walk on.

43 - Existential suffering

Q: You wrote about Hui Neng who overheard a man reciting a line from the Diamond Sutra: "Depending upon no-thing, you must find your own mind," and was enlightened instantly.

Later, competing against Shen Xiu in a poetry contest, he wrote a poem that said:

The mind of Bodhi has no tree.
There's no support for mirror bright.
Buddha-nature is ever self-clearing.
So where could dust alight?

I am confused about the emptiness aspect. To me, the mirror is the stuff accumulated through life. But are you saying that in essence there *is* no mirror, because there is no "myself?"

It's all so confusing, even though it isn't supposed to be. I get that all we have is right now. The difference between you and me—in my perception at least—is that, at this moment, my experience is influenced and even dominated by concerns for the future, most likely generated by painful aspects of my past.

My understanding of your experience is that you live each moment and feel each moment for what it is in that moment. You don't live in the future (although I'm sure you still appropriately plan and such). I can't seem to transport my attention from the future to the current. Thanks so much for the discussion.

A: There is no future. What you are calling "future" is imaginary. Not *somewhat* imaginary, but totally and completely imaginary. You may stop breathing in the very next moment, and if that were to happen—as one day it will, since everything alive must die—every bit of your fantasized future would have been entirely non-existent. This is obvious and undeniable. What, you might ask yourself, stops you from accepting the truth of it right now?

I don't know how to help you to see that, from my perspective, what you are calling "future" is constructed entirely of your own anxieties, replayed again and again like a low-grade horror movie.

You see that or you don't. If you see it, then you are able to say:

> *Wow! All that grief about what bad things might or could happen is just a story I keep telling myself. Actually, I have no idea what will happen, or how I will feel even in the very next moment, to say nothing about the fantasized far away future. So obsession with possible catastrophe is just a form of mental masturbation that distracts me from the only life I really have, or ever will have, which is here and now.*

As the poet Annie Dillard said, "How we spend our days is, of course, how we spend our lives." If you spend your days worrying about what *might* happen or *could* happen, you will be spending your life embroiled in worrisome fantasy, while missing out on the only reality a human being can ever experience—which is the perceptions, thoughts, and feelings of *this* very moment. Right here and right now, I mean. I can reply to questions about this, but I cannot make anyone accept it. You can lead a horse to water, but that's the limit.

Regarding Hui Neng's poem, the "mirror" is a metaphor for consciousness or awareness, and the "dust" stands for such items as what you are calling "painful aspects of my past." That metaphor was used commonly in the spiritual teaching of those times. Hui Neng's awakening showed him that "myself" is not like a mirror. A mirror is a *thing*, but "myself" is not.

"Myself" is not a thing, but a pastiche, a medley, a potpourri confected from unrelated parts: a physical body; thoughts and feelings; conscious awareness; perceptions; an apparent outside world based upon perceptions; and many other factors which are really separate and quite unrelated, but which we combine into a supposedly unitary "myself"—an object, a thing.

This process of reifying or "thingifying" seems to produce an apparently solid, autonomous "myself", but if we look more deeply, "myself" will be seen as empty of independent existence. We say that it is "empty," because it is dependent upon all those various unrelated, separate factors that create an *illusion* of a unitary, independent, stand-alone "myself". That, I imagine, is what Hui Neng came suddenly to apprehend.

I can tell you the same. I can tell you that you are not a thing but a *flow*, so you don't need to clean anything up or fix anything. Just let it be. But unless you somehow come to feel this in your bones, such words will not help much, if at all.

If you are troubled by worries to the extent that they intrude constantly upon your present life, psychotherapy may be needed, not simply hearing about Hui Neng or about how Robert sees these matters. My words here are not psychotherapy, but only an expression of the way I see the world.

Q: I see a therapist now, so I recognize that my issue goes beyond a typical person who may be questioning "life." My issue with the future is that I don't see how you can avoid considering it.

For example, if you are undergoing medical testing, I don't see how you *can't* fear the results—which will obviously come in the future. Or if a child is struggling somehow, worrying that their future may be hindered by their present condition.

I am not saying I am right by any means. Logically, I totally get that the future isn't here right now. But in my addled mind, what the future holds is bad. It's a feeling of dread and impending doom, even dread over what used to be considered innocent situations. No matter how great today is, I know tomorrow could be bad, and that impacts today because I have to plan and prepare for the future at all times.

A: Yes, from the point of view of a "myself" that imagines itself to be a thing, the future *is* bad: old age, illness, and death. A *thing* is mechanical; therefore, its future is predictable. On the mechanical level, predestination is the rule. If you know the velocity and angle of the cue ball as it strikes the object ball, you can know in advance if the object ball will go into the pocket or not. Total predictability. That is the Newtonian universe of *things*.

So, to the extent that you see yourself as a fixed "person," an *object* to whom things happen, you are in a pickle: the same difficult, embarrassing, existential dilemma that Woody Allen lampooned so well. "Life is filled with misery, loneliness, and suffering," he would say. "And it's over much too soon."

That existential dilemma motivates your questions. You suffer psychologically from feelings of dread and impending doom, and, on a certain practical, material level, your feelings make perfect sense. As much as some try to paper it over, there really is no denying mortality.

This same matter of existential pain was under discussion way back in the seventh century in Daman Hongren's temple, when Shen Hsiu opined that the way out of the dilemma was to understand that mind is like a mirror, reflecting everything equally without being altered itself. Since that is the case, he asserted, spiritual practice entails keeping the mirror free of the dust of wrong thoughts and feelings. So Shen Hsiu was asserting a "myself" that does not care what happens since, like a mirror, it *has* no feelings and emotions. Our fears and desires, he was saying, are just the dust on the mirror. Keep the mirror clean, and one will have "transcended" suffering.

In that view, Shen Hsiu was in the traditional "spirituality" place. I mean the place where existential suffering motivates goal-seeking and perfectionism by means of practices and methods aimed at attainment of the imagined goal, "enlightenment." Shen Hsiu, the top student, meant to win a poetry competition with that poem by proposing a method of constant vigilance or "mindfulness," as it might be called nowadays.

Hui Neng, on the other hand, upon hearing the words "depending on no-thing, you must find your own mind," had snapped out of a lifelong trance, and he knew it immediately. He found himself suddenly awake. So, unlike Shen Hsiu, who saw "practice" as a continual janitor's job, Hui Neng could flow along, mind as free as light on water, taking things as they came, the apparently good along with the apparently bad.

So Hui Neng, illiterate and untutored, heard a few words and snapped right out of it. The difficulty here is that I cannot know what words, if any, would get *you* to snap out of it. You seem to understand as well as I do that your fears are obsessive, but I have no "snap out of it" magic.

Since we are speaking personally, I have had medical testing myself and did not much fear the results. The physical condition, whatever it was, already existed, and results were going to be what they were: information. Once I had the results, I would feel what I felt, and deal with the situation then. Meanwhile, I was not going to a waste a day in useless fantasies of a bad diagnosis that might not be in the cards anyway. If anxieties bubble up, OK, they do—and then they die out. Our time here is better used celebrating the brief gift of this aliveness than mourning in advance the inevitable loss of everything.

If you can, try to replace your worrisome fantasies with the *real facts of life*. You may be using this chronic anxiety in a vain attempt to paper over and cover up those facts with apprehensions and forebodings. Mortality and the loss of all one holds dear is inevitable. No one knows when or how accident or illness might strike. No one knows when or how one's death or the death of loved ones will occur. As soon as that obvious, undeniable fact really sinks in, most of what I say here will be as clear as a mountain stream. My words are not esoteric. I am not hiding anything. Impermanence is the human condition. Those who know that are free to live until they die.

Q2: Robert, as I've been working for some time on an essay whose point is that there is no future, I am, as you might have guessed, completely in accord with your view. However, explaining this is complicated, because the process of evolution has created the capacity to imagine the future as a matter of survival. And this capability, present to varying degrees in many creatures, is very highly developed in humans, partially because of the developed trait we call "self-consciousness." The natural occurrences of imagining the future generate the illusion that we can "know" the future, and this illusion will often persist even after other illusions have been abandoned. It doesn't help that often our "future plans" actually work out, reinforcing the idea that "we" are in control of events.

A: Yes. I'll be interested to read your essay.

There's nothing wrong in imagining a future, as long as the images remain on the practical level where they can function, as you say, to further survival. That, after all, is how DNA-encoded traits evolve and persist in the genome: if they serve survival, the bodies that bear them live long enough to reproduce them sexually.

Now, if I plant some beans and tend to the young shoots with weeding and watering, I may do it because I imagine a future in which I harvest beans and eat them to survive. Most likely, that imagining of the future was strengthened with the shift from a hunter-gatherer culture to agriculture; and presently to money-culture, in which present actions may bear financial dividends. So, if my imagining helps the beans to flourish, and I get to eat them later, *mazel tov*.

A problem arises when the useful faculty of imagining the future jumps the shark, and rather than being used to further material goals—for which it may have some utility—instead purports to predict what I might think or how I might feel at some supposed future time. Only when the so-called future remains psychologically unknown and *blowing in the wind*, as Bob Dylan put it, does one enjoy the freedom to experience in its fullness and unrepeatable essence whatever comprises *this* moment.

This is what artists and lovers know in their bones.

42 - A therapist's misconduct

Q: This is in response to your earlier writing on compassion. I want to ask you, what is compassion? You say what compassion is *not*, but what *is* it?

This has become an even more resonant question in my own life in the last few months. At the end of last year, I started to see a psychotherapist, not so much because I wanted someone to help me with my suffering, but because my own psychotherapy training required it. I do not feel inclined to ask anyone for help in making me feel better, and in subtle ways, I also encourage my patients to be more free of depending on people and things.

Given my experience of knowing therapists and working with them in the past, both as a patient and as a colleague, I did expect that there might be a deepening of my awareness of life through this therapy that was really a training requirement, but I was not sure.

Over the next six months my psychotherapist and I developed intimate, romantic feelings for each other, albeit this was never explicitly stated—until, one day, she expressed her feelings very powerfully just before our session ended, and I said I felt similarly for her. We did not have an elaborate conversation about this because the hour was over. The week after that, she disappeared from my life, canceling all sessions indefinitely, and evoking a lot of anxiety and confusion in me.

She remained out of touch entirely for a month and returned with an e-mail announcing termination, because she did not have time for this relationship anymore. She changed her mind a few days later and said we could resume—which I think was out of fear of my making a complaint to the ethics committee of her affiliating organization.

However, in the sporadic sessions she has offered since then, over the past two months, including several long, unexplained absences, she has shouted at me in almost every session, and humiliated me, using sensitive things I had shared with her previously. She has completely denied having had any intimate feelings for me, and also portrayed me as a psychopath and herself as a victim of my "rage" and "threats," even though I never raised my voice once or used attacking language, despite her provocations.

I believe she changed into this emotional monster because her boyfriend, also a therapist, came to know about her feelings for me, and threatened to leave her if she did not eliminate me from her life immediately. What followed has been my having to listen to her boyfriend's dictates and her trying to minimize the impact of an ethics complaint, in case I make one.

I have decided to end this relationship, and in a few days, we will have our last session. I have written a complaint to the ethics committee of her affiliating body, an elaborate document that brings together evidence to show convincingly that what I wrote above is true.

Here, I have offered only a summary of what has happened in my life over the last year, the traumatic part of it being the last four months. It is probably impossible for you or anyone to know whether I am portraying things correctly—although, for myself, I know that I am. That will be a question for the ethics committee to investigate.

But the question I am asking now, Robert, is a different one. You have spoken of "self-compassion," so what is the compassion for me, the self-compassion in this situation?

I will not deny that I cared deeply for her and still do. For me, the romantic feelings were a concomitance, something that I do not feel were central to the way I felt about her; and they were probably a lot more powerful on her side than on mine. However, I shared my inner life with her intensely, with all its sorrows and beauties—it is rare that one is able to share things so deeply with another person—and for such a relationship to be brutalized in this fashion is deeply, deeply wrong. Therefore, I feel it will be totally wrong if I do not make a complaint.

The complaint is likely to result in her being censured. In all this, as grandiose as it may sound, I truly believe that it will be helpful to her if she comes face to face with her vulnerability, her terror of losing her partner (which has made her do these things to me), her own brokenness. It may demolish part of the facade of lies and aggression she has built up around herself to protect herself from these things.

I do not feel that my making this complaint is in any way devoid of compassion. Perhaps it *is* compassion. On the other hand, I would have to repress my conscience if I did nothing, and allowed her to walk away after shattering something beautiful that we had together. I think justice is not incompatible or in contradiction with compassion.

I wonder what you think about this, both as a psychotherapist and as a person concerned with the real nature of things. Thanks.

A: As Lao Tze is alleged to have written:

> *When the Way has been lost, there comes virtue*
> *When virtue has been lost, there comes ethics*
> *When ethics has been lost, there comes morality*
> *When morality has been lost, there comes justice*
>
> —*Tao Te Ching, Chapter 38*

I have sworn off dealing with relationship questions like yours since the old "Ask Dr-Robert" days, but I will reply here for two reasons. First, you are a worker in the field of psychotherapy and need to get your own head straight about these issues before continuing trying to help others. And second, the difference between compassion and ethics has been on my mind since being subjected to a brouhaha the other day by a woman who wanted to instruct me fanatically about "ethical veganism," as if *ethics* were the highest manifestation of human understanding. It isn't. Ethics are needed, as Lao Tze pointed out, only after the *Way*, as he called it, has been lost.

And what is the Way? The Way is the triple jewel of patience, humility, and compassion. This is not something to be "practiced" as if it were ethics or morality, but to be discovered through one's own suffering. Having suffered truly, do I really need someone to preach to me about ethics and the Golden Rule?

You want me to define compassion for you, but that I cannot do. It falls to each of us to *find out* what compassion is—not by having a spiritual teacher, a psychotherapist, or an overheated "ethical vegan" *tell* us what it is, but by discovering the depths of *self-compassion,* which then extends automatically and naturally to all sentient beings.

Now, let's get to your question about your failed therapy and your desire to report your therapist to the authorities.

The ancient Greeks, who were devoted philosophers, liked to keep their philosophizing down to earth. An old saying of theirs went like this:

> *You can throw nature out with a pitchfork, but she will always come back again.*

As human primates, animal attraction is a major governor of our attention—perhaps *the* major governor—so it is not surprising when sexual feelings arise in the confines of a small room where two people who feel naturally attracted in the first place, in complete privacy, unseen by others, look into one another's eyes and speak about intimate matters. How could such feelings *not* arise?

The therapy situation is a perfect background for feelings of attraction to unfold and deepen. If you are to be any good in your profession, you must acknowledge that plain fact, and learn to handle such feelings without either denying them or acting them out. A good beginning is to remove the word "romantic" from your vocabulary when referring to such feelings. Fuck "romantic!" That is a circumlocution and a euphemism that obscures what really occurs: you imagine touching your shrink, and she imagines getting her hands on you.

Those fantasies arise frequently in the therapeutic milieu and must be *analyzed,* not acted out—which is why there are *ethical standards* forbidding them from being realized in the flesh. If those desires were not often front and center in your profession, ethical standards would not be required.

Now, this particular therapy was not something you desired, and perhaps not something you needed, but a required part of your training. Nevertheless, you were the patient and your therapist was the doctor. That means that you two were never on an equal footing. You had your obligations, and she had hers, but they were entirely different. As the patient, your obligations were to refrain from being physically threatening to the doctor and to pay her fees. That's all. Her obligations were much more extensive, and, according to your account, she failed to meet them.

If she felt sexually attracted to you, the way to deal with that would *never* be to tell *you* that, but to discuss her feelings—both as a potential threat to the treatment and a potential source of useful information—with *her* therapist or supervisor.

Without getting too deeply into the weeds: here, her sexual "counter-transference" feelings could, if properly understood, tell her things about *your* sexuality. But that could happen only if she were able to analyze her own feelings and keep them to herself. Confessing her feelings to you was a major error, a fatal error, that destroyed the therapy. That she raised the issue at the very end of the hour, so as to leave no time for discussion, makes it worse, but there was never going to be a good time for her to raise it. She would have been in the wrong whenever she raised it.

You were not similarly enjoined. You had the right to talk about any of your thoughts and feelings—no limit—and if you had said, "I think about the two of us in bed," she would be professionally prohibited from replying, "Yes! I do too," regardless of her feelings. The proper therapeutic response would be, "Say more about that." If a therapist cannot handle that end of the work, she needs to find another gig. Simple as that.

As far as reporting her, I heard no compassion at all in your question to me about that. Clearly, you feel hurt and damaged by this relationship—and that is *her* failure, not yours. She bungled this therapy entirely. Not only did she raise false hopes in the part of you that did not want to be a dependent *patient*—which is what you were—but an equal, an intimate, and a lover, but she destroyed the possibility of making proper therapeutic use of your feelings for her. She ruined the chance of helping you to investigate those feelings, which would have included, for example, exploring this question: what is attractive about a woman in a position of authority over you? (Think "Mom"—the ultimate sexual forbidden fruit.)

If I were in your shoes, I'd learn what I could from this—which might involve getting a qualified therapist to help you work through it; you could find out a lot that way, not just about your feelings, but about how a *real* doctor does this work—and then let it go. But even if you want to follow through on the ethics complaint, don't imagine that *compassion* has anything to do with it. It will be feelings of injury and the need for *justice*, not compassion, at the heart of that procedure.

You may imagine that you will lodge your complaint partly to protect future patients from this incompetent shrink, and that might be partially true. But the real reason, I suspect, is a desire for avenging her betrayal, although you probably will reject that idea. Reading between the lines of your question, I can see how defended you are against the idea that an ethics complaint would have a personal aspect. I encourage you to consider the idea.

I want to close by saying that I have only your report to go on, so anything I have just said is based entirely on that.

Q2: "Tough love" is the challenging side of compassion, or so it seems to me, because some of us obviously want to be kind and find it difficult to say no or to withhold approval.

The classic example is, of course, the tough love that's advised for people caught up in others' addictions: this means not enabling their addiction by covering it up and not facilitating it by direct or indirect means. The same applies to abusive behaviors. Is it compassionate to facilitate this therapist's continuing train wreck? It's unlikely, although possible, that this is the first time she's been up to these tricks.

Reporting the therapist might prevent her from manipulating and exploiting other "innocent" analysands, so there might be an element of compassion. This is the sort of ethical dilemma that comes up for anyone in the "caring" professions, and is usually included in the education leading to a qualification. All my comments are meant to be practical on the level of living life as stuff happens, and I am not implying or inferring any critique of compassion in general.

A: I do not see compassion as having *practical* applications. In my view, practicality calls for *ethics,* not compassion. Compassion is like love. It just *is*. It cannot, in my view, be learned or created on demand. Compassion may work well in the world of ethics or not. Who knows?

For example, in the brouhaha about "ethical veganism", I raised the case of indigenous people who hunt to live—but that was passed off immediately as, "Well, nowadays they can have food *shipped* to them." Really? And are you volunteering to pay for that?

That woman's zealotry is a perfect case of ethics gone awry. There was no love in her comment and no compassion either—just single-minded obsession and the obtuseness of someone who believes herself to be standing on the moral high ground.

She may be a lovely person otherwise and may mean well, but that does *not* constitute compassion, nor ethics either. Compassion is *not,* I am saying, a bleeding heart, and ethics requires considering all stakeholders, not just one's favorites.

In case it matters in understanding my view of that dust-up by the way, I am not a meat eater, and I love and protect many animals.

43 - Loosening the grip of ego

Q: Hello Robert. Thanks for your wonderful book that I have been diving into over the last fortnight. I have a question for you. You have stated a number of times that you did absolutely nothing to awaken, that in your experience we have no free will, and that the clinging to this belief in free will is what binds us to attachment and desire. Does this mean that when I practice self-inquiry, sit in witnessing, and read your book, I am wasting my time? Will this type of practice not loosen the grip of ego in any way?

How to let everything go when the mind is not comfortable when I find myself alone, which is often now? I have almost stopped all of my labeled spiritual practices, yet I find my mind more chaotic than ever before, and in a state of desperate aloneness.

A: That's a good question. If you will try to make clear to me what you mean by "practice self-inquiry," and what you mean by "sit in witnessing," I will reply as best I can. Please be as specific as you can. I don't want to assume anything.

Q: For a while, I practiced meditation and silent sitting, asking questions such as "Who am I?" and "What am I?"; and rested as the space of the observer. In this, I was influenced by people such as Ramana, Adyashanti, and especially Mooji. Then I stopped reading or watching anything related to Advaita Vedanta, because every time I watched Mooji, for example, something inside wanted to renounce everything and run away.

When I came across your message initially, I felt relaxed and flowing with life, but now my ego is digging in his heels, and I become anxious whenever I contemplate choicelessness.

I guess what I'm attempting to state here is that I'm struggling like never before just to be comfortable in my own skin. I'm also a men's coach and I facilitate men's retreats. Now I'm starting to think it's all a big waste of time.

A: To begin with, unlike those guys you mentioned, my work is self-expression, not "teaching." Like my photographs, my words constitute a kind of report about my own experiences, not instructions for others to follow in order to be "free like Robert." I am an artist and retired psychotherapist, not a spiritual teacher. Anyway, no one can be "free like Robert." You can only be free like yourself.

I do say that I find myself awake, but what "awake" means to me might be very different from what you imagine it means; and different from the way others, such as the people you mentioned, have viewed these matters.

For me, "awake" entails seeing that the character called "I" or "myself" is not in control of what seems to turn up moment by moment—not thoughts, not perceptions, not feelings. None of it. Everything one sees, hears, feels, thinks, or otherwise experiences, just materializes as it does, and the *apparent* "myself" becomes aware of it automatically, without trying or *needing* to try.

"Myself" is not something I "do." "Myself" just is, just *exists* as a confection of physical attributes, awareness, feelings, emotions, thoughts, and a point of view, all of which flow and change ceaselessly. If you doubt that this flow is ceaseless, try to *stop* being "myself" for even a moment. Don't take my word for this. Try it.

Suppose you have been sleeping, and the morning sun awakens you. As you awaken, you become aware that you had been sleeping and are now awake. You don't have to *ask* yourself if you are awake—you just *know* it. That is what I mean by the phrase "choiceless awareness." Nor do you have to create the world around you—the objects in your bedroom, the sounds you hear, the scene that appears when you look out the window. All of that is just *there,* without your having to do anything to *make* it be there.

This should be obvious. If, for example, you go to the window and see a cloud in the sky, you did not put it there, nor, having seen it, can you "unsee" it. You have no control in the matter. None. Zero. I wonder if this is clear to you. If not, please don't read further. Instead, contemplate it, until it becomes clear. Unless you see that you are not the creator of sights and sounds, there is no understanding the deeper question about loosening the grip of ego.

OK. Suppose you accept that you are not the creator of sights, sounds, feelings, emotions, thoughts, dreams, etcetera. Suppose you see that all of that information just arises, just presents itself, and then you have to deal with it. The "you" who has to deal with it is what you are calling "ego." It is an imagined "you." When I say "imagined," I am not suggesting that it does not really exist or that it is not real. Of *course* it exists, and is just as real as any other thought or feeling—but not *more* real.

On this point, my perspective may differ from those spiritual teachers you mentioned. I don't know much about Mooji except that he seems to be posing as a holy man and sells photographs of his feet in the gift shop. I guess that is so people can kiss the photographs when Mooji is not around to have his actual feet kissed. But Ramana, as I understand it, was all about distinguishing the real from the unreal, and I think Mooji, Rupert Spira, and others are in that camp as well.

I am not. I consider that task hopeless and useless. In my view, it can lead only to splitting and delusion.

The "myself" that feels itself to be in the "grip of ego" *is* ego, I say. There is no way to choose to loosen that grip. The grip *is* you. The "myself" who is "struggling just to be comfortable in my skin like never before" *is* ego. That's what "myself" is: a point of view that prefers thoughts and feelings to be one way and not another, and that dislikes thoughts and feelings that are difficult, uncomfortable, or otherwise fail to satisfy. Try to see this clearly. The very wish for things to be different from the way they are in this moment *is* ego.

In writing *The Ten Thousand Things*, there was no way to avoid discussion of "free will." That question was raised in some of the conversations upon which that book is based. But the endless debate about free will is a kind of red herring that really has little to do with these matters. So-called "free will" is not some absolute power that you either have or you don't. That is a misunderstanding. Perhaps you are free, for example, to move your hand if you "will" it to move, but that still leaves the question of what caused you to *want* to move your hand in the first place. Where did *that* desire originate?

Contemplate this, please. "Free will" is a fantasy. We do not choose our thoughts and feelings. They simply arise, from whence we do not know, and "ego" is left to cope with them. If you really could choose thoughts and feelings, this entire question would be moot. You would simply *choose* or *decide* to feel comfortable in your own skin, and maintain that choice endlessly. If an uncomfortable thought—such as "old age, illness, and death"—arose, you would simply erase it, banish it, and never think it again. But it doesn't work that way, does it?

Now you say that, since reading my book, you "have almost stopped all of my labeled spiritual practices, yet I find my mind more chaotic than ever before and in a state of desperate aloneness." Yes. Perfect. Now you are getting the idea. You *are* in a state of aloneness. We all are. That's what being human entails: born alone, die alone.

No one will ever understand you fully, and you will never understand yourself fully either. As I put this in *4T*, "The 'I' of enunciation never thinks just what it thinks it thinks, and never simply is what it thinks itself to be." That is my perspective as a depth psychologist, and I have found good evidence for it in psychoanalytic practice.

Self-described jnanis, like Sailor Bob for one, hate that point of view which says that one will never fully know "myself," and try to discredit observations that suggest the existence of an unconscious mind. But they cannot erase human psychology, nor escape it, merely by reiterating the weak logic of Vedanta.

The practices you mentioned are used by many people to distract themselves from remembering that they were born alone and will die alone. For example, if I occupy myself with "witnessing," I may get lost in the process, and overlook the facts of what sooner or later must be "witnessed:" physical annihilation often preceded by plenty of pain and suffering.

The supposed "witness" is part of what is dying. There is no permanence in it. "Myself" is a goner—no staying power. "Myself" is short-lived, transitory, ephemeral, and entirely powerless to be otherwise, except, I say, in spiritual fantasies like "Heaven with Jesus" or "You are the unchanging Self."

Unfortunately, you picked up my book, and now those tactics of denial offered by the "enlightenment" gurus are not getting the job done: "I am *not* an animal like any other with a heart that must keep beating in order for me to remain alive—I am the unchanging, deathless 'witness' of all that." No wonder your anxiety has deepened since reading *The Ten Thousand Things*. In that book, I do not look kindly on such tired-out spiritual tropes. I say *how it feels to me* to live without them.

From my perspective, you have been living in an hypnotic trance—the trance of transcendence—and now you may be snapping out of it. The snake may be shedding its skin. Of *course* that feels uncomfortable, particularly at first.

So, to answer your question, there is, I say, no method for "loosening the grip of the ego." The "myself" who imagines wanting that grip to loosen *is* ego. That which prefers one condition to another *is* ego. The more you try to loosen the grip, the stronger the grip becomes, because that which *tries* is ego. If you see that, perhaps you will feel like living in the suchness of each moment as it comes, without always aiming at betterment of thoughts and feelings, or trying to escape into religious fantasies.

In each moment, we are what we are—perceptions, feelings, thoughts, and emotions—and *that is what we have*. That is all we ever have. Like it or not, this is it.

By the way, you probably know more about Ramana Maharshi than I do, but according to his own testimony, he had a kind of panic attack as a teenager in which, although young and in good health, he somehow began to imagine that he was dying. To deal with this, he lay down on the floor and shut his mouth tight, stretching out his limbs "as if rigor mortis had set in." He then said to himself, "This body is dead. It will be carried out to the burning ground stiff, and there burned and reduced to ashes. But with the death of this body, am I dead? Is the body 'I'? It is silent and inert, but I feel the full force of my personality, and even the voice of the 'I' within me."

He then concluded from that "inquiry" that he could not be the body because the body was "dead," but he was still present; and for him, that confirmed the entire Hindu metaphysics with which he had been surrounded culturally since the day he was born.

I wonder if you see the preposterousness of that story, the blatant absurdity of it. And if you don't, I wonder *why* you don't.

In case you don't, let me give you a clue: Maharshi *assumed* himself dead because he imitated the posture and manner of a "dead person," and reasoned from that false premise that any sense of self that remained could not be originating normally in the body/mind, but must be separate and apart from the body. That was just a child's naive reasoning. In plain fact, Ramana was *not* dead. His body, including its brain, was functioning just fine—so on what basis could he possibly conclude that the "self" existed apart from the body? This is ludicrous on the face of it.

Based on this very shaky teenage "inquiry," he decided that all of Vedanta had been confirmed, and spent the rest of his life preaching it, chapter and verse. That preaching was dogma, not "Truth," and his popularity subsequently, and the idea that he was some kind of "master," in my view, is a case of the emperor's new clothes. I do not mean to say that this man never uttered a word of wisdom. That's not the point.

People like to have their religious upbringing confirmed, of course, and he did it well, and without talking a lot, which leaves much to the imagination. As for why he is taken as some kind of spiritual genius, when actually the story is one of a rather conventionally religious fellow, I leave to you to determine, assuming you are interested. Ramana, of course, had every right to believe whatever he believed and to preach whatever he preached, but I have little interest in that kind of teaching, none at all for the legend that is being whipped up and promoted in regards to it.

Some people have said that my reports are not very different from what Ramana taught, or what his imitators teach, but I disagree. Yes, to an extent there is agreement—we both advise not striving, and to "be as you are," as he put it. And I like this from him:

Let come what comes, let go what goes. See what remains.

But often, this so-called *jnani* lapsed into the kind of silly religious preaching for which I have no use, and which is no different from the dogma of any middle-of-the-road Christian church. For example:

> *The Lord of the universe carries the entire burden of this world. You imagine you do. You can hand all your burdens over to His care. Whatever you have to do, you will be made an instrument for doing it at the right time. Do not think you cannot do it unless you have the desire to do it. Desire does not give you the strength for doing. The entire strength is the Lord's.*

Is there really a "Lord of the universe?" No one, I say, could possibly *know* such a thing. And yet this is stated as a fact. It may be comforting to believe in a benign "Lord" who is in charge of everything that occurs, but comfort is not the same as awakeness.

As for your work in facilitating men's retreats, it seems to me that you owe it to yourself and to your clients to ask yourself what exactly you are facilitating. If you are not comfortable in your own skin, what do you really have to facilitate? This is not a judgment, just a question. Be well.

44 - Are we only just flesh and blood?

Q: I studied with the Huichol Indians for a time, and felt a moment of transcendence while dancing the Deer Dance. I was befriended by a Huichol shaman in his 80s. These men and women study for at least 25 to 30 years and claim many powers, including the power to heal. When my shaman friend, TaTa, fell ill, he went to the mountains to consult the most famous and powerful of all the healers, but his kidneys still failed. On his death bed, he expressed surprise that he too would die.

A: I have heard it said that "reality is that which does not go away even if you *don't* believe in it." This case sounds like a perfect illustration of that epigram.

Humans do have abilities as healers. I did some healing work myself for years, which is largely about *clearing away obstructions* to the natural process of healing. What we do *not* have is the ability to live a life that is not a *human* life, or to help someone else to live such a life, with all that entails: old age, illness, suffering, and death. We humans are a species in the animal kingdom, and all animals age, become ill, and die (unless they die before old age and senescence set in, due to early illness, war, murder, accident, suicide, or other misadventure). Certainly, none of that can be denied.

Some people try to create two separate categories:

1. Humans
2. Animals

with the intention of claiming that humans are the specially created "Children of God," different not just in appearance but in kind from our non-human brothers and sisters. But as we learn more about the intelligence that other animals besides us really possess, that is increasingly untenable.

In fact, we may not even be the most intelligent among animals on this planet. We already know that whales, for example, are highly intelligent, and possess exquisitely evolved modes of communication among themselves. But because they have no need to work for a living or invent and build things, we are limited in our ability to assess their level of intelligence.

So, when someone harbors beliefs that require denying any of the above, I consider such a person to be engaged in wishful thinking, which is a type of self-created, delusional escape hatch.

Based on what you wrote, it seems that TaTa was deluded in that way. And, of course, the medicine man who taught that stuff to TaTa was deluded just like his teacher, and his teacher's teacher, etcetera. This nonsense is passed down from parent to child, and enters our minds by osmosis from the wider cultural surround.

The roots of that delusion lie, I say, in fear, superstition, and aversion to impermanence.

Anyone reading this may disagree. And given the intense religious conditioning to which the majority of children are subjected from birth, I am sure that some *will* disagree, and perhaps even feel insulted. That's fine by me. Feel what you must. I say what I see and seek neither agreement nor approval.

Q2: Robert, you say, "What we do *not* have is the ability to live a life that is not a *human* life, or to help someone else to live such a life, with all that entails: old age, illness, suffering, death." My question is this: what if we do have that ability, but just don't know about it?

A: Your approach last week seemed more about wanting to debate and pin me down with words rather than wanting to understand what I am saying. But let's give it another shot.

Dreaming up "what ifs" will never end, no matter what I say. There will always be the next "what if?" What if there really is a fairy living at the foot of the garden, but I can't see her? What if I *would* be able to see her if only I had sufficient faith in her presence there? What if Jesus really does await me in Heaven, assuming I don't fuck it up by bad behavior or failure to have faith?

I have zero interest in such hypotheticals myself, nor do I have any way at all of "proving" the things I say, although to me they are not hypothetical. To me, they are phenomenology. But I understand that others—and you may be one of them—enjoy fantasy, and like to keep all options open. Fine by me. Knock yourself out.

Q2: I feel that you are trying to avoid my question. Why can't you just answer directly? What if we do have the ability to be more than human, but just don't know it?

A: I am not trying to avoid your question. I just don't understand what you are asking. I can offer nothing but simple, down-to-earth answers, so any questions must be simple, down-to-earth questions. If you have one like that, please state it plainly, and I will give it my full attention.

Q2: I can see I will not get an answer. I really asked a very simple question. Are we—humans and animals and everything else—just flesh and blood? Is that good enough?

A: Oh. "Are we just flesh and blood?" is the question. Now I think I understand. I will reply without equivocation and with all the honesty at my disposal. But before I do, indulge me in a short exploration of the natural history of questions such as that.

Suppose I gave you what you are asking me for, a yes or no answer to that question. How would that help you? I can't see how it would.

Suppose I said, for example:

> *No. We are not just flesh and blood, bodies and brains. That is just blatant materialism. How can anyone deny that we live in a world of spirits? Carl Sagan may have called the world of spirits the "demon-haunted world," but he was a materialist and a scientist to boot. He may have felt energized, thrilled, delighted, and enthralled to find himself present in a universe beyond measure, but at heart,*

> *he was an atheist, lost in scientism.*
>
> *He and his scientific cohorts may* claim *that our bodies and brains evolved in a natural way from older, more basic life-forms. They may* claim *that all life on Earth has one common ancestor, and that human consciousness evolved in the same natural way as brains, beginning with the initial chemical sensitivities of our most distant, microscopic forebears.*
>
> *They may* claim *such things, but those claims show their ignorance of* spiritual Truth. *Bodies and brains don't* really *exist. We are only* dreaming *bodies and brains. This world is Brahman only. We humans only* seem *to exist. The fossils that undergird the common ancestor theory are only dream-fossils, and the theory of evolution by natural selection is only a dream-theory put forth by dream-scientists. Our real nature is pure consciousness, and nothing* really *exists but God.*

Then, on hearing that—and assuming that you had really *wanted* an answer and were not just trying to begin a debate—you would either believe me or not.

If you believed me, you would *know* nothing more for certain about this question than before you asked it. You would only have made an authority of me, whom you have never even met, except as a voice on a Facebook page. "Robert says that we are more than just flesh and blood." That is credulity. What makes you think that Robert knows anything with certainty about any such question, or that the Dalai Lama does?

Or, suppose I said:

> *God? That's just some idea humans once cooked up and now dish out to account for the power of nature, and to paper over their doubts and fears. You and I are flesh and blood like any other animal—a bonobo, for example—except that the stories we have in our minds are most likely somewhat different from the stories a bonobo has in its mind, but perhaps not very different. After all, a bonobo's brain is very much like ours—we share 98.7 percent of our DNA*

with the bonobo, and, like us, they are tribally organized and show remarkable social intelligence, as well as physical and mental abilities of a high order.

Then you would either *believe* me when I said that bonobos and humans could sit down to dinner together if the humans weren't so *speciesist*, or you would have some esoteric reason to *disbelieve* it—for example, the holy books say we are made in the image of God and were given dominion over the animals, so it can't be that we and the bonobos are really such close cousins. Or you might say, "All that about DNA is only the *physical* world—the world of flesh and blood. But what about the *spiritual* world, Robert?"

If you went that way, you would be defacing my reply with the second-hand beliefs you already entertain and love to advocate, which would have nothing to do with hearing my reply or anything else I have ever said. That defacement would *stop* you from hearing me fairly in the first place—which, by the way, you have yet to do.

I wonder if you get this. If you look to any outside authority at all in questions such as this, you would still not have a definitive answer, because no one *has* such an answer to give. Instead, you would have an "authoritative" answer to stir into the disorder in your mind already produced by soaking up answers from others who have no *real* answers to give. Having solicited a fresh answer and received one, you will have either to denigrate and discount it, or accept it and deal with it. Thus, you will be forced into a posture of either greater disbelief or greater credulity, a posture based not on any real evidence or lack of it, but upon your own psychological needs (some of them, by the way, demonstrably—demonstrated by twin studies—encoded in DNA).

I promised a straight answer. Here it is. Are we only flesh and blood? If you mean, "Is there a 'myself' that goes on existing when one's flesh and blood have been consumed by other organisms, as is the way of nature?" I have no inside information on that, but if you press me for an *opinion*, very likely no. I assume—but do not *know*—that when the brain dies, the lights go out for good and all.

To me, and with some reliance on Occam's Razor, it seems most likely that "myself" is something that a brain does—*part* of what a brain does while running the rest of the organism as well, astounding and mysterious as that may seem. This view is not mere fantasy, like the beliefs of Christianity, Islam, or Hinduism—for which there is no *evidence* at all, but only testimony (people can *say* anything) and tradition (old does not equal true). I have no interest in either religious fantasy or traditional explanations.

Admittedly, there is no way to *prove* that a brain is needed for consciousness and not the other way around, but it *is* suggestive that, as parts of the brain are damaged or die, parts of "myself" disappear along with those selfsame organic structures in predictable ways. Data like that cannot be dismissed out of hand. Still, if consciousness really *were* prior to brains as per the metaphysics of the Hindu jnanis, then we really *would* be dreaming up brains and bodies, when actually there are no brains and bodies. In that view, this world is only a dream in the mind of God, and no one can *prove* that it isn't.

You may be surprised to hear that I don't actually care which way all that shakes out. It makes no difference to me at all. I am in *this* moment, always. My *be*-ing is freefall in apparently endless space. If, at death, the lights go out and freefall ends, fine by me. In that event, nothing remains to be dealt with. If, by some chance, good old Robert—or the old boy's *essence* anyway—is still around, that will be the same dharma as right now: *deal with it* moment by moment. What else *is* there?

From this perspective, ego and its natural desires to survive, and even to fantasize transcending biology, do not trouble me. In seeing that now is all we ever have, questions such as yours are unmasked as moot, and die away by their own negligibility.

Does that satisfy?

45 - A human life ends

Q: Robert, you have said that the idea of killing the ego or vanquishing the ego is naive. But many spiritual traditions put that forth as a goal—as *the* goal. Please explain.

A: Traditions cut no ice with me. To me, the idea that tradition is somehow authoritative in the realms of cosmology and metaphysics seems absurd. From my point of view, traditions are just what we ordinary human animals have had passed down to us by our ordinary human caregivers, and will pass on to our ordinary human offspring in turn. It's unavoidable. We are *swimming* in tradition.

Certain elements of that unchosen endowment may be useful, particularly in the realm of practical matters: how and when to plant a garden, how to deliver a baby, how to bandage a wound, etcetera. But other elements may be entirely false, superstitious, and counterproductive. People believe all kinds of nonsense. They always have and always will.

In the physical world, methods and beliefs that fail empirically don't *become* traditions, but sooner or later are discarded as erroneous and useless. But in the realm of concepts and idealism, all kinds of foolishness can survive just fine, because in that regime, conjectures and imagined "truths" resist reality testing.

If I tell you that everything happens for a reason, how can you prove me wrong? A statement like that can neither be validated nor falsified, but even if totally false, it could become a traditional belief. In fact, it has. The wise among us know better than to believe anything without good evidence.

I have no use for religion or spirituality at all, but I am not saying that others shouldn't. There are parts of what is wrongly called *spirituality*—but is better regarded as *wisdom*—that can be useful for certain people at certain times, as I see this. However, that wisdom is only useful if one can differentiate it from the great mass of nonsense that comprises most spiritual discourse. Unfortunately, however, that differentiation usually occurs only as one is already shaking off the hypnotic trance. Then it can be seen as clear as a bell.

I regard ego as a normal aspect of this aliveness. Donkeys have egos too—donkey egos; but since they cannot speak up for themselves, they express self-centeredness by, for example, pushing one another out of the way when food appears.

So *ego* seems to be a point of view ordinarily necessary for economic and social survival—an assertion of "myselfness." I am not saying that a donkey has the same self-reflective point of view as a human primate, but that looking after one's own needs is not an aberration, but a natural part of this aliveness.

Perhaps a so-called "god-intoxicated being" can survive entirely without considering her own welfare and/or his own necessities, but he or she will have to be fed and carried around by worshippers and disciples. We ordinary people do have to earn our livings, pay bills, keep appointments, and manage countless ordinary matters that amount to self-care.

Now one may understand "myself" in a different way, apart from likes and dislikes, fears and desires, and all that; so there may be a way of regarding myself non-egotistically. One may notice that "myself" was never chosen but just arose as a spontaneous organic process, for which no "myself" is responsible, and for which no ego deserves either credit or blame.

From that awake perspective, one does not *need* to walk around identified with ego, but can just flow into self-centeredness if and when required, like wearing business attire at work. I have gone into that in detail in *The Ten Thousand Things*, and I suggest you read that.

From that point of view, one may see ego for what it is: an unchosen, spontaneous survival mechanism that is not really the kernel of "myself" at all, but a kind of required standardized framework that is a normal part of this aliveness—not a problem to be "transcended."

If you see that, there is nothing to kill or vanquish. It's all part of this mystery we call life.

Q2: Hey there, Robert. I really enjoyed hearing you tell someone to fuck off. I am amazed actually at your patience and how much you put up with before getting angry. I loved hearing about the dream in which you were in a little boat, rowing away from a crumbling old building that you knew in the dream to be ego.

Your dream reminded me of a dream I had as a child. But in my dream, there was no structure crumbling behind me ... Which leads to my question: was the structure necessary? Did it have to exist before it could dissolve? Is a healthy ego a prerequisite to the awakening you experienced? It seems many of us lucky enough to live at a time or in a place where we can get good counseling or therapy spend much of our lives *repairing* the structure, with the ultimate goal, ironically, of eventually letting it go. Also, why not have your cake and eat it too? I mean, can the structure *serve* what we truly are rather than *distract* from what we truly are? Please comment. Thanks.

A: That's a good question.

I have heard it said that "you have to be someone before you can be no one," and I suppose there is some truth in that, at least as a warning to the young not to jump into "spirituality" too soon—before finding ordinary sanity, I mean.

It is hard to define what constitutes a "healthy ego." The psychologists don't have all the answers about that, and their definitions keep changing. The latest handbook of mental illness—*The Diagnostic and Statistical Manual*—no longer even mentions Narcissistic Personality Disorder, which was a major category in all previous editions. Why? Because what used to seem "disordered" (self-absorption: a grandiose sense of self, a serious miscalculation of one's abilities and potential, often accompanied by fantasies of greatness) is rapidly becoming the new normal.

And the cultural component is huge. For example, what would seem a normal, healthy individualism in the USA, France, or Germany, might, in Japan, seem a loutish self-centeredness and a worrisome inability to go along with the crowd.

The implication in your question—that someone can "let go" of ego—needs investigation. I have no idea who that "someone" letting go of ego would be, if *not* ego. This seems like pulling yourself up by your own bootstraps. You can talk about doing it, but it is physically impossible.

If your question is about me personally, I never think about ego. All of this is just here, changing constantly according to no rhyme or reason that I can discern, with no *doer* or creator at the center managing any of it. Things just are as they are, and in this moment can be no different. I find myself responding to necessities without feeling the need to take responsibility for anything or blame myself either.

For example, when you saw my reply telling someone to fuck off, you assumed that I must have felt angry—otherwise, why would I use those words? But I did not feel angry at all. It seemed clear that this guy would never be satisfied with anything I said, and that I'd already wasted too many words trying to meet his unending fears. He wasn't looking for clarity—which I *do* have to offer—but a way out, an escape hatch from the realities of biological existence—which I do *not* have to offer. He'd started out idealizing me, and expected me to hand him the keys to the kingdom. As soon as I would not play spiritual teacher for him, he felt compelled to tear down that idealization, so I found myself helping him with that tear-down. See how quick we got to "Sayonara?"

Vulgarity is sometimes useful in this world of reverent spirituality, which is 99 percent pure fucked up horseshit. It was no different in the 10th century:

Q: "What is Buddha?"
A: "The shit stick in the latrine."

I respond honestly to any question put to me in earnest. That is the commitment. Though not unique, my perspective *is* unusual, so most of the time my replies are misunderstood, often by people who imagine they have understood perfectly. I have no magic powers to make anyone understand anything. I just say what I see, and the questioner has to take it from there.

I have a personal life where people know me and see me as the ordinary human being I am. In that milieu, I am open to being set straight if I need it. But here, with thousands of friends and anonymous followers, I am not looking for appraisals and reviews, and certainly not instruction. Unless I make a factual error, don't even *try* to correct me, much less "teach" me. That would be as much of a waste of time as trying to give me tips on improving my photographs. As if.

Q: Great! I like your response. Thanks. So interesting about the *DSM* and Narcissistic Personality Disorder being tossed out. Those with the disorder must be hugely pissed. What a perfect insult: you no longer exist. Ha, ha.

In terms of your response, when you wrote, "I don't even think about ego," perhaps back in 2013 you did think about it, or perhaps I misunderstood, because when you recounted your dream you mentioned that the structure was perceived by the dreamer (not your exact words) to be the ego. Anyway, I'm very confused by this word "ego," period. I guess it's the belief that you're a separate being? It seems fraught, whatever it is.

I am off and on in Jungian analysis and find that analysis helps me when I'm in a kind of ET mode, wanting to return home. This leads me to another question. Your discussion with Robert K. Hall about a dream of yours back in the 1980s makes me wonder what you think of dreams. Who is the dreamer? What is a dream? Thanks for listening.

A: Oh well, the rather sudden awakening I experienced occurred not in a dream, but in broad daylight, while sitting in my pickup truck at the edge of the Rio Grande Gorge in New Mexico, looking out at that amazing landscape. The dream of rowing away from a crumbling mansion had occurred earlier—by several months, I think—and the symbolism was entirely and instantly clear to me, which made it feel quite different from the usual kind of dream that has to be discussed and analyzed. Perhaps it was what the Jungians call a "premonitory dream." But nowadays I don't ever think about ego unless someone asks me a question about it.

You are right. The entire subject is fraught. The feeling of being a separate being is a *kind* of dream, but so is the idea that no separate person really exists. Both are inaccurate in my view. These written conversations are like dreams—ones that I do not trouble myself to analyze. My perspective is simple and requires very little thought, so all that theory—what Carl Jung made of dreams, what Ramana Maharshi made of them, what the ego is and isn't, etcetera—to me lacks interest. I don't mean to belittle your questions, your Jungian analysis, or anything else. It's all valid. If you find something helpful anywhere, *mazel tov*. I'm only talking about my own feelings.

For me, *mortality* is the chief feature. Each of us will lose *everything*. The sand is running through the glass. A human life *ends*. And being "enlightened" doesn't change that fact one iota. If one can get the sense of that, the rest kind of falls into place, I find, Jung or no Jung, ego or no ego.

46 - I am afraid of non-existence

Q: Good evening, Robert, and Happy New Year! Your Facebook page is packed with so many great questions and answers, and *The Ten Thousand Things* is brilliant. But something came up in Chapter 25 that doesn't sit well with me, and I wonder if you could comment on what you said there. Here it is:

> *There may be thoughts about the body—many of them anxious and fearful—but the body does not need those thoughts. The body needs air, water, food, and shelter, not thoughts. From the standpoint of the body, thoughts are superfluous. "But," you might object, "if I don't care for my body, which involves thought, the body might die." Yes, that is true, but the body does not care about dying—"myself" does. The body has no interest in continuing. The body does not want to continue. You want to continue.* You *don't want to die.*

I don't understand how it could be said that the body has no interest in continuing. Isn't self-preservation a response that the "I" has little part in? Isn't it a survival instinct? Or do you mean to indicate that the concept of a body having an interest is irrational? Thanks.

A: Thank you. I wish you all the best too.

Even the most basic single-celled organisms are forced by constant selective pressure to evolve ways of avoiding damage from their surroundings. So "self-preservation" is the name for packages of evolved responses that refer to physical bodies, even a body of the most basic variety, and is not particularly a *human* trait, but a universal feature of living entities. A one-celled bacterium cannot "care" about anything, but still actively avoids harmful situations as best it can.

But that level of automatic, unthinking avoidance is not anything like the desires of the conscious ego—that which calls itself "I" or "me"—to control its environment by means of thought. For example, if I convert to a vegan diet because I have come to believe that I will live longer that way, that has nothing to do with any evolved means of bodily self-preservation, but with the desire of the *"I of enunciation"*—everything I *call* "myself"—to keep existing for as long as possible. That same desire—the desire to continue *as* myself—may drive someone to speculate about an individual existence prior to or subsequent to the observed life of the body. But that has nothing to do with "self-preservation" in the biological sense. It is *myself* that wants to live forever, not the body.

I am not saying that there is something wrong with desiring to keep on being oneself and to continue enjoying what one enjoys. All of that is entirely natural, and those who advise "transcending it" by means of effortful renunciation are, in my opinion, speaking from ignorance. Living provides its *own* renunciation. Youthful vigor—assuming one is fortunate enough to have it at all—does not last. Even *with* vigor, physical existence can be difficult, and the difficulties tend to compound as one ages. That's just direct observation speaking—observation of myself and others. That's the kind of plain, fact-based understanding that I mean by the word "sanity."

If one is willing to pay the price in terms of the efforts needed for feeding, clothing, sheltering, and otherwise caring for this body, plus the price in terms of physical pain and suffering—and with a bit of *luck*—the body may go on for quite a while. But sooner or later *it will end*. That is mortality, and *that* is the source of many anxious and fearful thoughts. Not that the *body* will end. If one is around long enough, bodily death may come to seem desirable—a relief from pain, suffering, and disability. The anxiety and fear centers around "myself" ceasing to exist.

Q2: About fifteen years ago I experienced a big shift in consciousness. I felt suddenly that I was not separate from anything, and everything was happening inside me, and even *was* me.

I had by then let go of so many beliefs. As best as I could tell, my thoughts and feelings came from conditioning and biological wiring, so I wasn't identified with them. I was still meditating, mostly because I found it enjoyable.

One day I sat to meditate and within a few moments I had a thought: "Just rest in awareness." Then another thought: "No. Rest *as* awareness." So I did, and what seemed to be my consciousness floated out of my body and hovered above my body for a moment. I thought, "This is scary!" And then, "Oh well."

Then, consciousness floated away into the darkness. For some time—I really don't know how long—there was nothing: no self, no darkness, no thoughts, no feelings, nothing. Then I floated back into my body.

I was very disturbed by this, as it seemed to imply that there *was* nothing, no continuation, nothing beyond this existence, no bigger intelligence, nothing. I went to several teachers asking about this. Their answers left me unsatisfied.

Within a year or so my marriage ended, and I moved from Florida to California. That's a long story. But most importantly, I had left my home town of over 30 years, my private psychotherapy practice, the old house I loved, and my friends, while losing most of my financial resources.

I moved in with my daughter and son-in–law, so I wasn't alone. But I fell apart emotionally. I became frightened, overwhelmed by sadness, and lost any sense of peace. I felt separate and alone. I was forced to see the beliefs and attachments that had been swept under the rug while I had imagined falsely that I'd already let them go.

I moved to Asheville, North Carolina about four years ago, and slowly my life has come together. Something lovely is beginning to arise in me again: joy, peace, awareness of life flowing, acceptance, etcetera.

I came upon your interview with Rick Archer on his *Buddha at the Gas Pump*[22] internet program, and it captured my attention. Fifteen years ago I was drawn to the nondualists, but later concluded that they were missing something, something human. In the video, you seemed very human and yet more. So I got your book, and in

22. See https://BATGAP.com/robert-saltzman

reading it, I realized that I had always understood my big shift in consciousness as feeling no separation between myself and everything else, but that was not quite right. There still was a separation, because I was still the one it happened *to*.

So here's my question. Can you help me understand all this? And can you give me any guidance that might allow this shift in perception from myself as the center that everything happens *to*, to a viewpoint more like yours, that seems to come from actual oneness without separation?

What you say rings true, Robert. It's like I've always known these things. But it's scary. I am afraid of non-existence.

I started my spiritual search in my teens. I'm now 68. Thank you so much.

A: You are most welcome. You closed by mentioning having started a spiritual search in your teens. Apparently, despite your dramatic experiences, that search continues. You went to "teachers," but weren't satisfied by what they told you, and now you are looking to me for answers.

You have read *The Ten Thousand Things*, so when you ask for help, I assume you understand that any help I can offer must begin by questioning any supposed boundary—any imagined difference—between ordinary human primate life and so-called "spiritual experiences."

I mention this because, with the growing popularity of *4T*, I have been receiving some rather boorish messages from aggrieved magical thinkers. The latest one said, "I hope that seekers will not be injured by your writing." That "hope"—which is really a nasty, passive-aggressive complaint—is sad to hear. "If my writing is too raw for you," I might have replied, but didn't, "that's *your* problem—not a problem for some generalized class of 'seekers.'"

The sooner we human beings stop looking to others to explain the world to us, the better, I say. If someone hears my words and is "injured," in the sense of losing faith in magical thinking, fine by me. That so-called "faith" is nothing more than a self-hypnotic belief in rumors and second-hand prattle anyway.

Fair warning to magical thinkers: if the debunking of the "I will never die" fairytale would for you comprise "injury," you might indeed be hurt here, and may wish to put these questions out of your mind entirely. Just close the book and stop reading. Of course, injury is a matter of definition and point of view. I had a cancerous lesion cut from my arm last week. There was pain, bleeding, and all that. Did the doctor "injure" me?

As I understand your story, you had come to see that the doctrine of nonduality was being used to denigrate and deprecate the personal aspects of our humanity, and so your fascination with that theory came to an end. Nevertheless, you had an experience that some people imagine is "nondual"—a sensation of, as you called it, "resting *as* awareness." You even had the dramatic out-of-body experience—right on the edge of what the Hindus call *nirvikalpa samadhi*, which means losing self-awareness entirely—which so many people imagine is the ultimate in "spirituality" and yearn to undergo. But now, years later, you have come to see that, all that drama notwithstanding, "there was *still* some separation," and you ask for help in arriving at *no separation at all*.

OK. I will comment, but I don't promise any help beyond just saying what I see.

After your encounter with what you called "nothing, no self, no darkness, no thoughts, no feelings, nothing," you felt disturbed because "that seemed to imply that there was nothing, no continuation, nothing beyond this existence, no bigger intelligence, nothing."

I wonder why that seems *disturbing*. I don't find it disturbing at all. I like that idea a lot better than roasting in Hell; or just floating around in a world of desires without a body to fulfill them; or any of the other punishments that people have dreamt up for lives lived like mine, free of obeisance to Big Daddy in the sky or more nuanced versions of the same inane hierarchy. Yes! By all means! Bring it on! Laugh, love, suffer, and die, and then... nothing. I'll *take* it!

I hope you don't hear that as satire. I really mean it. It sounds lovely. Like a dreamless sleep after an extended day of hard work. And that may be the way things really are. I have no way of *knowing* that, of course. "I may be a Zen master, but I am not a *dead* Zen master," as the story goes. But that is my assumption: you stop breathing, the brain dies, and the lights go out for good. Unlike the life-after-death fairy tales—which, since no dead person has ever spoken, are *totally* unsupported—I have at least some evidence for it.

Some years ago, I had abdominal surgery. I was wheeled into the operating room, already pretty stoned on whatever anxiolytic drugs the doctors had been dripping into my arm, and then they induced general anesthesia. I was asked to count backward: *"Cien, noventa y nueve, noventa y ocho..."* And that is all I remember until awakening in my hospital bed, slowly twigging where I was and why. I had experienced no interval at all between the induction of deep anesthesia and awakening. As far as I knew, I might have been out like that for five minutes or five hundred years.

I don't *know* it, but I can *assume* easily that a body called "Robert" existed for that interval of which I have no recollection; and based on logic and general knowledge, I feel justified in making that assumption. But by my own lights, I do not *know* that such a body existed. I don't know anything about that time that existed for my caregivers and others, but not for me. I assume that people were doing things to that unconscious body, but I could know that only on their word. So apparently the body can exist without awareness, but can awareness exist without a body? Good question. The experience of total chemical anesthesia suggests no: with the higher brain functions in hiatus, awareness apparently does *not* exist. But still, I consider all of this an open question.

Now, suppose my assumption is correct. Suppose there is no "afterlife." Suppose there is no "Supreme Being." Suppose what we call the universe is not conscious in the way that many who consider themselves spiritual like or need to believe. Suppose that human consciousness is neither a derivative nor a reflection of some so-called "higher consciousness," but is, in fact, the resultant of physical processes—neurons and all that—and that ordinary human primate consciousness *is* "higher consciousness," the highest on this planet at least.

I can almost hear some readers slamming their minds shut on that idea. But automatically rebuffing ideas that feel dissonant with one's preferred world-view is how one remains stupid.

I am not saying that my suppositions *are* true, but they certainly *might* be; and the evidence seems to be mounting for the idea that intelligence is not something non-physical, but an emergent characteristic of complex systems like large animal brains. A growing number of researchers predict that machine intelligence, which is based on purely physical processes (quarks moving around in silicon), may one day equal or surpass human intelligence, including possibly attaining *self-consciousness*. That idea may be debatable, or even sound far-fetched, but certainly cannot be discounted out of hand.

So, given my suppositions, this question arises: if nothing continues after death, and if living has no destination, no ultimate object or aim, no *telos*, then what do *you* want to do right now?

Alan Watts wrote:

> *We thought of life by analogy with a journey—with a pilgrimage... but we missed the point the whole way along. It was a musical thing and you were supposed to sing and to dance while the music was being played.*

Suppose Alan had it right—then what?

You mentioned the "nondualists" and said they seem to be missing something human, while I, Robert, seem to be "human and yet more." That seems to be the crux of your question. You want to be *more than human*. You want to be more than you are *right now*. You want to live as if there were some ideal state—the state of so-called "nonduality"—in which, like a successful "nondualist," you achieve "no separation" between "myself" and "everything else." And the motive for wanting to succeed as a nondualist is that "the body" will die, but "I"—triumphant "realizer," being "one with everything"—will *not* die. Whatever I am after death, this story goes, it will not be *nothing*.

Your problem is, as I see it, that your dramatic episode of "leaving the body" did *not* reveal a non-corporeal "myself" that continues without necessity for a body, as most of spiritual dogma complacently claims, but quite the opposite. On "leaving the body," which is what you imagined had occurred, suddenly there was *nothing,* and you found that disturbing. *You* don't want to die.

In the *BATGAP* interview[23], and in *4T* as well, I referred to Donald Winnicott's two primal fears. The first is falling forever. That's a toughie. Just watch a baby cling so hard with her little hands soon after birth. How does one get over *that*? But the other one is a toughie too, the one you are asking about: *the fear of not being at all.* Winnicott called "falling forever" and "not being at all" *primal* fears because, as an observer of thousands of women and their babies (he was a pediatrician by profession), he believed that babies were born with them.

Be that as it may—primal or not—the way to deal with fear, I say, is not by dreaming up or coming to believe in some alternate story, but by confronting the fear head-on; by assuming, I mean, that what one fears most might be exactly the way things really are.

To wit, the acquired beliefs that are part of your psychic support system—part of the glue that makes "myself" cohere—tell you that there *is* something beyond bodily death: a continuation, a bigger intelligence, something. How do I know this about you? I know it because the disturbing aspect of your bout with *nirvikalpa samadhi,* or whatever it was, entailed actual personal experience failing to support those beliefs. If you had not been inundated with all that spirituality jive in the first place, total unconsciousness after death might seem just peachy, as it does to me.

So, assuming that "just nothing" is an accurate vision of "reality," how do you want to live *right now* at age 68, much closer to the end of a human life than to the beginning, and subject to an inexorable biological clock, facing only increasing senescence followed by death, and then... nothing? To continue with Alan Watt's metaphor, what kind of singing and dancing appeals to you? Because that may very well be the whole deal: sing and dance right now.

You say that I seem to be "very human and yet more." I don't see myself that way. I am *not* "more than human," but just *fully*

23. See https://BATGAP.com/robert-saltzman/

human—by which I mean awake and aware here and now, entirely liberated from dependence upon beliefs that cannot be corroborated within my own mind, and open to each moment as it occurs, without centering on the concept of "myself."

Quoting from Chapter 5 of *The Ten Thousand Things*:

> *When the path peters out, and you find yourself alone and without assurances of anything, this aliveness, unmitigated, is apparent. Unless you find yourself alone like that, without taking refuge in second-hand notions, no matter what their source, you will never be free, but will remain always an adherent, forever a disciple or an epigone.*

Alone and without assurances of anything *is*, I say, the fully human condition. The rest is just wallpaper.

Q3: Robert, you said recently that you rarely find yourself lost in thought. Couldn't being lost in thought be a kind of dance like the one Alan Watts pointed to? What's the difference from your point of view?

A: Well, you could rightly see the whole thing as a dance, and if you do, then let's say that some dancers are sleepwalking through this aliveness, half-hypnotized like the marathon dancer played by Jane Fonda in *They Shoot Horses, Don't They?*, while others find themselves wide awake and open to full participation.

47 - Faith, hope, and prayer

Q: Since meeting you years ago, Robert, I have lived without the idea of a future, and without hope, trust, faith, and prayers that apply to the future. But as these things were taught to me as a child, they still come up often in my mind. Does that make sense? It has been years since I have taken refuge in hopes for a better future. This is difficult socially since everyone I know believes in positive thinking, hope, trust, and a "better" future.

A friend tells me how she is approaching the New Year: "I just have to hope and trust in the universe," which is the new word for "God." I see this as a way to avoid facing one's fears about this next unknowable year. I see her mind racing off into the future as just a form of psychological avoidance. And yet, what if prayer and hope *are* a better way of facing life than despair? What if I am seen as a grumpy, troubled bore?

I bring this up because I have noticed there is a bogeyman hiding out still in my mind, a latent thought from childhood, that maybe I am wrong about this and need to get started praying. My friends ask me, "What if one gives up hope?"

"Well then," I reply, "if that is what occurs, I just have to live with it, don't I?" To date, this has not gone over very well with others.

A: From my perspective, prayer is a form of superstitious magical thinking, but that does not mean that I think no one should pray. Living and dying as a human animal can feel difficult if one is honest, so if prayer helps someone to cope with that difficulty, fine by me. It's certainly better for the body, including the brain, than many methods people use to cope with anxiety, such as overdoing drugs and alcohol, overeating, etcetera. But if asked directly, I will neither lie nor dissemble. *I refuse to lie about anything.* As I see it, when you pray to "God," you are praying to a groundless concept.

When I say "from my perspective," I mean a vision which does not *want* to be comforted by magical thinking or any other form of unfounded belief. For me, despair and hope are the extremes of the same spectrum, like nihilism and eternalism. I have no interest in being stuck on either side of that see-saw. What is, *is*. And that is rarely exactly what one *wants* it to be, or what one *hopes* or *prays* it will be. It is what it is.

Reliance on magical thinking is disempowering. It is a way of saying, "I am not ready to deal with myself and my own mind, so I want some 'greater power' to step in and save me," whether that outside power is a spiritual teacher, or "God," or the man in the moon. If that's the best someone can do, I understand, but that way of being has nothing to do with an awakened life.

A friend recently reminded me of this epigram from Idries Shah:

> *Q: What is a fundamental mistake of man's?*
> *A: To think that he is alive when he has merely fallen asleep in life's waiting room.*

So to me, an *awakened* life is one in which you are *not* asleep in the waiting room, appeased by faith while praying for things to get better later, but *embracing* this aliveness called "myself" right *now*, in this very moment, in all its pain and glory—and to hell with the fantasized, far-away future that never comes.

Faith, hope, and prayer are strategies for remaining *in* the waiting room, killing time with fancies of future goodness. Instead of embracing *this* moment, and participating in *this* moment—which is the only moment in which one really *can* participate—the magical thinker tries to convince herself that somehow things will "get better." Really? When?

"Better" is very much a matter of point of view. If you need brain surgery, probably things are a lot better now than when the Stone-Age Egyptians treated headaches with trepanning. But if you like a natural Earth, with pristine rivers, and balanced ecology, those same Egyptians had it much better than we do.

Countless people pray day and night for the endless violence to stop, for our fellow sentient beings to be treated respectfully, including the ones we call "animals" (as if we human primates were *not* animals), and for the ending of the insane rape of our dear Earth. How's *that* working out?

> *In primate behavior, we can see they have a sense of fairness. They have empathy: they enforce rules among themselves, they can delay gratification and they can control their impulses. So many of these tendencies that go into our moralities can be found in other animals, but instead of their coming from logic and reasoning, they actually come from our primate psychology most of the time.*
>
> *The human brain's capability of abstraction has produced a move toward universal standards combined with an elaborate system of justification, monitoring, and punishment. At that point, religion comes in.*
>
> —Franz De Waal

I have seen you pass through some radical changes. Change can be scary. Each of us, at root, is totally and completely alone with our thoughts, emotions, and beliefs. No one else will ever know what one really feels, what one really suffers. That absolute solitude can seem a burden, and one craves relief.

But since you ask for my take on this, I would much rather hang out with a grumpy, troubled bore than a bliss-ninny who imagines that "God" will fix everything as soon as "He" gets around to it, or when enough humans have sufficient "faith." That point of view, to me, is not only boring but sad.

At least the grumpy one has some actual material to work with. The bliss-ninny is hypnotized by nonsense and will not snap out of that trance no matter what, for no one can ever *prove* that "God" is a fairy tale, or that prayer is useless except as a tranquilizer, albeit there are scientific studies to that effect. And most often the "bliss" is really only a beard to cover up fear—the fear of living in a world without a "God" running the show.

Q2: But who is happier, the bliss-ninny or the "grumpy, troubled bore?" You have mentioned Alan Watts' analogy of life being like a dance. Dancing is about theatre, music, fantasy, and transcending the dreary daily routine. It is a form of escapism. I recently saw a clip of a talk by Watts in which he encouraged people to take part in all the religious practices and to enjoy them without taking them too seriously. To be like children playing a game. Because the human mind is so much more complex than that of other animals, maybe constant creation of stories and reliance on escapism is necessary.

A: Well, if happiness is the goal, neither the bliss-ninny nor the grumpy bore has attained it. I love Alan's explanations of Zen and such, but he was not at all a happy man, so why imitate him or take his advice about religion?

Happiness, by the way, is not *my* goal at all. As I experience this dance, happiness just comes and goes like the breeze in the trees while we are otherwise involved and not even thinking about happiness.

Q2: Happiness is always the ultimate goal, otherwise why do anything at all? Following a spiritual path has happiness as its goal. Leaving a spiritual path and trying to just "experience the moment" also has happiness as its goal. Letting go and "just being" is aimed at being happy. Happiness does just come and go, of course—you can't guarantee it no matter what you do—but who doesn't want to be happy?

A: Well, that is your perspective, and you have every right to it, but it is not mine, as I tried to make clear. I have no such goal. A goal implies a future to be attained. That is what I call "fantasy." I have no interest in that. Psychologically, now is enough—and it had better be, because it's all we ever have.

You are proving a point I have made often: most people don't really want "truth," although many they say they do. Most just want to feel better. If you just want to feel better, I respect that need, which is entirely human, but you are mistaken in believing that everyone has the same needs as you.

That is a classic mistake made by those who have not understood themselves in depth and who have not come to terms with their existential aloneness in this aliveness. It is simply *not true* that "everyone" is just like you. Other people have different ways of viewing self and mind—ways of which you may be entirely ignorant. Unless you see that, you will *remain* ignorant, hypnotized by your own futile desires to attain some fantasized emotional state, which you justify by saying that "everyone" has that same desire. This is like a child who imagines that "everyone" likes cotton candy and circuses.

Happiness is lovely. There is nothing wrong with happiness, unless one is a happy idiot. Happy idiocy is entirely boring. But some of us are interested in seeing things as they are—not twisting them around in ways that will make us feel happy.

Q2: I still say that the search for happiness is the force that underlies all human activity. But isn't stopping seeking, as you recommend, just another way of continuing the search?

A: As I say, you seem determined to remain ignorant. I am speaking clearly, but you refuse to listen, wanting instead to debate and "win," just as you have done before. This is a poor approach, and I have no intention of debating anything. I see what I see. Even if I reply to your questions forever, unless you are able to open your mind and stop justifying and advocating for your present world-view, my replies will fall on deaf ears already baffled by misapplied logic.

I will give it one more shot, but after that, you are on your own. Yes, if "calling off the search" became just another practice or method aimed at attaining something special, that would be a sneaky way of continuing the search. But there is another way that seeking stops. That is called "awakening," or snapping out of the bewitchment of becoming. Nothing is *becoming* anything.

When awake, I am saying, there *is* no seeking, including seeking happiness. There *is* no future. If feelings of happiness are part of the present moment, fine, congrats, *mazel tov.* If one is not feeling happy, that's OK too. Each moment has a suchness of its own, to be experienced in its brief turn upon the stage of attention. This aliveness is utterly transient, you can't hold on to a second of it. Fortunes can change at the drop of a hat. There is joy in this aliveness and sorrow as well. They cannot be separated. If you just want to be "happy," you are only half alive. Not even half.

And please do not reply by saying that my observation of transience is a strategy for making myself happy. It isn't. There is an element of tragedy in seeing the transience of "myself"—a kind of nostalgic sadness that the Japanese call *mono no aware*: "the pathos of things," or "a sensitivity to ephemera"—that goes right over your head. Because there is no "happiness" in emptiness and evanescence, you reject them. To notice and honor the transitory nature of existence is what I meant earlier by "seeing things as they are," which you also disparage.

Seeing things as they are is not about the pursuit of happiness at all. It is about openness to impermanence, including a gentle wistfulness, a gentle poignancy about how transience and non-abiding are the basic facts of existence, and all we love is lost. That same grasp of evanescence can be a wellspring of a beauty unrelated entirely to "happiness."

When I say that this seems to go right over your head, I do not mean to be insulting, but I would be doing you no favor by silently acceding to your world-view—which, to me, appears narrow and terribly well-defended. You have engaged me twice now, and both times clumsily. Your attitude is demanding and entitled, as if I *owed* you an explanation. Now it is time to get down to brass tacks.

Your generalization about "happiness" is arrant nonsense. The desire for happiness does *not* "underlie all human activity." It underlies nary a moment of my activity, for example; and there are others just like me, people who meet each moment with open arms, whatever its particular character and without wishing that things were otherwise. "Otherwise" for me does not exist. Except as a fantasy obscured from critical inspection by whatever psychological defense mechanism one uses to pull the wool over one's own eyes, there *is* no "otherwise," and never will be. I am not writing a prescription or proselytizing. I am *reporting.* This is *my* experience I am discussing—not what *you* should think or do.

You presume far too much, including that your way of seeing things is "true." You seem desperately eager to sell yourself on the idea that being human is all about being happy and nothing else. And you seem dead set on proving me "wrong." Perhaps my words about bliss-ninnies triggered this as a reaction?

Q2: For someone who claims not to like arguments, you seem addicted to throwing gasoline on the flames. If only "Robert" is awake and the rest of us aren't, then "Robert" seems to be putting himself on a pedestal along with Ramana Maharshi, etcetera. In that case, we should listen respectfully and not "answer back." If, on the other hand, "Robert" admits to being just an ordinary human, because he claims it is ridiculous to idolize anyone for being awake or enlightened, then surely the conversation should be a two-way one between equals. Which is it?

A: You have not shown yourself to be an equal. Equals of mine do not debate these matters aggressively as you are doing. They listen to one another respectfully, with open ears, grateful for the opportunity to hear some sanity for a change, and for the gift of really being listened to and heard when it falls to them to speak.

Here, I am just saying what I see, and I speak as forthrightly and candidly as I can. If someone sees things differently, I am fine with that. I make no claims to superiority of any kind. I am an ordinary human being just like all of us primate human animals. This is self-expression. This is *my* experience and *my* perspective. I make no claims to "truth," except to be speaking truthfully. This is a report. Take it for what it's worth or reject it entirely. It's all the same to me.

Your idea that a desire for happiness is the chief motivator of *all* people is narrow and restricted, to say the least. It's really absurd that you are so sure of yourself about this foolishness. You actually imagine that whatever motivates you, motivates everyone else in the world. You even want to debate it—crudely, by the way: either Robert is up on a pedestal with the consensus demi-gods, or else stuck in the muck where the rest of us pitiful mortals are all pitifully equal. I am sideways to all that hierarchical hodgepodge. I just see what *I* see, and when I speak, I *say* what I see.

I don't care what you think of me. Your opinion on that is utterly inconsequential to my work here, which I see as a space for philosophical awareness, for *human* awareness of our *humane* relations, whatever the word "humane" means to you.

Here the idea is not to carry on with the boring old top-dog, under-dog psychodrama, where someone is really debating with Daddy or some other imago, not even *seeing* "Robert," and desperately needing to win. This page is *not* psychotherapy. I don't need to work through anything with you, or explain myself to you. Since I already know that you will find a way to reject anything I say, I am indulging you, not for your benefit, but because this conversation is being read by others who don't have their heads so far up their own asses, and reading it might interest some of them.

Here, the work consists of debunking the automatic, uncritical *splitting* of so-called "matter" from so-called "spirit," as if teasing those two apart were really somehow feasible. The idea that it *is* feasible needs serious examination by anyone who is interested in these matters. I am not saying that such splitting cannot be done. You can install a barbwire fence right down the middle of a beautiful meadow too. That exact barbarity was visited upon a high-altitude meadow in New Mexico, where I used to love lying on my back looking up at the sky.

With the canard of a universal pursuit of happiness as your principal belief—an entirely self-justifying, self-contained falsehood, by the way— no wonder you don't get it. All you are really doing is trying to drag me down to your level of understanding, and I don't belong there. When you speak like an equal and listen like an equal, you will be treated as such.

This pedestal nonsense of yours is only a mindless diversion from what is being said here. I am *not* putting myself on a pedestal with Ramana Maharshi or anyone else, because I don't have him or anyone else *on* a pedestal. We are all human here. No one has the "final answers"—not Ramana, not yours truly.

Ramana was an ordinary human being just like me. He was, by all reports, a lovely, unselfish, gentle cat who loved to hug non-human animals, which always gets points from me. He and I have that in common. I don't know about his flaws. All that is being expurgated and eradicated by the stakeholders to that name. And he is not alive to disagree about anything or to set anyone straight. He saw things as he saw them, just as I do.

This hunger for hierarchy does not befit an intelligent human. Ramana might have told you the same thing about the pursuit of happiness as I just did.

And if we are going to play this silly game, I'm probably closer to Nisargadatta on the personality level. He did not suffer fools gladly, discouraged devotees, and would tell people to leave and not come back. I have already given you more space and time than he ever would have. You would have been thrown out of his attic room long ago.

I see Nisargadatta also as an ordinary human. Honorifics are just wallpaper. I would never address someone as "Maharaj," any more than I would call some rich woman in England "Your Highness." Those men whom *you* have on a pedestal had backgrounds in Hindu metaphysics, so that is their vernacular. I don't use that same lingo, but Nisargadatta and I might have lit up some bidis and had a lovely extended schmooze. Meeting me might even have been a relief to him—at last, one visitor not wanting to suck the marrow out of him.

I am willing to listen and learn from anyone, but only if they have something fresh to say. So far, you have not shown even a trace of anything like that. You have a bunch of characters on pedestals. You have nothing to show me, or, if you do, you are hiding it under all that body armor. You just have your happy-happy-happy *idée fixe* and want to argue and advocate for it. I have no interest in that level of discourse. There is nothing for me there.

I feel that I have indulged you long enough. You don't know it, I guess, but your approach is robotic and entirely disrespectful. Unless you can do better, I will not reply again.

Q2: OK. Well, would you like to clarify why the desire for happiness doesn't motivate humans? If you had done so earlier, when I suggested that this was the case, we could have saved ourselves a lot of time. If you are able to explain why I am wrong on this matter in a rational, intelligent manner without resorting to personal insults, then maybe I will learn something.

A: Good. Then just listen without trying to refute what I say. Just *hear* me the way an equal would: "That's *Robert's* experience. That's *his* phenomenology, *his* report." Give it your most open and favorable consideration as if you *want* it to be true. If it needs refutation, you can always do that at the drop of a hat. Refutation is easy. The refutation scripts are already written and right at hand. Philosophical awareness is another matter, demanding, as it does, a widening of horizons and the dissolution of habitual boundaries.

Be clear on this: I am not saying, and never have said, that wanting happiness does not motivate *some* humans. Clearly, it motivates you, although you seem to be going about it in a strange way. I am saying that the desire for happiness does not motivate *all* humans, which was your express assertion. In fact, you are *still* trying to assert it, *still* trying to convince me. Or else you can't help yourself, and you're just in it to win it, no matter what I say.

The desire for happiness does not motivate me in the least. Not at all. For me, happiness is a transitory feeling, not a goal. Feelings like that just come and go like the wind in the trees. Pursuing happiness is, from my perspective, like trying to catch smoke in a butterfly net.

I have said countless times that my words here are *personal confession*. That's what this page is about, the *first-person phenomenology* of someone who is awake and knows it. I am telling you what I experience—not what every human on the planet experiences. I know nothing about that. Nor am I equating myself to some demi-god fantasy, like those Hindu cats whose real lives and doings are now buried under a billion projections, and owned as intellectual property by people who may have no idea what was really being said.

From my perspective, one has seen through the fantasy of

improvement or becoming something that now one is not, and so simply experiences the suchness of each moment— happy, sad, or whatever else—without the least desire to fix, change, or pursue anything.

You may not believe this, or you may try to explain it away by saying that living in the eternal present is just my way of pursuing happiness. If you do, you will only be deepening the egocentric ignorance into which you have fallen by assuming that your feelings and perceptions apply to all other humans. Clearly, they don't, and it is rather amazing that you imagine they do.

Q2: Robert, to me that seems a rather evasive answer. If you were a scientist you would provide some evidence. Anyone can make claims about themselves: "I don't care about happiness, I have no ego, I am awake, etcetera." But those are meaningless without something to back them up. To give an example, in an earlier comment I asked you why you take photographs, wrote a book, posted on Facebook, etcetera. You didn't reply with any explanation as to why you do those things rather than not doing them. So, I am still in the dark about your motivations.

I don't assume everyone else is just like me. I actually asked a few friends yesterday what they thought about this topic and there was unanimous agreement that happiness is what motivates all human activity. It's hardly a controversial viewpoint.

Are there some rare humans who are missing the happiness-seeking drive? Maybe, but, if they exist, they would be living radically different lives to the one you appear to be living.

A: Oh, I see. You "asked a few friends." OK. Now I really am done. I don't have to explain myself to you or anyone else, and I have nothing to prove, scientifically or otherwise. And, by the way, I have said that I find myself awake, but I never said I have no ego. That's your fantasy. Have a nice life.

Q3: Robert, you say that "prayer is a form of superstitious magical thinking." That's a bit of a broad brush. Certainly, petitionary prayer may fall into the category of magical thinking, but there are other forms of prayer which are not so primitive.

A: Please specify.

Q3: Expressing gratitude would be one form of deeper prayer.

A: Well, in that case, I'd say that it is you, not I, who is painting with a broad brush. Gratitude is gratitude and prayer is prayer. In my mind, they are not identical at all, which is why two entirely different words are used. Prayer, as I understand it, usually involves petition—almost always, I think. Gratitude might figure into that or not. But even supposing prayer that is *not* petitionary, *not* an appeal of any kind, in prayer, there is a sense of "I-thou," an inclusion of the other, the "one" (*not* oneself) to *whom* one prays or feels grateful.

Gratitude, in the way I mean that word, is just a feeling, and has no "thou" to whom I feel grateful. I feel grateful for this astounding experience, grateful to participate in a world of such scope, variety, and sensitivity. I feel grateful that we get to play these mind games together and these love affairs. I am grateful to be this aliveness, is what I am saying.

To be. Not to be beholden, but just to be.

Beyond *I am (I be)*, I know nothing about any "thou" to whom I ought to feel grateful—or pray to, for that matter. I never chose to feel this way. This is just the way the cookie crumbles. If someone believes that a god baked the cookie, who am I to disagree? I can't prove that wrong, nor do I wish to.

Q3: It is said that there are no atheists in foxholes. When really up against it, most of us will pray, won't we? And so how can you say that prayer is useless?

A: I never said that prayer is useless. I don't think that way. Prayer may be useful to someone—just not to *me*, because I see prayer to a "higher power" as superstitious magical thinking, as I said. My words here are a report—*phenomenology*, not *prescription*. From my perspective, belief in the efficacy of prayer to affect outcomes appears to be delusional magical thinking, and there is scientific evidence for that; but belief is powerful.

If you believe in a so-called higher power, and if you need help in dealing with fear, stress, anxiety, etcetera, prayer may work just fine, or Xanax, or a long walk in the woods as well. And both prayer and Xanax generate measurable placebo effects, regardless of any actual potency—*as long as one believes*. If the doctor *tells* you that the "tranquilizer" is only a sugar pill, it won't work. Same with Jesus or whatever.

When it comes to coping with fear, anxiety, and all that, hypnosis can be useful too. After induction, unbeknownst to them, of a light trance, I often told distressed therapy clients something along the lines of "This will get better," although I had no idea if it would or not. So in a sense I lied, and I felt perfectly fine doing it. Often, I could see the anxiety evaporating right before my eyes. Whatever gets you through the night, right? Prayer, post-hypnotic suggestion, Xanax, cannabis, whatever. There are times for medicine of all kinds.

But we are not *in* therapy here. Here I have only one purpose: to speak with total candor about what I call "awake." I will neither lie nor hypnotize here, but only tell the truth as I see it. I have no choice in this.

As I see it, prayer may be a good crutch, but to be awake requires throwing the crutches away—*all* of them. The more you pray, the more self-hypnotized you will become, just as taking Xanax regularly will not awaken, but bewilder.

I am not an atheist. For all I know, there could be some overarching intelligence ruling the universe. But if there is, I don't know anything about it. And even if there is such an intelligence, who says it listens to prayers, or is good, well-intentioned, or benign in the first place? Belief is cheap. Knowledge is rare. Prayer confuses one with the other.

In my view, practices such as meditation, chanting, prayer, wearing amulets, and all the rest, are like medicine. If you are ill, taking a medicine—even a placebo—for a while might be just what the doctor ordered; but if you make a lifestyle out of taking medicine, there's no cure in that at all. Then you are an addict.

Q4: Hi Robert, I finished reading your book and I must say, thank you. *4T* is a work of art that enables the observer of that art to understand quite easily what the artist means and does not require speculation. I really never experienced this kind of directness before.

There is one question, though, I might ask: you write a lot about magical thinking, and I think I know now what it is, or what you mean by it. But there are experiences in my humble existence that are truly magic, and the only way to express those is by surreal art, for example. Any attempt at a logical explanation would lead to either endless text or ultra-big machines, I guess.

As a side-note: within that magic were voices and visible entities that forced my thinking to not try to repeat that magic, and it took weeks and months for me to put everything in place again.

I am talking about experiences I had with Salvia divinorum, where I somehow shifted to the perspective of a table in my room, and I felt and was like a table. My mind couldn't take that, so in an instant I switched back to my body, went to the table, and could bend it like rubber. Another time I saw a little green guy sitting where I just sat, and really intense "voices" told me not to do that ever again, and I felt really sorry.

I think you get the idea.

The question is, what would you do other than to admit that there is no way to understand what happened and let it be magic? And how is magical thinking related to that?

A: I am happy to hear that you like *4T*.

I have had various experiences with Salvia divinorum myself—a very amazing substance, unrelated chemically to any other psychedelic. The last trip a few years ago was a doozy! But the visions, hallucinations, or whatever one calls them, that one experiences with psychedelic substances are not what I mean by magical thinking.

Magical thinking, in my usage of that term, is the belief that thinking about events in the external world—somehow applying "mental power" to them, including prayers—can *affect* those events. For example, a child is angry at a pet and thinks, "I wish Muffy would just die," and the next day, Muffy gets sick and dies. A child of four or five would be certain that he or she *caused* Muffy's death. A child of seven or eight would have doubts, and by the age of ten or so, most children would know that they did not cause the death.

If an adult has such beliefs in non-material causation—for example, "If I pray to Jesus, events in the material world will be affected in my favor," or "When I throw my money in the collection plate, I am *planting seeds* for riches I will harvest later"—*that* is magical thinking: a regression to a childish belief structure that is both false and inappropriate to a sane adult human being, in my view. Magical thinking at delusional levels is commonly observed in schizophrenia. Often, obsessive-compulsive behavior involves magical thinking: "Step on a crack, you break your mother's back." And "spirituality" in general, including religion, comprises all manner of magical thinking.

In general, magical thinking entails the belief that one event happens as a result of another, without a plausible link of causation. For example: "I have painted a sacred symbol on my chest; therefore I am protected from harm," or "Rubbing this quartz crystal on my body will cure my cancer." Those are purely magical beliefs with no rationale whatever.

That is another aspect of magical thinking. Not only does one believe firmly in instances of supposed causation, without any idea of how they could occur; and not only does one explicitly feel that *faith*, not real-world substantiation, is of the essence—but one imagines *intervening* in that process through some practice, some ritual or whatever.

From that point of view, the world of woo-woo with powers and protocols of its own is just *assumed*, and the wherefores elided. *That* is what I call magical thinking. One person's certitude is another's delusion. What you see, I say, *is* you. That is all one has to deal with, and all one ever *can* deal with. If faith, however delusional, is part of that, it just is, and nothing I say is aimed at changing that.

The shift in point of view occasioned by Salvia, DMT, or other mind-manifesting substances, has nothing to do with magical thinking, as I use that term. Such altered mental states are not "magic"—which in general means physical events produced by non-physical means (Sai Baba produces "sacred ash" from his fingertips or gold rings)—but are clearly produced *physiologically,* by the interaction of a chemical substance with the normal chemistry of the brain. That chemistry is either understood at present or will be understood eventually, just as the germ theory of illness replaced the belief that illness could be caused by voodoo or other forms of sorcery.

To be clear, I am not saying that eventually every experience will be explained scientifically, or that a comprehensive understanding of brain chemistry will answer the enigma of how chemical changes in the brain produce *qualia*[24]. *That* puzzle, the "hard problem" of consciousness, as David Chalmers dubbed it, may defy decryption for a long time—perhaps a long, long, long time. Human intelligence, for all I know, may be insufficient ever to cope with that question. Nevertheless, that does *not* mean that *qualia* appear "magically." It means only that we do not know *how* they appear. Notice this distinction. Not having final answers is one thing, and filling that emptiness with made-up answers is quite another.

Since you ask my opinion, I think calling observations for which one has no explanation "magic" is a very bad idea indeed. "Magic" may be a word like "chimera"—a fire-breathing female monster with a lion's head, a goat's body, and a serpent's tail; a word that refers only to something that can be imagined, but does not really exist and never has (notwithstanding ancient cultures considered the chimera, along with the unicorn, to be a real animal, that was included in natural history books of the time along with lions, tigers, and elephants).

Once you assume that things or events happen "magically" just because you cannot see any mode of ordinary causality, any serious investigation is over. Then you are just making shit up. For example:

"What causes thunder?"

24. *Qualia*: phenomenal experiences such as the redness or tartness of an apple.

"Oh, simple—the gods are angry. It's time to sacrifice another newborn infant."

Even the almost axiomatic splitting of "reality" into two distinct worlds—matter and spirit —may be a kind of magical thinking that, like "You have a friend in Jesus," is so pervasive as to be swallowed whole by countless humans without ever being questioned.

In awakened awareness—which includes awareness of the great weight of conjecture and belief that has entered one's mind from the cultural surround as if by osmosis with little or no evidence to back it up—the idea of "spirit" as a separate force or even a separate *world* may be called into question, along with the rest of the axioms and certitudes. Then, for a change, the entire structure of metaphysics is opened up to skeptical due diligence that begins with the question, "This *thing* I assume exists—I *know* that *how*?"

If the answer to *how* you know it is akin to one or more of the following:

1. *Obviously*, it exists. Why even question it? Anyway, the idea of higher powers makes me happy.
2. This is ancient wisdom. These ideas have been around forever. Who are *you* to question it?
3. The Bible says so, or the *Bhavagad Gita*, or *The Tibetan Book of the Dead*. Are you saying you know better?
4. The spiritual masters all proclaim it. Who are *you* to doubt *their* word?

...then I'd say your epistemological rigor may need an upgrade, assuming *rigor mortis* has not already struck.

48 - Patience

Q: It is difficult for me to succinctly describe Robert's approach to life, because it is at once personal, authentic, simple and profound, and because I still have things to learn from him. He has been mistaken as belonging to various schools of spirituality, due in part to some of the similarity of some of his ideas with those schools.

Like many great teachers, he brings one to the current moment, including the idea that while there may be no unitary, concretized self, there are patterns of personality that operate regardless; and this is simply something to be accepted. As an intellect, Robert patiently and meticulously walks you through his position, consistently across his writings, in a way that, at least intellectually, brings you to what is obvious, to a simple acceptance of what is.

I believe most everyone, of any growth, healing, or spiritual practice, would benefit from his writings. *The Ten Thousand Things* resides on our coffee table. I have spent much time enjoying and being moved by his photographs, which also reveal pureness and presentness of humanity.

A: Thank you for the kind words. If I seem to have more patience, perhaps that is because, at 73, I have more aches and pains that *require* patience. That's how patience is acquired—by endurance, and by seeing that one really has no alternative to what is. When I see *this* moment for what it is, I feel no hurry about getting to the *next* moment. That is what I call *be*-ing.

Q: Perhaps, then, I will grow into more patience as the body provides the context.

A: As long as you can avoid feeling sorry for yourself, living itself is the best teacher of all.

Q: I am too blessed to feel sorry so far, and I believe that I have lived as well as I could. I believe I shared this with you before, and it is a response to life itself being a teacher:

One of my most brilliant professors through all of my education said, "Some people get wiser as they age, some have cumulated stupidity." So, although life is indeed the best teacher, it is up to the student to learn the lessons. You are a model of a student, and a TA, a teacher's assistant!

A: Thanks.

Q2: I loved your reply to the woman who said that you had inspired her to let go of her spiritual beliefs. I particularly liked this part,

> *Myth taken as myth informs, but myth taken as fact bewilders. Thus one can be deeply bewildered, while imagining oneself to be following the correct or true path. There is fear behind that dogged literalism I suspect, not wisdom.*

I was taken aback by the interview with John LeKay in *Nonduality Magazine*. Although disrespected, you kept replying with such patience. I have watched you do the same thing with others over the years. You seem able to hold your course without ever becoming annoyed. Patience like that is something I seem to lack. I wonder what gives you the ability to carry on such conversations. Is there a secret to practicing patience? Could you say something about that?

A: Hi. Thanks. As I said earlier, the ordinary aches and pains of life are the best teacher, if one can face them without feeling sorry for oneself.

But I do not consider that I have ever *practiced* patience. Frankly, I don't "practice" anything. If you see a lack of impatience in me, it's not that I am trying to *do* patience. You are seeing the natural outcome of the comprehension that in *this* moment things are as they are and can be no different, regardless of what one might like or dislike.

I see no reason at all to be hurrying on to the next moment, which is what is meant by impatience. If that "no hurry" perspective seems distant, take a walk in a graveyard sometime, maybe bring this book with you. Sit down on one of the graves, and read this chapter again. Ha, ha.

Except in fantasy, there is no alternative to what is—what actually *exists*. In recognition of that inevitability, I find myself choicelessly free to enjoy what I can enjoy and to endure the rest. And the line between enjoyment and endurance may be hard to draw. Sometimes, there is only a hair's breadth of difference between what one enjoys and what one must endure. From the outside, that attitude might look like patience, surrender, or resignation, but that is not how it feels to me at all. I simply feel awake, by which I mean "This aliveness *is*, and I, Robert, am not doing it."

I know there are metaphysical systems that view what I call "awake" as only one of the middle floors in a tower of self-realization, with total ignorance on the ground floor, and the big cynosure, "enlightenment," in the penthouse. That is what I mean by hierarchy. John LeKay pursues enlightenment through one of those systems, Theravada[25].

So I did not feel "disrespected" in my interview with John. I knew that he and I were carrying on one instance of a very old conversation in which there is no right or wrong, but only normal differences in point of view. Nor did I feel that I was being "patient." It was only a dialogue.

Each of us comes to any conversation with a different background and a different kind of mind from our partner in the colloquy, so it is not required—or even necessarily wholesome—that we all agree on everything. My intention in such discourse is not to convince anyone of anything, but only to illuminate the issues at hand. So a discourse that may seem contentious could be just the right tool to sharpen up one's own understanding. The important thing is to speak as gently as possible, and to listen to others with kindness and an open mind.

25. Theravada: literally, "School of the Elders", the most commonly accepted name of Buddhism's oldest extant school. The school's adherents, termed Theravadins, have preserved their version of the Buddha's teaching in the Pali Canon.

As a determined practitioner of Theravada Buddhism, John subscribes to a collection of core beliefs grounded on the notion that the words of Gotama Siddhartha, as reported in the Pali Canon, express not just Gotama's *personal* experience, but pure "Truth" of a kind that comes to only one special person—the one "Buddha"—in each eon. Therefore, for the Theravadin, those ideas take on an air of towering authority. Essentially, they are the voice of "God."

The basic ideas are these:

1. All of us have had many lifetimes before this one, and except for a very few humans who are on their final go-round, will have more to come.
2. Although daily life might sometimes *feel* enjoyable, day-to-day life (*samsara*) is essentially unsatisfactory (*dukkha*). However, there is a way to escape that feeling of dissatisfaction.
3. That way is to meditate assiduously while strictly following the eightfold path of rules controlling conduct.
4. If one sticks to that path—perhaps for many lifetimes—eventually one ends all craving, gains the status of knower (*arahant*), and attains nirvana, which means that one will not have to be born again.

My attitude towards what it means to be human is radically different from all that. I do not imagine that there is a "myself" that has lived before or that will be reborn. I could be wrong of course, but I see no good evidence for that dogma. When I look for "myself," I find no fixed entity. I see habit and conditioning, such that certain thoughts and actions tend to recur, but that's automatic—not any kind of a fixed self. I cannot even imagine what exactly would *be* reborn.

As for being a "knower," like an *arahant*, or a *jnani* in the Hindu systems, all I really *know* is that I, as an apparent focus of awareness, seem to exist. What that "myself" is or isn't, to me is undefined and undefinable.

I am not looking to escape from ordinary life into an envisioned nirvana. I'm not aiming at feeling better or happier. In a flash of awakeness to what *is*, unobscured by wishes for things to be different, any apparent insufficiency disappears. In a heartbeat, the incredible beauty of this world of ours shines brightly, whether "I" am suffering or not. Philosophically, this is the aim of stoicism, but I don't practice that either. Honestly, I don't practice anything. All of this just is what it is.

I see living as a privilege—a once-upon-a-once opportunity to experience this aliveness—not a prison sentence from which one wants to escape into nirvana (which literally means "blown out," the way a candle flame is blown out). This gratitude for being at all is quite opposite to versions of spirituality that claim that one would be better off never having been born at all.

As for *extinction*—which is another translation of nirvana—that, so far as I know, will occur inevitably for us all in due time: one stops breathing, and out goes the candle. If someone believes differently, fine by me.

So John LeKay, along with other Theravadins, secretly worried that all kinds of hells and suffering may await anyone who is not enlightened according to orthodox Buddhist dogma, doggedly pursues an eventual goal—the attainment of nirvana, to be realized through effort and strictly proper behavior, probably encompassing many lifetimes.

John believes what he believes, and he is quite certain that his beliefs correspond to facts in evidence. In that view, if a *sutta* purporting to be the words of Gotama directs one to do such and such, that is "Truth," and must be believed and obeyed. As for me, I do not have to believe *anything* in order to be alive. Like the stars in the sky, this aliveness is present whether noticed or not; and when the contraction called "myself" relaxes sufficiently, the aliveness appears obvious and indisputable.

That relaxation of the clenched "myself" feels like having been roused from a dream to find oneself alive and aware. What is, simply *is*, and cannot *become* anything. Each moment feels fresh, different from any other, and entirely unspeakable. The future never arrives. Enlightenment is a non-issue—not worth thinking about. One simply experiences what living human beings experience from moment to moment, and that's it. And that is sufficient.

This view of "awake right now" is grounded in my own experience, not on Pali scripture about what the Buddha supposedly said. Still, perspectives like mine can be found in Buddhism too, just not the kind John favors. And that is why I say this is an old conversation.

I have mentioned Hui Neng who, while delivering a load of wood, heard someone reciting words from the Diamond Sutra: "Depending on no-thing, you must find your *own* mind"—and, so the story goes, was instantly awakened.

So in that school of Buddhism, the idea is not to follow precepts in hopes of gradually purifying oneself of wrong desires, but to wake up instantly right now in a single moment of clear vision. Of course, speaking as a photographer, a moment of clear vision seems a delicious, highly desirable happening, and, for me, corresponds *perfectly* to facts in evidence. That is when I like to click the shutter.

Now, unlike Hui Neng, I had already read lots of books before my moment of clear vision into the emptiness of "myself," but in essence, my experience is not so different from his, which is why I love to tell that story. If I understand John's position, he sees that kind of awakening—in Zen called *satori* (which means sudden awakening or instantaneous comprehension of reality)—as a good beginning perhaps, but not the whole enchilada.

According to that way of thinking, Robert cannot really be awake like a "buddha," but is only a "mystic" (which for John is a derogatory term). And this cannot be my last lifetime, for if it were, I would be living as a celibate monk, not a married father and grandfather; and I would never say the kinds of things I do, such as, "*Samsara is* nirvana."

But I am not the first to utter those words. This style of dialogue has occurred for millennia, long before either of us was born—so I don't take any of it personally. And the talk will continue, but there is something beyond talk, beyond views and opinions, beyond religions and spirituality, including Buddhism or anything else that humans have invented to try to make sense of being here at all.

So conversing with John requires no patience at all. I am not looking for agreement or approval. I just say what I see, and allow John the same space as I do with anyone who can keep a civil tongue.

I like John. He's a good egg. He understands a lot, seems kind and generous with his time, and at least he has a sense of humor, which is not the case for everyone who wants to discuss these things. Far from it.

49 - A light unto oneself

Q: Dear Robert, I completed *4T*. Profound is the one word that comes to mind. My communication abilities cannot match yours and some of those who interact with you; nevertheless, I feel I should share my thoughts about *4T*.

When I was a young boy, I used to get these two thoughts recurrently: "If the world and all galaxies cease to exist, what will be there?" and "What I am seeing and perceiving—will it be the same for another person?" I never had the courage to share these thoughts with anyone. But now I feel the dots are being joined.

I was born in a Hindu Brahmin family in a sect that follows dualism. The man who propounded this philosophy strongly condemns Advaita Vedanta. His dualistic Vedanta philosophy is about an eternal hierarchy of Gods, Demigods, and Souls. Even though I was born in such a family, my father broke away to follow a "godman" who proclaimed himself an avatar of God, and he promulgated Advaita Vedanta.

So my conditioning was a cocktail. Initially, I used to follow what my father followed. When I was a young man, I was attracted to the Hare Krishna Movement, then I came back to the godman. I moved away again and tried Transcendental Meditation.

Like many of us, I also have fears and insecurities, self-doubt and what not, so I had been searching for solutions and a life free from all challenges. And that search took me further, into Past Life Regression (I got trained as a PLR facilitator too), crystal healing (which I learned to do), attending Family Constellations, etcetera.

Then I became attracted to Jiddu Krishnamurti. I read his books, trying to explore "choiceless awareness." Altogether a deadly cocktail, isn't it?

All this produced in me confusion, anxiety, and a constant pressure—till I read *The Ten Thousand Things*. When I read *4T*, a great calm descended on me. My "search" ceased. I understood, at last, the futility of aiming at enlightenment. And I noticed that the animosity I used to feel towards many people just left me. That is how my cookie crumbled.

This was an experience very different from my earlier experiences. Sometimes a PLR session or a Family Constellation session would be a powerful experience, but soon that was followed by anxiety: an anxious desire that the pleasant experience continue, or that I should be relieved of my woes permanently. But after reading *4T*, that pressure is off my shoulders.

You have beautifully explained that this is not about taking up the stance of a nihilist or becoming a limp noodle either. It is about understanding impermanence. It is about understanding what exactly we think of as "myself." It is about being with the flow.

I have just expressed this as best I could. I am now with the flow, completely aware that nothing is permanent. Perhaps some day I would like to meet you, but when we meet, I will not be asking any questions. I would love to just sit with you quietly, experiencing the wonderful flow of life all around and within.

Many thanks, Robert!

A: Thank you for sharing that with me. You write beautifully.

Q: Krishnamurti tried so hard to make people understand. Yet I feel that there was always a subtle hint of effort. While he said "Don't label," he used to label suffering; and he used to say that, through choiceless awareness, you can see the fear withering away, and so on. I've tried to raise this question, only to receive the wrath of my friends who are ardent followers of Krishnamurti. But *4T* just clarified everything. It's so beautiful.

A: How wonderful that you saw that. J.K. was a remarkable philosopher. I found his words unusually lucid when I first encountered them, and they were just what I needed at the time. I think of him with gratitude. But there are countless levels of understanding. On one level something can be useful, helpful, and, as I said, lucid; but for someone on another level, the very same approach might not work at all.

I have recommended Jiddu to many people, and only some of them got him at all. Some were highly critical of him personally, others found his approach dry and boring, and still others acted as if he had stepped on their toes, to say nothing of their guru's toes. I am often accused of that last "sin" myself. Ha, ha.

Some people, such as yourself, have said that a reading or two of *The Ten Thousand Things* left them in a calm, awake frame of mind, and with no further questions at all. I have heard that comment and others like it from numerous people by now. Some, like you, have expressed a sense of relief at the ending of a long search. But just as with J.K., my work has detractors of various stripes. Different strokes for different folks. I have never cared much about popularity.

The *bhakti* style of human is bound to feel challenged by *4T.* Some of those devotional types feel that guru so-and-so had it all down, so all they need to do is follow the yellow brick road of worship and adoration. That's OK by me. To each his own.

This *be*-ing, this aliveness, is an expensive ticket indeed. We all pay with blood, suffering, loss, and death. However, having found oneself already inside the theater, one might as well enjoy the show. And it is *your* show you must enjoy, not mine. I have *my* show and this is the third act already.

At first, I was frankly surprised at the rave reviews for *4T,* but I have come to understand what people see in it. I can see it that way myself now, like something I would like to have found when I was rooting around in bookstores looking for the key that would unlock real understanding. If *4T* goes beyond Krishnamurti's level of discourse—which I think in some ways it may—remember that I had the benefit of his wisdom when I needed it. We are all standing on the shoulders of those who came before.

J.K.'s very best words were, "Be a light unto yourself." That advice is as good as it gets. Once *that* light is noticed—and it is closer than your own heartbeat—teachers and "godmen," as you called your father's guru, are entirely superfluous. They are not just unnecessary, but intrusive and unwelcome: what the French call *de trop.*

At a certain point, one may have needed to look to an outside authority as a source of "truth"; but when that epoch ends, one sees clearly that there *is* no such outside truth, and never was. All of that so-called "truth" is just words. Someone else's "truth" can never be yours.

The *light* to which J.K. referred is quite beyond words and has nothing to do with spirituality, nonduality, or anything of the kind. Hearing good words may be useful on a certain level at a certain time for certain people, but until one sees the limitation in all that and begins to function not as a recipient of someone else's light, but as *a light unto oneself*, one will always be a disciple, a follower, an imitator—and to that extent, hypnotized.

Those who look to an outside authority fail to understand that the *teacher*, the exalted one, the "*source* of truth," most often is repeating old formulations that he or she learned as a *student*. That is not to say what is being taught is false—it may, in fact, contain worthwhile wisdom and understanding—but it is not "Truth" either. Truth is only ever fresh and alive in this very moment. That freshness is spoiled as soon as the so-called "Truth" is spoken. And by the time those words are *learned*, they may be something between pabulum and a lie.

In seeing this, one is totally and completely alone in the universe and must meet each moment—not based on what guru so-and-so recommends, or on how Zen master Joe Blow meets the universe—but only and solely upon a light that does *not* come from the outside: the light unto oneself. If one sees that light as all one ever really has, that might be a hard pill to swallow, but there is no going back. And that is why it is always recommended that if you cannot finish, don't even start.

At this point, almost inevitably someone will ask a question like this: "But Robert, if it's always now, what do you mean by finish and start?"

I will forestall it. Start, finish, and in between all takes place in *mind*. Seeing is instantaneous, but if a ritual is required to take it all in—and it usually seems to be—a ritual will be devised, and time will be part of it. That's the liminality, the waiting in the doorway. That's the death of one view and the discovery of another. How long does one have to wait in the doorway where doubts and fears abide? I don't know how long that takes. For me, it was a few years before it was all sorted out. Since then, I've had no now and later.

50 - Loneliness

Q: Hi, Robert. I'm taking another trip through *The Ten Thousand Things*, and it is interesting to see some things pop out clearly that I had not noticed the first time.

As you know, I've been whining about loneliness for some time. My old friends who are wrapped up in spirituality no longer like the things I say, and I don't get much from them either. Feeling so alone no longer takes me way down into the darkness of existential death as it used to, but still, there is the sense of a hole in space, an uncomfortable openness. It is something rather unnerving, a sense of nothingness that the wind blows right through.

In Chapter 5 of *4T*, you say:

> *Unless you find yourself alone like that, without taking refuge in second-hand notions, no matter what their source, you will never be free, but will remain always an adherent, forever a disciple or an epigone. When I say "find yourself alone," I do not mean alone socially. I mean alone in the comprehension that your indefinable presence in this mysterious stream of energy we call "life" brings your world into being—not the world, but your world.*

When I read this, it felt like being flipped into a deeper understanding; but now as I write, that understanding is lost. I think it has something to do with trying to fit in and to see the world as others seem to see it. What if this actually were *my* world as you say? Suddenly, I'd not be trying to live in someone else's world with their views and opinions, but I'd just be seeing what I see. I feel as if I might be coming through the back door on this.

Also, there was another flip into an even deeper place when you asked, "What if it's just OK to think whatever is being thought, whatever arises, without judgment or censorship?" Now that was a revolutionary idea, especially after all the meditation groups, the books, and the rest of my cultural programming.

Say what? Did I really just hear that? Just be OK with whatever thought was passing through my mind? To be able to experience this world on that basis would be completely liberating! I feel liberated by just hearing the idea. This constant judgment of thoughts, this incessant judgment. What the hell!

Would you give me a little feedback here on the empty hole of loneliness with the wind blowing through it?

A: Yes, I will. As Jimi Hendrix, guitar in hand, raging on psychedelics, once said, "Loneliness is *such* a drag." Jimi was right. It can feel like a drag or worse to admit that one will never be completely seen, heard, and understood by anyone, including oneself. But if we truly desire the unconditional freedom of awakeness, we must make peace with the plain fact that each of us, in the depths of our being, is very much alone, was born alone and will die alone.

No one will ever know the fullness of what we have gone through and what we find ourselves going through presently, moment by moment. I can't even know all that about myself, much less anyone else. If good fortune has provided an understanding friend or partner, we can, of course, discuss our feelings, perhaps share anecdotes, confessions, and commiserations with one another about the human condition in general and one's own sad state in particular—and this can be a beautiful side of friendship. But at some point, any conversation must end, and there one is, alone again.

My mother died recently at 99 years of age. We'd been great friends and I loved her. But I can't love her anymore. Love ends, and then what we love are memories. Memories of love are not love, nor is loving a memory anything like loving a living being, which happens only in the present.

Years ago, I told you that we humans are composed physically of the same stardust, atoms, and molecules from cosmic space (which fact I'd heard from Carl Sagan)—but, psychologically and philosophically, it seems to me, we can be as far away from one another as the stars in the sky.

Yes, we all share this aliveness, but the perspective of one mind could be light years distant from that of another. This is part of what I meant when I said, "Not *the* world, but *your* world." Each of us lives in a world of our own, because each of us sees what we see in ways that are self-centered and uniquely self-referential.

The idea of "objective consciousness"—which somehow is accorded axiomatic status: just *assumed* without evidence to exist—for me, has the ontological status of a unicorn. You can *talk* about it and *try* to imagine it, but objective consciousness does not exist, except conceptually. Please be clear on this. No matter what some "master" may claim, *objective consciousness does not exist*. You see what *you* see. You may disagree, and if you do, fine by me. Throughout this entire book, I am saying what I see, not trying to define "reality" for anyone else.

I used to tell the story of a bunch of teenage boys hanging out in the street and catcalling at the girls that pass: "Hey, baby. How about a taste? Come on, baby, give it up." They're all into this game, with clear referents in male-dominant mating rituals, until one particular girl approaches. This time, when the harassment begins, one guy dissents forcefully. "Hey! Shut the fuck up," he tells his amigos. "That's my *sister*!"

So that's *his* world he's asserting. *His* point of view. *His* consciousness. In *his* world, that young woman is not perceived as some random babe you'd like to take home and mess around with, but a member of his family who must, at all cost, be protected and respected. This example is not meant to illustrate the incest taboo, although it would serve well for that, but to demonstrate how each of us lives in a separate world of our own—primarily unconscious—making.

What you call "*the* world" is the world of *your own mind*. Still, assuming sufficient willingness and intellect, factual information—the kinds of statements that seem to correspond accurately to the material world—can be exchanged more or less easily with other minds: "It's raining," or "Humans have twelve ribs."

To a far lesser extent, views, opinions, and abstract ideas can be passed from one mind to another with at least some coherence.

However, *feelings* are not nearly so amenable to being communicated. And one's personal phenomenology is *comprised* largely of feelings, often barely expressible, or entirely inexpressible. So the *fact* is that you don't know *what* I feel or what I experience. You never will to the fullest, and I cannot explain it to you.

Describing my feelings verbally won't go far, because a word can mean only what the hearer *thinks* it means based on past experience. You may *want* to know what I feel. You may even imagine that you *do* know what I feel—but you don't. You really know only your *own* feelings—to the extent they have not been pushed into the shadows or eclipsed entirely—and what you imagine *you* might feel under the circumstances. What you hear in my words, I am saying, is your mind, not mine.

This inability to be outside one's own mind is one implication of my saying that each of us is essentially alone; that each of us resides, without objective knowledge or final answers, in the vastness and freefall of this mindspace that we call the "universe." Some of us, of course, personify and commodify it as "God," as an obeisance to or as actual participants in the superstitions of our ancestors, who, in the eons before science, had no other explanation for events, whether catastrophic or beneficent, other than that a powerful deity intentionally produced and controlled those events.

In their ignorance of *natural* causes, our forebears learned to propitiate and pray; and since sacrificing infants or praying in special words for what one desired sometimes *did* seem to work, they kept it up. That is how superstition is born and thrives. When those methods failed, they could always inculpate a member of the tribe as the cause of the deity's wrath, and drive that human scapegoat out of the village or stone him to death. Maybe *that* would help. Sometimes it did.

Artistic modes—poetry, music, dance, visual images—often work better than just ordinary speech for communication of feelings and emotions; but no matter how adept an artist might be, she or he will never fully bridge the gap between one mind and another. To be honest with ourselves and one another, we must admit that. Each of us is existentially alone with our own thoughts and feelings. Expressing some of them in words or otherwise may help to ease the sense of loneliness—but the *aloneness* is still there, and always will be.

Many of us cannot tolerate the implications of that fact—that essentially one is alone in the world of one's own mind—so we resort to papering that aloneness over, often by means of binding ourselves to an identity or, more likely, to an assemblage of identities composed of gender, nationality, social class, ethnicity, religion, so-called "race," political outlook, economic status... or the Michael Jackson Fan Club, for that matter. With every such identification, one asserts, declares, and affirms belonging to a *subgroup*, to a *regime* with rules, customs, and commandments of its own.

Recently, identifying "as" has become a *thing* and, for many people, the central focus of their lives, so this is a sensitive area to dissect. In looking into it, I am bound to step on toes, although that is not my intention—not at all. But questions such as yours cannot be considered properly without examining this matter free of the need to respect the prevailing cognitive biases with which many, if not most, people regard the human condition.

To be clear, I am not saying that "identifying as" exists *only* as a way of dealing with the essential human aloneness that cannot be denied (you were born alone into a world you never made or chose, and will die alone). That *is* part of it—a large part perhaps—but the matter of identification is more complex than that.

To begin with, not all identities are self-selected. Certain identities are imposed upon us by the attitudes of the wider social surround. If, for example, you live in Chicago and have dark skin, you really cannot avoid at least some identification as "a person of color." Others will view you that way, and some of them will judge you on that basis, which is racism. Refusing to identify as a so-called person of color will not make that kind of racism disappear. How you are regarded by ignorant others is not your choice.

But if you live in northwest Africa—in Benin, for example, where one can spend days without seeing anyone with light colored skin—you will *not* be seen primarily as "a person of color," and do not necessarily need to "identify" that way. There, you are just a *person*, or perhaps a Beninese, which is a *national* identity, not a *racial* one.

One way to deal with discrimination due to so-called "race," or gender, or sexual preferences, is to make common cause with others subjected to the same bigotry, for consolation, protection, connection, and the possibility that unified efforts might move the social order in the direction of greater justice. That may be important, or even a matter of life and death, so I do not mean that one can simply stop identifying entirely. That's not the idea.

Nevertheless—and surely this will offend some readers—identifying *"as"* is intrinsically a lie. It's a lie when imposed upon us culturally (for example, I have dark skin and someone calls me "black"), and equally a lie when we *internalize* the cultural surround and impose identities upon ourselves (I call *myself* "black"). Our true identity, I say, is this aliveness and the faculty of self-awareness that comes with it. All the rest is an add-on, largely a set of misconceptions and ignorant social constructions.

I refer to "race" in scare quotes and label it as "so-called" because the idea that someone is black or white is nothing but a myth, in the sense of an unsound, fallacious idea, a *false* idea. The idea of race is so deeply embedded within our culture, and all of our minds are so deeply conditioned to believe in it, that my calling race a myth may seem crazy, but it *is* a myth in the sense that "race" exists only conceptually. Since those concepts are *racist* by their very nature, using the words "white" and "black" to refer to *people* is a form of unwitting collusion in racism driven by *social compliance*: others say black and white and so you do it too.

Yes, it may seem convenient to use the words "white" and "black" to refer to people when you only mean to indicate one person or another—as in, for example, "That 'white' guy over there." I have said such words myself. But I have come to feel that it is worth the effort to avoid that mode completely and to find other ways to point someone out, just as one must do in a room full of people who all have a similar skin tone: "That tall guy over there. The one with the green shirt."

Race is a *concept* defined by society, *not* by genes. I am not denying that we human animals differ genetically due to ancestry, but *race is a myth* because the imputation of racial identity to one person or another based on ancestry is a fabrication, a canard and nothing more, regardless of how many people believe in it.

Believe what you will. Here is the science:

> *There is no genetic sequence unique to blacks or whites or Asians. In fact, these categories don't reflect biological groupings at all. There is more genetic variation in the diverse populations from the continent of Africa—who some would lump into a "black" category—than exists in all populations from outside of Africa, the entire rest of the world combined.*
>
> *Dark or light skin tells us only about a particular human's amount of ancestry relative to the equator, not anything about the specific population or part of the planet he or she might be descended from. There is not a single biological element unique to any of the groups we call white, black, Asian, Latino, etcetera... This is not to say that humans don't vary biologically, we do, a lot. But rather that those variations are not racially distributed.*
>
> —Agustín Fuentes Ph.D.

This is not just an opinion of mine or of Dr. Fuentes. The following are the words of a cutting-edge geneticist:

> *My laboratory discovered in 2016, based on our sequencing of ancient human genomes, that "whites" are not derived from a population that existed from time immemorial, as some people believe. Instead, "whites" represent a mixture of four ancient populations that lived 10,000 years ago and were each as different from one another as Europeans and East Asians are today.*
>
> —Dr. David Reich, Ph.D.

And another:

> *There is no definition of race that corresponds with variation in*

DNA. Race is not defined by DNA. We've known this for quite some time now, and we largely abandoned the term "race" in biology decades ago for this reason . . . "Race" most certainly exists as a social construct. But folk and colloquial racial definitions correspond poorly to human variation in DNA.

—Dr. Adam Rutherford

And another:

The concept of race has no genetic or scientific basis.

—Craig Venter, who led the first draft sequence of the human genome.

And finally:

Problems arise when meaning is made from superficial genetic differences. It's a fairly short leap to the incorrect conclusion that peoples, in addition to their similar surface-level physical attributes, might have different psychological, physical, or intellectual attributes. It's such a pervasive, simple idea that it can lead us to believe that it's actually true, normal, or natural. It's a powerful idea that, in many ways, we have structured our society around. This is so true that after 60 years of scholarship which says over, and over, and over, that it is not true, this simple idea may still be shocking.

—Paul D. Sturtevant, *Is "Race" Real?*

In that view—which is the consensus view of genetics—so-called "race" has no biological meaning at all. No one is "black." No one. To regard someone *as* black is a lie that tells us nothing factual about that person. This does not mean that *racism* is not real. On the social level, of course *racism* is real, as real as a heart attack. But racism is based on a *false premise*: so-called "race," which is a word like "mermaid," without any factual correspondence to the actual physical world.

The point of this chapter is not to deny that most people use terms like "white man," or "person of color," *as if* they referred to something real, but to indicate that in my view, to the extent that you *believe* such terms refer to something real, you, like most people, have been hypnotized by the erroneous, ignorant conceptions of the generalized cultural surround. And until you snap out of *that* hypnotic trance, you will never be what I call "awake."

In 20th-century USA, some states enacted into law the so-called "one drop rule," which asserted that any person with even one ancestor of sub-Saharan African ancestry—no matter how distant ("one drop of black blood")—was considered black, or "negro," as the word was back then in my youth. And the racism embedded in this "one drop" idea becomes even more obvious by the rule of *hypodescent*, which meant that children of a "mixed union" between different racial groups—the children of *miscegenation*, as it was called—would belong automatically to the group with the *lower* status, regardless of the proportion of ancestry in different groups.

No one is a "negro" any longer, but still, in the United States, a person is "black" if he or she has any sub-Saharan African ancestry at all—as if "blackness" were a kind of stigma, the slightest trace of which marked someone indelibly. In Brazil, this matter is seen and adjudicated along lines that are the polar opposite of the "one drop rule". There, a person is *not* "black" if he is known to have any European ancestry at all.

Why is Barack Obama "black?" Why is Mariah Carey "black?" Why is Tiger Woods "black?" Why is Halle Berry "black?"

They are *not* "black," I say, and neither is anyone else, even if they, having *internalized* the "one drop rule," now identify "as" black. If you have dark skin, others, *in their ignorance*, might refer to you as "black," but that doesn't mean *you* must call *yourself* "black."

Racism is toxic. It is a poison that has no legitimate use. Race is a lie. Let us not, I am saying, allow the racists to define reality for us.

This is not to say that one particular human population, somewhat isolated by geography and breeding mostly within its own members, does not evolve in ways different from another such isolated genetic concentration. Clearly, that has occurred and continues to occur. Height, for example, is a heritable trait so that, on average, certain population groups are taller and others shorter. Such variation can apply to any heritable trait. But that is the *average* we are talking about—*not the individual.*

An individual human is just that: a singular case with all kinds of traits that may diverge widely from the average. In fact, usually there is more variance *within* population groups than *between* them. To wit, the average Chinese is shorter than the average Netherlander; adult male height in China is around 1.72 meters (5 feet 8 inches), quite a bit shorter than the 1.81 meters (just under 6 feet) of the average man in the Netherlands. Nevertheless, the Chinese basketball player Yao Ming, at 2.3 meters (7 feet 5 inches) in height, is taller than *any* man in Holland, or in most other places for that matter. Averages say nothing about the individual.

Social scientists like to use so-called "race" and ethnicity to make generalized statements about populations—for example, "White people in the US commit suicide at nearly three times the rate of ethnic minorities." In my view, that procedure is bogus. It opens the door to errors of all kinds, including the encouraging and supporting of racism; and the statement itself is linguistically unsound. An *ethnic minority* is a population made up of people who share a common *cultural* background—not necessarily a common skin color.

I understand the desire to split people up that way, particularly for a certain kind of scientist for whom taxonomy is a major approach, but it won't wash. Drawing such boundary lines may be justified by convenience, but from my perspective, such splitting is entirely spurious. There is, I say, no valid racial taxonomy.

As a photographer who works almost exclusively in monochrome, I know every shade from darkest black to whitest white and how to put them on a page. The human face is one of my favorite subjects, so I see skin color just fine. Better than most, I'd reckon. Plain as day. But when I regard a face, I don't see "race"—and that's part of what I mean by "awake."

It doesn't take a genius to see people as I do. It's a plain fact—a direct report of my experience. When I look at your face, I don't see a "black face" or a "white face"—I see a *human* face: my own phenomenology of a certain human face. Every face is different. And when I look into your eyes, I don't see "white male pain," or "black lesbian pain," I see only human pain. The phenomenology of human pain.

Now, in my experience, this statement is just where an identity politics advocate might misconstrue my point of view as coming from either ignorance or white privilege:

> "Easy for *you* to say this, Robert. You are a 'white man' with an Ivy League education and a Ph.D. You are in like Flynn. You don't *need* to identify. You can have the luxury of ignoring 'race.' Your pain is *not* my pain."

I understand that point of view. And I accept my good luck in being well-educated and at peace with my gender. But I will *not* accept the "white" part. I refuse to collude in that. I am *not* "white," and I will not allow the history of racism and the unwitting internalization and embrace of racism to label me with that falsehood.

If you mean that getting stopped for speeding is a lot less scary for me than it is for a man with dark skin, yes—and just like all of us, I need all the luck I can get, so if the cops don't see me as a suspect, I'll take it. As for the rest, yes, "race" permeates the entire world-culture, and doors are open and closed based on that falsehood. Does that mean that my light skin opened doors that would have been closed to someone like me but with darker skin? Very likely, but that is not my doing.

This is a key point. To go any further into this requires admitting to oneself that justice is a Platonic ideal, not a condition that pertains to human actuality, where everything that can be turned to advantage *is* turned to advantage. Whatever can be corrupted already is corrupted. Every niche where there is money or privilege to be gotten, legally or illegally, morally or immorally, is filled.

You did not make this world. Certainly, you had no influence on this life before you were born. No matter what color your skin is, you are not responsible for any of that. This seems logically obvious but does not go down well with people who focus primarily on injustice.

It *is* unjust, this racism, but so is everything else. Yes, being born with dark skin may be disadvantageous in a milieu of racism, and that is totally unfair. But being born with a dull mind or a face people find unattractive is a disadvantage too. We don't get to choose any of this.

Guilt is a terrible burden. I have some Austrian friends much younger than me who, while knowing logically that they were never Nazis and had no influence on anything that occurred years before they were born, still feel somehow implicated. As I say, this is a key point.

If that is clear, the subject under discussion here is not racism, although that subject needs plenty of attention. The subject before us concerns identifying "as." In pointing out the fallacy of identifying "as," so-called "race" comes into it, because "race" is off-the-charts popular as an anchor for identification. I understand that, but here I am clarifying what I mean by "awake," which requires going much deeper into what "myself" is or isn't than just the luck-of-the-draw tribulations of personal appearance and personal history. I am not writing all that off, but pointing to perspectives that can *include* all that, without *fixating* on any of it.

So, having been born with the "right" skin tone, in a sense I *would* have the luxury of ignoring race if I really *could* ignore it—but I can't. Of all the stupid, self-inflicted wounds of humankind—and they are many—racism is among the worst.

My closest friend at Columbia had dark skin. He'd been born a mile from the campus, right in the middle of Harlem, where in those days you'd see nary a light-skinned face. I never thought of my friend as "black," nor did he, I imagine, think of me as "white," unless that dubious duality was imposed upon us from the outside such that it needed to be taken into account.

This was neither naiveté nor colorblindness. It's not that so-called "race" never came up—it came up frequently. How could it not in a world so permeated by racism, as we traveled together in strange and dangerous locales, sometimes finding ourselves in places where most people had light skin, and sometimes where most had dark skin? It's just that I thought of Joe as this really bright, beautiful friend of mine who could destroy me on a chessboard—not "black." Later in life, I played bass in a blues band in which I was the only light-skinned member of the combo.

You may not like my ideas on the subject of "race," but they cannot be dismissed as coming from ignorance or "whiteness." I have pretty much seen it all.

Of *course* I comprehend why the grandchildren and great-grandchildren of slaves would want to assert an historical identity. So much identity was stolen from them along with all the rest. It's a tragic history, and it's not healed yet—far from it.

This is a hard topic to discuss with candor. We are living in a world-wide bigoted culture. *White privilege* certainly exists as a major factor in that bigotry. But in stating the *facts* about so-called "race," I am not ignoring that. Rather, I am pointing out how, for those of us who are *not* racists, splitting the world's people falsely gets in the way of an awakened view of what "myself" really is. My topic here is not identity politics, but freefall with no handholds.

I am being as precise and careful as I can, because, once having identified "as," having that identification debunked might feel like having the rug pulled out from under you, and that is not my intention. Nor is my perspective in any way a repudiation of the racism afflicting us all. To be clear, racism is a chief feature of human life all over this planet, and that cannot be denied.

The loss of any identity, even a false one, can feel like a kind of death—ego-death. And if you are racially identified, here I am apparently criticizing that. But if you have read this far, and are still reading, perhaps there is something about my perspective on "race" that seems sane and worth considering. You are not likely to hear this point of view very often, so get it while it's hot.

This world can be hard and cruel, and I understand why people who feel marginalized would resort to splitting. If, for example, the "straight people" want to demean you because your way of being sexual or your sense of gender does not fit their narrow biases, well then—you can find a different type of gender that matches you better. That's OK. I'm all for expanding upon established ideas of male and female, and seeing gender more accurately as a spectrum than an either/or. If, for example, you tell me that your gender is "non-binary," I get that. Makes perfect sense actually.

But when the notion of gender is split into smaller and smaller subgroups that really have more to do with the need to identify "as" something special than with anything about sexual expression, the train has jumped the track. Last I heard, we are up to 63 genders—uh oh, someone just told me 80 is the latest number—that can be displayed on social media, which is, in my view, bonkers.

> *Aethergender—a gender that feels very wide, commanding, breathtaking, and powerful.*

> *Xumgender—a gender that is never satisfied with itself due to constant self-doubt or identity issues, causing one to compulsively search and seek out the perfect gender or the "one truth."*

Oh, please! What arrant horseshit. Gender, in my view, is not about whether you feel breathtaking and powerful or you don't. Gender is related to sexuality and its expression—not whether you feel breathtaking or have doubts.

To me, the word "gender" refers to one's own understanding about whether one is a man or a woman, something in between, or none of that. So in this view, your *sex* refers to actual physical organs at birth, and to which category biology caused you to be "assigned"—and *gender* is how you feel and think that applies to you. Gender is about how you think and feel about your sexuality, not about trying to fit into one of dozens of cubbyholes.

But it's not quite that straightforward. There are differences in brain structure between men and women that cannot be ignored, some of them major. Even fifteen years ago that idea was distinctly out of favor, but technological advances have revealed and measured those differences with clarity. I don't want to get too far into the weeds here, but the entire topic of sex and gender is already fraught and likely to become even more conflict-laden as the politics of gender identification meets neuropsychology.

So it falls to us—the *dissidents*, the *awake* ones, the lobsters who manage to climb out of the pot, out of the "identify as" chowder—to assert that we see individuals *as* individuals and not identified "as" anything. That is why you must not expect me to focus upon your chosen *identity* as a chief feature of your being. You may need, for one reason or another, to identify "as," and I will respect that—but I don't see people that way, and am I *glad* I don't.

Getting back to ethnicity for a moment: ethnicity means shared *culture*, not shared *appearance*. Ethnicity has nothing to do with so-called "race," although those who like to think in racial terms believe it does. "Ethnic" is unequivocally *not* an apt or proper synonym for "non-white," although some people, including even very bright, well-educated people, use it that way.

So, now that we have been around that block, who are these suicidal "white people" in the US that the social scientists are blathering about? And anyway, apart from statistics, your particular shade of skin color says nothing at all about whether *you* will commit suicide, regardless of how you "identify." There are plenty of so-called "black people" taking their own lives every day, I am sure. Humans are not averages, our deepest and most authentic being *has* no color, and most of us feel that.

This is a fraught topic, thrown completely off kilter by identity politics, which is founded on the expectation and requirement that one's views will unvaryingly support the agenda of "*our* side," including a kind of self-hypnotic ritual consisting of intentionally fanning the flames of one's own cognitive biases, while throwing shade on any idea to the contrary, regardless of how well-substantiated. As Susan Dunn wrote of the French Revolution: "Any distinction between their own political adversaries and the people's 'enemies' was obliterated." This is a prescription for ignorance.

In considering the matter of so-called "race," the easiest shade to throw is not that one view or another is erroneous or misconceived, but that—except for the ones on "our side"—anyone else speaking about "race" or gender *at all* is out of bounds right from the start. Behind this perverse desire to deem certain topics completely out of bounds (except for certain people who for one reason or another have the right to speak of them) resides the assumption, never openly stated, that a dumbed-down world, in which difficult information is elided so that no one *ever* feels unsafe or offended, surpasses *ethically* a world of open-eyed, open-minded intelligence that relies not upon ideas that make us feel *safe*, but upon the best facts available, regardless of *how* they make us feel.

Unfortunately, to the extent that ideas may be considered not just offensive but *too* offensive to be spoken, our ability to express ideas—or even just to cite plain facts—is compromised. Since ordinary sanity requires openness to honesty—anything less is a dumbing down—a dilemma ensues. Often the brightest among us keep their views to themselves, falling silent rather than risk arousing the self-righteous wrath and the witless verbal attacks or worse of the lesser lights who prefer emotional comfort to truth.

Nowadays, university professors run scared. If they say the "wrong" thing, even if factually correct, their words are likely to be in play on social media in a trice. Then there will be the call to the dean's office, etcetera.

Working to straighten out our ways of discussing gender and skin color seems a worthy project. Eliminating thoughtful views on those matters because the speaker of those views is somehow disqualified due to skin color, gender, or any other factor, is not the way, I say.

I have no intention of offending anyone, but in this space, I must say what I see, and you can always stop reading whenever you like. I will speak as plainly and clearly as I can, so that any objections at least stand a *chance* of being objections to what I actually say.

If you identify "as" Jewish, there is no biological or racial truth in that at all. None. No one is a Jew biologically or racially. Race does *not* exist. Observing the physical characteristics of another human standing silently before you offers no inside information about that human. Absolutely none. To imagine that skin color can offer such information is pure delusion. Regardless of the color of your skin or that of the person you are observing, if you imagine knowing something about that person based on physical appearance, that is a *racist* delusion. And that is the point.

If you have dark skin and, on seeing a light-skinned human, you think you are looking at a "white man," whereas you are "black," that is the form of impaired comprehension that I call "splitting." That split was *imposed* upon you, and now you accept it, embrace it, defend it, and even pass it on to your children. Unless you are able to see that culturally-imposed—and now self-imposed—limitation as the lie it is, you will never be what I call "awake."

If you live in the USA, for example, and your skin is dark, you may feel that, since "blacks" are a minority that has been oppressed historically, you are *obliged* to accept that identity. If you didn't, you would be "acting white." You may feel that you have not *chosen* to identify "as" black, but have had that identity forced upon you. I can't disagree with that. I know the history first hand. I traveled in the American South when Jim Crow was the law and "colored" waiting rooms and "whites only" water fountains were the rule.

So when middle-school teacher Julia Blount posted the following, I knew what she meant:

> *Dear White America,*
>
> *It is somewhat strange to address this to you, given that I strongly identify with many aspects of your culture and am half-white myself. Yet, today is another day you have forced me to decide what race I am—and, as always when you force me—I fall decidedly into "Person of Color."*
>
> *Every comment or post I have read today voicing some version of disdain for the people of Baltimore—"I can't understand" or "They're destroying their own community" or "Destruction of Property!" or "Thugs"—tells me that many of you are not listening.*

Yes, Julia, given the last 400 years of human history, how can you *not* identify as black in a culture of racism in which a rich, white-skinned *guilty* man stands a better chance in court than a poor, dark-skinned *innocent* one, and policing includes such imaginary "crimes" as driving in the wrong neighborhood while black? I get that. And I understand also why, faced with an ignoramus who denies that *racism* exists at all, you might need to *educate* and *orient* that racism-denier by saying something like, "If you were *black* like me, you wouldn't be talking that way."

But history, politics, and racism have nothing to do with *awake*. And *awake* has nothing to do with how others see you, but rather is about how and what *you* see. That is what is being discussed here—not social mores, which are what they are and change only slowly.

So even if you do find it necessary to say something like "black like me," I advise saying it with fingers crossed behind your back, because, like Julia Blount, you *really* know that *you* are *not* "black," unless some racist makes you be.

Awakeness sees with open eyes the history of racism and its crimes against humanity and sees the racism that infuses everything even today, but will not allow racism to be reenacted within one's *own* mind. In your deepest heart of hearts, you probably know you are not "black," and probably know that the light-skinned cat over there isn't "white" either; or, vice versa, you probably know, like me, that you are not "white," and that dark-skinned dude isn't "black" either.

If a clear-eyed outlook is desired, it's best not to *reenact* that split. Social pressures encourage reenacting it. If one can identify as human, and nothing lesser, the split will have healed within one's own mind. That will not, it is true, cure racism. Nothing you arrive at can do that. But at least, within your own mind, the trance of false identification will have run its course.

There may be comfort to be found in identifying "as" one thing or another. From the perspective of evolutionary psychology, the tribe is most conducive to genetic survival, not going it alone. So it is somewhat instinctive to want to fit in, to get with the program, to go along to get along. We all like to feel connected and accepted—it's just natural. But tribal days are over and cannot return.

In this interconnected world, tribal identifications are fictions imposed culturally upon the freshness, curiosity, and freedom of our minds, which then have to sort through those lies and discard them. In an *awakened* understanding, no identity applies but our identity as primate humans with the concomitant human faculty of self-awareness. That faculty is unrelated entirely to skin color or gender.

To be clear, I am not denying the phenomena of white privilege, economic privilege, male privilege, or gender discrimination. All four exist on this planet, and no one, I say, should pretend they don't. I am saying that one can see the injustice of those phenomena clearly, and work towards ending them, without having to identify "as" anything but human.

To stop identifying "as" is what I mean by not taking refuge in second-hand notions. I don't mean just the false notions of race and gender identification, but also religious and philosophical beliefs of every stripe—which are, by definition, second-hand. This is not to say that all beliefs are as unfounded or invalid as so-called "race." An idea may be more or less valid in proportion to how it agrees with or can predict events and conditions in the real world, including the psychological world. But regardless of validity, *beliefs* are second-hand *by definition*. If you know something *first-hand* because you experience it, you don't *need* to believe in it.

You may believe that existentialism is more valid than Christianity or vice versa, but I advise avoiding identification with either one. I strongly advise against saying, even to oneself, "I am a Christian," or "I am an existentialist"—or a nondualist, or a feminist, or a socialist, or a "white cisgendered male"... or you fill in the blank.

If identification "as" comes to an end, that leaves *you*, as you are in this moment, *depending on nothing*: not religion, not gender, not economic class, not nationality—none of it. No "thing." Yes, this abstinence from all identification may feel lonely, but it has the virtue of being honest, true, and *awake*.

Nevertheless, it takes plenty of gumption to stop identifying, because identification is the way most humans think and speak at all times. The news reports will continue saying that "blacks believe so and so," as if there really were such a group as "blacks." So great is the pressure to conform to racial (racist) terminology as "whites" and "blacks," that relatively few people will understand "race" as a figment of human misunderstanding, driven by the need to categorize what cannot be categorized: this aliveness.

So in most situations, unless I happen to be with eyes-wide-open people, or perhaps a group of geneticists (ha, ha), I will find myself *alone* in this view—completely alone. That might feel lonely, but what is the alternative—drink the Kool-Aid?

An old Sufi tale goes this way:

One day, the prophet Khidr met Moses, who told him that, before long, all the water in the world would dry up and be replaced with new water, but that the new water would make people insane. So Khidr began to preach:

"To save yourselves, you must stockpile all the water presently here on Earth. Save the old water, and you will be saved from madness."

But among the multitude who heard Khadr preach, only one very bright man heeded his advice. That man collected all the water he could. He went to rivers, streams, ponds, and pools, and drew water from every well in the area. He filled any container he could find and hid the old water in a secret cave.

Then one day, just as Khidr had foretold, the rivers stopped flowing, and the rivers, wells, ponds, and pools dried up. No matter where people looked, there was scant water to be found.

The one man who had heeded Khidr, taking care to make sure no one followed him, went to his cave and hid there, drinking the water he had accumulated.

Soon, it began to rain, and rivers were once again flowing. The people, who had been close to dying from thirst, were delighted and appreciated water as they never had before.

The man in the cave, confident that everything was fine again, left the cave and returned to his village. When he saw people drinking, he approached and called out, "Hello"—but no one responded.

Soon the man discovered that his neighbors had gone mad. They spoke an entirely different language from the one they had once spoken, and had no memory of the time before the drought. The man tried in every way he could to tell them, but when he spoke, no one could understand him. To them, it appeared that he had gone mad.

He tried to reason with them: "That riverbed was only rocks and dust. The well was dry. The lake was dust."

The people asked themselves, "What is he saying?" He could not understand their language, but he did understand the expressions on their faces.

They stared at him as if he were the one who had gone mad. They shook their fists and shouted. Soon, he became afraid. They would never remember the world as it had once been. They would never understand what he was trying to say. Khadr had been right. So he returned to the safety of his cave and back to his secret water. He refused to drink the new water that drove everyone mad. No. He would remain in the safety of his world, with his own water.

But as time went on, he felt lonelier and lonelier. No family. No friends. No one to talk to. One day, his loneliness became too much to bear. He returned to the village and took a big drink from the community well.

Instantly, he could understand the language that the others were speaking and soon forgot all about his cave and the old water. His old friends were happy for him. "You were out of your mind," they said. "But now you are OK again." And because he no longer remembered, he did not dispute it.

When you confess to "a sense of nothingness that the wind blows through," and speak of "the empty hole of loneliness," I see the promptings of an awakening mind that has had just about enough of trying to escape loneliness by seeking to define this indefinable presence "as" anything but what it is—a complete and total mystery. As for the friends who no longer like what you have to say, those lost friendships are just collateral damage to this awakening. Let them go.

Jump right into that hole of aloneness, I say, and see what it's like to be on your own without trying to define yourself as anything but this aliveness, this flow.

51 - Native trust

Q: A dear friend told me that I didn't "trust the bond" we had. I did not know how to respond. Until that moment, I had not noticed that the idea of needing to "trust" had disappeared from my mind some time ago. She kept alluding to this "bond" as if it were real. I was at a loss for words.

Tell me, Robert, does trust remain? Do *you* trust? Have I missed something? Maybe in my desire to see that what presently exists is perfect, and to leave hope and belief out of it, I have gone too far, so that even my close friend now finds me strange and disconnected. Please give me your thoughts.

A: Trust is *not* optional. Trust is *not* a decision. Look into the eyes of an infant, and you will see trust. You will see undefended openness and innocent curiosity, just as it shone from your eyes once when *you* were an infant.

In each and every moment we all trust innumerable things to be as they are. We must. If we did not trust in that way, we would be paralyzed, and could not act at all. If you did not trust the ground beneath your feet, you could not take a step. This is inherent trust.

When inherent trust is combined with freedom from belief and a distaste for dogma, one has returned to the condition of native innocence; not exactly like a child—those days are gone forever—but with something of a child's unalloyed enjoyment of simple things. Those of us fortunate enough to love life for what it is walk through a world of wonders wherever we go.

To live in a condition of inherent trust is what the seekers are seeking, whether they know it or not. In the condition of native innocence, love and compassion arise effortlessly. No one has to *try* to love. No one has to *try* to be compassionate. There is nothing to explain, nothing to justify.

Your desire to see that everything is *perfect* to me seems foolish.

"Everything is perfect" is one of those spiritual tropes that may seem inspiring at first glance, but won't hold up to scrutiny. Would a mother watching her child starving to death say that everything is perfect? What is "perfect" about the racism that dominates social arrangements on this planet?

How can one speak of perfection unless also knowing imperfection? Without imperfection, the entire concept of perfection is meaningless. One might equally well say that in this moment everything is *imperfect* and going to hell in a handbasket—which would then raise a similar objection: "imperfect" compared to what?

Q2: This native trust you talked about, Robert, seems to equate to a sense of well-being, the sense that all is as it should be.

A: I would not say that everything is as it should be. "Should" is a weighty word that implies the very idea of perfection that I just criticized. This sense of psychological relaxation is hard to pin down. Let's say that everything is just as it as and in this moment cannot be different, including what one thinks and feels. That's closer.

So native trust is like a kind of relaxation of the psyche upon noticing that *nothing* is optional. Apparent decisions and choices are not that at all, but the playing out of countless, mostly unrelated factors that one *calls* "myself," but which are not and never were a "myself."

With that understanding, one acts as necessary without dithering and delay, even in times of pain and suffering. This relaxation of the psyche is entirely human, not supernatural or so-called "spiritual." Native trust is apparent, part of the human endowment—the natural history of a species in which progeny arrive helpless and remain that way for years—and requires no belief or faith in anything. In fact, the dogmas of spirituality and spiritual materialism seem to interfere with direct perception of this natively trusting self; this "single bright essence," entirely real, but without any form.

> *This thing called mind has no fixed form; it penetrates all the ten directions. In the eye we call it sight, in the ear we call it hearing;*

in the nose, it detects odors; in the mouth, it speaks words; in the hand, it grasps; in the feet, it runs along. Basically, it is a single bright essence, but it divides itself into these six functions. And because this single mind has no fixed form, it is everywhere in a state of emancipation.

As I see it, there's no Buddha, no living beings, no long ago, no now. If you want to get it, you've already got it–it's not something that requires time. There's no religious practice, no enlightenment, no getting anything, no missing out on anything. At no time is there any other Dharma than this.

—Lin Chi, 9th century

52 - Our deepest desire

Q: Perhaps this is all too intellectual and irrelevant, but given that the sense of being a separate independent long-lasting entity is produced by the brain, what are the factors which facilitate its dissolution?

You said in an earlier post that you wouldn't bet on me making the leap. That assumes, in my head anyway, that there is someone to make such a leap. And your challenge, or goad, simply leads to a reinforcement of my position: "Who does he think he's talking to? I'll show him," etcetera. Well, actually it doesn't make any difference either way. So is there anything one can do to bring the shift about, or accelerate it, other than to simply entertain the possibility, and wait?

A: Good question.

When I said that I wouldn't bet on your making the leap, I was not referring to you in particular. I don't know you well enough to speculate on that. I meant that relatively few people actually see through the illusion that there is a "leap" to be made.

There is not, in my experience, any such leap. How can you leap from here to here? The "leap" is based upon the false idea that one can become something that one now is not. There is no leap other than to see that what you are, you *already* are.

No matter how often I have said this, or how many ways I have tried to express it, only a very few times have I seen it understood. I don't mean understood intellectually or logically, but pragmatically, empirically, matter-of-factually. When I say that nothing can be gained because you already are that which you seek, that is not intended as a clever remark, a riddle, or a *koan*, but the plain, down-to-earth essence of the matter.

And even in those few times when someone did seem to have grasped it observationally and operationally, so that the pious hope of a "self-realization" that occurs in some hypothetical future truly ended, I could never be sure of that. On the deepest levels, we are all entirely alone, and no one will ever know where someone else *really* is.

> *Nobody knows where you are, how near or how far.*
> *Shine on, you crazy diamond...*
> *Come on you miner for truth and delusion,*
> *You stranger, you legend and shine.*
>
> —Pink Floyd

That is why, after a rather brief go at it, I stopped teaching. I could no longer believe in it. What I share here might *look* like teaching, but it is only self-expression, like my photography or your painting. It's just what I do because I find myself doing it. I have neither an intention to awaken anyone nor, it seems to me, the means to do so. I feel compassion for the suffering I see, and sometimes I am moved to intervene on an ordinary level, but I don't know how much I can mitigate that suffering with words.

I had a mentor, and the tenor of our friendship helped to move me off a kind of stuck place. He showed me the ego-trip I had been on since childhood. Being around him could seem a serious challenge on many levels. Since my rapid awakening occurred in the midst of that period of challenge, at the time I attributed it to a kind of work he seemed to be doing with me—but in retrospect, I am not so sure.

In those days, I sometimes thought of him as my teacher, but perhaps he was just being himself and not ever "teaching": simply *be*-ing and expressing that *be*-ing, as I am now.

Just as you, a skilled and talented draftsman, understand that most people do not see faces as they really appear, most of us do not see other humans as *they* really are, but project our own material onto them constantly. So very likely I never saw my mentor as he *really* was, despite the intimacy and openness of our time together.

Ever since those days, I have had a high sensitivity to the thick layer of defensive sophistries and untruths behind which so many humans are hiding out—often without even knowing it. People lie to themselves and to others constantly, and this has become so habitual that, if you call them on it, they will feel righteously offended. So-called "spirituality" is rife with such lies.

Even if one particular teacher actually does manage to ignore the traditional spiritual commonplaces and see things afresh—and even if such a person can speak honestly and intelligently about what she or he sees, most of the students, in my observation—including the ones who go on to become teachers themselves—do not *ever* see things afresh for themselves. They turn out to be clones of the teacher, even parroting the teacher's very words, and claiming to be sure of whatever the teacher claimed to be sure of. That is *not* finding one's *own* mind.

Anyway, just getting off the well-defended ego-trip—which, with help from my mentor, certainly did occur—is only an ordinary realization. What you are asking about is extra-ordinary, and yet is the most ordinary way of being imaginable.

You ask if there is anything one can do to bring the shift in perspective about, or accelerate it, other than to simply entertain the possibility, and wait. Entertaining the possibility seems a good idea. So without becoming a starry-eyed believer, do try to notice that countless humans throughout time seem to have come to terms with living in a way that liberated them—if I can use that word without setting off a chain of grandiose associations—from the normal lives of quiet desperation that ails many humans psychologically. And notice, crucially, that their emancipation from disheartenment is not based upon belief of any kind—neither belief in so-called "God," nor scripture, nor traditional practices, nor hope of an improved, possibly permanent future, etcetera—none of that pie in the sky.

A friend who knew U.G. Krishnamurti intimately, and who says I remind him of U.G., sent me a link which includes these words from U.G.:

The search must come to an end before anything can happen.

That is precisely what I am trying to express: you will never, never, never find anything "out there"—not in scripture, not in gurus, not in practices, not in prayer, none of that stuff. As long as one is looking elsewhere, here and now remains invisible, overlooked, or undervalued.

Although some traditions do at times seem to address these matters, the actual marrow is far simpler than the countless traditional words about it, so making a lodestar or method of tradition immediately steals attention from that marrow and converts it into pre-digested sanctimony. I see this occurring right here on my page among the best-intentioned people, who love to quote Vedic aphorisms as if they were unquestionable, totally authoritative "Truth," thereby missing the only "truth" there really is for anyone: what you yourself see here and now.

A useful step, perhaps, is to *stop looking for proof*. This is not about "finding certainty" as some people imagine. Doubt is *not* the enemy. No one could possibly *prove* to you that you are already in the desired condition and always have been. In seeking something "else," something "more"—which, being a glorified fantasy, does not exist and never will—one misses *this*, the here and the now; or one sees it but rejects it as insufficient.

As my mentor, Walter Chappell, once said to me: "You are swimming in Lake Superior, dying of thirst."

And, as thirsty as you seem to be, you won't, I will add, actually *drink* that delicious water, because you fantasize that champagne would be more satisfactory, perhaps imbibed, in your case, from the navel of a supermodel, or somewhere close to the navel. So maybe all you need is to become even thirstier—I really can't say.

You might be able to bring your *fantasies* into being—many have; but even if you were able to do that, you would find in those realized fantasies not one shred of the liberation about which you are asking me. (I've not tried the champagne and supermodel bit myself, so I am generalizing here.)

You have a kind of honesty which is a good foundation—again, judging only from a distance—so I wish you well.

Q: Thank you once again. I re-read my questions and saw I already knew the answers, which I can't articulate. I then read your reply and burst into tears, because I *know* I am alone. I feel like Jesus on the cross saying, "My God, my God, why hast thou forsaken me?" And, just as you say, I have seen my fulfilled fantasies leave me empty time and time again. And at the back of it all, I still want you to be my father, and to love me. And that is so, so sad and so painful.

A: Yes. Yearning to be loved may be painful, but it is human as hell. Many boys had fathers who could not even *see* their essential goodness, much less properly love them. That does leave lacunae. It's best not even to try filling those in, I say. Let the spaces remain. Let the wind blow through them. The patience and wisdom you perceive in me have deep roots in the intuition of emptiness, non-fulfillment, and disillusion. That is why I often say it's not for everyone. Only a burning desire for freedom from the known could ever countenance this intentional suffering.

Although it may feel that our deepest desire is to be loved, I say that there is a desire deeper by far—which is not to *be* loved, but *to* love. By the light of love, the entire world is transformed right before one's eyes.

Coming to terms with being fully human seems always to be a hard slog—a long walk on the razor's edge: nihilism on one side, and the stupidity of idealism and eternalism on the other. It's never easy if it's real. As I wrote earlier, honesty is a good foundation, and you seem to possess that virtue. So have at it, amigo—I'm rooting for you.

Q2: You have mentioned your mentor several times, Robert, and said that he helped you to get off the "ego-trip" that you had been on since childhood. Could you say more about that, please?

A: The man who mentored me was not a spiritual teacher but a photographer with whom I was fortunate enough to study, the late Walter Chappell. Walter's mentor, Willem Nyland, was a close friend and associate of George Gurdjieff, who taught the idea of what he called "conscious labors through intentional suffering." Conscious labors, according to Gurdjieff, involved three items:

1. In each moment, to recognize what is needed.
2. To do what is needed without regard to any possible reward, including to become better, to become stronger, to be free of this or that trouble, to attain higher levels of being.
3. To be entirely content to have sown the seeds for a harvest that others will reap.

Walter told me that "intentional suffering" meant two things. First, to bear, without avoidance or complaint, the physical, emotional, and psychological suffering that is part of ordinary life; and, second, to accept and tolerate the mechanical behavior of others without resentment, and without calling their attention to it. This second part becomes, according to Walter, part of one's "obligatoire" as soon as one becomes aware of one's own mechanical behavior.

This "obligatoire" is necessary to "the work," because in the course of self-study one undergoes the profound shock of seeing that one's *own* behaviors are *not chosen at all, but entirely mechanical.* Naturally, at the same time, one sees that the behaviors of others are equally mechanical.

According to this perspective, the only way to stop being a kind of robotic person is to allow the "heat" of this noticing one's own mechanical nature to build up until it becomes an "intention." If one focuses on others and "blows off steam" by complaining about *their* foolishness or mechanical behavior, the heat needed to constellate a true intention cannot build up sufficiently.

Intentional suffering is also called voluntary suffering, and the willingness to suffer voluntarily is what distinguishes a conscious human from an unconscious one. Part of voluntary suffering involves giving up all desires to be popular, admired, useful, superior, wealthy, or spiritual.

Q2: "Part of voluntary suffering involves giving up all desires to be popular, admired, useful, superior, wealthy, or spiritual." Ouch. How does one do this without secretly hoping it makes one useful, superior or spiritual?

A: *You* don't do this. All *you* can do *at best* is to notice your own robotic nature. For example, I insult you, so you insult me back. The only possibility for non-robotic being, according to this view of human nature, is to undergo the profound shock that I referred to above. If you actually see that your own behaviors are not chosen at all, but entirely mechanical—that you *automatically* seek gratification and try to avoid suffering—you may begin to understand that whatever it takes to escape from that robotic programming will be better than to live your life as a robot, no matter how gratifying that mechanical life may appear to be.

Some of the most successful and admired people in this world—including the most "spiritual"—appear, from my vantage, to be entirely slavish to their robotic programming. In my view, the majority of human beings are living largely robotic lives in which fears and desires rule their every thought and behavior.

I'd like to say more about the influence of fear and desire. I am a pretty fair animal trainer, partly because I understand that trainable animals will do pretty much anything you want them to do if:

1. You can make them understand what you want of them; and
2. If they see an advantage in it for themselves.

When I say "see an advantage," I do not mean that a dog, for example, *thinks* about advantages and disadvantages in the same way you or I do. I mean that both dogs and humans are quite easily motivated if a reward is in the offing.

This drive towards satisfying desires—which humans share with other animals bright enough to have desires and to work towards fulfilling them—influences human thinking profoundly. So beliefs that promise rewards such as freedom from existential angst, or the abatement of the fear of not being at all, are embraced readily, even greedily, while ideas that *frustrate* such desires are quickly rejected.

If you see this, then it is a small jump to understand that human beliefs are not believed because they are "true"—far from it. They are believed mainly because they satisfy desires, relieve anxiety, and provide so-called "meaning."

This is why many ideas among the most believed are also among the most farfetched: it takes a farfetched idea to provide that kind of relief. The deeper and more basic the fear, the more voodoo and woo-woo is needed. This insight changes profoundly both the nature of one's beliefs and one's attitude towards them.

In the spirituality milieu, the preoccupation with ordinary human fears—the fear of old age, illness, and death is an example—is replaced by obsessive spiritual fears, such as the fear of not "getting it," of missing out, of not being "saved," of failing to find "liberation," or whatever the purported goal is called. Similarly, the panoply of ordinary desires—such as wanting to be popular, admired, wealthy, sexual, etcetera—is replaced by one unitary desire for "transcendence" of *all* desire. That way, the eggs of desire are all put in one basket—the desire for so-called transcendence; but that does *not* make the eggs disappear. Not at all. They are still sitting there whispering to us, waiting to be "transcended."

Regarding relinquishment of desire—not just ordinary egotistical wants and needs, but the yearning for "spiritual advancement"—years after hearing from Walter about George Gurdjieff, I came upon words of Nisargadatta in the book *I Am That,* which seem to echo Gurdjieff's injunction perfectly:

> *Stay without ambition, without the least desire, exposed, vulnerable, unprotected, uncertain and alone, completely open to and welcoming life as it happens, without the selfish conviction that all must yield you pleasure or profit, material or so-called spiritual.*

That's easy, right? A walkover. Piece of cake.

Back in 1976, I had a girlfriend who was just a knockout—a total peach. That was Catanya, the woman who is now my wife and the love of my life ever since those bygone days. But back then, we were new. My band was playing a gig at a local club, and backstage on a break, the owner, a rich, smooth, good-looking cat with a big rep as a lady killer, approached me with a question:

"Robert," he said, "Catanya is so beautiful, and I've tried every way to get her attention, but she has eyes only for you. I don't strike out often. What's your secret?"

"Well," I replied, "I don't have sex with other women, and if I am going to be late getting home, I always give her a call."

There was a long silence. I could almost see the wheels of calculation turning in his mind. Then he said, "Oh. I couldn't do that."

53 - No one can awaken you

Q: Robert, as the author of a book on awakening, what's your take on having a quick *satori*, a mini "seeing things clearly," and then quietly slipping back?

A: Everyone is different. What feels to one person like a profound insight might be missed entirely if it occurred in the mind of another person. When the fruit is ripe, it falls from the tree, but not before.

Perhaps what you mean by *satori* is not the same as what I mean. For me, a *satori* is seeing things—myself and the world—as they really are. In an opening like that, a tremendous "download" of information comes through clearly and without effort. It may be quiet or dramatic, but either way, it's *volcanic*—by which I mean that vast quantities of "lava" flow even in a brief time, leaving the landscape altered forever. There is no question of slipping back. What's seen is seen. That cannot be erased.

When I say "seeing things as they really are," I mean noticing that everything one sees, feels, thinks, or otherwise beholds and experiences—*including* the sense of self—is a kind of illusion.

This does not mean that the ordinary world is not "real" but only a pale reflection of a world of "spirit" that *is* real, so that our "ordinary world" is like Plato's Allegory of the Cave, in which people chained up inside a cave with their backs to the entrance perceive the "real world" outside the cave only as shadows on the cave wall in front of them. Nor do I mean that the world is only a so-called "appearance" in alleged "universal consciousness." That's not the idea.

I mean that what each of us sees as "*the* world" is a *version* that differs from others' versions according to countless factors, including the type and condition of the nervous system that is doing the beholding.

A hummingbird and I behold the same flower. We both see it. And as I watch the hummingbird, he is keeping an eye on me. The flower *looks* one way to the hummingbird and another way to me, but we both see it. Anyone who says that the hummingbird is just *dreaming* the flower, and so am I—or else that I am just dreaming the hummingbird *and* the flower—has a lot of 'splaining to do. Or, as Carl Sagan liked to say:

> *Extraordinary claims require extraordinary evidence.*

I know all about the claims of Vedanta and so-called *jnana* which now have penetrated deeply into the Western mind, so that many "spiritual" people regard them not as assertions but facts. But Plato's claim of a world of ideal forms of which *this* world is only an imitation or a shadow play, or the claims of the Hindus that the brain is only an "object *in* consciousness," are exactly what Carl meant by "extraordinary" claims.

So where is the extraordinary evidence? Surely scripture and testimony, including logic and reason, are *not* sufficient evidence—not according to my epistemological lights. Nothing is ever proved by logic, because all logic must begin with an axiom or two. Logic is *not* evidence.

So in true *satori*, I say, one sees that *something* is here, but we are not making it be here; and all the claims of "teachers" notwithstanding, we have no idea what this something "really" is.

Compared to the ordinary hypnotic trance that most people call "myself," noticing this could feel shocking, world-changing: "What? I am not doing this? It's all just happening, including myself?"

If it feels lukewarm, that is no *satori*, but just more wallpaper When I say "wallpaper," I mean *second-hand* seeing about which one has been told and which one now pastes over any ordinary experience to make it *seem* "spiritual."

It is not in society's interest to have its members be awake, and so the entire structure of culture tends to induce and deepen the hypnotic trance. If someone begins to awaken—perhaps with a mini-*satori* like yours—that entire automatic structure tends to pull that person back into the trance. As a fisherman friend of mine said: "Robert, you are the lobster who climbed out of the pot."

Now *you* have to climb out of the pot. No one will "awaken" you. No one *can* awaken you. The most I can do is point out the hypnotic trance that often goes unnoticed, or, if it is noticed, is not regarded as a trance, but viewed as something essential and valuable: "faith" or "hope" or "tradition."

54 - Call off the search

When someone like Papaji[26] says, "Just call off the search," that may sound like advice, but it isn't advice. No one can do that—just call off the search, I mean.

Telling someone to stop seeking is like telling someone to show you the sound of one hand clapping. Like the paradox inherent in that *koan*, the dilemma inherent in trying to stop searching sometimes provokes a kind of snapping out of the egoic trance. Suddenly, and as if for the first time, one might see that one cannot prevent being whatever one is in this moment—and if that involves searching, so be it. Searching is not a capital crime after all. Just human doings.

Others, hearing such words as Papaji's, *will* take them as advice, and *will* indeed call off the search—by "*will* power," naturally—which willful action simply hardens further the original egoic dilemma. "See what I did? I called off the search! I'm so glad I'm a Beta. The Gammas still have to search, the little fools."

That kind of person just declares herself or himself "awake"—just out and out asserts it—which ends, supposedly, "the search." But that is only a mind-game. A masquerade party for one.

Q: A friend and I were discussing your latest post about spiritual seeking. I commented that hearing your point of view really is freeing, in that it reasserts that there is nothing to seek or do: just be. Is that it in a nutshell?

A: No, that's not quite it. Each of us meets *this* moment naively. The so-called "truth" of the last moment, in this new moment, may not apply. To deny this is to be less than fully alive. This essential naiveté is true for the "master" as much as it is true for the student. In fact, relaxing into and honoring such naiveté may be most of what a real teacher has to impart.

26. H. W. L. Poonja, known as "Poonjaji" or "Papaji," was an Indian sage who taught self-enquiry as advocated by Ramana Maharshi.

Many humans act as if they were not naive about ultimate matters. They claim to know what cannot *be* known: what "God" wants or doesn't want, for example, or what "truth" is and isn't. Such people resist meeting each new moment naively—without tradition, without rules and regulations, without religion, without so-called spirituality, and without imagining that they know what "reality" is or isn't. For then they would see how naked and vulnerable they really are, falling through psychic space with nothing to grasp.

When one resists and denies the unique aliveness—the never-to-be-repeated suchness—of each moment, that is when one searches. Something, one feels, is missing. Something is incomplete, something requires improvement, something is not as it should be—so one searches for something *else*.

But there *is* no something else. This is it.

Because simply living out the completely natural, biological unfolding of this aliveness—birth, being, dying, death—feels frightening or somehow unsatisfactory, a search arises for that legendary "something else." But whether that something else is Heaven with Jesus, 86 virgins in *Jannah*[27] (they really believe it: imagine *that* sticky scenario!), "enlightenment," enduring fame, unmatched sexual conquests, or a big pile of money and power, there is, as I see it, no difference at all. Those things, and others, are what one searches *for*.

The end of searching for satisfaction is not achieved by trying to call off the search, nor is the end of searching a once and forever "end." The feeling of not *needing* to search—of having no questions the answers to which *require* searching—is a state of mind that can never be produced willfully but, rather, is one that arises naturally in any moment met openly and naively.

The only way to understand this kind of "non-doing doing" is to see the futility of belief in "something else."

I hope this is clear.

27. *Jannah*: meaning literally "garden", used in the Quran to refer symbolically to paradise.

Once you have recognized the donkey, to mount it and be unwilling to dismount is the sickness that is most difficult to treat. I tell you that you need not mount the donkey; you are the donkey!

—Foyan (1067-1120)

55 - Don't be a donkey

This conversation seems well worth sharing: it seems to get to the heart of what I mean by awakening.

Q: Hi, Robert. Thanks for all you do.

I've listened to and read some of your work, which has definitely had an impact on my perspective towards the "spirituality industry," as you called it. I've often felt impressed and inspired by some of the speakers in that industry, but have generally found those feelings not to last. And so I have always needed to get a fresh injection of inspiration from the next speaker with a different take on this awakening business. None of it seems to reveal the freedom, the *awakening*, that I am seeking.

This is a need that has always seemed nebulous and elusive, a bit like the donkey and the carrot. Something drives me forward, but I cannot say what it is. I began to get more doubtful about the teachings and practices I've done after hearing some of the Liberation Unleashed[28] writings about seeing that no actual "self" exists or controls things. However, even that point of view failed to permeate my being in any visceral or profound way, and I would just continue in the same old conditioned self-view and behavior, although perhaps I do have a less identified perspective towards an apparent "me."

Anyway, I feel I'm now at a stage, especially since coming upon your work, where I've lost the impetus to read or practice or take an interest in much of the "spirituality" out there, but at the same time fear I might just become a world-bound blob. So, to awaken and "Know Truth" still seems the only point of my existence.

I would much appreciate any comments you might have on what I've said.

A: Hi. I guess the best thing I can tell you is to keep going. You are not

28. https://www.facebook.com/Liberationunleashed2017/

done searching yet, and you should not let anything you hear from me talk you out of that search.

That said, "truth" is not what some spiritual teacher tells you it is. All of that may be his or her *own* so-called truth, but that does not mean it can be yours. Truth—not "the" Truth, but one's own truth—is here right now, always here right now. And it is *your* truth, *your* mind—not what someone else tries to *tell* you to believe.

So this is less about finding "truth," and more about *noticing* what is here right now.

I understand that such words from me may not seem helpful, and I am sorry about that. The real problem is that you are looking everywhere for "truth," when this unique moment is right under your nose. This is called riding a donkey in search of a donkey.

Q2: Hi, Robert. About your reply to Q, I seldom see, read, or hear anyone in nonduality circles say "Keep searching!" Yet you stated it in such a heartfelt manner, and in a way that relieves any stress about finding or not finding. Sometimes we search. If that is what's happening, it's perfectly fine. Until it isn't.

A: Well, I don't know if I really belong to any "nonduality circle." From my perspective, most of that Advaita talk seems rather dry and experience-distant. I certainly do not walk around thinking about nonduality. And I've said that if I talked that way I would want my mouth washed out with soap—which prompted a shit-storm of vituperation from a nonduality fanatic whom I had to ban for good from posting here.

I prefer to keep things on the level of ordinary human awareness—just noticing everyday happenings and everyday feelings, without trying to concoct explanations. Once rooted *there*, in the quotidian, and without wanting or needing anything to be different, better, or more "evolved," if someone gets a whiff of "oneness"—OK. But that's really not needed to live as an awake human being.

In fact, when people make "carrots" of nonduality, self-realization, oneness, and all those shibboleths, all they really do is make themselves into donkeys. Ha, ha.

"Be here now" means be *here* now—not hope to be someday *there,* where some "expert" tells you that you should be. So forget the carrot. Don't be a donkey. Find your *own* mind, and you will be done with carrots.

56 - Can you induce your state in others?

Q: This state that you are in, Robert—can you induce it in other people? I was watching videos of Papaji where he looks into other people's eyes and empties their minds. I saw one with some Indian people, where he said that his mind was emptied by staring into Ramana Maharshi's eyes. Then he realized that he had learned from Ramana how to look into people's eyes and empty their minds or arrest thought generation. Can you do that?

A: I don't think that way. I am an ordinary awake human, not a hypnotist. Well, that's not quite honest. I used hypnosis in my clinical work occasionally without ever calling it that, and sometimes I find myself using it in ordinary life when it's really needed. But it would never occur to me to hypnotize someone to be *awake*. That's an oxymoron if I ever heard one. Awake is the antithesis of an hypnotic trance. And since we are talking brass tacks, I am not in any *state*. I am just awake and aware of it.

Q: Well then, if someone helped you wake up, how did they do it? Have you helped anyone to wake up?

A: I had a mentor for a time, but he was no hypnotist either. He helped me by manifesting his own awakeness in a natural way. He was not *trying* to do anything about or for me. He was simply being himself. Awakeness was his natural condition, just as it is my natural condition. Something in me saw that awakeness in his eyes, recognized it, and interacted with it. To others, his awakeness was invisible, and since he did not suffer fools gladly, he could appear to be just some cantankerous, impatient character. He helped also by answering my questions candidly, just as I am answering yours right now.

Have I helped anyone to wake up? Perhaps. Some people have told me that. In fact, people seem to enjoy gazing into my eyes, and I have no problem with that. But I am neither trying to hypnotize such people nor "awaken" them.

Q: But Robert, if it was hypnotism that awakened Papaji, that's the most powerful technique of inducing hypnotism that I can think of: a permanent change. If it is fakery, these people were not getting rich from this fakery. Papaji was not rich; Nisargadatta was pretty ordinary; his teacher, Siddharameshwar, was from my town, and he was very ordinary. Ranjit Maharaj, another student of Siddharameshwar, was pretty ordinary. They did not charge money for helping seekers.

A: Well, I am just like that: pretty ordinary and not charging money to have these conversations.

I have little doubt that both Nisargadatta and Papaji believed entirely in their own ideas of the relationship of Self to the universe. In both cases, theirs was the traditional version taught in Advaita Vedanta, so they had plenty of support for their "certainty." I am not saying that those people were fakes. Not at all. They believed what they believed, found comfort in their beliefs, and seemed to be trying to encourage others to believe the same.

But just because someone believes that "I and Brahman are one" does not make that belief true, nor does it mean that such a person is "awake" as I use that word. For all we really know, "Brahman" or "God" may be no more than a bunch of nebulous concepts in the human noosphere, the milieu of thought in which we live; like the atmosphere, but consisting of ideas, not gases.

Those men were considered jnanis because they claimed to have "realized" the so-called "Truth" of identity with "God," which is the traditional definition of *jnana*. But that entire structure may be imaginary. If it made them happy, fine by me—but that does not make it *true*, nor is that kind of *jnana* any part of what I mean by "awake."

So that's the first thing. If they believed what they said, that is not fakery, but it might be erroneous.

Now the second thing is more to the point. The people who were influenced by these guys and spent time sitting at their feet may very well be hypnotized for life—*and* be fakes on top of it. Papaji said that they were all on ego-trips, each and every one of them. Nisargadatta said that only one person had ever understood what he was talking about.

I am someone who actually is eyes-wide-open awake, or so it seems, and I feel pretty sure that I do not have the power to wave a wand and make *you* be awake. I can discuss these matters with you, perhaps clear the ground a little, and that might be helpful—but I cannot "awaken" you. If I "awakened you" by hypnosis, you would not be awake, but hypnotized. Awake is a *natural* condition, not a *trance* state.

People have come to sit with me with the express intention of getting something "special" from me, and sometimes they do seem to "awaken" briefly by such contact, but contact highs don't last. Anyway, if you approach me already inclined to believe something special about me, I don't even *have* to hypnotize you. You will look into my eyes, see what you see, and hypnotize yourself.

You mentioned Papaji. I agree fully with his most famous line: "Call off the search." Yes. You will never find anything useful by searching outside of *your own mind* in this very moment. It's all about discontinuing the habit of imagining that there is something "better" or "more evolved" than *this* very moment, and just noticing without comparing. See what you see. Feel what you feel. Think what you think. Don't make a big deal out of any of it, or assume that you are supposed to get something special and exalted from this aliveness, from this natural living and breathing.

If you simply left it at that, if you stopped imagining any self-improvement, any transcendence, or any future state at all, you would apprehend and appreciate your own mind as it is in this moment. In that condition, you might not *like* what you see, or perhaps you would—but in either case, you would no longer be hypnotized by spiritual seeking, nor befuddled by the claims of others about what *they* have found.

I have just given you the "secret" in plain words, but the difficulty is that just hearing me say it will not make someone call off the search, any more than Papaji's saying it did. The would-be "realizers" will keep imagining some advanced "state," no matter what anyone says. It's like a joke, but they don't get it.

Q2: Induce? Does anyone really want to be "induced" into any kind of "state?" That's what we have been subjected to, each and every one of us since birth; and not just by other people, but, more importantly, by our own abhorrence of anything disturbing. We have been induced into a state of sleep, a waking dream. Why trade that for another waking dream? How about seeing the nature of the dream for what it is? That is not very complicated by the way. And then see what happens. Good lord! Do you really want to be spoon-fed? The wisest most "awake" person would send you packing with such a question, just as Robert is doing here. *Induce,* my foot!

A: Yes. Good comment.

Q2: I may have been a bit unfair to the questioner. You are more gentle. And I see your gentleness again and again, Robert. In any case, I hope it was helpful, but who knows? It seems that the blinders are actually necessary, and the whole world has been doing more or less OK with blinders on. In any case, there is no way to know when the blinders are to come off for anyone, right?

A: Yes. No way to know. And the "whole world" will continue just as it is. Awakening is an individual matter. As a group, the human race is profoundly hypnotized, and cannot snap out of it *en masse,* but only individually.

57 - Awareness and self-awareness

Q: Robert, just one question, please. You wrote, "I live with self-awareness without trying to make sense of it." Can you say a little more about what self-awareness is? I am aware of things, and sometimes I am aware that I am aware of things. How does that relate to self-awareness?

A: What do you mean by the word "I?" *Who* is "aware of things?" Who or what? That such questions could arise and be known at all is what I mean by *self*-awareness. My donkeys are exquisitely aware. Their hearing is phenomenal; they sense things that go right over my head. But I do not think they are *self*-aware in the way I mean that phrase.

Q: In *The Ten Thousand Things,* you discuss the phrase "I throw the ball." You say that, because of the limitations of language, we might imagine a thrower separate from throwing, separate from "doing" throwing, but that in reality there is only one "thing": throwing is happening. So in the case normally stated as "I am aware of this or that," it is not really that "I" am aware, but that "awaring" is happening. What is the value of inquiring into who or what is aware?

A: "Throwing is happening" seems a good way to emphasize the holistic view, the indivisibility of experience which has become natural to me and which is part of what I mean by "awake." When I am questioned, although I may use the word "I," that holistic outlook underlies my replies. Experience, if seen holistically, is all of a piece. Part and parcel. No doer separate or apart from events.

I say that this *all-inclusive* view "has *become* natural," because I can recall a feeling of separation between "myself" and the rest of the world that once was there, but now does not obtain. In fact, if I try to summon up that erstwhile feeling of a split between myself "in here," and the world "out there," I cannot. I can *remember* it, but I cannot *feel* it. I can summon up verbal descriptions of splitting, but not the feeling of separation of a "self" from everything else.

I understand that my referring to a holistic *personal* experience motivates questions such as yours, asking for resolution of a seeming paradox: can you pull yourself up by your own bootstraps or not?

On a physical level, obviously not. Nor on a logical one. But still one might feel a personal, individual "selfness" that can entertain intentions or conduct phenomenological investigations about who or what is aware. If you have that feeling, investigate it.

I do not mean necessarily that someone "chooses" to investigate—choice and free will is another kettle of fish—but that questions that arise can be *entertained*. You might ask, "What do you mean by 'entertained,' Robert? How can the faculty of attention investigate itself?" But don't get stuck there. That is a linguistic cul de sac. One can be stuck in logical inconsistencies forever without any way to resolve them. Walk on.

I first heard that idea about the oneness of seer, seeing, and seen from Jiddu Krishnamurti. It was useful to me at the time, and may be useful to you now, but don't let it hang you up. Oneness implies and *contains* the multiplicity—the ten thousand things—including twoness, threeness, fourness, and everything else. So don't make a problem where there isn't one. Forget nonduality. It's a false god. *This*—the unutterable, ineffable, non-definable suchness of each moment, precisely as it appears right now, like it or not—is all we ever know.

So-called "nonduality" is a philosophical conjecture, not an experience that can be known. But this suchness—the texture and tenor of this very moment—we *can* know without defining it, speculating on it, or trying to make it fit into a conceptual box.

You ask, what is the value of that inquiry into who or what am I? Perhaps it has none. Whatever one thinks about it, life passes quickly: "Like the morning dew in the rising sun," Gotama is reputed to have observed. OK. So *don't* inquire. Case closed. Does that take care of it? You have been told that "awaring is happening." So is that it?

"Awaring is happening," la-di-dah, la-di-dah. Are you now satisfied?

No. I assume that you are *not* satisfied. Why do I assume that? Because you are asking about it. If you'd seen for yourself that boundaries and separations are expressions of a particular point of view—and a changeful one at that, not actualities—you would be finished with questions about awakening. Awake, I say, is when you *have* no questions; when each moment, without answers, without *jnana*, is sufficient unto itself.

Plenty of teachers and their students seem disconcerted by that idea. Many teachers have nothing to teach *but* what they claim to know beyond any doubt. *Not*-knowing is a much harder sell: a product only for the sharpest students—not the garden variety-disciples who don't really want "Truth," however much they claim to want it, but only to feel blissful if possible, or at least less anxious.

My critique of a video sent to me for comment—a video of a popular teacher dishing up lame logic that he, ironically, called "higher reasoning," just to avoid saying, "I don't know"—led to various private conversations. One of those started out with, "Aren't you being too hard on him, Robert?" Then settled down into, "Well, yes, he does go too far—but still there is *some* value in what he says." And finally, after some further discussion, arrived at the admission that the entire *jnani* approach seems shaky.

When it became clear to me that boundaries between self and world are apocryphal, the "question factory" went idle on such matters. I did not *make* it go idle—it just did. No one, I say, has answers to ultimate questions, so asking them is just begging for some self-proclaimed teacher to fill your mind with nonsense. For me, all that noise has abated, leaving space for the beauty of *be*-ing. Is it not amazing enough that we are *here*, that there is something rather than nothing, and that we, running around like the animals we are, can be aware of all this, including aware of ourselves being aware?

When I say that I find myself "awake," I mean that I am free and content to regard a wonderful face without having to ask myself *who* is seeing that face—or if the face "really" exists or is just an "appearance"—or if what I am really seeing is "the face of God"—or fixating on any other of the countless questions and speculations that seem to obsess "spiritual" conversations.

I have no interest in such questions. If *you* do, there is a plethora of self-appointed teachers ready to supply answers based on scripture and/or "higher reasoning." To me, a wonderful face right now, whatever its ultimate ontological status, touches me more deeply than *any* question, and orders of magnitude deeper than any answer in theology, metaphysics, or so-called spirituality. Ninety-nine percent humbug is how all those "answers" appear to me.

Because I have tempted the gods, one might say, by referring to myself as "awake," and even authoring a book from that vantage, people ask me questions like yours. I get that. I am happy to reply candidly. But I don't have a bag full of *answers* to those questions. My replies compose themselves right before my eyes on the screen before me. From whence and how those words arrive, I do not know. And I find it astounding at times to read what I am typing, just as I am sometimes amazed by my own photographs.

I did not *make* the question machine stop. No one can do that. Seeing occurred. The question machine, this name and form, the seeing, and the stopping, are all one and the same indescribable arising. Those are just words. Don't get lost in words. Use them—don't abuse them.

Q2: I am the contents of awareness. Is that right?

A: No, I would not say that. The idea of separating awareness or consciousness from its so-called "contents" is a spiritual fiction that appeals to escapists who seek to finesse the pain and suffering of ordinary primate life by making themselves believe that, since the pain and suffering are only "contents," they are not "real."

In that view, only consciousness is "real," because, according to this view, *it* never changes—whereas the so-called "contents" cannot be "real" because they are *always* changing.

From my perspective, this is a religious idea resting upon absolutely no evidence, but only belief in what so-called "masters" have taught. But those supposed masters learned that idea from their masters, etcetera. So that notion of an unchanging consciousness that is the only "reality" is an article of faith and tradition, not experience. Clearly, no one can *experience* unchanging consciousness—since experience entails, after all, a change from one moment to the next.

58 - Knowing and choosing

Q: Natalie here, also known as Nacoca Ko, also known as the niece of Bill Gersh. I heard you guys were good friends.

Yesterday I was speaking to a learned Jewish man about the subject of soul and will. It was interesting to see that he believes in nothingness, and in will and consciousness as a wave; and it is all very compatible with the things you say.

I have a few concerns I'm working on. One is just quieting my mind so that I'm not spreading it out over different planes of space and time all at once, and focusing more on the now; getting some objective peace under the weight of responsibilities.

Another concern is what it means to be human, especially in the rise of the age of robots and artificial intelligence. What's the difference? The predeterminism you describe—the idea that my choices are all just the outcome of a long chain of physical and chemical reactions—sounds too much as though I'm a character in a video game, following a complex algorithm and the flashing of pixels.

Maybe you are right—anything is possible—but of all the possibilities, that one is still too sad to believe. To take away will and consciousness takes away all that makes anything truly alive. Plants, viruses . . . anything alive has a will and a form of consciousness, in my opinion.

I've read about choice being a reaction that you are informed about a split second later, but I kind of feel that misses the point. Certainly a physical wheel of cognitive blips and bleeps occurs to set a decision into place, and then your "actor" part takes the next step. But so what? That's just a broken down "how" that doesn't erase this entity I call "Natalie."

I think people have given up on will and individual consciousness too early—that there is still much to learn about the way physics interacts with universal consciousness, and how that consciousness and will arise on top of the skimpy material that is our mind and body.

And in humans, imagination plays a big role too. Infinite imagination was required to develop a complex social code of ethics and morality, in order to maintain a somewhat stable evolution and keep our wills healthy enough so that we could continue to evolve and not all just run ourselves into the ground. But that's maybe off on a tangent for now.

We can agree that everything is an illusion, and that we only see things from our little perspective—but that little perspective *is* our reality, and the sense we give it by communicating it is our reality as well. Perhaps that is why the word is so important (another thing I've been thinking about), because all that's left once you strip it all away is the story and meaning you pass on with the word.

And then there are the words, the concepts "I" and "you"—we couldn't even have this conversation if there was nothing the dust could rest on.

Regardless of religion, life makes little sense without will. Even animals who haven't been taught preconceived notions in their infancy make choices to survive or sacrifice, to perform acts of kindness, to honor their dead. Those choices, especially for a human, give you a sense of identity. If I am just an experience of emotions and feelings, I am also experiencing a sense of will and choice. Why would the feeling of sadness be any different than the feeling of choice? I'm sure even Zen people give individual names to their children, and guide their decisions respecting their sense of an individual making choices.

I am interested in finding truth and feeling "freer than light on water" in the midst of the chaos around me, but I'm also very weary of detachment and denial of the self. I am looking forward to reading your book, and loving the thoughts your words provoke.

A: Hi, Natalie or Nacoca Ko. Yes, Bill and I were good friends. I am sure he would have liked what you have written here. Clearly, you have thought deeply about these matters and still have unanswered questions, particularly about free will and determinism. I imagine that you will be a reader of *The Ten Thousand Things* when it is published, because it deals specifically and directly with many of the questions you raise.

Now, you said that you are "interested in finding the truth and feeling 'freer than light on water' in the midst of the chaos around me," but that you are also weary of detachment and denial of the self.

Freedom from the known, as Jiddu Krishnamurti called it, is not about detachment, nor about denial of the self. It arises with the understanding that the "self," as it is conceived by most human beings, is a fantasy. This does not mean that the self does not exist. It means that the "myself" that most people imagine and attempt to evoke when they use the word "I" does not correspond to the facts of the matter. So I am not saying that no "myself" exists: I am saying that "myself" is not what most of us think it is, and does not have the powers most of us imagine it has, and perhaps wish that it had.

Your message contains, from my perspective, various unexamined or under-examined assumptions; and like many people, you fail to allow that your assumptions may be entirely untrue or inaccurate. You simply state them as if they were obvious and undeniable.

For example, when you say, "There is still much to learn about the way physics interacts with universal consciousness," you simply *assume* the existence of some "thing" that you are calling "universal consciousness"—whatever *that* means—and that "physics" somehow "interacts" with it.

I am not saying your assumption is untrue, but it might be. What if "universal consciousness" and "God" and all the rest are nothing more than ideas in human minds? And what if consciousness is something that brains produce on a completely physical level, as the result of countless eons of physical evolution? No "God," no overarching "supreme consciousness" at all, regardless of what you feel or believe. That certainly could be the case And if it were, everything could appear just as it does right now, except that 99 percent of "spirituality" would be nothing more than fantasy.

And then you say, "Even animals who haven't been taught preconceived notions in their infancy make choices to survive or sacrifice, to perform acts of kindness, to honor their dead. Those choices, especially for a human, give you a sense of identity."

If you observe non-human animals—or human animals for that

matter—you can see them carrying out certain behaviors, but you will not have any way of knowing that those behaviors were "choices." The notion of "choice" might be just the projection of your fantasy onto what *really* exists: behaviors. The idea of "choice"—in the sense that some other behavior could have happened but didn't because of "will"—is your *assumption*. You do not *know* that, but you speak as if you do.

In fact, you quickly discount evidence that calls your assumption into question by saying that, even if the thought of needing to decide arrives *after* the actual decision has already taken place unconsciously in the brain (which is what numerous experimental findings, beginning with Libet[29] in the 1980s, have suggested), "that doesn't erase this entity I call 'Natalie.'" No, it doesn't *erase* it, but it certainly alters one's understanding of what that so-called "entity" is and is not, and the actual powers it has and hasn't.

This is the crux of the matter. You say that a world of determinism would be "too sad to believe"—that taking away will and consciousness would take away all that makes anything truly alive.

First of all, you need to separate will from consciousness. They are *not* the same at all, and when you bracket them, as you have done throughout your comments, you blind yourself. I may be conscious, but that does not mean that I have free will.

And secondly, just because an idea might be sad, does not make it untrue, any more than an idea is automatically true just because it makes you feel happy. One's emotional reaction to an idea says absolutely *nothing* about the facticity of that idea. Zero.

A kid who believes that Santa Claus loves her and brings gifts may be happy as a result of that belief, but that does not make it true. A person who understands the flow of life as culminating in the loss of loved ones, loss of physical powers, illness, and death, may feel sad about that, but that does not make it false. As Kurt Vonnegut said,

29. Benjamin Libet (1916-2007) was a pioneering scientist in the field of human consciousness. In 2003, he was the first recipient of the Virtual Nobel Prize in Psychology from the University of Klagenfurt, "for his pioneering achievements in the experimental investigation of consciousness, initiation of action, and free will."

"Likes and dislikes have nothing to do with it."

I cannot go into detail here. That would require an extended essay, and at the moment I am not up to that. But let me touch briefly upon what you are calling "predeterminism... that my choices are all just the outcome of a long chain of physical and chemical reactions."

I never said that choices are "just the outcome of a long chain of physical and chemical reactions," although that may be the case. I am saying that there is no little homunculus called "myself" sitting in the middle of my skull, *apart* from the flow of feelings, thoughts, and perceptions, somehow *directing* anything. That kind of "myself" is imaginary, nonexistent—a ghost in the machine.

It seems clear either that present events are the resultant of previous events, or present events arise randomly, or else that present events arise due to a mixture of the influence of previous events and randomness. Do you see that?

So if you have a feeling of willing something, either you are willing it now because the long chain of previous causes has led up to your willing it, has caused you to will it—or because the feeling and direction of willing arises at random—or else what you are calling "my will" is a combined outcome of the influence of the chain of causality plus randomness.

In any version of that, where do we find "*you*," the supposed "chooser" in charge of the operation? Don't be too quick to answer. This is a *serious* and *profoundly deep* question that deserves more than just a reprise of what you already believe, or a clutching at religious ideas. Please look into it, and get back to me with any observations.

Understand that I am not saying that the *sensation* of choice is nonexistent. That feeling does exist. Most of us experience it in one way or another, but not all of us experience it in the same way. For me, choice is *not* factual. For me, choice is like a unicorn. You can imagine it, you can name it, you can discuss it, but—in the way you use that word—choice, I say, does not exist. I do what I do because that's the way the cookie crumbles, and my "choices" are part of that crumbling, along with everything else in this world—along with the ten thousand things.

I did not *make* the cookie, but I have to eat the cookie *as* it crumbles and when it crumbles. I see no choice in that. I cannot even choose how to *feel* about it; we feel what we feel when we feel it. Nevertheless, when I am asked about choice, I reply, "If you feel you must choose, choose well." Although my own mind no longer works that way, and I do not find myself needing to choose anything, when I say "choose well," I mean it.

I am not advocating fatalism; I am not saying that when it is time to decide you simply flip a coin. The very effort of dithering and *apparently* choosing may be part of the chain of causality for all I know, so certainly suppressing such efforts, or avoiding them, or explaining them away is uncalled for. One may find oneself liberated, as I have, from that entire drama, but that "liberation"—if I can call it that—cannot be chosen either. As your uncle Bill once remarked to me, "You get what you get when you get it."

If you ask me if I'd like a chocolate ice cream cone or vanilla, I would "choose" chocolate. Why? Because I like it better than vanilla. So the supposed "choice" is not a choice at all, but only an expression of what Robert likes. But likes and dislikes, preferences and aversions, arrive mysteriously on their own. I don't choose my likes and dislikes. I never *chose* to prefer chocolate—I just do. I become *aware* of my predilections effortlessly, if and when I do, just like any other detail of the natural world.

From my perspective, choosing, chooser, and choice are all one and the same, and "Robert" is neither making nor producing any of that. Robert, I am saying, has no such power. Robert cannot choose what to think next. Robert cannot choose what to feel next. All of that comes upon one like fate—it comes, I mean, out of the *unconscious*, only becoming known if, when, and as it does, completely independently of any supposed "choice" by Robert.

Robert, I am saying, may be a conscious and self-conscious *knower*, but is not a *doer* of anything—not even a doer of knowing. Knowing without trying or needing to try, *is* "Robert"—not something any "Robert" *does*.

I am not producing the words appearing on my screen as I type, nor am I even "doing" typing. If Robert had to consciously choose which fingers to move and how in order to get these pixels to lighten and darken, writing this would take days, not minutes. And *clearly*—clear to me, at least—I have no idea from whence these words come. No idea whatsoever. Nor can I *choose* what word will appear next. I do not even know from whence come the movements that type these words, much less the words themselves.

Understanding that, I can get out of the way and let these words appear as they must. No dithering required. No agony. No so-called "choice." I have not, in writing this, *chosen* anything. Nor did I choose to reply to you. That's what I find myself doing at the moment. Some alternate "reality" in which I ignored your comment and never replied may or may not exist; but if it does, I have no access to it, and never did. *That* is what I mean by freedom.

You imagine this view of mine to be "sad." That's just your imagination—over which, by the way, you have no control. "Robert" is not sad in the least. He actually loves the privilege of *be*-ing, and participates wholeheartedly in the affairs of this world, however powerless to choose or decide on some ultimate level what to do or who to be.

I'd be happy to hear more from you, niece of my erstwhile amigo. Be well.

59 - Watching the movie of our lives

Q: A long time ago, I was introduced by Ken Kesey to the notion that *now* is a moot concept. At the time, it was my hope, as it was that of the Pranksters, that by ingesting LSD I would "catch-up to now" and actually live in the precise present. That, as I see, was a brave attempt, but a failed experiment. I still view the purest idea of *now* as a misconception. Right or wrong, I don't think there is such a thing, but only my "perceived-now." So when fellows like Tolle expound on it I think they're blowing smoke.

My experience, both from copious amounts of psychedelic drugs as well as countless hours of zazen meditation (the slow way around to an LSD trip, they say), is that in nothing short of a non-intellectualized experience (nearly infant-like consciousness, I imagine) can I experience the directness of those perceptions referred to as *now*. The very idea that one may "bring oneself to *now*" is absurd.

As soon as anything is "brought," the object or concept which one is bringing instantly evaporates or morphs into thought processes. Apparently, neurophysiologists are proving this. So, just relaxing into this being, not knowing, things-as-they-are, has become, quite without effort, my way.

> *A person has all sorts of lags built into him Kesey is saying. One of the most basic is the sensory lag, the lag between the time your senses receive something and you are able to react. One-thirtieth of a second is the time it takes if you are the most alert person alive and most people are a lot slower than that... You can't go any faster than that... We are all doomed to spend the rest of our lives watching a movie of our lives—we are always acting on what has just finished happening. It happened at least one-thirtieth of a second ago. We think we are in the present but we aren't. The present we know is only a movie of the past and we will really never be able to control the present through ordinary means.*
>
> Tom Wolfe, *The Electric Kool-Aid Acid Test*

A: Yes, each new "event" in the seemingly continuous self-saga (perceptions, feelings and thoughts) is a *fait accompli* before "myself" takes credit for what was never chosen in the first place—takes credit after the fact *biologically,* as the Tom Wolfe quote suggests, and *psychologically* as well: always playing catch-up, driven by a fear of missing out.

Ego is not some pollution to be scraped off the "real self" and thrown away as if it were some dog shit on a shoe. Ego is just a point of view, and we all have one. If one yearns for "nonduality," splitting experience into real and unreal will never avail, I say. Ego is as real as any other perception—not more and not less.

Q: Yes, right on! Ha! Although sometimes my ego reaction feels like dog shit on my shoe!

A: It may be dog shit, but you can't wipe it off and throw it away. After all, where would you put it?

60 - I still suffer

Q: Hello, Robert. I hope you are well. Would you mind if I ask you something? You have said that life is supposed to have suffering, and that we can't really escape it. But many teachers, including the Buddha, say that there is an end to suffering. You say that you are awake—so why do *you* still suffer?

A: I do not say that life is "supposed" to have suffering—I say that suffering is part of this aliveness, and that efforts to avoid suffering or escape from suffering are a *denial* of this aliveness. Some of that denial may employ belief in the words of so-called *masters*, including the Buddha—who, in the mind of modernity, is more than just a master, but an iconic, mythological character whose words are held by many to be absolute truth.

I do not think that anyone's words are absolute truth. We are all just human here, including Gotama, assuming that such a person actually existed historically. But even if there was once such a man, we cannot know what he *really* believed or *really* said, despite the insistence by some Buddhists—mainly the Theravadins—that the suttas in the Pali Canon are accurate historical accounts. Obviously they are not. Those suttas, which are said to be accounts of talks given by Gotama to the monks of his era, were preserved orally for around 450 years—passed from one person to another in the form of stories—until finally, after much debate, they were put into written form during the Fourth Buddhist Council in the first century BCE.

Four or five hundred years is a long time. It's easy to say "four or five hundred years" but difficult to imagine a span like that in human terms. If you ever played the game of telephone as a child, you will know that even a single sentence can be distorted—and possibly have its meaning changed entirely—in just a few minutes of being passed from mouth to mouth.

So the idea that those suttas are in any way an accurate accounting strains credulity. But so great is the desire of humans to have an infallible authority on whom to rely, that millions of Buddhists take every word of those scriptures as literally true and factual.

And it is not only Theravadins who believe in an end to suffering—that idea has penetrated modern spirituality so fully that contemporary teachers speak of it confidently, as if they themselves had experienced self-consciousness without suffering, leaving students to imagine that, as long as *they* still suffer, they have not yet come to "Truth."

That misunderstanding is what moves me to point out that, although I find myself awake, I still suffer.

I still suffer, for example, when I hear the American President, who, in my professional opinion as a psychologist, is seriously mentally ill, talking like a gangster, and lying about everything with no regard at all to facts, while the people who voted for him dote on every word of that hate-filled, racist, sexist verbal diarrhea. That cat is one sick kitty, and he is contagious.

I suffer from having to see that I am part of a race—the *human* race—that consists of a large proportion of nincompoops and that many of the habits and customs of this world of ours are fashioned by nincompoops for nincompoops.

Or I come upon a dog with a chain around his throat tied up in the sun with no water in his bowl, a look of despair in his eyes. He has been tortured beyond even looking for help from me, the way a normal dog would. He won't look me in the eye. And when I try to bring water to him, I find myself being threatened with physical harm by the dog's owner. It's *his* fucking dog.

If I did *not* suffer at such a sight, and did *not* want to alleviate the dog's suffering, I would consider that a form of spiritual bypassing. So, although I am not thirsty myself, I must suffer along with the dog—and that cannot be explained away by "awakening."

I guess it's hard for you to get over hearing that even the wide-awake ones among us must suffer. Suffering cannot be avoided. Trying to avoid or escape suffering just makes matters worse. I despise hearing from "teachers" that suffering is "all in your mind." *Everything* is all in your mind—but that does not mean it's not real.

I was talking with my friend, Dr. Robert K. Hall, an expert on Theravada Buddhism, a dharma teacher himself, and a lifelong meditator in the *vipassana* tradition, who, at the time of this conversation, was in hospice care, and in considerable physical distress. We were discussing suffering and the Four Noble Truths, which Robert had said were "kindergarten stuff, meant for beginners."

Robert recalled a conversation with Jack Kornfield[30] in which Robert said, "Jack, there's no *escape* from suffering. What *is* this bullshit?" And, Robert told me, Jack agreed. He doesn't know *anyone* who has escaped.

Now contemporary Buddhist teachers never claim to be "enlightened." A *faux pas* like that would put them beyond the pale. But they do commonly speak *as if* enlightened. Jack Kornfield, for example, is famous for saying, "Enlightenment is an accident, but spiritual practice makes you accident prone." Well, logically, how do you *know* that if *you* are *not* enlightened?

So even honored teachers may have two accounts: the *public* account, in which the teacher speaks about the end of suffering, and how to pursue it through "practice," such as Jack's books and lectures; and the *private* account that is shared only with a trusted friend (if at all), in which you come clean: if enlightenment means the end of suffering, you really *aren't* enlightened, and have never met anyone who was.

This is not guesswork on my part, but a factual account of my observations of teachers, and how they talk backstage when they are *not* teaching.

If you have an interest in spirituality and spiritual teaching, it is crucial to understand this point. Most teaching represents a conveyance of tradition—*not* a phenomenology of direct experience. So if you want the boilerplate version of spirituality—to be instructed in Buddhist dharma, for example, or nonduality—go sit at someone's

30. Jack Kornfield (born 1945) is an American author and teacher in the *vipassana* movement in American Theravada Buddhism. He is one of the key figures in the introduction of Buddhist Mindfulness practice to the West.

feet. There, as a supplicant, you can get all the "Truth" you like. But if you want to see things more as they are, forget all that hot air and find your *own* mind—which is yours to *live* with, like it or not, including suffering.

As soon as one really comprehends the thorny truth that, short of death, there is no exit from this aliveness, and the relentless, painful self-awareness that comes with it, freedom is apparent. *You are free to be you exactly as you are right now*—and not free to be anything else, no matter what some teacher tells you.

We all want what we want when we want it. Wanting what one does not have is a *form* of suffering. You may want a pain-free version of aliveness, with transcendence of suffering as the final condition, the *attainment*—but think of the countless people on the Earth who at this very moment are not thinking about transcendence at all, but only wanting some clean water to drink, or a safe place to sleep.

Q: What can one do then, when there is suffering? The mind resists it. Thoughts of wanting to escape come up unheeded. This wishing for the end of suffering can't be stopped. What can one do?

A: I advise forgetting what others say and allowing yourself to open your mind to *this* moment. Breathe in, breathe out. When you feel thirsty, drink. Be grateful that you have clean water to drink. Eat enough to keep the body healthy. Sleep, walk around, carry out tasks, laugh, cry. Each moment must be chewed up and swallowed as best you can. That's life.

Q: Openness like that seems too painful. And the tendency to resist suffering or escape seems unstoppable.

A: If that is so—if the tendency to resist seems unstoppable—then what is your option? If that frame of mind really is, for you, unstoppable, then there is nothing for it. You *will* resist suffering and you will try to escape it. That is what I mean by saying that you are free to be yourself exactly as you are right now, and not free to be anything else.

So of what possible use are words from me? I am someone who is *not* resisting—and I *still* suffer.

Q: When there is resistance, just chew it up and swallow it all too?

A: Yes, and try not to choke on it.

Q: When you say awakening never ends, what exactly do you mean? Do you mean that noticing that this present moment is just what it is, is a never-ending process?

A: Yes, I do mean that, and also that one's understanding of oneself and the world will never be final.

Q: That is true. You don't know if tomorrow all your so-called "understanding" and "realizations" will completely reverse or something. What we have, or know, and everything else, can change in an instant.

A: Yes. That's the idea. Don't get stuck anywhere. Just keep walking.

61 - The story of Han-Shan

Q: Hello Robert. I hope you can help me understand the story of Han-Shan from *The Ten Thousand Things* and your comment about it.

Han-Shan said: "This morning I face my lonely shadow and, before I know it, tears stream down." And your comment was that those tears require the flash of lightning. That sounds special, and not ordinary. Can you please explain?

A: I can try. So much of spirituality is couched in positive terms, in terms of *progress* towards a goal, in terms of *victory*, in terms of *gaining* something—including, as some people imagine, attaining a so-called deathless state, in which the ordinary conditions of biological life no longer apply. And this is considered "enlightenment."

In a flash of lightning like Han-Shan's, one sees that all those words are empty promises; and that no matter what one thinks, believes, or experiences, there are no ultimate victories in life. We all age, suffer, and die, no matter what; and even if we have good friends, sweet lovers, and supportive families, we are all ultimately alone.

To live without denying that aloneness or trying to finesse it is what Jiddu Krishnamurti called "the flight of the eagle."

The inability to escape impermanence and mortality is what Shunryu Suzuki meant when he said: "Life is like stepping onto a boat which is about to sail out to sea and sink."

The awakened mind, cognizant of its aloneness and evanescence, does not require rules, practices, ideologies, and procedures, but can simply bounce around unimpeded like a beach ball in a rapids, enjoying what can be enjoyed and tolerating what cannot. Meanwhile, what must emerge, will emerge.

Words cannot express the sweetness of such an emancipation from striving, seeking, and the fantasy of becoming.

Q2: Robert, the way you express your experience is exquisite. You demonstrate how much clarity is possible, and what we humans can do when there's no "I" in the way. Language can be such a healing instrument.

A: Thank you. Yes, I agree with you. When there is no "I" struggling for permanence in a world of impermanence, questions clear up quickly. Most questions—apart from practical ones like "What's for dinner?" or "How far from here to Alpha Centauri?"—are not really *questions* at all, but delaying tactics.

Q3: One thing I have heard you say is, "This moment is so rich." This sounds as if, to you, each moment is perfect in its own way, and as if you are appreciative and engaged fully in each of these moments.

I was just wondering, can you share how different that is from when you were not "awake" yet? I know your experience can never be my experience, but I am wondering if there was a marked difference for you. This is more curiosity than anything.

A: Curiosity killed the cat. The best questions come from a need that is deeper than curiosity.

In simplest terms, "awake" is when you don't take this aliveness for granted. Imagining a better tomorrow comes to a halt. The anodyne promises of "spirituality" do not obtain. We have *this* moment and all it entails.

You may like what you see, feel, and think, or detest it. You may fear what is in front of you, or desire it—maybe even a little of both. Likes and dislikes are not ours to choose. What is, is, including fear and desire. This, as they say, is *it*.

Awakeness is *not* "spirituality," in which one aims at an imagined "perfect" state that some saint or holy man attained, and to which that "great one" has marked the path. I have no need for such pie in the sky. The awakeness I know means being with whatever is *right now*, without explanations, justifications, or fantasizing about something better or "more evolved."

62 - Enlightenment and awakening theories

Q: Robert, you present a lot of reasons why we cannot make a legitimate claim to absolute truth. But the thing is, students of philosophy have known for a long time that we cannot successfully investigate metaphysical issues. And you offer good reasons why it's best not to glom onto theories and such as being absolutely true, or practices as being uniformly safe and effective. But nothing you have said, so far, seems to prevent people from having their own favorite theories, theories that they can't prove, but which they find very compelling.

A: Right. Many people love conjecture, pet beliefs, and "certainties," and live in a world of their own prized opinions, regardless of facts. Due to normal human cognitive biases—the *confirmation bias,* for example, in which information tending to support what one already believes is overvalued, while that which might to cast doubt on one's beliefs will be discounted or even forgotten entirely—a conjecture that meets emotional needs may quickly become a pet belief and then a "certainty," regardless of facticity.

Nothing I have said will forestall that. But there is a condition of human *be*-ing in which one lives *without* conjectures and pet theories about metaphysical matters, and without needing any. That condition—which is an aspect of what I am calling "awake"—is the point of view embodied in *The Ten Thousand Things.*

Some people say that a "Supreme Being" created the universe and everything in it; that is the "theory." But since that conjecture can be neither proved nor falsified, but only believed or disbelieved, I have no interest in it. It fails entirely to engage me. And, by the way, the "Supreme Being" conjecture does not deserve the name "theory." A conjecture or hypothesis can only rise to the stature of a *theory* if there are good ways in which it can be falsified—*and* after some of those ways of refutation have been tried and failed—which is not the case with religious dogma and never can be, as you pointed out.

To be perfectly clear on this point, a *theory* is not a guess or a belief, but an idea that has already stood up to investigation. The more it is investigated and continues to stand up, the more "robust," as this is said, the theory is considered. If, at some point, the theory *fails* to stand up to investigation, then it is discarded. In that use of the word "theory"—which is the *proper* use when speaking philosophically—"Supreme Being" or "Source" is not actually a "theory" at all, but rather speculation, conjecture, or article of faith.

However, if someone has a use for religious belief in the so-called "Supreme Being"—perhaps, for example, it takes the sting out of the idea of death, or provides a rationale for acting "morally"—fine by me. I am not proselytizing, but only saying how I personally see these matters.

Q: As a long-time critic of enlightenment and awakening theories, it seems to me that you would have some thoughts on which of the theories you have heard seem to you to hold water, or at least hold the promise of holding water.

A: I am not sure what you mean by "enlightenment and awakening theories." If you specify, I will try to respond.

Q: Also, your approach generally would seem to me to discourage others from putting forth ideas that they think would hold water.

A: It's not my intention to discourage anyone from anything. If you have ideas like that, please feel free to share them. Put forth whatever you like. My words and photographs are purely an expression of my *own* mind, with no further agenda or ulterior motive.

That is why I say that I am not a spiritual teacher. I share my point of view as a form of philosophical self-expression not very different from the self-expression conveyed by my photographs. This sharing of my perspective is not intended to teach anyone anything about "reality" or discourage anyone from beliefs that seem important to them. It is a frank report of how I see life and mind, not some dogma I am trying to foist off on anyone. I speak only for myself, and just say what I see. Take it for what it's worth or reject it out of hand. That's not up to me.

Nevertheless, some people are annoyed by my point of view and are moved to blame me for having my outlook and not the one they have. After I was quoted as saying that reincarnation is not a fact but a belief based on hearsay and fear of death, and that words like "destiny" or "karma" do not explain anything, someone commented that my view of reincarnation was "a stupid man's cop-out," and went on to assert that "denying reincarnation is similar to denying climate change and more dangerous."

Really? That is a perfect example of the confirmation bias in action. The writer of those words elevated his belief in reincarnation to the status of a scientific fact by bracketing it with real scientific observations about greenhouse gases and climate, while, at the same time, demeaning an idea that conflicted with his pet belief—now elevated to a "certainty"—by calling me "stupid," and my refusal to accept reincarnation as a fact, "dangerous."

Q: Also, as a therapist, tasked with helping others find health, peace, or healing, you must be working from some tentative theories about the nature of the mind. Otherwise, you would spend your entire career advising people about the folly of putting faith in just about anything.

A: I do think faith is a kind of folly, but I would not necessarily have said that to a therapy client. Psychotherapy is a specialized arena for emotional healing within artificially constructed boundaries, not the place for devil-may-care metaphysics or philosophy. One assumes that the client is wounded and hurting (otherwise, he or she would not be in the *consultorio* in the first place) and needs care and attention—not necessarily unadorned, blunt truth-telling, although that might figure in at the appropriate moment.

However, when people ask questions about "awakening" or "nonduality"—which is what arises in this milieu of public discourse—my answers are *not* therapy and make no claim to be. All I can offer in this forum—which has nothing to do with psychotherapy—is unvarnished, entirely candid replies, the more forthright the better. To do otherwise would be to disrespect the questions.

Q: Do you at any point go beyond criticism to suggest positive guidance?

A: If you are still speaking about psychotherapy, yes. Guidance may be part of that. My work was more psychoanalysis than guidance, usually leaving practical matters to the discretion of the client, but I did some counseling and couples work too where advice figured in. I have, for example, said to more than one client, "It seems to me that you are being abused in this relationship. Perhaps you should consider changing the arrangements."

One outcome of giving that kind of advice was a phone call from an irate husband, a gangster known to have killed personally at least two people, threatening to kill me. Fortunately for me, my client was ready to leave him and had a friend with whom I could collude to get her and her daughter away from her bodyguard and on a plane out of the country. The wife-beating husband had been wanting to muzzle me while she was still my patient, but it wasn't vengeance he was after. Once she was gone, I became a person of little interest. He knew she was never coming back.

But if you are speaking about "awakening," the best "positive guidance" I have to offer is to start from scratch. To the extent possible, let go of attachment to previous beliefs and childhood indoctrination. Stop focusing on what others believe. Leave off identifying as a member of a so-called "race," gender, nationality, school of thought, religion, tribe, or anything else. Then deal with *this* moment as freshly as you can.

You seem to imagine that suggestion as "negative." I don't see it that way, although it is related to the so-called *via negativa*, the traditional process of *neti neti*[31]. If someone actually *wants* to awaken—

31. *Neti neti:* in Hinduism, and in particular Jnana Yoga and Advaita Vedanta, a Sanskrit expression, meaning "not this, not that," or "neither this, nor that."

many more *say* they do than actually mean it—that begins, in my experience, not by learning and acquiring, but by discarding and becoming naked, alone, unprotected, uncertain, and open.

The word "negative" has in general speech a *negative* connotation. Being "positive" seems strong and "can-do." Compared to that, "negative" seems weak and downbeat. But weak and downbeat is not the connotation of the term *via negativa*. Here, it does not mean weaker or lesser—not at all. It means open-minded, not always looking to glom onto explanations, willing to assess ideas skeptically without smearing a bunch of power and respect on them like maple syrup on a pancake.

This is a negativity akin to the "negative space" of the empty chair in a Gestalt therapy session that will be one's interlocutor in a round of straight talk, without evasions and justifications.

This is the emptiness we find within our own minds if we have such luck; an emptiness willing to be filled, but only with the finest understanding available in each moment, not second-hand tropes or self-help truisms. On the *via negativa*, there are no believers, no disciples, no one kissing Mooji's feet, no one whipping up poor old Ramana Maharshi (now buried under a slab of concrete) into a myth that will feed many mouths. It's so easy and pointless to speak for him now that he is dead and cannot debunk a word of it.

On the *via negativa*, everything is out in the open. Each of us has our own fish to fry. The heart is a lonely hunter, as Carson McCullers put it. And the greeting when we meet is, "Walk on."

Q: If you absolutely had to pick one of the available spiritual schools of thought, which one would it be? Or would you recommend sticking to extreme Socratic doubt for everyone in all circumstances, including yourself?

A: Wowie! You *are* relentless. Personally, I no longer require the potent medicine of Socratic doubt. Since I am free of beliefs, nothing needs doubting. But certainly, I can recommend that you *try* that medicine. It might help to cure the delusion that "Robert" or any other human primate animal has answers to ultimate questions. That said, a little Taoism never hurt anyone, and Stoicism has a lot going for it as well. Ha, ha.

Q: Given that people are going to continue searching, sometimes randomly, for guidance in their beliefs and practices and to continue trying various things, do you feel at all obliged to offer some positive guidance?

A: The only "obligation" I feel on this page is candor.

Q: Earlier you said, "I am not sure what you mean by 'enlightenment and awakening theories.' If you specify, I will try to respond." I dodged the question then because I did not trust you to hear my answer fairly. Now I do, so let me try to specify. Up until a couple of years ago, I had considered myself a garden variety "spiritual aspirant" in pursuit of "enlightenment," the kind of spiritual enlightenment that emerged in the 1960s.

Then, a couple of short years ago, several things happened at once.

I experienced a spontaneous and completely unbidden *kundalini* arousal, which knocked me on my butt for a period of months. Also, I began to experience what I understand is referred to as "celestial perception," the perception of celestial or trans-dimensional or noumenal beings.

I was in no way ready for these things. I did not embrace them or make assumptions about them. They just happened. And I am not going to talk about that here, for fear of inviting comments I don't want to deal with.

The word "enlightenment" quickly fell by the wayside for me. It just didn't seem to refer to what had happened to me. And I quickly concluded that the term was at best outdated and at worst completely bogus.

I began reading stuff and watching videos, and found that the word "awakening" had come into vogue. However, the people using that word made it clear that there was no official definition for it; and lots of people defined it lots of different ways, some of which seemed relevant to what was happening to me, some not. Frankly, it didn't seem to have any really useful definition. And although, as I said, a lot of the stuff that was happening to me seemed to fit under the "awakening" umbrella, there was a lot of other stuff going on that didn't seem to fit anywhere.

So, by the time I encountered your work, Robert, there was a lot of stuff going on for which there was no language, and about which there is not a lot of intelligent discussion.

There are many in the broad and increasingly inclusive and varied meditation community willing to discuss at least some of these phenomena. But basically, I was at sea, forging my own personal approach to spirituality or religiosity, obviously fitting nowhere and no longer sure who my allies in the traditional meditation community might be.

I found your work attractive because I was reacting against the spiritual establishment, the meditation community, broadly defined, and you seemed to be a staunch critic of both.

I think there are a lot of us out here experiencing all kinds of stuff for which there is no name and no catch-all, no umbrella term.

In a way, that relates to your work, Robert. You seem to me to be critiquing a school of thought that is now kind of outdated. The reality has moved on, so your critique seems outdated also. No offense.

Meanwhile, nobody is addressing the new, emergent reality — the reality of people like myself whose experience is totally effing anomalous and who cannot readily find anyone ready or willing to discuss it; and to whom the meditation culture seems wholly outdated, irrelevant and archaic. The only thing I feel I can bring to the table are anecdotes that you have clearly signaled wouldn't hold up for you.

So, I understand that God is an unprovable theory or something like that, but a good *defensible* theory comes in very handy. I think most of us understand the limits of theories, but it would be nice to have a provisional explanation or two that, in the midst of a lot of unusual phenomena, we can adopt at least temporarily, until something better comes along.

A: No. "God" is not "an unprovable theory." It is not a *theory* at all. And the proper approach to an actual theory is not to defend it, but to question it by testing it against real-world conditions. To the extent that it resists attacks, the theory becomes more useful. Please try to be clear on that.

Now, with all due respect, you are asking me for something that I cannot give you—and no one else can either, in my view. I have no explanation, provisional or otherwise, for your experiences. Anyone who claims to have one is, in my view, either a liar or self-deluded.

Nor do I have any idea really of what you mean by "noumenal beings," unless you mean hallucinations, which I do not think is what you intend when you say that. And ditto on "*kundalini* arousal." I have no idea what that term means. I am not feigning ignorance. I have *heard* the word *kundalini* used countless times, but naming something does not indicate that it really exists. So far as I know, no one has demonstrated the existence of any "*kundalini*." I am not saying it doesn't exist; I am pointing out that the only evidence for it is hearsay and subjectivity—which are not actually *evidence* at all.

People see all kinds of things and have all kinds of experiences that may be interesting, compelling, enjoyable, or frightening, but experiences take place in the brain (or, if brain sounds too materialistic to your ear, experiences take place in "mind") —not "outside" somewhere. If we are honest, we do not even know if a tree we can walk up to and touch "really" exists, much less any "trans-dimensional beings."

There is an assumption in your question that is simply incorrect. The term "awakening" has not "come into vogue." It is an ancient usage. For example, in Zen, the word "*satori*" means a sudden awakening, such as occurred in my case, and that usage goes back more than a millennium. I avoid the word "enlightenment" only because, like the word "God," it is so overused now that no one knows *what* it means; and so it has become a screen onto which people project their spiritual fantasies. One must have some kind of word, I suppose, so I prefer the word "awake."

When I am with other people whom I see as awake—the few I

know—we recognize one another easily; and if we speak of these matters, it has little or nothing to do with any "special experiences," but with a kind of sane world view. No confusion there at all, nor any need to explain anything. It's as if the commonplace egoic view is present only as a kind of amusing guest. No arguments. No contention. No defending. No debate. None of that. Any conversation is coming from a different place entirely, and often a lot of smiling takes place.

The confusion about being awake in the present resides in the minds of people who *seek* to "awaken," which many imagine is a "state" marked by all kinds of phenomena like the ones you describe. But visions of trans-dimensional beings and all of that have nothing to do with what I mean by "awake." Nothing. If I started seeing a lot of that stuff, I might consider a neurological exam.

No doubt people experience all kinds of stuff, but I do not think you should assume that such happenings are something new, as you said. Nor should you assume that those experiences have anything to do with awakening. I am not saying they don't; I am saying that you should not jump to that conclusion. But you already have, I see.

You said that I seem to be "critiquing a school of thought that is now kind of outdated. The reality has moved on, so your critique seems outdated also." What school of thought is that exactly? And what "reality" has moved on from it?

Please clear that up. By the way, I was not offended in the least. Here you are free to speak from the heart, without consideration of the impact of your words on "Robert." All I ask is basic civility, and I do not ask that to avoid being offended—I won't be—but because name-calling and rudeness obscure communication.

Frankly, I do not see any "new, emergent reality." I see the same old thing being repeated endlessly, the same old wine in different bottles: human beings in a trance state trying to "explain" the inexplicable with religion and spirituality. Why? Because they are afraid to experience this aliveness, a total and complete mystery, *without* explanations; or if not afraid, dissatisfied by it.

You will never know what any of this "really" means, I say. You will never know the ultimate source of anything. The very trying to find out is *part* of the trance—a way of remaining *in* the trance—a way of *not* being awake.

Consider this, please. What if, instead of the foregoing, I had replied this way?

> *Great question. Yes, early in my meditation practice—which involved ten hours a day staring at the wall—I "broke through." I had a massive* kundalini *arousal. And then a voice—it could have been an angel—spoke to me, telling me:*
>
> *"Robert, your true nature is divine, and you were born to lead others to the knowledge that the noumenal beings that appear when you raise your* kundalini *must be honored as avatars of the unity of all life in the universe. And the phenomena that are causing you this anxiety are not hallucinations at all, but more real than the nose on your face. They are beings from another realm, advanced beyond our world, who see you as an awakening spirit and want to open channels of communication with you if you will only let them. You must never doubt this, because it is only your doubt that keeps you from knowing God.*

What would that do for you? Would that make everything just dandy? No insult intended. That is a serious question.

Q: I understood and related to the first part of your response better than the second part. The thing is, I made no assumptions and I still make no assumptions about what happened. I only used the words I used because I wanted to be understood—not to be believed. Nor was I looking for a particular response of any kind.

The second part of your response seems to imply assumptions about my possible response to events, or the response that I expected, that are inaccurate.

I do not think I am awake. In fact, I'm pretty sure I'm not. And with all I've seen and heard, I do not want to be awake in the sense you mentioned. Nor do I think that I am being tapped by some invisible agents or agency for some special purpose. I honestly do not know what is going on and I honestly do not care.

Also, I never imagined the kind of response you posit in the second part of your response, and I can't relate to it. In reality, I have withheld judgment on all of these things since it all started, and I am still doing so. It's just too confusing.

What you did do was illustrate why I don't like to talk about this stuff.

Also, with respect to the use of the term "awake," I was out of touch with this sort of discussion for many, many years. When I initially lost touch with it, "awakened" was not used in the sense one hears it today. When I started watching videos to see what was going on, everybody was using "awakened" all the time. In all kinds of different ways. "Enlightenment" appeared to have disappeared from the dictionary.

For the record, I have a doctorate in modern European history and had the empirical method drummed into me. So I understand about evidence and proof and such. So I always knew I was on very uncertain ground empirically, and I understood exactly why.

As for *kundalini*, I can only say that it seems quite real to me. I stopped meditating to avoid any further encounters with it. And when, once in a while, I go back to meditating to see if I can do it anymore, I experience things I associate with *kundalini*. So I always stop again.

For what it's worth, I do not want anything to do with awakening or with *kundalini*, and I am careful to avoid these things. I just find my life full of phenomena that I did not seek, do not indulge or enjoy, and try to avoid. And my tentative efforts to discuss them here hasn't changed my resolve.

A: Thanks. Now I get it. The last part of my reply was a kind of joke meant to illustrate that explanations are useless. I did not intend the joke to be at your expense.

As for *kundalini*, do you really imagine a serpent coiled up at the base of your spine that sends "energy" up the spinal column when you meditate, causing visions when that energy reaches the *"crown chakra"* in your head? Frankly, I don't. I see visions such as you describe as what happens when attention is turned inward. I see plenty of visions when my attention is removed from the outside world—at night, for example, when asleep and dreaming—and I can see them at times just by closing my eyes. I just do not assume that they are "beings." To me, it's all mind. I don't ask you to agree.

I sense that you are a bit frightened by what you have seen, so probably suspending those practices is a good idea. Please be assured that I have taken everything you said seriously. I just have a strange sense of humor.

Q: I don't think of *kundalini* in those terms. I can only attest that when I meditate, even for small periods of time, I experience strong surges of energy from the base of my spine. It doesn't look like a serpent, although whenever I have watched it, the surge of energy does have a certain sinuous quality to it.

On one notable occasion such a surge, an especially strong one, triggered months of anxiety and hypertension. This experience and the symptoms that resulted sounded a lot like what other people described when I went looking to find out. It took me months to calm down. That was a couple of years ago.

A similar thing happened during a workshop I attended this winter. The workshop was being conducted by the son of a close friend, hence my attendance.

The workshop experience was complicated. I'm still coming back from that one. I think the important thing to say here is that I do not seek these things out. I don't enjoy them when they happen, and now I studiously avoid situations that might cause these things to repeat.

I think I started having these experiences because I meditated more or less regularly for four or five decades, never thinking these things would happen to me. Now I realize that I was being naive and foolish, and I regret my past actions. I really badly disturbed my inner peace with all that meditation and I want it back.

By the way, I'm not big on inner or outer visions. And I don't recall my dreams very often. I do see some "subtle phenomena," and I can tell you that they don't seem imaginary. It seems like I am seeing something going on on subtle levels.

This might sound paradoxical or even contradictory, but I don't go looking for this stuff. I get a kick out of it when it happens, and other people usually enjoy the tale—but I don't seek this stuff out. And if it doesn't happen for a long time, I don't miss it. I might wonder about it, but I don't miss it. Something about the way I lived my life caused this stuff. All those years of meditation, I figure.

A: Aha. Yes, I have heard things like this from others, and often with the regret you seem to feel. I do wish you well, my friend.

Q: Thanks, Robert. For what it's worth, after several months of what I think of as recovery time, I am feeling a lot better. The symptoms have largely subsided. What I used to think of as normal seems to be returning. I will continue reading your book.

I am planning to avoid meditation practices, etcetera. They all seem kind of hokey and risky to me. And I might once in a while talk to people about what I think are the dangers of meditation, although nobody seems to appreciate my efforts in that direction.

After all of the above, I am not bereft of what I might very cautiously refer to as the comforts of spirit. It feels like I am developing a healthy "spirituality," or whatever the heck one can safely call it. Going forward, I will treat this whole category of phenomena with the caution and respect I now realize it is due, and humbly suggest that others do the same.

I think it is courageous and generous of you to put yourself out there as a critic of meditation culture. Somebody needs to be out there doing it. Thank you.

A: You are most welcome. As I said, I wish you well.

63 - Crystal healing

Q: Hi Robert, while I have been following your Facebook page for some time now, to be honest, I was not giving it too much attention. I am very suspicious about everything "spiritual" these days. Even from myself.

This suspicion feels strange, since I am one of those people who see themselves as spiritual. I enjoy quite a lot the idea that there is more to all this than there seems to be. I am energetically very sensitive, and I can feel and sense vibrations very well. I have been calling myself a "sensitive" and a "healer" for years. Most of the time, I feel that I have a mission in this world, which is to help people to rise from darkness and suffering.

I have been repeatedly searching and giving up. Moving back and forward. I guess when my search gets close to touching some of my deepest fears, that is when I feel attracted to moving on.

I am writing this because I'm frustrated by what life is like for me lately. Perhaps you can bring some clarity to it.

I use "spirituality" to earn my living. I love crystals. I love to do handcrafted works with them, and I feel intuitively the vibrations that come from the stones. I sell crystal arrangements for the purpose of healing. I love to make people feel better, so I do what I call healing, by working with the sun, the moon, the earth, and the energy of each crystal, to restore balance and remove dense energies from people. In this work I ask for intuitive guidance from other realms of spirit. I ask them to help me to heal people.

When I am doing this spiritual healing, it feels right. It makes sense to my heart. But then I see your views on these things, and I start to question. Am I truly helping people to awake into higher states of consciousness, or am I deceiving them and myself as well? Is it wrong that I am earning my living doing this?

I want to read your book. It is calling me. But I confess, I am afraid. I'm afraid to get even more confused.

Well, thanks a lot for your time, Robert. I love to gaze at your profile picture. You are very beautiful. Thank you.

A: Hi. Thank you.

You ask if your work with crystals is really helping people to awake into higher states of consciousness, or if you are only deceiving them and yourself as well. And given your doubts, you wonder if it is wrong to be earning your living this way.

Those are good questions. You are courageous to ask them.

While you are in this open, questioning mood—which I understand feels painful and insecure—you might also ask yourself what you mean by "higher states of consciousness." What if higher and lower states are only something you once heard about and believed? What if there really is no higher and lower consciousness, but only this *aliveness* existing exactly as it is right now, prior to all categories and judgments?

Everyone needs to make a living somehow, and if you can do that by helping people to feel better—by serving as a kind of healer of moods—why judge yourself? If you believe that crystals have powers, perhaps they do. Or perhaps they don't, and those "powers" are only imaginary. But human contact *can* heal bad moods; that is a known fact. So if relying on crystals is part of the way you work, maybe that's OK, even if you have your doubts, and even if crystals have no actual powers of their own.

Do you know the story of *Dumbo*? If not, here it is:

A cute little infant elephant is born to a circus-performing mom. Mama elephant adores her baby despite his one flaw—gigantic, oversized ears, for which he is teased and told he is ugly.

When Mom dies, leaving her baby an orphan with no means of support, Dumbo is forced to become a lowly clown elephant just to get by. But a helpful circus mouse points out that, if he opened up his giant ears he could fly, and thus become a star attraction: "Dumbo, The Flying Elephant."

Dumbo is afraid to try, until the mouse offers him a magic feather. If Dumbo will hold the magic feather in his trunk, open up his wings and jump off the high-dive platform, he will be able to fly, the mouse tells him. Desperate to get away from the nasty clowns, Dumbo gives the magic feather a go. His big ears catch the air and off he goes flying around the circus big top. Soon, Dumbo becomes a main attraction, drawing large crowds.

Weeks go by, and Dumbo continues his star turn, convinced that the magic feather is what keeps him aloft. Then one day, a gust of wind whisks the feather out of his trunk, and Dumbo starts to drop like a stone. The mouse, who was hitching a ride in Dumbo's hat, screams at the elephant that the feather was only a ruse and that he could fly just as well without the feather.

Could this be true? At the last possible moment, just before he and the mouse have a crash-landing, Dumbo opens up his giant ears and soars.

What if crystals are your magic feather?

It's good to have doubts, I say. They are a sign of open-mindedness, which I find sorely lacking among many people who like to call themselves "spiritual." Keep your doubts close to you as long as you need them. They are a powerful ally in finding *your own mind*, the natural awareness prior to belief in anything at all. Until you find an unencumbered awareness, you will never be at peace, "higher consciousness" or not. If you do find your own naked awareness—your *own* mind—doubt will no longer be an issue.

The finest, purest crystal in the world cannot give you peace of mind, I say. Only standing on your own ground, free of magical beliefs, can do that. As long as you cling to beliefs, you will always be troubled by doubts, because *doubt is the shadow side of belief.* And so doubt must exist as long as one believes or has so-called "faith" in ideas that may not be true.

As for reading *The Ten Thousand Things*, everything in its own time. Meanwhile, forget about "spirituality" if you can. It is your *own* mind you need to discover, without relying on the many things you have been told and believed.

Don't be hard on yourself. Try to let your beliefs go and concentrate instead on your actual feelings from moment to moment, allowing everything to be just as it is, including doubt.

I wish you well.

Q: When I dared to write to you, I knew this would probably happen. I spent the day processing your answer, and do you know what I came to realize? I realized that there is excitement in seeking and searching. Some kind of novelty or addictive suffering. Because when I stop to meditate without crystals, without focusing on certain chakras or light visualizations, I feel a deep dissatisfaction with meditation, and boredom. It seems that there is a huge desire to keep the mind busy, and I actually become too afraid of what will happen next. Can you say anything about this? Thanks a lot.

A: The first thing I want to say is how much I enjoy witnessing the opening of a mind that had been clinging to pet beliefs and outgrown self-definitions. Although it might feel uncomfortable, this *liminality* is rare and special, so try to appreciate it for as long as it lasts.

Liminality means the condition of uncertainty, ambiguity, or disorientation that occurs in the middle stage of a rite of passage, when participants no longer retain their earlier pre-ritual status but have not yet entered into a transition to the status they will possess when the rite of passage is complete. During a rite's liminal stage, participants "stand at the threshold" between their previous way of defining their identity and a new way that completing the rite will establish.

As I see it, you may be on the threshold of an important understanding that I will illuminate if I can. Since you have demonstrated such unpretentious, honest mettle, I will just say it straight up.

Yes, there can be excitement in seeking and searching—like a treasure hunt, isn't it? You aim to find the pot of gold at the end of the rainbow. But there is no end of the rainbow, nor any pot of gold, I say. This right now is it: all one ever has or ever will have.

In each moment, what is is, and, except in fantasy, cannot be different. If this moment feels insufficient or unsatisfactory, that cannot be repaired, but only seen and noticed.

Seeing and noticing is what real meditation is about—not focusing on crystals, or so-called "chakras," or trying to produce any state or condition at all. If you go at it with some self-improvement purpose—to balance chakras, to raise *qi*, to commune with fantasized "higher powers," etcetera—that is not what I call meditation. Meditation in the best sense is motiveless, clear-headed noticing of whatever one *can* notice in this very moment—not about fixing or improving anything.

Anxiety is part of life. Whether we admit it to ourselves or not, we really know that, in the next moment, anything at all can happen. Any breath might be our last. We are all subject to events beyond our control, and there is no protection from that uncertainty, only ways of papering it over. This fragile body we call "me" is going to die, and we know it. And when it does, that may very well be the end of "myself." We may like to *believe* otherwise, but we do not *know* otherwise.

One might try to sugarcoat the anxiety of ordinary living with religion and spirituality, but fixes like that don't last. Eventually, doubts must arise, because doubt, as I said earlier, is the shadow side of belief. *Belief and doubt are two sides of the same coin.* You cannot have one without the other. So if you embrace beliefs, you must live with doubts that you will always be trying to sweep under the carpet.

You could live in a house constructed entirely of the most perfect crystals, drinking from a crystal goblet, eating from a crystal bowl, and sleeping on a bed of perfect crystals—and still be searching for the peace of mind that eludes you. Your belief in "higher consciousness" and "guidance from other realms of spirit" may be as imaginary as chakras for all we really know.

The human mind can believe all kinds of things, but belief, no matter how firm, does not make any of them true. And what you are calling "intuition" is not some kind of flawless power either, but just another word for thoughts and feelings that come to mind, we know not how or why.

What one really *knows*, I am saying, is almost nothing, and part of the anxiety you feel stems from clinging to beliefs while doubt waits in the wings.

Your questions indicate that peace of mind is what you really want, and the humility with which you express that desire is a gift.

That is why I am speaking so directly.

This aliveness that we call "myself" is a mystery and always will be, regardless of traditions and magical thinking. We may nibble around the edges of that mystery, but the core of it, I say, is beyond our ken. That is what I call human limitation. No matter what any system or religion may claim, no one really *knows* anything at all about ultimate matters, including higher powers, higher forms of consciousness, life after death, or whether being alive has any inherent meaning at all, except that which we have been taught to project onto it.

I understand your fears. They are natural enough. Abandoning beliefs that have seemed like certainties can feel like a loss of something precious. But there is, I say, something far more precious, and that is up to you to discover.

In that, I wish you well.

Q: Thank you so much, Robert. Seeing the truth can be very painful at times. I have experienced a mixture of anger, sadness, happiness, and gratitude during our conversation. I don't want to take more of your time, but I feel you are guiding me into something here, so I ask if it's OK to ask more questions as they arise.

I have been reflecting on all you have said, and after the storm of feelings and emotions, there is definitely a sense of relief and a relaxation into being present, being me. I have seen so much from your replies to my questions. I can't even express how deeply blinded I have been by my fantasies. That blindness is a part of the anger I was feeling. I've seen so much arrogance and ugliness attached to this spiritual identity with which I meet the world. I became like a dictator. By clinging to the idea of how perfect and divine this world *should* be, and how people *ought to* behave, I forgot to see how beautiful everyone is just as they are.

I feel so grateful for your advice. I have no words to express the love I feel for your open, compassionate, nonjudgmental teaching. Thank you. I feel there is a lot more in me that needs opening to reality. But it seems I have found a door to what I am really searching for, here and now.

Thank you, Robert.

A: You are most welcome. Honesty and humility always touch my heart, so feel free to ask questions if they should arise.

A moment like this of walking out from under an outworn identity can feel exciting. It's as if one had been carrying around a useless burden that now can be set aside so that one walks more freely. And walking more freely feels lovely. Just remember that an insight—no matter what insight—is never the *last* insight. Awakening never ends, so keep on walking.

64 - Things are as they are

Q: Hi, Robert. I've been thinking about what it means to awaken. From what I understand, you are saying awakening means accepting how things are without judgment of good or bad. So, for example, are you saying that if one is awakened and a hurricane is coming, you plan for it as you should, but you don't live there ahead of time? You don't worry about the animals being harmed, but you do all you can to make sure they are safe? That those worry-type thoughts just don't come your way, but you are more than able to properly plan and execute?

A: Hi. No. That's not quite it. Awakening, as I use that word, is my name for the dawning of the understanding that things are always just as they are, whether you imagine accepting them or not; and that your feeling of accepting or non-accepting is just another one of those things that are just as they are—neither a choice, nor something that a "you" does.

That "myself"—the chooser, decider, acceptor or rejecter—exists only in fantasy, and its imagined powers of choice and doing are *part* of that fantasy. No matter how strange this idea may seem to you, there really is no "you" with the power either to accept or reject anything—except, I say, in the fantasy story you keep telling yourself about "myself."

"Myself" may *imagine* feeling feelings, thinking thoughts, dithering over choices, and coming to decisions, but that "myself" is an illusion supported by the false belief that, when thoughts are present, some "person" must be "doing" thinking.

No one is doing thinking. No one is making thoughts. Thoughts just arise when and as they do, just like everything else of which we become aware choicelessly and automatically.

Thoughts and thinker are two different names for the same process, the same flow: the stream of consciousness. There is no "myself" *apart* from that stream. "Myself" is a thought *in* that stream—not different from nor more privileged than other thoughts, none of which has any staying power at all. That's why it is called the *stream* of consciousness; it is forever flowing and never the same from one moment to the next. No one can stop it, and no one can make it be the way it was even one moment earlier.

In that ceaseless flow, every now and again an "I-thought" arises, and when such a thought is noticed, "myself," comes into being. When the "I-thought" is absent, there *is* no "myself." When, for example, one is stunned by natural beauty like the night sky, the eyes of a child, or the bray of a donkey, the "I-thought" is overwhelmed and silenced, allowing seeing with fresh eyes or hearing with fresh ears. So "myself" is a thought like any other thought, a concept, a creation of culture—sometimes present, other times absent—not a fixed entity that *has* thoughts.

When I use the word "concept," I mean a notion like the boundary between Nebraska and South Dakota that is symbolized by a straight line on maps. No such boundary exists in the physical world, but only in the thought-world upon which some humans have been taught to depend, as if thoughts were actual facts just because someone believes in them.

In the same way, the borderline between "you" and "events" is an artificial boundary that you have been taught to believe is real. If you look for that borderline, you will not find it. Are "you," for example, separate from the microbes that are digesting the food you ate earlier? If so, how? Did the ideas you call "mine" really originate with you, or have you learned from others what to think?

If you make this about self-help and feeling less anxious, you will never understand it. Here I am speaking not of personality, but of *be*-ing. If you are interested in this, it is important not to confuse the habits and tendencies we call "personality" with simply being at all. They are not the same. People with all styles of personality can be awake in the way I mean that word.

On a practical level, I find myself doing whatever seems necessary or desirable in each moment, and so I am acting as I must. But there is no ultimate judgment of those actions, no justification for them, nor any feeling of separation between "Robert" and Robert's thoughts, feelings, perceptions, and behaviors. Myself and "my" actions are one and the same flow.

No one ever *chooses* what to *do* next, any more than one can choose what to think next, or what to feel next: anxious, relaxed, worried, in love, etcetera. All of that just *arises*—including what you find yourself "doing," whether the "you" you imagine yourself to be likes it or not.

When the hurricane approached, and a direct hit looked likely, I found myself stowing loose objects and going out to the store to buy bottled water. Those actions were not "choices." They just occurred. Yes, I felt concerned about the donkeys. When the winds howled and tree limbs were flying around, I worried that they might be injured. Those feelings were irrelevant. There was nothing I could offer them. If there had been, most likely I would have found myself offering it.

I wonder if you can see how natural all this is, if you are able to get out of your own way and just be as you are from moment to moment—*including* worrying, if that is what occurs.

65 - Aware of your own enlightenment

Q: Robert, I know you like Eihei Dogen[32]. Do you have any comment on these words of his?

Do not think you will necessarily be aware of your own enlightenment.

A: When I hear the words of some of these middle ages Zen cats, I feel cut out of the same cloth. And in that feeling resides the core of a mystery. After all, to say "cut out of the same cloth" is like saying that we—the old Zen cats and I—embody certain essential qualities in common.

So do we humans have essential qualities? And if so, do I have certain ones, and the next person different ones? This is a good question, I think, to bring to the matter of so-called enlightenment.

One proclivity I seem to share with Dogen and some of those other old school dharma dudes—Hui Neng, Foyan, Lin Chi, Huang Po, et al.—is a love of language, and particularly a love of cooking up contradictions, quandaries, and koans.

Many here bemoan the limitations of language and imagine that those who speak and those who heed such speech automatically limit themselves, but if your inner child is like mine or Eihei's, perhaps you know better than to demean the best means of communicating with our fellow hairless apes.

It's fun, I say, to talk about the mysteries of *be*-ing as long as one knows how to forbear conclusions. After all, awakening never ends, so why pretend anyone will *get* to the end?

Without desire for culmination, the flow proceeds as it will, timeless, endless and unimpeded. To feel that one is not just *in* that flow, but part and parcel *of* it, is the true heart's desire—of *my* heart, at least—not "enlightenment" or "awakening," which is only the

32. Eihei Dogen (1200-1253), also known as Dogen Kigen, Dogen Zenji, Koso Joyo Daishi or Bussho Dento Kokushi—priest, writer, poet, philosopher, and founder of the Soto school of Zen in Japan.

McGuffin in this movie.

Enlightenment, I say, is not the point; *flowing* is. This is so simple. What is, is, and I am not the doer. What more does one need to know? From there, everything just unfolds naturally.

So, let us regard "Do not think you will necessarily be aware of your own enlightenment" as I imagine Dogen meant it—as a *koan*, a kind of riddle, a contradiction that by baffling the mind brings the background chatter to a dead stop, including spiritual chatter:

> *How's your aura, baby? Nonduality is lit. Everything happens for a reason. "Universal consciousness" is awesome. It takes plain old ordinary consciousness outside and kicks its ass.*

OK then. When Dogen says that you might not *"necessarily"* be aware of your own enlightenment, does he mean to imply that you *might* be aware of it? That seems to be the simplest and clearest reading of that sentence. But that clashes with the universal spiritual bromide that she or he who claims to be enlightened isn't.

And what does Dogen mean by "your *own* enlightenment?" If "myself" does not really exist, as all these neo-advaita cats like to point out—*ad nauseam,* in my view—then who is the "own" in the *koan*?

According to my reading of his words, Dogen is saying that you *might* be aware of your own enlightenment—but if you are, I say, best keep it to yourself. Look how much perturbation I have whipped up merely by remarking that I find myself "awake." Just imagine the repercussions and afflictions if I'd slipped and used the E-word! Ha, ha.

66 - Star gurus

I received a question asking me if I thought human beings could "shed the ego," in which the questioner said that Eckhart Tolle claimed to have shed his. After replying that I thought the idea of "shedding" the ego was confusing, I added this:

> *Without accusing Tolle of anything, I do wonder about people who claim to be "enlightened" but seem to want to amass big piles of wealth beyond what is needed for ordinary living.*

That comment aroused a firestorm both here on this page, and also in several private messages I received. So let me try to respond once and for all on this subject, and then, I hope, never again.

I do not know much about Tolle. My comment was not directed at him personally, but at the entire spirituality industry, which, to me, is a travesty. This is not a new idea to me. I saw my first star guru at work in Taos, New Mexico, in 1969, a nasty piece of work called Yogi Bajan—and that was all I needed to see.

I understand that Tolle teaches "presence," by which he means "Be here now." Fine. Good advice. My only question is, why would someone pay hundreds or thousands of dollars to hear it? If you have the money and want to spend it that way, fine by me. I just say what I see.

This is not about Tolle specifically. I feel exactly the same about the entire crop of American gurus who charge big fees to parrot the teachings of people like Ramana Maharshi, Nisargadatta, and Papaji, who gave their teachings away for free. Everything those three had to say was out in the open and still is. Their words are in the public domain, and now contemporary teachers want to be paid for repeating them, sometimes with a little pop-psychology blended in for the self-help fans.

I know a scam when I see one. If you disagree, fine by me. You have every right.

As for the people who tried to convince me that Tolle might be unaware of how much his retreats cost, or that he is not in control of all that, or that charging big bucks is a teaching tool to show people how attached they are to their money, or that rock concerts with big stars are expensive too—give me an effing break. Elsewhere in this volume[33], you will read a personal observation of Tolle, sent to me during the firestorm by an old friend of his, that puts the kibosh completely to the idea of "innocent little Eckhart."

One more thing. As I said in *The Ten Thousand Things*, what is, is. In this moment, things are as they are and cannot be any different. I accept that completely, so I know very well that the enlightenment industry will continue to thrive, just as any efficient way of separating customers from their money continues.

So why do I comment on it? Very simple: that is what I find myself doing. And perhaps, on hearing what I have to say, someone will find him- or herself *not* paying through the nose to hear ordinary advice like "Be here now."

Here is an excerpt from an interview in *Nonduality Magazine* which talks about my first experience with a star guru:

> NDM: Did you practice or study Zen, zazen meditation, Shikantaza[34], koans, or undergo sesshins in a monastery or some kind of retreat setting with a Roshi (master)?
>
> Robert: I never studied Zen with a master. My first interest was not Zen but Taoism, which I approached by reading *Tao Te Ching*, and attempting to understand what was being said. I began reading Zen soon after, having seen that the essence of Zen was in the same ballpark as Taoism—which had made sense to me immediately.

33. See Chapter 68, "*The Power of Now*."

34. Shikantaza is a Japanese translation of a Chinese term for zazen introduced by Rujing, a monk of the Caodong school of Zen Buddhism, to refer to a practice called "Silent Illumination" or "Serene Reflection" by previous Caodong masters. In Japan, it is associated with the Soto school.

This was the 1960s. I liked reading Alan Watts during that period, and Jiddu Krishnamurti. I was pretty much turned off entirely by the entire guru trip and kept my distance from it. Here's a bit of memoir on that theme:

In the summer of 1969, I went to visit some old friends in Taos, New Mexico. There was a whole group of friends there—all people who were native New Yorkers and had that kind of New-York-style practical skepticism. Taos was beautiful in that era. I recall days of eating peyote—someone arrived at the house with an entire pickup truck full (I think it was still legal in those days)—and walking to the hot springs, where dozens of beautiful young people cavorted naked and happy.

People were always giving things away: food, marijuana, clothing, whatever. Although I was reading Zen and Taoism, most of my companions were not "spiritual" at all. Because I would come forth with Taoist ideas, they began to call me "Cosmic Bob." There was one astrologer in the crowd who later became famous as a best-selling author on astrology, but I completely discounted astrology along with all the other mysticism in the air. I considered myself a realist.

Anyway, in that house, I was probably the most open to "searching for truth." The others, my best friends, were more occupied with love affairs, sex, drugs, R. Crumb comix, etcetera.

The house was a rented house, and one day a group of very serious-looking young people arrived and asked what we were doing there. My host, George Weiss, explained that he had the house rented for the summer.

The head guy of the other group became quite upset. Apparently, the house was the New Mexico ashram of Yogi Bajan (none of us had ever heard of him), and the Yogi was expected to arrive at any time. We would have to move out. "Impossible," said George.

A long negotiation. Finally, it was agreed that we NY people would use one part of the house, leaving the other part, including the kitchen, to the 3HO people, as they called themselves. Since

Bajan was expected to stay only three or four days, this seemed workable. We would cook outside, and spend most of the day in the garden, and they could have the house for their doings. All of us city people were learning to relax and be "far out," so it seemed to be the least we could do.

OK. Yogi Bajan arrived. A large, powerful-looking man with a nasty look in his eyes. He could have been a hit-man or an undercover cop. He wrote all of us off with a single glance and sat on the throne that had been prepared for him, surrounded by his adoring disciples. We retreated.

Over the next three days, I eavesdropped a lot. What I heard was totally shocking—and eye-opening—to me. Here was this guy with a gold Rolex on his wrist, giving orders to a bunch of poverty cases sitting at his feet: who would marry whom, who would get to rub his feet (considered a prime privilege), who would fetch his tea—just like some kind of pasha or potentate.

Later, I found out that he was a complete fraud who, in India, had not been a "yogi" at all, but some kind of corrupt government official.

67 - The chatterbox mind

Q: Thank you for *4T.* I resonate with the philosophy, for lack of a better word, embodied in it.

The one thing that vexes me is that I rarely dwell in the here-and-now because my mind constantly narrates events, ruining the direct experience. "Wow, what a beautiful day! Look at the clouds—they look like little sheep! And what is that guy doing over there?" Blah, blah, blah. I am definitely *not* in the zone, for when you are in it you don't know it. You can't say, "Hey, I'm in the zone."

Alan Watts has written: "You can only live in one moment at a time, and you cannot think simultaneously about listening to the waves and whether you are enjoying listening to the waves."

This is the problem of the "divided mind." As it seems that I cannot just will it to cease, do you advise giving no attention to the chatter and just getting on with it?

A: Hi. So you have become aware that your mind has a chattering aspect, and that vexes you because it keeps you, you say, from dwelling in the here-and-now.

I cannot agree with that statement. If the chatter is in the foreground, that *is* the here-and-now, *your* here and now. The "other" here-and-now—the one you *imagine* is being obscured by the chatter—is a fantasy; completely non-existent. Your here-and-now *is* the chatter. And what *might* or *could* be your here-and-now if only that effing chatter would stop, is the fabled pot of gold at the end of the rainbow.

When you fully acknowledge that—when you notice it and really *see* it—you *are* in the here-and-now. You may not *like* chatter. You may not like the headache you have either, or the bad diagnosis you just got from the doctor, but that's the way the cookie crumbles. You may not *like* this moment of awareness, but likes and dislikes have nothing to do with it.

You do not get to wait for a here-and-now you like and live in that one. That scheme is delusional. The only here-and-now is *this* one, in which you are reading words on a page—unless, of course, your mind is wandering and the squiggles on the page are not being translated into ideas. If it is the latter, your *eyes* may see the squiggles, but your *mind* is elsewhere.

No one is in control of this. Not you and not "Robert." But Robert *knows* that he is not making any of this be the way it is, and so he just takes what he gets, moment by moment, like it or not. Poor old simple-minded Robert. Ha, ha.

Awakeness is *not* "spirituality" in which one aims at an imagined "perfect" state that some saint or holy man attained and to which that purported "master" has marked the path. Awake means being with whatever is *right now,* without fantasizing about something better or more evolved.

It may be useful to notice the chatter, and to understand that chatter is not helping you. But if chatter is there, it is. Ah, well.

68 - The Power of Now

Q: I've read all your posts about spirituality on your webpage and elsewhere on the internet. Thanks for the great work, Robert. Thanks for your outstanding work in psychology too.

I've found some nuggets of wisdom in *The Power of Now*, but you dismiss it. Please tell me how it is an unworthy read.

A: Hello, and thanks. You are most welcome.

Except for a few brief quotes, I have not read *The Power of Now*, so I cannot criticize its content. My remark was not about any particular book, but about the way people like Eckhart Tolle sell themselves and their so-called "enlightenment" as a product: "You want to be enlightened too? Pay me."

I was only pointing to a book purporting to be about so-called spirituality with the word "Power" in the title as a flagrant example of the commercialization, commodification, and merchandising of so-called "Truth."

At that juncture, I am saying, any possible "truth" goes right out of it, no matter how good it might sound. Why? Because anything that might depress sales must be left out.

Too much actual "truth"—old age, illness, and death, for example—is unpleasant to hear, and will not sell books to the masses. *Power* sells to the masses—not the *absence* of power. Not the facts of the matter, not adumbrations of emptiness, and not the acknowledgment of existential ignorance and possible meaninglessness. No one is going to pay hundreds or even thousands of dollars to hear some guy on stage speaking *that* kind of truth. Only the best stand-up comedian can get away with that act, and he or she better be damn funny. George Carlin could get away with that.

Don't get me wrong. All of us must find ways of surviving in a material sense. It's in our DNA. So if selling water by the river's edge is someone's niche, well, we all have our niche.

Tolle, Deepak Chopra, and others like him are essentially entrepreneurs working the niche of "self-help." Perhaps they were once onto something profound, but that was long ago and far away, apparently. Presently, they are like showmen, in competition with others in the same game, driven by ambition, repeating platitudes, and lying to themselves about their motives all the way to the bank.

Forget those guys. They have their own problems, and you have yours. Awakening is not about hearing the next pointer from an "enlightened" expert—it is about noticing something yourself here and now.

I am not saying that Tolle, or Chopra, or whoever, never uttered a sensible word. Those two and others like them are well-versed in the classical truisms, and that same old wine can always be poured into a new-looking bottle. I'm saying that the entire style of presentation—biased towards sales—elides, however subtly, the tough stuff, and offers promises, self-help, and hope instead of hard facts. That may *feel* good, but usually, it just *deepens* the hypnotic trance that one needs awakening *from*.

I know some people imagine that my words about one guru or another amount to personal attacks, and feel that "teachers" should not be criticized. But that's not the intention. I couldn't care less about Eckhart Tolle personally. If I call these self-described teachers out by name, it's because, by promoting and commodifying their names, they have become public figures with powers of hypnosis. Pointing out their merchandising of perennial truisms, along with the hypnotic nonsense they teach on top of it, is my way of inviting people like that and their listeners to *SNAP OUT OF IT!*

To flesh out what I am talking about, you may be interested in this personal account from an intimate friend of Tolle's, who watched the whole Eckhart becomes Eckhart show from backstage:

> "Hi, Robert. I don't know where to begin to comment here. I am not exactly versed in this site and rarely do I participate in chat rooms. I just want to add some information about Eckhart Tolle here. I have read over some of the discussions with much interest.

I am delighted to see so much good common sense at work! For many of these suspicions are right on target.

"I have known Eckhart since the fall of 1993. I met him through mutual friends back in England. At the time, Eckhart was a nobody. But a nice man and extremely intelligent. He lived very modestly, after moving from London to Glastonbury where I met him, and he was just the nicest person. He went by this name way back then. As far as his real name goes, it is Ulrich and he changed it after that life-altering experience he had, during the many years that went by when he started to study spiritual thinkers like Meister Eckhart. I think he changed his name because he was drawn to that teacher. And he also wanted to break from the former, unhappy person he had been.

"As far as speculation about his past, he did attend Cambridge as a Ph.D. candidate in Comparative Literature. His emphasis was on Latin American Literature. We later reconnected when he came to Northern California, where I got to know him much better. His father, now deceased, lived in Mallorca. His mother, also now deceased, lived in the Black Forest, in Baden-Baden. He went to see them every year at Christmas. His dad was a real character—a free-thinker, a former journalist, who left Germany after he divorced Eckhart's mother, when Eckhart was about twelve or so.

"Eckhart is a very emotional and complicated person. Believe me, I knew a whole different side to him. Kind, thoughtful, and very sincere in his rich interest and devotion to spirituality. I recall, at a mutual friend's, he and I ended up having a five-hour conversation on everything from Latin American fiction writers to various mystics and eclectic thinkers. That conversation flew by. He is a very engaging, humorous and social person; and that came as a surprise because, normally, he seems so reticent and shy.

"Anyway, I remember when he was writing his first book. We were talking on the phone and he told me that he had started writing this book—all in long-hand, mind you. We continued to have a very pleasant friendship and, a year or so later, he ended up moving to Vancouver, BC, because it was difficult for him to emigrate to the US. He had no relatives here, and no real external purpose for coming here. He just wanted to try out the 'new world.'

"Again, he was such a pleasure to be around in those days. We also kept in touch when he moved north to Canada. He was funny, he was a joy to talk to, even on the phone.

"To cut a long story short, Tolle started out very modestly. Truly. A woman he met in a small class he was giving to business people in downtown Vancouver ended up speaking with him after class, and one day, Tolle asked if she would read his book, which was still in manuscript form. She did, and later he asked her if she had ever thought about going into the publishing business. She considered what he said, and they pooled money together. (He owned a piece of property in London, and I remember him going back to London at some point, so he could have some money to live on. He never really lived on park benches, by the way, but he did drop out of that graduate program and meandered around, with not a lot in the till, so to speak.)

"Once this woman had brought out his first book, things slowly picked up. Tolle made as many appearances as he could at every Canadian bookstore. He very gradually achieved his success. We kept in touch and, always, in the early days of his success, he was happy to get together with me when he was in the area.

"Without saying too much about myself, I too, am a writer, but I am not in his field. I am a fiction writer. Though Eckhart and I shared an interest in things spiritual and in literature, I would disagree with my old friend on many things, and I still do. Not that I outright told him this, but I never thought highly of the New Age/'feel good' genre. I am not a fan of these books, although I do think there are some exceptions, and I absolutely loved his first book, *The Power of Now*. I still think it's his best. I also think Eckhart is gifted in the way he gives his talks; some of them are amazingly brilliant.

"But I have to say, the last time I heard from my friend was several years ago, before things got to where they are today.

"Here it is: things have changed, and Eckhart has become obsessed with his own success and—I have to say it—monstrously so. He has shown a side of himself that scares me. He is determined to get as far up the mountain as he can go, surpassing his competitors like Deepak Chopra, Gary Zukav, and all those other souls who crank out these books,.

"I am afraid for him, and a little afraid of him. He is no longer recognizable to me. Some say this is not unusual for these guru types. That, sooner or later, things come tumbling down, thanks to a lot of hubris and just ego-overkill. That's right. Ego-overkill.

"Tolle and I were out one day and ended up walking into a bookstore where Tolle knew the guy behind the counter. I busied myself browsing the books, but Tolle came across with an arrogance and know-it-all-ness that surprised me. I had never seen this side of him before—but I blew it off and didn't give it a lot of thought, as he rarely acted this way with me. (I am a woman, by the way.)

"Now it seems Tolle is all ego. And yes, it is horrendously ironic how he has made the ego anathema, when he has become an ego-maniac himself. I am sad to see it all unfold the way it has. Sadly, being a true friend, a real friend, was not as important to Tolle as his voracious ambition.

"Let me tell you something. According to my own modest experience at being human myself, Tolle is very unhealed. I do believe he had that spiritual experience, that that's true—but the weird thing is, it didn't really change the core person. It seems that Eckhart was one of those 'knows it all' students; he is extremely smart, and that is the problem. He is arrogant if given the ground on which to become so. Know what I mean? When he was outside that academic milieu of a school like Cambridge, he was a nobody—and that was probably better for him.

"Let me put it to you this way: Hitler could have had a spiritual experience, but would his nature really have changed? I realize that sounds like a strange question. And, normally, people will assume that the person having these beautiful spiritual experiences is a good person—but you know what? It's not necessarily so. And I know this from so many years of knowing Eckhart. But I also know this about other spiritual teachers and their dark sides, and I am sure many of you out there know a bit about this, too.

"For example, Krishnamurti could be very curt with people on the subject of morality, especially young people. But also, there's a book that was written by the daughter of a woman who was Krishnamurti's secret mistress for many years and whom he treated abusively, punitively. There are people who will refuse to believe this—and I am sure there are those who will not want to see the truth about my old friend, Eckhart.

"But if I could continue, about this aspect of him being unhealed: in all my years I have come to see that there is a huge discrepancy between this 'spirituality' so many seem to be seeking, and unhealed inner emotional issues. It's strange. But the two shall never meet or mix. This seems to be very true about people, no matter what their spiritual path. And it's true about Tolle. He had a very complex relationship with his mother. His father was a much better parent to him, but his mother was another story. There were times when he spilled his emotions out to me, and what's become of him saddens me because he's really a very lonely person. An extremely, and I want to say, dangerously isolated individual, who has become worse, far worse, since he achieved fame.

"Eckhart tells the public that this woman Kim Eng is his 'partner.' She's not. She is more like a pupil and disciple. There is no relationship there except this 'arrangement.' She has been with him for many years, as an assistant and contact person for his trips and talks; and in exchange, he has shown her the ropes. Now *she* goes out and does these talks and seminars. It's odd, but I think Eckhart doesn't like women, or men, or anyone, really. Not enough to shack up with. Some have speculated about his past relationships. I know of a woman in London, I believe he lived with her when he was in his twenties. He is afraid, though, of women coming after him. And I really know about this. I am not just making it up. He has made some kind of arrangement with Eng, an agreement of sorts, so he could feel comfortable on a public level.

"He did seem to have an interest in me back in the early days, but nothing ever came of it. But it was very sweet and nice. Until fame got the better of him and he showed me that he was not going to do anything for anyone, unless it benefits him. This is all I can say.

"I think, though, that his unhealed issues are at the root of what motivates him in what has become a monstrously unfathomable ambition. ('Napoleon complex', anyone?) Frankly, he's a homely fellow. He looks like 'Despereaux the mouse.' He's a little guy, in a little body, with stooped shoulders, that no woman would bat an eye at back in the old days. Yes, he was a nice friend, but I had no interest in him otherwise. And I think he had a lifetime of that. He was 45 when I met him.

"The heart is a lonely hunter, 'spiritual teachers' notwithstanding. Ya know? Anyone remember the 'man behind the green curtain?' As in: 'I am Oz. And I am the all-powerful, Oz! No one dares go against the all-powerful Oz!' Now don't pay attention to that little man behind the green curtain! Of course, we all know what happened next."

69 - "Be here now"

Q: Robert, if our attention is on the senses, we are in the moment. If our attention is on thoughts, we are not in the moment. In human evolution, the brain expanded dramatically. With this new brain, we started having more thoughts, and more advanced thoughts. Our attention was drawn to those thoughts. So we evolved to be more not in the moment. If we want to be more in the moment, we just need to retrain ourselves to put our attention more on the senses.

A: I cannot agree. "Be here now" is an injunction against being lost in thought—not any kind of ultimate "truth". One may be lost in thought to be sure, but one may also be lost in sensing. I see no superiority to either of those two conditions. Lost is lost. The best case is when you are lost in neither, but simply open and present to whatever may arise, be it a thought, a perception, an emotion, whatever. That is when one is most alive, I say.

My friend Joan Tollifson has said that if we give "open attention to sensations rather than ideas, impermanence is quite obvious, not as an idea we logically understand, but as our direct experience." As I understood her, Joan was not recommending that one ought to *prefer* noticing sensations to noticing thoughts. She meant only that, for many of us, it may be easier to notice the fleetingness of sensations than it is to notice the transitory nature of thoughts, many of which, being habitual, seem "stickier" than sensations. This is particularly true of certain kinds of thoughts such as self judgments, anxieties, and fears, etcetera.

However, one might equally well sit quietly and observe the flow of thought—how a thought rises, unbidden, only to be replaced by the next thought, and the next, and the next... That flow is no different from the flow of sensations. They are, in fact, parts of the *same* flow, the stream of consciousness.

Sensations, perceptions, feelings, thoughts, emotions—all of it—are occurring constantly, whether noticed or not, and cannot be divided.

The idea here is to open one's eyes to the impermanence of all experience—including the experience of being "me."

70 - Source

Q: I was forced to attend a Protestant church till age fifteen. Around the age of twelve or thirteen, I realized that I couldn't believe in the stuff they told me. I had no idea if there was a God or not, and I found the rituals boring and painful (the singing was fun, though). For many years I avoided all religious institutions until I realized, maybe in my forties, that something was missing in my life, and I began my exploration of Eastern spiritual traditions, finally arriving at Advaita. I am aware that I'm aware, but not sure of much else.

After more years of exploration and confusion, I really enjoy your down-to-earth and clear writings about these matters. There is a question about a unifying factor in all we are, see, and experience. Many use the word "Source" for this. Do you have anything to say about that, Robert?

A: Yes. I see what I see and avoid "explanations" that are not explanations at all, but only hanging names on the unknown. Naming is *not* knowing. This is very important to keep in mind.

I don't know if there is a "unifying factor" or not. I am not sure what that would mean exactly. Things seem pretty well organized and entirely intermeshed on the organic side of life; and so far as we know, that reciprocal enmeshment was not "created" according to some "factor," but evolved by means of natural selection, independent of any "outside force" or "intelligent design." It evolved randomly, as what worked survived and multiplied, and what did not work died out.

Anyone can, of course, believe differently. People believe all kinds of things.

All of this is here, and no one knows anything further about that. The notion that whatever exists must have a source seems naïve, or just another pretext for getting the deities back in the picture, particularly Jehovah (by whatever of his many names) who "created the Heavens and the Earth," or that trio of heavy-hitting Hindu hipsters whose dreams sustain our world: Brahma whips it all up, Vishnu tries to keep it happening, while Shiva plays bad boy and keeps tearing things down.

And don't call those guys or Jehovah "metaphors." Metaphors for what? Why do you need a metaphor for what's right on the table in front of you?

But for the moment, suppose that all we see, feel, think, etcetera, does have one unified "Source." Then where did that source come from? What was *its* source? Oh. It was *always* here. Gotcha.

In that case, why not just forget all this speculation and supposition about "Source," and just say that all of *this* is always here?

71 - Wash out your bowl

Q: Hi Robert, I keep going back to this Zen koan that I read in *Zen Flesh, Zen Bones*. It goes something like this:

> A Zen student approaches his master dismayed at not being enlightened, and asks to know the meaning of Zen. The master looks at him and asks the student if he has eaten lunch yet. "Yes," says the student. "I have."
>
> "Well then," the master replies, "go wash your bowl." And the student became enlightened!
>
> I feel like this is a great pointer—would you agree?

A: Yes. I have quoted a version of it myself, but without the last five words, which are an unfortunate add-on that was not there in the original.

Q: Ha, ha. And that's the part that is most enticing to the mind.

A: Yes, like catnip to a cat. Awake is *right now*—not later, when I am "enlightened"—whatever the hell *that* is. That one *word*, the *E-word*, has confused countless people and continues to confuse.

Q: I'm one of them.

A: Well, snap out of it. Read my book.

Q: Now I see this and it cuts through the bullshit which obscures experience! Yes, I have your book and have started reading it. I am determined to finish it. I just have to see it through. Thank you again, Robert. Next time I reach out I will have read it all.

A: Enjoy yourself, amigo. You will never be any younger. Old age, illness, and death await us all, enlightened or not. One day you will wash out your bowl for the last time.

72 - *What is spiritual unfoldment?*

Q: I came across a piece of yours from 2005 in which you were asked about spiritual enlightenment and offered advice on certain practices. But in your newer writing, you seem to say that spiritual practices may be useless or even harmful. I wonder how you reconcile these two apparently conflicting points of view.

A: You are referring to an article on the old "ask dr-robert" webpage[35]. For those who are interested, I will include it at the end of this chapter.

So how do I reconcile two points of view, both written by me, that seem to contradict one another? There are so many good answers to a question like that. Walt Whitman just killed it with this:

The past and present wilt—I have fill'd them, emptied them,
And proceed to fill my next fold of the future...
Do I contradict myself?
Very well then I contradict myself,
(I am large, I contain multitudes.)

"The past and present wilt." Like cut flowers. I love that. And "I contain multitudes." That's equally wonderful.

Since that is my view to a letter, I could stick with old Walt, but I will be more specific. "ask dr-robert" was intentionally and unambiguously a page of *advice*—midway between self-help and psychotherapy, with a bit of philosophy thrown into the mix. People would write with questions about problems in living, and I would offer my best counsel from the standpoint of a clinical psychotherapist.

Nowadays, that is not my focus. If asked specifically about one issue or another, I might offer some advice, but that is rare and seems to be getting rarer. If the advice requested is "how to wake up," I have *nothing* to offer. I mean that literally. My advice is, "Depending on

35. www.dr-robert.com/questions.html

nothing—including what I say—find your *own* mind." You may find something in *your* mind about which I have never even dreamed.

"ask dr-robert" was very much in the mode of therapy, an outreach making use of my training to serve others who, for one reason or another, were without access to face-to-face therapy. That's not my focus now. In therapy, as in all the healing arts, the first commandment is *primum non nocere*—first do no harm—and I followed that injunction explicitly as "ask dr-robert."

Nowadays, I don't think that way. My current readers are not patients, and I do not intend to treat them as such. My writing these days is radical self-expression and unfiltered personal confession—a phenomenology of "Robert awake and unbound." I just say what I see, and the Devil take the hindmost. Many readers find that unvarnished candor refreshing, and some have even found it liberating.

Someone may feel injured by my words, but that's not my problem. It's not that I intend to hurt anyone—I'd rather not—but total, unadulterated honesty is all I have left these days. I cannot lie to myself, and don't want to dissemble, so true believers in this or that guru, path, method, or metaphysics might indeed end up feeling upended, lost at sea, and out of their depth. My own skirmishes with awake people used to leave me feeling that way sometimes. As I wrote those last words, my dear old friend, Bill Gersh, now departed, came to mind. Great artist. Wild spirit. We had some exceptional encounters that left me at times quite bemused.

Working at *helping* is a delicate task that deals with people who are somehow wounded and want to heal those wounds. We are all wounded in one way or another, it appears to me, but many of our wounds heal naturally, especially if one is lucky enough to have friends and lovers in this life. The psychotherapist sees cases requiring more specialized help, or provides a kind of friendship for people who otherwise are alone.

The worst thing a therapist can do is reinjure places that are already wounded so, in that work, there are limits to candor. A prime limitation demands that the therapist not reveal too much of his or her personal views and opinions. If, for example, the patient is religious, the last thing the therapist should do is manifest the skepticism towards belief in so-called "God" that is a routine aspect of my work here. If there are doubts about the deity, they must originate with the patient, not the doctor. Nor should the doctor be quick to agree with the patient's views, even if they comport quite well with his or her own.

A somewhat nasty joke on this point is heard in therapy schools everywhere:

> A patient is going on and on about his girlfriend and her faults. The therapist listens for a while, and then, nodding his head in agreement, says, "Yeah. I know, I know. They're all a bunch of bitches."

Actually, the first time I heard that joke, the final word was not "bitches," but you get the idea.

So clinical invisibility is a must, and I worked in that manner for years. But now that I am retired from that work, I find myself dealing not so much with especially wounded people who come to me for healing, as with bright, experienced people who come to me, it seems, to have their minds relieved of the idea that there is a "path" from here to here, or that "awake" is some exalted "state" that can be attained only by special people through great efforts.

Certain efforts applied in the right way at the right time may be useful, but may also delude. And as for the so-called "path," forget about it. If one exists, I've never seen it. You can do all the self-observation and self-inquiry in the world, or follow all the rules in the Eightfold Noble Path of Buddhism, and end up more self-hypnotized than before you began. From my vantage, that seems to be the condition of many of the self-appointed "teachers" of spirituality, nonduality, etcetera, and I am not afraid to say so.

This does not mean that the advice I gave back in 2005 was *wrong*. Actually, in retrospect, it seems good advice for someone who is just beginning to be aware that "myself" may be more than just the second-hand religion and acquired attitudes one was taught and now holds close as if they were "Truths." There's really nothing wrong with self-observation and self-inquiry, but just as I said fifteen years ago, they are not a one-size-fits-all prescription—and there is more to living—a lot more—than being "spiritual."

That said, here's the article in question:

ask dr-robert
Sunday, May 1, 2005

Dear Dr. Robert,
I have been following your advice on diet. I began this change ten weeks ago and recently noticed feeling much better than when eating in the old way. I am just happier, and I feel physically and emotionally lighter, just as you said. My thoughts are not so often depressive as they were before. So thanks for the advice.

Now I have another question. I noticed on your homepage that your site is dedicated, among other things, to "spiritual unfoldment." I would be very interested in learning more about that. Would you please explain what you mean by spiritual unfoldment, and please give some suggestions for spiritual unfoldment as you did for diet?

—T.H.G., Lahti, Finland

Dear T.H.G.,
Thank you for your letter. What I mean by "spiritual unfoldment" is the possibility of finding a center which is more than just "myself," a center which seems to embody a level of wisdom, empathy, creativity, humor, and joy that is missing in the ordinary, everyday personality; a center, I mean, that is not the outcome of thoughts, attitudes, and ideas, but that seems to exist *prior to thought.*

Once this center is somehow intuited by the ordinary self, "unfoldment" refers to the ever-expanding experience of finding meaning and value in living more from that greater center, and less from the demands of the everyday personality as it expresses itself in thoughts, fears, and desires. To put this in somewhat grander terms, that which is finite, time-bound, and subject to death, becomes aware in some way of the underlying ground of being, which feels infinite, timeless, and everlasting.

I say that this center must be *intuited* by the ordinary self because intuition is a faculty that functions beyond the regions of conscious thought, and so may provide a kind of bridge between thought and the underlying ground of being. I like to use the word "unfoldment," because it suggests that this process involves the unfurling or unwinding of something that is already present but needs to be opened up so that it may function to the fullest. If you have ever seen the leaf of a large fern uncoiling, this may provide a good visual metaphor.

Unfortunately, general advice on nutrition is easier to offer—and much easier to convey in words—than advice on fostering spiritual unfoldment. This is because dietary advice can be based on scientific research, and so can be demonstrated *factually* to the human intellect, while spirituality or spiritual unfoldment cannot even be *understood* intellectually, much less *proven* scientifically.

For example, we now know that substances in the cocoa bean provide a powerful antioxidant action that slows the oxidation and breakdown of HDL cholesterols, causing them to remain longer in the bloodstream. This is a *fact* which can be shown by means of exact measurement. Since HDL cholesterols are beneficial to the circulatory system, adding cocoa to the diet should benefit total bodily health; and recent studies demonstrate that this is true. Therefore, I would feel confident in suggesting that one consider adding a tablespoon or so of unsweetened cocoa powder to the daily diet, and unless someone is allergic to cocoa, this practice ought to work well for anyone.

But even assuming that one accepts that spiritual unfoldment exists and that trying to encourage it is desirable, and that advice on how to promote it can be conveyed at least to some extent in words—without knowing where you are in your *own* understanding and without hearing about your own specific attitudes towards the human experience of living and dying, it is difficult for me to suggest what *you, in particular,* might do next to "unfold" spiritually.

This difficulty in generalizing about inner life is one of the chief reasons why individual, personalized psychotherapy is so valuable. In private, and in an atmosphere of safety, acceptance, trust, and understanding, these subtleties may be entertained so that their finer nuances become apparent without the necessity of resorting only to words on a page, or to a one-sided talk to a general audience.

Numerous gurus, guides, and spiritual teachers—to say nothing about the gang of self-help authors eager to sell books—offer advice on this matter, but many of the people who come to me for therapy have not found such advice to be particularly helpful. In fact, some have found such advice to be demeaning, misleading, or confusing, and have come to psychotherapy partly in order to try to sort out the confusion or heal the damage.

This happens, I believe, because the advice of such gurus and spiritual teachers almost always refers either to some traditional religious practices which are to be followed more or less blindly, regardless of individual temperament or individual need; or else depends on what that particular teacher believes has been helpful in his or her own approach to spirituality.

But my experience tells me that each person must find his or her own way to "unfold," and that following a doctrinal religious system or the generalized advice of a guru is not likely to do the job. As Jiddu Krishnamurti put this, "Truth is a pathless land."

In my advice on dietary changes, I said, "Everybody is different, and every *body* is different, so without a private consultation, I cannot give you person-specific advice. But I will offer some general principles that can help almost anyone."

I will try to do the same here as regards to your question about spiritual unfoldment, but only with the understanding that—unlike my generalized nutritional advice—this advice about how to approach spirituality will certainly *not* apply to everyone; and that, without knowing you personally, I am able to speak only in the most general way. In fact, my suggestions, being generalized, may *not* be the best thing for you. Indeed, this is the point I have just made about the methods imparted, usually in an authoritative tone, by so many gurus, guides, self-help authors, and spiritual teachers. Therefore, please take what follows merely as suggestions to be tried out in the spirit of experiment—certainly not as gospel.

That said, one way involves working with two practices at once. The first requires an ongoing, honest, non-judgmental observation of one's own life, behaviors, and personality patterns, with a view towards feeling and noticing barriers to further psychological and emotional development—not, by the way, trying to *remove* the barriers, but just feeling and noticing them. The second practice is to ask oneself: "Who am I? Who is seeing, feeling, and thinking these things?" So I am recommending that you might like to combine two practices that seem to be helpful for many people: *self-observation* and *self-investigation*.

By "self-observation," I mean watching oneself as if one were watching a friend for whom one feels a certain affection, but whom one can see also with a certain detachment and objectivity.

For example: suppose that someone makes a remark that I find insulting, and I begin to feel angry. In *self-observation*, instead of focusing attention on the insulting remark and upon the motives of the person who made it, I will instead simply watch anger itself, as if observing a phenomenon that I want to understand better. So it is not the insult that I wish to focus upon, nor do I wish to prove to myself that the insult does not apply to me, nor do I want to focus upon the personality, motives, or possible character flaws of the person who made the remark. But rather, I want to *watch* anger as it manifests in my own habitual process of responding to perceived insults with anger and self-justification. That is why this practice is called *self*-observation.

And I will apply this same attitude of non-judgmental self-observation to all of my behaviors, thoughts, and emotional states whenever possible.

You might begin this practice by, for example, noticing your own tone of voice when speaking. Just *notice* it, without judging. Try this for an entire day, and see what happens.

By "self-investigation," I mean discarding the conventional and normal ideas that "myself" is my body, my name, my personal history, my membership in a family, my profession, my nationality, ethnicity or so-called "race," and approaching the question of who or what I am afresh. Simply ask, "Who am I?" without accepting any final answers. Just keep asking.

Perhaps these two procedures seem simple-minded, and, from a certain point of view, I suppose they are. But like my nutritional advice, you can try them for a while, and see if you like the results.

Be well.

73 - Isn't a teacher irreplaceable?

Q: You are the only person I've read and listened to who seems to be able to cut through my own peculiar brand of bullshit, so I'm hanging in, and I apologize for the odd rant or irrelevant comment.

My question is this: I've seen art that instantly moved me to tears, made my heart sing, transformed me somehow. However, when someone describes a work of art they've seen personally—not on a screen but in real life; a Van Gogh painting, for example—I can hear about their enjoyment, but I'm not moved at all by their description into my own enjoyment. Intellectually yeah, I grasp it. Aesthetically, I can see the painting online and appreciate it. But my heart hasn't leapt. I haven't felt that work of art loosen the moorings and set free something in me. Sorry, I can't even find words.

I can admire your photography. I can admire your words too, and those of a few others like Alan Watts, etcetera. But I'm not sure all the reading in the world makes it sink in—makes it *live* in the way I'm struggling to compare with art.

I found some words of yours discussing studying with Walter Chappell, the photographer and mystic known for his association with the work of George Gurdjieff:

> *The best a teacher can do is show, not tell. This awareness belongs to no one. It cannot be dissected or explained. Rather, I am that. We all are, if we only knew it. I suppose Walter always imagined this would happen, just as it happened for him after meeting Willem Nyland, and for Willem when he met George Gurdjieff. This understanding stays alive as it passes from living person to living person in ways that are beyond comprehension. The wheel turns, and we, the living, occupy the places of those who came before.*

I know you say, "Teachers—pfft!" and that you're a non-teacher (a play on words, I realize) —but you had Walter, Walter had Willem,

Willem had George Gurdjieff, and on down the line. It's clear that your writing does help us a bit to loosen the moorings to our antiquated ideas and false prophets, both in the external world as well as in our own heads. But truthfully, Robert, isn't getting knocked about personally by a teacher who is the real deal irreplaceable? Do you understand what I'm trying to say about art, and by extension, spiritual awakeness?

Thanks for tolerating my rather relentless inquisitions. I'd like to think that, on this remote island in the middle of the northern wilderness—where I'd get locked up for saying the words "I'm not a separate being"—I might just "fall forever" and get it, *really* get it. But maybe not. Thanks.

A: Good question. As you say, calling myself a "non-teacher" is wordplay, an old habit of mine, for better or worse. The interviewer asked me about nonduality, so I said I was a "non-teacher" of it. At the time of that interview, I had a few students but was feeling ambivalent about that entire setup, and so that wordplay involved a measure of ironic self-deprecation. Nowadays, I really am a non-teacher, in the sense that I do not see myself *teaching* anything, but only *reporting* phenomenologically on how it feels to *me* to be awake and know it; and what I see from that perspective.

My writing and conversations with people do not feel to me like "teaching," but more like self-confession or unbridled self-expression. It's almost embarrassing sometimes to be so candid, to strip myself so naked. Referring to oneself as "awake" can be seen as audacious—I get that; but I have found no better way to reply to questions than with the phenomenology of what I call "awake."

I do understand that people may learn things—or, even better, *unlearn* them—through hearing my words, but *what* they learn and *how* they learn it is a mystery to me. I have no method of conveying *my* experience of this aliveness to anyone else so as to alter *their* experience. I can talk about my experience, but cannot *transfer* it. Nor could Walter transfer his understanding to me. What I got from him, I got through observation, and a few words from him every now and again—not instruction or emulation.

Even if I do have something to teach, as others tell me I do, it is *not* "nonduality." Not only can I not teach nonduality, but nonduality is a term I would never even use, except to reply to someone who has used it first. Nonduality is fraught terminology, like the word "God." No one knows what it means, and yet people "believe" in it, and talk about it as if they did know. They even call their beliefs "Truth" with a capital T. That, in my view, is ignorance—not knowledge.

Regarding "I'm not a separate being"—a statement for which you say you might be locked up—that depends on how one regards "myself." For me, there is not a question of separate or not separate. I don't think that way. I have no idea what any of this is, how it got here, of what it consists—none of that. Yet I find myself *here*, willy-nilly.

We humans—some of us at least—are endowed with enough brain power and self-awareness to wonder deeply about life and death. We may pose questions about who or what "I" am, how to find meaning in the face of mortality, and all that jazz. But we are not, it seems, gifted with sufficient intellect to *answer* such questions in ways that truly satisfy. So, to reduce anxiety and fear in the face of the apparent lack of any overarching meaning, we find ways of occupying our minds with trivialities, false certainties, and bootless conjectures that becloud and obfuscate our existential questions. Carrying on about God, universal consciousness, Source, or nonduality is one of those ways of obfuscation, as I see it.

No one, I say, can actually *teach* you *anything* about what you "*really* are." That is the crux of my critique of spirituality in general: a hodgepodge of claims and conjectures with little or nothing to back them up. I cannot even show you the way out of that moronic mish-mash of mental models, or how to ferret out your *own* mind. But that is not to say that all mentoring is futile.

At the right time, some guidance might help, but not the kind of half-baked religious twaddle that has been imposed upon an entire generation of credulous seekers in the name of nonduality. I find all that talk a bit sickening. I can't listen to it. And the ones spouting it, although they may be surrounded by admirers, to my eye, most often appear obtuse, self-satisfied, and hypnotized—not "awake."

I understand that you would like to "*really* get it"—to feel, as I do, awake and free to live and die in each and every moment; to feel that "myself" is not a separate, freestanding being, but more like a flow composed of countless impressions, both conscious and unconscious, from which the faculty of mental self-consciousness confects a false sense of unity and permanence.

But what if you "really" get it already, and only elevate Robert's understanding and discount your own because you are expecting something "special" to occur when you *really* get it? That point hangs lots of people up. No one is coming around to pin a merit badge on you. No superpowers are conferred either. It's stark, this aloneness, and without fixed form, but beautiful.

Your metaphor about the difference between being moved by art and only having a work of art explained to you is perfectly apt. I can describe *phenomenologically* how "awake" *feels* to me. I can say that the suchness of each moment is all that exists as far as I know, and that "myself" is neither making it nor controlling it. But even the most accurate phenomenology cannot evoke the lightning bolt of direct understanding.

Suppose you'd never had an orgasm. Would the phenomenology of my orgasm do much for you? Nor could I help you experience the taste of a wild mango except by offering you one to eat yourself.

When I say "Teachers—pfft!" as you put it, I am not referring to everyone who ever opined on the question of who and what are we anyway. There have always been voices worth hearing on that question. I have mentioned some such voices that I have found meaningful, including personal friends whom I have quoted in these pages.

Since the publication of *4T*, I have heard from a number of people who said reading that book was the *causa finalis*—the last straw—that broke the camel's back of belief in "nonduality" and similar so-called "Truths" bandied about with preposterous certainty by so-called teachers. Yesterday, I had a long video chat with someone like that, a well-known author who told me that, since reading *4T*, his feelings of certainty and "Truth" had flipped upside down, leaving him quite at sea, and wondering if he has anything to teach at all. Honesty like that is admirable, so perhaps he can teach *that*, instead of propositions about "Love" or "God."

Referring to a letter that a reader of *4T* had posted on my Facebook page, saying that exposure to my work had "capsized his boat," this author confessed that his encounter with my ideas had been similar. He read the book, saw an interview on *Buddha at the Gas Pump*[36], and that was the finale: quite suddenly, he found himself *here*, without actually knowing *anything* or depending on the metaphysical ideas of others as if they were "knowledge."

As I have never met these people personally, those reports seem to suggest that being "knocked about by a teacher" is *not* irreplaceable. Perhaps "getting it" is not as difficult as it seems. Perhaps words alone—*if they are rightly understood*—can be powerful enough.

This is not to discount the value of a mentoring friendship. If there is real heart in it, that can be an amazing gift that comes around only rarely, like a great love affair. Now, having mentored others, I understand how deeply Walter and I inspired *each other*. Real mentoring is a two-way street. Walter has been gone for almost twenty years now, but I still recall the look in his eyes—serpent wise, with just barely enough kindness to make his gaze tolerable. So yes, that was a special friendship, but I wouldn't say that such relationships are *indispensable* to awakening. We have all heard tales of people who snapped out of the trance on hearing a bird singing or stalks of bamboo clicking together in the wind. No teacher needed.

When I mention that kind of spontaneous awakening, it's funny how many people hasten to discount it. That doesn't *really* happen, does it? Yes it does—often, I think. Sometimes it's just the briefest flash of a radically different perspective, lasting but an instant or two. In other cases, it seems to stick around longer.

One cannot, I am saying, *produce* that flash by trying. That is completely unfeasible. One might be able to *notice* such openings if and when they occur, apparently spontaneously. Openness to noticing them when they occur *without seeking* them or trying to *make* them

36. See https://BATGAP.com/robert-saltzman

occur is what I called, in the introduction to this book, "intention." I can't *make* the flash of awakeness, but perhaps I can intend to *notice* a "burst of reality"—a moment of non-hypnosis—if one should occur. A great deal of information flows freely in even a short episode of that kind, I find. Such "states" do not have to be constant or ever-lasting to be highly worthwhile.

By the way, this unnamed author is a close friend of one of the famous leading lights in the current spirituality scene and had always considered that fellow's teaching to be "Truth," or at least *pointing* to "Truth," but that's all down the drain now. He still regards his friend as apparently sincere, but feels now that the so-called "Truth" he teaches—that all *you* really are is only a reflection of universal consciousness—is more religious dogma than truth.

This is nothing personal against the famous teacher in question. He does seem sincere, which is a good beginning—but one can seem sweet, kind, compassionate, and all the rest, and still be hypnotized by beliefs masquerading as facts. Here in Mexico, the Virgin of Guadalupe hears sincere prayers and responds magically by personally protecting the supplicant against evil. Some of Guadalupe's devotees would give you the shirt off their back if you needed it. In that sense, they are lovely people, but I would not call many of them "awake" in the import of your question.

So when I say, "Teachers—pfft!" I mean teachers who have convinced themselves that *their* teachers or their teacher's teachers knew "Truth" and were able to pass it on to them; and that now they should *sell* to you what was *given* to them. It doesn't work that way. Find your *own* mind.

It doesn't really matter *what* a teacher like that has to say. If you *believe* it, so much the worse for you. Belief in the beliefs of another human animal is the death of intelligence, I say. The only actuality is what *you* think, feel, or otherwise perceive for *yourself* in the suchness of *this* very moment. Second-hand won't cut it. It's the orgasm we *really* need—not a movie of someone else's orgasm. The mango—not a painting of a mango.

This is not to cast blame on the famous teacher whom I have never even met, unless watching him ply his trade on video is considered a kind of meeting. But it is to affirm that *awake* is when you follow neither that guy—who is just another guy after all—nor anyone else.

The only "reality" is your *own* mind here and now. There is where sanity is found, I say, or it isn't. And please make no mistake about this: if you come to actual sanity first, and then want to explore the speculations of spirituality, no harm, no foul. But if you get that order reversed, you may spend a lifetime in a deep trance without even knowing it.

As for Walter, I never followed or imitated him. When we met, I was already a recognized photographer myself—New York shows, numerous publications, and all that—but Walter was a master of the black and white print and that's what I needed to learn. So, in the darkroom with him, I listened and observed with a beginner's mind.

It was much the same on the philosophical level. I'd thought and read a lot by then, but I was willing to listen and observe as if I knew *nothing* about anything. So yes, all that was helpful. The direct line to Gurdjieff was helpful, because there was wisdom there. And yes, a friendship like that can open vistas. But Walter would never have called himself a spiritual teacher, and *certainly* would *never* have claimed to know "Truth." He would never have uttered such foolishness, and I would not have listened if he had.

It's a joy and a privilege to hang out with an awake human being—someone who is open entirely to the never-to-be-repeated, once-upon-a-once suchness of *this* moment. My friendship with Walter was a revelation to me, always to be valued. But as to whether meeting Walter was *indispensable* to my own particular awakening, I cannot say. Such questions are purely hypothetical.

You have heard this before, but apparently have yet to see it in yourself: we are all awake *right now*.

That which is reading these words *is* "awakeness." It is only our searching for something "else"—something more "evolved," something that will allow us to transcend biology, and so evade mortality (as if one really could)—that occludes *noticing* the awakeness that is always present in us all, but often buried in a farrago of nonsense.

As for the last words of your question, I do not simply "tolerate" your relentlessness, but applaud it. If you are not easily satisfied by the stupidity that passes for "spirituality," I consider you fortunate.

74 - The artist versus the art

Q: Hello, Robert. You once said in an answer to me that the idea that "the messenger is not the message" is bullshit. If a teacher or guide, you said, isn't living what they preach then they should shut up, or words to that effect about walking the talk.

Now, you have quoted Alan Watts, and I love his words. Who couldn't? Yet the man died most likely of alcohol and tobacco-related heart failure, young, and, according to his son, apparently depressed at the time. Not so much about his diseases, but about an event he'd attended, plus perennial disappointment in the stupidity of people, the war… the stuff that depresses all of us who have the intelligence to see it.

Alan cheated on various wives. He tried to stop alcohol, apparently signing up for an LSD method of stopping drinking, but couldn't. Anyway, Alan seems to be a perfect example of what I'm trying to ask.

Beautiful art has been made by people whose lives were a mess, and now I learn that beautiful words were spoken by a guy who, according to those close to him, was quite a mess.

The world depressed him. It depresses me too. But he didn't write that way. His writing is so clear—"like a diamond" as you said.

So it seems the messenger and the message weren't entirely congruent. I'd love your feedback on this, please.

A: This is a great question, which must occur sooner or later to anyone who thinks about these matters.

A perfect example of the "artist versus the art" issue is the case of Richard Wagner, whose musical compositions many consider among the best of his era, but who coined the expressions "Jewish problem" and "final solution," by which he meant the mass murder of Jews and the complete destruction of Judaism; and whose work itself—for example, his ultra-nationalistic opera, "The Ring"—provided a substrate for Nazi ideology.

So, is one able to listen to the music itself without thinking about Wagner's anti-Semitism? I am no big fan of Wagner anyway, so for me, that question is moot. But suppose the answer is no—then what about Chopin? He was a rabid anti-Semite too. Personally, I would not spend half a minute listening to the *words* of a bigot, but I love Chopin's *music* and listen to it often. In fact, although I have heard them many times, if I am in the mood for a good cry, his Nocturnes can move me to tears.

I have no problem watching a Woody Allen movie either, or looking at a Picasso, but both of them, according to reports, had serious sexual abuse habits. Woody is alleged to have abused his adopted daughter, Dylan Farrow. As for Picasso, according to his granddaughter Marina, Picasso "submitted women to his animal sexuality, tamed them, bewitched them, ingested them and crushed them onto his canvas. After he had spent many nights extracting their essence, once they were bled dry, he would dispose of them."

As for Alan Watts, yes, he was an unhappy man. People tried to make a paragon and guru out of him, but he knew his weaknesses and was having none of it:

> *I want to make one thing absolutely clear. I am not a Zen Buddhist, I am not advocating Zen Buddhism, I am not trying to convert anyone to it. I have nothing to sell. I'm an entertainer. That is to say, in the same sense, that when you go to a concert and you listen to someone play Mozart, he has nothing to sell except the sound of the music. He doesn't want to convert you to anything. He doesn't want you to join an organization in favor of Mozart's music as opposed to, say, Beethoven's. And I approach you in the same spirit as a musician with his piano or a violinist with his violin. I just want you to enjoy a point of view that I enjoy.*

So, just as I am not a teacher or a guide advising people on how to live, or how to "awaken," Watts was not either. If I quote Alan, it is for his easy way of illuminating certain philosophical principles, not because he had it all figured out.

Now, you might ask, if I can separate Chopin's music from his bigotry, or Watts' understanding of Eastern thought from his alcoholism, why doesn't Bentinho Massaro, who came up yesterday, get the same treatment?

Very simple. When I listen to Chopin, I am not hearing any hate-speech. When I read Alan's exposition of Eastern wisdom, I am not hearing recommendations and instructions, nor anyone claiming to be enlightened. But Massaro, as well as many other self-described "teachers," are claiming precisely that: "I am enlightened, and I can teach you how to be enlightened too." In fact, Massaro goes a lot further than that. According to him, he is not just enlightened, but, having attained a level far beyond any previous enlightened being, he is totally infallible. This is extreme megalomania, a serious, dangerous mental illness.

As Carl Sagan said, "Extraordinary claims require extraordinary evidence." Good old Carl. A bright light *he* was. If you claim to be enlightened, walk the walk. *Show* me the enlightenment. And that you will never do—not by my lights anyway—by abusing and demeaning the people around you, by imagining yourself superior to them, by telling them that you came from another galaxy to save humanity, and, least of all, by devising ways of sucking as much money as you can out of them.

I love to be around people who would never claim to be "enlightened" but who are *awake* to their humanity and mortality and know it. In those folks, you see humility, generosity, and benevolence towards others. You can *trust* someone like that. As far as most of these internet gurus go, keep your wallet in a deep pocket, I say.

Q: Thanks for a great explanation, Robert. I also appreciate Watts, and never viewed him as a teacher, or thought he claimed to be one. But to take the conversation further, how do you feel about Trungpa in this respect? I know you appreciate his words, but his behavior toward his students was allegedly appalling; and he, being a Vajrayana Buddhist, advocated total obedience to the guru, i.e. himself.

A: Yes. That is a good question that does take this a bit further, for now, we must get into personality types, and what they can handle.

When I said that, in regards to spiritual teachers, it is foolish to separate the message from the behavior of the messenger, that was a kind of warning against imagining that other human beings are worthy of worship and emulation, and thus blinding oneself to plain bad behavior by imagining that anything the teacher says or does is part of the teaching. That kind of warning is particularly important for the natural *bhakti* type of person, who feels drawn to putting teachers on a pedestal, adoring them, and submitting to their whims.

For other types, that kind of warning is unnecessary. In my case, as a natural skeptic, I have never been tempted to worship anyone. The very idea seems absurd. Therefore, my essence-friend, Walter Chappell, who, like Trungpa, was a "crazy-wisdom" kind of guy, was a good fit for me. Walter drank and smoked himself to death. I emulated neither habit.

But I was never looking for a spiritual teacher, and Walter never claimed to be one either. He was very much like me in a certain way: he saw deeply, brooked no bullshit, and *that* was the wake-up. Sometimes he talked what to me seemed nonsense—the kind of stuff I call "magical thinking"—but I could, as the defeated Japanese said of the Christian missionaries who tended to them after WW II, "eat the rice, and leave the religion on the plate."

So if someone imagines that Trungpa was advocating drinking as much *sake* as you can and having sex with everyone you meet as a means to spiritual awakening, that's just pure misunderstanding. Those were *his* bad habits, not the teaching.

What I got from Trungpa was never "how to attain enlightenment"—which is what his lazy followers were trying to get—but a powerful warning against spiritual materialism which, for me, came just at the right moment.

I consider Vajrayana Buddhism to be a variety of superstitious nonsense, and would never advocate obedience to any "master." In this, I concur with Jiddu Krishnamurti: "Be a light unto yourself."

Q2 (*Anne Watts*): Thank you, Robert. I so appreciate your perspective on my father. I completely agree with you. I have always felt that Alan's work stands solidly on its own. People around the world have had life-changing experiences from reading or listening to his words. I know, because people tell me this all the time! He truly was gifted. I particularly like the comparison to Chopin, as he was a favorite of my father's too. His music was played often in our home. Alan was also a kind, caring, and deeply compassionate man. He loved life, good food (he was a gourmet cook), wine, women, and song! He loved to dance and to play.

He felt enormous pressure to support his large family and worked hard to do it. He became exhausted from all his traveling and lecturing. He was very human. As you say so well, he never wanted to be put on a pedestal.

Ram Dass once said to me, "Alan knew *it,* and knew that he, Alan, *wasn't* it." That landed well for me. Humans seem to have a need to idolize people. Then they are disappointed when they discover that those people's lives do not match their picture of who they should be—so then they knock them off the pedestal. Well, they never should have put them there in the first place!

It is my hope, that like the music of Chopin, Alan's words will continue to touch and expand people's consciousness for as long as humanity continues to exist.

Again, I really appreciate what you have written.

A: Anne, welcome. How lovely to hear from you. Thank you.

Your father was a wonderful influence in my life. I will always appreciate his clarity and sense of humor. We crossed paths, probably often—his houseboat, *The Vallejo,* in Sausalito was only a stone's throw from a boat I was living on in those days—but that was before I had much of a clue about any of these matters, and before I'd ever heard of Alan Watts.

I am happy to say that I never idealized your father at all. I just saw and loved the brilliance in his expositions of Eastern philosophy. Perhaps that is why I was able to glean so much from his words: I knew the whole time that Alan was human, just like me.

Q3: Robert, here is something I copied out of Alan's book *This Is It*, and have cherished for decades:

> *These experiences, reinforced by others that have followed, have been the enlivening force of all my work in writing and philosophy since that time, though I have come to realize that how I feel, whether the actual sensation of freedom or clarity is present or not, is not the point—for, again, to feel heavy or restricted is also IT.*
>
> *But with this point of departure, a philosopher is faced with a strange problem of communication, especially to the degree that his philosophy seems to have some affinity with religion.*
>
> *People appear to be under the fixed impression that one speaks or writes of these things in order to improve them or do them some good, assuming, too, that the speaker himself has been improved and is able to speak with authority. In other words, the philosopher is forced into the role of preacher, and in turn, is expected to practice what he preaches. Thereupon the truth of what he says is tested by his character and his morals—whether he shows anxiety or not, whether he depends upon "material crutches" such as wine or tobacco, whether he has stomach ulcers or likes money, whether he loses his temper, or gets depressed, or falls in love when he shouldn't, or sometimes looks a bit tired and frayed at the edges.*
>
> *All these criteria might be valid if the philosopher were preaching freedom from being human, or if he were trying to make himself and others radically better.*

Thank you, Anne, for contributing to this rich thread. And Robert, thank you for... everything.

A: You are most welcome, my dear friend.

Q4: I love this conversation as I have wondered the very same thing regarding Trungpa and Alan Watts. For me, Trungpa resonated, until

I read about his rather bizarre proclivities. Then the glass shattered and his message goes nowhere with me. That is true for me with people in general, be it authors, co-workers, etcetera. If I don't respect someone, I have a hard time hearing them. I am not saying that is right—it is just how it goes for me.

However, I think when it comes to spirituality, many people need their teacher to be perfect. That perceived perfection provides an anchor, and the justification for following the words and beliefs. I think that is why some people get fiercely defensive when it comes to criticism of Eckhart Tolle and others. If the glass shatters, then they may be left with nothing.

Q5: And methinks that's the beauty of the shattering: to be left with nothing. I sense this is the starting point, or the ending one, depending on the person. Often, they can't handle the "nothing" and jump like fruit flies onto the next juicy teacher, alas. But I'm not pretending to be holier than thou. I've landed on many a juicy "nothing fruit" myself.

Q6: Robert, regarding megalomania:

> *I am higher than Jesus.*
>
> —Adi Da

> *I am going to build a city.*
>
> —Osho

> *I am in contact with aliens.*
>
> —Marshall Applewhite (Heaven's Gate Leader)

It took years for these gurus to get to their full psychotic state—Bentinho has done it so quickly. Highly impressive.

75 - Ring around the rosie

Q: Hi Robert. I hope it's OK to contact you again. If you want to post this on your page, could you do so without my name, because it's a bit of a vulnerable share?

After our conversation recently, I realize how much I have held on to numerous beliefs about the meaning of life and the spiritual journey. You said, I think, that *The Ten Thousand Things* is a dangerous book (you might not have said it that way). Now I get that. I am left with nothing to grasp onto, a sort of sense of freefalling; or another way of putting it is I am left with no escape.

I find myself in a place of both grief and some liberation—although, in this moment, more grief than liberation. I scroll down Facebook and find post upon post about the so-called spiritual path, the soul's purpose, using astrology to make sense of where we are at in this time of evolution, etcetera. And I find myself seeing through all that as just more ways of escaping the fact of not knowing who we are and what is the meaning of this life.

So this leaves me with nothing to grasp onto. My whole adult life has been oriented towards a spiritual path. I mentioned I felt scared, a feeling of not being in control. It feels so primal. I am finally meeting the place I have always run from in my search for meaning. When I allow myself to just be here, I find some peace and deep acceptance of the groundlessness and uncertainty of being human, and even a sweet tenderness.

One of the ways the thoughts show themselves is trying to hunt for a future direction. I feel almost frantic when I can't find a way out or a way forward. I am here again with feelings of fear and not knowing. I am not even sure what I want to ask you. Perhaps I just want to hold your hand as I fall. If only to remind me that fear is OK, not knowing is OK, and everything passes.

Sending you much love and gratitude.

A:"I find myself in a place of both grief and some liberation," you wrote. Yes. Freedom and a kind of sadness go together, like love and tears. This is the kind of sadness that is called, in Japanese, *mono no aware*: a sensitivity toward the ephemeral. At first, this may feel like grief; but with understanding, grief is replaced by acceptance, and an appreciation of the gift of being at all. It is the feel-good stories aimed at *explaining away* tears and sadness from which one must be liberated—not the feelings.

I did say that *The Ten Thousand Things* could be dangerous if one is not ready to feel the emptiness that must arise when those feel-good stories are seen as the childish nonsense they are. Clearly, my perspective is not for everyone, but still, *4T*—which is about what Jiddu Krishnamurti called "freedom from the known"—had to be written.

I do not know your background, but let us suppose that you were raised to believe that Jesus loves you and awaits you in Heaven, so that your present life here on earth is only a kind of rehearsal; only a brief period of suffering and difficulty, after which you will live forever in a place of joy and endless happiness, accompanied by all the people you love now (and even, some people believe, all your old pets). The only requirements are that you believe this story by taking it on faith and that you follow certain rules, mostly about sex and other ordinary behaviors.

That may sound silly—but remember that countless human beings believe that story, and find, they say, deep meaning in following the rules, and in banishing from their minds any doubt or even the faintest suspicion that the Jesus story might be a human fabrication; that it has nothing to do with what awaits us after old age, illness, and death.

I know personally many people like that. I would never talk to them this way unless asked.

I cannot *prove* that the Jesus story is a human fabrication—after all, there *might* be a Heaven, and the son of God *might* be waiting there to reward you for a life of belief and rule-following—but you would need to be completely hypnotized and deluded to imagine that there is no doubt about that story. There *might* be a fairy at the foot of the garden too, or a unicorn in the next meadow.

That's just an example. The same applies to those who imagine that they are on a spiritual path that leads to "liberation." Liberation is only a name for and idea, like Heaven. All we ever know is *this* moment—not some imaginary future time in which one is free entirely of pain, grief, and sorrow. Such a state of complete isolation from ordinary human suffering may be as imaginary and unreal as eternity in Heaven with Jesus; or it might be psychological dissociation, an indicator of mental illness.

So here I recommend that you put the idea of "liberation" out of your mind entirely, and in each moment, be as you are. Just see what you see, feel what you feel, and think whatever you think. That is the best liberation I know: forget the high-flown ideas, and just be yourself.

If you live for the future, you will never find the ground of your *own* being, which is always only now. And if there is any "liberation," it must, I say, be founded on *that* ground—not upon some fantasy put in your mind by others about a so-called "spiritual path."

The grief you feel is the price one pays for snapping out of the hypnotic trance, the belief in some ultimate meaning that is not here now but which will come to us eventually. Sooner or later we must grieve everything, for everything will be lost—our youth, our friends, our loved ones, our physical powers, and eventually this aliveness itself.

You say that perhaps you wrote to me as a way of just holding my hand as you fall. We are all falling:

Ring–around-the-rosie,
A pocket full of posies,
Ashes! Ashes!
We all fall down.

We are all in the same boat, it appears to me. Perhaps seeing *that* is a *kind* of liberation. In my view, we are all human beings who have no way of knowing the ultimate "Truth" about anything, or even if there is any such thing as ultimate truth. And so, as we are all in this together, we might as well be holding hands.

You are doing just fine, it seems. Just hang in there. Clarity is always right here for the seeing. Let it be. I wish you well.

Q: Thanks for not holding my hand, Robert. I have fallen into my own seeing and authority.

A: Aha! Brilliant!

76 - A teacher exploring his sexuality

Q: Hi, Robert. Recently you came into my life, and I have read your book. I am currently reading it aloud to my husband, who is similarly blown away and grateful for the freedom it is revealing in us. The navigation markers of subtle beliefs in spiritual concepts we had not even considered questionable are collapsing. The cozy warm blankets of beliefs in *sangha*-family, the future enlightenment carrot, and even life after death have dissolved, leaving us sort of blinking, as if walking out of shade into sunlight.

I am 51 years old and have a lifetime of being involved with the spiritual search and gurus. I took *sannyas* with Osho/Rajneesh when I was 18. I married a man who became a guru/cult leader after an "awakening experience" soon after we got married, and I stayed with him for twenty years because—well, I thought he would outgrow it, and I wanted to protect my kids from his brainwashing, which I couldn't do if I wasn't there. Behind the scenes, I saw that this little emperor had no clothes and I told him so frequently, but it never made much difference.

I maintained a separation from that whilst living in that situation for years. However, now I see I was just as gullible in my own spiritual journey, giving away my power to other teachers I considered more worthy, clear, and enlightened. I was involved with an American woman teacher in an Indian lineage. That made for a lot of confusion, as my sincere, deluded heart wanted to be such a good disciple. But taking on the beliefs and customs of the traditional Vedic Indian culture that she taught never sat right with me, so I felt two-faced a lot of the time—I was there for the parts that did resonate, and sitting in cognitive dissonance with the rest.

I have also been involved for twenty years in the neo-Advaita lineage through a particular teacher who I always felt was very free of cultish behavior. He always said he was not a teacher, and always seemed so clear and free to me. Recently—and this is what probably led me to your book and your Facebook page—I have become disillusioned as this teacher explores his sexuality through members of his *sangha*, particularly with much younger women. While he is transparent about it, and says that this exploration and inquiry is valuable in our repressed culture, I find it hard to reconcile this behavior. But I'd put him up on a pedestal in the first place, and there he would have stayed forever if not for this. So in a way, his humanness is setting me free.

So the whole spiritual construct is collapsing and dissolving now. *The Ten Thousand Things* seems to have that effect. I feel grateful to fall back into *this* moment as home, after being "out there" searching so hard for so long. What a relief! I was so lost in concepts and the momentum of a spiritual path that gives so many amazing experiences that I had forgotten what I was even searching for. I remember now: freedom.

A whole lot of searching has just dropped away. I keep catching the tendrils of belief in this illusory spiritual path that are still lurking in me. I am no longer interested in spiritual experiences, or highs, or energy release, or any of it, not even "healing." Even the ideas of becoming more loving, more aware, more accepting—which seemed so obviously important and motivating before—now are seen as toxic in a way. No more becoming.

Thank you, Robert. It seems that the message of freedom you naturally live and are now sharing in your own way, is needed and wanted, by some of us at least, and the time for gurus is ending. I had heard that before, even my teachers had said it, but I didn't really know what that meant for me before. I'd been thinking that I was already pretty free. Thanks for being here, just by being yourself, so that this can keep disintegrating.

A: What a beautiful letter. Thanks for that. I am so glad to hear that *The Ten Thousand Things* has found its way into your world.

There is no freedom in any aspect of that guru trip, but only the continuation of subservience to the same old hierarchical structures one sees everywhere in human culture: the main guy or gal—the one with the supposed power, the charisma, the magnetism, the authority, the mystique; there are many names for it—ensconced at the top, and the miserable wannabes clinging to their particular rungs on the ladder ("At least I'm not at the bottom"), trying to satisfy themselves with the fantasy that all this rigmarole is "leading somewhere."

Nothing is leading anywhere. Nothing is becoming anything. This is it. Here and now.

Depending on nothing (no-thing) may feel sweet and free at times, and lonely and difficult at others. Perhaps the "amazing experiences" are not so enticing once real understanding dawns and they are seen to be passing phenomena, but at least the lies and self-deception about life after death and all that have come to an end.

The promise of walking a path towards an improved future may feel exciting at times, but the better future is only an aspect of the hypnotic trance in which one is always aiming at goals. The "amazing experiences" are part of that trance. When awake from the trance, every moment—the mere fact of being at all, and that there is something rather than nothing—is *beyond* amazing or any other adjective. Whether they know it (the scoundrels) or not (the self-deluded), *the trance itself* is what spiritual teachers have to sell, and the promises, procedures, and instructions are the techniques of hypnotic induction.

To be clear, there are and have been teachers who do not fall into either category. People like that are not profiteers, nor are they self-deluded. But those are rather rare birds in my view. I have mentioned a few like that in this book.

As for your teacher who is collecting the sexual benefits that accrue to those who sit at the top of any particular hierarchy—artistic, athletic, economic, political, spiritual, whatever—I don't know if he is a scoundrel, or just confused and self-deluded, but either way you seem to be cutting him too much slack.

That behavior is not what I would call "exploring his sexuality through members of his *sangha*," as you have characterized it. Such verbal delicacy often obscures what is really going on, so let's call a spade a spade. Old guys with clout can always arrange to exploit for their own pleasure as many nubile women—or handsome young men for that matter—as they desire. Exploration is one thing, and exploitation quite another.

I wish you well.

77 - Hypocrisy in India

Q: I am from India, belonging to an Indian orthodox community called Brahmin. I have seen all that *bhakti, vedanta, dvaita, advaita*, yoga, etcetera. I have grown up hearing Vedic mantras everyday chanted graciously loud at home. I love Sanskrit for its musical mesmerizing sounds. I know what it means too. Most of us know in India.

We call our country "*punya bhoomi*"[37], so it should be a land of awakened minds. I feel extremely sad and guilty to say that it is not a land of awakened minds, but a land of hypocrisy and perversion. Is that not evident from the number of visa applications being launched every year to leave India and live elsewhere? Many Indians do not want to live in our *punya bhoomi,* our sacred land of grace, including me myself.

In just an hour, if one happens to be an Indian among Indians, one can see so much hypocrisy, so much deceit, competition, envy, materialism, comparisons, bragging, and what-not, in every single statement they make. Can we then say such Vedic practices and religious rituals, and all the religious books, have helped these poor individuals to awaken themselves?

Decades of such practices. God-fearing minds. Yes, they fear God, but it's all mere conditioning. A herd of sheep *they* are. Nothing more.

They treat their fellow human beings so badly and then go to the temple. Do you think they confess there? No. They pray for more wealth and prosperity—not for others, but for themselves. None of them has a proper understanding of anything they do. They chant mantras, do *puja*, and worship—not to say thanks to their God, but only to ask for more for themselves alone. Incredibly spiritual souls *they* are.

So I see Robert talking only realism, not condemnation. I don't hear him imposing disbelief but only sharing his perspective on belief

37. *Punya bhoomi*: the sacred land.

and disbelief. I am not blindly condemning spirituality and religion either. I have seen it all, but by choice have kept away from it since childhood because I saw the hypocrisy. I saw that they were cheating themselves, and I felt angry at that. When I first saw that, I was only a child, but I strongly felt so, and I don't repent a bit now for that understanding.

A: Thank you for that. You have understood my intention perfectly.

The Westerners traveled to India in search of so-called "spirituality," and somehow ignored the poverty, the violence, the subjugation of women of all castes, and both men and women of lower castes, as if none of that hypocrisy existed; as if all that ugliness were not connected at all to the religion that underlies it and justifies it. The Western seekers, besotted by the images of jnanis and masters, saw only "transcendence," which they clutched at the way an addict clutches at drugs. Some of them brought the "transcendence" home with them and began teaching it to others—for money, by the way, although they had paid little or nothing to receive it. As you said so well, my friend, "Incredibly spiritual souls *they* are."

I should add that I grew up in the USA, and saw, even as a young child, the same hypocrisy among so-called "people of faith," Christians and Jews, as you saw among the Hindus. I know that India is a sad place in many ways, but insincerity, double-dealing, and sanctimony are a problem among religious people worldwide, not only in your troubled country.

I wish you well.

78 - The grammar of awakening

Q: I love you, Robert. I really do.

Gravity has laws, and there is a grammar to language. So does awakening have any grammar? A guide like you probably modulates energies and helps with awakening. But what does the one *seeking* to awaken have to do? Is there an equation X+Y=Z, or is it just like a game of roulette? It happens if it happens, and you can buy lottery tickets or not buy them. And if you hit the jackpot, you were supposed to hit it.

A: It happens by luck, or what people foolishly call "the law of attraction"—which is another name for the same thing, but a poor, misleading name.

It is a poor name because it suggests that one can *manipulate* luck by following a so-called *law*. That nonsense was monetized up the kazoo in the bestseller called *The Secret*. For promoting such drivel, Oprah Winfrey should be sentenced to ten years on Wiseacre Island in solitary confinement—alone except for Deepak Chopra, who will give her lessons in quantum mechanics to help kill the time.

Luck *has* no laws except the laws of probability. No matter how my luck goes, it is highly improbable that I will live to be 110 years old. And regarding the supposed "law of attraction," *visualizing* myself at 110 will not make living to that age one whit more probable. Sorry, too late to ask for your money back from the bookstore, but *The Secret* might make a decent doorstop. And the Deepak book you are using as a doorstop now can be moved to the table. It'd be perfect as a trivet.

I call my present situation "luck" because I did not choose my genetic inheritance, the country where I was born, the historical era of my birth, my parents and other earliest influences, the neighborhood where I grew up—none of it. All of that came upon me like fate. There is no *choice* involved in any of it, nor any basis for praise or blame. If you find yourself at the moment in a favorable situation in life—lucky!

What is, is, and arises as it does.

When I say that our luck seems to come upon us like fate, I do not mean that some supernatural power is in charge of events, like the preordination of the Calvinists or the predestination of the believers in karma. I would never say that you hit the jackpot "because you were *supposed* to hit it." That word "supposed" could be confusing to someone such as yourself who wants to explore these matters, implying, as it does, a kind of metaphysical causality that may not pertain at all.

I just said, "someone such as yourself who wants to explore these matters." Why do I assume that you really desire to explore this; that your luck, the luck of DNA, your family of origin, later influences, and all the rest includes being *attracted* to exploration? I assume it because when you said you loved *me*, what I heard was, "I love what you are *saying*. I love hearing the *words* you speak." See? That's what I mean by luck. Most human beings will never even *hear* words like these; and of those who do, most won't understand them. You cannot *make* yourself understand. Nor can you make yourself stop believing in balderdash with blinders on. If you do stop believing in nonsense, it's just good luck.

I'd prefer to say that, if there are jackpots to be hit, *someone* is going to hit them. If it's you, you were lucky that way. If it's the other person, she or he had the luck this time around.

Nevertheless, you would have to be a lot more than just lucky to win the lottery without even having *bought* a ticket. What would that entail? You just find a loose ticket on the street *and* it turns out to be the winner? Well, I suppose that *could* happen, but what are the odds?

That's what I mean by probability. You *could* hit the lottery that way, but buying some tickets every week would increase the odds markedly, I'd say. However, buying tickets cannot *cause* you to hit the lottery unless you buy them all. This may seem a fine distinction, but *causality* is right at the heart of your question, so ponder it.

Finally, I am not "modulating" any energies, nor managing anything else here. This page is an honest record of my own musings on life and mind—not a set of instructions for others. If you are helped by this page, I am happy to hear it, but that is not my intention. I worked for years in a helping profession, so I do know the difference. For me, this page is an art space, a play space—a kind of scrapbook open to inspection and commentary by the public. That's how I use Facebook.

Q2: As usual, Robert, clear and simple. One thing could be confusing: buried in this is the idea that probability can be improved—buy more tickets and improve your chances of hitting the lottery; take certain steps in your lifestyle and improve your chances of living until 110. Many of your readers honestly want to know what they can do to improve their chances of "awakening," and an awful lot of the conversations here pertain to that question. I think you know my answer, but I'm not sure—despite all the different ways you have said it—that they all comprehend *your* answer.

A: Good old Lao Tze pointed to the contradiction involved in speaking of these matters, and here I am 2,500 years hence screwing it up even worse than he did. A lot worse. Lao Tze had the virtue of being vague and ambiguous and of speaking in generalities, not about himself—whereas I seem to gravitate toward subjective phenomenology and personal confession. And yes, it's a conundrum: no one will *ever* understand except those who already do or, at least, are just on the verge of understanding.

Q3: Hi again Robert. I trust life is treating you well.

My own path has been one of facing and dissolving emotion, making it conscious. And I suppose that would be like buying a lottery ticket to increase one's chances, instead of just hoping to find a winning ticket lying around somewhere. Perhaps the more one faces and dissolves emotion, the more lottery tickets one is buying.

Despite your many assurances that it would be fine, I don't feel it's appropriate to be seen to be contradicting you here in your own group. And if I was persuasive enough (ha, ha)—and anyone in your group liked what I said—surely it would only confuse them.

So I just wanted to touch base with you here, to again offer an alternative experience: that there is indeed something one can do to further so-called spiritual development.

What do you think?

A: Hi, and thanks for the good wishes.

From time to time, an urge to stop lying to yourself may arise—not that you *make* it arise: it just does. Then, instead of brushing it away, you notice yourself honoring that urge and entertaining that urge until it becomes an *intention*. This is an extremely subtle matter, and I don't want to imply that one can *choose* or decide to have an urge to stop lying. The urges we feel are not something that "myself" *does*. But if the urge should arise, perhaps it can be noticed, honored, and entertained, until it changes from an *urge* to stop lying to oneself into an *intention to* stop lying to oneself. And perhaps the noticing, honoring, and entertaining of that urge is akin to buying a lottery ticket instead of just hoping to find one. Who knows? I don't. I am just spitballing here.

As for contradicting me, no worries. I have no desire to express my views in a sheltered milieu. Surely not everything I say is perfectly true and error-free. If someone can show me where I have gone astray, so much the better for me. So feel free to tell me what you see.

I won't debate these matters, but as long as you aren't preaching or talking absolute rot, I *will* listen. The few times that I have blocked someone from posting here were not due to disagreement with me but to disrespect or lack of ordinary civility, which I do not tolerate.

As for someone in my "group" becoming confused if your objections happened to sound persuasive, I don't have a group. I have readers and fans of my photographs but—unlike you—I have no students, and don't want any. This page is a space for the expression of my views on life and mind and replying to questions, not tuition.

I am willing to say that I am awake and to go into what I mean by that but—other than clearing the ground of the hype of so-called spirituality—I do not have the foggiest idea of how to *teach* "awakening."

From my perspective, much of what people call "spirituality" appears as fear-based nonsense, and I am willing to specify, including naming names if that seems warranted. If hearing my perspective provides a "snap out of it" for someone who is lost in the bewitchment of becoming something that one now is not, wonderful. But beyond that, I have no wake-up magic to offer.

To be clear, I was not saying that *awakening* occurs only through luck. I was saying that *everything* occurs only through luck. To put awakening in a separate category only beclouds the matter.

Now you might disagree with the idea that whatever occurs is due to luck alone. Perhaps you object on the grounds that, without effort, nothing that one desires to happen will happen. You might say that, even if effort will not *ensure* the occurrence of some desired outcome, surely effort will make that outcome more likely than if one made no efforts.

That is a familiar argument among spiritual teachers whose stock in trade, after all, is offering their students methods and procedures aimed at "awakening." The noted Buddhist teacher, Jack Kornfield, made that argument quite cunningly when he wrote, "Enlightenment is an accident, but spiritual practice makes you accident prone." That may be true, or perhaps not. Elsewhere in this book, you will read the backstory of that epigram[38].

Frankly, I have known many spiritual practitioners, both students and teachers, and only a very few of them were what I call "awake." The rest seemed hypnotized by the quest and the special feeling of meaning that following a path seems to provide in a life that otherwise might seem to lack meaning.

In my experience, religion and spiritual practice seem often to serve as a hiding place for people who are disinclined to notice the apparent emptiness and existential pointlessness of the human condition; a defense, I mean, against finding oneself *here* without knowing how or why, with the "meaning" of this aliveness blowing in the wind. So, if so-called "spirituality" provides a way of avoiding that rather obvious observation, perhaps spiritual practice works *against* awakening as much as or even more than it does to foster it. But that is

38. See Chapter 60, "I still suffer."

a different question.

The point of the post about which you are asking was this: you may find yourself seeking enlightenment, or, as in your case, teaching others how to be enlightened. But if you do, that role in life came to you entirely by chance, as I see it. You never *chose* it, although you may be convinced that you did.

Seeing choicelessness is the very essence of what I mean by "awake." If you don't see that—that there is no *doer* of all this, no *chooser*, no decider—I don't know how to make it clearer.

Do you not see that, if you had been born into different circumstances, you might be making other efforts entirely, and making those efforts would seem natural—as natural as your effortful career as a spiritual teacher does now?

Perhaps you would be a one-star general in Iraq, or a drug dealer in Bolivia, or a woman giving birth to her tenth child in Somalia. It's *all* luck. Can you really not *see* that? How can you possibly *miss* seeing it? If you desire to be "enlightened," that desire is nothing you ever *chose*. You either have that desire or you don't. I don't know how to make this any plainer.

79 - A Course in Miracles

Q: Hi Robert, thank you for your book: I am halfway through it and I like it.

I am an alcoholic and addict. I went through 12 Steps in "The Big Book" of Alcoholics Anonymous, and found God for the first time in my life.

I used to call myself an atheist before my spiritual searching began. When reading your posts and your book, I find myself back where I began—without a God.

I pray and read and do the lessons in *A Course in Miracles*. Am I self-hypnotizing? I have read plenty of other "spiritual" books, but lately mostly *ACIM*.

A: I'm happy to hear you are enjoying *The Ten Thousand Things*.

I don't know anything about *ACIM*. I know it is a book used for self-help, but I have not read it, nor have I ever spoken with anyone about it.

If you were being harmed by drugs and alcohol, and now have found a way to live without them, good for you. If belief in God is part of that, I would not judge it. Even if that belief is only a magic feather—like the one Dumbo held in his trunk in the conviction that the feather allowed him to fly—magical thinking like that may be preferable to a life impaired by drugs and alcohol. Perhaps one day you will find yourself as neither an atheist nor a believer, but just here in *this* present moment—which is what *4T* is all about, God or no God.

As for self-hypnosis, most of us are at least somewhat self-hypnotized. Lying to oneself is a common and ordinary human manifestation. I have known only a very few people whom I considered *wide*-awake, by which I mean living with a "beginner's mind"—living without beliefs of any kind and not lying to themselves.

Just as you used alcohol and drugs to deal with the pain and fear of being a human animal in an insecure world, people use *ideas* as drugs. Knowing what those ideas are without judging them will allow them to fall away naturally in their time.

I wish you well.

Q2: Early on, about 40 years ago, I was asked for my opinion on *ACIM*. I was provided the original manuscript prior to copyright. I met the author, Helen Shucman, and was invited to participate in the first small group to try it out as a class, hosted by the J. B. Rhine parapsychology folks at Duke. Later, I was a key witness in a trial over copyright infringement and was witness to the greed and infighting as the lawyers got involved.

A Course in Miracles is Advaita Vedanta in Jesus-speak. It is now a big book business competing with the Bible. *ACIM* is the same old wine in a brand new bottle with belief in a brand new version of Jesus. The material is not subject to editing, even though it had to be edited in many ways during the legal battles.

Robert's book, *The Ten Thousand Things*, is a far better book in my opinion. Robert doesn't mind removing the spiritual pacifiers without providing replacements.

A: Thank you for that, John Troy. You really are the Zelig[39] of modern spirituality. Always on the scene in one way or another. Yes, that's the idea: no escape hatch.

Q3: I don't want to offend anyone here, but I read the book about Helen Schucman and her so-called "scribing" of *A Course in Miracles*. From what I have read, it appears to me that most of the teachers, the writings, the courses, and the books are all somewhat mad. I mean *loco* to a degree beyond just a bit fucked up, which no doubt we all are some days, but truly mad. The emperor is butt naked from where I'm standing. Am I too cynical, tainted by my own hubris? Perhaps. But hey, I just checked and the emperor's butt is shining like the autumn moon.

39. *Zelig*: a 1983 American mockumentary film written and directed by Woody Allen, in which Leonard Zelig is a nondescript enigma, who seems always to be on hand for important events with famous people.

Anyway, soon after he'd published *The Power of Now,* the Jungians in Toronto invited Tolle to talk to them, not in public, but in a closed meeting of Jungian analysts (that's a scary thought—ha, ha). And afterwards, they all concluded he *was* genuinely mad. Then he got famous.

I'm wondering, if enough people believe you're awakened, can that *make* you awakened? Some people say all of reality is a kind of collective projection, an invention of mind, so could the "enlightenment" of a guy like Tolle be due to the power of group-think? My gut feeling is that fame, and perhaps the need to play the role of a celebrity so as to keep the ball rolling, makes those poor mad souls even madder, and even lonelier.

Once the teacher has been outed, those who want to defend him say, "The messenger is not the message." Really? I'm curious what others think. Does it matter if the emperor is butt naked? Should we just "take what speaks to you and discard the rest?" Isn't that a big waste of energy, and wouldn't we be better off looking up at the real moon? What are your thoughts, Robert? My copy of *4T* is in the mail which is slow here, so perhaps all these musings will be addressed in its pages, and hopefully no photos of emperors' butts.

A: That's a really good comment, replete with meaning and important questions for those who follow teachers they imagine are "enlightened."

To see that a human being who calls herself or himself "teacher" behaves not just in a manner that belies any claims of mastery or knowing "Truth," but in ways that would not befit even an ordinary human—and then to argue that the messenger is not the message—is pure denial fueled by attachment to a fantasy figure. We are, I say, all just human here. Yes, there are some of us with real understanding and useful ideas to share, but no gods walk the Earth—not even demi-gods.

There are some self-proclaimed experts in so-called spirituality—Ken Wilbur for example—who assert that someone can be spiritually advanced (whatever *that* means) but childish on an emotional level. I don't buy that for a minute. That view is what I call "splitting", which is an archaic psychological defense mechanism, not a reasonable way of regarding human psychology. If "advanced spirituality" is not about sanity and know-how in the art of living, including regarding self and other with compassion and kindness, then what could it be about?

If the teacher's message cannot even heal the teacher's *own* mind, how can it ever help the poor hypnotized student? This is not a moral judgment, but a practical question.

Q4: Well, I learned a lot from *A Course in Miracles*.

A: Please say briefly what you learned. I have no idea what is in that book.

Q4: Yes. Where to start? There is one mind and we are dreaming a dream of separation. Like a pane of glass that shattered into billions of fragments. We are the dreamer. Time is a concept of the mind, as well as space and all the rest. To undo the separation, the *Course* uses the process of "forgiveness"—which basically means seeing that, in the dream, there is an illusion of a right mind (love, oneness, peace, "Jesus," "Buddha") and a wrong mind (ego, guilt, fear, sin) and a decision maker, which is the mind deciding how to interpret the events that seem to be happening "right now."

As we let go of guilt, judgment, fear, etcetera, we spend more time identifying with the peaceful, loving part of ourselves. But there is lots of resistance to this because we are letting go of the *ego*, which is also an illusion. It's *all* an illusion, that gently and naturally dissolves as fear abates, and we realize we are home in our Self and we never left.

I'm not sure I answered your question. Basically, it's we are One—including a chair, a rock, everything we perceive. There is no hierarchy of illusions. We all come from the same source. So everything we do or think or see *is* us. Man, this is hard to articulate. Basically, the fundamental metaphysical teaching is "Nothing happened" and "The world is a maladaptive solution to a non-existent problem."

A: Well then, you have come to the right place. If someone can talk straight about these matters, as you have, she is always welcome here. So, based on your explanation, *ACIM* is a message familiar to many humans of various backgrounds, and agrees with a great deal of mainstream contemporary "nonduality"—which in itself is the old Advaita Vedanta poured into new bottles with fancy labels and set out on the shelves of the spiritual supermarket.

So *ACIM* seems to be a kind of restatement of Hindu metaphysics, stirred and shaken with some Christian "love" stuff, presented with the gloss that the writer—who obviously knew about Vedanta before writing her book—got her words direct from "God," the same claim often applied to the Bible. This does not make the metaphysics of *ACIM* wrong, but the author's claims as to the origin of her work are beyond fishy. Clearly, it is a sales gimmick. Since all of that metaphysics existed in written form long, long before *ACIM* was conceived, suggesting that the book came from "God" is a bit much, as Q3 was saying.

I do not agree with that metaphysics, by the way, wherever it came from. I find it full of unsubstantiated claims and rickety logic.

Earlier, Q3 mentioned Eckhart Tolle, whose origin myth relies on a similar stratagem: never even *mention* the sources who spoke of these matters long before you were born; just say it all came to you magically while you spent two years sitting on a park bench—which is Tolle's claim, debunked entirely elsewhere in this book by an intimate friend of his[40]. Because I have read some of the earlier sources, I recognized Tolle's writing as theft as soon as I saw it—which it would not have been if only he had cited it properly, instead of pretending to have pulled it out of thin air. And judging from what Q2 said, I guess *ACIM* belongs in that category as well: a rip-off.

Nevertheless, that does not mean that you were not helped by something you found in *ACIM*. Addicts and others in psychological need seem to gravitate towards Tolle too. I would never presume to judge that. Apparently, there is something in that message, a kind of mishmash of ancient philosophy and pop psychology that attracts

40. See Chapter 68, "*The Power of Now.*"

people who are in various stages of confusion, or emotional or physical disarray. Still, there is a problem—a big one—in attributing a book to "God," and pretending to have *"scribed"* it rather than to have *written* it.

When I write about my own experience, everyone is free to take it that way: Robert, an ordinary human, sees it like this. If, conversely, I say that the information comes from "God" and I am just jotting it down, that is a different claim entirely, and one that opens a huge can of worms. To begin with, no one has the foggiest idea *what* "God" is or even if such an entity exists, so that is rather shaky sourcing. But the real problem lies in painting one's *own* words, stolen or not, with a brush of ultimate authority: the voice of "God."

If *ACIM* helped you, fine, but I'd advise being clear on where those ideas came from—which was *not* "God," but ancient Hindu philosophy plus a bit of "Jesus-talk" with a 20th-century psychological spin. The author pulled a fast one, alleging a supposedly "divine" author whom she only "scribed" as a way of selling books, when really she was only stealing something that already existed in its entirety. Anyone with the intelligence your writing shows would be better off, in my opinion, in having a look at the original sources, and leaving the rip-off artists, like Shucman and Tolle, to their commercial enterprises.

80 - Faith

Faith is confidence or trust in a particular system of religious belief, in which faith may equate to confidence based on some perceived degree of warrant.

—Wikipedia

Q: Hi, Robert. I promised myself that I wouldn't write to you until I had finished reading your book. A few times I was tempted, but a promise is a promise, especially to oneself.

Anyway, now I have finished reading twice through. Wow, very good. *The Ten Thousand Things* did for me what others have said it did for them: it lifted the spiritual fog from my eyes. What a relief. I had a few weeks of: "Oh no, what am I going to do now? What will I do without my favorite hobby, spirituality?" But since then, I've found myself coming from a much healthier and more authentic place. And, overall, I seem to be OK, quite fine. So thank you, Robert.

Actually, ironically, I consider myself a true seeker now. Why? Because I am not afraid to see truth and go there. I am not afraid to drop spiritual concepts that I had previously thought true. Your book crashed my world, and that is so fine with me. Well, *now* I can say that. Ha, ha.

It's quite funny really. I saw your interview on *BATGAP*[41] and I was intrigued straightaway. I thought to myself, "Oops, I am going to have to look at this! If I am honest in seeking the truth, I am going to have to look into this place where he is pointing." But many, I speculate, watching that same interview, will have done so with the same degree of intrigue and fascination—and then carried on as if nothing had happened. Too much at stake for some, perhaps. Thankfully, I don't have much at stake. Just me and my beloved, and we pretty much always travel the same path.

Anyway, that's the preamble. Here is the question:

41. See https://BATGAP.com/robert-saltzman/

So all this stuff—you break it down to thoughts, feelings, and perceptions—is registered on our one screen of awareness inside, but it's so many things, from planning a dinner to deep insights into the nature of life; from worrying about the future of our planet to being angry at somebody at work; from feeling a sore knee to seeing and appreciating a beautiful scene in nature; from having some kind of deep intuition about some person or relationship to worrying about money; from solving a math problem to feelings of eroticism; and so on, and so on. It seems to be one continuous amorphous mess of stuff. So much and on so many levels, if there are levels.

Where does it all come from? What is it all? And, further, although the overall themes are probably very much the same, everybody has their own flavor of inner experience. And as we get older, the type of content shifts. The contents of my inner world were very different at sixteen than they are now. When I meditate, after about 40 minutes, pretty much on the dot, the stuff gets less and it goes quiet in here. Then, when I go back into the world and do my thing, after a while—there it all is again. Pretty much the same stuff. I don't mind it being there—it's just there.

What is it really and where does it come from? Probably, if I know you by now, you will say, "I don't know." And I agree—nor do I.

A: I am glad you enjoyed the book. If any spiritual fog lifted, that's wonderful.

The Ten Thousand Things was written from a perspective that sees the world of religion and spirituality not only as largely irrelevant to comprehending what "I" am, but in many cases as an absolute impediment to comprehension. Why? Because when you take someone else's word about who or what you are, no matter how supposedly authoritative that person seems to be or is said to be, you are then blinded to your *own* experience, debarred from coming to your *own* understanding. You have become a believer, a disciple, a follower; and so events will always be seen and understood not directly, but through the screen of concepts and beliefs you have acquired and accepted on no real evidence but testimony.

Someone might then ask, "But what about scripture—the Bible, or the Bhagavad Gita, and all the rest?" Isn't scripture a kind of evidence apart from testimony?" No! Scriptures *are* testimony, *human* testimony. Does anyone seriously believe that "God" wrote them? And, by the way, they are testimony from pre-scientific times, when deities and other invisible presences were the only explanations for many aspects of life and mind that we now understand as natural, not "supernatural."

You may have misunderstood *4T* a bit. I am *not* saying that perceptions, feelings, and thoughts are "registered on our one screen of awareness inside." In my world, there *is* no "screen of awareness." That movie screen metaphor comes directly from the dogma of Advaita Vedanta, and has confused countless people. An actual movie screen is entirely separate from the movie projected upon it. And both the movie and the screen are separate from the viewer of the movie sitting in the theater. Applying that schema to human *be*-ing seems pretty lame. Unlike a theater in the physical world, in the realm of simple *be*-ing, the "movie," the "screen," and the "viewer" in the audience are all one and the same indescribable *be*-ing. Not three "things," but one inseparable happening.

Nor can awareness be split into inside and outside. That kind of splitting is proposed by religious teachers to encourage people to believe that so-called "true self" exists *prior* to the events and happenings of this aliveness; that there is a "you" that is totally and completely uninvolved in perceptions, feelings, and thoughts, but somehow above that whole show and superior to it. In that view, "myself"—being identical with Brahman or God—is "real," whereas perceptions, feelings, and thoughts are not "real" because, unlike "God," they are always changing.

As I see it, that entire schema is defective and erroneous from the get-go. A "myself" separate from and superior to perceptions, feelings, and thoughts does not match the psychobiological facts of this aliveness. In my opinion, the metaphysics of Vedanta are merely a form of learned ignorance not much different from the hierarchal structure of Christian or Muslim metaphysics.

As I see this, perceptions, feelings, and thoughts *are* you—not "things" projected on a screen that "you" are watching as if separate from all that. In my experience, there *is* no separation between myself and "my" perceptions, feelings, and thoughts. None at all. That's what "me" is: perceptions, feelings, thoughts, a body, intellect, etcetera, plus the conscious and unconscious awareness of all that.

To be clear, as I experience "myself," I feel no splitting. No inside vs. outside. No sacred vs. profane. No "realized being" vs. ordinary unenlightened being. There is only *this*—undefinable, mysterious, and beyond human conception.

Vedanta goes wrong, I say, when it imagines a permanent, undying self. In my experience, there is no such self. One might have the *feeling* of a fixed "myself"—what the monotheists call "the soul"—but that, I say, is an illusion arising from the mixing together of countless bits of information and perception, including the perception of one's own physical body, which comes to be viewed as a "self."

I feel no separation at all between thoughts and the thinker of thoughts, between perceptions and the perceiver of perceptions, between feelings and the feeler of feelings. It's all one incomprehensible happening. That is the very essence of "awake," as I use the word.

Hindu philosophy—which aims at "realizing" the self as an eternal, unchanging *presence* to which thoughts, feelings, etcetera, occur, while *it* remains unchanged—created that movie screen analogy, thereby splitting the *perceiver* (assumed to be eternal and unchanging) from *perceptions* (which are always changing). I reject that kind of splitting entirely. In my view, that one idea, taken on faith, has confused countless seekers who imagine that Nisargadatta, Ramana Maharshi, or whoever, had "Truth." Why should *you* believe *that*?

As for your question about what is this world, this experience called "myself," and where does it originate, yes—you have predicted my answer perfectly. I do not have the slightest idea. But neither, I am saying, does anyone else, although many claim to.

Why should anyone put faith in a claim like that? If reading *The Ten Thousand Things* has really "crashed your world," then you will understand that there is no reason to believe those so-called experts who claim to "know" things. They had *their* lives and their points of view, and you have *yours*. Why is their perspective "truer" than yours? One contemporary spiritual teacher says his perspective is truer than yours because he has attained "higher reasoning." Oh, *please*!

The abilities of human beings to be hypnotized and remain that way is, I say, apparently boundless. This is not to say, I want to add, that Ramana, Nisargadatta, and others never said anything worth hearing. Both of those men expressed a kind of wisdom, as I understand their words. However, when claiming to know "Truth" about human consciousness, they both jumped the shark.

The particular "Truth" of which they were sure—and of which the present-day teacher I mentioned is certain beyond a doubt as well—holds that the human brain cannot be the origin of human consciousness, because the brain is not "real," but only a so-called "appearance" *in* what they call "the Absolute" or "universal consciousness."

That is the claim, but why should you take it on faith? After all, Christians believe that Jesus is the "Truth and the Way," and they are just as sure of that as Vedantists are sure of their "Truth."

Q: Okay, I kind of see. Two more questions then, but this is only curiosity really, because I am now understanding that it doesn't really matter what *your* experience is—I am best served by looking at *mine*. But anyway, do you have moments where nothing is going on, where the experience is just empty? If so, would you call that just aliveness? And also, how is it for you when you sleep? As I say, just curious.

A: Exactly! You are best served by looking at your *own* experience. You may get inklings from what others say—perhaps from what I say—but your *own* experience is the only first-hand material you have. Peace of mind, I say, is the absence of self-generated mental turbulence, such as questions about what some other apparent person experiences.

As for a moment when nothing is going on, if that happened, I wouldn't know about it, would I? Ha, ha.

When I sleep, sometimes I am visited by dreams, and sometimes not, but I can't recall the times between dreams. Judging from what others say and what I have read, my sleep is middle of the road normal: periods of deep, dreamless unconsciousness, punctuated by so-called REM sleep in which dream imagery arises, including the occasional nightmare. Two nights ago I was passing through airport security and the agent found psychedelic drugs in my carry-on. Last night a tall woman in a nun's habit passed by me on the sidewalk, but where her face should have been, there was nothing but blackness.

It's *all* just aliveness. What else is there?

81 - The snipe hunt

Q: I love *The Ten Thousand Things*. Thank you for this exciting and unique book! Your take on spiritual awareness is incredibly genuine, uncompromising, and revelatory. I would compare the way you roll it out with the technique of photographic development in the dark room. The blank paper slowly but definitely starts unveiling details of a raw chunk of reality that may strike the eye and mind by unexpected shades, contrasts, and meanings.

Going to specifics: you imply that the state of awareness in your case occurred spontaneously, and in the absence of any intentional spiritual pursuit and systematic "work" such as meditation, prayer, yoga. I have no doubts about the sincerity of this affirmation. Nevertheless, something interesting could be noticed on the backstage, something that can be construed as an intense and effective exercise: the identification with the *now* of the photographer when shooting a photo.

The process of capturing a picture with a camera requires visual focus, sharp attention, a keen desire to find the perfect angle, the appropriate amount of light, the intended visual effect, plus effort—all of which eventually turns into *the* moment. The impassioned photographer is more prompt than other professionals to develop a sense of here and now.

Does this mean that all photographers are on the verge of enlightenment? Well, perhaps it's not *that* easy. There were for sure some other favorable circumstances in your case. So, I believe that the practice was there, and applied in the most effective way, by *not* "hunting" an ultimate spiritual goal, but doing something else. Your thoughts on this?

A: Thanks for the kind appreciation of *4T*.

There *is* no "ultimate spiritual goal," I say, so anyone who is chasing after that fantasy is on a snipe hunt.

I would not say that all photographers are on the verge of enlightenment. Most of the ones I have known certainly weren't. Ha, ha. And anyway, the idea of "enlightenment" is *part* of the snipe hunt.

This is such a simple matter. Sages over the years have laid it out clearly, but most of their listeners—those with an informed interest in these matters, which already is only a small fraction of humanity—usually misunderstand what is being said.

Awakening is *not* a religious proposition and has nothing to do with believing in anything. If one regards the sage as a prophet, understanding is obstructed. The sage is *not* a prophet, but an awake human being.

In her sapience, the sage has seen that the sense of self is a kind of illusion—smoke and mirrors. That illusion has a source, which is the human nervous system. The countless data from the trillions of sensory cells are assembled moment by moment into a "world." That assembling is automatic: an involuntary process that takes place entirely unconsciously and preconceptually. It can be neither noticed nor controlled. No one is "doing" it. No "*myself*" is doing it.

The imagined "myself" that arises as the supposed center of that confected world does not exist, except as an apparent center of habitual thoughts and feelings. This aliveness is a *process*—not a *self*. When the "I-thought" is not there, "myself" is not there either. That is what is meant by the word *shunyata* in Eastern thought, which is translated as "emptiness" and is understood to mean empty of "own-nature," empty of *independent* existence.

So it is not that one has no *feeling* of "myself"—we all do—but that one recognizes that even the feeling of "selfness" is dependent on countless non-self factors.

Since thought requires a brain, and a brain depends upon a living body to support it, when the "I-thought" *is* present, one understands—and perhaps fears—that "myself" (the myself of thought) has no permanence and will not survive death.

This fear of impermanence, of ceasing to exist, of *not being at all*, drives much of so-called spirituality, which is fixated upon *realizing* a "myself" that will not die. But that presumes some imagined "thing" that *already* does not exist—except as an apparent focus of perceptions, feelings, and thoughts—will later *cease* to exist.

So, the fear that spirituality tries to remedy is that something that never existed in the first place will later *become* nonexistent. But there *is* no "later," and nothing is "becoming" anything. This is it. When the "I-thought" is present, "you" are there. When it is not present, there is only this aliveness doing what it must (or doing what it does, in case "must" seems a bit too deterministic for your taste).

Bodies die, of course. That is just natural. But apart from a body, all that dies is thoughts—such as those about "myself" dying. There *is* no "me" *apart* from thought. There *is* no "myself" that must go on living. All of it—the recurrent thoughts of "myself" and the efforts to realize a permanent "myself"—is just an automatically spinning wheel of no consequence.

This can end right now, and nothing is lost. As the warriors say, "Today is a good day to die." When that is seen—and it is fairly obvious—one finds oneself *awake*.

At this point, those committed to the snipe hunt will voice objections. Someone will say, "But Robert, if there is no 'myself,' then who is the one who finds oneself awake?" Such sticklers fail to understand the limits of language. They fail to see how words have baffled them—not because words are *inherently* baffling, but because they *want* to be baffled. No matter how many times they hear me say "This is it," they will find a way to believe that something "better," something more "evolved," something "spiritual," is later to be attained.

The real point of their objections is that the snipe hunt must never be allowed to end.

Most of what I am saying has been said before by certain famous sages and many nearly anonymous ones. Those men and women have been widely misunderstood. When awake—by which I mean free of self-bafflement, free of the denial of impermanence, and free of the desire to live forever—it is easy to grasp everything those sages said or that I am saying. I will repeat it:

Nothing is hidden or esoteric, so there is nothing to attain. This is it.

This is simple, not complex in the least. But in the usual human condition of culturally-induced hypnosis, the words of the sages are twisted to fit labyrinthine religious concepts with which they actually have nothing to do at all.

Someone told me that, for her, spirituality was "a useful map reference." I suppose it could be, or it might be only an excuse to keep on dreaming the same old hypnotic dream of something that lasts in a world where nothing lasts. From my perspective, it usually is the latter. I am not saying that one can avoid dealing with "spirituality," but I do advise being over and done with it as soon as possible. Right now, perhaps.

The sages to whom I refer, both famous and unknown, were clear on this. Religion is mostly an excuse to remain hypnotized, a tool of self-bafflement, a way to keep going with the same old, same old—the snipe hunt.

> *If you live the sacred and despise the ordinary, you are still bobbing in the ocean of delusion. If you want to perceive and understand objectively, just don't allow yourself to be confused by people. Detach from whatever you find inside or outside yourself—detach from religion, tradition, and society, and only then will you attain liberation. When you are not entangled in things, you pass through freely to autonomy.*
>
> —Lin Chi, 9th century

82 - I am afraid of death

I received a long letter about free will and the search for lasting peace. Here is part of my reply:

Yearning to feel everlastingly happy or perpetually at peace can be a barrier to really living. Few people I have met really see that. Most humans I have known seem to assume that a continual quest for enhanced physical and emotional comfort is the norm, and that one should pursue those ends until they are attained. Then, they imagine, "I will be satisfied."

As for physical comfort, I don't say ignore it. I am not recommending putting on a hair shirt—which is, after all, just a mirror image of the same preoccupation. Bodily ease is welcome enough. But animal life has its discomforts after all, and since they are inevitable, why set oneself up to feel victimized by them? Next time you feel uncomfortable, ask yourself what it would be like to feel that way *and* be living in the middle of a war zone (assuming you are not living in one now). That should put things in clearer perspective.

Emotional comfort is more complex, because for many or even most people it rests upon a bed of second-hand beliefs—other people's beliefs, I mean—that one has heard about and perhaps been taught, which seem to neutralize the fears and uncertainties of human primate life, but for which one has no first-hand, immediate experience. If one's foundation for emotional comfort is an article of faith, a second-hand *belief*—"Everything happens for a reason," for example—then the counter-idea, that maybe all of this is just arising with no rhyme or reason at all, must arise and be *denied, defended* against, and *pushed* into the shadows.

No one *really* knows *why* things happen as they do, or even if there is a "why." And, horror of horrors, our being conscious as the latest scions of an inconceivably long line of variously conscious ancestors—harking back to the minimal consciousness of primitive worms, or even to the one-celled bacteria that somehow evince awareness of their surroundings—may have no overarching "meaning" at all, and no "force" or "Source" controlling it.

Unless belief is total, doubtless, and seamless, banking on second-hand beliefs as a means of assuaging ambivalence and anxiety will become a *source* of anxiety in and of itself. That was a theme of *The Ten Thousand Things.*

If belief is strong enough, there will be no struggle with ambivalence—not consciously, at least. If trance induction begins early and is carried out skillfully enough, the subsequent enthrallment may be so unshakable as to feel rock solid. "Give me the child until he is seven," the Jesuits say, "and I care not who has him thereafter." In a mind like that, someone like me will be pitied for missing out. For those who *truly* believe in the glories of Heaven with Jesus or Jannah with Mohammed, skepticism may not be what they like hearing, but it's no big threat either.

It's the others, not so deeply hypnotized, who feel troubled and upset; the ones with doubts about the dogma, be it Christian, Islamic, Hindu, Buddhist, New Age, or whatever. Betwixt and between they are. They don't *fully* believe it, and yet cannot quite bear to regard all that dogma as the nonsense it is. They may *doubt* the axioms of religion and spirituality, but seem compelled anyway to afford them the culturally assimilated, automatic *respect* said to be owed to anything deemed holy, no matter by whom or why.

Minds like that may *want* to keep believing in fairy tales, perhaps by telling themselves—the bright ones anyway—that *behind* the fairy tales is some actual benign, omniscient, supernatural "reality" of which our world is but a reflection. But they can't quite get that boulder to the top of the ontological hill. And the fear is not only that they will never get the boulder to the top, but that even if they did, their "faith" would require constant vigilance, protection, and renovation to keep it there. And that even with all that attention, sooner or later the boulder might roll back down the hill again, a so-called "crisis of faith."

In their hearts, they aren't *really* convinced by Heaven or Jannah. If it was really *that* good, a fatal diagnosis would be greeted with celebration by the one soon to be in "Jannah," rejoicing amid the envious congratulations of friends:

Abdul: *Good news, Zafir. The doc said I have only around six weeks left to live.*

Zafir: *Really? Cool! Some guys have all the luck.*

So-called "self-realization" is just another version of "Jannah." No one who speaks of Jannah is *in* Jannah. What the *self* is, or what *consciousness* is, isn't something that can be *realized* as if it were a question with a known answer. What other self can there be, apart from that which is reading these words in this very moment? It's here already, and does not need "realization" to *make* it be here. You can't touch it. You can't change it. You can't define it. And neither can anyone else.

Whether the cynosure, the promised land, is Jannah, Heaven or self-realization, the mechanics are identical: the preacher or "teacher" promises some mythical Shangri-La, arrival at which will make everything entirely and eternally groovy; and you *believe* that—except for the voices in your *own* mind that don't.

Fear of death and dying—which implies a fear of fully living—is the mainspring of this credulous grasping for answers where there are none, but only conjectures, beliefs, and dogmas; nothing but escapist fantasies for frightened minds. If you see that *nothing* lasts forever, including "myself" *with* all its fears and desires, all will clarify quickly and without effort. This is it.

Once impermanence is grasped as obvious, every moment is your teacher, and you will not need to believe anything about God, truth, consciousness, or Self. Then you are a light unto yourself, and will not depend on "teachers" and their beliefs.

Q: Hello, Robert. I don't want to die—I'm frightened of it.

A: Yes. Many people are. Or if not that, something else—perhaps being incapacitated and dependent on nursing care. We all have fears.

Q: Scares the shit out of me.

A: Yes. The idea of not being at all—ceasing to exist—can feel that way. But every night you lose consciousness, and you are not frightened of dreamless sleep, I suppose. Perhaps that is what death is like. One minute you are self-referentially conscious, and in the next, you aren't. Years ago, I was deeply anesthetized for a surgical operation. On awakening from that, after having been entirely *unconscious* for an indeterminate period of time, with no sense of time having passed, I knew all I needed to know about death. "You," quite likely, aren't there anymore.

Q: I want to escape. My mother is dying in hospital and she said, "I just want to run away across the fields." I knew what she meant. I just want to run away across the fields.

A: Yes, very understandable, but you do not have to deal with physically dying until it's actually happening. And you have no way now to imagine what that will be like. It could be far worse and more difficult than you imagine, or far better and easier than you imagine. It might even happen in your sleep.

But all of that is only fantasy and leads nowhere useful. When your time to die arrives, you won't have to *do* anything about it. One way or another, you will stop breathing, and that's it. Don't let your mother's fears be yours. You can see her drama with compassion and comprehension, but neither of those requires taking on her fears as if they were yours. All lives end. Now it is your mother's life ending, not yours. Your turn will come.

All you ever have to deal with—and all you ever *can* deal with—is this self-awareness right now. That can be difficult, given that part of that awareness comprises knowledge of impermanence and mortality, which means dying moment by moment. But on the other hand, you also get to *live* moment by moment—which, speaking personally, I find interesting, even when things are not quite going my way.

Would you really prefer to not be at all?

83 - *Dementia*

Q: Hi Robert. I have an elderly neighbor who has dementia. He spends the majority of the day just looking out of the front window of his house, staring into the street. He doesn't appear distressed, although his family always seem to. In fact, he always has a subtle smile on his face. I know it's none of my business, but I can't help wondering what goes through his mind, and whether any conscious awareness can exist there.

My own parents, now deceased, spent their final years with dementia. Ironically, my mother—who, after being orphaned, spent much of her life suffering from anxiety and depression following a very troubled childhood, spent in the care of and strictly disciplined by Roman Catholic nuns—seemed to lose much of this anxiety as dementia took hold. Maybe her forgetfulness (she had no idea who I was) made her forget her troubled past, and freed her somewhat from the mind-created prison.

I guess this is why I ask the question about my neighbor. I wonder if my mother—who seemed, outwardly at least, more relaxed about life with increasing dementia—also achieved more conscious awareness. Or would the opposite be true in your opinion and experience?

A: I don't know. There are many flavors of dementia, and it is hard to know what someone besides oneself is actually experiencing. So much of what one imagines seeing in others is fictional. And all the more with someone who cannot speak and explain.

Q: That's what I thought too, but I am always interested in your opinion. I'm halfway through *The Ten Thousand Things* by the way. It's encouraging me to question a lot of things and to realize that not knowing answers to everything is OK, because that's the truth; and I am feeling at peace with that. Thank you.

A: You are most welcome.

Honesty about not knowing is, in my experience, where equanimity is to be found. What we actually *know* is precious little, so many of us fill the apparent emptiness by pretending that believing is the same as knowing. When one believes without actually knowing, then there is always lingering doubt to deal with—even if only unconsciously—and there is never peace in the struggle between belief and doubt.

Q: Indeed. Thanks again. I don't necessarily always agree with what you say, but your honesty and insights are proving valuable.

A: Good. No need to agree or disagree. I see what I see, and you see what *you* see. That understanding is the essence of what I mean by "awake": what I see is my *own* mind, and I know it.

My experience with voicing my ideas about what I call "life and mind" is that most of the disagreement—I am not saying *all*, but most—seems to come from people who have no idea what I am actually saying, but only *imagine* they do; or who have some preexisting belief system or cherished teacher's ideas to which they feel attached and which they feel compelled to defend.

Just the other day, someone who'd bought my book on the recommendation of Joan Tollifson quoted this from *The Ten Thousand Things:*

> *I have conversed with people who called themselves jnanis, and heard all about what they say they know, of which they seem convinced beyond all doubt. I have read some accounts of Nisargadatta, the acclaimed 20th-century* jnani. *From my point of view, that kind of knowing is akin to what the Bible calls knowing a woman, meaning to have sex with her. OK, you spent the night with her, and you call it "knowing her." You know what you experienced, but you do not know that woman, and you never will. You have no way of knowing her. You know you, and that's the limit. You know your impressions of that woman—your images of her—not the "truth" of her.*

> *In the very same way, despite any claims to* jnana, *you do not know the "Supreme Being" or even if the term "Supreme Being" refers to anything more than a cultural shibboleth with which you were indoctrinated before the age of reason, and which you now project onto what you call "the world." Naturally, that is my point of view. I understand that you have yours.*

And then replied to the quote with a protest in defense of his bidi-smoking *jnani* hero: "That sounds like Robert is saying you can't truly know that which is aware, which is true. I'm puzzled, though, because he seems to suggest that Nisargadatta didn't know what he was talking about. There are certainly many teachers whose claims seem larger than their realization—but Nisargadatta?"

This is just what I mean. This ticks both boxes #1 and #2—no idea what I was saying, and compelled to defend a cherished teacher—a double play.

In the first place, I never said Nisargadatta didn't know what he was talking about, so this fellow has no idea what I am expressing in that chapter, but only *imagines* he does. At this point, Marshall McLuhan steps from behind a curtain and says, "You have no idea what Robert is saying."[42]

In the second place, a basic question: was Nisargadatta some kind of infallible, omniscient god? If you're in that bag, you *won't* understand what I am saying. This comprehensive view has the god demoted to ordinary human animal status, just like you and me—well, just like *me* at least. Ha, ha.

To a Nisargadatta worshipper, that would feel like a *self*-demotion. If my god—the hero I emulate—is diminished, then I am diminished too; suddenly I am the child of a *lesser* god.

It could also feel quite unsettling—or worse—to be reminded that the "Truth" about these questions of "What does it all mean? Where is it all going?" was *not* defined once and for all by some deceased guy from India who taught what his teacher had taught him, which is what his teacher's teacher had taught him, etcetera.

42. Refers to a scene in Woody Allen's *Annie Hall* - see https://mediatropes.com/index.php/Mediatropes/article/view/1771/1482

I am not saying there is no intelligence at all in that, but to me, most of Nisargadatta's rap does seem short of brilliant. It is, in large measure, a cut and dried restatement of the dogma of the sect of Hinduism called Advaita Vedanta. If that appeals to you, fine—but why make a god or even a faultless authority out of the guy? I like some of what he said and quote it when appropriate. He was, as I see it, on to something—but an omniscient seer of reality? That's a tall order. And assuming you believe it, what are your credentials for judging seers of reality? Doesn't it take one to know one? How does that work?

This is *not* complicated. If Nisargadatta was correct in everything he ever claimed was "Truth," then the Buddha was incorrect. Why? Because they disagree on some major points. So if you want to believe in one "expert" as infallible, you will have to reject the other's imagined perfection. More generally, if you want Hinduism, you don't want Buddhism, and vice versa. They don't mix well at all, and all paths do *not* lead to the top of the same mountain. That is only a canard.

Why get bogged down in all that? Controversy between one system of thought and another is a dead letter. Things are *as* they are, regardless of what anyone believes or disbelieves. Belief does not make something true, nor disbelief falsify it.

If you find someone like Nisargadatta worth hearing, fine. Just listen to the words, take it all in as best you can—and keep walking.

Q2: I live in Nisargadatta's home city. It is known that he smoked like a chimney, fucked women in a brothel, kicked people out of his house, and changed his teachings often. We have been programmed since childhood to distrust our own experiences. We were often wronged and abused for being ourselves, so no wonder we seek others as a source of truth to tell us what is true and what is not.

For instance, recently someone was amazed and in deep praise of Meher Baba's 44-year silence. My reply was: "Did you live with him 24/7 for those 44 years to validate that?"

We are addicted to hearsay and we are terrified to trust our own experience and knowledge. We use others to continue living in denial and escapism.

Q3: I am Indian too. In his early days, Nisargadatta gave spontaneous talks to anyone coming to his shop seeking his spiritual wisdom. Some brought their sick relatives to him, hoping for cures. He sent the afflicted to a café at the street corner, telling them to drink a glass of water therein—and in doing so, they were often healed.

Siddharamesvar, Nisargadatta's guru, instructed him to stop participating in such healings, which he said were trivial compared to the need for spiritual awakening from the ultimate disease of identifying with the body-mind-personality. Nevertheless, over the years, many miracles and synchronicities still occurred.

A: I have heard stories that seem far more dramatically synchronistic and logically inexplicable than a glass of water that apparently heals ills. An event like that could be touted, foolishly, as a supernatural "miracle," when in fact it might have been only a *natural* outcome of an interaction with a powerful person who was obviously hypnotic, plus *expectations* of miraculous intervention. Since the *natural* version—the placebo effect—has demonstrable, testable scientific validity, I'd be more inclined to give it preference than to call upon any *supernatural* explanation that has no substantiation, other than certain events occurred and someone *called* that a miracle.

For many people, *not knowing* feels so anxiety-ridden, and the desire that life have a definite meaning and definite destination so pressing, that they glom on as soon as possible to an explanation that allows them to "*know*" that life has a telos—which is "God" or "universal consciousness."

According to Gustave Flaubert:

> *The rage for wanting to conclude is one of the most deadly and most fruitless manias to befall humanity.*

I observe that rage in many others, but I cannot find it in myself, not even to the slightest degree. That absence of the rage to conclude is certainly an aspect of what I mean by "awake." I feel content sitting here breathing, drinking good Mexican coffee, and typing, with zero desire to hear about Shambhala or any other such "place."

I think it likely that the only real difference between me and a gorilla is a bit of DNA eventuating in a slightly thicker prefrontal cortex; and that, otherwise, my destiny is precisely the same as his: birth, survival, reproduction, death. And I doubt that anything I think or feel about that inexorable process makes any difference at all, except to the "me" who wants it to *mean* something, to feel *gratifying*, or whatever the desire may be.

Humans hate that idea: the idea that the other primates are really very much like us and we like them. Darwin was despised when his work first came out. He was misunderstood by the public as asserting that humans were descended from apes—when what he was really saying is that we and all other forms of life, both animal and vegetable, have a common ancestor; and that all lifeforms are part of the same family tree, with humans and the other primates comprising a certain branch that, in turn, is an offshoot of the branch of vertebrates, etcetera.

The distaste for admitting our animal nature, and so wanting to draw a bright line between humans and animals (humans *are* animals), persists even today, undergirded by religion and polluting the regimes of science.

No so many years ago—perhaps fifteen—a primatologist who spoke of having observed primate *culture*—or even worse, that primates have *personalities*—would have wandered beyond the pale of academe where grants dry up, publishers aren't interested, and professorships never include tenure. Nowadays, culture and personality are the hottest buzzwords in primatology.

We humans have severely underestimated our primate cousins, as well as many *non*-primate animals rather far from us on the evolutionary tree, like crows or octopi. The primatologists may be catching on, but most of the rest of us still don't get it. In our ignorance, we have injured and continue to injure countless intelligent, feeling beings with our mechanized powers of building, killing, manipulating, and enslaving.

This barbaric abuse of non-human animals continues even now, when many of us know better. Even this late in the game, when words about how "God" gave humans dominion over the animals won't quite cut it anymore, we play along. We need our barbarism justified, legitimatized, absolved, and forgiven. Permission from God to *use* "animals"—as if *we* weren't animals ourselves—is just made-up shit, just like most of the Bible. Lots of us don't believe a word of it, but most of us still play along in one way or another.

Good old boy God was. Put us right smack dab at the top of the mother-fuckin' food chain. Survival of the fittest, baby. It's so cool to be an Alpha.

By failing to see intelligence *biologically* as an emergent quality of neural complexity, and always wanting/needing to put some supernatural spin (like "Source" or "The Absolute") on the ball, we have damaged ourselves severely and directly. By failing to recognize our *natural* history as *the* basic existential fact—the one fact that fair observation should make tantamount to undeniable—we humans are far too disposed to dreaming up and believing fantasized supernatural explanations.

A lot of that dogma is simply preposterous—*most* of it is preposterous. No wonder the purveyors of it enjoin you not to think too much, and certainly never skeptically and critically. "Your mind is not your friend," they say, or "This is only relatively real." And they say it with such confidence.

That is why I find the reliance of human beings on supposed spiritual experts a sad spectacle indeed. Fortunately for me, I can see the absurdity in it. Otherwise, it would seem unremittingly tragic.

Years ago, in a flash, I found myself what I call "awake." I kept silent about that for a long time. Now I find myself speaking about it. But no one, I say, myself included, knows anything for sure about any of this. Each mind is a world unto itself. And the universe is vast beyond human conception. I would never imagine that some cat chain-smoking bidis in an attic room in Bombay had the keys to *that* kingdom.

84 - True human nature

Not long ago, I posted an article about a performance by the artist Marina Abramović, in which, according to the article:

> *She told viewers she would not move for six hours no matter what they did to her. She placed 72 objects one could use in pleasing or destructive ways, ranging from flowers and a feather boa to a knife and a loaded pistol, on a table near her and invited the viewers to use them on her however they wanted.*
>
> *Initially, Abramović said, viewers were peaceful and timid, but it escalated to violence quickly. "The experience I learned was that if you leave the decision to the public, you can be killed. I felt really violated: they cut my clothes, stuck rose thorns in my stomach, one person aimed the gun at my head, and another took it away. It created an aggressive atmosphere. After exactly six hours, as planned, I stood up and started walking toward the public. Everyone ran away, escaping an actual confrontation."*

This piece revealed something appalling about humanity, similar to Philip Zimbardo's Stanford Prison Experiment or Stanley Milgram's Obedience Experiment, both of which also demonstrated how readily people are disposed to harm one another.

I received a response from one of my correspondents which said, among other things, that "it's always possible to summon evidence for any point of view. Other studies seem to indicate that people are inherently compassionate and altruistic. On an experiential level, I've found that when I treat people with kindness, compassion, and respect, they reciprocate in kind. From my experience, I would say that our true nature is inherently happy, peaceful and loving, and so-called bad people have been strongly conditioned away and disconnected from this essential 'Buddha' nature."

Here is my reply:

Yes, of course. I never try to *prove* anything. As I have said often, I have no answers to ultimate questions such as "true nature," and I do not expect that either scientific inquiry or mysticism will ever penetrate a question like that in sufficient depth to achieve certainty.

We human beings are *limited* in our ken, and there is no way, I say, to remove those limitations. I am aware, however, that confirmation bias is a powerfully entrenched feature of human psychology; and so, when presented with any proposition, regardless of my own views, I always look for the contrary evidence. And if I am going to err, I prefer to err on the side of skepticism than on the side of belief. Skepticism is a much more open and welcoming stance, I find.

Like you, I also have found that treating others with respect often improves relations—but *not* always. The psychopathic mind knows how to manipulate such "weakness"—as that kind of mind perceives it—and such a person can go from apparent kindness to cutting your heart out in an instant.

I'm not just speculating here. I have treated psychopaths in my therapy practice, including a murderer who felt nothing when he carried out that crime. It is not useful to call that way of being "mental illness" or to blame it on "conditioning," because it exists everywhere on Earth, and in roughly the same proportions, regardless of cultural conditioning.

Psychopathy, which contains not a shred of altruism, is not an anomaly, but a normal personality variant that remains with us presumably because it serves the perpetuation of the species. And this is not the result of a defective modern culture that wrongly conditions everyone away from their inherent loving natures. Many of the ancient Greek gods were total psychopaths, so this is old stuff. The same is true of aggression and aggressive sexuality. They are part of us. We may not like them, but that does not mean that they are an aberration just because you think so. Even our current gods, like Jehovah, who we created in the same way that the ancients dreamed up Zeus and Thor, seem psychopathic in some ways. Our gods, for example, are jealous gods who demand total fealty, enforced by threat of punishment.

If human beings were really inherently as happy, peaceful, and loving as you seem dead-set on believing—even to the extent of disparaging out-of-hand evidence to the contrary such as I just educed—then why do we need so much "fear of God," moral codes, police, harsh laws, and prisons? And how do we account for the wars and violence which are entirely central to thousands of years of human history?

Based on fair observation, not idealism, it appears that human nature is most likely very much like the nature of the other primates who are our closest genetic relatives. To say that there is some *other* kind of "true nature"—above and beyond that which we observe directly all around us, as manifested in human behavior and in that of other primates—is a kind of idealistic religious idea. One may *want* to believe in it, but that requires ignoring lots of evidence to the contrary. I am not willing to ignore that evidence.

I am not saying that such evidence *proves* that human nature is not as peaceful as you imagine. I simply say that such a large mass of evidence cannot simply be ignored out of hand or disparaged by saying, as you did, that "it's always possible to summon evidence for any point of view." That's about as effective as discounting plain facts by calling them fake news. I did not just "summon up" the findings of Zimbardo's and Milgram's experiments. Those findings are central to social psychology and have been replicated often. You may not *like* those findings, but you cannot just wave them away with a word.

Nor am I saying that altruism does not exist. In my world, it does, and science backs that up. But I strongly doubt that altruism *alone* constitutes true human nature. In my view, human nature is many-faceted, and to imagine that "our true nature is inherently happy, peaceful and loving, and so-called bad people have been strongly conditioned away and disconnected from this essential 'Buddha' nature," to me, appears to be a form of naive idealism for which you show *no* evidence but your desire to believe it.

You say that the strife and evil we see all around us occurs only because people have been conditioned away from "Buddha-nature," and that without that conditioning, we would all be in Heaven. That is a big claim. A *huge* claim. Show me the big evidence for it.

By the way, where does the "conditioning" come from—another universe? Do you not see that your point of view relies on creating a split between what is and what you want to imagine could be, if only humans were not "conditioned?" But we *are* conditioned, and always have been, including conditioned from birth by our human primate DNA.

According to noted primatologist Frans de Waal, speaking of his long studies via immersion in one group of chimpanzees and another of bonobos:

To have two close relations with strikingly different societies is extraordinarily instructive. The power-hungry and brutal chimp contrasts with the peace-loving and erotic bonobo—a kind of Dr. Jekyll and Mr. Hyde. Our own nature is an uneasy marriage of the two. In fact, we are one of the most internally conflicted animals ever to walk the earth.

85 - On suffering

Q: Happy New Year Robert! 2017 turned out to be a good year for me, in large part due to *The Ten Thousand Things* as well as your generous sharing on Facebook.

Here is a question: in some recent posts there was a discussion about the suffering of billions of people on earth. You said that an aspect of the nonduality scene that you see as delusional is the implication that suffering does not really exist. I agree with you on that. But you've also said that, since this is all just passing anyway, we might as well enjoy ourselves while we are here.

In my view, we should be aware of suffering and do what we can to alleviate it. But if we put too much attention on suffering, won't that interfere with our ability to enjoy ourselves?

When we open our eyes in the morning, we see whatever is in front of us. We can live in places where, when we open our eyes, we are more likely to see beauty as opposed to suffering. I'm assuming that you are living in a location you love with the people and animals you love. So is that not a kind of choice to pay less attention to suffering?

Please comment. Thanks again.

A: Thanks, and I wish you everything lovely in the year to come. I am glad you like the book.

Yes. I am living in a place I love—Todos Santos—with people and animals that I love. That is my great good fortune. But I cannot say that I see more beauty here than suffering. Frankly, I see lots of both.

I cannot *choose* to avoid attention to suffering. The visual sense is far too quick for any "chooser" to intervene in what is seen and noticed. Seeing is instantaneous. I see what I see—and that seeing, that noticing, that awareness *is* me. There is no going back in time. What is seen is seen. It may be repressed or papered over with explanations, but nothing is ever entirely forgotten. Likes and dislikes have nothing to do with this. Likes and dislikes kick in long after the fact, and can have no censoring effect on what is already seen.

What is seen is seen, and the arrow of time points in one direction only. The unavoidable loss of innocence involved in biological maturation is a form of entropy, which is not a local event or something peculiar to oneself personally (although it can be taken personally), but the most basic condition of the entire observable universe.

Entropy means that things tend to become less organized. For example, an egg might roll off the kitchen counter and break, but a broken egg lying on a kitchen floor is not going to "unbreak" and hop up onto the counter intact. This is an example of how, from the human point of view, the arrow of time points in only one direction.

I may "wish I didn't know now what I didn't know then" (Bob Seger), but that wish must remain unfulfilled. This aliveness does not stand outside the universe and its conditions. This aliveness we call "me" is part and parcel of the universe and its conditions—no separation, no splitting. This is a key point. According to the best cosmology—which is not just guesswork, but theory based on countless observations—our world began around 14 billion years ago in a condition of minimum entropy, and entropy has been increasing ever since. In our blindingly brief human lives, we experience this increase in entropy as ageing, illness, and death.

When I look into the eyes of the humans and other animals I meet in my daily rounds, I see plenty of suffering. I see stress, confusion, fear, anxiety, yearning, the tracks of physical pain, and all manner of inquietude. And I see that whether or not my fellow humans know the word "entropy." The *awareness* of entropy and its implications is never far from any mind.

I see beauty and dignity too in my brothers and sisters—both human and non-human—some of whom manifest great understanding, generosity, tranquility, fearlessness, and joy. So I see both. I see it all. I think my photographs show that.

There is no little homunculus sitting in the cerebral control room, nor some "enlightened Robert" standing *apart* from seeing, who can simply "decide" to ignore suffering and "enjoy himself" (by binging on beauty, I suppose, or burying his brains in the sands of Nepenthe). The *fantasy* of such a chooser is, I am saying, a *form* of suffering in and of itself—a heavy burden to carry.

Years ago, I worked with a load of camera gear which I would carry on my back on long treks—mile after mile in the high mountains of the Sangre de Cristo range in New Mexico. Nowadays, a couple of pounds is all I am willing to tote around, and I am lucky to have a good camera that weighs less than that.

There were lightweight cameras back then too. Good ones like Leicas and Nikons. But I wanted my work to look a certain way, and as good as a Leica might be for street work, it would not have done the job for me out in the landscape, nor a Nikon either. So I needed to carry the burden of much heavier gear for purposes of my own that could never be understood fully by anyone else.

A viewer of my images, knowledgeable about photography or with a quick eye, might have noticed and appreciated the wealth of textures and details in those images; features that would not have been made visible if I'd shot with a Leica. But even a viewer like that, for whom my efforts *were* visible, could never comprehend the *suffering* such efforts entailed. Not just the extra weight to carry—that was not always easy, but I was young and strong at the time—but the *striving* and the *perfectionism* I brought to that work, a kind of obsession. I never *chose* to need my images to look a certain way, but I *did* need them to look that way, and was willing to jump through hoops to achieve that look.

At some point there may have been rational, fact-based choices and decisions about what kind of camera to use, or what kind of film, or how to develop the film, or what kind of paper to print on, etcetera. Those are important matters from one perspective, but inconsequential from another. However, I am certain there was *never* a moment when I *decided to care* so deeply about those images. Caring that deeply just happens, like falling in love. And there is *nothing trivial* about it.

I am pointing here to a kind of suffering involved in coming to terms with the facts of what one *really* wants and needs—not necessarily what one might prefer, but promptings prior to likes and dislikes.

The recognition of one's own particular drives and desires, the finding of one's *own* mind—however difficult to accept—may involve all kinds of discomfort, embarrassment, and anxiety. But *that* is the suffering of awakening: of seeing what *is*—not what might have been or could be, and particularly *not* what one wishes were.

That is the suffering of having one's face rubbed in the understanding that "myself" is not in control of such matters and never was; and that all one can ever do is be what one is, *whatever* that is. There's no avoiding *that*.

If being oneself includes struggling against what one is and trying to alter it, then part of what one is might be named "a struggler trying to avoid oneself." There is, I say, *no escape* from this inevitability. One way or another, "myself" *will* be expressed. As the ancient Greeks had it, "You can try to throw nature out with a pitchfork, but she will always come back again."

So that's one kind of suffering: the inevitability of what one is, which will be expressed one way or another. I am involved in that kind of self-expression right now as I type, without having the slightest idea of what the next word will be or from whence it emerges, or why—if there even *is* a why. So calling it *self*-expression is only a manner of speaking. I have no way to put my finger on the provenance of the actions I call mine.

But another style of suffering involves not self-*expression*, but self-*identification*. By this I mean hanging a frame around one's own neck—for example, calling oneself "a Buddhist," or "a socialist," or "non-binary," or any one of numberless categories. A label like that may seem necessary—may seem to be a vital feature of what you feel you *are*. If so, that is what I mean by self-identification.

Having read *4T*, you may understand that I am not saying one can just *decide* to *not* identify. It doesn't work that way. I am only pointing out that, to the extent that one "identifies *as*," the ability to see things as they are is occluded.

To be blunt, among the people I consider awake—I have quoted some of them in this book—not one of them identifies "as" anything but this *aliveness*, as I call it, or this *awareness*, as some put it. Based on that rather small sample, it appears that one can have the safety net of group identification, tribal identification, racial identification, etcetera, or the freedom of freefall—but not both.

I am not asking anyone to agree, but in my experience, a certain kind of suffering ensues when the unspeakable, ineffable suchness of this aliveness is forced into a framework of self-identification—*any* framework. This is far worse than trying to force your feet into the wrong size shoes.

You may imagine that to live without such a framework would be difficult, but I find it almost effortless. From my vantage, living without self-identification is easy. The opposite—needing always to frame oneself—is difficult, even if—or perhaps *especially* if—the frame hung around one's neck involves identifying with a god of some kind, or "universal consciousness," or nonduality, or some such shibboleth.

Q: Thank you, Robert. I think I get that. Now, you speak of seeing suffering in others, so in that context, I would like to explore whether the way you see suffering is different from how I see it.

I suggest three possible ways of regarding the suffering of others:

1. Empathize.
2. Sympathize.
3. Accept suffering, by rationalizing it as the inescapable, universal human condition.

I tend to deal with suffering predominantly with the acceptance approach. I can't help it. That's the way I am wired up.

I see the past as past. Over and done. For example, due to the gap of space and time, I have no emotional reference to the Holocaust. I *know* about it, but I don't *feel* it. Those events have no living reality for me presently. We move on. There is nothing anyone can do to undo the Holocaust. No amount of empathy or sympathy has value, except to perpetuate that suffering by keeping it alive in memory.

So my point is that my way of dealing with suffering, the third way, is not less valid than empathy or sympathy. Just because all that past suffering means nothing to me presently does not make my way of seeing things invalid or inhuman. Bygones are bygones: it's a matter of common sense.

My question to you, however, is this: from a nondual perspective, how do *you* regard suffering of that magnitude from the past?

A: I will reply not from "a nondual perspective," but from the perspective I have.

I see humanity in all its agony and confusion; the Holocaust is part of that. Time, for me, has nothing to do with it. I have known people who were in the Nazi concentration camps and survived. All of that is real to me, in a way that apparently it is not for you.

It would not occur to me that I have to *do* anything about empathizing, sympathizing, accepting, or any other style of managing the perceptions, feelings, and thoughts that constitute my world. I am not trying to avoid anything. One way or another, I find myself responding to whatever arises, and I cannot predict any of that.

I do not feel separate from what I see, feel, or think. I do not fear my thoughts and feelings. They are what they are. None of that is up to me. I am not *controlling* anything. I am not *becoming* anything. I have *no idea* what may be seen next, felt next, thought next, said next, or done next.

I am not standing apart from biology and the mortal situation. Impermanence appears obvious to me, and I feel no temptation to paste some religious wallpaper on top of it. No escape hatch. No fingers crossed behind the back. This is freefall, most likely into oblivion.

While editing the video meeting from last Saturday for YouTube, I viewed it with the kind of objectivity that can arise when working technically. In that mode, the "Robert" on the screen appeared transparent and clear. I saw no heavy agenda. Nothing greedy. Each moment seemed good enough, including "I just embarrassed myself"—which the "Robert" on the screen declared after holding forth for what had felt to me at the time to have been an excessively long time, but which, when viewed in retrospect, seemed fine. Nothing embarrassing about it.

Regarding a "nondual perspective," I feel totally and completely unconcerned with what any philosopher or teacher from the past ever said about nonduality or anything else. My vision is simplicity itself and has nothing to do with "nonduality."

From this vantage—the vantage of my own mind—I see that many immersed in the faddish world of so-called nonduality have lost themselves entirely, so eager are they to distance themselves from the ordinary experience of being an ordinary human primate animal. Dissociation and depersonalization are symptoms of psychological splitting, an archaic ego defense mechanism—not "spiritual progress." When a metaphysical conjecture has bested ordinary experience, there is no sanity in that condition.

I see an unseemly thirst to comprehend nonduality logically, to defend it, advocate for it, to view it as a so-called "path," and even to teach it to others—as if "You don't *really* exist" were a precept to be followed; as if acquiring that doctrine would somehow immunize one against suffering the slings and arrows of outrageous fortune.

To my eyes, this passion to see things from a "nondual perspective"—whatever *that* means—appears to be a kind of madness. I wonder what anyone hopes to gain by being taught that. It's still old age, illness, and death, any way you slice it. I have called this nondual infatuation an hypnotic trance, because to me it often resembles the kind of delirium in which the mesmerized one seems intent upon gazing at a far away, fantasized landscape, while the facts of life are right here on the table in front of us, where they always are.

I do not intend to teach anyone what to think or believe about anything. I just say what I see. If this moment is filled with speculation and conjecture, or yearning and craving, that is what one will have.

That is *not* what I have.

86 - Existence precedes essence

A common religious idea holds that there is an essence that precedes existence. That idea is stated in numerous ways by different religions and philosophies. The Hindus, for example, say that the world is a drama staged in the mind of Brahman who is engaged in *leela,* divine play. For true believers, this is *not* a metaphor, but serious metaphysics. The Christians say that God made the heavens and the Earth.

Jean-Paul Sartre famously said the opposite: "Existence precedes essence," he declared. He meant that *being here at all* is the primary fact upon which *all* notions—*including* religious, spiritual, philosophical, and metaphysical ideas—are grounded. In that view, without *being*—which means the actual physical existence of us human animals—there *is* no "God," there *is* no religion, there *is* no spirituality.

To take as axiomatic the belief that a god, spirit, or universal intelligence consciously dreams up and creates all we see, feel, and think, is a bridge too far, I say. That is a religious conjecture, not a *fact*. Taking the "God" idea as axiomatically true immediately isolates the mind from coming into direct contact with things as they are; the reality of finding oneself conscious and aware, without *really* knowing anything about the source of all this, or what any of it means.

All we really *know* is that there seems to be something rather than nothing, with myself as the apparent center of perceiving that something. But we do not know what that something is or from whence it comes.

Seventy-something years ago, I awoke in my crib. Looking out the window, I saw the stars of the night sky. That was before I ever heard a word about "God."

We exist first, before trying to make sense of things via religion, science, philosophy, etcetera. And no matter what one believes, the world of sensory experience will not disappear. But when I say that "we exist," I do not mean that we humans are simply objects. We are *objectified* by the gaze of others because they see us, at least partially, *as* objects, but we do not have to see ourselves that way.

Q: In a letter dated 16 November 1959 to Valentine Brooke, Carl Jung writes:

> *When I say that I don't need to believe in God because "I know," I mean I know of the existence of God-images in general and in particular. I know it is a matter of a universal experience and, in so far as I am no exception, I know that I have such an experience also, which I call "God." It is the experience of my will over against another and very often stronger will, crossing my path often with seemingly disastrous results, putting strange ideas into my head and maneuvering my fate sometimes into most undesirable corners or giving it unexpected favorable twists, outside my knowledge and my intention.*
>
> *That strange force against or for my conscious tendencies is well known to me. So I say: "I know Him." But why should you call this something "God?" I would ask: "Why not?" It has always been called "God." An excellent and very suitable name indeed. Who could say in earnest that his fate and life have been the result of his conscious planning alone? Have we a complete picture of the world? Millions of conditions are in reality beyond our control. On innumerable occasions, our lives could have taken an entirely different turn. Individuals who believe they are masters of their fate are as a rule the slaves of destiny.*

A: I understand that point of view very well. It is shared by countless people. I am not one of them. We are *all* the "slaves of destiny," if you want to call it that. I see no way of getting around that. And I agree with Jung's saying that "Millions of conditions are in reality beyond our control." But just to say that one cannot subdue reality with will power does not mean that some "god" is in charge. Carl asks, "Why not call reality 'God?'" Very simple, I say. Such personification only obscures matters, and Jung, in my view, for all his brilliance, was often an obscurantist, too eager to concoct mystical explanations for ordinary events; and rather besotted with Christianity too.

I am more in line with Sartre's idea that existence precedes essence. The God idea of Jung and others has that reversed, holding that there is some universal essence from which human consciousness derives, and which we can come to know via religion or spirituality.

The problem with the word "God" (or its stand-ins such as "the universe" or "Source," etcetera) is that—once it has been *assumed* that essence precedes existence; once that is just taken as a given—any investigation is already polluted by that preconception, so that any claim to be experiencing God phenomenologically (such as the claim in Jung's letter to Valentine Brooke) has no epistemological validity at all.

To me, this seems a simple matter, but I understand that fear of God—strangely, to call someone a "God-fearing man" is considered a compliment on his character—which is taught to us from childhood, debars many of us from any actual phenomenological investigation in the real sense of that word. If something occurs, "It was God's will."

Another foolish aspect of Jung's statement is his imputation of a "will" or intentionality that is "greater" than human will and desire to a character, "God," who may not exist ontologically, except in human imagination.

Physics has said that random quantum fluctuations occur constantly but become "real" only in the presence of an observer. That view—which began at the turn of the 19th century with the ideas of Max Planck, and matured in the 1920s with the work of Erwin Schrödinger, Werner Heisenberg, and Max Born—is more like Sartre's and mine.

We humans *exist*—we must, for if we do not, none of this conversation makes sense at all on any level; and what we see, feel, think, etcetera, for *us*, exists. All else is beyond comprehension, and hanging a name, "God," or Brahman, on the incomprehensible explains nothing at all—zero. In fact, that very naming of something that may not exist outside of human imagination obfuscates and confuses, as I have just laid out.

You can say the word "unicorn," and even sing bhajans to the "Universal Unicorn," but that word has no significance except in the realm of myth. Outside the realm of myth, in the factual world, the word "unicorn" is utterly meaningless—a sound that refers to nothing real. If, on hearing that word, someone goes searching for a unicorn, that will be a long search. If, in the midst of that search, someone says, "I have not found the Great Unicorn yet, but I am certain he exists," that will be delusional.

87 - Might as well enjoy the show

Q: I just read a post about an awakening experience written by someone you helped. Why are these awakening events associated with a tremendous physical reaction, which often times is painful rather than pleasurable or neutral?

A: Pleasure lulls one to sleep whereas pain awakens. As the British playwright, Howard Barker, put this: "You emerge from tragedy equipped against lies. After the musical, you're anybody's fool."

Suffering is the royal road to understanding. The wise among us embrace suffering as a gift, albeit, like a rose, a thorny one. Not that one *wishes* to suffer—this is not about masochism—but we all *must* suffer in this long goodbye called life. So, when pain arrives, the wise among us don't ask why.

Q: Freedom lies that way, but you have to walk on embers without shoes on. Either stay enslaved, or take the leap and step on hot coals. I hate you, Robert—but I really mean I love you.

A: That "take the leap" claptrap is just another way of lying to yourself about being in charge. There *is* no leap. In each moment, you see what you see and feel what you feel. That is *not* optional. To imagine that you *could* decide to see more clearly and honestly than you do now, but are only postponing that clarity until you are ready for the shock, is just another way of falsely bestowing upon ego powers of choosing and deciding which it does not have and never will.

We are all walking on embers, no matter what. Do you imagine that avoiders, escapists, and magical thinkers never feel anxiety, never feel loss, never feel pain? You ought to know. Ha, ha.

Mortality—old age, illness, and death—is *the* central fact of human existence: a fact that cannot be denied, albeit most of us try and try. We all live with mortality and total impermanence, whether we imagine ourselves to be "enlightened," or claim, as you are doing, to be "enslaved." Enslaved by what? Living and dying? Welcome to the club. Your membership card is your navel.

Do you really think that you are enslaved now, but can *decide* at a certain moment to *stop* being enslaved? You may imagine that you can blind yourself to the truth of impermanence by covering your eyes with your hands, but you are already peeping through your fingers, like a child playing peekaboo.

You can call it "leaping" if you like, and therefore imagine postponing self-honesty until the fictional "later" when you are *ready* to leap. That's only a mind-game. You *really* know the facts of life right now as you read this. There is no "choice" in this. No one "leaps." Understanding happens for each of us as and when it does. No one can choose to understand, and no one can forestall it.

If, after hearing that, you still think you need to take the leap, then why not leap into full participation in this aliveness? One's health and physical freedom are soon enough diminished and degraded as the days dwindle down, and then this aliveness is depleted entirely.

So stop cowering on the porch like a frightened puppy, and come down to run in the meadow with the big dogs. Just come clean with yourself. Admit that you *already* see things as they are, that you already *know* the facts of life, and that this business about leaping is only a way of pretending you don't.

Then you won't need this charade about choosing and deciding; this agonizing dither will be over and done. You and this aliveness will be seen as one and the same happening, that can be neither sourced, nor split and dissected, nor explained, nor guaranteed, nor controlled.

This show we call "life" is the most expensive ticket on this planet. You pay, willy-nilly, with blood, suffering, and death. But hey! Since you are already in the theater, and the policy is "no refunds," you may as well enjoy the show.

And relax. It will all be over soon enough.

88 - Spontaneity

Q: Good day, Robert! A little history, and then I would love to hear any insight you may have.

During meditation in my early twenties, on four different occasions I experienced a sense of being pulled backward by my britches into a black tunnel that got very small until it disappeared. Instantly, in its place, was a beautiful white/yellow light which simultaneously seemed both to pulse and vibrate, like a gentle but powerful electrical current.

All this sight, sound, and vibration was also accompanied by an intense and powerful sense of love. I cried tears of joy as it literally took my breath away, leaving me feeling that there was no person called Donna, but rather that I *was* this light, sound, vibration, and love, which was everywhere and in everything ("things" were no longer, in fact, visible, yet there was a knowing that they were still there somewhere, way in the background).

Next, in my mid-thirties, I had a four-year experience of feeling total peace and joy and gratitude in the midst of this ever-changeful life of being a human being on planet Earth. It was very clear that, though there was a sense of being a person, it was also seen that "I" was not doing any of this. I felt very much like an instrument or willing puppet; and I called the animating power of that instrument "God" at the time. I had no other word for what was happening.

There was a definite sense of "me" in partnership with an all-powerful God, and I was a more than willing servant. Through thick or thin, good or bad, I felt like everything was meant to be just as it was, and I didn't want to change a thing. I woke up excited and grateful to be alive and couldn't wait to see what God had in store for me that day. I felt like the eye of the hurricane, safe and secure in the love of God.

Looking back at that experience today, it sounds so similar to what you speak of, which is this aliveness here and now.

Sadly, following some emotional trauma, I no longer felt this; and over the past sixteen years, I have done everything I can think of to get that experience back. I had no idea why it happened to me, where it came from—or what to do to get it back.

I retraced all my footsteps prior to that experience, and still nothing. I have spent all these years getting angrier and angrier that I lost this peace and gratitude for being alive. I have kicked and screamed; I have hated everyone and everything; I have gotten very depressed, and even suicidal. Life without that peace and love was meaningless and I wanted no part of being on Earth without it. Being human became a burden, and I hated to be here any longer.

In the last four years, nonduality has grabbed me faster than anything; I soaked it up like a dry sponge thrown into a lake. This did provide some relief and peace, as I could see that I was not the doer of my actions—yet I still could not explain the suffering I felt. And mostly I still felt the lack of peace and love and gratitude for this aliveness that we are, and the beauty of compassion for my fellow men.

After reading your book (which I have not quite finished yet), I feel like I was a locomotive speeding along at warp speed—and now I have come to a sudden and abrupt stop. I feel that I need to turn around, or even easier, just drop everything I've learned—which is a bit of a juggling game at the moment!

I am grateful to you for this "smack in the face" or "pulling the rug out from under me," because I am left sitting here thinking, "All this time, I thought I had all the answers that the nondualists were feeding me!" I really do feel that I was a wiseacre, and now I don't know anything. At first I laughed at this predicament, but now, a few days later, I feel a little numb.

In a way, this feels good: no more being fooled and having the carrot of everlasting bliss waved in my face. But I did experience *something* at one time, and now I am not experiencing things the way I would like it to, the way I remember it, and I know I have no influence over that ever happening again.

I am not sure how I feel most of the time, since recently finding you. But there is still the desire for that experience to return—to feel and know that I *am* that aliveness, with its freshness, newness and exciting spontaneity. Oh, how I miss waking up that way every day!

A: Hi. Yes, I will give you my thoughts, but you may not like hearing them.

1. You seem entirely attached to a few experiences that you imagine indicated something "spiritual" that you called "God." When I say "attached," I mean that you want to "get it back." But you can never get anything back. Everything is once-upon-a-once. Here today, gone tomorrow.

   As long as you are fixated on memories of some "better" time that you want to "re-experience," you are closed off to *this* very moment, which is all that actually exists. The idea that experiences, however pleasant or spiritually fulfilling, last forever is pure fantasy. No, experiences don't last. You feel what you feel when you feel it.

2. A "partnership with an all-powerful God" has nothing to do with what I call "aliveness." Aliveness actually exists and cannot be denied. "God" is an idea that was injected into your mind at some point, and, for some reason, you bought into it. You have no way of knowing whether such a thing as "God" exists or not. And even if it does exist in some way, you do not have the foggiest idea what "God" would be like. What you are calling the "love of God" is a particularly damaging notion. If someone desires to see things as they are, that idea will destroy clear-eyed seeing before it even starts.

   Even supposing that some all-powerful entity called "God" actually does exist, what makes you think there is any "love" involved? If "God" is pure love, why is there cancer, or children born blind, or people starving to death, or incessant wars being fought? What kind of "love" is that?

   In reply to that question, a popular answer is, "The Lord works in mysterious ways." I wonder if you can see the inanity of that reply. Why not just say that *events occur* in mysterious ways, and leave the conceptual "God" out of it?

3. "Aliveness with its freshness, newness and exciting spontaneity" is not some lovely feeling from the past to which you can return. Freshness and spontaneity are *not* memories. Freshness is only *right now,* not in the past.

   Spontaneity is the polar opposite of what you are wishing for. Spontaneity means that thoughts, feelings, and perceptions simply arise as they do, whether you like them or not. Likes and dislikes have nothing to do with it. As long as you keep seeking feelings that you desire, while seeking to avoid ones you dislike or fear, there is no spontaneity in that. And you are only deepening the self-hypnotic trance that conjures up a "myself" apart from feelings—a "myself" that "has" feelings and can wish for better ones.

If you really want to awaken to life as it is, that requires radical openness to what is—not the pipe dream of continual happiness and peace. I mean openness to feel *whatever* may arise for as long as that lasts. "Myself" does not "have" feelings. "Myself" *is* feelings (and thoughts, and perceptions and much more), peaceful or not, pleasant or not. Feelings *are* "you"—a big part of you—whether you like them or not.

All those supposedly happy memories to which you want to return are as dead and dry as dust. You have what you have *right now,* and that is all you ever have. Until you see that, you will always be *wanting* something. There is no *end* to wanting, unless you see that "you" are whatever you see, think, feel, etcetera, *right now*—not some separate, split-off "person" who has desires to fulfill and aversions to avoid.

This aliveness may include a great deal of suffering, both physical and psychological. Until you stop looking for the pot of gold at the end of the rainbow (call it "the love of God" or whatever), you will always be dissatisfied and searching for something better.

I've given it to you straight because you are dreaming of something that does not exist. You have been hypnotized by religion, is how it looks to me. *Snap out of it!*

Q: Thank you! So right! I have been scolded before for hanging onto the past and wanting only the good stuff. I guess I am a professional escape artist at avoiding unpleasantness. I truly appreciate the inspiration you are offering to be totally open to whatever appears now!

I had no idea that I was terrified of the pain and suffering that life would open me up to. Nondualism was a wonderful skirt to hide behind. Since reading your book, my mind has been cornered and has nowhere to go. I sit dazed and a bit numb as I absorb your words. "You are whatever you see, think, feel right now—not a separate, split-off person who has desires to fulfill and aversions to avoid." I know this, I agree—and yet something still has a hook somewhere in a promise of eternal bliss. Let go, I say. Let go! Freedom! Thank you! Hugs.

A: You are most welcome. It is never too late to awaken to what is.

89 - Hopelessness

Q: Robert, you said this:

> *Whatever you perceive, feel, and think is you. There is no* other *myself. In each moment, things are exactly as they are, and can be no different. The fantasy of becoming, supported by the false notions of time and progress, is an attempt to escape from this moment by replacing it with hopes for an improved future. Seeing this is an aspect of what I call awake.*

Well, Robert, that makes me think of an Alan Watts book title, *This Is It*, and I find myself struggling with that idea, the idea that there is nothing else *but* this. Maybe not struggling exactly, but hoping—hoping something special will happen. I guess the "special" is that I am here and aware. Is that it? Just this? Of *course* this is it. What else *could* be here but what *is* here?

Nevertheless, I feel some need to still believe in a future where, who knows how but somehow, things will be "better" and I will "wake up." On the one hand it seems silly, but yet I still notice myself engaging in this wishful thinking. I'm still meditating, hoping somehow to "jump." But hope seems to be fading. The idea of having no hope seems appealing in a way. I find myself just waiting and watching what arises. Thanks again.

A: You cannot decide to be *hopeless*. As my amigo John Troy has said, "The remedy is exhausting all remedies." I don't think John meant that you have to try every possibility under the sun, but that you try enough of them—meditation, prayer, faith in Jesus or some other godman, nonduality, sex, drugs, rock and roll, etcetera—until discovering that no matter *what* you try, ordinary human life still feels somehow unsatisfactory. The feeling of *needing* to try is unsatisfactory in and of itself. *Satisfactory* is when you aren't trying—you feel grateful for things as they are.

This is not to discourage you from meditating if you find that useful, but only to indicate that one can meditate from now until the cows come home, and still be hoping for something "better," something "more evolved." Which means that the present—which is all we ever have—is still felt to be unsatisfactory.

What makes it feel unsatisfactory is not just the pain and suffering of ordinary life, but that the moments of ordinary life—which are all that one really *can* experience—are constantly compared to a fantasy that one can *never* experience, and ordinary life suffers by comparison. Waking up means seeing the obvious: there is no alternative to now.

This, as Alan said, is *it*. On seeing *that*—really *seeing* it—one makes what one can of each moment, and that is the best any of us can do.

In my time corresponding with you, I have seen you grasp this *intellectually*—Watts said it, etcetera—but intellectual understanding can be a way of avoidance *disguised* as increasing comprehension. If you fully grasped the terror of the situation, even for a brief moment, you *would* wake up without having to *try* anything. And the feelings of dissatisfaction with ordinary *be*-ing would somehow have left, replaced by gratitude.

When I say *terror*, I mean that the very next instant of this life might not only not be "better" but could be devastatingly worse. We are all subject to events beyond our control. That obvious fact may be difficult to fully take in, particularly since we humans are so well defended against existential anxiety. But in my world, there are no guarantees of *anything*. One might be walking around feeling out of sorts because one wants to "wake up" and can't. Well, how would it be in the very next moment to trip and fall, ending up on one's back, paralyzed, *still* wanting to "wake up?"

I don't mean to preach, but how often do you count your blessings? Among the people I consider awake, every one of them, without exception, is filled with appreciation for the life they actually have, not wishing for something "else." That's why we awake ones enjoy one another's company so much. We all *get* it. We are all skating on the thinnest ice. No one has any questions about anything.

Even if nothing horrible ever happens, even if one has the great good fortune of a calm and gentle kind of life, perhaps one with real love and understanding in it, there is still old age, illness, and death waiting in the wings for us all.

In the light of *that* indisputable fact, the luxury of sitting at a keyboard posing questions, or in my case, replying to them, might seem just lovely. What else do you really want? What more has to happen for one to feel that the awareness one has right now is an opportunity, not a curse?

Q2: Hi Robert, what thoughts come to you about all of the chaos around the school shootings that seem to occur more and more frequently? I have a daughter aged seventeen in a public school, and the reports she brings of daily threats are shocking. I see it all as love screaming to know itself as tears fill up in my eyes also.

A: Hi. Since you are familiar with my work, I assume that you are asking for my thoughts because you want a candid view from an apparently awake human, but probably you won't like what I have to say. I understand that you are in pain about this and might be looking to me for comfort, but I have none to offer.

As I see it, saying that you see all that horrifying, murderous violence as "love screaming to know itself" is both foolishly idealistic and psychologically naive. To my ears, a statement like that embodies the worst aspects of "spirituality," which require blinding oneself to the animal nature of us human beings, who are actually very much like our close genetic relatives such as the chimpanzee, the bonobo, and the gorilla. If you observe those species alongside ours for any time at all, the resemblance is undeniable.

Yes, humans have the capacity to love, but we also have powerful capacities of aggression and instinctive sexuality that motivate a great deal of ordinary behavior, however much we may wish to deny it. Adolescent boys are particularly motivated by thwarted sexuality and by the need to establish themselves in the pecking order of aggression. Think, for example, of a middle school playground. Do you see a lot of "love" there?

The mindless aggression and pathological sexuality imposed upon Americans every day in the communications of their profoundly disturbed President give both impetus and cover to these tendencies towards violence.

If we looked into the histories of these mass shootings, I would bet that the perpetrators are mostly boys who could not attract girlfriends, were neither appealing physically nor athletic, and who were not even especially competent intellectually—which, while not as prestigious as either good looks or football skills, is another means of gaining a place in the pecking order.

The shooting sprees function, I imagine, as a means of *revenge* on those who did not recognize the shooter as a "somebody," while at the same time establishing his credentials as a person of note.

I feel for you. I would not like to have a child in an American public school at this juncture. But I strongly advise you to discard your delusive idea that humans are "loving" by nature. That is far too simplistic and rosy a view, and while you cling to it, you will not see things as they are.

Be well.

90 - What about protest against oppression?

Q: Robert, is protest, marching, fasting, useful or even pertinent, given your unique perspective? I ask because you post *very* little in that regard. Just to add, from my point of view, those activities will only have an effect when they cause financial difficulty for the perceived oppressor. Thank you, again, amigo!

A: You are most welcome, my friend.

I would not say that my perspective is "unique," except in the sense that no two snowflakes are ever *exactly* the same. My understanding, which is godless and devoid of piety, is neither singular nor original. The simple fact that an old Zen story or a quote from Epictetus can illuminate the ideas we discuss here demonstrates that my perspective is *not* unparalleled. It may be uncommon, but certainly not unheard of. This is worth noticing. There is, for example, no appreciable difference between my outlook and that of Huang Po from 1,300 years ago:

> *The ignorant eschew phenomena but not thought; the wise eschew thought but not phenomena.*

That said, let me address your question about the expression of dissent.

For me, certain injustices are so pernicious that they positively *demand* dissent, and that dissent might be anything from writing an editorial to carrying a picket sign, to blocking a highway, or, under certain circumstances, much more dramatic measures. As you say, hurting the oppressor's pocketbook often proves effective.

As a child, I felt that the most pernicious injustice was racism, which was institutionalized legally in the Southern states, and existed less formally, but not much less noxiously, everywhere else in the USA. All these years later, that racism is still baked into US cultural arrangements, and, except by those on the receiving end of it, goes largely unnoticed or even denied. Although race itself does not exist except as a fallacious concept, and the idea that humans can be divided into so-called "races" is a complete canard (21stcentury genetics confirms this[43]), racism *does* exist, and I oppose it in all instances.

So I was encouraged at seeing Colin Kaepernick take a knee on the sideline instead of standing at attention during the playing of the supposedly "sacred" US national anthem. And that style of protest is nothing new. In the 1968 Olympics, gold medalist Tommie Smith and bronze medalist John Carlos protested with a raised fist black power salute on the podium after the 200-meter final. I recall being encouraged by that sight too—thrilled by it actually. Of course, that kind of theater is always roundly denounced by the self-described "patriots." And that dialectic will never end.

Patriotism is the last refuge of a scoundrel, according to Mark Twain, and racism is related to patriotism, although few self-styled patriots will want to see it that way. When Muhammed Ali was drafted to fight in Vietnam, he famously said, "I ain't got nothing against no Viet Cong. No Viet Cong never called me nigger," and that's what I mean.

If you think I should not have used the so-called "N-word," I disagree. I would never call someone that, but I certainly refuse to bow to political correctness by bowdlerizing someone else's words when quoting. If you called someone a fuckhead, I would never say that you called someone "an F-word head." Since you are asking about protest, the dumbing down of language is one thing I *always* protest.

Other injustices I consider worthy of dissent and protest are the oppression of the poor by the rich and powerful; institutionalized misogyny and the imposition of gender roles; the abuse and exploitation of non-human animals; and the defilement of the Earth itself, which humans seem dead set on exploiting to the point of non-habitability.

Now, you and I may see the same injustice, but that does not mean that we will respond in the same way. No one has any choice in that.

---

43. See Chapter 50, "Loneliness."

My response *is* me; your response *is* you. As I have said often, the apparent cleavages between doing, do-er, and done, are, in my view, entirely imaginary.

More generally, no one is *making* this world be the way it is, or else *all* of us, whose aliveness is a feature of this universe, are making it be this way—which is the same thing. Each of us simply expresses what we understand, or fail to understand, and no "choice" about it.

Whether the dramas of protest and counter-protest (like Trump calling brave Mr. Kaepernick "ungrateful"—and where else can you make millions of dollars for being a second-string quarterback, so salute the flag and don't complain or else get out of "our" country!) are useful in some cosmic sense, I have no idea. But we human beings *will* express ourselves, which means expressing one's present understanding, both conscious and unconscious, for better or worse.

Personally, I love to see dissent against injustice and support that dissent without judging as "evil" the apparent perpetrators of the injustice. They are no more choosing their reprehensible roles than you and I are choosing ours.

Quite a circus, I'd say, and although it does have clowns, the totality is really not very funny.

91 - Alive and direct

Q: Dear Robert Saltzman, would you consider holding live meetings via Zoom or any live interactive video program? That would be much more alive and direct.[44]

A: That has been suggested to me often. I am not really drawn to it. Understanding that I have something useful to share, I am happy to offer candid replies to questions here, and anyone can read *The Ten Thousand Things*. So I don't know what would be gained by creating a group dynamic with yours truly as the cynosure.

I am not a spiritual teacher. I don't have any method to urge upon you. Nor can I say that "awakening" will solve all your psychological problems and leave you feeling just peachy. I have no special power to "awaken" anyone, so I don't know what any meetings would really be about.

You don't *need* a meeting with "Robert." I have only one thing to share, one message, and you can hear it right now for free without having to wait for any meeting:

Spirituality and religion are largely nonsense, based on promises of some supposedly "transcendent" state that you will obtain later after adopting some belief system, path, procedures, proper worship, or whatever. *Don't believe it*. Don't be misled. *You are here now,* I say, and this is it.

There is no guarantee that you will even be alive tomorrow, much less that tomorrow will somehow be better than today. Embrace what is here now, for, like it or not, now is all you ever have, and that is passing away like the morning dew right before your eyes.

In case that is not clear, these words of mine from an old interview express quite well what I call "awake:"

44. Robert has since held such meetings via Zoom, which are currently available on YouTube.

> *Freedom does not entail leaving anything behind, or splitting "good" from "bad," but in opening completely, without resistance, to whatever is seen, felt, thought, and otherwise experienced moment by moment as the one and only "reality." There* is *no* other *"you," and no* other *reality except in your imagination, which is only changeful thought.*
>
> *The freedom you desire is here right now and consists of being exactly what you are moment by moment, with no idea of improvement or of attaining or becoming anything else. There is no impediment, I say, to this radical self-acceptance except in imagination. That impediment is whatever you* imagine *you* might *be or* could *be "if only." Just stop!*

Please do not imagine that "Robert" has some unique "teaching" that you can get only from me. Here are some words from the middle-ages that say it all:

> *Friends, I tell you this: there is no Buddha, no spiritual path to follow, no training and no realization. What are you so feverishly running after? Putting a head on top of your own head, you blind idiots? Your head is right where it should be . . . Stop turning to the outside and don't be attached to my words either. Just cease clinging to the past and hankering after the future. This will be better than ten years of pilgrimage*
>
> —Lin Chi

If you think that seeing and hearing me on a screen would "enliven" this message, I did a two-hour interview with Rick Archer on his program *Buddha at the Gas Pump*[45] that is available on YouTube. It's been viewed a lot.

Q: Your response raises some questions. If live interaction is really of no use and has no effect at all, then how could you explain spending years and years with your mentor, and he with his, and he with his,

45. See https://BATGAP.com/robert-saltzman/

etcetera? I can feel the gratitude in you when you speak of your mentor. Would you say all those years you spent with him did not help strip from you the many delusions you held in your head about awakening? Did your mentor tell you that meeting him live was useless, and so you understood that and stopped going to him?

I do certainly understand that you have no desire to guide or mentor anyone, as perhaps that is not what you like or prefer. Perhaps you are weary of us, the idiots. Ha, ha.

It has been said that the greatest help of an awake person is to be with them. Please, I would love it if you would expound on the above questions.

A: OK. Ask and ye shall receive. Ha, ha.

When I met the man in question, Walter Chappell, he had just returned home from an exhibition of my photographs to find me waiting for him there at his house. I'd not gone there seeking guidance, but because a woman at the opening of my exhibition told me that another serious photographer was living just down the road, and I should meet him. At the time, I had not heard Walter's name and had no idea who he was.

It was just my good luck that Walter turned out to be one of the great photographers of the 20th century, who took me under his wing and imparted to me the arcane intangibles of black and white printmaking. When we met, I was not looking for a spiritual teacher, nor was I thinking much about "awakening." That just occurred. Who knows how or why? And we did not spend "years and years" together. That friendship was not at all what you seem to imagine.

Most of what I learned from my association with Walter was learned through our darkroom hours together, or traveling for hours in silence in his beat-up old car, or showing our photographs at some museum or university art department, or staying up all night along with my wife, Catanya, drinking Armagnac (which Walter favored because George Gurdjieff always used it for his toasts to the idiots). There was never any specific "spiritual teaching" involved. Whatever his quirks—and they were many—Walter was *awake*, and

I recognized that when others missed it entirely. If you see that in me, make use of it.

Finally, it is not that I am reluctant to be a guide. If someone finds guidance in what I am sharing here, I am OK with that. I am *reluctant*, if you want to put it that way, to form a group with myself at the center of it. Very reluctant. The results of that procedure are all too predictable: people act out their own historical family dynamics, and Robert will be "Daddy." I don't need to see any more of that. I paid my dues to the psychotherapy union for years, and now I am retired.

If you want that kind of thing, just google "spiritual teachers" and you will find countless possibilities. My message is not about that. I am telling you that your "true self"—the one you imagine has gone missing and has to be recovered—is here right now. It always has been. What do you imagine is reading these words and making sense of them right now? That's *it*, amigo!

There is, I say, no pot of gold at the end of the rainbow. The notion of *transcendence*—of being "elsewhere" than this, or being something "other" than this—is a product of superstition and priestcraft. Priests, whether they are called that or not, are paid to disseminate religious fantasies. If they spoke honestly—meaning only about what they really *know* personally, not what they believe on *faith* or what the teacher ahead of them in their "lineage" believed—no one would want to pay them. I have no use for that foolishness.

I am not withholding anything. I am speaking publicly, and this is my second book on these matters, so obviously I am not hiding. I reply to all questions as honestly and open-heartedly as possible. If someone finds guidance or mentoring in that, fine by me.

Earlier, a friend said, "Robert, your open Q&A availability, as you know, takes you dangerously close to 'play guru' territory." He's right. However, all the real sages (such as Lin Chi, whom I mentioned above) had to get "dangerously close," because that is where the rubber meets the road; and I am like that. I am not a guru with some perfectionistic fantasy to peddle. I am telling you, just like Lin Chi did, to get your head out of your own ass and try to see that *this is it*! Right here, right now, as you read these words. There isn't anything "else."

Lin Chi said it more politely. He didn't mention your ass.

Stop turning to the outside and don't be attached to my words either. Just cease clinging to the past and hankering after the future.

Q2: I know I have asked you this before, Robert, but I am just not getting it. Regarding the notion of not clinging to the past, don't thoughts of the past just happen? The past just resurfaces on its own, and you get caught up in thoughts about the past automatically. I don't know how you "stop it," as Lin Chi stated. And the same goes for the future. For those for whom this "stopping" has happened, it sure sounds great. But in reading Lin Chi's words, it sounds like a choice, and I don't see that it is.

A: That's a good question. From my perspective, it's like this: there is no choice; in each moment things are as they are and cannot be different. So you are not "choosing," but you are influenced by everything you see, hear, feel, etcetera. And all of those influences become part of the present "you." If you happen to pick up a book about Lin Chi, for example, and you read where he says "Don't cling," that enters into the mix. Thus, we humans influence one another.

Now, you cannot *choose* either by whom you want to be influenced. You came upon some words of mine long ago now and felt attracted to them, and so you went on to read more. And now you find yourself understanding what earlier had been incomprehensible to you. But you did not *choose* to keep following this page; you simply followed your attractions *as we all do*. Nor can anyone *decide* to understand my words. You either understand or you don't. You get what you get when you get it.

Another person might come upon this page and think, "This guy is all wet. What does he mean by saying no one is choosing anything? I make choices constantly. I'm not going back to his page again." And that would not be a *choice* either. She would just be following her attraction—or in this case her aversion, which is the backside of attraction.

Q2: So is all this, as you say, just the way the cookie crumbles?

A: Yes, you've got it! You can't *do* anything about this. The apparent *choice* to stop avoiding this moment—to stop escaping into regrets about the past or worries about and hopes for the future—is the outcome of innumerable processes taking place mostly invisibly and outside of conscious awareness. One day you might just find yourself no longer looking to the future for anything. And if you told someone about that and they said, "That sure sounds great. Teach that to me," you couldn't.

Lin Chi reminds me of myself. Perhaps I am his reincarnation, ha, ha. He said, "So far I have not found anyone who can set himself free"—by which he meant that he could *mention* freedom, but no one could get it by trying.

Q2: I guess I am wasting my time here. Ha, ha.

92 - This is not a test

Q: It is remarkable how many seem to share the common experiences and shift in perception that *The Ten Thousand Things* has constellated.

I'd like to share a bit of a personal update, if I may. I now find myself past the very powerful initial flush of realization that occurred just a few weeks ago, and settling into this spinning gyroscope of newfound perception. I find myself without a "fixed point" from which to take my bearings. As once I struggled to realize, there is a sense that this is "uncontainable-open-sky."

Some sort of surrender occurred when this shift took place, but it has become clear that there was no willingness on my part to surrender. More accurately, my position had been overrun.

Primarily, I feel a sense of equanimity, but occasionally this sharp sword of discernment (Manjusri riding a lion with a sword in his hand is the Buddhist image of it) gives rise to shreds of confusion and frustration. At times the ice is thin. The most noticeable difference, if one were to compare, is that these sensations and emotions are no longer recognized as a "state" or identified as "myself," but rather a passing cloud, blossoms blowing across the snow. Yet this is somewhat troubling.

The telling of your tale has come forward with profound effects, and I imagine, to be truthful, for you this is something of a burden, at times. I and many others deeply appreciate your honesty, your sharing of ideas and clarifications.

I would like to inquire if you would share with me some of the experience shortly after your initial realization. All sensations, fabricated mythology, and "past" remembrances are clearly just that; grasping at straws. But, as I said, standing in the light of realization casts a deep shadow as well. Does it seem that such a shadow must necessarily fall upon one's former sensibilities?

Have you ever seen the book *The Mountain Poems of Stonehouse,* translated by Red Pine (Bill Porter)? His translation of "Cold Mountain" is recognized as one of the better ones. Perhaps your friend Robert K. Hall may know about him. Stonehouse was purported to have said:

> *Where there's a Buddha you can't remain. Those are dead words. Where there's no Buddha, hurry past. Those are dead words too. Now I understand living words.*

When questioned about his understanding, he replied: "When the rain first clears in the late spring, the oriole on the branch sings out." A very lovely metaphor, pointing to appropriate action as it arises without complication. So it is! This, just *be*-ing, has become the reality of what I formerly called "myself". The flow of perceptions at times seems incomprehensible, their presence unbearable, often leaving me stunned.

Your comments are most deeply appreciated.

A: Interesting that you mentioned Manjushri and Robert K. Hall in the same letter. Robert and I used to meet weekly for several years to discuss these matters, and often those meetings were not entirely peaceable. In those days, Robert was an ordained Buddhist priest, a traditional teacher of *vipassana* meditation, and the charismatic leader of a *sangha* here in Todos Santos. He is still all those things, except that the word "traditional" no longer fits. His vision lately has turned radical.

Robert has devised a kind of meditation retreat that is unparalleled as far as I know. This combines days of silent meditation with evenings of Gestalt psychotherapy. It's powerful, and "Buddhist" in name only. I've never attended one, but Robert invited me to the farewell dinner of a ten-day silent retreat with his favorite students, who came to Todos Santos from the Mexican mainland—I was the only outsider. He had instructed the students in advance that they could ask me questions. The questions were coming from a notably turned-on place. Remarkable, really.

But, as I was saying, during the time we met weekly, Robert was teaching straight-ahead Theravada Buddhism, which I regard not as

"Truth," but as a kind of philosophy informed by acute psychological insights, with some unfortunate piety and even more unfortunate worship attached to it. For me, some of those teachings ring true, and some don't. But I seem to be skeptical by nature. Robert, as he will tell you, is more the *bhakti* type.

So we were two very different types hashing out our perspectives, and it wasn't always easy, particularly for Robert, who later told me that a few times he left our meetings ready to call the whole thing off. But by the skin of his teeth, I suppose, Robert hung in there with me, and nowadays we find ourselves like two birds if not in the same tree, at least in the same little part of the woods. Robert read *4T* and got it all, one hundred percent, no questions asked—which, since he was the first reader, was an excellent hit for me.

Anyway, one day when Robert and I were sitting under a tree conversing, I said something along the lines that such and such a Buddhist idea did not comport at all with my understanding—except that, to be honest, I used the word "bullshit," and other such language. Robert looked at me and said, "Oh, *now* I get it. You're Manjushri."

Robert is quite ill now, and I love him a lot, so I enjoyed being able to write that remembrance. Yes, as you say, "remembrances are clearly just... grasping at straws." So I just found myself grasping at one.

Well, with that out of the way, let me try to reply to your question.

I was fairly young when that unmistakable "initial flush," as you called it, came over me. It was 1984, I think. I saw what I saw, and there was no going back, but it was not always easy. Regardless of my seeing that nobody is "doing" anything—all of this is just arising as it must, or "arising as it does," if the word "must" seems unduly deterministic—I was still attached to my image and identity as an artist, and struggled for years trying to accommodate both modes, having to live together in the same body and speak through the same mouth. I would not say that equanimity was my most common condition in those days. I was on a mission of some kind, I can recall that much, but honestly, I cannot remember what the mission entailed. Vanity, self-promotion, and self-importance had something to do with it.

The struggle between name and form as an identity—as opposed to what one "really" is—was never resolved by anything I did, but by *force majeure.* I was struck down by a devastating illness just on the eve of an exhibition and book signing at which I was to be the star—and that was the kind of lesson you never forget. This body I call "my" body has a life of its own. I may *call* it my body, but it is not "mine" at all.

> *Like a falling star, like a bubble in a stream, like a flame in the wind, like frost in the sun . . .*
>
> —*Gotama the Buddha*

So, if your body is not "yours," what, if anything, is? I understand you when you say that it can be "somewhat troubling" to suspect that the answer is "nothing at all." That is what I call "freefall."

I got used to it. But I have had a lot of good luck. I was in love with a beautiful woman when the freefall began, and she has stuck with me all these years, including the year of that illness, during which I was useless, and ever since; while I, falling forever through vast vistas, immersed myself in study, art, and my work as a psychotherapist, almost at times like a monk.

Fortunately, I avoided blathering about my "awakening" as I see people do, so that vision wasn't wasted and exchanged for status, money, or otherwise debased. And because it wasn't ill-spent, and because, except for a brief foray, I wasn't "teaching" awakening, these ideas have been free to flow and change as they will, without considerations of consistency, marketability, or what people might think of me.

I am not a spiritual teacher, but just an ordinary awake human. I feel beholden to no one. I don't feel obligated, so I do not regard you or anyone else as a burden. Put that out of your mind. Everything I do or don't do is pure self-expression. There is no avoiding it. It issues forth as it does, and I am not judging it.

It's good that I am not a spiritual teacher, because I have said things that a year or two later seemed questionable, or at least sophomoric. Thank god I'm not on a pedestal and so don't have to apologize for being human. Some of that imprecision and error was just pure laziness; sometimes, when asked about "awakening," instead of diving in totally to my own experience, I'd resort to catchphrases and boilerplate. I think those days have passed. This all feels utterly honest now; perhaps that accounts for the "common experiences and shift in perception that *4T* has constellated," as you put it. Honesty is a powerful clarifying agent.

But this "nonjudgment" of self and others is not some stance I have affected because someone told me that judgment is "bad." If I don't judge, that's because I am in no *position to* judge. Yes, I am awake, and I know it, but awakening never ends. Something I say today might need revision tomorrow. There are no experts in the art of living, which is an art of improvisation, not certainty. We are all in this together. If there is to be a goal at all, let it not be "enlightenment"—that will o' the wisp—but ordinary adult sanity.

I don't know the poems of Stonehouse, but that sounded like something I might say myself. I appreciate your candor, so I will give you some advice:

Now that the scales have fallen, don't worry any further about this stuff. Just let it all flow, like water in an arroyo making its way to the sea. Ideas are just ideas, whether they come from some "master," from Robert Saltzman, from the man in the moon, or right out of your own mind. Meanwhile, this aliveness simply is, and if that feels uncomfortable at times, it just does. We are, after all, human primates alive in a universe so vast that no human can comprehend it; we are not "gods." Our mentality evolved for survival and reproduction, not for comprehending ultimate metaphysical so-called "Truths" to the point of total confidence and freedom from all anxiety. The desire for *that* may be a false lodestar indeed.

That is why I have no use for emulation of the "masters" of Vedanta so beloved by "spiritual" people who imagine that imitation is a "path" to selfhood or "self-realization." It isn't. Quite the opposite in fact. To find one's own mind requires killing *all* Buddhas. The so-called "Truth" of the Indian sages, whose shadows still fall upon

21st century minds, is only a variety of *ontological idealism*, as this is known in Western philosophy: the idea that nothing exists but consciousness. Really? And one knows that how?

That idea can be considered and arguments made for it, but never demonstrated factually. To assert that one *knows* this by means of personal experience—which is *precisely* the claim that jnanis make—seems an empty claim indeed: "Truth is what I say it is." Such unmitigated certainty about ultimate matters may inspire, but by that very feeling of being inspired, people lead themselves astray. They are beguiled by the Ramanas and Nisargadattas of this world, and nowadays their epigones as well, who claim to be certain of so much. I, on the contrary, who feel wide awake, cannot be certain of anything except I know I'm here.

In my view, the key point is this: being near Ramana Maharshi seemed to produce a sense of stillness and peace in people, and that is why he was loved. I have no doubt of that. But inducing peace and stillness is not a test of the facticity of his metaphysics, which were just party-line Advaita Vedanta, like that of Nisargadatta, Papaji, and their present-day copycats.

I have known more than one person whose religious certainty about "no death" seemed to provide them with a deep sense of peace and stillness that was felt by others, including me. There are photographs of two aged women like that in *The Ten Thousand Things*. Those women, and others I am thinking about in this regard, were not Hindus, but neighbors here in Mexico who embrace straight-ahead Catholic theology, including God, Jesus, Heaven, the Devil, saints, angels, etcetera.

There is no question that beliefs can influence mood and behavior, and that belief in certain religious propositions might reduce anxiety about impermanence and mortality. But that's not the point. I am writing here for people who are wondering about a sense of peace and stillness that does not hinge upon believing *anything* about ultimate matters. If someone finds relief in the idealism and eternalism of religions such as Advaita Vedanta or Christianity, fine by me. To each his own. Whatever floats your boat. I am not proselytizing here, only saying that, by my lights, belief is one thing and knowledge quite another.

Saying this openly may seem audacious, but in all honesty, I find myself wide-awake and entirely present—which for me, I am saying, requires *no belief* in anything idealistic or eternal at all. To feel alive, including aches and pains both physical and psychic, is a *fact*—not necessarily a problem to be solved like a Rubik's cube. Each moment dies as soon as it is born, and can never come back again. Nothing is *becoming* anything. "You" are not becoming anything. This is it.

As Ramana Maharshi put this, "What you are, you *already* are;" or, in another version, also attributed to him, "You already are that which you seek."

Notice, please, that I am able to agree wholeheartedly with the *phenomenology* of Maharshi's self-observations, which are not dissimilar to mine—the *suchness* of each moment, the *equanimity* of silence—without needing to agree at all with the traditional metaphysics taught to him since childhood, and preached in turn to his followers. Whatever may have been his *experience* of being this aliveness, verbally he was mostly just affirming the certainties that his followers had heard countless times before, or read in the Bhagavad Gita or other "sacred" books. Boilerplate.

Ramana always said, as I do, that silence is the *real* teacher, and that his verbal instructions were for those who couldn't access that directly. In the same way, if I had been born and raised Catholic like my neighbors here, and then found myself equanimously awake like this, I might very well be talking about "the peace of God that transcends all understanding," and working within the constraints of Christian conceptions like the myth of Jesus.

Thank god I'm not! I feel fortunate to be entirely free of that entire trip. For me, living and dying is sufficient in and of itself. No afterlife encore required. Beliefs are *de trop*, superfluous, just excess baggage, at best misleading.

We are not required to attain *anything*, I say. Nothing. This is not a test. When that is seen, one can relax.

93 - Tabula rasa

Q: I just learned the meaning of the term *tabula rasa* that you used in the last Zoom meeting, when you said that some babies are born with a confident disposition and others with an anxious disposition. The last day or two, I became aware of the idea that inculcation of religion can have traumatic effects on the nervous system, and if one is born with an anxious disposition, can traumatize the entire organism.

One of the things I noticed from your book—and this is my third reading—is its quiet influence in these matters. During these last two days, I have come across Peter Levine's work on somatic experiencing and trauma release, and I saw how the "not-knowing" of which you speak can help with that release of old wounds. Today, I found my body taking it real easy, and requiring quietness.

I lay there, sensing various areas, and just allowed release. I let it flow, and this was very subtle. I came to your book with few expectations, but I find *4T* working in interesting ways and filled with deep clarifications, beyond even, as you say, my ken.

A: Yes, the human being is not born *tabula rasa*—not born a clean slate. That is an undeniable fact, and an important one to understand. So much of what we suffer was there on the day we were born—not as ideas and concepts as we adults speak of them, but as inborn tendencies that developed over eons in African grasslands radically different from the highly structured environments in which we humans increasingly live and must survive.

That is one reason why the search for understanding cannot be satisfied fully by a one-size-fits-all answer. If you feel satisfied by someone else's words and ideas, you have sold your birthright for a mess of pottage, or is it a pot of message (sorry, couldn't hold back). Awakening never ends. Walk on!

Q: Yes! *4T* is a bit of a mystery. I noticed when reading it that, as images come up, your way of expression seems to strip away the concreteness of the images, leaving no solid objects, but just this ineffable now. This is *not* a woo-woo observation. In my reading of your words, even the woo-woo buggers off. I observe this also in your responses to people's questions. You seem to leave them with nothing to grasp.

A: That is what John Troy says about my work. It leaves no "escape hatch," as he calls it. That's probably because I have no escape hatch. This is it! And all I can do is deal with *this* moment as best I can. That's not always been pretty, but sometimes it's been entirely beautiful.

94 - Philosophical awareness

Q: Warm wishes from Northern Ireland, Robert. I discovered you through Joan Tollifson and am on my second reading of *The Ten Thousand Things,* as are several of my friends, and I have passed details on to others. You don't leave a rug under anyone's feet.

A: Thanks, and I wish you well from Mexico. Joan and I met through *The Ten Thousand Things*. Julian Noyce, who publishes *4T,* gave Joan a copy to read, and she got in touch to discuss it with me. Since then, we have become friends.

You know, I don't have the intention of pulling the rug out from anyone. I have no ambition, goal, or design for anything like that. What may appear to be intentional iconoclasm is really just my point of view—just the way I see things—which is philosophical, but not in any way religious. I am a life-long artist by nature who has always found modes of self-expression, and this writing and my photographs are the present work.

My interest has never really been "spirituality" but what I call "life and mind." Those two may intersect sometimes, but they are not the same. There is so much of life and mind that most spirituality seems bent on excluding or denying; or, if it cannot be denied entirely, then cleaning up, "improving," and putting to good use.

I kept silent about the whole "awake" thing for years and felt no need to discuss it, except with one friend, Robert K. Hall, the noted Buddhist teacher, who could understand my words. Robert and I have great conversations. A few years ago, we decided to have one publicly at a weekly meeting of his *sangha*. It's on my YouTube channel—worth a gander, I think. Robert is very ill now, but this was Robert at his best.

The issue of spiritual teaching came up when a therapy client I was seeing twice a week said, "Robert, whenever I come here, you are always the same. Always relaxed, always open, always smiling. How do you do that?"

Well, I found myself answering from the heart, as I am doing here and now. But later, I began to feel that my candor might have wandered beyond the therapeutic pale, so I spoke with Robert, an ex-psychiatrist, about it. Robert said, "You did no wrong. You are a natural teacher of nonduality, and that's all it was. That's what you should be doing."

Soon after, he sent me someone from his group whom he said he was not able to help, and I started working with her. So that's how I got into spiritual teaching. That lasted a couple of years, and then I'd done all of that I wanted to do.

If I am doing some kind of teaching here, let's call it philosophical clarity, not spirituality. As I tried to make clear in *The Ten Thousand Things*, I have little interest in spirituality *per se*, but only to the extent of its intersection with human actualities.

There are some teachers of what is called "spirituality" whom I can and do respect. Joan Tollifson is one of them. Before she shared my work with you all, I did not know about her, but *Nothing To Grasp* is a beautifully written, honest book. Joan brings a frankness and integrity to her work that is rare indeed.

But teachers free of dogma seem to be in the minority. In my view, to perform the role of teacher properly requires that one be fully human, with no desire to escape from the ordinary facts of ordinary life. Unless the teacher can offer that, I can't get with it. Nowadays, people ask my opinion about one teacher or another. It's rare that I can offer a positive review, so Joan is an exception. Mostly, I see too much speaking *about* "Truth," and too little speaking truthfully.

Thanks for getting in touch. Be well.

Q2: Hello, Robert. You said that the entire spiritual dilemma comes down to denial. What is that denial? It does not seem to be something from modern times. It is there in traditions sanctioned as coming from God, or whatever name they give it.

A: The denial to which I refer is the resistance to seeing that everything alive must die; that time cannot be stopped; that all you think you are and all you think you have will be lost, and that this cannot be "transcended" except in fantasy.

Q2: So is the denial just the effort to live as if we had an immortal self, a soul? To leave something behind that makes us immortal?

A: So far as anyone knows, oneself is not immortal, and the "immortal self" or "soul" is a religious fantasy with absolutely nothing to back it up.

Q2: But the personal self, which we call "me," wants to survive the body, right? And is it not true that we are immortal as life, which exists always and does not disappear just because of the passing on of a body?

A: I never think about "surviving the body." That idea doesn't mean a thing to me. Couldn't care less.

You ask if you are not "immortal as life." That depends on what you mean by "me." First, discuss with yourself what you mean by the word "I," and then you will understand what I have been saying.

Q2: Yes, life is the force that animates all this, and "me" is just a construction in the brain of images, memories, thoughts, and the process of conditioning. I understood that, and I understand that just repeating an affirmation that we are immortal as life does not do anything until we really see it; and this seeing just happens or it doesn't. There is nothing I can do about making it happen.

A: No. I am *not* saying that this is about coming to see that "myself" is immortal. Quite the opposite. This is about coming to see that "myself" is *not* immortal—not as "life" and not as anything else.

The "myself" that has raised the idea of immortality as a defense against fear of meaninglessness and extinction is not "life" at all, but a collection of programs that were pushed upon the child from infancy: ideas such as "God," salvation, Heaven, reincarnation, transcendence, etcetera, that are imposed upon the physical and mental structures of a primate animal. There is nothing immortal in any of that, nor in the idea that one is only *dreaming* of being a separate self.

Suppose you got the "just a dream" idea from some Hindu *jnani* or a Western imitator, and now you believe it. Then how do you know that the *jnani* is not just a dream figure, or that his or her words about Brahman or whatever are not just more dream nonsense?

Further, it may not even be true that life in general is immortal. We have no way of knowing that. After all, eventually our Sun will go nova, and Earth will be incinerated. There may be life elsewhere in the universe, but if there is, we know nothing about it. And your reference to "the life force" is a prime example of denial. That assumes that there is some outside, superior "force" that "animates" the body, as you put it. The body *is* alive in and of itself. Why split this aliveness into a body and a so-called "force?"

The "life force" is a *religious* idea: "God" fashioned man from clay and then breathed "life" into that lifeless clay man. The English word "spirit" is derived from the Latin *spiritus*, which means breath. But the body *is* life. It is *born* alive and does not need any "spirit" to be breathed into it in order to be alive.

I am suggesting that you stop imagining that there is some eventual "understanding" that will take the sting out of the facts of living, ageing, and dying. That is a desperate fantasy. The pinprick of impermanence is part of our actual condition as primate animals with brains developed enough to afford a measure of self-consciousness. *There is no escape hatch from mortality.* You can play around with words like "spirit" as much as you like, but when the time comes, you will have to turn your face to the wall and die just like any other animal.

That is what is being denied in whatever form the denial may take, religion and spirituality being one of the most popular, along with drugs and alcohol; promiscuous sex and other forms of hedonism; constant distraction and entertainment; collecting huge piles of money and property; attaching oneself to long-lasting institutions; or creating "legacies" that will carry on one's name after cessation sets in. As for the money and property gambit, some country and western star—I forget who—said, "I never saw a hearse with a U-Haul trailing behind it."

The wise, I find, *acknowledge* the sting, *live* with the sting, and may even come to appreciate that impermanence brings the piquancy and the beauty to this situation we call "living."

95 - To see that you are awake right now

Q: Hi Robert. In our conversation in the last Zoom meeting, you said, "To see that you are awake right now, just extend 'I don't know' to 'I know *nothing*.'" For someone such as myself who doesn't know I'm awake, how does this knowing nothing extend into daily working life? Is there no division? Does one really not know anything at all? Is "myself" just natural choiceless awareness throughout?

A: You can know how to tie your shoes or do a calculation in mathematics, but you will never know what "I" am.

Q: You talk about never knowing what "I" or "myself" actually is; that "I" or "myself" is simply here, or simply arising without any say-so. You also mention the ever-changing in the changeless. Do you see any distinction between the changeless field of awareness, and the flow or changing within that? Or is it one and the same? What is this perspective that feels so personal? Do such questions matter, or are these just thoughts to be discarded, no longer useful ideas, so that it is better to, as you said, "just relax?"

A: I don't think I ever used the word "changeless." That does not sound like something I would say. Perhaps nothing is changeless. How could I ever *know* such a thing? Assuming there even is such a condition, from what perspective could *changelessness* be observed? What, for example, if something is changing incredibly slowly—over thousands of years, or millions of years, like the changes that occur through evolution by natural selection or changes in the geography of Earth? How could a human who lives for such a brief span of time ever notice such changes?

"Changeless" is an idealistic religious concept—not a fact. Concepts about ultimate matters have nothing to do with *knowing*—not by my epistemological lights. Those concepts are *beliefs*, not knowledge.

Others may have less stringent standards than mine—for example, "I know it because it's in the Bible," or "The Dhammapada said so."

Q: So, aside from the "how" of one plus one equals two, or where to buy good coffee, is "*this*" unknowable in every way, or is it a felt sensation? Is it both tangible and intangible? Is "*this*" only knowable as "myself" in present form appearing in each moment? Does this question make sense?

A: We can know what it is like to be human, including ideas, theories, feelings, and intuitions about ourselves, the universe, and this aliveness. But we cannot ever know how, or even if, those ideas and feelings correspond to some theorized "greater reality." Details of a supposed "greater reality" are conjectures, not facts. If you take those concepts as facts and imagine that they point to an ultimate goal to be realized or attained, you will only impede the kind of useful noticing and comprehending that is, I say, possible for us human beings.

For example, I can notice easily that I, Robert, am not the author of my thoughts and feelings. That kind of noticing is part of what I mean by "awake." So I can be aware of thoughts and feelings, but I cannot know the ultimate *source* of thoughts and feelings. That is beyond my ken. Calling it "Source" or "God" or "the Divine" or "the Absolute" explains nothing, and only creates yet another devotional mental image that, for all we really *know*, may refer to nothing actual at all. Our minds are *filled* with such images that were put there by others. Image pollution.

Q: Your way of seeing seems ungraspable. Your manner of expression and the outcome of what you are conveying is most rare. So, if I understand anything you are saying: although one can know that one is *not* the maker of the arising of the inevitable flow of thoughts, and that "myself" simply arises of its own accord, one can never know anything about any ultimate source.

OK, so seeing that one can never know of ultimate matters, and that one can notice that "I" am not the author of the arising of thoughts and feelings, is this knowing—or rather this "not knowing"—the space in which the flow of "myself" arises and is not separate from?

It is 4.30 a.m. here, so I am giving this my best shot, Robert!

So, is "*this*" unknowable, ungraspable, even to someone like you who knows he is awake? Is *this*—which you say exists prior to any and all explanations—really an utter and total mystery?

A: Yes, it is ungraspable, and words cannot do it justice. The condition in which I find myself may appear unusual, and my expressions from that perspective may seem rare. But as soon as one really *notices* one's *own* mind—not what someone else *tells* you about this aliveness, but your *own* mind right now—this "condition" is not unusual at all, but just the way we humans are; a flow of perceptions, thoughts, and feelings: aversion and desire, fear and attraction, pain and pleasure. All of it. You see me as different from you, but I do not see you as different from me. It's *all* ordinary—although utterly amazing—and not rare at all. *Be*-ing is natural and commonplace. *Noticing* seems to be the uncommon part.

To be clear, self-awareness is not at all unusual. I see it everywhere I look. I suppose what seems remarkable in my words is the idea that there is nothing hidden or esoteric, nothing "spiritual" to be sought. From my perspective, awakeness has nothing to do with "God," or any supposedly final answers to ultimate questions, which can only be fairy tales and lies. It simply means meeting each moment wholeheartedly, without resistance, without centering on "oneself," and without dependence on the ideas that others have been putting in your mind since birth.

I find myself awake, calm, and aware at all times, completely disposed to do whatever is needed in each moment, including dying. I feel no resentment, no regret, no desire for this *be*-ing called "myself" to be different. To some, that might sound boring or resigned—and that's fine by me. Ultimately, it's both completely ordinary, and also often lovely to feel this way.

I cannot teach this perspective—which is, after all, not some super-human, transcendent attainment, but something entirely natural—but I can speak from or about that perspective. Now and then someone will tell me that my perspective is worth hearing about; and I have nothing better to do, so I continue to speak and write. Before he died, my old artist friend Bernard Wisser told me that my tree had flowered, and now the seeds are just falling everywhere.

Many who hear words like mine misunderstand and make awakened self-awareness into something it is not. Some foolish ones even try to debate this with me, as if their opinions mattered. I might listen to an opinion on politics or aesthetics, assuming that the speaker has some actual experience to relate and not just a parroting of the thoughts of others. Ideas like that might be worth consideration. But an opinion on ultimate matters—on religion and metaphysics—means nothing to me.

In my world, such opinions are not worth discussing, and certainly not worth debating. *Be*-ing simply is, and the explanations come later on a lesser and far less certain ontological level, just as seeing the Grand Canyon with your own eyes is on a level radically different from having the Grand Canyon described to you. Actuality cannot be described, but only alluded to.

I do not know which to prefer,
The beauty of inflections
Or the beauty of innuendoes,
The blackbird whistling
Or just after.

—Wallace Stevens, from "Thirteen Ways of Looking at a Blackbird"

One day, I found myself awake. I *noticed* it. I have written elsewhere about how that blew my mind initially, and how gradually and with difficulty I came to see that *awake* is an ongoing condition—a condition not of "Robert," but of what we call intelligence, consciousness, or awareness.

Awareness really *is* aware. No one has to produce that. No one can. Nor does anyone have to *do* something about it. Robert can *notice* that, but Robert is not "saved" by noticing that. We are all on the same wheel, regardless of what we understand. There is no salvation from what is.

Noticing that now cannot be otherwise does tend to reduce anxiety, which can be pleasant, but this awareness—so far as we know, and by the evidence of our own eyes—seems inseparably intermingled with senescence, illness, and death. If permanent survival of the mind one has now seems important, one can *hope* that awareness survives organic dissolution; or someone with epistemological standards far looser than mine can have *faith* that it does. But hoping, believing, and having faith are *not* knowing. If I *know* something, I don't *need* to hope for it or have faith in it.

I have told this tale before, I know, in *4T* and elsewhere, but many readers of this book will not have seen it, so it belongs here too. Last time I spun the story out in its full glory, but here I will just cut to the chase:

> The Emperor of the North, terrified by the idea that he will die, has summoned before him a Zen master said to be the sagest human in the realm.
>
> "I hear you are a great teacher, a Zen master," intones the potentate from his throne.
>
> The old man just bows.
>
> "They say that you are the wisest man in the realm," continues the Emperor in a hopeful tone.
>
> Again, only a silent bow.
>
> "Well, if you are such a great Zen master, tell me this," commands the Emperor. "What happens when you die?"
>
> "I am sorry, sire," replies the old man, "I cannot say what happens when you die."
>
> At this the Emperor, never a patient man, and at the limit of his comprehension, blows his top. He glares down from his throne at the old man, and demands angrily, "If you are such a great Zen master, why can you not tell me what happens when you die?"
>
> "I am sorry, sire," says the old man. "I may be a Zen master, but I am not a *dead* Zen master."

Now *that,* I say, is the epistemology of awakeness. Because I am *not* dead, I know nothing about any so-called afterlife. I have no *way* of knowing anything about that. And just like that fabled Zen master, I *notice* that there is a *limit* to human knowing. This may sound simple or entirely obvious, but is it? If there really is such a limit, then why are the Hindu jnanis and their Western counterparts not laughed off the podium? And take the flowers, the mala beads, and the feet-kissing groupies with you.

Why, I always want to ask the fans of such "enlightened ones," do you believe what these people say? By my lights, they claim to know too much. Far, far too much.

If you hear that as a *judgment* on such and such a self-described teacher, like the ones I have named elsewhere, and if you consider "judgment" to be something nasty—something to be avoided at all costs—try replacing the word "judgment" with the word "discernment." Is that better?

Without skepticism and discernment, one is just a fool, bumbling one's way through life, influenced by any nonsense that makes you "happy." And the people listening to so-called spiritual teachers describing "reality" to them are just that: fools, many of them at least.

There is, I say, something to be *discerned* here and now—for me, as I write, and for you as you read: the suchness of *this* moment, that has nothing to do with the nattering of the gurus. Religion is the *death* of understanding, even if it is not *called* religion. Set all that nonsense aside and be free—free to be as you are *right now,* without aspiring to something theoretically better, holier, or more evolved.

Noticing the bounds of human limitation—noticing, I mean, that one may be able to understand *certain* things but *never everything*—for me, put an end to all questions about ultimate matters. I cannot sufficiently express in words the freedom I feel when I look into my own mind and find no questions there at all.

Now, two years after its publication, I understand that *The Ten Thousand Things* may comprise a kind of teaching, but it's not *spiritual* teaching. Quite the opposite. My words will point, for those who want it, to the *end* of so-called spirituality. To be naked and alone in the here and now with no escape hatch, without the false comforts of religion and spirituality, *without* the light at the end of the tunnel.

Speaking so candidly is fraught. Certain people measure my words against the words of their spiritual heroes on the basis of which words make them *feel* better. They misunderstand entirely. Plain talk is not intended to make you feel better or feel worse. It's just straight talk about ordinary matters, and the hell with how it makes you feel.

Some think I am blowing my own horn, others try to put me on a pedestal, and yet others—those with more open minds—might have a *feeling* for what I am saying, or even *imagine* that they understand what I am saying, without *actually* understanding it.

You are one of the few in my current circle who does not pretend to understand, but who seems to intuit that you are looking at the real thing: an ordinary human being who somehow, through no doing of his own, has come to know "awakeness," and who wants neither credit nor blame, and certainly not emulators.

To speak this way may appear pretentious, but in this awakeness I feel humble and naked. Defenseless. Entirely mortal. Exposed to the elements. And, yes, *this* is unknowable, I say.

Q: You read me well, Robert. You are one of the most human and open people I have ever come across. It is a pleasure to talk with you and make your acquaintance. I must ask you, in your "condition," do you feel everything, including being physically sensitive, and yet nothing sticks?

A: Yes. Nothing sticks. I feel with immense gratitude this mortality, this joy, this pain, and this suffering—perhaps I feel it more intensely than many others—but it all passes. It's all a flow, like water over a dam, and I can catch none of it. Not a drop. That is why I say there is nothing to *get*. I am here now, and that is all I ever know. In this, I am without protection, as vulnerable as a child.

There's nothing in why or when,
There's no use trying,

You're here, digging again, and ov'r again.

—The Rolling Stones, "She Smiled Sweetly"

This is why I find it hard to respect some of the self-described spiritual teachers I am always asked about (I won't mention names here). I see that they have some insight—certainly more insight than their followers—and I do not mean to impugn their motives. But they don't go deep enough, and by claiming special access to inside information through so-called "higher reasoning," or the words of *their* teachers, in whose supposedly august lineage they claim membership, they discourage serious scrutiny—deep scrutiny—of their metaphysical assertions.

If a serious questioner raises doubts, he or she is overpowered and defeated with false logic, or the parroting of traditional metaphysics, or palaver about "Love." But these matters are quite beyond logic, and just because something is old and widely accepted does not make it true. Much of the "knowledge" they are retailing is second-hand, not fresh. It's just the same old wine—of doubtful virtue to begin with—in 21st-century bottles. If those teachers noticed their *own* human limitation, they would not speak as they do, claiming that their words point to "Truth."

If such self-appointed teachers really saw things as they are, I say, they would not appear so pleased at being believed, but would do everything they could to *not* be believed. A true teacher, as I see it, does not give you answers or try to convince; she or he raises the questions, and leaves *you* to struggle with them. That is how you find your *own* mind.

At root, such lesser lights are relying on what *their* teachers claimed to know, which they got from *their* teachers, etcetera. All that Vedanta or whatever it's called may seem profound, but it isn't. It's just the verbal foam on the surface of an unknowably deep ocean.

Some things *can* be taught, including certain aspects of wisdom, and some cannot. The suchness of *be*-ing *cannot* be taught. So the problem is not, as many imagine, that "Truth" cannot be put into words. Words or no words, the real issue is that we human beings have no way to see entirely freshly, radically, and without self-interest. Residing in a world of habit, memory, and prior conditioning, we foolishly imagine finding "Truth" there. There is, I say, no such "Truth." There is only this right now.

Q: Well, the way I see it, it's as though they are all speaking, no matter how eloquently, from a ground of belief. So whatever they say is arising from a cup that is not continually emptying itself of its own volition. The root of their being is still sucking dregs.

What I get from hearing you is similar to hearing Jiddu Krishnamurti. You speak from a place that is beyond the known, without volition, an unfathomable emptiness that, as you said, is beyond even your ken, and prior to any explanation. I noticed that, when listening to Krishnamurti talk, the dynamo of my mind would slow, and pause, and I would find myself present with my whole being.

I get the same sense of no separation between formless and form when listening to you. No agenda, nothing to prove. As Krishnamurti said, "A bird just sings," or something like that. Also, it helps to have a brain that lends itself to speaking well, like Krishnamurti's or yours. As you said, you have no beliefs, and as far as I am concerned, I got fucking lucky and stumbled onto a top bloke and a straight shooter, who has been a true friend. I am not a sentimental bloke and most people are fools. But in my view, you ain't no fool, Robert.

A: Thank you. The bird just sings. I like that. I like it a lot. Robert K. Hall once said that the two of us were like birds on a wire chirping at one another.

This bird is going to age, weaken, stop singing, and fall off the branch, just like any other bird—assuming, of course, that a hawk or a snake doesn't grab him first. That is why I say that there is nothing to get, nothing to hold on to. Continuing to say, "This is *it*" probably won't awaken anyone, but it's the best I can do verbally. And as long as this bird can still sing a bit, why not? Ha, ha.

Q: Yes, radical seeing. That is what was great about U.G. Krishnamurti as well. I remember asking you about U.G. on BATGAP[46], and you said that U.G. is not the only game in town. I appreciate you reintroducing me to *Verses on Faith in Mind, Tao Te Ching*, and some of the other Zen readings. My experiences in reading *The Ten Thousand Things* seem to have allowed me to read those other sources with a new clarity that doesn't seek to grasp, only to hear.

I remember reading Chögyam Trungpa's book, *Cutting Through Spiritual Materialism*, years ago. It was great, but ever so much better now. And Alan Watts, who has a great way of talking about the Tao and Zen. Really lovely stuff if you are not *clutching* at it.

A: Those are my brothers, although Chögyam, I must observe, was a bit off his rocker—more than a bit actually. The first time I came upon Jiddu and began reading, it was like a door opening up wide; a door that I had not even known was there. "Is it all right, sir?" he would ask in that thin voice. What a mind!

Got to take off now. Doctor's appointment. Find out if I am still alive. This has been a fine chat. It feels rather personal, but I might share some of it with your name removed, because it says something that others might like to hear. Thanks for your friendship. Be well.

Q: Glad I got to perch on the telephone wire with you, Robert, for as long as it lasts in its own way. Who knows who will go first? Reminds me of a small book I read years ago about another bloke's quiet conversation with Krishnamurti called *Two Birds on one Tree*.

Anyway, it's almost 5 a.m. here, and I'm going to crash as well. Share whatever you like. It's no worries by me, Robert. Cheers much.

46. See https://BATGAP.com/robert-saltzman/

96 - Nisargadatta and you

Q: Robert, the way you talk and answer questions with a brutal candor reminds me of Nisargadatta. I do not know whether the guy was truly in the "Absolute" state, whatever that may be, but you and he are similar, in the sense that he stated his points of view honestly and with a fiery intellect and sharpness.

One of the reasons *4T* is so lovable to me is because the simple logic and sense of your words make me laugh. I mean, the things you say are so obvious, so simple, and so true that it's actually funny. I also laugh at the way you just honestly tell the people what you see in their words and behavior, with no attempt to soft-pedal anything.

Nisargadatta was the same.

A: Those of us who find ourselves speaking of these matters, not theoretically, but from living experience—empirically, pragmatically, phenomenologically—will express that experience in our own terms and in whatever language we have available, all of which is inexact and inadequate. Frankly, I do not expect to be understood. I speak this way, who knows why?

I like to say, "Nothing is becoming anything. What is, is, and can be no different." Nisargadatta, I think it was, said, "What you are, you already are."

Nisargadatta came of age in a cultural milieu in which terms like "the Absolute" were commonplace, more or less like the word "God" in my childhood. But those are just words for the incomprehensible "continuous arising" (also just words) that Nisargadatta felt as himself, and I feel as "myself." *That* defies words entirely.

Words are *part* of that continuous arising, part of *mind*, as I might name it. But the word "mind" is only a placeholder symbol for the incomprehensible, just like the word "Absolute." Words are nothing but meaningless sounds, until the hearer of them *invests* them with meaning according to his or her *own* experiences. Ergo, words are subject to human limitation.

To be clear, to utter the word "mind" or the word "Absolute" is easy—a piece of cake, a walk in the park. But to *fathom* the infinity that a word like "mind" or "Absolute" attempts to evoke is not humanly possible.

My childhood intellectual diet included a large helping of rationality and reliance on the scientific method, and those influences can be seen clearly in my style of discourse, but did not figure much in Nisargadatta's. Nevertheless, language and childhood influences are just a fraction of the picture. If those influences are seen for what they are—elements of cultural indoctrination that are not the gist, not the kernel, not the marrow of these matters—then Nisargadatta and Robert appear to be very much on the same page:

> *In nature nothing is at standstill, everything pulsates, appears and disappears. Heart, breath, digestion, sleep and waking—birth and death—everything comes and goes in waves. Rhythm, periodicity, harmonious alternation of extremes is the rule. No use rebelling against the very pattern of life.*
>
> —Nisargadatta

97 - Does psychotherapy reinforce the ego?

Q: Hi Robert. You mentioned that psychotherapy can be useful for some issues. Wouldn't that reinforce "I" in the subject? Kindly clarify.

A: The issues *are* "I." The issues are not happening *to* "myself"; they *are* "myself". There is no way to distinguish "myself" from the *issues* by calling them "my issues," as if there were a "myself" separate from the issues—a "myself" that "has" issues. One can talk that way, but that does not change the facts of the matter. "Myself" and the issues are one and the same happening.

To imagine a separation between "myself" and "my issues" is to draw an imaginary boundary line in a territory that *has* no boundaries. That territory—*be*-ing or existence or reality—is a mystery that no human being understands, or can, I say, understand, despite the dogmas of religion or spirituality. This false boundary line is a central tenet of the Hindu metaphysics that has influenced Western thought to its detriment, and you have been persuaded by that metaphysics. That is why you even see this as a question.

"Myself" is not some fixed, unchanging, unitary *entity,* from which so-called "ego" can be split off, but an aggregate of physical properties, consciousness, awareness, physical feelings, thoughts, perceptions, emotions, and all the rest. There is no "I" apart from all that. If a session of psychotherapy changes outlook and understanding—which means that new ideas are now part of the mix—then "I" will have changed. "I" is always changing. The purported "unchanging I," which is a feature of the idealism of certain schools of Vedanta, is a matter of faith, belief, and conviction—not fact.

The condition you hint at and presume—"myself" without a "reinforced I"—is, I say, imaginary. "I" is *constantly* reinforced by the very fact of breathing, feeling, thinking, and all the rest of human experience, no matter what one does or avoids doing. Talking this way reinforces it. Psychotherapy reinforces it. Spiritual practice reinforces it. Advaita Vedanta reinforces it. Trying to *not* reinforce it, reinforces it. *Everything* reinforces it. If a non-reinforced "I" were available to you, you would not be asking this question.

Here, I am just dealing with this question logically, but if this were psychotherapy, our conversation would be very different. Then, we might look into how important it feels to you to be able to split off "I" from experience; to imagine an "I" that is pristine and untouched by everything ever seen, felt, heard, thought, or otherwise encountered and undergone in the course of a human life—*your* human life. We would explore your view of "ego" as a dirty word.

You may believe in "nonduality," but that does not make the world go away, nor the "I." If an idea in your mind seems to make the world go away, that is not understanding, but self-hypnosis.

Spiritual seekers talk about these matters as if words about so-called nonduality could inoculate them against the anxiety and sense of loss that characterize our shared human experience—as if doing without "ego" would just fix everything. No more fear, no more longing, no more sexuality, no more loneliness, no more mortality, no more death.

If that works for you, who am I to call it into question? Ha, ha.

That reminds me of an old poker joke: "If you look around the table at all the faces, and can't tell who the sucker is, it's *you*!"

98 - *No evidence for "universal consciousness"*

Q: Hi Robert. I received *The Ten Thousand Things* a little while ago. It's beautiful! I love the photos too. I've started reading. It's a beautiful, beautiful thing to read. Thank you, Robert, you're brilliant. I'm drinking every word. Love this book.

Three weeks later:

Q: Hi Robert. Obviously, I've been out of touch for a little while. It turns out I got only so far in your book and then started feeling a lot of negativity about Advaita, which has been a path for me for a very long time; so it became difficult for me to read. I don't really understand the difference between what you're saying and the jnanis, which you say you are not. I hung out with Robert Adams for about three years in LA and in Sedona. Wayne Liquorman, Ramesh Balsekar too.

I see that many people are feeling liberated by *The Ten Thousand Things*. I would like to be one of them. All I know is everything has been crashing for a very long time. In spite of everything, you seem to be part of the crashing. It's just that sometimes I experience severe pain and feelings of depression that make it difficult to continue functioning, which I must do to survive. I speak to a mentor once a week or so, a complete unknown whom I would call a *jnani*. Your thoughts?

A: Hi. Sorry to hear you are in pain. By definition, a *jnani* is someone who has "realized" the identity of self and Brahman. I don't think that way, so I have nothing to add to that. I consider Robert Adams (I have never met him, but I did read a bit of a book of his) to be an example of a wild fox spirit. In case you have not gotten that far in the book, it is Chapter 36. That phrase comes from an old Zen story about a teacher who became a wiseacre, and so was condemned to be reborn 500 times as a wild fox.

Advaita is one kind of metaphysics among many—not "Truth." I don't see how Advaita could be a "path," but if it is that for you, fine by me.

My book is not meant to help anyone to feel better about life. Nor does it provide any kind of path or shortcut. I am simply proposing that the reader, for once in his or her life, drop all ideas of progress, spirituality, salvation, hope for the future—all that terribly heavy weight of tradition, concepts and beliefs—and simply experience this aliveness just as it is in each moment, without imagining that there is anything "else" to achieve or attain. In a word, simply *be*.

Some people have found that approach liberating, and others are frightened by the very idea that the self-described spiritual teachers might be spooning up pie in the sky. I don't ask anyone to believe me. I am just sharing a certain perspective.

Q: The word "path" is only for convenience. I will read the chapter. When I say things are crashing, what I mean is concepts, structures, belief, and hopes. It's only a word—*jnani*. No one I know really used it except Robert Adams, because he was around Ramana.

He was only fourteen when he woke up spontaneously in a math class. He sprinkled in a little bit of language that other people used, but he was my favorite of all, mostly because to me it made no difference what he said. I just adored and loved him and had amazing experiences in his presence, whether it was friendship experiences or *satsang*. (In the last year or two, I really spent a lot of time reading Joey Lott, who also sounds like you. But he is still struggling, it feels like to me.)

Robert didn't even have any framework. Someone told him about Joel Goldsmith, and he used to take a train for two hours to go have a chat with him. Before that, he had no idea. Joel recommended that he go to Yogananda in California. He was there for two years. And then one day Robert said, "OK, I guess I should join the ashram." But Yogananda said, "No, you don't belong here. Go see Ramana Maharshi in India—because, like you, he had no guru."

So he did, and that was pretty much the size of it.

I appreciate your message. I always open to new pointers towards freedom. However, I think you pretty well dissed Robert. I have no clue why anyone would diss Robert or Ramana either. Neither one of them proclaimed a damn thing. Robert certainly never said he was a *jnani* or anything else. He just liked to teach. He was the most innocent creature I have ever met, other than an animal. I'm really not sure why you have to put him down.

Is there anything you feel like saying about that? Why besmirch innocence any more than you would besmirch a tree or a flower?

A: I think you have misunderstood what I am saying in *4T*. I am not "besmirching" anyone. I am saying that people who claim to tell you what "you" are in some ultimate sense, or anything at all about "Brahman," are living in fantasyland. They have every right to their opinions, of course. They may be interesting, friendly, intelligent people. I am not putting them down in the least. I am simply saying that their religious beliefs are *not* "Truth," so anyone who takes those words as if they were, will very likely end up hypnotized.

That is the meaning of the wild fox story. It applies to people who make definitive statements about the unknown.

So the problem is not that people like Robert Adams like to teach. The trouble, I say, is that when they claim that their words refer to some ultimate, indisputable "Truth," you believe them. The problem is not the teacher, but your uncritical acceptance of the doctrines being taught. If you disagree, I will understand.

Q: They also say the words they say are not "Truth," Robert. Maybe if you had met one of them, you would have a better way of talking about it. It feels very derogatory towards the person, which to me just simply feels unkind. Unnecessarily unkind. And puts you in an elevated status, because you're the only one who can speak about it correctly.

Talking about the unspeakable, naming the unnamable, conceptualizing about the inconceivable, is just language, and language is language. Every word is a concept. On Earth, we talk to communicate.

A: The *details* of what is being communicated matter crucially. Communication is not all of the same value, just because it can be written with the same 26 letters. And I am far from being the only one who can speak about consciousness without proclaiming that "God" or Brahman precedes consciousness, and is the "source" of human consciousness. That is a religious idea based on scant evidence or no evidence at all.

Many researchers who understand more about consciousness than Robert Adams or any other religious teacher can speak factually about these matters on the level of biopsychology. I can speak phenomenologically about this. Neither the researchers nor I will be slinging around a lot of capital T "Truth." They and I will admit freely that we do not know the "source" of consciousness. No one knows that. Some people are not comfortable with not knowing, and so they just make stuff up. Others hear the made-up stuff and for one reason or another believe it or have faith in it.

To be clear, I am not saying that "God" or "universal consciousness" (which is another name for the same thing) does not exist. I am saying that, apart from scripture and testimony, there is *no evidence* for that at all, so surely no evidence that brains are only objects *in* consciousness. You said that those men you mentioned never "proclaimed" anything, but that is precisely what they *did* and do proclaim; and on no evidence but scripture and the assertions of their teachers.

As for my attitude toward the Vedanta crowd, it is not *personally* derogatory in the least. For the most part, I have not even met those people. My open-eyed view only seems derogatory to you because you have them on a pedestal. I just see them as the entirely ordinary human beings they are. There is nothing derogatory about pointing out that claiming to have "Truth" is a big claim, and that big claims require big evidence. My approach to such claims is skepticism, not credulity, no matter how charming or even apparently kind the person making the claims.

Q: Those people that I've spoken to directly continuously point out that they don't have the truth. Robert had a cute way of saying it: if there was ever a *jnani* convention, anyone who showed up would automatically be disqualified.

A: That's clever, but Robert was a bit of a twit in my view. "Your body is not your friend," he wrote—and that's when I threw the book, sent to me by a well-meaning friend, in the trash. Literally. I threw it in the wastebasket. Didn't even want it around for a doorstop. What nonsense. What is the meaning of such a statement?

I think my book has frightened you, and instead of dealing with that, you want to kill the messenger. Why not read the book a couple of times nonjudgmentally, your old *jnani* buddies temporarily muzzled, and then see where you are?

Q: What happened was I enjoyed the beginning a lot, assuming you were an illusion-smashing teacher like the ones that I have known. But then somehow everything you were saying seemed so unbelievably negative, and to no purpose that I could comprehend. So reading it just made me feel bad. The pain of life and the ego breaking down is enough. I don't read things that cause more pain, but I'll see if I can do what you're asking.

A: OK, please do give it a try. But if your goal is to feel good, then there is no chance of "smashing illusions." If you just want to feel good, you are sure to find something that makes you feel that way and cling to it. You say that you have known illusion-smashing teachers, but if they were that, they did not get the job done with you.

If you really want illusions smashed, that will be a terribly painful process. Having illusions smashed and avoiding "feeling bad" do not go together. I do not know how to say this more plainly. If your goal is to feel good, by all means, *stop* reading my book. The book is for people who really want to inhabit this aliveness directly, without rumors and hearsay about Brahman—not for people who just want to feel good.

So this is entirely up to you, and has nothing at all to do with me or what I say about Robert Adams.

Q: My goal is not to feel good. There are far easier ways.

A: So what is it you want?

Q: The only word that ever gave me any hope for a reason to live is "enlightenment." My dad died before my thirteenth birthday. We had been very close. My remaining family did not understand or, in my opinion, love me. I had a very narcissistic mother who actually never loved me from birth, I've come to understand. I seem to have a lot of pain from the rejection from family, and originally from the despair of losing my father, especially not knowing what death meant or where he went.

What I want is the kind of understanding that is complete. If that means the personal "me" who thinks she's *doing* everything must be seen through and therefore dissolved, so be it. There's been a struggle in that direction. It was either go for enlightenment or the unthinkable—which I decided not to do right after he died, believing there must be something. Because life had been so beautiful up until that point.

So I have always wanted the bottom line. But I had to keep living. Being and feeling alone in the world has been an issue. Although I have met beautiful people and have some beautiful friends, I never had kids, never got married. Just the spiritual search.

A: OK. Thank you for your honesty. That does clarify matters. First, I am sorry for your suffering. To feel unloved by one's own mother must be an ongoing pain, or at least must have been way back then. So in a very real sense, you were set up: "It was either go for enlightenment or the unthinkable." But "enlightenment," as some future state that will be attained "eventually" by following some so-called path, is a fantasy, I say.

The people who teach that are only parroting the words of religious scripture or the claims of *their* teachers, who were only parroting *their* teachers, etcetera. There is absolutely nothing to achieve by following that kind of "path," I say, except self-hypnosis. I don't ask you to believe me—just to hear this with an open mind.

If you imagine that Robert Adams knew "Truth," he has hypnotized you, just as he was hypnotized himself. That is what a wild fox spirit is: someone who speaks as if he *knows* something about ultimate matters beyond any doubt, when in fact he is only repeating hearsay or personal opinions.

If you, for example, believe that there is such a thing as "universal consciousness," and that the brain is just "an object *in* consciousness"—which is exactly what all those people you mentioned teach—you are attached to an idea for which there is no evidence at all; unless, unfortunately, you consider scripture and the testimony of godmen to be evidence. If you do regard scripture and testimony as evidence, that really is a mess from which extrication is unlikely.

On the other hand, evidence for the opposite view—that the brain is the *source* of consciousness—exists already, and more evidence for that view is emerging as science marches on. What do I mean by "evidence?" Very simple. If a part of the brain is damaged, the functioning of consciousness is impaired. This is not some belief or speculation of mine. It is a plain fact.

Among scientists and philosophers—not self-proclaimed jnanis—much is known about consciousness biopsychologically; but how the electricity, chemistry, and structure of brains eventuate in feelings, thoughts, and all those *qualia*[47] is not known. That question is considered a hard problem, and was even named "the hard problem" by David Chalmers in 1995:

> *It is undeniable that some organisms are subjects of experience. But the question of how it is that these systems are subjects of experience is perplexing. Why is it that when our cognitive systems engage in visual and auditory information-processing, we have visual or auditory experience: the quality of deep blue, the sensation of middle C? How can we explain why there is something it is like to entertain a mental image, or to experience an emotion? It is widely agreed that experience arises from a physical basis, but we have no*

47. *Qualia*: phenomenal experiences such as the redness or tartness of an apple.

> *good explanation of why and how it so arises. Why should physical processing give rise to a rich inner life at all? It seems objectively unreasonable that it should, and yet it does.*

Some informed people imagine the problem never being solved, even after science has figured out the biology and all that in detail. Some say that a solution will involve finding that the entire universe is somehow conscious. And others say that consciousness is an emergent quality of complex systems such as brains, so that human intelligence is part and parcel of animal nature at its most evolved. I see little hope of getting to the bottom of this question.

Yes, it may be difficult to be without hope, and given your background, it might be, for you, impossible—but *hope is a lie*. No matter what you may think about it, this life culminates in old age, illness, and death. We lose *everything*. Someone may walk around feeling "enlightened," and may repeat such silly formulations as "Nothing is born and nothing dies," or "You are not your body"—but those are just words.

The only place of "enlightenment" is here and now, without reference to spiritual traditions or the words of so-called "masters." If you rely on others in this regard, you will never find the ground of your *own* being, I say. Again, don't take my word for this or anything else. Just examine it with an open mind, because you may never have heard this perspective before.

You have heard the injunction to "kill the Buddha." That is *not* just words. Get those guys off the pedestal on which you have put them. Until and unless you do, you will not understand anything I am saying. You only imagine that I am dissing them because you have overvalued them.

Try to understand this. Try. I am not "dissing" anyone. I am not saying that those guys were bad people. I am just pointing out that your "heroes" are not some breed of special humans like no others. They are, in a very human way, clinging to certain unsubstantiated beliefs that eased *their* pain and fear. If you use *their* beliefs—their world-views—to ease *your* pain and fear, it won't work. You will just end up confused, and without any real ground of your *own* on which to stand.

If you need therapy to feel better, get it. Spirituality is not therapy. It is religion. I say this with love and respect.

Q: I have seen at least a dozen therapists who have all told me there is absolutely nothing wrong with me. It's obvious that you've never spent a minute in the company of any of the people I referred to. I will take your advice to get them off the pedestal as best I can. I feel very sad that you just believe they are parrots. You clearly have never met a sage. As far as what I have experienced, they are the only originals among mankind. They have no agenda. They have no purpose in teaching anything—except compassion.

A: I have never met a sage? Oh, *please*. You have every right to your ideas, but you don't see me at all. Do you not suspect, even perhaps a little, that what I have to say might be something *new* to you, something that you have never heard before or even suspected?

If you consider Adams a "sage," you have every right. I do not. I see someone desperate to divide mind from body, and to find something "eternal." The guy spoke of reincarnation as a *fact*. Come on! That's absurd. No one could possibly know such a thing, and teaching such superstition has nothing to do with being a "sage."

If you like that kind of "path," fine by me. To each his own. Because of your earlier apparent enthusiasm about my work, I am making this effort. But if you don't understand, no worries. Feel what you feel. That's fine by me. I have nothing to sell.

From my point of view, you illustrate exactly what I mean by an hypnotic trance. It is *hypnotic* because you don't see it. Anything that might cast doubt on the trance is explained away, however farfetched those explanations must be. Robert Saltzman has never met a sage—"clearly," you said—because if he had he would not speak that way about "the only originals among mankind." It's like a joke, but you don't get the joke, and I am sorry you don't.

Q: Hi. Back to my house at work. It was a very long day yesterday. I will try again with the book. It may be that we are just not a match. Not everyone is for everyone. Your comments about sages don't match my experience. And it sounds like you don't really have any personal experience with sages. But that's because you don't have any interest. Perfectly understandable. Most people don't. You may end up also writing me off as a sadly deluded spiritual train-wreck doofus. We'll see.

The main reason I wanted to read your book so badly is because of the beautiful things people are saying about it. That doesn't necessarily mean it's for me.

A: Yes. My ideas are not for everyone. I won't write you off as anything. I don't see people that way. Every mind is a universe. As for sages, do you actually imagine that I have not known people of wisdom? For all you know, I might be one myself.

You, I am saying, are blinded by your ideas and do not see the people you call "sages" as they really are: human beings just like you, with fears, desires, ideas, a childhood, etcetera. I am not saying that Robert Adams had nothing to offer. If you got something from him, fine. But whatever you got wasn't sufficient, because if you *really* get it, your search ends, and you *have* no more questions. You said, "Many people are feeling liberated by *The Ten Thousand Things.*" Yes, and that "liberation," if we must use that word, is freedom from the *search* for "enlightenment"—the freedom to be as they are without having to believe anything.

Your assumptions about me as "an illusion-smashing teacher" like the ones you have known are entirely incorrect. If I relieve you of an illusion, I do not replace it with a new one, like those "jnanis" you like so much. It's time, in my opinion, for you to kill the Buddha—to kill *all* the Buddhas, and stand on your own two feet for a change.

As my friend, John Troy—a marvelous sage, by the way—put this, "Robert removes all beliefs and does not replace them with new ones. He leaves you without an escape hatch." Yes. "Enlightenment" at some later date is one of those escape hatches, along with "God." If you can, let it go. It's only a story you tell yourself, abetted by those "teachers" you love so much.

As it stands, you seem befuddled by delusions, the worst among them being that those men you mentioned are "the only originals among mankind." There are seven billion humans on this planet but the ones you happen to know are the only originals. A little clique of sages. Oh, please! Do you not see the absurdity in words like that? I guess you don't. If you did, you would not be talking this way.

I will smash an idol or two if that is needed, but that is not my favorite work. I'd rather talk about the *beauty* of impermanence than dispute the words of a bunch of true believers. You love Vedanta, I understand, which I consider a form of dogmatic religion, not "Truth." But it's not my intention to hurt or insult you. I just say what I see, and have no way of predicting how someone might react.

In my view, Robert Adams and others like him make claims about "reality" that require skepticism, not hero worship. Adams stated something that did not ring true to me at all, and he asserted it as a fact; not as his perspective or his opinion, but a *fact.* As soon as I read it, his confusion was apparent. I wonder if he ever said anything to *you* that did not ring true, or was it all just perfect, and beyond question?

The chief flaw I see in Vedanta and its teachings is the belief that anything that changes is not "real," or is only "relatively real," whereas there is something—Brahman—supposedly "unchanging" that *is* totally "real." Once someone drinks that Kool-Aid, it's only a short step to where Robert Adams goes: "Your mind and your body are not your friends."

Really? Besides mind and body, what else *is* there? If a statement like that seems sagacious to you, fine by me. You have every right to your beliefs and opinions. To me, it appears to be a kind of life-denying, fear-based splitting or dissociation that replaces this *aliveness*—body, brains, and all, which is about as real as real gets—with dead, dry religion.

In any case, I feel for your situation, and I wish you peace.

99 - *Money and beauty*

Q: In one of your Zoom meetings, you spoke about how your wife had stuck with you during a long illness when you were "useless." On hearing that, it struck me hard that women are valued just for their being, while men are measured by their ability to provide. I understand that's how the world works, at least here in India, and that there are evolutionary reasons behind this too. But coming from you, hearing this was discomforting.

A: Please say what you mean by "coming from you," and what you find discomforting about those words.

Q: I mean that I felt that you, an awakened human, wouldn't draw your self-worth from your ability to provide, and that your and your significant other's relationship would be above these evolutionary and socially conditioned requirements, but only about sharing love.

Some women say that the pain and unfairness of men being judged by their ability to provide are balanced out by the pain and unfairness of women being judged by their looks. During your years as a psychotherapist, you must have seen many couples in which women were supported by their partners, and very few in which the woman paid the bills. I really feel bad for those men who are at the bottom of the socio-economic ladder. They are wretched. Unless they are especially good-looking, they have little or no access to sex. I wonder if this explains, at least in part, why men commit suicide at a rate three or four times that of women.

The fact that women are valued for their "being," but men are valued for their "doing," is discomforting, along with biased law for child custody, alimony, and zero reproductive rights for men (if he has sex, he is automatically consenting to fatherhood and has no choice about it, whereas a woman can take a pill, abort, or give the baby for adoption).

A: I understand that your country is still quite traditional regarding such matters, and that you might feel discomfort at being forced automatically into a conventional male role whether you like it or not. But I find it hard to imagine that Indian men have it harder than Indian women. I have never visited India, but I have read reports of women subjugated and misogyny taken for granted, legally as well as socially, so that rapes and other violence against women take place with impunity.

Nevertheless, it seems true among us humans that women are seen more often than men as objects of sexual desire; and that if a woman is attractive and inviting, she will be able to find a man to support her, whereas the opposite is less common. I understand that you see this as unfair.

I do not expect life to be fair. If "fair" means everyone on an equal footing, I see fairness nowhere on Earth. Perhaps this obvious inequality explains the attraction and popularity of the doctrines of karma and reincarnation—and all the more so in your country, where the caste system had somehow to be rationalized and justified. Life may *seem* unfair now, so that story goes, but in the end, it all comes out in the wash. We all get our just desserts. Really? I see no evidence for that at all, and so I reject it as superstitious wishful thinking. Judeo-Christian culture has its own version of just desserts: Heaven and Hell. We humans are a sad lot, constantly lying to ourselves, and eager to impose those lies on others.

Of *course* human life is not fair. The idea that it could be or should be is a misunderstanding of life on Earth in general, not just among human animals, but among all animals. One baby is born with a clever brain and good looks, and another is born with a dull brain and an unattractive face. That's just for starters. It can get much worse than that. Some babies are born severely handicapped right from the start, or into families that abuse them, or into a poverty so pervasive that almost no one escapes it.

As I see it, we all do the best we can with whatever hand we have been dealt. I mean this literally: we *all* do the best we can, and for some of us—billions of us, in fact—that is not very well at all.

Some people disagree with me on this, arguing that those who make the best efforts are the best rewarded, while others who don't try hard enough fail. That may be true in part, but if it is, what *causes* one person to try while another in apparently similar circumstances does not? Does anyone *choose* to try, or choose not to? Or is trying or not trying just part of an entire "myselfness?"

I say the latter. From my perspective, each and every one of us is doing as well as we can. That is why I don't sit in judgment, but just see things as they are, without always arriving at rulings and verdicts.

The apparent unfairness of a woman being able to get by on "just being," as you put it, while a man must labor to provide economically for a woman if he wants sex, reminds me of a story.

> One night, an older man is out to dinner with a voluptuous young woman in a low-cut gown, and they are discussing the very matter you raise: the various bases for attraction and sexual involvement.
>
> "If I couldn't take you out to places like this," the man asks, "buy you clothes and jewelry, and pay your rent, would you still want to be with me?"
>
> At this, the woman gestures towards her breasts and says, "And if I didn't have these, would *you* still want to be with me?"

I think that little anecdote pretty much nails it on the biological level. But we humans are more than just biology, so it is important, it seems to me, not to generalize in the way you are doing.

Bluesman Tiny Grimes used to sing that "romance without finance is a nuisance." He may have had a point, but there are many styles of sexual relationships, and usually the reasons people have for being together are complex, and not based entirely upon either looks or money. I imagine this is less true in traditional cultures, where brides are purchased or must bring a dowry to the transaction, than it is in Western cultures, where many women earn money. And many more women than you seem to imagine bring home the bacon, not just for a man, but for an entire family.

Be that as it may, you misunderstood the meaning of my saying that I felt useless during my illness. I did not mean that I was useless as an earner, but useless as a *partner*—which is not the same thing. My sweetheart had to care for me and take on most of the responsibilities that had been mine, including many physical tasks for which I had been better suited, while at the same time, there was little I could do for her.

You say that you would not expect me—as an awakened human—to draw my self-worth from my ability to provide. Indeed, I do not. *I never think of self-worth at all,* although if I found myself thinking about it, that would not trouble me. No no-nos. Thoughts are just thoughts, and usually mean much less than we imagine they do.

If you imagine that awake humans have *transcended* their ordinariness, including insecurities, anxieties, and the like, you will continue to misunderstand what I mean by "awake." For me, awakeness involves not perfection, but *full participation* in this aliveness.

I regard this aliveness as a natural happening that has nothing to prove to anyone, including itself. I feel that I have as much right to be here as any other part of nature—a tree, a flower, a springbok, or the Pacific Ocean.

100 - Are we just tourists in our little lives?

Q: I am reading *The Ten Thousand Things*. What a beautiful piece of work. I enjoy your photography so much, as well as the verbal content of this book that has brought me to a different perspective regarding the concept of so-called "universal consciousness".

Rupert Spira and Francis Lucille concede that "universal consciousness" is an unverifiable hypothesis. It can't be known, so it requires a leap of faith. Or as Francis Lucille says, "Try them both out—individual consciousness and universal consciousness." So yes, I agree with you that, as far as we know, this is it. I am totally OK with that.

On a separate note, I have a question about personal responsibility. Aside from bizarre circumstances, I have always felt very strongly that we are responsible for the choices we make and create most of what happens to us. Responsibility seems to imply control, but my present understanding, gleaned from your book, about how thought arises spontaneously, suggests a *lack of control* about what one thinks next; and so *no element of choice* and personal responsibility.

So are we just tourists in our little lives, watching the world go by and witnessing our minds and bodies subjected to the compulsion of thoughts and feelings?

A: Thank you. I am glad you like the book and I feel particularly happy to hear that you see the images as part of the work.

I wonder why people simply *assume* that those who claim to be teachers of nonduality—you mentioned two—have some kind of inside information the rest of us do not have. On what basis are those people viewed as experts? Because they *say* they are? Because they have "made a name" for themselves? Because they attract followers? Why?

At some point, I say, one must reclaim one's *own* authority, or all is lost. To make another human being an authority on these matters is to enter voluntarily into an hypnotic trance in which one might spend the rest of one's life.

It should be obvious that the term "universal consciousness" is meaningless. No one has the foggiest idea what *ordinary* consciousness is, much less a "universal" version of it.

Setting the purported "universal" variety aside, you have no idea what plain old everyday consciousness is, and neither do I. We know feelings, perceptions, thoughts—that kind of thing—but of what feelings, perceptions, and thoughts consist, and how they come to arise and be known, we do *not* know. *No one knows*. Anyone who claims to *know* such things is, I say, either self-deluded, intentionally deceitful, or a blend of both. I include in this the two men you mentioned.

That whole late 20th century and early 21st century Advaita Vedanta "lineage" is, in my view, a disaster of belief purporting to be factual knowledge. The beliefs espoused by those claiming membership in the lineage are *not* knowledge, but merely traditional metaphysics passed from one disciple to the next. You can believe in their claims if you like, but you cannot *know* them to be true.

Words go only so far—not very. I have never heard any words that went far enough to explain this undeniable aliveness, this entirely mysterious universe, this incomprehensible *be*-ing.

The truly wise, in my opinion, do not speak authoritatively as if they could not possibly be mistaken. There is, as I see it, far too much certainty and self-assurance coming out of those mouths—to say nothing of the vacuous truisms they sell to followers: "Try them both out," see which one makes you feel better, and that will be "Truth." Baloney! I am put off entirely by such displays of inanity, ensconced in false logic and double talk. How do you "try out" "universal consciousness?" Just *declare* yourself "universally conscious" and assess how that makes you *feel*? Oh, *please*!

Hui Neng, illiterate himself, overheard someone reciting from the Diamond Sutra, so the story goes; and when the words, "Depending on no-thing, you must find your own mind" were uttered, Hui Neng came awake. Explanations of reality and other people's metaphysics are precisely the *"things"* upon which one must not depend. It is one's *own* mind that must be found—not what some self-described "teacher" has to say about anything. Your *own* mind.

That said, I am happy to reply to your question, but with the proviso that neither you nor any other reader of these words view me as an authority in these matters. I am *not* an authority. I enjoy a point of view that I consider awakened, but that point of view is certainly *not* all-knowing. I can share what I see, but as for ultimate truth, I don't have any.

I do not agree that I am responsible for most of what happens to me. Leaving aside the very thorny question of what I "really" am, which Francis and Rupert seem delighted—overeager, actually—to answer with certitudes, let us ask ourselves instead whether the kind of "myself" that you imagine—a "myself" with the power to make choices and take decisions—really exists at all.

If it does *not* exist; if all of *this* (including one's perceptions, thoughts, feelings, and apparent "decisions") simply arises as it does without any little controlling homunculus residing behind one's eyes, separate somehow from that arising and with the ability to censor thoughts and shape behavior, then the entire drama of *apparent* choice and control is really only an inevitable playing out of fear, desire, and all the other drives and emotions.

I am not saying that one can avoid that drama—one cannot *avoid* anything. That's my point. All you can ever be is *you*. There is no choice about that. If "you" includes the idea of choosing, perhaps after painful dithering—going around in circles of self-blame, guilt, the need to be in control and get it right, and all the rest—well, it just does. That's the way the cookie crumbles. There is no alternative to what is.

My own experience of "self" is more like an amorphous, formless flow of thoughts, feelings, perceptions, etcetera, that keeps moving and changing in ways never chosen at all, beyond control, and far too complex for logical analysis.

I do not know *why* there is something rather than nothing, but that seems to be the case. This world seems to be here of its own accord without my willing it. I open my eyes in the morning, and everything is just here. I did not make it be here or put it here. As this reply is written, I am not willing or choosing the next word to appear. It just *does* appear, and I have no idea at all whence that derives, much less any choice about it or control over it. Words just come to mind and I type them.

From that perspective, any apparent decisions and choices simply occur as they do, and if "I," in a kind of ignorance of the big picture, take unmerited credit or blame for them, that is a narrow view.

But even assuming an "I" with enough stability, cohesion, and temporal persistence to act responsibly—assuming, that is, that there really were a fixed "someone" to *be* responsible, as you want to believe—when does that accountability begin? Am I responsible for the time and place of my birth? For my body type and all its details? For the capacities of my brain? For the family and larger social surround into which I am born, along with all its attitudes and cherished beliefs imposed upon me before the age of reason? What about the people I happen to meet by chance, not by *choice* at all—my kindergarten teacher, for example, and the other kids in that class with whom I spent hundreds of hours?

None of that is chosen, I think you will agree—and yet, in a very real sense, all that, beginning with the DNA inherited from my progenitors, *is* what "I" am. *All* unchosen. So how can I be "responsible" for it?

Does that mean that we are, "Just tourists... watching... and witnessing?" I would not say that. I do not feel in the least like a tourist. I feel like a *participant* in a dance entirely beyond my comprehension. The "witness" is one small element among many others in that dance, and certainly too narrowly focused to constitute a useful definition of "myself." As Walt Whitman put it, "I am large. I contain multitudes" (and the "witness," Walt might have added, is just one face in the crowd).

I have written elsewhere in detail about so-called "witnessing," a perspective that some consider a mode of spiritual practice, but which looks to me like "splitting": marking out a spurious borderline between the so-called witness and that which is *being* witnessed.

That splitting, which is false on the face of it, creates an imagined division of perception, in which the so-called witness is considered "real," permanent, and "changeless," whereas that which is witnessed is deemed not "real," because it is transitory.

From my vantage, the witness is equally transitory, but seeing *that*—seeing "myself" die from moment to moment, powerless to hold on to anything, or reconstitute itself as it was even a split second before—is more than many people can bear to notice. And so they resort to so-called "witnessing" or "presence" as a means of denial of impermanence. From my psychologist's perspective, that kind of splitting is a defense mechanism, not an awakened understanding.

If you feel like a tourist and a witness, perhaps you should give the spirituality thing a rest and just get into the game—the game of *aliveness*, in which one knows neither the rules nor the ultimate meaning of anything, if indeed any meaning exists apart from the suchness of each moment.

This scene from a Woody Allen movie, *Hannah and Her Sisters*, just came to mind (how or why I do not know). When his doctor tells him he's got a slight hearing loss, Woody, in his uber-hypochondria, immediately believes he's got a brain tumor. By the time he gets back to his office, he's a basket case. His assistant asks what's wrong, and when he explains, she says, "You *don't* have a brain tumor. Maybe you just need to get laid."

Are we "pure awareness?" No, I would not say that either. I would prefer to say that I have no *idea* what I am and never will. That is honest.

And in the face of that total uncertainty, you say that Francis Lucille advises "a leap of faith"—meaning that you try to "leap" into believing what *he* believes, I suppose. Faith? Give me a *break*. And Jesus will be there to greet you in Heaven with the angels singing hosannas.

On a practical level, if you feel responsible, then I strongly advise acting as responsibly as you can.

101 - The denial of suffering

Q: Hello, Robert. I find that I am often aware of the mind and acutely perceptive of what arises in consciousness. However, this does not mean that I do not suffer in these times of awareness. Feelings of pain, fear, grief, and frustration may emerge, but arise and die, usually in just in a few seconds or less. They may arise again the next moment, but they die away again. And when they die, often something beautiful emerges in their place, like a feeling of affection and care.

This is different from how many people I know seem to experience suffering. For them, fear or grief is fought with, denied, and they look for alternatives to their experience of each moment.

It seems that we have an immense reservoir of painful feelings, like an ocean on whose surface things unceasingly appear, and this reservoir is never empty. Our only freedom, perhaps, is to watch those feelings and let them die their natural death. Also, certain situations can make this reservoir send up more suffering. Someone being violent to us or betraying our trust can be such a situation, perhaps.

I don't understand when people say that suffering ends when one is spiritually awake. Rather, it seems that being awake is something that happens every moment, and transforms suffering in that moment. But the next moment, the reservoirs of the unconscious may bring out new suffering.

What is your experience and understanding of this?

A: I find that the kinds of feelings you mentioned—pain, grief, and the rest—arise and pass away again on their own schedule—not according to anything I do—leaving in their wake feelings of compassion. Compassion for others, who have their own suffering to deal with, and self-compassion for "Robert," who must live in a world he never made, having no choice but to deal with its demands and challenges improvisationally, as best he can.

From my perspective, awakeness is not a condition free of suffering. In fact, in some ways, one suffers all the more, including having constantly to behold the ignorance with which we human beings treat one another; use and abuse the fellow sentient beings we call "animals" (as if we were not animals ourselves); and despoil this beautiful planet on which we reside.

So it is not that suffering *ends* when one is awake, but that one endures and engages with the inevitable suffering intentionally, and with at least some measure of wisdom.

I have discussed these matters with a wide variety of people over the years, both in my work as a psychotherapist, and otherwise. In my experience, those who claim that suffering ends with spiritual "realizing" are lying. In this context, by "lying" I mean expressing a *belief*, no matter how sincerely believed, as if it were an actual experience, when it is not. The suffering of such people is often evident and obvious to me—along with fear and denial. Conversely, I have never heard anyone I considered awake claim to be immune to suffering—which, the more one thinks about it, is a bizarre and heartless claim.

You are fortunate to be in the condition of openness to suffering without attachment to suffering or to avoidance of suffering. I suppose you understand that those who are afraid to suffer and who look for ways to deny suffering, or those for whom suffering provides an identity to which they are attached ("Poor, poor pitiful me!"), cannot help themselves any more than you or I can choose to be different from the way *you* are or I am.

We human beings have a very difficult time comprehending our powerlessness. It is not something we want to see. We have been carefully trained in countless ways of avoiding that idea, and even have ways of "proving" to ourselves that it is not true.

Part of what I call "awake" occurs when avoidance of the facts of mortality and human limitation comes to an end—who knows what makes it end?—to be replaced with humility and compassion.

Q2: I'm going to copy this, dear Robert, and share it or relevant extracts (with attribution of course) from time to time, if that's OK.

I feel disturbed and unsettled when people who claim to have some form of awakening experience—such as no-self, liberation, energetic shift, transcendence, and all that—seem to have a jaunty "I'm alright, Jack" attitude to "the ignorance with which we human beings treat one another; use and abuse the fellow sentient beings we call 'animals' (as if we were not animals ourselves); and despoil this beautiful planet on which we reside."

A: Yes, of course. Feel free to use anything I say as you see fit, attribution or not.

And really, in my view, all that you are calling "awakening experiences—such as no-self, liberation, energetic shift, transcendence" is beside the point entirely. All that is imaginary—a hanging of labels on the incomprehensible. When students of the late Charlotte Beck paraded their "attainments," she would say, "Don't tell me about all that. How are you getting along with your mother?"

Q3: In my experience, the relationship to an event or emotion may change, but there will still be what might be called less than preferable feelings, thoughts, emotions. It's only a *belief* that those kinds of conscious and unconscious inputs will not affect us ever again.

A: Yes, clearly we swim in a soup of perceptions, thoughts, feelings, emotions, and the rest of our many psychophysical milieux. I say "*we* swim," but that is just a manner of speaking. Really we *are* that soup, not just swimming in it. There is no swimmer separate from the soup. The swimmer *is* the soup, and the swimming is just part of it.

This is more than just a belief on my part, so when I say (borrowing language from Yeats' poem "Among School Children") that I cannot know the dancer from the dance, I am not lying, in the sense of asserting a second-hand "truth" as if I knew it first-hand—although I would never expect anyone to accept the unity of dance and dancer purely on my testimony.

From that perspective, there really are no *preferable* feelings, thoughts, etcetera. The matter is much more direct: what is, *is*. And, as Kurt Vonnegut observed in *Cat's Cradle*, "likes and dislikes have nothing to do with it." Not that likes and dislikes are *absent*; they are just part of what is.

Q3: I love this because it's so honest, but I feel like I'm clinging to the top of a cliff with bleeding fingers and don't know how to let go. I cannot accept the horror of accepting the notion that we are totally powerless to do anything other than to let go, even if I knew how to.

A: Yes, I understand that. To cling is an instinct present at birth, one of the few true instincts we human animals possess. The youngest newborns will grasp and cling, and their grip can be surprisingly strong. So clinging is natural, and this is not a question of accepting or rejecting, nor of clinging or letting go. I would not say that letting go is a matter of knowing how. I don't imagine that anyone can choose or decide to let go any more than one can decide to fall in love. To imagine that one can *choose* to let go arrogates to oneself a power one does not really possess.

This all boils down to seeing things as they really are—to *noticing*, which no one can choose or decide to do either. In each moment, you notice or you don't. *Trying* to notice is a way of not noticing. No one does noticing. No one can.

On this level, so-called "mindfulness" is just more commercialized twaddle aimed at *not* noticing—not noticing one's powerlessness. Mindfulness, as it is marketed and sold in corporate culture, is a strategy aimed at efficiency and productivity, which has nothing to do with seeing things as they are. And practices have a way of becoming habitual—which is the death of noticing, I say.

If you think you would prefer a different way of seeing these matters, and a different feeling about yourself and this life, just *choose* it. Oh, you can't? Sorry about that.

I don't mean to make light of your suffering. I feel for you, but seeing things as they are, including human limitation, may *reduce* that suffering, not add to it.

Q4: If I understand this, your theory is that we humans never really choose anything. Is that right?

A: Yes, that's right, except that my writing here is not *theory*. I have no use for theory in regards to human *be*-ing. What I write is reportage—phenomenology, not conjecture. If I am going to advance a theory, I will label it as such and put forward the *evidence* for it. Otherwise, my replies to questions will never be *theory*, but personal expression: my *own* experience as best I am able to put that into words.

To be clear, I am not denying the *feeling* of needing to choose and decide, but, as a friend of mine put this, the apparent chooser is like the sports announcer up in the press box. No matter what the announcer thinks or says, the events on the field are not affected in the slightest.

Readers have been telling me that reading *The Ten Thousand Things* provides a mind-opening experience. That may have to do precisely with the book *not* being theoretical, but entirely down to earth. When the chips are down and one has real skin in the game, theory—particularly metaphysical theory—does not go very far at all. Not in my world anyway.

Mindfulness practice may be an initial goad for one who is habitually unaware, and might be useful for a time, but "observing" can quickly degenerate into splitting and dissociation, both of which are symptoms of a disordered mind. Sanity, I say, requires that pain be felt and acknowledged—not kept at a distance or explained away with a "theory."

Although we know very little, if we *stick to what we actually know* and take things moment by moment, we can, I say, remain awake and aware with equanimity and sanity.

102 - A teacher in disguise

A reader recently shared with me this bit of history pertaining to his current understanding of teachers and teachings:

"I was a tree planter those days, and in-between contracts I would spend a few days in Vancouver. As was my habit at the time, I would go and sit with one spiritual group or the other on those days off. At the time I was sitting with a Zen monk who presided over what appeared to be an always empty *zendo*, at least when I was there. Interestingly enough there were always twenty or so cushions where we sat, so other people must have been sitting when I was not. I never saw anyone else there except him. If I remember correctly, I only went there maybe three times, and our conversations when we were not sitting were brief. The last time I went he said an interesting thing which, for reasons I will get to, stayed with me all these years.

"As I was leaving, he stopped me at the door. He looked at me and smiled and said, 'I have to tell you something. It won't do you any good but it is my duty to tell you this.' He then said, 'You already are enlightened. You were enlightened simultaneously with Shakyamuni Buddha, because Shakyamuni Buddha is the entire universe.' I, of course, knew he was yanking my chain, because I certainly did not feel enlightened, whatever that meant.

"I went off to do another tree planting contract, but this time I designated some of the money I would make on this contract to be a donation to that Zen center. What that monk had said was very close to my own experience earlier on in life, and that was something. I mean the Buddha oneness thing, not the enlightenment part.

"On my return to Vancouver, I set out for the *zendo* on the exact night of the week I knew would be available for visitors to sit. Well, on that night, for some reason or other the *zendo* was all locked up and no one was there. I walked away thinking I was sure this was a scheduled night for sitting, and how curious no one was there.

"As I walked a little further along, down a particularly dark stretch of the street, still thinking how curious this was, a huge man came out of the darkness from behind some bushes. He was very tall, had a trench coat on, and was not only very drunk but also had the front part of his head shaved with a visible series of stitches on a large wound there. He was asking me for money.

"I recognized him instantly. Here was the Buddha himself in a very clever disguise. Here was the temple to which to make my offerings. I took the Buddha to a restaurant where I fed him. I then took him to a store where I got him vitamins and a few other items. Later I took him to a hotel, got him a room, and made sure he had some money for coffee in the morning. All the money I was going to donate to this Zen center I gave to him instead, this Buddha in disguise. It was one of those moments of clarity where, if you are open to it, a teaching is recognized for what it is.

"I never went back to that *zendo*, or any *zendo* for that matter. Whatever it was I was supposed to get from that Zen monk I got. The drunk turned out to be a cleverly disguised great teacher and he never knew anything about it."

I love that story in its own right, and all the more since it reminds me of this old fable:

Once there was a goat who was walking into town to meet his friend the llama for dinner. In the course of his walk, the goat came upon a man who looked like he was about to scream, or perhaps begin to cry. The goat stopped and asked the man, "What's wrong?"

The man replied that his wife had just left him for another man. The goat said, "Well, that's nice—gotta go." But the man said, "Wait! I sense that you are an enlightened master who has come to teach me the path to enlightenment in my time of need.

Please teach me whatever I need to know." Reluctantly, the goat agreed and took the man on as a student.

The man followed the goat for many days, often trying to talk about spiritual things, but got nowhere. Every time he mentioned enlightenment, the goat would bite him on the arm or leg, whatever was closest. The man understood the wisdom in this and began to enjoy the journey itself.

However, one day, feeling unsatisfied with the situation, he pleaded with the goat to teach him the nature of reality. The goat agreed, and, after finding a good place for conversation about deep matters, in the shade of a tree beside a river, began to instruct the man:

"Tell me, man, if the sun stops shining, can these this tree continue to grow?"

"No, Master, it cannot. Without the sun, this tree will die."

"And what of the river? Can it continue to flow without the rain?"

"No, Master, it cannot. Without rain, the river will dry up."

"And what of the path to enlightenment? Can enlightenment occur without someone to teach the path to enlightenment?"

"No, Master, I do not believe it can. Without a master, no one would be able to attain enlightenment."

"Wrong!" the goat bleated sharply. "In the case of the sunshine and trees, and in the case of rain and the river, there was always a cause and an effect. For each effect within the world, you can be sure there is a cause, and for each cause, there must, by definition, be an effect. But the path to enlightenment does not exist, and so is subject neither to cause nor effect. Why not? Can you tell me why not?"

The man looked confused, and said, "Master, I don't understand. Why do you say that the path to enlightenment does not exist?"

The goat sighed deeply, and said, "OK, let me try my question in another way. You say I am an enlightened master. How did I get to be an enlightened master? Relax, take your time, and answer me correctly."

The man closed his eyes and thought deeply. Many different answers came to mind, but none felt correct. Finally, he thought of an answer that seemed so obvious, he wondered why he had not thought of it right away.

"You attained enlightenment through your past lifetimes, Master. You practiced for many lifetimes and, finally, you were able to overcome all obstacles and reach enlightenment."

"Wrong!" the goat said again. "Please, think about the answer and try again."

The man took a deep breath, closed his eyes and began to think deeply. Again many answers came to mind, but most were the same answers as before. He was filled with doubt. He had a nagging feeling that something was wrong, but could not quite put his finger on it. Perhaps, he thought, his first answer had been correct, and the goat was just testing him. With an effort of will, he banished all doubt from his mind, and began to think again, but got nowhere. Then, he said to himself, "In order for me to come up with the correct answer, I should stop thinking about anything at all."

Immediately, an answer came into his head:

"Through the power of the *universe*! You attained mastery through the power of 'universal consciousness,' which knew all along that I would need you. Now I get it! Everything works out perfectly! Everything happens according to a plan! Everything happens for a reason! I understand now, Master! I understand!"

"Wrong again!" the goat said in the same sharp tone as before. "This is your last shot, man. Please consider the question to the best of your ability and try again."

The man began to sweat. His head ached. He felt discouraged and distressed. He couldn't imagine what the correct answer could possibly be. He closed his eyes and tried again to ponder the question. Something in the back of his mind was bothering him. He tried to find some new approach to the question, but now his doubts were back again, stronger than ever. He tried and tried, but he couldn't ignore his doubts or push them away as he had done before. Then, all of a sudden, it hit him, and he shouted out:

"Goats can't talk!"

The goat got up from where he was sitting, bit the man on the arm, and walked away.

103 - The whirlpool

Q: Hi, Robert. Is it really your contention that no "I" exists apart from perceptions, thoughts, and feelings? This goes against a long history of spiritual teaching that sees "I" as pure awareness, that which is *aware* of perceptions, thoughts, and feelings without being involved in them.

A: My words here are not *contentions*, but simply *report*s of personal phenomenology. If I look for an "I" split off from perceptions, feelings, and thoughts, I don't find one. For me, awareness *is* perception. To be aware *is* to perceive.

I vastly prefer the findings of my own mind to belief in the dogmas of traditional religion, however "historic" or long-standing, and notwithstanding how many "teachers" teach them.

When "myself" is defined as pure awareness, that is what I call "splitting," in which an undivided, all-embracing *experience*—the experience of *be*-ing, of this aliveness, of existing at all—is broken down the middle conceptually, positing awareness or consciousness on the one hand, and the supposed "contents of consciousness" on the other. But consciousness and its supposed contents cannot *be* separated like that. They are, I say, one and the same mysterious happening.

Yes, without awareness, there is no experience of objects; the experience of objects *is* the awareness of them. But without objects, there is no experience of awareness. Ask *yourself* if you have ever felt "aware" without being aware of one object or another, one feeling or another, one thought or another, etcetera. If you have not—but want to argue for it—you are hypnotized by second-hand religious doctrine, and will never understand what is being said here until you wipe that slate clean.

"Objectless awareness" is a perfect example of how anyone can cook up any old concept and hang a name on it, whether the concept relates factually to the real world or not. Once named, the concept is thus *reified*, which means "thingified"—made into a "thing" that is *presumed* to exist in *fact*, when it may exist in name only.

Q2: But what about the body, Robert? You haven't mentioned that. I may be walking around in a dream, but if I walk into a tree, suddenly I really know that "myself" is real. I can imagine walking through a wall, which is thought or belief, but I—the real I—cannot walk through walls. You yourself have told the story of the student who was bragging about his understanding of esoteric matters, whereupon his teacher kicked him in the shins to remind him that he was really here.

A: Well, you seem to have missed the point of that story, which is not that "myself" is only a body, but that the student was so caught up in concepts and overwrought with his new "attainment" that he forgot that he was alive, which is not an attainment, and which is entirely beyond concepts.

Defining "myself" as a body and its autobiography is a way of looking at this, to be sure, but a limited way that leaves out too much. A human body is not like a rock that can sit there, more or less unchanging, for thousands of years. Everything about "myself," including the body, is always changing, and most of those changes and the rapidity with which they occur are obscured when "myself" is confined by definition to name and form.

Here is an analogy. I am familiar with a particular stretch of river and can tell you that just around the bend is a whirlpool. Although I can speak of the size and shape of it, that whirlpool is not a material object. "Whirlpool" is the name for an organization of water into a *pattern* powered by the flow of the river. Beyond its appearance as a recurring pattern, the whirlpool has no independent physical existence. Nevertheless, I can describe the whirlpool to you and predict that it will be there for you to see.

Yes, there is a physical substance—water—involved in this structuring, but it is never the *same* water; and if one observes carefully, the shape of the whirlpool is never quite the same from moment to moment. So, although I can predict that you will see it when you walk round the bend, the whirlpool cannot quite be said to exist in a material sense. It is a pattern, not an object.

That is how I regard the constantly changing pattern we call a human being, *including* the body. The cells in the body are always changing. The relationships among the organs of the body are always changing. Thoughts are always changing. Emotions are always changing. Understanding is always changing. Are you really trying to say that thoughts and emotions do not exist, or that understanding does not exist? That all "I" am is a fleshly body that cannot walk through walls? That's a hard case to make, and I don't even know why you would want to make it.

Just as a whirlpool has no separate existence apart from water and energy, there is no freestanding "me." You may define "myself" as this body and leave out thoughts, emotions, and understanding, but if you do, you will never grasp what I am saying. You can define a whirlpool as an object or a *thing*, but that will be inaccurate at best, and it will end the conversation. If someone simply *decides* to call the body, an apparent physical object, "me," most of what it means to be human is ruled out of consideration.

Q2: You have said that "person" is only a legal and social designation, and that "myself" is not a person. How does that figure into this?

A: A *person* is something quasi-physical, like a whirlpool, plus the autobiography of the whirlpool—the story the "whirlpool" tells itself ("I was born last spring when the rains came. As more water filled the riverbanks, the river got deeper, and I grew taller," etcetera.) When the story stops, the person disappears, and all that is left is seeing, hearing, feeling, etcetera.

That direct seeing, free of commentary, often occurs momentarily in a kind of hiatus or gap between perception and conception. For example, I am dumbfounded by some sight or sound that I cannot identify. In that instant, "myself" goes unnoticed, and only the sight or sound exists. Then the gap closes, and "I come back to myself," which means that direct, unmediated seeing stops, and the story—the conceptions, the *concepts*—resumes.

In that hiatus, no person existed, but only seeing or hearing. Yes, if observed from the outside, some kind of physical body is always present—although what that body *really* is defies understanding, even scientifically—but the *person*, the *story*, was not present when the unmediated seeing occurred.

When the person is there, unmitigated seeing is not, but only memory, description, and commentary—which are not *seeing*, and have nothing to *do* with seeing. It is the "person" from whom seekers of liberation long to be free. As long as you keep imagining that my words refer to bodies, you will never comprehend this.

104 - The price we pay

Dear Robert, you said, "Suffering is the price we pay for embodiment," and that, "we must continue to suffer what we suffer, including the sadness one may feel when witnessing the suffering of others." But in my understanding, the Buddha said that there is an end to suffering. Would you please explain?

A: Thank you for your question. It is a deep one, and I would have to write a book, not a few paragraphs, in order to address it. Actually, I have written such a book, *The Ten Thousand Things*, but for now, I will try to give a briefer answer.

In the first place, although I find much wisdom in what the Buddha reportedly said—especially his explanation of how the sense of self arises emergently as a pastiche of various thoughts and feelings, plus other factors that do not actually constitute any coherent "self"—I am not a Buddhist believer, nor do I take the words of the Buddha as authoritative in any absolute sense. I know, however, that many do, and you may be one of them.

According to inconclusive reports, Siddhartha Gotama was born in the 5th or 6th century BCE in what is now Nepal, the son of a potentate. His father, so the story goes, went to great efforts to raise the boy in total luxury, and to keep him shielded from any awareness of either religion or ordinary human suffering.

Until the age of 29, to continue the traditional account, this spoiled rich boy knew nothing much of actual life, but only the life of a prince with a "helicopter father." One day, being curious about life outside the palace walls, which he had never seen, he bribed a charioteer to take him into the village. There he saw for the first time what life was like for ordinary people: the constant struggle to acquire the ordinary necessities, illness without treatment, the disabilities of old age... And finally, upon seeing a corpse, he saw death, which had always, so the story goes, been hidden from him.

Now, this account seems unbelievable on the face of it, doesn't it? How could a grown man actually be *that* naive? So I suggest taking it metaphorically: not as if it were an actual history, but as a myth. And I suggest taking the rest of the Buddha story the same way. I understand that this attitude will not sit well with many of those who call themselves Buddhists, but that's one of the problems with signing on to scriptural accounts and a structure of beliefs as if they were indisputable facts. Once a belief is adopted, views to the contrary, however sensible, often are defended against and dismissed out of hand. This is the famous confirmation bias.

During his brief sojourn outside the walls of the palace where he had been shielded from reality, Gotama had seen an ascetic wandering nearly naked with nothing but a staff and a bowl. When Gotama asked about the *sadhu*, the charioteer told him that the man had renounced ordinary life in order to search for an end to his fear of old age, illness, suffering, and death.

Since we are now in the realm of myth, where stories carry meta-information planted in the interstices of their narratives, let us notice that the charioteer said that the man wanted to search for an end to his *fear* of old age, illness, suffering, and death—*not* the end of old age, illness, suffering, and death themselves, but an ending to his *fear* of them.

Following this probably fictitious initiation into the tribulations of actual life, Gotama returned to the palace, only to find that his wife and the other women who had pleased him so much no longer appeared so attractive now that he had to imagine them and himself ageing, becoming ill, and dying. Nor could he take pleasure in the endless entertainment, music, food, and drink that was his daily fare. Suddenly, a life that had seemed endlessly sweet and perfectly gratifying began to feel unsatisfactory and even distressing.

This man of almost thirty, who had never before known suffering, was awakening to ordinary *reality*—what life is *really* like. And so, feeling for the first time his own fears and anxieties, he determined to imitate the path of the *sadhu* he had seen in the village. In secret, he fled the palace with only his man-servant and his horse, and began to wander.

Leaving kith and kin to roam in search of one's *own* mind seems to be a fixture in this kind of story. It certainly has been in mine.

Before long, his fine robes, his horse, and his servant were gone by the wayside, and Gotama fell in with a band of other mendicant wanderers. From them he learned religion and meditation, but his doubts, fears, and anxieties were still not put to rest. At that point, the story says, he left his companions just as he had left the palace and all the comforts of home.

Setting off into the unknown alone, eventually, he found a place to sit in the shade of a tree, vowing that he would not leave that place until he found the answers to his questions and an end to his chronic unease. Finally, it is said, he attained "unexcelled perfect enlightenment," after which he went on to preach for many years until, in this version of the story, he died an old man in agony, after a meal of poisonous mushrooms, either poorly selected or intentionally fed to him. There is always jealousy around greatness, the myth reminds us.

Now myth is myth, whether the hero of the myth actually lived or not. There are mythic characters of both kinds. We don't really know if the Buddha existed as an historical person, nor is there actual contemporary evidence for Moses, Jesus, Muhammad, or Zoroaster either. But whether their stories are *only* fictional or based on some actual once-alive cat—who, like other boys, had nocturnal emissions as he came to puberty, made love to his penis, and had to work it all out from there—a myth, in any case, is not the man, but largely psychological commentary.

Psyche—after whom psychology is named—was a mythological character herself, the goddess of the Soul, who lived on Mount Olympus and who enraged Aphrodite (Venus) when all the guys began to hit on sweet young Psyche instead of Her Highness.

Out for vengeance, Aphrodite commended her son, Eros, the god of Love, to make Psyche fall in love with and marry the ugliest man on the mountain. Instead, in the course of that mission, Eros himself fell in love with Psyche. After a long backstory worth reading, they were married, and—whoo boy! A-kissin' and a-huggin' and a boom-boom! We humans, who are not gods and goddesses living on a magic mountain, but just ordinary people without superpowers, are left at that point to work it all out for ourselves.

So the hero of a myth might once have lived in the flesh, or not. That matters little. Myths are not true, except sometimes on the level of psychological narrative. The *story*, larger than life, is all the public has access to anyway. Backstage, things are entirely different.

I have tried in this book to illustrate that difference, which someone is sure to interpret as attacks on some of the people I mentioned—but that was never the objective. The intention is to demythologize the word "awake," not to demean the memory of poor old Jiddu Krishnamurti because he lied about his secret sex life. Perhaps we can understand these matters better if we understand that perfection is *never* part of the story, and so allow *ourselves* to be awake *imperfectly.*

Now, I am not saying that Gotama never existed historically. Some scholars, but not all, believe he did. But I think it highly unlikely that the purported *teachings* of the Buddha—which were recorded only hundreds of years after his death—can be taken as gospel. Nevertheless, I have enjoyed those teachings, so it is not my intention to disparage them, but only to put them in what I consider proper context.

Here is an example of what I mean by proper context. A friend of mine who is devoted to the Pali Canon (the earliest written reports of the Buddha story, recorded hundreds of years after the events which they are purported to chronicle) firmly believes that because, according to those reports, the Buddha abstained from sex, and reputedly told others to do the same, only a celibate monk can attain "full enlightenment." My friend, who otherwise seems quite bright, is one hundred percent convinced of this.

To me, this sounds fishy. Remember that Gotama was perhaps the most spoiled boy in history (or one of them at least), who spent his days in complete self-indulgence, in whatever pleased him at the time, including a wife and who knows how many girlfriends. So perhaps to come to a real understanding of what it means to be human, Gotama needed more *voluntary* austerity than someone like you or me who had not been so shielded from ordinary life. Spoiled children, if they hope to reach actual psychological adulthood, often have to create obstacles for themselves in one way or another.

Speaking for myself, I have been married to a beautiful woman for more than forty years, and sex never got in my way at all. In fact, in my view, the bonding experiences and intimacy of ordinary human love and family have only added to my understanding of what it means to be a human primate animal capable of self-referential self-reflection.

I am not saying that no one should practice celibacy. That's an individual matter, and that's my point. Anyone who imitates Gotama or anyone else in hopes of attaining "liberation" is missing the boat, I say. The only *viable* boat is your *own* boat. Gotama had his boat, and welcome to it. But you cannot sail *that* boat. You can only sail your own. If you become a Buddha-imitator, you will always be a disciple, and will forever be in the position of having to defend your acquired beliefs in reincarnation, monkhood, and all the rest.

If you live without premature cognitive commitments, but rely upon your own experience, and see things by the light of your *own* mind, you will not need to defend anything, but will be free to live here and now, moment by moment by moment, without focusing on attaining so-called "Buddhahood." This is the meaning of the saying, "If you meet the Buddha in the road, kill him"—which is capital advice in my opinion.

With that as background, let me get to your question directly.

In the first place, when you look at this world with open eyes and observe the terrible suffering that surrounds us, even if one prefers to deny it, how could you possibly imagine ending your own suffering? Is that not the height of selfishness?

If humanity and the rest of the sentient animal kingdom are suffering in this way, what would it even mean for you to say, "Yes, they are all suffering, but I am not; I am 'liberated' from all that?"

When I say "suffering," I do not mean just such kinds of suffering as lacking the possessions one desires, or the experiences that one craves, or the pain of loneliness, or the knowledge that one will age, sicken, and die—although one may suffer all of that. Here, I am referring primarily to being subjected to brutality, enslavement, rape, war, starvation, etcetera.

And I am not referring only to human suffering but to the suffering of all sentient beings, such as the farm animals that humans use for food without the slightest thought about their comfort, while they await a usually pitiless slaughter. That is the sadness one may feel when witnessing the suffering of others. You may love bacon, but a visit to a corporate pig operation might change that forever. Or, by the time they serve it up on the BLT, perhaps others have done all the suffering for you.

In the face of all that, how could adopting some religious philosophy, no matter how highly touted, possibly lead to an end to one's personal suffering? And if it could, would you not suspect that the philosophy must be somehow bogus or inhumane?

This is the problem, I say, with religions that promise an end to suffering through so-called "enlightenment." And make no mistake about it: some equivocators try to claim that Buddhism is not a religion, but if the Buddha is seen as omniscient—which is how my friend regards him—that is *not* a human attribute but the attribute of a god; and the kinds of Buddhists who regard every word of Buddhist scripture as absolute "Truth" are his fundamentalist worshipers.

If you like to believe Gotama to have been omniscient, or that a Buddha only "takes birth" once in thousands of years, fine by me. I am not selling my point of view—only expressing it, just like the bacon thing.

This is not to demean the teachings of the Buddha, which, as I said above, I consider a source of useful wisdom—primarily, in my view, the understanding that "myself" is not a fixed "thing," but an endlessly impermanent flow of experiences that we cobble together unconsciously, to create the *illusion* of a unitary "self." That is Abhidharma, early Buddhist psychology, said to be the teaching of Gotama. The five skandhas[48] and all that. If you don't know about

48. Skandhas (Sanskrit) or khandhas (Pali): heaps, aggregates, collections, or groupings. In Buddhism, the five aggregates of clinging are the five material and mental factors that take part in the arising of craving and clinging: form (or material image, impression), sensations (or feelings), perceptions, mental

that, it's worth a look.

So, if the Buddha reputedly said that there is an end to suffering, how do I square that with my saying that we must continue to suffer what we suffer, including the sadness one feels when witnessing the suffering of others? That was your question, and here is my reply: the Buddha never said that all life is suffering and that there is an end to that suffering.

Not being an English speaker, obviously, Gotama could not have used the word "suffering." The word he did use—reportedly, of course, hundreds of years after the lectures he is purported to have given—was a word in Pali, *dukkha*. To translate that word as "suffering" is an outright mistake that has rendered the Western versions of The Four Noble Truths in a distorted way that has misled, and continues to mislead, countless people who call themselves Buddhists.

A much better translation of *dukkha* would be insufficiency, anxiety, disquiet, distress, unsatisfactoriness, a sense of unease. A helpful image for understanding that word—I read this somewhere, but can't recall where—is that *dukkha* is like riding in a cart that has one wheel with a flat spot. It *feels* like a smooth ride, and one enjoys the ride complacently until the flat spot comes around again, and suddenly—klunk!—not so smooth after all. This is why even those who have things pretty cushy can still feel anxiety. As much as they try to ignore it, they know that nothing lasts forever and that what goes up must come down again.

So, the message is not that *suffering* comes to an end. The cartwheel still has a flat spot no matter what you think, and that cannot be repaired. That's life. A toothache still hurts, the death of a loved one still produces grief, and seeing the greed, the violence, and the abject, seemingly limitless ignorance of humanity still hurts, perhaps profoundly.

If it did not hurt, you would be, I say, a kind of cold-hearted monster, not "enlightened" in the least. It is certain monsters like that who can look at human suffering—not just psychological suffering, which is one thing, but torture, starvation, child abuse, racism, and

---

activity or formations, and consciousness.

the rest—and feel just peachy because, in their trance of religious ignorance, they imagine that none of it is "real."

So suffering continues and cannot be denied. Nevertheless, one can, I say, come to grips with feeling that life itself is unsatisfactory or that one must live in a state of perpetual anxiety. That is part of what I tried to address in *4T*, and why I say now, "Depending on no-thing, find your own mind."

105 - The sense of self

Q: Early in *The Ten Thousand Things*, you spoke of "I, being a flow of consciousness." I understood this to mean that I am aware somehow of what appears to be a spontaneous flow of life or the universe without knowing who I am. Do I have this right?

Then you say, "In accordance with that observation, one can just be, and let the stream of consciousness flow where it will. That is what I mean by awake."

A: The "I" of enunciation—the "I" that calls itself "me"—is *part* of one's actual being, but nowhere near all of it. In fact, most of one's *actual* being operates behind the scenes, below conscious awareness. Think iceberg.

For example, you are not normally aware of your internal organs, unless there is a problem indicated by pain or discomfort. Nevertheless, those organs are in constant conversation with the brain, sending and receiving information second by second via nociceptors. So a great deal of the generalized feeling of being an entity, a "self," derives from the sense of aliveness generated by that continual, unceasing communication, which is entirely nonverbal and ordinarily entirely unconscious. Even if there is a problem—a sharp pain in the gut, for example, or a heart arrhythmia that gets one's attention—most of that nonverbal communication still remains unknown to the "I" of enunciation.

If one can get a feeling for this cognitive/informational limitation of the "myself" that ordinarily fancies itself the doer of perceiving, feeling, thinking, and acting (when, in actual fact, most of that occurs behind the scenes and out of sight), then this aliveness will flow more naturally and freely. From a wisdom perspective, the "I" of enunciation will stay out of the control room, and do what it does best: experiencing and participating on the everyday human level, without presuming itself to be the doer and decider of this aliveness. Otherwise, the controlling, choosing, deciding "myself" that one *believes* oneself to be, and calls "I," will dither and struggle, impeding that natural flow.

This is not a black and white, "either/or" matter, so perhaps it is better to say that one can go with the flow *to the extent* that one can understand consciously that no "myself" actually exists as a discrete unitary being. And therefore, although it may *feel* that "I" am deciding, choosing, and doing, that is largely an illusion, and can be seen as such, by some of us at least.

I don't know if you are familiar with the five skandhas[49] idea in Buddhism, but that concept can be helpful in understanding my saying that the ordinary experience of a unitary "myself" is largely an illusion. But since it is an illusion that we are taught from birth, widely-shared, and difficult to contradict, awakening—in the way I mean that word—seems to happen only for some of us. The others remain firmly *attached* to the "I" of enunciation. It's what they identify "as."

Ordinary "spirituality" is not helpful in coming to this understanding, I say, and can even be counterproductive, if one imagines that choosing to undertake some practice will lead to "awakening." No, I say—it won't. Practices that are felt to be "chosen" for the purpose of transcending ordinary biological existence only deepen the illusion of "myself, the do-er."

Does that help?

Q: Yes. Just hearing you say that diffuses much suffering. Still, when I look outward, the world seems to consist mostly of causes of suffering, even if those might appear to give pleasure; but, on the other hand, when I look inside, I feel peace and stillness. Slowly, the list of outward objects I crave seems to be dwindling. Is this what you call progressive awakening?

Other than the experience you had of suddenly awakening, is there any other way of snapping that list altogether? If yes, what can I expect? I find resistance from family, as they see me less and less passionate about things. I used to teach yoga and meditation, and felt quite enthusiastic about all that. I still attend satsangs, but I have stopped teaching as I have lost the desire for it.

49. See footnote on p.578.

A: A kind of dispassion often seems to go along with seeing things as they are. I don't mean not caring about things: I still care, in a way more than ever, but with equanimity.

From my perspective, there *is* no inside and outside. That is a false dichotomy, a split where none actually obtains. I understand that experience can *appear* to be split like that, but this may become clearer if you ask yourself *who* is seeing all of this—both the apparent "inside" and the apparent "outside." How is the seer different from what is seen? Is there a difference? And is there truly a little homunculus "inside" somewhere *doing* all this looking inward and outward (the "I" of enunciation, perhaps)—or does it just *feel* that way?

From what you have written, I'd advise not worrying about snapping anything together. Just live as you must until you die. Whatever wisdom and understanding you can bring to that process will be yours to enjoy.

Q: Thanks. So *nirvana* is also part of what you call "the hypnotic trance?"

A: You are most welcome. Yes, if *nirvana* is conceptualized or commodified as a *future destination to* be sought in hopes of transcending the biological and emotional suffering of human existence, I'd say that is a feature of the trance.

It may be hard to accept each moment as it is without hoping or searching for something "more evolved," but seeing the lie in such hopes for the future, in my experience, allows freedom, sanity, and reality in the present. And you only have to take it one moment at a time. Without hope, imagined future glories—familiar hiding places—disappear. *This* moment is all one ever has to deal with, and all one ever can deal with. With that understanding, *samsara* is *nirvana.*

Q: Ha! Maybe your "freedom, sanity, and reality" got translated into "*nirvana*" by whomever.

A: As for *nirvana*, that's a tricky word. I think it literally means extinguished or blown out like a candle. That's not my experience at all.

Q: By the way, why is your book called *The Ten Thousand Things*?

A: "The ten thousand things" is an ancient term for the manifest universe. In the epigraph to the book, I quoted Eithei Dogen:

> *To study the self is to forget the self.*
> *To forget the self is to be enlightened by the ten thousand things.*

Q: I see. Thank you. So since I don't and can't know who I am, why bother? Is that it, Robert? In fact, stop wasting time and enjoy whatever appears to be here and now? I think I get the gist, but giving up doesn't come easy to the brain. Failure to know who I am feels like death.

A: Yes. Whatever one thinks or has been taught to believe—perhaps in one of those satsangs you attend?—each of us is *mortal*, and will age and die like any other animal. Nothing trumps biology—not, at least, so far as we know.

In fact, you will never be this young again, so enjoy it while it lasts. I would not see that approach as "giving up," but more as embracing the true existential situation of "myself." If I see things as they are, I may find that simply being at all—even if I don't know how or why—feels more like a gift than a burden. Would I really prefer that none of this be here: the stars, the oceans, the flowers, myself?

Q: So no euphoria, no bliss, no oneness with the universe. And even if I did get those experiences, like so many others those too would fade away, and I would be left with whatever *here* is. Perhaps the best teachers are those who never said anything.

A: Yes. I said nothing for years. But a friend I trust kept urging me to share my point of view. Finally, I gave in. Perhaps euphoria is a bit over the top, but in my experience there *is* joy, there *is* love, and there *are* feelings of oneness. It's just that no feeling is permanent. Everything is in flux. To be honest, I *do* have feelings of unity, but I don't cling to them conceptually as an explanation of anything. Freedom is the key.

Q: I am already free. So it must be that I start to feel this freedom in my day-to-day living in the body?

A: Be as you are. If that includes feelings of oneness, lovely. If it doesn't, that's fine too. The point is to stop looking for something "else," something "better" than right now. One can spend an entire lifetime hoping to "transcend" ordinary human primate life. I consider that a crying shame, a waste.

Q: Anticipation of some bliss in the future seems to be so hardwired. Nearly all my life I have been trying to fix things so I would be happier tomorrow. I understand now that I missed out on many todays in the process. Thanks for that, Robert.

A: You are welcome. This life is so very brief. It's sad to see someone always on to the next thing, while the suchness of *this* moment goes unnoticed. And anyway, the expectation of being happier tomorrow may be misplaced.

Q: One thing keeps coming back. If some, like you, have this expansive experience, it must be physical/mental. That too is impermanent. So why does it seem so special? The Zen masters advise ignoring such experiences. That too, they say, is clinging and hence suffering. "Why invite more suffering?" they say. But a voice inside says, "Sour grapes!"

If I were really convinced that there is no "aha!" moment, I'd stop thinking of enlightenment. What would be the point?

A: I am not saying that there are no "aha!" moments. I would never say anything like that. I am saying that wishing for one will only get in the way of noticing one if it arises, because an "aha!" moment may be entirely different from what one had been imagining. That seems to be the case for many of us. I have little "aha!" moments frequently, but most of them are undramatic, subtle, and quiet, so if I were always on some kind of mission to have my mind blown, I might miss most of them.

You just thanked me for reminding you that in your search for happiness tomorrow you "missed out on many todays in the process." That's a kind of "aha!" moment, isn't it? It would be for me.

I don't use the word "enlightenment" myself because, in my view, it is fraught and carries too much baggage. But I do use the word "awake." I observe that lots of us really *are* awake, or could be at least, but miss it because we were expecting to feel, "Eureka! Now everything is solved!" And that isn't necessarily the feeling—although it might be, I suppose. I am saying that if it can be noticed that you — the "I" of enunciation, the feeling of "myself" you call "me"—are neither making thoughts, feelings, and perceptions nor controlling them once they arise, you *are* what I call awake. It just has to be noticed and called that.

Q: You have deconstructed every other religion, what do you think of Kabbalah?

A: Kabbalah is the mystical side of Judaism, focused squarely upon what I criticize as magical thinking: the entirely false belief that humans can influence and alter the course of natural events by uttering the "secret names of God;" intoning magical incantations; wearing amulets; working with sorcery, seals, and symbols; resorting to thaumaturgies; and the rest of that superstitious twaddle.

As you know, I reject the "God" thing entirely. Humans have cooked up gods since time *immemorial*. For me, it's just not an issue.

Once people prayed to Zeus and "knew" what he wanted from them: lots of sacrifices. Nowadays people pray to Jesus, Jehovah, or Allah, and "know" what "He" wants. I see no difference. None. Mythology is mythology. The gods used to be painted on the walls of caves, and children and animals sacrificed to them. That was pre-science, so it may have been all they had. But nowadays, to believe in all that godlore requires a different *kind* of sacrifice: the sacrifice of good sense and reason.

Q: Well then, a final question, please. If I can see "myself" as a construct, can "I" be *part* of the construct? If I knew that, then I would know who I am. Do I have any attributes?

A: Of course you do. A questioning, questing mind seems to be among them.

Q: I love it. The *construct* is my attribute. Who is under hypnosis? Isn't it the body/mind? The construct can never know, but I can see the construct. Or is that the construct looking at itself?

A: The part of the mind of which you are aware is hypnotized by the notion of *becoming* something one is not now.

Q: If there is nothing else, then perhaps there is no value in seeking, but it does seem that I found considerable insight into my stupidity along the path, though.

A: What you are calling "the path" is seen only in retrospect as a history of certain memories. "Path" is a poor name for *be*-ing. It's a name that can only confuse. A *path* is a track that is already laid out—perhaps marked by stones or the footsteps of others. If one is really living, and not just following and imitating, that is not what this aliveness is like. Some people seek and follow until they find what they wanted—Jesus, nonduality, whatever. Others live in the spontaneous present.

Q: Isn't spiritual seeking similar to Freud's self-analysis? Forgive me if I am paraphrasing him incorrectly. Isn't much of the Buddha's teachings the earliest form of psychology?

A: Judging from the words attributed to Gotama, he was a great psychologist. If his work could be understood that way, much confusion would subside.

Q: I understood your book, Robert, but it is really tough to accept that I cannot know the answers to ultimate questions.

A: Yes. I get that. The spiritual teachers are trying to claim that you *can* know, and that they will show you how to know. Perhaps they have been hypnotized themselves, or maybe they want to add you to their roster of followers. It takes a strong mind to resist hypnosis, and to live only for what one really *can* know—which is nothing about Brahman and all that, but only one's own mind in this moment.

Q: What do you think of this saying, Robert: "The reason you can't know Brahman is because you're it?"

A: Nah. Clever nonsense that means nothing much. As far as I *know*, what I *really* am is a primate human animal whose ancestors evolved from the same original one-celled ancestor from which all life on Earth evolved, beginning billions of years ago. The evolved brain is capable of complex conceptual thought, including concepts about non-existent items—items that exist only in imaginary ontology—and to me, Brahman seems to be one of those concepts.

I am not saying the Brahman of the Hindu scriptures does not exist, but I see scant evidence for it. There may be a teapot, too small to be detected by telescopes, orbiting the sun somewhere between the Earth and Mars, as Bertrand Russell said. No one can *prove* there isn't. Those who are "certain" of religious metaphysics, from my perspective, seem terribly overeager to take ideas on faith and deem them "Truth."

I have no use for "faith." I see what *I* see—not what some "teacher" or scripture *tells* me to see. So I am free, not because I believe one thing or another, but because I don't need to believe *anything* in order to live and breathe, laugh and love.

Q: What do you think of "I am not the body" or *neti neti*[50]?

A: I do not agree at all with "I am not the body." What is the meaning of such an assertion? Without a body, including a brain, there *is* no I, is there?

Neti neti. Yes. That seems a good approach. Why not give it a shot?

Q: Do you feel that consciousness is an emergent property of the body? Or do you just not care?

A: You do know the right questions to ask. Ha, ha.

The jnanis and the Vedic scriptures claim that consciousness exists prior to brains, and that brains are only objects *in* consciousness. But that seems a far reach, and they offer no evidence, but only tradition, testimony, and shaky logic. Tradition is not evidence, nor is logic. Zeno "proved" that an arrow could never reach its target.

As for testimony, anyone can claim anything while feeling totally certain of what he or she is saying, but that does not make it so. If some contemporary spiritual teacher has *evidence*—not scripture, not belief, not faith, not talk, but observable *facts*—put them on the table. I would be interested to see them.

There is a great deal of evidence to suggest that consciousness is an emergent property of brains—for example, if part of the brain is damaged, consciousness is impaired. The 1985 book *The Man Who Mistook His Wife for a Hat*, by the neurologist Oliver Sacks, speaks in detail of such cases and is a lovely read.

I will never accept any unsubstantiated ideas about consciousness or anything else, regardless of how many humans before me believed them. Ancient does *not* equal true—only old.

Q2: How do you know the difference between awakening and just being in a dark place? I read your report of Sonam Kazi's[51]

50. *Neti neti:* in Hinduism, and in particular Jnana Yoga and Advaita Vedanta, a Sanskrit expression, meaning "not this, not that," or "neither this, nor that."

51. Sonam Topgyal Kazi, or Sonam T. Kazi or Sonam Topgay Kazi (1925-

remarks about your past lives and how you rejected all that. Like you, I totally don't care about past lives. I don't care about religion. I have zero interest in pursuing any "spiritual truth." I have no way of discerning truth. But I don't think my lack of interest in those things is a sign of being awakened. I think it is because I have no faith in anything anymore.

My life-long belief system is just plain gone, like shattered glass. But what is left in its wake is fear. Maybe the fear is based on the loss of my sense of security. Regardless of its validity, I once had a sense of security, but that is gone. I don't even know why I am sharing this with you, Robert.

On the other hand, something smacked me right in the forehead last night. I've always liked the movie screen analogy, even though I didn't really get it. It made logical sense, but not *felt* sense, I guess you could say. But last night it just hit me. I got it deeply. It was suddenly clear and obvious. The screen—which is my awareness—just is. It has no choice about what movie plays, what feelings arise, what scenes are seen. The screen *lives* the show. The events happen on the screen of awareness, and become part of "me," is how I see it now.

The losses of loved ones I have faced—there was no choice but for that to play out. The screen took it all in, and that *is* "me" now. I can't rewind, I can't edit, and I can't fast forward. At least, that is how things appear at present. Tomorrow may be different, and probably will be.

A: Good. You have seen that no one gets to *choose* the movie, because the movie is this aliveness itself. To see—not just on a logical level, but empirically—that this wild aliveness is the deepest referent of the word "myself," leaves no choice but to *deal* with that movie minute by minute. The movie *is* me. The sense of *be*-ing flows unstoppably—a river of perceptions, thoughts, and feelings springing up spontaneously; already water over the dam before anyone can judge them, control them, or fix them. Like it or not, the would-be doer or controller lags behind, if only by a split second. Something seen cannot then

2009), a Tibetan writer and translator and specialist in Dzogchen.

be made "unseen," nor a thought erased.

To call this aliveness a movie is not to trivialize it, or to suggest that it is not "real," as some foolish people imagine. It is a "movie" in the sense that it keeps playing, and you are already in the theater watching it, with a "no refunds" policy at the box office. You can try to turn your face away, but the movie just keeps playing. Each moment of that movie—which will end presumably at death—comprises a never-to-be-repeated suchness on its own.

Awake, one notices the suchness of each moment. Each moment is precious precisely because it is ephemeral and transitory. One meets that suchness with open arms, chewing up perceptions, thoughts, and feelings, and swallowing them bite by bite. Any particular moment may taste sweet or bitter, but we all must keep eating.

106 - The myth of Sisyphus

Q: From my point of view, we human beings appear to be striving constantly to gain or achieve something. This is just the human condition, isn't it? Although this striving does not provide much equanimity or long-term happiness, it does provide motivation. Believing that there is a future in which we may find or arrange something that will make us happy, is what motivates us to earn money, find friendships and romantic relationships, and a whole host of other ordinary things.

If one sees things exactly as they are—thoughts as thoughts and fantasies as fantasies, etcetera—then what's the point? Where is the motivation? You have said that your photographs are a form of self-expression. Could you elaborate on that? If one is accepting of this moment, and is aware that there is only *this* moment, it seems a paradox that one could exert him- or herself with any concept of an end goal, such as creating art.

I hope this is clear—I'm finding it difficult to find the right words. I think you'll understand, nevertheless. Thanks.

A: I thought you stated the question clearly. I suppose the answer is that, if you need motivation, you need it, and will have to dream some up—perhaps in the way that some people use pornography to arouse themselves to have sex.

I follow no far-reaching goal such as "creating art." A morning of camerawork for me is a satisfaction unto itself, and I don't even *need* to see the pictures later. I still have some rolls of exposed film around from years ago that I never managed to develop, and now I have no darkroom. I like printmaking too, which I now carry out on a computer instead of a chemical darkroom. I have made some lovely versions of images no one else has seen and that I probably will never show. I made them for *myself*, just to see what they would look like. I find myself working with a camera in the same spirit in which I am typing right now on this laptop. Writing is what I find myself doing. I feel no sense of what you imagine is "exertion" at all.

I could construct an entire narrative about *choosing* to write, or *deciding* to write, or being "creative," and I understand that such a narrative would comport with the conventional perspective. But that is not how this aliveness *feels* to me. I do not *choose* the next word that I find myself typing. The word just emerges—from whence I do not know—and fingers move as they learned to do long ago, not as I *decide* to move them now. I don't know *what* mixture of desires slings a camera around my neck whenever I leave the house, or *why* I am so in love with the viewfinder and the click of exposure. All of that is a mystery to me. But it's not much about "creating art."

Q: So then, Robert, I'm thinking that nobody knows what the point is. So if someone is fortunate enough not to need a point, then there's one less fib to tell yourself before bed. So let me ask you this, was there ever a time where you realized there's no point, and found it terrifying?

A: I wouldn't say that there is no point. Although that thought has crossed my mind more than once, it never solidified into anything terrifying. Nowadays, I never ask, "Why am I here? Where is it all headed? What's the *point* of living?" Questions like those just don't arise. Simple *be*-ing seems sufficient—a gift actually. Perhaps the only point to life is to live; and the meaning, assuming there is one, must emerge moment by moment, visible only to oneself, prior to preconceived notions, or the explanations, justifications, and value systems of others.

Each of us *feels* like a "myself," alive and conscious. Alive and conscious are the primary facts of the matter. Questions about a *point* to this aliveness—a *purpose* to our being here—are attempts to justify or explain these primary facts.

Given our evolutionary lineage, seeking explanations seems entirely reasonable and natural. Of *course* we would like to be able to explain that mysterious noise in the night. Was it a hungry predator on the prowl, or just a gust of wind in the brush? The survival of ancient DNA into subsequent generations depended upon the accuracy of such discernment, and it is deoxyribonucleic acid, whether we admit it or not, that does a lot of "my" thinking. In a real sense, the human individual is the mortal means for the reproduction and immortality of DNA.

Looking for explanations of phenomena is central to the capacity for survival, and we humans are programmed to survive—therefore, we are always thirsting for reasons and explanations. We want explanations and sometimes feel we need them. If, for example, I feel a pain that persists, I may need a trained physician to *explain* it to me so I can decide what to do next.

However, seeking explanations on the level of cause and effect for events in the physical world is one thing, and a demand to know the *purpose* of this aliveness or the presumed "source" of consciousness is quite another. No doctor in the world can explicate *reality* for me, nor any self-appointed spiritual teacher either, although I have met one or two who tried.

The late James Broughton, poet, and member of the Sisters of Perpetual Indulgence in the San Francisco Renaissance of the mid-20th century, said this so well:

Do not ask where
we go from here
Nobody knows
Some think they do
but nobody really knows
anything
about anything
We are only gurgles
in the stream
and the stream doesn't
know where it's going
either
It is just going

It is just
going with its nature
as far as that
will take it
And with its nature
it has to take along
a horde of
gurgles
who are forever asking
where they are
gurgling to
Everything
is going beautifully
nowhere

Q: I apologize. I have not made my question clear. Please let me try to explain what I meant. You have discussed a time when you were in a different condition than you are at present—a time *before* awakening. I assume that, during that time, you believed there was a future and that there was a point to living, a reason to live. At some stage, you no longer needed a reason; any concept of a "point" was seen as an illusion, a fantasy, a distraction from the here and now.

It seems to me that even being able to say that there *is* no point might be in some ways comforting. At least, in that case, there is still the feeling of an "I" who can know things, and who understands the boundary line between hope and hopelessness.

But if I understand you, you are not saying that there is no point. You are saying that you never even think that way; that for you the question never even arises. You have no hopes but are not troubled by hopelessness either. For you, there is no way of knowing *anything* for sure.

I won't lie. Sometimes I feel terrified by that idea. I'm sure that many others experience that terror too.

A: Yes, of course. I have been through all kinds of razor's edge ruminations about hopelessness, but apparently I am more inclined to depression than terror. I cannot actually recall any time at all when I felt *terror* at the thought of "meaninglessness," but I can recall many times when I dealt with depressive thoughts such as "What's the use?" by immersing myself in work and projects, ingesting drugs and alcohol, or losing myself in risky physical behaviors (particularly the latter, which used to be a habit of mine).

Q: Thanks for your honesty, Robert!

A: My pleasure. I find *meaning* in honesty—honesty with myself, and, by extension, honesty with others—not because honesty necessarily *leads* somewhere meaningful, but because participation in the human capacity for candor, openness, and unbridled self-expression lightens my heart in *this* moment—even if *this* moment is a sad moment or a painful one. In a case like that, I feel that at least I am not *lying* to myself, that I can face the ebb and flow of thoughts, feelings, and perceptions with sanity and ordinary human wisdom.

Nevertheless, there is nothing eternal to be gained by speaking honestly. However we speak—candidly or with forked-tongue—in the end there is still only death and the loss of everything one calls "myself." That is how it appears to me: a time for everything, including the ending. However, since there are alternate hypotheses about mortality in which death is not the end of "myself," it is fair to ask if I *know* that.

Do I *know* that? Do I know that when the heart stops and the brain dies that "I" die? No. I do not *know* it. But to assume otherwise leads immediately to fevered fantasies of an onward and upward "journey" on the stairway to Heaven, until we are "one with God," or "realize" so-called nonduality or "universal consciousness," after which one is in a so-called "undying" state.

Lots of people live in such fantasies without ever admitting such ideas might be no more than wishful thinking, but I can't. The only approach that works for me is open-hearted participation in *this* moment, without regard to speculative metaphysics and conjectures about ultimate matters.

I know my approach will not be understood by those who seek happiness, self-satisfaction, or so-called bliss, and all that. I do not seek *any* emotional state. *I seek nothing.* This is freefall: no seeker, no doer, no explanations, no nothin' but *be*-ing.

This dependence on nothing, on no "thing," is what I call *awake*—by which I mean openness to whatever arises, without focusing on the fantasy of future fulfillment, or fixating on fears and desires, likes and dislikes. To be clear, to me "awake" does not mean superhuman or *more* than human—it means to be *fully* human. From that vantage, I regard what you are calling the human condition—which is *my* condition—as a blend of the tragic and the absurd.

The *tragic sense of life* should be obvious. Sooner or later, one will lose everything: friends, loved ones, possessions, bodily health—and then, finally, this aliveness itself. Whatever you think you possess, you have only on loan. Sooner or later, all is taken, all is lost. That's what Bob Dylan alluded to in his song, "Buckets of Rain."

Life is sad
Life is a bust
All you can do is do what you must
You do what you must do and you do it well

As for the sense of the *absurd,* Albert Camus examined that approach beautifully in *The Myth of Sisyphus,* written around the time of my birth in the 1940s. Camus pointed out that the human condition revolves around an unavoidable central conflict, a kind of fatal flaw. We want to find meaning in life, some purpose, some order, some knowable system of values—but if we are honest, we find uncertainty and chaos, not meaning.

For many of us, this conflict feels psychologically unbearable—riddled with anxiety, or even, as you say, terror. A mind in that condition simply cannot and will not tolerate living with incertitude, perplexity, and ambiguity. The anguish of quandary is too much for people like that. In a muddle, their sense of self will not cohere, and the first commandment of ego is "Thou Shalt Cohere."

Some banish the anguish of quandary by bringing "God" into the picture. Once "He" is there, I *know* my purpose: it is to *obey* God, *worship* God, *find* God or, in extreme cases, to *identify* with God, even to the extent of *becoming* God—"I and the Father are one," or "I Am That."

Forgive me the bilingual pun, but God is the ultimate *deus ex machina*. From the lofts of the theater, the stagehands lower an effigy of the deity, and instantly the central conflict of the drama is resolved. Doubt disappears. The meaning of life is perfectly defined, and the apparent messiness and bedlam of ordinary existence is seen as that which must be *transcended*.

For others—some of the ones who cannot derive sufficient satisfaction from a religious philosophy—the qualms of quandary are quenched by immersing themselves in a position radically opposite to that of devotional certainty: *nihilism*. In that view, this life is meaningless, so nothing matters. Through either maneuver—idealistic devotion to spiritual fulfillment or total nihilistic materialism—the fearsome ambiguity of *not knowing* is taken off the table.

I assume that you do not rely on fantasies of God and the transcendence of ordinary life as an answer to "What's the point of living?" If you did, you would not be asking these questions. Apparently, you have found no overarching meaning in living, and for you, that feels terrifying. And as you rightly say, it's not just you. Others experience that same terror as well. If life ends in death; if there is no known meaning to this existence; if unconditional love is *not* the basis of reality; if no "greater intelligence" watches what we think, do, and say—then we are living without rules and without limits, except the limits of our own biology. Then, each of us is alone in the universe—alone with our own mind.

Perhaps all of us, as Freud opined, survive psychologically somewhere along a kind of spectrum of life/death, with pure Eros, the life principle, at one end, and pure Thanatos, the death principle, at the other. If asked, one might say, "Of *course* I want to live"—but often it's not that simple. There is in all of us, whether we recognize it or not,

not only a desire to go on living but also a desire to *not* go on living—to be relieved at last of this suffering, both physical and emotional. To get it over with. To be done with it. To be at peace.

If life is meaningless and doesn't lead anywhere but to the grave, what keeps us from suicide, if not right now, then the next time one is in serious pain or otherwise terribly distressed? That, I believe, is the *source* of the terror you feel: the absolute loneliness of being without comforting truisms about future glories. If there is nothing permanent to gain, and if my factual observations indicate that what lies ahead is decline and the incapacities of senescence, then what keeps me alive right now? If transcendence, God, and eternal life are fantasies, and if life has no inherent meaning, then why *not* suicide?

Camus raised this issue often, sometimes in an ad-lib remark such as, "Should I kill myself or have a cup of coffee?" but also in total seriousness and academic formality as well:

> *There is but one truly serious philosophical problem and that is suicide.*

In pondering the extremes—the impossible ingenuousness of religious faith on the one hand, and the powerlessness of nihilistic resignation on the other—there was, Camus thought, a third possibility: an outlook neither mawkishly devotional nor cynically bleak, which is to dig into the *absurdity* of being self-consciously alive, while *knowing* that death lies ahead.

So, instead of finessing the conflicted and fraught human condition by burying one's head like an ostrich in the sands of religion and spirituality, or clinging to the nihilistic delusion that nothing matters anyway, Camus wants to *embrace* the absurdity of the contradiction between the desire for meaning and the inability to find it. This view seems quite like Peter Zapfee's view[52] that we humans have sufficient brain power to *pose* ultimate questions about the meaning of existence, but not enough to answer them.

---

52. See Chapters 7, "Do you feel an oceanic connection?" and 16, "The abysses of vanity and meaninglessness."

His proposed embrace of absurdity is made possible, according to Camus, by living in continual revolt and rebellion against suggested explanations and justifications for this aliveness. By steering clear of explanations, one may learn to enjoy the freedom of *not knowing* and *not seeking* answers to ultimate questions. Without hope of salvation and future fulfillment, one is *liberated* to live as fully and freely as possible from moment to moment. Camus illustrates this position by a reconsideration of the Greek myth of Sisyphus.

Sisyphus, the mythological King of Corinth, was infamous not just for his many murders, rapes, and other crimes, but for an unmatched cunning and ability to outwit any opponent. By various ruses, Sisyphus managed to stay ahead of Death for many years. Once, on the verge of being captured, he managed to bind Death up in chains, so that no one anywhere could die. People who should have had the release of Death were forced to go on living, maimed or ill, wandering the streets in all manner of injury and disease. Finally, Ares, the god of war, whose work depended on Death's collaboration, unchained Death and delivered Sisyphus to him directly.

It looked grim, but Sisyphus was not done scamming. He instructed his wife, Merope, to not bury his body; to not carry out the usual sacrifices to Hades and Persephone, the King and Queen of the Underworld; to not give him the customary funeral feast; and definitely not to place under his tongue the silver drachma used to pay Charon (son of Erebus, the god of deep darkness and shadow, and Nyx, the personification of night), whose job it was to ferry the dead across the River Styx to the Underworld.

So when Sisyphus arrived at Hades' castle in the Underworld, he appeared to be not a king at all, but a wretched, unburied derelict. Entreating Queen Persephone, Sisyphus argued that he should not be there at all. As one of the unburied, and without the drachma for Charon, he never should have crossed the Styx in the first place, but should have been abandoned and left to decay on the far side of the river.

Persephone was not moved by this argument, but when Sisyphus added that allowing Merope's neglect of the funeral rites—and especially the required sacrifices to Persephone herself—might set a bad example for other bereaved wives in the future, the Queen was convinced.

Sisyphus then asked Persephone to allow him to leave the Underworld and return to the surface of Earth for just three days. In that brief time, he would arrange for a traditional funeral and properly chastise his wife for her neglect of protocol. This request made sense to Persephone, particularly the part about teaching Merope proper respect for herself, the Queen of the Underworld, so she arranged for Sisyphus to be carried back across the Styx.

Once safely back on the other side, Sisyphus reneged on his promise to return and lived for many years more, until, finally, he died of old age. At that point, his life of fun and games having run its course, there was no further escaping Hades. Once back in the Underworld, Sisyphus was condemned to descend to Tartarus, the lowest of all the regions, there to be punished for eternity.

Hades decreed that Sisyphus must labor to roll a massive boulder to the top of a steep hill. He then contrived, however, that the job could never be completed, for just as Sisyphus neared the summit, the rock would roll right back down again, leaving the condemned one to walk down after it and begin the endless task anew.

Now this situation might seem like eternal damnation itself and, indeed, punishment, vengeance, and retribution were Hades' intentions. Sisyphus had defied the power of the deities and must now pay forever. To awaken each morning with a bone-breaking task on the agenda, while knowing in advance that you are destined to fail at it, seems a terrible fate. But nevertheless, Camus wants us to imagine Sisyphus happy.

The period of pushing the rock up the hill may be pure suffering—a straining of muscles and tendons trying to achieve an unachievable goal; but in the easy walk *downhill,* with no burden to carry, we can imagine Sisyphus feeling free. He is free to contemplate the absurdity of his situation, and free to *participate* in that absurdity without hope; without looking for the non-existent escape hatch. No improvement, no salvation, no transcendence, no overarching meaning, no *deus ex machina*. Just what *is* right now.

Alone on that hill, Sisyphus—a life-long deceiver, crook, and conniver—comes to awareness of *himself*. There is nothing but the man, the hill, and the rock. Depending on no-thing, Sisyphus finds his *own* mind. And we can imagine that in this opening of his eyes to what *is*—not what he wishes *were*, or what he believes *could be*—Sisyphus is as liberated as a human being ever can be.

> *The absurd man, when he contemplates his torment, silences all the idols. In the universe suddenly restored to its silence, the myriad wondering little voices of the earth rise up. Unconscious, secret calls, invitations from all the faces . . . There is no sun without shadow, and it is essential to know the night. The absurd man says yes and his efforts will henceforth be unceasing. If there is a personal fate, there is no higher destiny, or at least there is, but one which he concludes is inevitable and despicable. For the rest, he knows himself to be the master of his days . . . This universe henceforth without [an outside] master seems to him neither sterile nor futile. Each atom of that stone, each mineral flake of that night filled mountain, in itself forms a world. The struggle itself toward the heights is enough to fill a man's heart. One must imagine Sisyphus happy.*
>
> —Final words of Albert Camus' *The Myth of Sisyphus*

So Sisyphus finds himself in a kind of *Groundhog Day* from which there is no exit. He must get up every day and do it again.

One sees immediately the resemblance to our own psychological lives as self-conscious primate animals called human beings, who—while we may strive to achieve our material, social, and philosophical goals—happen to know all about decline, decay, and death. We may *want* to explain death away, but that is just whistling in the dark.

This view—no exit—may be entirely *hopeless*, but it is not in the least nihilistic, although in many minds those two quite different ideational realms are conflated as if there were no distinction between them.

Those with a taste for Hollywood happy endings might think the absurdist view devoid of happiness, to say nothing of joy, but the phenomenology of the absurd does not preclude happiness—not at all. At times that very absurdist view might be a *source* of happiness—a kind of love affair with what *is*, however seemingly humble—since what is, is all we ever get.

Frankly, from my perspective, to embrace the understanding that right now is all one ever gets seems so obvious, and so entirely liberating, that I still wonder at the apparent difficulty so many have in coming to it.

I wonder if at least some of that difficulty derives from the thought of actual *effort*—like the daily labors of Sisyphus—without any final victory, seeming impossibly daunting. Effort, after all, implies exertion, and some of us perhaps would like to think that freedom means never having to exert oneself. I see it a bit differently. Once Sisyphus said yes to his situation, thereafter his efforts were unceasing.

Q2: But Robert, you have often said that "no effort can avail." That's a direct quote. So what do you mean about efforts being unceasing? What efforts?

A: That's a good question. I could take the coward's way out and just fall back on Ralph Waldo Emerson's little epigram, "A foolish consistency is the hobgoblin of little minds, adored by little statesmen, philosophers, and divines," but a good question deserves more than cliché for an answer. As I see it now, I'd have done better to have put it this way:

> *Before one has said "yes" unequivocally to the mortal realities of the human situation, efforts are likely to go awry* regardless *of good intentions.*

When I say "mortal realities," I mean that—regardless of what one believes or does not believe, wants or does not want, practices or does not practice—each of us human animals must age, sicken, and die just like any other animal. Unless we don't last long enough to die aged and infirm, but are murdered, fall prey to accident, contract a fatal illness early, commit suicide, or are otherwise preempted. From this mortal finale, I say, *there is no escape*—including identifying with "universal consciousness," which is, after all, but a concept in limited *human* consciousness. If it were more than just a concept, no one would be talking this way.

It may be comforting to make oneself believe in "Nothing was ever born so nothing ever dies" or some such cant; and if that is what one wants, those concepts are well laid out. But ideas like that are *not* factual, not by *my* epistemology. My theory of knowledge and what can be known requires not that I hear someone *talking* about "universal consciousness" and believe it, nor that someone "prove" it to me with so-called higher reasoning, but that I *experience it directly.* "Universal consciousness" is *not* my experience, so when I say that I am awake, that has nothing to do with nonduality and the rest of those riffs; the religious metaphysics, I mean.

To me awake means this: I am not on any kind of *journey.* I have no *destination.* There is *nothing to attain.* I am not *becoming* anything. This is it.

I will cut to the chase. If you subscribe to a metaphysics that imagines other worlds, other levels, a hierarchy of non-material guides and masters, earthly gods whose feet you want to kiss or whose photograph you worship and perhaps wear around your neck, from my point of view you are living in an hypnotic trance, expecting all that devotion to pay off somehow, probably by moving you higher in the imaginary hierarchy of so-called "spiritual realization"—or maybe just by making you feel better.

The real payoff, I am saying, is *death*—ordinary human animal mortality. That's the end of the whole deal, *your* deal. That deal ends when it's time for *you* to turn *your* face to the wall and die—just as *my* deal ends with *my* demise, *my* last breath. And everything else will still be here.

Do I *know* that with epistemological certainty beyond any shadow of a doubt? Nope. But my experiences with total anesthesia have been highly suggestive. One minute I'm there counting backward—and then, with no sense of interlude, I find myself awakening in an unknown bed in an unknown room. Ten seconds could have passed in that interlude or ten years. I would not have known the difference. In that interval, there is just *nothing,* no-thing.

Does that constitute overwhelming evidence? Not really, but it is, I say, highly suggestive. Anyway, to imagine otherwise is sheer fantasy—the kind of pull-it-out-of-your-ass metaphysics that the human race has favored since our far less intellectually well-equipped ancestors gained brain power sufficient for *fabricating* explanations as they gazed up at the stars.

We may want to believe otherwise. We may yearn to believe that awareness is an ongoing account that is not canceled and emptied out at death. But in our hearts, we suspect that our efforts at transcendence of the mortal realities are bootless attempts to be *rescued* from mortality. We want to have our cake and eat it too. We want to *be* here, to *exist,* but we bridle at the price of this human existence, which is ordinary suffering, physical *and* emotional—*including* prior awareness of death.

If one is looking for a way to get around this—looking for "the escape hatch"—any "spiritual" efforts will aim at trying to regard this human animal life as a "journey" that *leads* somewhere. That kind of effort, an effort aimed at transcending or escaping ordinary human suffering, I say, will not avail.

That is Camus' point. It is only *after* contemplating his ongoing hopeless fate and saying "yes" to it—not yes with fingers crossed behind his back, but a *categorical* yes—that Sisyphus's efforts become focused. He participates *fully,* happy simply to live and breathe, Camus wants us to imagine, albeit knowing that he will *never* gain the summit. Getting that boulder to the top of the hill won't happen, any more than a human animal will become a deathless "presence," or attain "oneness," except conceptually.

But what about the profusion of philosophies, paths, and methods? Are they all just nonsense? How can the weight of all that be ignored? What about meditation, prayer, repetition of sacred words, spiritual retreats, embracing nonduality, bowing to masters, killing the ego, dosing oneself with psychedelics, cleansing the chakras, etcetera, ad infinitum? Do not those established, well-trodden paths, if taken in earnest, all lead eventually to the same desired destination: self-realization?

If you believe that one path or another does, you will have to try it for yourself, of course. Far be it from me to tell anyone what to do or not do, believe or not believe. I speak here only of my *own* experience, my *own* mind—not yours, dear reader, about which I know nothing. From my personal point of view—what other kind is there?—the only "path" I know is to chew up and swallow one's experience bite by bite. I may suffer, but I don't fret. It may feel hard at times, but I feel pretty sure that, unlike Sisyphus, I won't be at this forever. Meanwhile, life can be beautiful, at least in the interstices, in the brief, unencumbered walks *downhill.*

In a real sense, we human beings *are* all one. We share a common fate. We all end up, each and every one of us, inanimate lifeless corpses pushing up the daisies. Ashes to ashes, dust to dust. There are no winners in the game of life.

But *meanwhile,* while hearts beat, loins throb, and bellies call out for sustenance, there *is* a difference—an absolutely crucial one, I say—between saying *"yes"* to each moment, unequivocally, like it or not, or else pussyfooting around with rumors of transcendence: "I don't like *this* now, so I will wait for a now I like better and be in *that* one," as Eckhart Tolle quipped. That difference mattered to Sisyphus, and it matters to me.

If here you want to inject God, or Love, or "universal consciousness" as the riposte to my assumption that death is the finale of this "myselfness"—the annihilation of all I know, love, and care for—go right ahead. You have as much right to your perspective as I do to mine. But in all honesty, I say that out of pure civility—not because I consider any one point of view as good as any other.

According to Hafiz, "Everyone is trudging along with as much dignity, courage, and style as they possibly can."

Yes. I agree. It may not always *look* that way, but we are all, in my view, doing the best we can—the *only* thing we can. So if "universal consciousness" for you is a "thing," OK. For me, it isn't.

I have no interest in the profusion of methods and beliefs claiming to lead to endless happiness and ultimate self-realization. For me, *this right now is it,* and there *is* nothing else. If you see that, the rest looks like blowing smoke. So, like others before me, I say:

This is it!

Now suppose someone has heard "This is it!" thousands of times and never got it, but this time *does* get it. The penny drops. Eureka! I'm *alive*! This is *it*!

"So what. Big deal," Nihilism says, and thereby foregoes in advance any need for effort. When the answer is *always* "no," effort is never required. That's life on autopilot. And so is the apparent opposite of nihilism, the dogmatic certainty that answers to ultimate questions exist *a priori* in some Platonic world of "Truth," known only by experts: "Just tell me what to think and do next, Oh Great One."

You ask about effort. If the effort is to embrace nihilism, it's effort gone awry. And so are efforts aimed at "realizing" the supposed spiritual "Truths" proffered by pundits and self-appointed "masters" in the art of living. There *are* no masters in these matters. This is *terra incognita* for us all, I say.

If there is to be effort, it does not end in simply finding out that "this is it." That trope is so commonplace that it has lost all power, and should be obvious anyway. So if you are still dithering over *that* question, snap out of it. Of *course* this is it. What other "it" do we have?

"This is it" is not the *end* of anything. It's where effort begins. No more fingers crossed behind one's back. No more mouths parroting nonsense. Be *here*. If not now, when?

Depending on no-thing, find your *own* mind.